Life in the *Limes*

Lindsay Allason-Jones

Life in the *Limes*

Studies of the people and objects of the Roman frontiers

Presented to Lindsay Allason-Jones
on the occasion of her birthday and retirement

edited by
Rob Collins and Frances McIntosh

OXBOW | books
Oxford & Philadelphia

First published in 2014
Reprinted in paperback in 2020 in the United Kingdom by
OXBOW BOOKS
The Old Music Hall, 106–108 Cowley Road, Oxford, OX4 1JE

and in the United States by
OXBOW BOOKS
1950 Lawrence Road, Havertown, PA 19083

Paperback Edition: ISBN 978-1-78925-385-6
Digital Edition: ISBN 978-1-78297-254-9 (epub)

A CIP record for this book is available from the British Library

Typeset by M.C. Bishop at The Armatura Press
Printed in the United Kingdom by CMP (UK) Ltd

For a complete list of Oxbow titles, please contact:

UNITED KINGDOM
Oxbow Books
Telephone (01865) 241249
Email: oxbow@oxbowbooks.com
www.oxbowbooks.com

UNITED STATES OF AMERICA
Oxbow Books
Telephone (610) 853-9131, Fax (610) 853-9146
Email: queries@casemateacademic.com
www.casemateacademic.com/oxbow

Oxbow Books is part of the Casemate Group

Front cover: Tombstone of Regina from South Shields (photo: Society of Antiquaries of Newcastle upon Tyne)
Back cover: The reconstructed commanding officer's house at South Shields (photo: Rob Collins)

TABLE OF CONTENTS

CONTRIBUTORS

PAUL BIDWELL, Tyne and Wear Archives and Museums.

MIKE BISHOP, Writer, publisher, and archaeologist

DAVID BREEZE, Honorary Professor of Archaeology, Newcastle Univerisity

ROB COLLINS, Portable Antiquities Scheme and Newcastle University

HILARY COOL, Barbican Research Associates

JON COULSTON, St. Andrews University

ALEX CROOM, Tyne and Wear Archives and Museums

NINA CRUMMY, Small finds specialist

IAIN FERRIS, Independent consultant, researcher and writer

ELIZABETH GREENE, University of Western Ontario

BILL HANSON, Glasgow University

IAN HAYNES, Newcastle University

MARTIN HENIG, Honorary Visiting Professor, Institute of Archaeology, UCL

NICK HODGSON, Tyne and Wear Archives and Museums

FRASER HUNTER, National Museums Scotland

RALPH JACKSON, The British Museum

SIMON JAMES, Leicester University

REBECCA JONES, Historic Scotland

MARK LODWICK, National Museums and Galleries Wales

BILL MANNING, Emeritus Professor of Archaeology, University of Cardiff

FRANCES MCINTOSH, Newcastle University and English Heritage

ALEX MEYER, University of Western Ontario

EMMA MORRIS, Balliol College, Oxford University

ANDREW PARKIN, Tyne and Wear Archives and Museums

JENNIFER PRICE, Durham University

ROGER TOMLIN, Wolfson College, Oxford University

CAROL VAN DRIEL-MURRAY, Leiden University

TONY WILMOTT, English Heritage

ACKNOWLEDGEMENTS

This volume is a result of a career of curiosity, enthusiasm, and good-will demonstrated by Lindsay through her life, endearing her to people around the world. This resulted in very high interest in contributing to this volume; however, the decision was taken to accept papers that focused on the primary themes found throughout Lindsay's research: Roman frontiers, the people of the Roman world (especially women and children), and material culture. The contributors are to be congratulated and warmly thanked for their prompt delivery of interesting papers.

There are many people to thank for their help in making this volume possible, not least those organizations providing grants that contributed to the cost of publication, namely the Mark Fitch Fund, Newcastle University, the Royal Archaeological Institute, and the Society of Antiquaries of Newcastle upon Tyne. English Heritage kindly provided permission for reproduction of images of objects in their collections and the use of survey data free of charge. Tyne and Wear Archives and Museums and the Society of Antiquaries of Newcastle upon Tyne kindly provided permission to reproduce images of items in their collections.

LIST OF ABBREVIATIONS

AA	*Archaeologia Aeliana*, journal of the Society of Antiquaries of Newcastle upon Tyne.
BAR	*British Archaeological Reports*.
Britannia	Journal of the Society for the Promotion of Roman Studies.
CSIR	*Corpus Signorum Imperii Romani*.
GMA	Kotansky, R. (1994) *Greek Magical Amulets: The Inscribed Gold, Silver, Copper, and Bronze* Lamellae, Part I, *Published Texts of Known Provenance*. Opladen.
ILS	*Inscriptiones Latinae Selectae*.
JRA	*Journal of Roman Archaeology*.
JRS	*Journal of Roman Studies*.
JRMES	*Journal of Roman Military Equipment Studies*.
LIMC	*Lexicon Iconographicum Mythologiae Classicae*.
MAMA 9	*Monumenta Asiae Minoris Antiqua* IX: Cox, C.W.M., Cameron, A., Cullen, J. and Levick, B. (1988) *Monuments from the Aezanitis*. London.
ORL	Fabricius, E., Winkelmann, F., and Stade, K., various dates, *Der Obergermanisch-Rätische Limes des Römerreiches*.
PGM	Preisendanz, K., *Papyri Graecae Magicae. Die griechischen Zauberpapyri* I, II (ed. Heinrechs, A. 1973–74). Stuttgart.
PSAS	*Proceedings of the Society of Antiquaries of Scotland*.
RIB	*The Roman Inscriptions of Britain*.
*Suppl. Mag.*I, II	Daniel, R. and Maltomini, F. (1990, 1992) *Supplementum Magicum* (Opladen)
TAACW	*Transactions of the Antiquarian and Archaeological Society of Cumberland and Westmorland*.
Tab. Sulis	Tomlin, R.S.O. (1988) *Tabellae Sulis: Roman Inscribed Tablets of Tin and Lead from the Sacred Spring at Bath* (Oxford) = Cunliffe, B. 1988 *The Temple of Sulis Minerva at Bath*, II, *The Finds from the Sacred Spring* (Oxford), 59–269.

1

INTRODUCTION: A WALL FOR ALL

Rob Collins and Frances McIntosh

Lindsay Allason-Jones has been a 'fixture' (or perhaps a fitting?) of small finds and Roman frontier research for 40 years, ever since she completed her undergraduate degree in Newcastle in 1974. She immediately threw herself into research, first for the Classics Department at Newcastle, before a brief stint in a cemetery in Chelmsford with the Excavation Unit. She soon returned to her native *Britannia Secunda*, specifically to work for the Tyne and Wear Museums Service on the assemblage of small finds from the fort at South Shields.

Following the completion of the South Shields volume, Lindsay was employed at the Museum of Antiquities through the 1980s and '90s, working closely with the collections of the Society of Antiquaries of Newcastle upon Tyne, and managing the museum on the retirement of David Smith in 1988. In 1998, her role expanded to include the Shefton Museum of Greek Art and Archaeology as the Newcastle University Director of Museums. Lindsay held this position, managing a small but dedicated team until 2009, when the Newcastle University Museums closed and their collections joined those of the Hancock Museum in the ambitious Great North Museum project. While the majority of time was dedicated to working on material from *Britannia*, brief forays to North Africa and the Near East also led to important work exploring the archaeology of Roman frontiers at the opposite end of the empire.

The Museum of Antiquities, following the example provided by its parent organisation the Society of Antiquaries of Newcastle upon Tyne, always provided an 'identification service' for public finders of archaeological objects. With the growth of the metal-detecting hobby, the Museum and Lindsay became a regular port of call for detectorists. This willingness to speak with public finders was important, and has resulted in a number of discoveries in the North East of England that might otherwise have been unknown. It was her familiarity with the importance of outreach that led Lindsay to host and manage the local Portable Antiquities Scheme officer in the Museum of Antiquities from 2003.

While managing the Museum of Antiquities, Lindsay also maintained strong links with the Archaeology Department (now part of the School of History, Classics and Archaeology) at Newcastle University, teaching, training, and educating a generation of budding archaeologists as Reader in Roman Material Culture. From 2008 until her retirement in 2011, Lindsay was the Director of the Centre for Interdisciplinary Artefact Studies, a formal recognition of a career spent forging links with professionals and specialists outside the field of archaeology.

In addition to the numerous achievements gathered over the course of her career, Lindsay has also devoted considerable time and effort to a number of organisations and committees, regionally and nationally. While it would be impossible to name each position held, a brief list demonstrates Lindsay's enduring commitment and enthusiasm. Lindsay has been a trustee and/or member of the Clayton Trustees, the Trustees of the Corbridge Excavation Fund, Hadrian's Art Fund, Heritage Lottery Fund North East, the Marc Fitch Fund, the Royal Archaeological Institute, the Society for the Promotion of Roman Studies, the Sudan Archaeological Committee, and last but certainly not least, the Society of Antiquaries of Newcastle upon Tyne, which celebrates it bicentenary during her tenure as President. In addition, Lindsay has provided conspicuous leadership and support to three important traditions in Roman frontier studies – the decennial Hadrian's Wall Pilgrimage, the International Congress of Roman Frontier Studies, and the Roman Military Equipment Conference. Further service has been rendered to an incalculable number of committees and organisations dedicated to Hadrian's Wall and the World Heritage Site.

Throughout her career, Lindsay has been a prolific writer, and Emma Morris has kindly prepared a bibliography of Lindsay's work up to the date of publication that can be found at the end of the volume. This bibliography amply demonstrates an impressive array of research interests: notes dedicated to specific artefacts; small finds reports accompanying site excavations; journal articles and papers in edited volumes on interpretive and theoretical issues; and last but not least a raft of single- and co-authored monographs and edited volumes. Whatever the scale of publication, Lindsay's interest in Roman artefacts is apparent, but this appreciation for the small details has frequently been employed to address the big issues, drawing attention to women and children and emphasizing the human elements of living in the frontiers.

The contributions to this volume all represent at least one aspect of Lindsay's research interests, but there are a number of cross-over themes between the papers. We start with a selection of papers that considers the frontiers and the people living within them. Bill Hanson's paper revisits the debate on the intended function of Roman frontiers, while Bill Manning considers evidence for blacksmiths in the Roman army. Nick Hodgson critically questions where and when soldiers' wives were provided with accommodation inside the fort walls, followed by Beth Greene discussing evidence for women and children from inside the early fort(s) at Vindolanda. Alex Croom rounds up this section with a consideration of the activities represented in the *vicus* at South Shields.

The next group of papers presents evidence specific to the military communities of Britain, Romania, and the Near East. Paul Bidwell, David Breeze, and Jon Coulston use the reliable inscribed and sculptural stones to present three thought-provoking ideas. In a site-specific study, Paul Bidwell considers the inscribed and written evidence for the name of the fort at South Shields prior to its association with *Arbeia*. David Breeze reminds us of the importance of antiquarian observations in regards to some rather unique sculpture from the Wall zone, hinting at monuments now lost to archaeologists. Jon Coulston argues for an insular tradition in military-figural stones, drawing on the excellent record of such stones in Britain. Mike Bishop takes us back into the realm of small finds, reconsidering the Corbridge Hoard in light of more recent discoveries of Roman armour, and reminding us of the value of reassessing established 'understandings'. Ian Haynes takes us out of Britain to the site of Apulum, where intriguing evidence sheds light on religious practices involving soldiers, and Simon James provides us with a detailed discussion of a military helmet from the Near East, revealing tantalizing evidence of cultural and technological interplay between Rome and Persia.

Returning to *Britannia*, the next section looks at individual objects and classes of finds to emphasize the economic and ideological penetration of *romanitas* even in the frontiers. Iain Ferris provides us with a brief discussion of a pseudo-Venus figurine from Binchester and its significance, with Alex Meyer critically examining the Vindolanda 'calendar' and related pieces to give us some insight into Roman temporal constructs. A polychrome bead from Housesteads, dubbed by Hilary Cool as 'Lindsay's birthday bead' or 'LBB' is another small but important indication of the late and possibly post-Roman material that is increasingly found in Roman forts sites in northern Britain. A seemingly simple decorative key handle from the Vale of Glamorgan is then revealed by Nina Crummy and Mark Lodwick to be an elaborate and subtle interweaving of a number of mythological and religious motifs. Rounding out this section are Martin Henig and Jenny Price, offering papers on some of the finer things to be found in the frontier, gemstones and mould-blown glass, respectively. While Henig reminds us that the military community could be highly literate and educated, Price considers the sources and implications of discoveries of mould-blown glass from military sites.

The tantalizing evidence of trans-frontier interactions and invisible people are addressed in the next group of papers. Fraser Hunter presents a detailed assessment of the jet and jet-like objects of Roman Scotland, suggesting important contributions from the peoples north of Hadrian's Wall to the Romano-British fascination with shiny black things. Following this, Rob Collins looks at the data gathered by the Portable Antiquities Scheme to explore connections between the military communities and natives north of the Wall. Beccy Jones reminds us of the discrepancy between remains on the ground and the evidence for their occupants, hypothesizing on the nature and scale of life in the temporary camps that provide evidence for campaigning and the establishment of frontiers. The final paper in this section is provided by Tony Wilmott, who has captured a curiosity of historiography in the Housesteads amphitheatre.

Contemporary with speculations about an amphitheatre at Housesteads, John Clayton was purchasing vast tracts of land and exploring the archaeological remains of the Wall, establishing the collection that now bears his name. Frances McIntosh reminds us of the debt that we owe to Clayton and subsequently the Trustees of his collection. A unique museum piece, an Estrucan mirror in the collection of the Society of Antiquaries of Newcastle upon Tyne since the late nineteenth century, is explored by Andrew Parkin, who considers the significance of the Classical scene depicted.

The final three papers provide detailed consideration of objects of significant interest. Roger Tomlin presents a detailed discussion of a Greek amulet made of pewter from Roman London that indicates the dissemination of literate Greek culture into far-flung Britain. Closer to the skin, if not the heart, Carol van Driel-Murray examines the evidence of leather bikinis found from a handful of Roman sites, and considers the implications this has on our understanding of physical concerns such as body size and social concerns in the world of the Roman woman. Last, but certainly not least, Ralph Jackson provides a provoking discussion of the widespread occurrence of mice in Roman art, connecting the small finds with contemporary views of alternatively pesky and cute little critters.

Lindsay Allason-Jones (BA, MLitt, FSA, FSAScot, MIFA, FMA, FRSA), we humbly present this volume to you in the hope that you find it stimulating and entertaining. It is but a small token of the time and energy you have given to your colleagues, friends, and the discipline in general.

2

THE NATURE AND FUNCTION OF ROMAN FRONTIERS REVISITED

W. S. Hanson

Some 25 years ago I attempted to summarise how and why frontiers came into being, their form, development and intended function (Hanson 1989). I still stand by much of that paper today. However, given the passage of time, with its inevitable new discoveries and re-assessments of evidence, the opportunity to make some revisions or further clarifications is timely.

One such new discovery of considerable significance is that of the Roman town of Augustan date at Waldgirmes to the east of the Rhine in the Lahn valley in Germany (von Schnurbein 2003). This very short-lived settlement clearly indicates Augustus' intentions to occupy territory beyond the Rhine. It also provides strong archaeological confirmation of Dio's much doubted remarks about the activities of Quintilius Varus as he set about the process of turning a newly conquered area into a Roman province (Dio 56.18). However, this all came to nothing as a result of the disastrous loss of three legions under his command in AD 9, which also effectively brought to an end any ambitions to extend direct Roman control as far as the river Elbe.

This event was clearly a turning point for Augustus and there can be little doubt that it influenced his deathbed advice to his successor, Tiberius, to restrict the empire within its limits at that time (Tac. *Ann.* I, 11). Nonetheless, that Augustus was basically an expansionist, very much in the tradition of the generals of the Later Republic, is clear both from his earlier actions and his own account of his achievements. Indeed, he boasts of extending 'the borders of all the provinces of the Roman people which neighboured nations not subject to our rule' (*Res Gestae* 26). I originally suggested that over the next two centuries or so certain emperors attempted to resurrect this traditional expansionist policy. I would now reverse that emphasis and assert that, with the notable exception of Hadrian, most emperors in that period harboured and, within the constraints of the circumstances that they faced, actively pursued that desire to expand the Empire. Thus, even emperors like Gaius and Nero, who are not normally associated with such attitudes, can be seen to fall into the same general mould and to have harboured expansionist tendencies. Gaius annexed the client kingdom of Mauretania and seriously contemplated an expedition to Britain (Barrett 1989, 116–20 and 129–32); while Nero annexed three small client kingdoms and planned an expedition against the Albanians (Kolendo 1982; Isaac 1990, 43–4). These views, with which I am pleased to note Whittaker now concurs (2004, 8), are elaborated more fully elsewhere (Hanson 2002).

Nonetheless, as the forward movement stalled, the definition of frontiers became inevitable and their character increased in complexity over time. The major European rivers continued to play an obvious role both as natural demarcators of territory and as simple geographical reference points. What is clearer now is that this formal recognition of their frontier role came earlier than had been thought. The discovery of several timber watchtowers of Claudian date along the lower Rhine, as for example at Valkenburg-Marktveld and Utrecht (Langeveld *et al.* 2010), indicates that control of movement along and across the river was a matter of early concern and brings forward by two decades or so the date of the appearance of such close control, which was previously seen as primarily a Flavian development. What is also becoming clearer, however, is that such developments were not necessarily synchronous across the empire.

Nonetheless, the earliest examples of such dispositions which define entirely 'artificial' frontier lines still fall in the Flavian period, assuming that the Roman road along the

Gask Ridge in Scotland, with its associated forts, fortlets and regular system of watchtowers, continues to be accepted as a frontier rather than a protected supply line (*contra* Dobat 2009). Traditionally this system has been seen to fit into a phased withdrawal from Scotland (Breeze 1982, 61–5), a view still espoused by some (e.g. Hodgson 2000, 19). But this dating is difficult to sustain if all the forts north of the Forth–Clyde isthmus were abandoned at the same time in the late 80s AD, as seems to be indicated by the coin evidence, with a *terminus post quem* for both Inchtuthil and Strageath provided by coins of AD 86 (Hobley 1989). Alternatively, recent attempts to push the date earlier than the campaigns of Agricola simply cannot be substantiated (Hanson 2009, *contra* Woolliscroft 2009). Rather, the logical chronological context for the Gask system, as I have argued elsewhere (Hanson 1991, 1765–7), is the halt on the Forth–Clyde isthmus in Agricola's fourth campaign (Tac. *Ag.*23). Thus, it may be no coincidence that the dispositions mirror precisely those demarcating the limit of Roman direct control in the Antonine period when the Forth–Clyde isthmus was again the focus of Roman military attention and outpost forts extended the Roman presence as far as the Tay.

The second example of an early artificial, open frontier system, the Taunus and Wetterau frontier in Germany, is now thought to have a much more complicated history than was understood 25 years ago. Though some garrisons were established beyond the Rhine under Domitian as a result of his successful war against the Chatti, the sequence of forts and fortlets in the Taunus Mountains and the northern Wetterau appears to date to the Trajanic period on numismatic grounds (Kortüm 1998). Indeed, there are now suggestions of phases of its development in the pre-Hadrianic period, with an inner line between Ober-Florstadt and Hanau-Salisberg a few kilometres to the west of what subsequently became the established frontier line from Altenstadt to Gross-Krotzenburg (Hodgson 2000, 13–16; Reuter 2004). There do not, however, appear to be any watchtowers associated with the inner line, only with the outer (though see below for a possible turf rampart associated with the former). A broadly similar layout, but less complex chronology of development, is attested along the Oldenwald *limes* between the lower courses of the Main and the Neckar to the south (Thiel 2009a). Such arrangements emphasize the more *ad hoc* character of developments along frontiers linked to the different tactical and strategic demands of different regions. They need not show the regularity and consistent planning that all too often we assume in our desire to understand the logic of the overall system.

Closing these artificial frontiers completely with the construction of a linear barrier is a logical progression, serving to demarcate and define boundaries more precisely in areas which lacked natural features to fulfill that function. Thus, linear barriers should be regarded as broadly the equivalent of rivers, for the two are never found in use together except as complementary parts of the same system. This is strikingly illustrated by the relationship between the upper German *limes* (through the Taunus, Wetterau and Odenwald) and the rivers Rhine, Main and Neckar, for the palisade is constructed only where the line of the river is not being followed. This fact has long been recognized, but integrating rivers and linear barriers in this way emphasises that the two served similar functions in relation to the operation of the Roman frontier, a principle whose significance is considered further below. For the most intensively studied frontiers, this final evolutionary stage can be seen to be a gradual development from what had gone before. Thus, on Hadrian's Wall, the curtain Wall with its fortlets and towers, traditionally if confusingly referred to as milecastles and turrets, was originally constructed to augment the previous open frontier based on the Stanegate, the east–west Roman road with its standard auxiliary garrisons and occasional smaller forts or fortlets and possible watchtowers (Breeze and Dobson 2000, 16–28 and 148–49; Hodgson 2000). So too along the upper German *limes* in the Taunus, Wetterau and Odenwald we see the addition of a timber palisade immediately in front of the pre-existing line of timber towers, behind which a series of forts and fortlets had already been variously established (Baatz 2000, 46–7; Thiel 2008, 83–5).

This final phase in the creation of fully fledged artificial barriers with associated garrison provision is still seen as a Hadrianic innovation. The intimation that this was the case in late Roman sources referring to both Britain and Germany (*SHA* Had. 11.2 and 12.6) is confirmed by a recent dendrochronological date of 119/120 AD from the German *limes* palisade in the Wetterau (Schallmayer 2005) and the consistent epigraphic evidence from the Wall in Britain, which seems to have been known as *vallum Aelium* from the outset (Tomlin and Hassall 2004, 344). This fits well with the picture of Hadrian as an emperor who focussed on the consolidation and maintenance of the empire within its established borders, as alluded to above.

Nonetheless, there are hints that small stretches of linear barrier in Germany are pre-Hadrianic in date (Thiel 2009b, 979–83), raising the possibility that localized solutions to frontier problems subsequently came to be applied in a much wider context, further emphasising the *ad hoc* nature of developments. Thus, the so-called Sibyllenspur or Lautertal *limes*, a short stretch of palisade and ditch between Köngen and Donnstetten on the border between Upper Germany and Raetia, may have served to help close the gap between the headwaters of the Rhine and Danube basins (Planck 1987). Similarly, the inner line of fortifications between Ober-Florstadt and Hanau-Salisberg in the northern Wetterau, noted above, may also have incorporated a linear barrier, as a 200m length of turf rampart and ditch of early second century date has been identified immediately in front of two adjacent fortlets at Hanau-Mittelbuchen (Reuter 2004).

Linear barriers were also constructed *de novo* in some areas. Antoninus Pius was responsible for two, one in Britain and one in Germany, both demarcating a limited extension of Roman held territory. As noted above, the Antonine Wall was constructed after the re-advance into lowland Scotland along the same strategic line as the Flavian halt on Forth–Clyde isthmus, but re-used probably only one of the earlier installations (Hanson 1980). In its original design it reflected the layout of Hadrian's Wall in its developed form, though, at least on present evidence, apparently lacking any provision of watchtowers. It rapidly went through substantive modifications, resulting from a reassessment of local circumstances (Hanson and Maxwell 1986, 104–12; Breeze 2006, 81–95). The German outer *limes* represented a completely new frontier, whose structural elements mirrored those of the Odenwald *limes* located only some 30 km to the west which it replaced (Baatz 2000, 218–51). Its creation incorporated good agricultural land in the Neckarland region and rationalized the link between the upper German and Raetian frontier lines. Its more bureaucratic conceptualization as the demarcation of the limit of Roman territory is indicated by the straight line it follows for some 80 km between Miltenburg and Lorch without regard for topography or local military tactical advantage. Most recently, a complex, multi-phase linear frontier system has been rediscovered, or rather re-dated to the Roman period, in eastern Romania (Hanson and Oltean 2012). It cuts across Dobrogea at its narrowest point between the Danube and the Black Sea taking advantage of a natural topographic feature, the Carasu valley. The frontier is defined by a large earthen rampart later replaced on a slightly different line by a stone-revetted rampart, both fronted by a large ditch. Both barriers have a regular series of attached forts, variably but quite closely spaced, but only the earthen rampart has attached fortlets. Like the Antonine Wall, whose form the system most resembles, neither barrier seems to have associated watchtowers, but the close spacing of the installations, at least on the earthen rampart, might have made them superfluous. The precise chronology of the use of these barriers is still to be determined, but an origin in the Hadrianic period is a strong possibility. However, their location clearly relates to the control of movement, for Dobrogea was a natural north–south route-way throughout history.

Despite all the work on frontiers over the last two decades, debate about their intended function and *modus operandi* is no less heated, particularly with respect to linear barriers. It remains my contention, however, that we can use the development sequence of frontiers, in combination with comparisons between different frontier regions, to indicate Rome's attitude to their function. Thus, in areas of zonal occupation, as seen for example in upland areas across much of northern Britain, Dacia and Mauretania, or in the desert fringes in Tripolitania, forts are consistently located in strategic positions. They are disposed along natural route ways, such as in river valleys or mountain passes, or at oases or river crossings, usually linked by roads, which suggests that both control of indigenous movement and protection of Roman communications were seen as fundamental. The closer the spacing of garrisons and the more dispersed the troops, heralded by the appearance of networks of fortlets, such as in the uplands in south-west Scotland in the Antonine period (Maxwell 1977; Hanson and Maxwell 1986, 72–4), the greater the concern that is implied for localised control of relatively small scale movement.

As is clear from the history of development outlined above, artificial open frontiers precede those closed by linear barriers. The former are recognised by the spacing of garrisons along a lateral line at closer intervals than the nominal day's march seen in areas of zonal control, often involving the deployment of fortlets to reduce the spacing and spread the garrison. This may be augmented by provision of a regular system of watchtowers, as seen in the pre-Hadrianic stage of the Upper German *limes* or the Flavian installations along the Gask Ridge. These dispositions suggest a concern for even closer control of movement, but in this case across a lateral line which is usually at or close to the limit of Roman occupation at the time. As noted above, closing these artificial frontiers with a linear barrier is a logical progression and indicates concern to increase the level of control across, and the intensity of security on, that lateral line. But the question remains, was that control primarily for the purposes of exclusion and defence, or was it more for administrative and economic convenience?

Debate in recent years has focused on whether or not linear barriers, particularly Hadrian's Wall and the Antonine Wall, were intended to be defended perimeters, and specifically whether they were regularly patrolled along their entire length rather than just manned at focal points, such as towers and fortlets. New evidence has been recovered in recent years which may cast some further light on this question. It now seems more than likely that additional defensive provision was provided as a regular feature on the berm along both Hadrian's Wall and the Antonine Wall. A series of staggered rows of pits have been discovered along long stretches of Hadrian's Wall at its western end, with parallel, but much less extensive, discoveries at various points along the eastern sector of the Antonine Wall, similar to the well-known *lilia* outside the fort at Rough Castle (Bidwell 2005). These newly discovered pits were designed to house branches with sharpened ends and create a near impenetrable entanglement, the Roman equivalent of barbed wire (thus, *cippi* rather than *lilia*). In addition, detailed architectural analysis of Hadrian's Wall, including full-scale reconstruction of a section at Wallsend, has confirmed that the Wall could readily have accommodated a walkway (Bidwell 2008). This evidence has then been used to argue that the two Walls were, indeed, designed to be defended along their entire length. Such a conclusion is, however, unnecessary. It could just as readily be argued that additional obstructions in front of the Walls were needed precisely because there were no troops strung out along the Wall top ready to repel attackers. While provision of a walkway on Hadrian's Wall is possible, even likely, on structural grounds, the argument that that was the norm on linear barriers is undermined because the analogy cannot be extended to other frontiers. A walkway on the Antonine Wall would have required a well-founded palisade to the front, but we have no evidence that the turf rampart was provided with any form of timber superstructure, which makes the traditional reconstructions problematic (Hanson and Maxwell 1986, 81–3). Moreover, clearly neither the main phases of the German frontier, with its free-standing timber palisade, nor the later narrow (1–1.2 m wide) stone wall in Raetia, can have sustained a walkway. Nor is the defensive logic of such a facility readily apparent, as it flies in the face of normal Roman practice which was to respond to threats or attacks by undertaking a campaign against the aggressors. What is indisputable, however, is that these additional defensive provisions on both Hadrian's Wall and the Antonine Wall clearly indicate considerable concern to prevent, or at least discourage, unauthorised crossing of the mural barrier.

This brings us back to the functional equivalence between linear barriers and rivers, which is important because the latter were the most common geographical features employed within Roman frontier systems. Twenty-five years ago, following the prevailing view at the time (e.g. Mann 1974, 513), I emphasized the role of rivers as geographically convenient lines of demarcation, drawing attention to their greater effectiveness as lines of communication than as natural barriers because they are far too easy to cross. This view has almost certainly been overstated and the importance of the major rivers of Europe as barriers should be re-emphasised. Rankov (2005) has surveyed a range of literary and epigraphic sources which show that the Romans regarded great rivers as protecting the empire and has drawn attention to the difficulty, in the absence of regular bridges, of crossing them in the face of an organised force which controlled river traffic. Meanwhile, Sommer (2009) has emphasised the consistent positioning of forts and fortresses along the major rivers at points of change in topography from where it was easy to control traffic along them. Finally, in some areas, such as along the Danube in Raetia in the pre-Flavian period, fortlets provided virtually the only garrison posts for long stretches (Symonds 2009, 957), which implies that the river itself was considered a sufficiently good security cordon not to require major garrisons.

Nonetheless, it remains the case that, in purely military terms, artificial linear barriers were not strategically effective. Their construction would not help the Roman army to combat any major incursion, since external forces could mass at whatever point they chose, outnumber the local defenders and, thus, readily breach the barrier before sufficient defensive reinforcements could be summoned to the spot. We know that this did, indeed, occur on Hadrian's Wall in the early 180s when several forts were overrun and destroyed, after which a major campaign under Ulpius Marcellus was necessary to restore peace on the northern frontier (Breeze and Dobson 2000, 133–35). Such substantive threats were far better dealt with by concentrations of forces with the ability to deploy quickly beyond the barrier. It was precisely for this reason that when forts were moved onto the line of Hadrian's Wall during the course of its construction, they were configured so that multiple gates opened to the north. This provision was later done away with, but is best seen as a response, a knee-jerk reaction, to an earlier perceived inability rapidly to deploy troops beyond the Wall.

Linear barriers could slow down such an attack and were impressive, highly visible, physical statements of Roman power and authority whose demotivating impact on potential aggressors is likely to have been considerable. Probably more importantly, however, they would effectively have excluded small-scale illicit movement such as border raiding or rustling. That this level of infiltration was a concern on other Roman frontiers is confirmed by a series of inscriptions from the Danube bend in the reign of Commodus (ILS 395), each of which provides an unusual level of information about their function, stating that towers (*burgi*) and fortlets/garrisons (*praesidia*) were being constructed to prevent the secret crossing of the river by robbers (*latrunculi*).

But what then was the strategic function of the provision of a regular series of gateways at fortlets located every mile along both Hadrian's Wall and, probably, the Antonine Wall? If, as argued above, the primary intention of these linear barriers was to exclude, such provision would have been both unnecessary and potentially disadvantageous, since gateways are a weak point in any defensive circuit. It was this over-provision of gateways which led to the suggestion that linear frontiers may have had a different, more administrative function: that they were intended to facilitate the closer control of peaceful small-scale local movement across the frontier (Breeze and Dobson 2000, 39–40; Hanson and Maxwell 1986, 164). Thus, it was argued that funnelling all legitimate movement through regular gateways under military supervision would have facilitated security control and eased the levying of customs dues. In 1989 I quoted several examples of such control being exercised along major European river frontiers (Hanson 1989, 60), but I have grown increasingly unhappy with the assumptions on which this more socio-economic interpretation of the operation of linear barriers is based.

Firstly, it is clear that the original function of the milecastles (fortlets) on Hadrian's Wall was to house the garrison for the turrets (watchtowers) and to allow the army readily through the barrier when they were housed in forts along the Stanegate to the rear. It is only the continued use of milecastle gates once the main garrison had been moved up to the line of the Wall, and the inclusion of similar fortlets in the blueprint for the Antonine Wall, which supports the wider socio-economic administrative function attributed to them. However, it is clear that the need for milecastles on Hadrian's Wall was much reduced when the forts were moved up to the Wall line. Most had their northern gateways reduced in width or entirely blocked by the end of the second century (Breeze and Dobson 2000, 146); causeways across the Wall ditch seem to have been largely removed, probably on the refurbishment of the Wall in the later second century (Welfare 2000); while construction of the Vallum had already effectively cut off access through the barrier via the milecastles in the Hadrianic period. Though a regular sequence of fortlets does seem to have been provided on the Antonine Wall *de novo*, this may simply reflect the fact that in its original form it was modelled on the plan of Hadrian's Wall. It should not be forgotten that the Roman army was still in the process of amending the former when they gave it up to build the latter. Nonetheless, the fortlets on the Antonine Wall also seem to go out of use very quickly when more forts were added to its line during construction. Thus, though the fortlet at Duntocher continued in use, it was incorporated into the new small fort there, while the interiors of the fortlets at Wilderness Plantation, Kinneil and possibly Seabegs Wood seem to have been cobbled over (Breeze 2006, 94–5).

Most significant for the present argument, however, is the situation on the German and Raetian frontiers. Over and above those known at or near forts, there is no regular provision of gateways through the linear barrier. The system of fortlets is generally less regular than along Hadrian's Wall; they consistently sit 20–50 m or more behind the frontier line; and they are not necessarily associated with gateways through the barrier (Symonds 2009, 961). The occurrence of gateways varies considerably, both in terms of size and distribution, on different stretches of the frontier. The most common are quite constricted, usually located by watchtowers, suggesting that they are most likely to have been provided to facilitate maintenance of the frontier by the military garrison (Hodgson 2005). These crossing points contrast markedly with some on the Raetian frontier which carried roads through the mural barrier. It would appear that Rome did not envisage regular, frequent controlled crossing of the linear barrier in either Germany or Raetia, except possibly in very limited areas. Thus, the primary purpose of the linear barriers in those two provinces was to discourage or prevent access to the empire. Though it may be the case that some areas beyond the frontier were not densely populated, that certainly does not apply everywhere and there would have been little point expending the huge resources necessary to construct and garrison such a frontier if the population beyond it was so limited and widely dispersed.

It has always been accepted that Roman frontiers were primarily military in character as they were built and operated by the army and housed the troops who defended the empire against external threat. However, we should also now accept that the requirements of exclusion and military defence at different scales of operation were the primary criteria applied in determining their location and design. This is not to suggest that no movement in or out of the empire was envisaged. Obviously, Roman troops needed to be able to access areas beyond the frontiers to undertake campaigns or respond to threats, and there is strong archaeological evidence of Roman material culture finding its way into the settlements of the indigenous population outside the empire, as the 'Corpus der römischen Funde im europäischen Barbaricum' is gradually elucidating across Europe. However, that is not the same as arguing that Roman frontiers in their most developed form were intended to be highly porous, or that one of their primary emphases was on economic regulation and control.

Classical and epigraphic sources

Dio Cassius, *A History of Rome* (Translation: Cary, E. 1914–27 *Dio's Roman History*, Cambridge/London).

ILS *Inscriptiones Latinae Selectae*, Dessau, H. (ed.) 1892–1916, Berlin.

Res Gestae Divi Augusti, The Achievements of the Divine Augustus, Brunt, P. A and Moore, J. M. (eds), 1967, Oxford.

Scriptores Historiae Augustae (Translation: Magie, D. 1921–32 *The Scriptores Historiae Augustae*, London/Cambridge).

Tacitus, *De vita Agricolae* (Translation: Birley, A. R. 1999 *Tacitus, Agricola and Germany*, Oxford).

Tacitus, *Annales* (Translation: Jackson, J. 1931–1937 *The Annals of Tacitus*, London/Cambridge).

Bibliography

Baatz, D. (2000) *Der römische Limes. Archäologische Ausflüge zwischen Rhein und Donau*. Berlin.

Barrett, A. A. (1989) *Caligula: the corruption of power.* London.

Bidwell, P. (2005) The systems of obstacles on Hadrians Wall: their extent, date and purpose. *Arbeia Journal* 8, 53–76.

Bidwell, P. (2008) Did Hadrian's Wall have a wall walk? In P. Bidwell (ed.) *Understanding Hadrian's Wall*, 129–43. Kendal.

Breeze, D. J. (1982) *The northern frontiers of Roman Britain*. London.

Breeze, D. J. (2006) *The Antonine Wall.* Edinburgh.

Breeze, D. J. and Dobson, B. (2000) *Hadrian's Wall* (4th edn). London.

Dobat, E. (2009) The Gask 'system' in Perthshire: the first artificial frontier line of the Roman empire? In D. J. Breeze, L. M. Thoms and D. W. Hall (eds) *First Contact: Rome and northern Britain*, 39–48. Perth.

Hanson, W. S. (1980) Agricola on the Forth–Clyde isthmus. *Scottish Archaeological Forum* 12, 55–68.

Hanson, W. S. (1989) The nature and function of Roman frontiers. In J. C. Barrett, A. P. Fitzpatrick and L. Macinnes (eds.) *Barbarians and Romans in north-west Europe: from the later Republic to late Antiquity*, 55–63. Oxford.

Hanson, W. S. (1991) Tacitus' 'Agricola': an archaeological and historical study. In W. Haase and H. Temporini (eds) *Aufstieg und Niedergang der römischen Welt* II 33.3, 1741–84. de Gruyter, Berlin.

Hanson, W. S. (2002) Why did the Roman Empire cease to expand? In P. Freeman, J. Bennett, Z. T. Fiema and B. Hoffman (eds) *Limes XVIII. Proceedings of the XVIIIth International Congress of Roman Frontiers Studies held in Amman, Jordan (September 2000)*. British Archaeological Report 1084, 25–34. Oxford.

Hanson, W. S. (2009) The fort at Elginhaugh and its implications for Agricola's role in the conquest of Scotland. In D. J. Breeze, L. M. Thoms and D. W. Hall (eds) *First Contact. Rome and northern Britain*, 49–58. Perth.

Hanson, W. S. and Maxwell, G. S. (1986) *Rome's north-west frontier: the Antonine Wall* (2nd edn). Edinburgh.

Hanson, W. S. and Oltean, I. A. (2012) The 'Valu lui Traian': a Roman frontier rehabilitated. *JRA* 25, 297–318.

Hobley, A. S. (1989) The numismatic evidence for the post-Agricolan abandonment of the Roman frontier in Northern Scotland. *Britannia* 20, 69–74.

Hodgson, N. (2000) The Stanegate: a frontier rehabilitated. *Britannia* 31, 11–22.

Hodgson, N. (2005) Gates and passage across the frontiers. In Z. Visy (ed.) *Limes XIX. Proceedings of the XIXth International Congress of Roman Frontier Studies,* 183–88. Pecs.

Isaac, B. (1990) *The limits of empire: The Roman army in the East* (rev. edn). Oxford.

Kolendo, J. (1982) Le projet d'expédition de Néron dans le Caucase. In J. M. Croisille, and P. M. Fauchère (eds) *Neronia 1977*, 23–30. Clermont Ferrand.

Kortüm, K. (1998) Zur Datierung der römischen Militäranlagen im obergermanisch-rätischen Grenzgebiet: Chronologische Untersuchungen anhand der Münzfund. *Saalburg-Jahrbuch* 49, 5–65.

Langeveld, M. C. M., Luksen-Ijtsma, A and Graafstal, E. P. (2010) *Wegens Wateroverlast. LR 39 De Balije II:*

wachttorens, rivierdynamiek en Romeinse infrastructuur in een rivierbocht van de Heldammer Stroom. Utrecht.

Mann, J. C. (1974) The frontiers of the Roman principate. In H. Temporini (ed.) *Aufstieg und Niedergang der Römischen Welt*, II, 1, 508–33. Berlin.

Maxwell, G. S. (1977) A linear defence system in south-western Scotland. In D. Haupt and H. G. Horn (eds) *Studien zu den Militärgrenzen Roms, II*, 23–30. Cologne/Bonn.

Planck, D. (1987) Ein bisher unbekannter römischer Limes im Lautertal bei Dettingen unter Teck, Kreis Esslingen, *Fundberichte aus Baden-Württemberg* 12, 405–29.

Rankov, B. (2005) Do rivers make good frontiers? In Z. Visy (ed.) *Limes XIX. Proceedings of the XIXth International Congress of Roman Frontier Studies,* 175–81. Pecs.

Reuter, M. (2004) Die römischen Kleinkastelle von Hanau-Mittelbuchen und der Verlauf des östlichen Wetteraulimes under Domitian. In E. Schallmayer (ed.) *Limes Imperii Romanii. Beitrage sum Fachkolloquium 'Weltkulturerbe Limes' November 2001 in Lich-Arnsburg*, 97–106. Bad Homburg.

Schallmayer, E. (2005) Zur Frage der Palisade am Obergermanisch-Raetischen Limes im 3 Jahrhundert n. Chr. In Z. Visy (ed.) *Limes XIX. Proceedings of the XIXth International Congress of Roman Frontier Studies,* 801–13. Pecs.

Sommer, C. S. (2009) Why there? – The positioning of forts along the riverine frontiers of the Roman Empire. In W. S. Hanson (ed.) *The army and frontiers of Rome. Papers offered to David Breeze on the occasion of his sixty-fifth birthday and his retirement from Historic Scotland*, 103–14. Portsmouth, Rhode Island.

Symonds, M. (2009) Fortlets and their adaptation for artificial frontiers. In A. Morillo Cerdán, N. Hanel and E. Martín (eds) *Limes XX: XX congreso internacional de estudios sobre la frontera romana*, 955–63. Madrid.

Thiel, A. (2008) Innovation and perfection: Antoninus Pius' frontier in Germany. In P. Bidwell (ed.) *Understanding Hadrian's Wall*, 83–90. Kendal.

Thiel, A. (2009a) The Odenwald *limes* and its relation to Antonine Wall. In W.S. Hanson (ed.) *The army and frontiers of Rome. Papers offered to David Breeze on the occasion of his sixty-fifth birthday and his retirement from Historic Scotland*, 134–41. Portsmouth, Rhode Island.

Thiel, A. (2009b) Der limes wird geschlossen. Zum Begin durchgehender Grenzbefestigungen in Südwestdeutschland. In A. Morillo Cerdán, N. Hanel and E. Martín (eds.) *Limes XX: XX congreso internacional de estudios sobre la frontera romana*, 977–87. Madrid.

Tomlin, R. S. O. and Hassall, M. W. C. (2004) Roman Britain in 2003. III. Inscriptions. *Britannia* 35, 335–349.

von Schnurbein, S. (2003) Augustus in Germania and his new 'town' at Waldgirmes east of the Rhine. *Journal of Roman Archaeology* 16, 93–107.

Welfare, H. (2000) Causeways at milecastles across the ditch of Hadrian's Wall. *Archaeologia Aeliana* (ser. 5), 28, 13–25.

Whittaker, C. R. (2004) *Rome and its frontiers: the dynamics of empire.* London.

Woolliscroft, D. (2009) 79 AD and all that: when did the Romans first invade central Scotland? In D. J. Breeze, L. M. Thoms and D. W. Hall (eds) *First Contact: Rome and northern Britain*, 33–8. Perth.

3

THE ROMAN ARMY AND THE ROMAN SMITH: SOME EVIDENCE FROM BRITAIN

W. H. Manning

The army was one of the major consumers of iron in the Roman world, but its most obvious iron equipment, the armour and weapons of its soldiers, represented only a fraction of the iron which it required. Most soldiers were equipped with a variety of entrenching tools; their heavy equipment and *ballistae* were carried on carts which had iron fittings, and all of the units, both legionary and auxiliary, had large numbers of trained craftsmen who used iron tools, as well as wide range of agricultural implements, cooking equipment and the like. When the army arrived in Britain in AD 43 it brought all of this equipment with it. In the Roman world metals were far too valuable not to be recycled, and the army will have continued to use the iron which came with it through the centuries which followed, not in the form in which it arrived but as a major source of scrap which could be used repeatedly to manufacture new equipment. Indeed it is probably true to say that most of the iron which was used by the invading army of AD 43 is still in use today. Newly smelted iron will only have been necessary to top-up this the endless cycle of use and re-use. But there was one area, construction, where, at least for the first century of the Roman occupation, the army will have required large quantities of new iron, most of it almost certainly newly smelted. Even in the early years of the conquest the army had winter quarters and in these early forts almost all of the buildings were of wood. The amount of iron which was used in such timber buildings was dramatically shown in 1960 by the discovery of a pit in the late first-century legionary fortress at Inchtuthil containing some 10 tons of nails, many of them bent and distorted as a result of their being withdrawn from timbers during the demolition of the fortress (Pitts and St Joseph 1985, 109–13, pls xix–xx; 289*ff.*)

Much of the iron needed for the construction of the first forts to be built after the invasion probably came from the Continent, for although iron figures in Strabo's list of exports from Britain to the Roman world at the beginning of the first century AD (Strabo 4.5.2.) it is unlikely that the Iron Age iron industry had much spare capacity. However, within a few years of the conquest the demands, not only of the Roman army but of the rapidly developing urban structure of the new province, will have led to a commensurate increase in iron smelting. No fewer than 10 legionary fortresses, not to mention scores of smaller forts, were built in the 60 or so years after the invasion of AD 43. Then came the construction of Hadrian's Wall with its associated forts and a few years later the Antonine Wall. But after that only a handful of new bases were built, perhaps most notably the forts of the Saxon Shore, suggesting that after the mid-second century the army's demands for iron for use in construction work will have declined rapidly. In fact this reduction probably began before then for as each old fort was demolished much of the iron used in its construction will have been reused elsewhere.

The demand for iron created by the developing urban infrastructure of the province will have run in parallel with the military requirements, and from the end of the first century when the cantonal capitals were developing, civilian consumption probably greatly exceeded the military. A major factor in the growth of the iron industry will have been the developed economic infrastructure of the Roman Empire. In the largely *laissez faire* economy which prevailed in the Roman world, the greatly increased demand for iron which followed the Roman conquest will have resulted in a corresponding increase in its production. Cleere and Crossley estimated the annual production of the iron industry in the Weald of Kent before AD 100 at around 150 tons a year rising to 700 tons a year in the first half of the second century (Cleere and Crossley 1985, 81). Such figures cannot be exact, but they probably give an idea of the quantities involved.

The furnace normally used in Roman Britain was a simple shaft furnace. A few larger forms are known, such as those found at Laxton in Northamptonshire which Peter Crewe has suggested could have produced up to five 20 kg blooms at a time (Crew 1998, 51), but these appear to have been exceptional and we still await experimental confirmation that they were capable of producing blooms on this scale.

In recent years there have been a number of experiments in smelting iron using reconstructions of Roman shaft furnaces. Of these the work of the Americans, Lee Sauder and Skip Williams is among the best quantified and it is instructive to apply their figures to the Inchtuthil nails (Sauder and Williams 2002). They found that the production of an artefact weighing 1.0 kg required 8.3 kg of iron ore. All of the stages in this process used charcoal, which was the only fuel suitable for metallurgical processes available to the Romans, and the creation of their 1 kg artefact consumed no less than 82 kg of charcoal. The estimated weight of the Inchtuthil nails was 10 English tons but it was an estimated weight and it is possible to substitute the metric tonne of 1,000 kg without creating any significant error in the calculations. Taking the figure of 82 kg of charcoal being required to produce 1 kg of finished artefacts, the production of ten tonnes of nails will have consumed 820 tonnes of charcoal. Some 6.5 kg of wood are needed to make 1kg of charcoal, which means that around 5,330 tonnes of timber will have been consumed in the production of the Inchtuthil nails. In medieval and later times the wood used was almost always coppiced. Whether this technique was used in the Roman period is uncertain, but if it was not practiced the major iron smelting industries, which, for obvious reasons, were concentrated in the areas where the ores were found, would rapidly have destroyed the suitable timber in their area. In fact the evidence from the Weald of Kent, which is the mining area which has been most extensively studied, suggests that production continued unabated for several centuries (Cleere and Crossley 1985, 60*ff.*). The evidence for the type of charcoal used is limited, but Sim and Ridge cite work which suggests that oak was the wood preferred in the Weald of Kent in the Roman period (Sim and Ridge 2002, 38). In modern practice, a hectare of coppiced oak trees, which are harvested on a cycle of between 25 and 30 years, will yield around 3 tonnes of wood each year. If that figure is applied to the Inchtuthil nails the area required to produce the required 5,330 tons of wood is 1,777 ha or 4,390 acres. This is an area almost 13 times the size of Hyde Park, and Inchtuthil is only one of at least 10 legionary fortresses built in the 50 years after the invasion of AD 43. David Sim and Isabel Ridge (2002, 115), who have made replicas of the types of nails found at Inchtuthil, estimate that forging the nails in the hoard would have taken some 60,000 hours of work.

A question of fundamental importance is whether the army produced the iron objects which they used or simply bought them from contractors? The answer provided by literature and archaeology is that they probably made quite a lot of their own equipment, but by no means all of it. There are two key documents; the first is in the *Digest* which, although compiled in the sixth century AD cited many earlier authorities (*Digest* 50.6.7). The relevant passage dates from the late second century and refers to *immunes*, men who were exempt from some routine military duties because they were specialists who had more important commitments. It begins: 'Certain soldiers are granted by their conditions of service some exemption from the heavier fatigues.' Then comes a long list of craftsmen: 'Glaziers, craftsmen (the word used is the generic term *fabri*), arrow-makers, coppersmiths, helmet-makers, wagon-makers, makers of wooden roofing shingles (*scandularii*), sword-smiths, trumpet-makers, horn-makers, bow-makers, lead-workers, blacksmiths, lime-burners, wood-cutters and charcoal burners.'

The number of trades involved confirms that the *Digest* was referring primarily to the legions, which, with around 5,000 men, had the capacity to maintain a large number of specialists, many of whom would already have had a trade when they were recruited. Most soldiers were in their late teens or early 20s when they enlisted and, as they came from the working class, most of them will have been working for several years before they entered the army. One of the interesting points about the list in the *Digest* is the high degree of self-sufficiency which it reveals; not only are there metalworkers but there are the woodcutters and charcoal burners necessary to ensure a constant supply of the fuel needed by the smiths. It also reveals a high degree of specialisation; the copper smiths do not make the trumpets and horns which the army used to communicate commands. Nor did the ordinary blacksmiths make helmets or swords, these were the preserve of specialised craftsmen.

The second source, Vegetius, wrote at the end of the fourth century AD but referred to an earlier period. In his day the production of military equipment was concentrated in great factories run by the state and his work reflects his rather futile longing for the glories (as he saw them) of the past. He wrote:

> 'The legion also had workmen, carpenters, masons, wagon-makers, blacksmiths, painters and other craftsmen for the construction of buildings in the winter-quarters (i.e. the legionary fortresses) … to make new arms, wagons and other kinds of torsion-engines, or repair them when damaged. They also used to have workshops for shields, cuirasses and bows, in which arrows, missiles, helmets and arms of every type were made.' (Vegetius II, 11)

A papyrus from Egypt, probably written in the second or third century AD, provides some confirmation of what Vegetius and the *Digest* tell us. Although fragmentary it is a record of two days' activity in a legionary *fabrica*; 100 men were employed making among other things swords, two sorts of shields, iron–plates, bows, and catapult fittings (Bishop 1985).

The *Digest* and Vegetius were concerned with the legions, and the question of specialised craftsmen within the auxiliary units remained somewhat obscure until the discovery of the Vindolanda Tablets. Indeed it was possible to argue that the auxiliary units, which usually had no more than one-tenth of the number of men in a legion, did not have the necessary craftsmen to have been self-sufficient in more than the most basic of tasks. But the Vindolanda tablets, which date from between AD 90 and 120, are concerned with auxiliary units. Most are no more than tantalising fragments and even the better preserved ones are rarely complete, but a few contain references which are directly relevant to the question of workmen in the *auxilia*.

The first is fragmentary but it contains a specific reference to the *Fabricae* – the workshops (Bowman and Thomas 1983, 81*ff*.).

> April 25, in the workshops, 343 men. Of these shoemakers, 12; builders, to the bath-house 18; for lead …; to the kilns …; for clay …; plasterers …; for rubble …

None of these men were concerned with smithing, but the list does indicate a degree of specialisation not only in the building crafts but also in shoe-making, a craft omitted from the *Digest* and Vegetius. It is interesting to note that although the list begins with a reference to *fabricis*, translated as 'in the workshops', most of these men were actually working outside on kilns (probably producing tiles) and building a bath-house. In effect, the word was being used to refer to men who were exercising their crafts rather than a specific building.

The second reference (Bowman and Thomas 1983, 81*ff*.) is even more fragmentary but it contains a number of significant words including three references to *faber*, the generic Latin word for a craftsman, and one to a […]*utarius*. Although the word is incomplete almost certainly it was *scutarius* a shield maker; a suggestion which is strengthened by references in other tablets to *Lucius scutarius* and *Crescens scutarius*. (Bowman, Thomas and Tomlin 2010, 207). Another word is *gladi*[...], again incomplete but a word which can be safely identified as a swordsmith, a craft mentioned in the *Digest*. This tablet leaves little doubt that the unit then in garrison at Vindolanda had specialist craftsmen including swordsmiths and shield makers, and by a logical extension, facilities for them to work in, a *fabrica*.

Perhaps the most informative of the Vindolanda tablets is No. 862 (Bowman, Thomas and Tomlin 2010, 210*ff*.) which provides details of the work done in the *fabrica* by the century of Firmus on 20 April in an unknown year.

> 20 April, craftsmen for
> The work of the workshop (*fabricae*),
> Century of Firmus.
> A *uocros* made for a vehicle,
> By order of Musurunus, centurion
> [*c*]*ircolas* made … to the number of 8.
> Huennius (?) craftsman (*faber*).
> Cross-bars (*trauersaria*) made, to the number of 5.
> Also iron drawn out. (*item ferrum [p]roductum*)
> Andauer craftsman, (*faber*)
> Tagomas craftsman (*faber*)

Some of the technical terms are extremely obscure and one of them, *vocris*, is otherwise unknown. It probably refers to part of the framework of a wagon which could have been made of wood but was more probably of iron. Roman wagons could have a surprising number of elaborate iron elements in their frames, as the pieces found in the great deposit from the Rhine at Neupotz showed (Künzl 1993,Teil 1, 257*ff*.), and the *vocris* may be one of them. The *circolas* were obviously circular and the editors suggested that they were tyres, but if we are dealing with the products of a single day, as the provision of the date, 20 April, suggests, eight tyres seems an improbably high number and some other circular fitting such as nave hoops may be more likely. The line *item ferrum [p]roductum*, translated by the editors as 'Also iron drawn out', probably refers to the preparation of bars and rods from the billets. All of the workmen are called *faber* which in this context probably means master craftsmen. That they were smiths may be deduced from the reference to the working of iron.

The evidence for smiths within both the legionary and auxiliary elements of the Roman army is clear, but what does archaeology have to tell us of the *fabricae* in which they worked? Both legionary fortresses and auxiliary forts contain buildings of fairly standard types which were almost certainly either workshops or store buildings or, quite probably, both (Petrikovits 1974, 82*ff.*). The British legionary fortresses of which we have the most complete plans are Caerleon and Inchtuthil. Recent geophysical surveys undertaken by Dr Tim Young and the Department of Archaeology at Cardiff University have filled most of the major gaps in the plan of the masonry phase of Caerleon and we now know of no fewer than four large buildings which can be identified as workshops and stores within the fortress (Burnham and Davies 2010, 163, fig. 7.3). Too little work has been done on most of them for any useful discussion of their precise functions but they provide ample space for all of the crafts listed in the *Digest*. The only thoroughly excavated part of any of them is one of the outer buildings of the complex to the east of the granaries which was excavated by Andrew Gardener and Peter Guest, who showed that it was probably a stores building. The discovery of fragments of *lorica segmentata*, spearheads and other military material in one of the rooms would accord with its having been a store for material collected for recycling but abandoned with the building (Chapman 2011, 324).

The late first century timber-built fortress at Inchtuthil in Scotland had a characteristic *fabrica*, with three great basilical halls around a central courtyard which was fronted by four large rooms. It was there that the pit with the great deposit of nails was found, no doubt because the *fabrica* was the place where scrap metal was stored ready for reuse (Pitts and St Joseph 1985, 104*ff.*). Continental fortresses contain very similar buildings although few of them have been sufficiently thoroughly explored to have produced firm evidence of smithing, or indeed of any other craft (Petrikovits 1974, 82*ff.*).

The Vindolanda Tablets leave no doubt that auxiliary units had their own skilled craftsmen, and possible *fabricae* have been identified in a number of auxiliary forts. Such buildings are usually similar in size to a barrack block but have far fewer internal partitions. Perhaps the most complete ones are the four pairs of double workshops, each 72 ft (22 m) long and 10 ft (3 m) wide, in the Severan military works compound at Corbridge. They contained small water tanks and furnaces but there was no obvious sign of hearth bases. However, the evidence of sculpture and frescoes indicates that the Roman smith, like his modern successors, did not crouch on the floor when working but had both his hearth and work-bench raised to a convenient height so that he could work either standing or sitting. The floors of the Corbridge *fabricae* had been flagged and later robbing, which removed many of these flags, will have destroyed the evidence for any masonry bases which stood on them.

A number of questions remain. What were these military smiths using as their raw materials? What were they producing? Were the military units actually self-sufficient in making the multiplicity of iron tools, weapons and fittings which even the smallest unit required? It is clear that in the ancient world (as in later periods) it was normal practice to recycle scrap metal. This is shown by the Inchtuthil nails and it can also be seen in the fort at Newstead where James Curle's excavations discovered a mass of equipment buried in a pit (Pit XVI) outside the fort (Curle 1911, 119). In almost all cases this equipment was either hopelessly damaged or in need of repair, often perhaps no more than the replacement of a wooden handle but, none-the-less, a repair which required some degree of expertise. The obvious explanation is that it was material which had been returned to the fort's *fabrica* as scrap or for repair and was still there when the fort was dismantled early in the second century.

However, newly smelted iron will have been needed not only to top-up the scrap material but to make the great number of iron structural fittings needed when a fort or fortress was built, and here again Newstead provides the evidence for this in the form of five billets, blocks of iron each weighing between 6 and 7.5 kg (Curle 1911, 288, pl. lxv, 9). Such billets are rare, although a few others are known including four from the fort at Strageath (Frere and Wilkes 1989, 176), but they must represent the form in which newly smelted iron reached the Roman army.

At the end of his list of craftsmen in the Roman legion, Vegetius wrote of the *praefectus fabrorum* who was in charge of the legionary workshops, 'His main responsibility was to ensure that nothing which the army was thought to require should be lacking in camp …', which implies that the legion (and he was writing of the legions) was capable of producing all the equipment which it needed. Was he correct? After all, he was writing at least a century after the disappearance of the large legions of the early empire. The answer appears to be not completely.

To modern eyes it seems somewhat surprising that the Roman soldier had to buy his own equipment and clothing. The most specific statement on this occurs in Tacitus' *Annals* (I, 17) where he has the leader of a mutiny in AD 14 say that one of their grievances was the fact that out of their daily pay of 10 *asses* they had to buy their clothing, their weapons and their tents. That this was indeed the case is confirmed by a number of texts from Egypt which record deductions for weapons and clothing (Watson 1969, 103; 220). That it was normal practice with the auxiliaries as well was confirmed by a recently published tablet from Vindolanda which lists the men who had bought spears and clothing and the prices they paid. The inclusion of a table and cloak in this list suggests that the transactions were between the soldiers and a civilian entrepreneur, as the editors suggested, rather than purchases from an official source. But whatever their source the key fact is that the men were paying for their weapons (Bowman, Thomas and Tomlin 2010, 204*ff.*).

A.m[ ]tus
Spears, denarius 1, asses 2
Goua[ ]us
Table (?), denarii 2
Spears, denarius 1
Alb[ ]us
Spears, denarius 1
Liber
Cloak, denarii 2
Tagomas the vexillarius
Spears, denarius 1
Victor, the huntsman
Spears, denarii 5

If such weapons were the personal property of the soldier one might wonder why so few are marked with any form of identification. Some are, a spearhead from Newstead, for example, has an inscription formed of punched dots which firmly states that it was the property of a cavalryman, one, Trinus (or Trinius), of the troop of Bassus (Curle 1911, 188, fig. 20, pl. xxxvi, 5; Frere and Tomlin 1991, 51, 2427.3). But the answer probably lies in the fact that all spears originally had wooden hafts where a name or identifying mark could have been cut.

Further evidence that soldiers owned their equipment is provided by an Egyptian papyrus of AD 143 which records the refunds for a soldier's equipment, including his share of a tent, which were made to his mother after his death (Bishop and Coulston 2006, 262). The *Lex Julia de vi publica* forbade the carrying of arms by civilians, save for spears which were used for hunting or necessary for self-defence on a journey (*Digest* xlviii, vi, i), and when a soldier retired or died his equipment was probably sold to his fellow soldiers, although it is clear that some of the cavalry were allowed to retain their elaborate parade armour. Successive ownership of military equipment is shown by the fact that several helmets are known from Britain and elsewhere which bear a series of ownership graffiti (Frere and Tomlin 1991, 44*ff.*, 2425.2 from London; 2425.3 from Verulamium; 2425.6 from Ribchester). To take one example, a cavalry parade helmet from the fort at Newstead has a series of graffiti on its neck-guard (Manning 2005, fig. 12). The longest one reads: *Rufi t(urma) Atinia(na)* '(Property) of Rufus, (former) troop of Atinus'. But there are four others. Three are simply numerals IIII, X, and XII, while the fourth is the beginning of a name, probably originally six letters long, reading IMA... Taken together they suggest that this particular helmet had had at least five owners before it became so dilapidated that it was scrapped (Frere and Tomlin 1991, 46, 2425.4; revised readings by R. S. O. Tomlin and the writer).

In addition to their clothing and weapons, a soldier had a number of tools; including an entrenching tool, the *dolabra*, as well as, at least in some cases, craft tools, and it is clear that some of the tools used at Newstead were the work of civilian smiths for they are stamped with the maker's names. Thus two *dolabrae* bear the names of Atticus and Vindissus, while an axe carries the stamp LGR, the initials of the maker (Frere and Tomlin 1991, 58, 2428.3; 62, 2428.18; 59, 2428.4). This latter also has a punched inscription giving the name of its owner 'The century of Barrus, (property) of Compitalicus'. Tools stamped with the maker's mark are rare in Britain. The relevant section of *The Roman Inscriptions of Britain* (Frere and Tomlin 1991, 58*ff.*) records, in addition to the Newstead pieces, stamps on three chisels, two leather-worker's awls, two styli and eight knives, the great majority coming from London. No doubt some stamps have been concealed or destroyed by corrosion, but it is clear that most smiths never stamped their products, and the evidence suggests that after the first century AD stamping effectively ceased, at least in Britain. Given this, the absence of maker's marks does not imply that they were not the work of civilian smiths. All in all the evidence which we have indicates that some tools at least were acquired from civilian smiths and owned by the soldiers who used them, but whether this was the norm remains uncertain.

From all of this it would seem that the soldiers, both auxiliary and legionary, bought much of their own equipment, but the various texts make it equally clear that the *fabricae* of both the legions and at least some of the auxiliary units were capable of producing a wide range of equipment. Much of it, such as the carts being made at Vindolanda, would have been the property of the unit, but other things, for example the work of shoe makers, or of the shield makers Lucius and Crescens, and the probable sword smith, was equipment which one would have thought was of the type which the soldiers would have been expected to buy. Did the troopers at Vindolanda have to buy the work of their fellow soldiers, or did these things fall into the category of equipment which was issued?

One thing which is clear is that even the auxiliary *fabricae* were extremely well equipped. Perhaps the best evidence for this from Britain comes from the fort at Newstead where we find examples of tools used in most of the processes involved in working iron, including the smith's rake, tongs, hammers of various weights, chisels, punches and files (Curle 1911, 285 *ff.* pl. lxiii). Carpentry, which will have been another major element of the work of the *fabrica*, is equally well represented with axes, chisels, gouges drill bits, saws (Curle 1911, 280*ff.*, pls lix, lxi, lxviii) and even the blade of a moulding plane, indicating that the carpenters of the fort were producing some relatively sophisticated work (Curle 1911, 281, pl. lix, 2). A similar blade from Vindolanda was found to have a steel edge (Sim and Ridge 2000). Many of these tools are of the highest quality and they are only a tiny fraction of those which must have been used in the fort. Clearly even in auxiliary units we are dealing with skilled specialists.

The use of tools which were produced by civilian smiths has already been discussed but there were probably other areas where specialists working outside the army regularly supplied equipment. The first is the production of chain mail, perhaps not the mail routinely used mainly by the auxiliaries, but the fine chain mail produced both in copper alloy and iron. The production of mail such as that found in the mid first-century fortress at Usk, with rings measuring around 2.5 mm in diameter, must surely have been the work of a specialist (Manning, Price and Webster 1995. 12*ff.*, pls i & ii). Another specialism may have been the production of the elaborately inlaid scabbards of the first-century legionary daggers (Manning, Price and Webster 1995, 22*ff.*). But the most likely of all to be the work of specialist craftsmen are the splendid parade helmets worn by the cavalry (Garbsch 1978).In describing these helmets in the *Ars Tactica* Arrian makes it clear that they were not standard issue:

> 'Those of the troopers who are distinguished in rank or are outstanding in horsemanship, come past armed with gilded bronze or iron helmets, so that in this way they draw the gaze of the spectators upon themselves. These helmets do not, like those made for battle protect only the head and the cheeks, but coincide completely with the faces of the horsemen with openings at the eyes' (Hyland 1993, 72).

Since they were private property which was not used in battle, such helmets could have been either sold to other troopers, as probably happened with the Newstead helmet referred to above, or retained when the owner retired from the army; a fact which is confirmed by the number which have been found in graves in the province of Thrace (Garbsch 1978; Manning 2005).

Acknowledgements

In preparing this paper I was greatly helped by the advice of Dr Tim Young and Dr Roger Tomlin, to both of whom I am most grateful.

References

Bishop, M. C. (1985) The Military Fabrica and the production of arms in the early Principate. In M. C. Bishop (ed.) *The Production and Distribution of Roman Military Equipment. Proceedings of the Second Roman Military Equipment Research Seminar,* BAR International Series 275, 1–42. Oxford.

Bishop, M. C. and Coulston, J. C. N. (2006) *Roman Military Equipment from the Punic Wars to the Fall of Rome.* Oxford.

Bowman, A. K. and Thomas, J. D. (1983) *Vindolanda: The Latin Writing-Tablets*. London, Society for the Promotion of Roman Studies.

Bowman, A. and Thomas, P. (1994) *The Vindolanda Writing Tablets (Tabulae Vindolanenses)* II. London, British Museum.

Bowman, A. K., Thomas, J. D. and Tomlin, R. S. O. (2010) The Vindolanda Writing-Tablets (*Tabulae Vindolandenses* IV, Part 1). *Britannia* 41, 187–224.

Burnham, B. and Davies, J. (2010) *Roman Frontiers in Wales and the Marches.* Aberystwyth, Royal Commission on the Ancient and Historical Monuments of Wales.

Chapman, E. M. (2011) Roman Britain in 2010: Wales. *Britannia* 42, 320–28.

Cleere, H. and Crossley, D. (1985) *The Iron Industry of the Weald.* Leicester, Leicester University Press.

Crew, P. (1998) Laxton revisited: a first report on the 1998 excavations. *Historical Metallurgy* 32.2, 49–53.

Curle, J. (1911) *A Roman Frontier Post and Its People. The Fort of Newstead.* Glasgow, James Maclehose and Sons.

Digest. The Digest or Pandects of Justinian.

Frere, S. S. and Wilkes, J. J. (1989) *Strageath. Excavations within the Roman Fort 1973–1986.* London, Society for the Promotion of Roman Studies.

Frere, S.S. and Tomlin, R. S. O. (1991) *The Roman Inscriptions of Britain.* II *Instrumentum Domesticum. Fascicule 3.* Stroud, Alan Sutton.

Garbsch, J. (1978) *Römische Paraderüstungen.* Munich, Verlag C. H. Beck.

Hyland, A. (1993). *Training Roman Cavalry. From Arrian's* Ars Tactica. Stroud, Sutton.

Künzl, E. (1993) *Die Alamannenbeute aus dem Rhein bei Neupotz.* Mainz, Verlag Römisch-Germanischen Zentral-museums.

Manning, W. (2005) The Newstead Parade Helmet. In N. Crummy (ed.) *Image, Craft and the Classical World. Essays in honour of Donald Bailey and Catherine Johns,* 119–41. Montagnac, Editions Monique Mergoil.

Manning, W. H., Price, J. and Webster, J. (1995) *Report on the Excavations at Usk 1965–1976. The Roman Small Finds.* Cardiff, University of Wales Press.

Petrikovits, H. von (1974) *Die Innenbauten römischer Legionslager während der Prinzipatzeit.* Opladen, Westdeutscher Verlag.

Pitts, L. F. and St Joseph J. K. (1985) *Inchtuthil. The Roman Legionary Fortress.* London, Society for the Promotion of Roman Studies.

Sauder, L. and Williams, S. (2002) A practical treatise on the smelting and smithing of bloomery iron. *Historical Metallurgy* 36.2, 122–31.

Sim, D. N. and Ridge, I. (2000) Examination of a moulding plane blade from Vindolanda. *Historical Metallurgy* 34.2, 77–82.

Sim, D. N. and Ridge, I. (2002) *Iron for the Eagles.* Stroud, Tempus.

Strabo *Geography.*

Tacitus *Annals.*

Vegetius *Epitome of Military Science.* (Translated Milner, N. P. 1993) Liverpool, Liverpool University Press.

Watson, G. R. (1969) *The Roman Soldier.* London, Thames and Hudson.

4

THE ACCOMMODATION OF SOLDIERS' WIVES IN ROMAN FORT BARRACKS – ON HADRIAN'S WALL AND BEYOND

Nick Hodgson

Introduction

One of Lindsay Allason-Jones' most important contributions has been to remind us (Allason-Jones 1999) how numerous and important women were in Roman military life, a familiar sight within the walls of forts and fortresses as well as in the extra-mural settlements. Her paper employed mainly epigraphic and archaeological evidence, but the Vindolanda writing tablets found from the 1970s onward have provided documentary evidence for 'the presence of women in the military ambit, some of them surely below the equestrian officer level' (Bowman and Thomas 1994, 29).

Despite a ban on soldiers contracting legally recognised marriages in the first two centuries AD, the discharge certificates ('diplomas') issued to some auxiliaries show that unofficial marriages were contracted and families raised, with the issue receiving citizenship on their father's discharge down to AD 140. After that only children born after his discharge and grant of *conubium* (legal right to marry a non-citizen) became citizens. The ban on soldiers' marriages was dissolved by Septimius Severus in AD 197 and shortly afterwards citizenship was extended to virtually all free inhabitants of the empire.

Everyone now accepts that the wives of equestrian officers lived with their husbands in the *praetoria* of first- and second-century forts – if there was ever room for doubt on this question, the Vindolanda tablets have removed it. Lindsay Allason-Jones argued that centurions were always immune from the marriage-ban and that their families lived with them in their accommodation at the end of barrack-blocks.

Others have gone even further and have claimed that, before the dissolution of the marriage-ban as well as after, the wives of the ordinary soldiers lived in the barrack *contubernia* rather than in the settlement outside the fort where archaeology has always found it most convenient to place them. Leading the way on this has been Carol van Driel Murray (1995, 12; cf. 1997), basing her conclusions on female-sized footwear found in certain rooms of a building interpreted as a barrack, in use *c.*AD 105–120 at Vindolanda, and on the analogy of the Dutch colonial army in nineteenth-century Indonesia, where native concubines cohabited with soldiers in barracks. She has argued that an officially sanctioned system of 'camp-concubinage' would have been usual in the Roman imperial army. This idea has been widely accepted, sometimes uncritically, sometimes with varying degrees of caution:

> '... it was C. van Driel Murray who showed through her analysis of the small finds contubernium by contubernium in one of the barrack blocks at Vindolanda that, here at least, women and children were accommodated within an auxiliary fort. And if at Vindolanda, why not elsewhere? ...'. (Hassall 1999, 39)

> 'Detailed examination of finds from barracks at Vindolanda has revealed an interesting level of artefacts relating to women and children ... If women were living in barracks designed for the lower ranks of an auxiliary unit, this suggests that the demarcation between soldier and civilian was rather more fluid than the normal fort and vicus model'. (Mattingly 2006, 170)

> 'The soldier ... might have a wife and children living outside the fort, or even in the barracks, on evidence from Vindolanda ...'. (Breeze and Dobson 2000, 190)

For more critical assessments see Rudán and Brandl 2008; Reuter 2008.

More recently Penelope Allison has studied the distribution of artefacts with female associations in a number of Roman forts in Germany and concluded that at two auxiliary forts, Oberstimm and Ellingen, 'there seems a prominent pattern for female residency within the barracks of ordinary soldiers ...' (Allison 2009, 1199; cf. Allison *et al.* 2005; Allison 2006a; 2006b).

The basic purpose of the present paper is to examine the structural and finds evidence from barracks in Roman forts to see whether it supports or goes against the idea that they accommodated soldiers' wives. The difficulties of attributing objects to purely female use (discussed in Allason-Jones 1995) are acknowledged, and in what follows LAJ's own working criteria of ear-rings, bracelets, hairpins, jet artefacts and in some circumstances beads have been adopted. Most of the examples will be drawn from Hadrian's Wall, because more barracks have been excavated on a large scale and using modern techniques on the Wall than anywhere else in the empire. It is worth looking at this question closely, for it was not specifically pursued in a recent discussion of barrack-life in the Wall-forts (Hodgson and Bidwell 2004). This is not a discussion of all the spaces in Roman forts in which women might have worked or lived. These were abundant and the recent attention paid to this neglected aspect of Roman fort life is welcome: for example writing tablets show that women operated drinking establishments by the baths inside the first century fortress at Vindonissa (Speidel 1996, 55; 80; 186–7). Rather the attempt here is to focus on the specific problem of whether there is evidence that women were accommodated in barracks (whether in the centurions' and decurions' houses or in the *contubernia*) on a day-to-day basis, and if so in what time periods.

First- and second-century AD barracks

The footwear evidence from a building of *c.*105–120 excavated in early wooden fort Period IV at Vindolanda has attracted so much interest because of its early-second century date. If females were present in barracks at such an early stage, surely their presence must be commonplace throughout the high empire. The references to this building refer to it as a definite barrack, often implying it is one of a regular series: 'One of the barrack blocks at Vindolanda' (Hassall 1999, 39); 'Detailed examination of finds from barracks at Vindolanda' (Mattingly 2006, 170). In fact the building in question is the only one ever to have been claimed as a barrack in the pre-stone fort levels at Vindolanda, and its identification is not certain. The published reconstruction of the building plan (Birley 1994, 109, fig. 30, also shown in van Driel Murray 1995, 18, fig. 1.8 and 1997, 59, fig. 4) needs to be compared with Birley 1994 (94, fig. 29) which shows how fragmentary is the evidence on which the reconstructed plan is based. The reconstruction is imaginative, but said by the excavator to be only 'relatively orthodox' as a barrack plan; elsewhere (Birley 2009, 92) the identification is qualified: 'almost certainly a barracks'. The discussion does not specify whether the ranges of rooms reconstructed to either side of a spine wall represent two barracks placed back to back or a single barrack, but as it is reconstructed with a frontal colonnade to either side the former is implied. In this case the individual *contubernia* in each barrack would lack the usual front-back division (which would surely have survived in the conditions of preservation at Vindolanda). The number of *contubernia* (seven) is also a problem: the discussion invokes a 6-*contubernium* third-century barrack excavated inside Vindolanda stone fort 2 but this is of a late-Roman type and grossly untypical for the first and second centuries (Bidwell 1991; Hodgson and Bidwell 2004, 147–50). We have no knowledge of the general plan into which the Period IV building fits; there are no fragments of accompanying buildings to place the 'barrack' in a general context – it is not in a known area of barracks within the fort. In short, there is no strong evidence to support the identification of this building as a barrack as opposed to an administrative, residential or stores building. The plan in Birley 1994 (94, fig. 29) surely suggests the possibility that the range of rooms represents the west side of a courtyard building, as did the two preceding building periods. In any case the use of the building had changed from its original purpose by the time that the crucial shoes were deposited, since the frontal colonnade was walled up. Reuter (2008, 94–5) approaches the problem from a different angle, suggesting that the shoes were imported with levelling material.

Is there any evidence that women could have lived in firmly identified second-century barracks on Hadrian's Wall? The only extensive excavations on barracks of this date have been at South Shields, Wallsend and Housesteads.

The barracks excavated at South Shields and Wallsend were of the stable-barrack type where each *contubernium* accommodates three horses in the front part and three troopers in the rear room, with the whole block occupied by a single *turma* or subdivision ('troop') of the unit (for the type see Hodgson and Bidwell 2004, 131–6). Each *contubernium* is an ideally arranged unit for three men and horses, unvarying throughout the life of the buildings. The arrangement is not one which can easily have accommodated even small

Barrack XIII						*Contubernia*					*Centurion's house*	
	11	*10*	*9*	*8*	*7*	*6*	*5*	*4*	*3*	*2*	*1*	*0*
Unstrat? Not listed in structural report	Glass bead **454** **476**	Glass bead **444** **451** **453** Melon bead **498**		Glass bead **467** **468** **475**	Glass bead **437** **474** **487** Melon bead **490** Jet bead **617**		Glass bead **482** Cu alloy bracelet **42**		Glass bead **436** **447** ?Shale armlet **627**	Glass bead **440** **449** **450** **472** Jet bead **618** ?Cu alloy bracelet **46**	Glass bead **448** **480** Jet bead **619** Shale armlet **626**	Glass bead **485**
'Dereliction layers'							Jet bead **614**			Glass bead **443**	Jet pin **516**	Shale armlet **629** Glass bead **431** **469**
Modifications to chalet phase	Shale armlet **623**					?Glass bead **432**					Shale armlet **625** Glass bead **434**	Glass bead **442** **464**
Early chalet phase						Glass bead **460**	Glass bead **484** **492** Melon bead **491**			Glass bead **446**		
Later barrack phase (AD 200+)											Silver ear-ring **4** Cu alloy ear-ring **38**	Glass bead **452**
Second-century barrack											Melon bead **494**	

Numbers refer to finds catalogue in Rushworth (2009)

Table 4.1 Incidence of possible and probable 'female' finds in Housesteads barrack XIII by contubernium *and phase. Officer's house material indicated by bold border. Data from Rushworth 2009*

numbers of women in addition to the troopers, their horses and their grooms, who perhaps lived in the roof space: the *contubernalis* of the cavalryman Tagamas mentioned on a Vindolanda tablet was probably such an attendant rather than his wife (*contra* Bowman and Thomas 1994, 130; cf. James 2006 on the ubiquity of such boy attendants in military life). What the cavalry barracks do demonstrate, because (on Hadrian's Wall and elsewhere, throughout the first and second centuries) the horse accommodation occurs in every *contubernium*, is that there was not routine provision of one or two *contubernia* for married or women's quarters, as van Driel Murray suggested at Vindolanda on the basis of the concentration of the shoe-evidence in two rooms.

What of the officers' houses at the ends of these second-century barrack blocks? At Housesteads it has been stated that 'Barrack block 13 … has revealed artefacts that may be associated with women in all occupation levels of the centurion's quarters but none in the rest of the barrack block' (Allason-Jones 1999, 45; cf. 2009, 431: 'an identifiable preponderance of female artefacts ... within the area of the centurion's quarters ... enough to indicate the presence of women at all periods of the fort's history'). However, when the final excavation report (Rushworth 2009) is used to plot all finds with even possible female associations from barrack 13 by room and phase, even including glass beads, which LAJ herself dismisses as liable to have been trailed in on muddy boots, it is clear that, with the exception of a single melon bead, there are no such finds recorded from second-century contexts in this barrack, either in the *contubernia* or the centurion's house (Table 4.1). When the contexts of those finds (two ear-rings and a glass bead) found in the centurion's house of the pre-chalet phase barrack are examined, they are all found to be modifications of later than AD 200 in date. There is no significant occurrence of female associated finds in the pre-AD 200 levels of the barrack, including the officer's house.

The number of *contubernia* in the Hadrianic-Antonine cavalry barracks offers another means of approaching the question of whether the auxiliary decurions were accompanied in their accommodation by wives and families. The number of *contubernia* in all cases is nine. With an absolute maximum of three horses per room it will have been impossible for nine *contubernia* to hold more than 9×3, that is 27 men and mounts. Yet the documentary evidence is consistent in suggesting a size of at least 30 for a *turma* (for the archaeological, literary and documentary evidence see Hodgson 2003, 71–90). The only solution to this problem that has been proposed is that the three *principales* (junior officers) of the *turma* were accommodated in the spacious, multi-room end-block with the decurion – giving a total of 30 *equites* plus decurion. If this was the case there would hardly be room for the decurion, let alone the junior officers (all with horses stabled in the end-block), to be accompanied by a family. The arrangement makes it very unlikely that regular accommodation for women and children was envisaged in a plan that remained unchanged until the end of the second century at South Shields and which was still current for some decades of the third century at Wallsend.

Third-century AD barracks

At Housesteads Barrack block 13 the statement that there are artefacts associated with women in the occupation levels of the centurion's quarters only (Allason-Jones 1999, 45) is borne out for the first time in the third century by the mapping of the finds (Table 4.1). The only two ear-rings to be found in this barrack occur in contexts in the centurion's house which must be of third century date. There is a complete absence of female-associated items from the *contubernia* of this period. However, the absolute number of finds is extremely small, and a similar exercise in the many excavated barracks at Wallsend and South Shields fails to show a correlation between 'female' finds and officers' houses, at any period.

Turning to the Wallsend cavalry barracks, those described above were replaced in the course of the third century by a new type – with fewer (5) *contubernia* each perhaps holding six men and mounts. But the decurions' houses are much larger than previously: 100–120 m^2 as opposed to 70 m^2. In one case, the report noted 'the expansion during the course of the third century of the Officers' House ... absorbing the neighbouring *contubernium*, which still has the appearance of a separate unit, though with a connecting doorway' (Hodgson 2003, 109–12; 118). This might be explained if as well as his junior officers, the decurion now had to accommodate a wife and family. To gain more space and privacy for the latter, the junior officers may have been relegated to an annexe.

At around 66 m^2 the centurions' houses of the third-century (Period 6B) barracks at South Shields are around the same area as the decurions' houses of the second-century cavalry barracks, but in one case (Barrack II, Hodgson and Bidwell 2004, 128, fig. 4) a *contubernium* at the end away from the officers' house was converted to form what is best interpreted as junior officers' suite, with rooms leading off a lobby and a latrine (never found in ordinary barrack rooms), perhaps hinting that junior officers were moved out of the main centurions' house. Junior officers' houses, again identified by latrines and distinct from the centurions' quarters, are apparent in the barracks of Period 5B/6A at South Shields, of Severan date (Hodgson and Bidwell 2004, 125–7 and fig. 2). Unidentified 'end rooms' at the other end away from the officers' suite are however known in some first- and second-century barracks (Johnson 1983, 173–4).

One of the two centurions' houses (Building 1A) belonging to the 6-*contubernium* barrack introduced in the 230s into stone fort 2 at Vindolanda (1980 excavation) is larger than earlier norms, at some 95 m^2, although its companion in the neighbouring barrack (1B) is only 65 m^2 (Bidwell 1985, 60 and fig. 25).

There are therefore some structural changes of the period after AD 200 that might mean that *principales* formerly accommodated with the centurion or decurion were sometimes moved out into their own quarters, and that centurions' and decurions' houses varied more in size, perhaps suiting the requirements of individual officers. This is not inconsistent with some centurions and decurions having families living with them.

As for the ordinary *contubernia* in the third century: the striking thing here is how conservatively they retain the front-back division, with a passage running along the side of the front room to give access to the back in infantry cases, and the now-familiar drainage arranegements for horses in the front rooms in the cavalry cases (Hodgson and Bidwell 2004). There are no documented cases anywhere of individual *contubernia* or groups of *contubernia* being converted to some other kind of accommodation.

Fourth-century barracks

Lindsay Allason-Jones' own work has suggested that artefact distribution supports the presence of women in the centurion's houses of the fourth century barracks but not in the ordinary *contubernia*: at Housesteads, Barrack block 13 in the fourth-century artefacts that may be associated with women occur in the centurion's quarters more than in the rest of the barrack block by a factor of 2:1 – the figures are eight finds in the centurion's house and four scattered in *contubernia*; three and one if we exclude the beads (Table 4.1).

Structurally, the conservatism of *contubernium* plans is maintained for at least the first half of the fourth century. In barracks that are well-preserved and extensively excavated at South Shields (Hodgson and Bidwell 2004, 148) and Vindolanda (1980 excavation: Bidwell 1985) there is no deviation from this plan, whose archetype, at least in the infantry case, lies in the Hyginian tent arrangement, before the mid-fourth century.

Removal of partitions and an increasingly irregular look to the barrack accommodation (which *might* signal the breakdown of the traditional *contubernium* unit, reduction in overall numbers, and the permanent presence of women, children and other civilians) is something that comes in at Vindolanda (1980 excavation) and South Shields only in the second half of the fourth century, and possibly not until after *c*.370 (Hodgson and Bidwell 2004, 154). At South Shields, however, there is no corresponding increase in the incidence of finds with female associations; the absolute number in the wholly excavated fourth-century barrack is as low as in earlier periods (Table 4.5), although in this case the occupation levels in the officer's house had been removed in Victorian excavations. At Housesteads the unstratified 'female' finds from over Barrack XIII, possibly derived from the latest occupation, are as common over the *contubernia* as they are in the area of the officer's house (Table 4.1).

Finds

The significance of the finds of female association from Housesteads has already been noted. At Wallsend all finds with possible female associations (bracelets, ear-rings, hairpins, beads and certain jet objects) have been plotted out across the fort for the forthcoming report on the Daniels excavations. The finds occur in very small numbers. There is no particular correlation with the barracks and the number of finds is too small to make a meaningful comparison between deposition in centurion's houses and *contubernia*, for example. The only significant concentration (bracelet fragments) occurred at the *porta quintana*, thought to have been the site of a market in the fourth century. More than 50% of the 72 possible female artefacts were unstratified. When we remember that the fourth century occupation levels at Wallsend have been largely ploughed away, this must raise the possibility that there was a greater occurrence of such objects in later levels.

The occurrence of such 'female' finds in barracks at South Shields is tabulated here (Tables 4.2–4.5). What is most striking is that they occur in extremely small numbers. They show no increase over time, and there is no increased incidence in the officers' ends at any period. A gold ring, probably a woman's, from over the centurions house of Period 6B (third century) Barrack V, is suggestive (Table 4.4). This was one of three gold objects found in the burnt destruction deposit that ended this period. One of the others, an ear-ring, did not occur near a centurion's house, but the fire deposit had been much disturbed and redeposited. At South Shields pins and beads predominate in all periods. These might have alternative uses: beads could decorate horse trappings, pins could be used in garments and as *styli*. Ear-rings (three in total) and bracelets (two) are extremely rare, the five examples associated with the third-century barracks, but a tiny haul from nine totally excavated buildings.

Moving briefly away from Hadrian's Wall to Allison's mapping of artefacts associated with women and children in forts in Germany, these provide useful hints at the presence of women *in certain areas* of some military sites, such as the early legionary fortress at Vetera I. But there are only two cases where her distributions are said to identify the presence of women/children in buildings that are identifiable as barracks: at Oberstimm and Ellingen (Allison 2006b; 2009).

At Oberstimm (early second century) one of the barracks (6) is a stable-barrack (although not recognised as such in the excavation report). We have already noted the inherent unlikeliness of *contubernia* specifically designed to house three men and horses also accommodating families. Here the relevant finds are categorised as only possibly female/child associated; most were melon beads, concentrating particularly in the decurion's house area. As Allison concedes, melon beads can decorate horse harnesses, of which we might expect the officers' to have been most richly decorated. The excavation report is cited as stating that from their small size the beads are unlikely to have been used for this purpose, but there can be no certainty about that. Melon beads could also be used to adorn other items of military equipment, such as dagger-sheaths (example illustrated in Campbell 2010, 53).

No finds categorised by Allison as definitely female came from the interiors of the three excavated barracks (6, 12, 14) at Oberstimm. Even if we accept the definition of what was 'definitely' female, such material concentrated in buildings 1, 3 (definitely not barracks) and 7 (the *praetorium*).

The case at Ellingen (Zanier 1992) is somewhat differ-

SOUTH SHIELDS PERIOD 4 BARRACKS, *c.* AD 160 – *c.* 205

Barrack B6	*decurion*					*contubernia*				
	10	*9*	*8*	*7*	*6*	*5*	*4*	*3*	*2*	*1*
4B occupation	Bronze pin **1191**			Bone hairpin **485**						
4B construction			Melon bead **1398**	Melon bead **1394**						
4A occupation						Glass bead **1395** **1396** Bronze pin **1154**			Glass bead **1388**	

Barrack B8	*decurion*					*contubernia*				
	10	*9*	*8*	*7*	*6*	*5*	*4*	*3*	*2*	*1*
4B occupation	Melon bead **1507**	Bronze hair pin **1266** Bone hair pin **548**			Glass bead **1524**					
4B construction		Bronze hairpin **1276**							Melon bead **1531**	
4A occupation						Bronze hair pin **1314**				

Table 4.2 Incidence of possible and probable 'female' finds in South Shields Period 4 barracks B6 and B8, c. *AD 160–*c. *205. Officer's house material indicated by bold border. Data from excavation archive at Arbeia Roman Fort, South Shields*

ent – this is not an auxiliary fort, but a '*numerus*' fort for some unknown and irregular formation(s) operating on the Raetian frontier line in the second and part of the third century. Few of the internal buildings can be identified with certainty, including one (C) which has produced most of the finds and infant burials that interest Allison. Building B undoubtedly represents a pair of barracks, but here there are no indisputably female finds and only one infant burial. There was very little stratigraphy and the finds were associated with buildings spatially rather than being recovered from well-understood occupation deposits. The report suggests that much of the material was imported in make-up dumps, though this cannot be the case with the articulated infant skeletons. There was no destruction or demolition deposit – we do not know that human occupation ceased when the site was abandoned or neglected by the military in the years before the '*Limesfall*'. There were eight infant burials in total, one from a known barrack. These were interspersed with adult human remains – otherwise almost unknown in Roman fort or barrack interiors and a clear sign that Ellingen is hardly typical of Roman forts in general. It seems unwise to use the infant burials at this fort inductively to support the idea that women raised children in barracks in general in all periods.

Infant burials

A straightforward view would be that infant burials in barracks indicate that some soldiers' families were present, although ritual explanations are possible – there are known examples of ritual placement of infants in civilian contexts in Roman Britain. Whatever the significance, it is not a constant phenomenon in barracks, but one that increases over time. The best known examples of multiple infant burials in forts in Britain (Malton, Portchester) are of late-

SOUTH SHIELDS PERIOD 5B – 6A BARRACKS, *c.* AD 205 - *c.* 225

Barrack I	*Contubernia*						*Centurion's house*
	1	*2*	*3*	*4*	*5*	*6*	*7*
6B construction	Glass bead **1126** Glass bracelet **1379**						? Bone pin **462** ? Glass bead **1286**
6A demolition							Br pin **1058**
6A occupation			Br bracelet **822**				
Barrack rearranged in Period 6A with new officer's house at NE end (7)							
		Junior officer in 5B?	*Contubernia*				
6A construction							
5B demolition				Br pin **1110**			
5B occupation	NOT BUILT	Glass bead **1338**			Glass bead **1343**		NOT BUILT
5B construction		Br pin **1075**					

Barrack VIII	*Contubernia*				*Centurion's house*
	1	*2*	*3*	*4*	*5*
6B construction	? Bone pin **200**				Bronze ear-ring **549**
6A demolition					
6A occupation					Bone pin **278**
6A construction					
5B demolition					
5B occupation					
5B construction					

Table 4.3 Incidence of possible and probable 'female' finds in South Shields Period 5B–6A barracks I and VIII, c. *AD 205–*c. *225. Each building represents half of a split barrack. The other 'halves' excavated (IX, X, II, III) had no 'female' finds. Officer's house material indicated by bold border. Data from excavation archive at Arbeia Roman Fort, South Shields*

Roman date (Bidwell 1991, 12–14; 2007, 71–2). Despite these examples, what is most notable is the general rarity of infant burials in fort interiors, even at a late date. Two infant burials apparently from a centurion's house in the first-century fortress at Vindonissa (Trumm and Fellmann Brogli 2008) at present stand as an exception. Of course female slaves of the legionary centurion, or even his wife, if he was of equestrian rank, might have lived here.

The only fort in the Hadrian's Wall area to produce a sizeable sample of infant burials from dated contexts in barracks is South Shields. Here there are no infant burials in the two second-century barracks to be totally excavated or in the fragments of others dug. There were single isolated examples in each of the third century AD periods (Severan, in a junior officers' house; Period 5B/6A; 3 barracks excavated in total), and after AD 225/35, in an ordinary *contubernium*; Period 6B; 5 barracks excavated in total). In the barracks of Periods 7 and 8, spanning the fourth century (one completely and nine others fragmentarily excavated in modern times) more than six infant burials have been found. Generally they cannot be closely dated, although one is possibly but not necessarily of the first half of the fourth century. It is possible but by no means certain that most of these fourth century infant burials relate to changed conditions after *c.* AD 370.

Conclusion

To summarise, the structural and finds evidence from the few well-documented barracks on Hadrian's Wall, offers no support for the routine accommodation of women in barrack *contubernia* or in centurion/decurions' houses in the second century (no strong reason to identify the Vindolanda building cited in the former connection as a barrack; arrangement of cavalry barracks makes accommodation of families with decurions unlikely; no suggestion of this from Housesteads barrack XIII). Certain structural trends might indicate that in the third century the quarters of some centurions and decurions became more spacious and private, and there is some

SOUTH SHIELDS PERIOD 6B Barracks, *c.* AD 225 - *c.* 300

From 7A construction levels over barracks			
Bronze pin 594	Area of VI? Redeposited destruction deposit.	9005	
Bronze earring 618	Area of VI?	9036	
Bronze pin 915	Area of II?	23800	

Per 6B II	*Centurion*	*Contubernia*				
	6	*5*	*4*	*3*	*2*	*1*
6B demolition				Bronze pin **957**		Gold ear-ring **6**
6B occupation						
'6B'						Bone pin **462**

Per 6B III	*Centurion*	*Contubernia*				
	6	*5*	*4*	*3*	*2*	*1*
6B demolition						
6B occupation			Bronze pin **826** Glass bead **1021**	(Infant burial)	Jet bead **32**	
'6B'						

Per 6B V	*Contubernia*					*Centurion*
	1	*2*	*3*	*4*	*5*	*6*
6B demolition						Gold ring **2**
6B occupation					Bronze pin **519**	
'6B'						

Per 6B VI	*Contubernia*					*Centurion*
	1	*2*	*3*	*4*	*5*	*6*
6B demolition					Gold necklace **5?**	
6B occupation	Bone pin **323** Jet bead **23**					
'6B'						

Per 6B VII	*Contubernia*					*Centurion*
	1	*2*	*3*	*4*	*5*	*6*
6B demolition			Bone pin **326**			DEPOSITS DESTROYED
6B occupation						
'6B'						

Table 4.4 Incidence of possible and probable 'female' finds in South Shields Period 6B barracks, c. *AD 225–*c. *300. Officer's house material indicated by bold border. Data from excavation archive at Arbeia Roman Fort, South Shields*

finds evidence which suggests the presence of women there (Housesteads barrack XIII) – but still no such evidence from the *contubernia*. This situation prevailed during much of the fourth century. Structural deviations from the traditional *contubernium* plan, and an increased incidence of objects (many found unstratified) with female associations and infant burials *might* indicate an increased presence of women in barracks, including *contubernia*, in the later fourth century.

SOUTH SHIELDS PERIOD 7-8 BARRACK, FOURTH CENTURY

South Shields, Fourth Century barrack NW of courtyard house		*Contubernia*					*Furnace room*	*Officer's House*
	0	*1*	*2*	*3*	*4*	*5*	*6*	*7*
Later fourth century modification (8 construction)			Bone hairpin **83**	Jet bead **6** 7 Bone hairpin **135**				NO SURVIVING OCCUPATION LEVELS
Modifications (7B construction)							Bone hairpin **164**	
Earlier fourth-century occupation (7A occupation)							Jet bead **9**	

Table 4.5 Incidence of possible and probable 'female' finds in South Shields Period 7–8 barrack north-west of courtyard house, fourth century. Officer's house material indicated by bold border. Data from excavation archive at Arbeia Roman Fort, South Shields

Whether this paucity of evidence for female occupation of barracks would be changed by further study of the available finds assemblages is doubtful. All the studies cited above and the tabulation of finds at South Shields remind us just how few finds even a large scale modern excavation of Roman fort barracks will produce. The idea that there are large bodies of finds with clear gender attributions that can be clearly associated with barrack occupation levels is misleading – many of the few finds are from construction or demolition dumps, or unstratified. The distributions at South Shields, Wallsend or Housesteads are about as good as they get. The numbers and distribution by phase and room of 'female' finds from the recent (2009–11) excavation of third- and fourth-century barracks at Vindolanda will provide a useful comparison when published. Unless some future excavation reveals a barrack that has perished in a sudden disaster with its day-to-day contents intact and well-preserved, it is unlikely that future studies of finds distributions will get beyond the conclusion that there were women about somewhere in the vicinity (itself a significant advance of recent times). It is notable that the destruction deposit that ended the third century Period 6B at South Shields, excavated over the area of five barracks, produced only a tiny handful of objects (six in total) with possible female associations (Table 4.4).

On the question of whether centurions and decurions were exempted from the marriage ban, the simple truth is that we do not know for certain. The most likely solution, favoured by Phang (2001, 129–32) in her study of soldiers' marriages, is that centurions of equestrian rank (some legionary centurions) were exempt, others (presumably all of our auxiliary centurions and decurions on Hadrian's Wall) were not, but that the latter tended to contract *de facto* marriages more frequently than ordinary soldiers because of their greater means and social standing. In this view the fact that there are more pre-AD 197 epitaphs mentioning wives of centurions than ordinary soldiers is not because the former had any legal right to marry but because they married more often. Where we get a case of a legionary centurion accompanied by a wife on the Antonine Wall (i.e. *c.*AD 140–160: RIB 3504), if he was of equestrian rank (or possibly of long service: Phang 2001, 132) he would have been exempted from the marriage ban and might have had his wife with him the fort. But the evidence as examined above is most consistent with it only being after the dissolution of the marriage ban in AD 197 that auxiliary and most legionary centurions and decurions, non-equestrians, were allowed to introduce families to the fort – and even then there is no case where finds from the officer's house of a barrack prove beyond doubt that this occurred.

Although the diplomas show that first- and second-century soldiers could and did contract *de facto* marriages, epigraphic studies have suggested that many of them did not and that those that did married late in life, presumably when they had acquired the means as well as the inclination to enter into such a contract (Phang 2001). For the ordinary soldier it remains entirely possible on the evidence above that the Augustan marriage ban did not merely prevent the legality of any marriage he might contract, but that it was actively and deliberately reflected in the traditional kind of accommodation in which he was made to live: in a *contubernium* with his fellow soldiers (*contubernales*). Within the fort walls the soldier was expected to live in an idealised and celibate state, conducive to military *virtus*, with his *contubernales.* There is to date no substantial archaeological evidence from *contubernia* that the enforcement of this separation from the female and the civilian ceased with the dissolution of the marriage ban – the latter made no practical difference, it merely gave legal recognition to contracts and relationships certain soldiers had long been entering into outside the world of the barracks. After the dissolution the privilege of cohabitation inside the fort was apparently extended to the centurions/decurions on the model of the earlier privileges accorded to equestrian officers, but this still needs to be placed on a firmer archaeological footing.

In antiquity 'military affairs were gendered as a masculine world' effected through *disciplina militaris* – 'the complex of practices that promoted and maintained *virtus* in soldiers' (Phang 2001, 354). In the literary sources of the first and early second centuries, women were seen as corrupting and debilitating to the military ideal of *virtus* – especially if they moved in with soldiers. From a twenty-first century perspective such views seem repugnant and misogynistic (Allison 2006a), hence the accusation that it cannot have been like this and that once we strip away our male and modernising nineteenth-century perception of the Roman army we will find women in barracks. But to describe a past ideology is not to agree with it, and to recognise that there is no evidence for the accommodation of wives in barracks is not to deny the vital role of women in Roman military life.

On the archaeological evidence discussed here it seems likely there was a ruling or a presumption for most of the imperial period against soldiers' unofficial wives – and after AD 197 ordinary soldiers' legal wives – living in barracks. It would be naive not to expect local variations in practice and exceptions to this, but as things stand the counter-assertion that there was widespread accommodation of wives in *contubernia* lacks any substantial archaeological basis. Despite large numbers of women being present in forts (including numerous slaves and attendants from the *praetorium;* wives of centurions/decurions (after *c.*200?); their slaves and attendants; soldiers' slaves; female *vicus* inhabitants brought into the fort for specialist work or marketing activities; the daughters of all concerned) it is arguable that certain areas and aspects of the fort maintained the idealised character of an all-male community (cf. James 2006). Even in the third and fourth centuries, when wives may have been present in the officers' ends, the *contubernia* may have preserved an all-male character. In the Wall forts the barracks may have been inhabited by families in the changed conditions of the later-fourth century, but the nature of the Wall-fort communities in that period is still very poorly understood.

Postscript

This article was submitted before I saw Ian Haynes' *Blood of the Provinces: the Roman Auxilia and the Making of Provincial Society from Augustus to the Severans* (Oxford, 2013), which points out (p.90) that the dissolution of the Augustan marriage ban in 197 evidenced at Herodian 3.8.5 may be a myth, as there are later examples of the granting of *conubium* to auxiliaries on discharge. As Haynes concludes, Herodian may have alluded in general terms to a relaxation of discipline which led to more routine co-habitation, whether or not in barracks. As a source Herodian is hostile and unreliable, but it is worth considering whether he alludes in part to the introduction of centurions' and decurions' wives to barracks, which we tentatively suggested above may date from this time.

This paper is offered to Lindsay Allason-Jones in gratitude for a 30 year friendship and for her contribution to Roman archaeology.

Bibliography

Allason-Jones, L. (1995) 'Sexing' small finds. In P. Rush (ed.) *Theoretical Roman Archaeology: Second Conference Proceedings*, 22–32. Aldershot.

Allason-Jones, L. (1999) Women and the Roman army in Britain. In A. Goldsworthy and I. Haynes (eds) *The Roman Army as a Community*, 41–51. Portsmouth, Rhode Island.

Allason-Jones, L. (2009) The small finds. In A. Rushworth (ed.), *Housesteads Roman Fort – The Grandest Station,* English Heritage Archaeological Report, 430–87. Swindon.

Allison, P. M. (2006a) Mapping for gender. Interpreting artefact distribution inside 1st and 2nd-century A.D. forts in Roman Germany. *Archaeological Dialogues* 13.1, 1–20.

Allison, P. M. (2006b) Artefact distribution within the auxiliary fort at Ellingen: evidence for building use and for the presence of women and children. *Bericht der Römisch-Germanischen Kommission* 87, 387–452.

Allison, P. M. (2009) The women in the early forts: GIS and artefact distribution analyses in 1st and 2nd century Germany. In A. Morillo, N. Hanel and E. Martín (eds)

Limes XX: estudios sobre la frontera Romana, Anejos de *Gladius* 13, vol. 3, 1193–1201.

Allison, P. M., Blackall, C., Ellis S. and Fairbairn, A. (2005) Extracting the social relevance of artefact distribution within Roman military forts. *Internet Archaeology* 17, http://intarch.ac.uk/

Bidwell, P. (1985) *The Roman Fort of Vindolanda.* London.

Bidwell, P. (1991) Later Roman barracks in Britain. In V. A. Maxfield and M. J. Dobson (eds) *Roman Frontier Studies 1989*, 9–15. Exeter.

Bidwell, P. (2007) *Roman Forts in Britain*. Stroud.

Birley, R. (1994) *Vindolanda Research Reports, New Series vol. I, the Early Wooden Forts.* Bardon Mill.

Birley, R. (2009) *Vindolanda, a Roman Frontier Fort on Hadrian's Wall.* Stroud.

Bowman, A. K. and Thomas, J. D. (1994) *The Vindolanda Writing Tablets* (Tabulae Vindolandenses II). London.

Breeze, D. J. and Dobson, B. (2000) *Hadrian's Wall.* Fourth edition. London.

Campbell, D. B. (2010) Women in Roman Forts: residents, visitors or barred from entry? *Ancient Warfare* 6 Nov–Dec 2010, 48–53.

van Driel-Murray, C. (1995) Gender in question. In P. Rush (ed.) *Theoretical Roman Archaeology: Second Conference Proceedings*, 3–21. Aldershot.

van Driel-Murray, C. (1997) Women in forts? *Jahrbuch der Gesellschaft pro Vindonissa 1997*, 55–61.

Goldsworthy, A. and Haynes, I. (eds) (1999) *The Roman Army as a Community.* Portsmouth, Rhode Island.

Hassall, M. (1999) Homes for heroes: married quarters for soldiers and veterans. In A. Goldsworthy and I. Haynes (eds) *The Roman Army as a Community*, 35–40. Portsmouth, Rhode Island.

Hodgson, N. (2003) *The Roman Fort at Wallsend: Excavations in 1997–8*. Newcastle upon Tyne.

Hodgson, N. and Bidwell, P. (2004) Auxiliary barracks in a new light: recent discoveries on Hadrian's Wall. *Britannia* 35, 121–57.

James, S. (2006) Engendering change in our understanding of the structure of Roman military communities. *Archaeological Dialogues* 13.1, 36–3.

Johnson, A. (1983) *Roman Forts of the 1st and 2nd centuries in Britain and the German Provinces.* London.

Mattingly, D. (2006) *An Imperial Possession: Britain in the Roman Empire.* London.

Phang, S. E. (2001) *The Marriage of Roman Soldiers (13 BC–AD 235)*. Leiden.

Reuter, M. (2008) Frauen in römischen Militärlagen? Eine archäologische Spurensuche. In U. Brandl (ed.) *Frauen und Römisches Militär: beiträge eines runden Tisches in Xanten vom 7. bis 9 Juli 2005*, BAR International Series 1759, 92–101. Oxford.

Rudán, B. and Brandl U. (2008) '... *intrare castra feminis non licet'* – Tatsache oder literarische Fiktion? Ein kritischer Literaturüberblick. In U. Brandl (ed.) *Frauen und Römisches Militär: beiträge eines runden Tisches in Xanten vom 7. bis 9 Juli 2005*, BAR International Series 1759, 1–19. Oxford.

Rushworth, A. (2009) *Housesteads Roman Fort – The Grandest Station*, English Heritage Archaeological Report. Swindon.

Speidel, M. A. (1996) *Die römischen Schreibtafeln von Vindonissa*, Baden-Dättwil (Veröffentlichungen der Gesellschaft Pro Vindonissa, Band XII).

Trumm, J. and Fellmann Brogli, R. (2008) Mitten in Lager geboren – Kinder und Frauen im römischen Legionslager Vindonissa. In U. Brandl (ed.) *Frauen und Römisches Militär: beiträge eines runden Tisches in Xanten vom 7. bis 9 Juli 2005*, BAR International Series 1759, 102–119. Oxford.

Zanier, W. (1992) *Das römische Kastell Ellingen*, Limesforschungen 23. Mainz.

5

IF THE SHOE FITS: STYLE AND STATUS IN THE ASSEMBLAGE OF CHILDREN'S SHOES FROM VINDOLANDA

Elizabeth M. Greene

Introduction

Some of the most significant and emotive evidence for the presence of non-combatants in military environments is the presence of children's shoes in the archaeological record. The footwear of children, especially those indicating that very young individuals were in residence, cannot be misidentified, nor explained away, for instance as adult shoes having shrunk or as having belonged to adolescent recruits. These artefacts form a category of their own that clearly demonstrate the presence of children, individuals that were rarely recognized in the archaeological record of the Roman army until recently (Allason Jones 1997; 1999a; van Driel-Murray 1995; 1997; 1998). The presence and role of women and children have become a greater focus in military studies than ever before. Families in Roman Britain generally, and more specifically as part of Roman military populations, were first considered in any depth by Allason-Jones (1989; 2004; 2005), after it became clear in the archaeological record that women and children were a significant part of military communities (van Driel-Murray 1993; 1998; Maxfield 1995; Roxan 1991; Wells 1997). The topic has been carried forward since by scholars considering every type of material evidence from infant skeletons (Allison 2006; 2007), to brooches (Böhme-Schönberger 2008), inscriptions (Brandl 2008), military diplomas (Greene forthcoming) and literature (Moore 2010).

The very definitive nature of children's shoes as evidence for the habitation by these individuals makes them a special group of artefacts that are not exposed to the usual rounds of scepticism and doubt. It is difficult to show, and often doubted, that small finds such as brooches, beads and hairpins, can be 'sexed' and proven to have belonged exclusively to women (Allason-Jones 1995; 1999b). However, arguments have been made convincingly about certain types of finds such as distel brooches (Böhme-Schönberger 2008) and small melon beads (Hoffmann 2006). The presence of children, however, cannot be misunderstood, particularly when their footwear is present. Children in the archaeological record of the Roman army stand as a proxy for the habitation of women, in many cases the wives of soldiers and mothers to soldiers' children. In some cases we can conjecture that these individuals lived within the fort walls rather than outside in the extramural settlement; but we are now beyond studies revealing merely the presence of women and children in the military environment and must move toward understanding social roles. By studying the details of children's shoes conclusions can be drawn in some cases about their status and role within the fort.

This contribution focuses on the children's shoes in the archaeological record of Vindolanda. It provides an introduction to this aspect of dress for children and considers the sartorial manifestations of status for the children living in auxiliary military communities. The Vindolanda Museum in northern England houses the largest assemblage of footwear from a Roman military site, with over 4,000 shoes currently in the museum collection. Many of those shoes belonged to children of a rather young age and have been found in all settlement phases (*c.*AD 85–fourth century). They come from a variety of occupation contexts including domestic spaces, official military structures, and rubbish deposits. Though children's shoes usually cannot reveal sexual dimorphism, they betray the presence of families of some form, whether legal or *de facto*, in the military environment. Footwear also allows some reconstruction of social hierarchy at the fort and the role of dress in expressing status. This is particularly salient when shoes are found in their original domestic deposits and the function of spaces can be identified. A good example is the *praetorium*, the commanding officer's residence, found in the central range of buildings in almost every Roman fort. Children's shoes from all contexts are considered here towards a better understanding of their habitation in military settlements.

Conservation and analysis of archaeological leather and shoes

A few points should be made about archaeological leather and its conservation. Shoes that are now known to have belonged to children, were once thought to have shrunk either during taphonomic processes after deposition or during the conservation process. It is clear now that these processes do not alter the shoe dramatically. Calculated with modern conservation techniques, there is a small amount of shrinkage in leather goods of about 3–5% (Rhodes 1980, 101–2). This would result in an overall difference in shoe size of less than 1.0 cm overall. For shoes of about 18–21 cm, the shrinkage would amount to just over 0.5 cm. Rector reported a loss of between 3–6% from medieval shoes at Blackfriars (1975, 36; Rhodes 1980, 101), while Thornton performed an experiment in 1959 that showed shrinkage of 4.33–5.5% (unpublished lecture reported in Rhodes 1980, 101). When dealing with footwear from Germany, Busch (1965, 160–1) reported a loss of up to 2.0 cm, but on shoes that were excavated around 1900, which indicates that leather continues to shrink over time. Though certainly necessary to render in size calculations, the overall result would not allow one to mistake an adult-male's shoe for a child's. It is important to keep this basic figure of shrinkage in mind when calculating the original size of a shoe, particularly on those examples nearing the largest end of the children's scale. This investigation uses caution where necessary, presuming that shoes could have lost up to 2.0 cm of their original size during conservation.

The age and sex of an individual is always estimated from the size and style of the insole, not the outer tread sole or walking surface (van Driel-Murray 1993, 42; 2007, 360). The tread sole of a shoe is in many cases at least 1.0 cm larger than the insole, sometimes 2–3.0 cm larger depending on the style. Just as in shoes worn today, therefore, the insole most effectively reflects the actual size of the wearer. In cases where only the tread sole is preserved a rough size of the owner's foot can be ascertained, but should be used with caution. The width of the waist of the shoe, which corresponds to the arch of the foot, can also potentially help identify its original wearer. Females tend to have a much narrower foot than men, and this difference seems to be reflected in the Vindolanda footwear assemblage. There is a large group of shoes that are in the size bracket corresponding to the upper end of the adult female spectrum, *c.*21–22 cm in length (post-conservation), in which the waist is very narrow at 4.0 cm or smaller. Conversely, another group of shoes of around 21–22 cm and above in length have a waist width of over 5.0cm, a significant difference (*c.*20%) for such a small area of the foot. Thus these narrow shoes of roughly 20–22 cm in length are considered to have belonged to a female individual, and sometimes the width may be used to differentiate a shoe on the 21–22 cm cusp. Children's shoes are those that are below 19.0 cm in length, with many of the Vindolanda examples discussed here much smaller at 14–16 cm in length. The insole of an infant shoe is 10–12 cm.

Two distinct peaks are detectable in most size distributions of large assemblages of footwear from ancient and medieval contexts, as well as in comparable data from a modern shoemaker (Groenman-van Waateringe 1978, 184–9, using data from the Swift shoe factory in the Netherlands; van Driel-Murray 2007, 360–1, for discussion and graphs of shoe size distributions). These data can be used to determine the probable owner of an individual shoe. When dealing with the Vindolanda assemblage all dimensions are post-conservation measurements. To take into account the variable shrinkage from the conservation process, this investigation assigns a shoe smaller than 19 cm to the ownership by a child; those of 19–22 cm were worn either by an adult female or an adolescent male probably under the age of 14. Shoes over 22 cm represent adult males. In the assemblage from Billingsgate in London the shoe size considerations are more generous, using pre-conservation measurements; a shoe up to 20 cm is considered as having belonged to a child, 20–24 cm were categorized as female adult shoes, while anything larger is presumed to have belonged to an adult male (Rhodes 1980, 102). The footwear analysis from the Rhine fort at Valkenburg also considers the female spectrum to continue up to *c.*24 cm, and anything above is male (Hoevenberg 1993; cf. Groenman-van Waateringe 1967, 1975).

Van Driel-Murray has done the most work on leather and footwear from the northwest Roman provinces and her size calculations are used as a guideline. She assigns continental European shoe sizes to her discussion, suggesting that men fell within a range from 24 cm and larger, with an average of 25–25.5 cm. The overlap for female and male shoes is around 23–23.5 cm (pre-conservation). Therefore, the female range is between 20–23.5 cm, and children's shoes are smaller than 20 cm (van Driel-Murray 2007, 360; 1993, 43). The analysis of the Vindolanda footwear remains conservative and presumes that anything above 22 cm could represent an adult male, allowing for up to 2 cm of shrinkage during conservation. A shoe considered to have belonged to a female, therefore, is now between 19–21 cm, and below 19 cm represents a child. This conservative standpoint does not stretch the evidence beyond its use, and even with this cautious approach the number of shoes that represent women, adolescents and children living at Vindolanda is significant.

There is an obvious issue with the overlap between the shoe sizes of fully grown females and still growing adolescent males. For this reason in many cases a shoe must be classified as female/adolescent, except when the style suggests a feminine owner and the waist of the insole is very narrow. There is not a great problem with such ambiguity for this study, particularly because the largest female shoe, except in rare cases that simply remain undetectable, seems to coincide with the foot size of a male under the age of 12, at most age 14 (Boys are typically a full adult shoe size by about age 15, van Driel-Murray 1998, 343). As the population of children in the military context should also stand proxy for the presence of adult females, there is no great methodological issue. In spite of the fact that 12- to 14-year-old Roman boys likely would have taken care of themselves, at the same time, a significant population of pre-adult boys or girls living in military contexts is not a part of our current image of Roman military settlements and needs to be kept in mind for future inquiry.

Shoe style does in some cases indicate the age or sex of the owner. The *carbatina*, a shoe which utilizes one thick piece of cowhide leather without iron studs and is secured with a single lace over the top of the foot, was favoured for children, though adult examples are also found (van Driel-Murray 2007, 353–4, 360). The simplicity in securing the shoe and the ability to change the size as an individual grew is the obvious reason for their popularity amongst children. For this reason it can be difficult to obtain an exact size measurement, but it is very clear when the shoe had belonged to a child rather than adult, and quite often the impression of the walking surface can be seen on the leather itself. Similarly, in the early Vindolanda periods, sandals were reserved for girls and women, only becoming popular in a slightly different style for men later in time (van Driel-Murray 1993, 32). The best example of this shoe type is the sandal from the Period 3 *praetorium*, labelled the 'Lepidina slipper' because of the identification from the writing tablets that this was the residence of Sulpicia Lepidina, wife of the prefect Flavius Cerialis (van Driel-Murray 1993, 44–6).

Children's shoes at Vindolanda: Context, style and status

Children's shoes generally incorporate the same stylistic features as adult shoes, an interesting fact in light of the role played by sartorial symbols in defining and advertising social status in the Roman world. What an individual wore, and how they wore it, meant everything in determining one's rank, status, wealth and role in society (Bonfante 1994, 5–6). Senators, for instance, were allowed to wear gold rings and their choice of footwear very much marked them as senatorial in rank (Goldman 1994, 101). In Rome itself a clear distinction was made between the *calcei equestres*, the high black boot of the equestrian class, and the *calcei patricii* and *calcei senatorii* of the noblest men (Goldman 1994, 116). The patrician shoe may have been similar to the equestrian boot, but was bright red in colour to easily distinguish social status. This sartorial detail was of the utmost importance, similar to the wide purple band (*latus clavus*) worn on a senatorial tunic, as opposed to the narrow band of the equestrian (*clavus angustus*). Such considerations of status and rank would most certainly have carried through to the military world, an environment that was by its very definition hierarchical. For the most part an auxiliary population would have lacked men of senatorial rank, but even still, to show one's status in the military hierarchy with visible markers would surely have been a necessity.

With this in mind, the shoes found in the *praetorium* of the period III fort at Vindolanda (*c*.AD 97/100–104/5) seem to adhere to the desire for visual cues about status. The children's shoes indicate that the prefect's family, even the youngest members, had become subject to the sartorial expectations of their class from a very young age. This fact is even more interesting considering the Batavian origins of Flavius Cerialis and his wife Sulpicia Lepidina, the prefect and highest ranking family in residence in the fort at this time. They must have been of equestrian class in order for Cerialis to have held the military rank of prefect, and they had clearly also adopted the social expectations of that rank in the Roman world. The most high-end shoe found at Vindolanda comes from the period III *praetorium* context, the so-called "Lepidina Slipper" with the maker's mark of Lucius Aebutius Thales (van Driel-Murray 1993, 46, pl. iv). This was certainly an expensive shoe and one that was worn by a high status individual; in this case quite likely Sulpicia Lepidina, the wife of the prefect.

The children's footwear from the *praetorium* also suggests that the youngest generations of an upper-class household were subject to the visual expectations of dress. The assemblage includes *calcei* of various sizes, the closed shoe that was popular around the empire. Most striking in this context is a tiny shoe of an infant of the exact same style that we have come to expect from a high-end adult male shoe, with detailed decoration in the cut-out leather of the upper portion of the shoe (Plate 1). Even though the child was probably not yet walking, with a foot size of *c.* 10 cm, the shoe is furnished with a full set of iron studs on the tread sole (van Driel-Murray 1993, 45). This type of footwear was clearly meant to reflect the status of its wearer, even though it was owned by a small infant of roughly 8 months to just over 1 year of age. The fishnet decoration and the expensive metal tread suggest that the individual was a valued member of society at this point in life already. Moreover, in order to utilize the visual marker of social status it may be suggested that he or she would have been a part of the public appearance of the family. In a military context we might imagine the family of the prefect being part of public life through parades or other state-level official events. This image of familial participation is not one that has been explored in military studies, but as we learn more about the presence and role of family in the Roman military world, it may become more commonplace. A public role of the prefect's wife is possibly revealed in the Vindolanda writing tablets (Greene 2013), and is certainly present in the late archive of Flavius Abinnaeus, a fourth century *praefectus alae* at Dionysias in Egypt (Bell 1962). Perhaps such a public role extended to the whole family in certain circumstances.

The other children's shoes from the *praetorium* may have also reflected elite ownership with an emphasis on showing that social status visually through dress. A style that seems to be especially favoured in the *praetorium* contexts is the highly decorative boot with 'fishnet' uppers. This is certainly an expensive shoe with its cost shown in the detailed decoration and time consuming process of the cut-out leather. This style would also allow the owner to wear any colour sock beneath, which would allow for the colour distinctions clearly present in visual messages of status in the capital. One shoe belonged to a large adult male, suggested by van Driel-Murray (1993, 46) to fit our expectations of the luxury that the commander would wear. This is most interesting because many of the shoes belonging to children, nearing the range for adult shoes (*c.*18 cm foot) for an individual between *c.*10 and 14 years are of the very same style. It would certainly be expected that the prefect's son would indeed follow the conventions expected of his class and status, particularly as he nears his teen years and would possibly enter the military himself. Perhaps we see this process and the expected public role to come, becoming apparent in footwear choices. The infant's shoe is also quite similar to this style with the fishnet upper and above ankle height, and suggests, even if this shoe was nothing more than a single memento of infancy saved by a mother (van Driel-Murray 1993, 45), that children of every age in the prefect's household were bound to the sartorial expectations of class.

The *carbatina* is another shoe favoured by children, or perhaps more precisely, preferred by their parents. A shoe made of a single piece of thick cowhide and closed by a lace that wrapped around holes on the top of the foot, the *carbatina* was easy for a child to manoeuvre and the shoe could be loosened or tightened depending on growth, within reason. The shoe was preferred for children, but adult examples are also found, probably having been worn by both men and women. The *carbatina* was used as an indoor shoe; therefore it never had metal studs on the bottom sole. It appears to have been worn by individuals at all social levels; however, there are certainly more and less elaborate examples. A few *carbatinae* from the *praetorium* have more ornate decoration on the sides of the ankles with long loops to take the lace, rather than a simple closed shoe with a series of triangular loops extending from the upper edge of the shoe. Other examples from the *praetorium* appear the same as those from elsewhere on the site, but we might consider those with greater decoration to be of slightly higher quality due to the time investment necessary in making these (van Driel-Murray 1993, fig. 16 for line drawings). The simplest *carbatinae* with solid leather sides and a simple row of triangular lace holes at the upper edge over the top of the foot are found in abundance on the site.

It is interesting to compare this assemblage of children's shoes from the *praetorium* to other shoes found in period 3 contexts outside this elite residence. A further ten examples of children's shoes from which one can make conclusions about style come from other buildings within the period 3 fort. Some are basic soles without discernible characteristics such as maker's marks and without the uppers any conclusions about style would be dubious. However, half of this group of children's shoes are *carbatinae*, none of which reveal any special details that would mark its owner as elite. This may mean very little, but it is clear that the very high-end nature of the *praetorium* assemblage does not exist elsewhere in the period 3 fort so far excavated. The 'fishnet' uppers discussed above appear almost nowhere on site outside of this elite context.

We might also conclude that the higher expectations of visual cues in footwear and dress only became apparent in the beginning of the second century AD, after the initial phases of Roman occupation of the northern British frontier. A comparison of the children's shoes from two contexts in period 2 (*c.*AD 90–97) show rather different results from what was seen in period 3. Shoes from the period 2 *praetorium* and a building across the street that does not have certain identification show similar stylistic patterns. Considering its location this structure could be a barrack, but also may have been the centurion's quarters at the end of the building, which would be the home of a lower level officer and his family if in residence. This structure held twenty-six shoes, of which 50% belonged to children and women or adolescents. The *praetorium* had only five shoes that can be certainly associated with children. What is striking about the assemblages from these two contexts is not the difference between the two, but the overall standard nature of the shoes, even from the *praetorium*.

The preservation in these two spaces was not as good as that in the period 3 *praetorium*, with only the sturdiest shoes such as *carbatinae* predominating. The sole layers are excellent for identifying the type of individual that originally wore the shoe, but style can only be evaluated in a few cases from the sole alone, such as with sandals, when the uppers are not preserved. Even so, it is quite apparent that these shoes did not form an assemblage of high end footwear as was found in period 3. The soles seem to conform more closely to standard changes of style through time, as was suggested by van Driel-Murray when first examining this material (1993, 31–2). She noted rapid changes at the end of the first century, particularly between the footwear at Castleford and Vindolanda; though only a decade apart and about 100 miles (*c.*161 km) between them the sites show very different groups of footwear.

What predominates in the children's shoes of both period 2 spaces, though possibly all from contexts of officer's residences (*praetorium* and possibly centurion's quarters), are wide shapeless shoes with a broad base and rounded toe. As van Driel-Murray has shown, this type of shoe was standard in the late first century, before footwear trends shifted towards a more 'shapely' sole in the second century (van Driel-Murray 1993, 32; cf. van Driel-Murray 2001). However, the adult shoes from the space are similar to what was found in period 3, particularly the 'fishnet' uppers that are found only in the high status contexts such as the *praetorium*. Perhaps at this point, or at least within this particular household, there were not yet expectations of dress placed upon the younger generation, even in the household of the prefect.

Another interesting approach is to compare the period 3 *praetorium* shoes to those found in the barrack block of the next phase, period 4 (*c.*AD 105–120). We should expect the shoes from the *contubernia* of the regular foot soldiers to reflect a lower social status if indeed the auxiliary population was subject to the standard visual cues of dress and rank, in addition to the obvious consideration of differing pay scales. Shoes were found throughout the period 4 barrack block and those belonging to women and children were found clustered in four rooms. This material was determined to have been localized domestic debris left around the spaces after the unit departed (Birley 1994), rather than infill containing rubbish brought into the building to level the area for subsequent building in period 5 (*contra* Reuter 2008, 94–5). Of the 16 shoes that were definitively worn by children and have at least some evidence remaining about style or general expense of the shoe, almost all follow an expected pattern. The basic 'Fell boot', the standard military marching boot found ubiquitously in the Vindolanda assemblage, predominates in the group of children's shoes from the barrack (Plate 2). The boot is a simple enclosed shoe that reaches above the ankle, with a single line of holes along the top of the foot and front of the leg for fastening the shoe. The stud pattern on the bottom usually reflects a utilitarian purpose – large studs covering much of the sole of the shoe – or is in a basic pattern that is found widely in the western provinces. The children's shoes found here use studs sparingly with large gaps in the coverage on the tread sole, another indication that the shoe was of a lower quality. Often basic utilitarian shoes have fewer studs with larger heads, presumably to spare the expense of the iron. Almost none of the children's shoes found here have any decorative embellishments such as cut-out decoration, leather stamps, or stylized stud patterns.

Two shoes stand out in the corpus of children's footwear from the barrack block. A single *carbatina,* with a more complex pattern in the leather cut-out than is typical, was found within the centurion's quarters. If this shoe was found in its original depositional location, it speaks precisely to the expectation of an officer's child wearing a shoe that reflects the status of a well-heeled individual. At the same time, this is still the simple *carbatina* that does not require studs or very much more than a single piece of cowhide; it is only in the more decorative leather cut-outs that a visual cue of status might be found. An infant's sandal found in room 4, which was a basic *contubernium* room near the middle of the barrack, goes against the expectation of what would be found here. It is highly decorative with intricate laces wrapping around the foot (Plate 3). Though a very different type of shoe, in terms of style it is surely comparable to the characteristic suggesting affluence in the *praetorium* assemblage of period 3. Its visual cues suggesting prosperity are found in the intricate and time consuming nature of the decorative work, with small triangular tabs and rosette shaped protrusions around the narrow laces. Saying that, there is very little leather involved in the entire shoe, with the most substantial material usage in the single layer of leather for the foot pad.

Another conclusion not yet considered is the material markers for the presence of slaves within a household. Their existence within the prefect's residence is quite certain and also quite probable in the residences of other officers, or even the households of the foot soldiers. It is quite possible, if not probable, that some of the footwear found within the fort structures belonged to these individuals. The consideration of slaves within the population living inside the fort itself has not been fully explored yet, because of the lack of definitive archaeological evidence. However, the Vindolanda tablets make clear the presence of slaves, for instance an individual named 'Privatus' associated with the *praetorium* (*Tab. Vindol.* 190) and 'Primigenius' and 'Rhenus' corresponding with each other (*Tab. Vindol.* 347). Certainly there would have been slaves and servants of both sexes working inside the households, as well as slaves under the age of eighteen, which should also be considered carefully when discussing the masculine nature of the military camp. Slave ownership is a possible conclusion for the less than spectacular footwear from the period 2 *praetorium*, though it would be quite difficult to prove this with certainty. Excavations in the period 3 *praetorium* clearly turned up the elite footwear of the prefect's family based on style, but perhaps the use of space was different in the period 2 structure and the footwear found was from the slave quarters of the household.

The *schola*, or officer's mess hall, found in the period 4 fort is another space where shoes that may have belonged to slaves could be found. This structure was located near the period 4 *praetorium* and was full of shoes belonging to women and children (Birley 2003, 18–35). A *schola* is the sort of structure which one might expect to find some sort of staff, whether slaves or paid servants, and based on the footwear it appears that children were also a part of the daily life of this space. The building burnt entirely and the finds within have been interpreted as the daily implements left behind in the moment of conflagration. The children's shoes found within are fairly basic *carbatinae*, with the simple triangular lace holes at the top of the foot and no further embellishment. This type of shoe would have been worn by children at all social levels. The adult footwear, however, does not correspond with what we might expect slaves or servants to wear. One female sole is the exact style of the Lepidina slipper from the period 3 *praetorium*, and others have embellishments of maker's marks and decorative cut-outs that only typically belong to high-end shoes. Therefore, caution should be used in assigning the children's shoes to this lower class category as well. The interpretation of the use of this space is also up for debate, with the potential that it was used not only by officer's but also their wives and even children. As always, these are tentative conclusions and ones that cannot be proven by footwear alone, but this evidence brings provocative possibilities to the forefront.

Conclusions

The archaeology of children has always been somewhat fragmentary and therefore our knowledge about their status and role in society is also incomplete. The material presented here may suggest that children living within the environment of the Roman auxiliary army may have been held to similar sartorial expectations of class and status as adults. The Roman world abounded with expectations of dress and personal adornment that would visually announce one's role in society and general level of affluence. One of the most important rituals for a boy was his acceptance into manhood, made visible by donning the *toga virilis*, to show that the individual had a new role in society. Certainly the available sculptural evidence of children in Roman art suggests that their dress should follow the expectations of their class.

It is not surprising to see the continuation of the visual cues used to maintain the social hierarchy in the military environment. Rank and status, and the physical advertisements of this social position, were of the utmost importance in the Roman army. What is of note, however, is that the auxiliary population seems also to have followed these cues to some extent, even in the period 3 fort of the *coh.* VIIII *Batavorum*, a unit commanded by one of their own. In the late first or early second century, on this newly formed Roman frontier thousands of miles from Rome itself, the visual manifestations of status were maintained, even within a mostly non-citizen environment. Even more striking is the suggestion that a child as young as one-year would be held to this expectation. The infant's boot with fully studded tread sole is a fabulous example of a shoe that one can imagine was worn in a public setting with the prefect's family on display as the highest ranking individuals on site. This image of families taking an active role in the daily life of a military fort is becoming more prominent in Roman military studies. The footwear of children offers interesting insight, though unique, into their role in military communities and on the Roman frontiers.

Bibliography

Allason-Jones, L. (1989) *Women in Roman Britain.* London: British Museum Publications.

Allason-Jones, L. (1995) Sexing small finds. In P. Rush (ed.) *Theoretical Roman Archaeology: Second Conference Proceedings,* 22–32. Avebury, Aldershot.

Allason-Jones, L. (1997) The women of Roman Maryport. In R. J. A. Wilson (ed.) *Roman Maryport and its Setting,* 105–11. Maryport, Cumberland and Westmorland Antiquarian and Archaeological Society.

Allason-Jones, L. (1999a) Women and the Roman army in Britain. In A. Goldsworthy and I. Haynes (eds) *The Roman Army as a Community,* 41–51. Portsmouth, Rhode Island.

Allason-Jones, L. (1999b) What is a military assemblage? *JRMES* 10, 1–4.

Allason-Jones, L. (2004) The Family in Roman Britain. In M. Todd (ed.) *A Companion to Roman Britain,* 273–87. Oxford, Oxford University Press.

Allason-Jones, L. (2005) *Women in Roman Britain* 2nd edition. York: Council for British Archaeology.

Allison, P. M. (2006) Mapping for gender. Interpreting artefact distribution inside 1st- and 2nd-century A.D. forts in Roman Germany. *Archaeological Dialogues* 13.1, 1–20.

Allison, P. M. (2007) Artefact distribution within the auxiliary fort at Ellingen: evidence for building use and for the presence of women and children. *Bericht der römische-germanischen Kommission* 87, 387–452.

Bell, H. I., V. Martin, E. G. Turner, van Berchem, D. (1962) *The Abinnaeus Archive. Papers of a Roman Officer in the Reign of Constantius II.* Oxford: Clarendon Press.

Birley, A. (2003) *The Excavations of 2001–2002. Volume I.* Hexham: The Vindolanda Trust.

Birley, R. (1994) *Vindolanda Research Reports, New Series. Vol. I: The Early Wooden Forts.* Hexham: The Vindolanda Trust.

Böhme-Schönberger, A. (2008) Die Distelfibeln – Sind sie Männer- oder Frauenfibeln? In U. Brandl (ed.) *'Frauen und Römisches Militär': Beträge eines Rundes Tisches in Xanten vom 7. Bis 9. Juli 2005,* 140–54. Oxford, Archaeopress.

Bonfante, L. (1994) Introduction. In J. L. Sebesta and L. Bonfante (eds) *The World of Roman Costume,* 3–10. Madison, University of Wisconsin Press.

Brandl, U. (2008) *Uxores, coniuges, libertae.* Frauen in Inschriften römischer Legionäre – Versuch einer numerischen Bestandsaufnahme. In U. Brandl (ed.) *'Frauen und Römisches Militär': Beiträge eines Runden Tisches in Xanten vom 7. Bis 9. Juli 2005,* 52–61. Oxford, Archaeopress.

Busch, A. L. (1965) Die römerzeitlichen Schuh- und Lederfunde der Kastelle Saalburg, Zugmantel und Kleiner Feldberg. *Saalburg Jahrbuch* 22, 158–210.

Driel-Murray, C. van (1993) The leatherwork. In *Vindolanda Research Reports. Volume III, The Early Wooden Forts: Preliminary Reports on the Leather, Textiles, Environmental Evidence and Dendrochronology,* 1–75. Hexham, The Vindolanda Trust.

Driel-Murray, C. van (1995) Gender in Question. In P. Rush (ed.) *Theoretical Roman Archaeology: Second Conference Proceedings,* 3–21. Avebury, Aldershot.

Driel-Murray, C. van (1997) Women in Forts? *Jahresbericht – Gesellschaft Pro Vindonissa 1997,* 55–61.

Driel-Murray, C. van (1998) A question of gender in a military context. *Helinium* 34 [1994], 342–62.

Driel-Murray, C. van (2001) Vindolanda and the dating of Roman footwear. *Britannia* 32, 185–97.

Driel-Murray, C. van (2007) Footwear in the north-western Provinces of the Roman Empire. In O. Goubitz, C. van Driel-Murray, W. Groenman-van Waateringe, *Stepping through Time. Archaeological Footwear from Prehistoric Times until 1800,* 336–76. Zwolle, Stichting Promotie Archeologie.

Goldman, N. (1994) Roman Footwear. In J. L. Sebesta and L. Bonfante (eds) *The World of Roman Costume,* 101–29. Madison, University of Wisconsin Press.

Greene, E. M. (2013) Female networks in the military communities of the Roman west. In E. Himelrijk and G. Woolf (eds), *Gender and the City: Women and Civic Life in Italy and the Western Provinces.* Leiden, Brill.

Greene, E. M. (forthcoming) The Families of Auxiliary Soldiers in Military Diplomas. In P. Bidwell (ed.) *Proceedings of the XXI International Limes Congress.* Oxford, Archaeopress.

Groenman-van Waateringe, W. (1967) *Romeins Lederwerk uit Valkenburg Z.H.* Groningen, J. B. Wolters.

Groenman-van Waateringe, W. (1975) Römische Lederfunde aus Vindonissa und Valkenburg Z.H.: ein Vergleich. *Gesellschaft pro Vindonissa, Jahresbericht 1974,* 62–84.

Groenman-van Waateringe, W. (1978) Shoe sizes and palaeodemography. *Helinium* 18, 184–9.

Hoevenberg, J. (1993) Leather artefacts. In R. M. van Dierendonck, D. P. Hallewas, and K. E. Waugh (eds) *The Valkenburg Excavations 1985–1988,* 217–338. Amersfoort, ROB.

Hoffmann, B. (2006) Melonenperlen und das Militär in Grossbritannien, am Rhein und an der oberen Donau. In G. Seitz (ed.) *Im Dienste Roms. Festschrift für Hans Ulrich Nuber*, 227–230. Remshalden, Greiner.

Maxfield, V. A. (1995) *Soldier and Civilian: Life Beyond the Ramparts. The Eighth Annual Caerleon Lecture.* Cardiff, National Museum of Wales.

Moore, R. (2010) Roman women in the *Castra*: who's in charge here. In C. Deroux (ed.) *Studies in Latin Literature and Roman History, vol. XV. Collection Latomus 323*, 49–78. Bruxelles, Éditions Latomus.

Rector, W. K. (1975) *The Treatment of Waterlogged Leather from Blackfriars, City of London.* Belfast, Ulster Museum.

Reuter, M. (2008) Frauen in römischen Militärlagern? Eine archäologische Spurensuche. In U. Brandl, (ed.) *'Frauen und Römisches Militär': Beiträge eines Runden Tisches in Xanten vom 7. Bis 9. Juli 2005,* 92–101. Oxford, Archaeopress.

Rhodes, M. (1980) Leather footwear. In D. M. Jones (ed.) *Excavations at Billingsgate Buildings 'Triangle', Lower Thames Street, 1974*, 99–128. London. London and Middlesex Archaeological Society.

Roxan, M. M. (1991) Women on the frontiers. In M. J. Dobson and V. A. Maxfield (eds.) *Roman Frontier Studies 1989*, 462–7. Exeter, University of Exeter Press.

Wells, C. M. (1997) 'The daughters of the regiment': sisters and wives in the Roman army. In W. Groenman-van Waateringe, *et al.* (eds.) *Roman Frontier Studies 1995*, 571–4. Oxford, Oxbow.

6

A GROUP OF FINDS FROM OUTSIDE THE SOUTH-WEST GATE OF SOUTH SHIELDS ROMAN FORT

A. T. Croom
with a contribution by M. Henig

Introduction

These finds come from a small area between the ditches outside the south-west gate and the edge of the fort park along Baring Street, excavated in 1987–8 (Fig. 6.1). The excavations in 1987 revealed the road leading up the gateway, the terminals of the outer ditches and a number of quarry pits (published in Snape 1994; see figs 4.18–9; fig. 4.1, area marked 1985–7). A new area of excavation was opened up in the same year, covering the zone beyond the ditches (*ibid.*, fig. 4.1, area marked 1987–8). The most noticeable feature of these excavations was a large area of metalling, which may have been used as a market-place in the late Roman period. As most of the finds come from the area beyond the ditches they were left for publication as part of the assemblage of the *vicus*, rather than of the defences.

Excavations in the *vicus* on the other side of Baring Street (Fig. 6.1) have revealed occupation dating from before the construction of the stone fort to the abandonment of the *vicus* in *c.*260–70, followed by cultivation until at least the late third or fourth century (Snape *et al.* 2010, table 1). However, the road into the fort remained in use throughout this period and into the late fourth century, while activity in the fifth century included a new ditch, re-use of the gateway, and the development of a small cemetery (Snape 1994, 131; figs 4.18–9).

The assemblage as a whole had a high proportion of copper alloy pieces (making up a third of all the small finds), but only small quantities of iron or bone. The catalogue entries include description, measurements, location and date of context, context number and small finds number.

Religion (Fig. 6.2)

1. *Stone bowl* (D: 500 mm H: 120 mm wall B: 60 mm shaft D: 210 mm). Make-up layer, fourth century, 15275, S209.

Five fragments from a large, shallow sandstone bowl with scalloped edges (Fig. 6.3). Underneath there is the remains of a circular shaft, expanding at the point where it is broken, with a roughly circular iron rod (W: 50 mm) set in a central socket. The interior of the bowl rises towards a central boss (D: 80 mm) with a smaller projection on top, now missing (D: 30 mm). The surface of the interior of the bowl has the remains of a thick black residue apart from a band at the junction between wall and base about 50 mm wide and 20 mm deep. The residue was analysed using gas chromatography mass spectrometry, but the results were inconclusive (Stern 2011). The interior of the bowl is quite roughly worked with visible peck marks and grooves, in contrast to the scalloped edges and the exterior wall, which are very smooth until close to the shaft.

The black residue could be the remains of a deliberate pitch lining or perhaps the residue of incense burning. Pitch has also been found in a stone bowl (from a *mithraeum* at Koenigshoffen/Strasbourg) identified as a charcoal burner (Clauss 2000, 121; fig. 84). A shallow bowl with a central boss reminiscent of the South Shields example was found outside the temple of Mithras in London and identified as a laver (Wardle 1998, fig. 212). Stone basins were part of the 'basic equipment' of *mithraea* and have been found in a number of them (Clauss 2000, 73). They held the water used to purify the hands of the initiates of the lower grades, although some might also have been used for the honey used to purify the higher grades, which might explain the range of different designs and depths of the basins. Unlike the South Shields examples, those from *mithraea* all appear to be portable, and

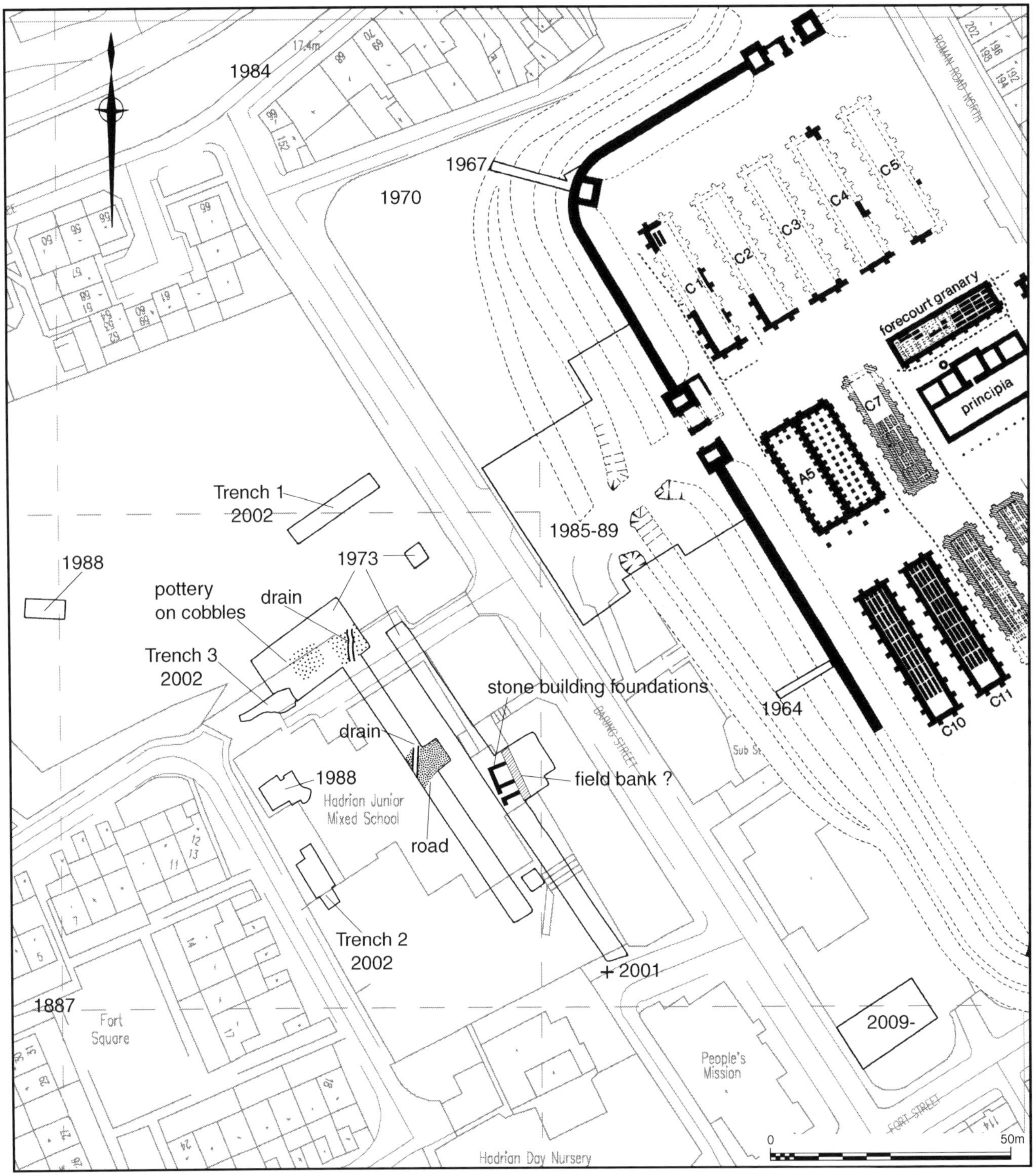

Fig. 6.1 Excavations in the vicus *south-west of the fort. The finds come from the western end (bordering Baring Street) of the trench labelled 1985–1989*

rather than coming from a *mithraeum*, this piece may have come from some other form of temple, with similar ritual requirements for cleansing or incense-burning. If it was intended for burning incense, the bowl may well have been set up in the open air, since the amount of incense burning in a bowl of that size would have produced large quantities of smoke.

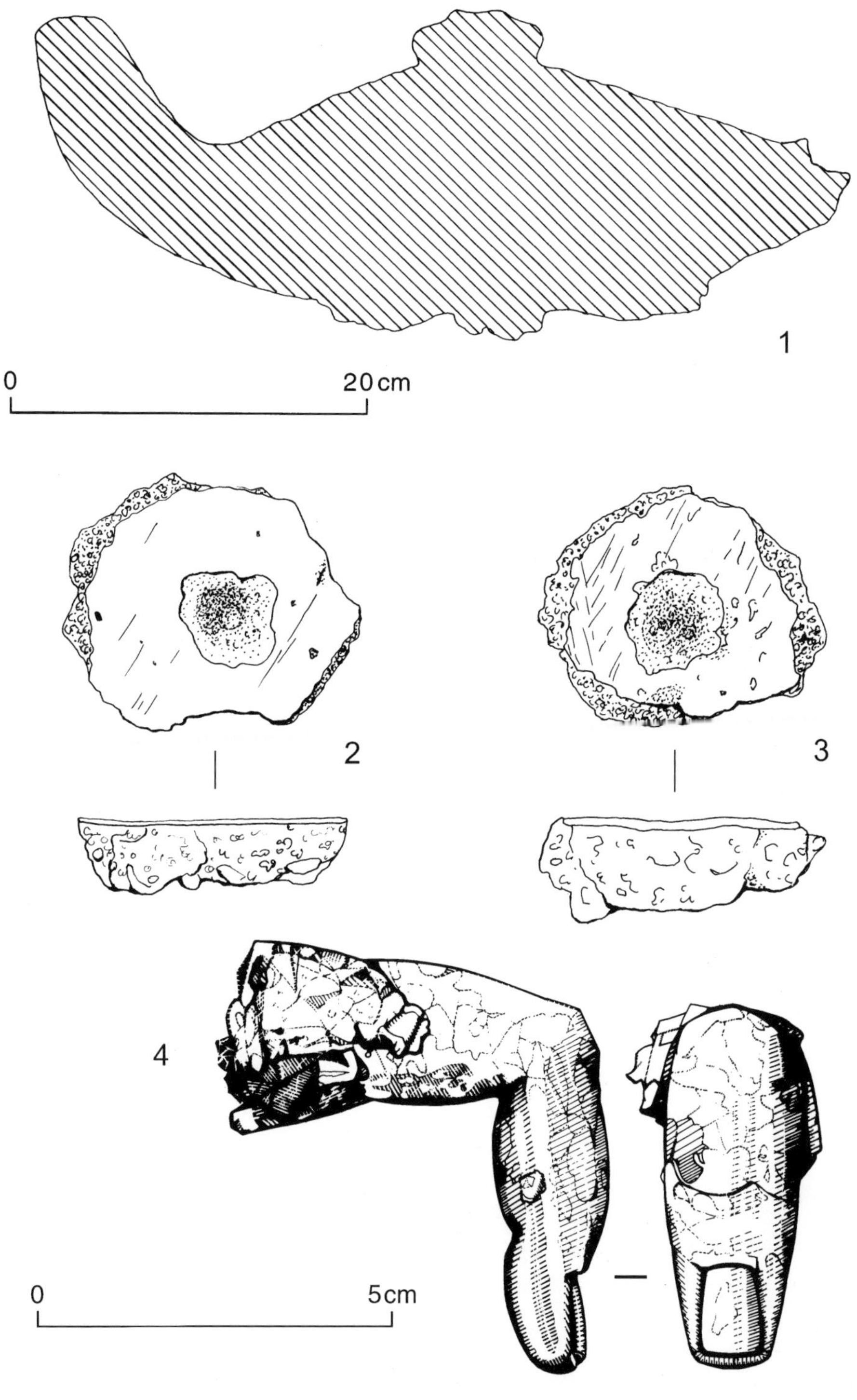

Fig. 6.2 Artefacts relating to religion. 1: scale 1:4; 2–4: scale 1:1

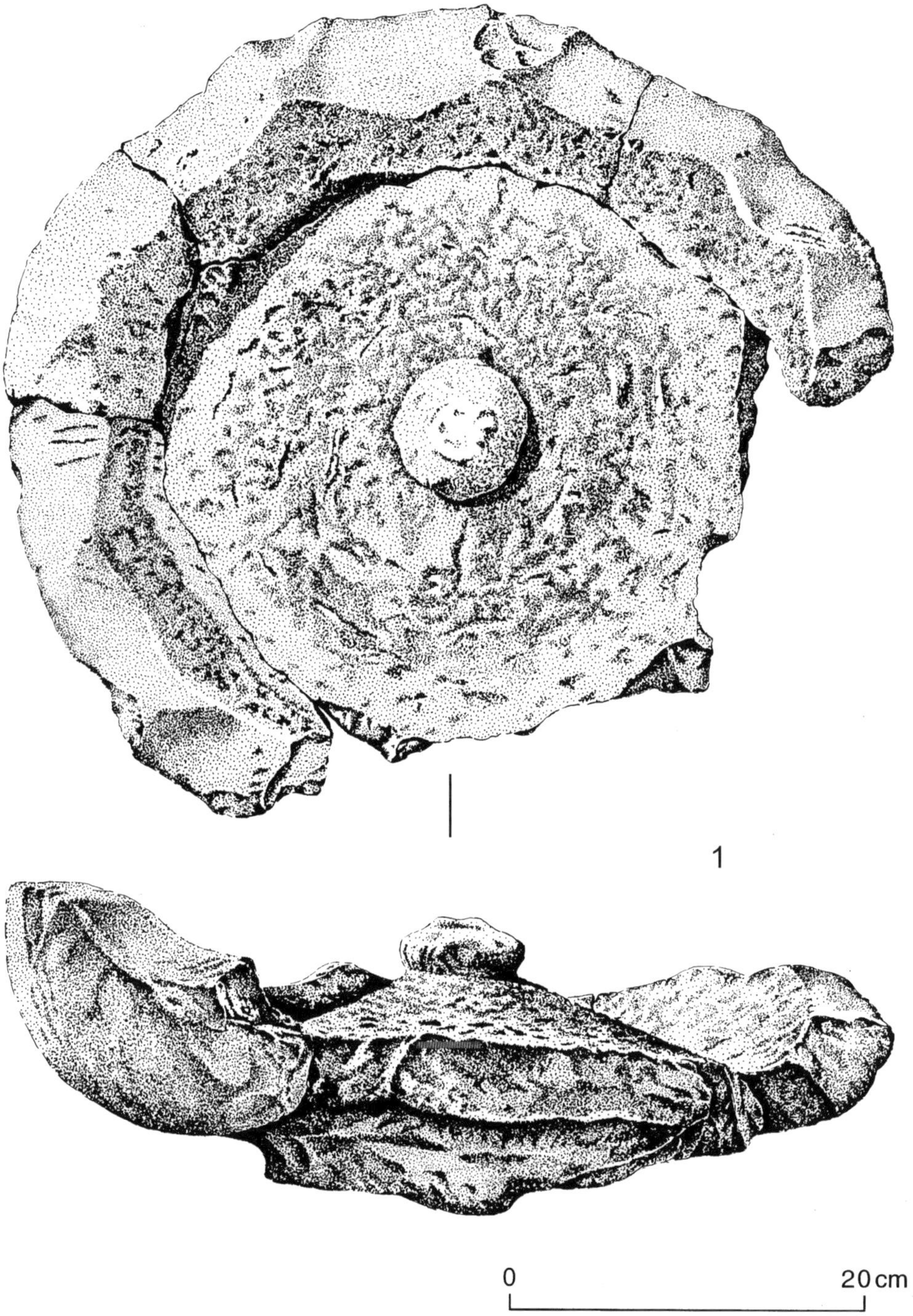

Fig. 6.3 Stone bowl. Scale 1:4

2–3. Plaster votive eyes *(Figs 6.2, 6.4)*

2. (L: 40 mm W: 38 mm B (max): 11 mm). Modern, 15004, Misc58.

Disc cut from fragment of wall plaster, with original surface surviving, cut by a small depression. Lower surface thin round edges and thicker in centre.

3. (L: 41 mm W: 32 mm B: 9 mm to 15 mm). Modern, 15003, Misc59.

As above. The lower surface is rough and thicker on one side than the other.

A large number of such votive eyes, which are chipped from re-used fragments of wall plaster rather than made from scratch, have been found at the basilica site at

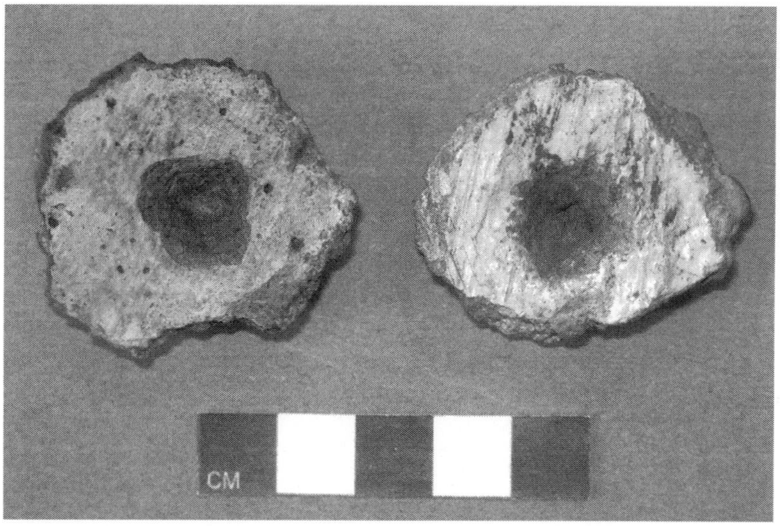

Fig. 6.4 Plaster eyes (cat nos 2–3)

Wroxeter (Barker *et al.* 1997, figs 312–3). It is thought they could be offerings for the relief of eye disease or cult objects from a nearby shrine (*ibid.,* 215–6). The Wroxeter examples came from make-up layers and could only be dated vaguely to the fourth century or earlier. These two examples are unfortunately unstratified, while another possible example from the courtyard house inside the fort comes from a robber trench.

4. *Bronze statue finger* (L: 52 mm W: 50 mm B: 22 mm). Modern, 15013, BR270.

Life-sized finger bent at the first joint, with the second joint and finger nail carefully depicted. The lower end of the finger is torn; it was apparently joined to other fingers on one side only making it the first or little finger of the hand, and most likely comes from a hand with gently flexed fingers (cf. Bayley *et al.* 2009, fig. 4). The metal is a bronze rather than a brass (test by P. Oakley, University of Newcastle upon Tyne).

The statue had no doubt been broken up for recycling, but Croxford's study of statue fragmentation has shown that fingers and hands from bronze statues are over-represented in the archaeological record, and it is possible they were kept as amulets or tokens (Croxford 2003, 89). At least eight examples are known from both military and civilian sites in Britain (*ibid.,* 89; Bayley *et al.* 2009, 158, nos 4–5), but many of them come from old excavations and details of their context are unknown, although over-life-sized fingers from Caerleon were found in a barrack and next to a statue-pedestal in the basilica of the headquarters building (*CSIR 1.5*, nos 45–6). Life-size bronze statues were most likely to come from either the headquarters building inside the fort or a temple outside the fort.

Temple

The plaster eyes were presumably intended for a shrine or temple as votive offerings in hope of, or in thanks for, a cure. Eye problems were rife in the Roman world, and were enough of a concern to the Roman army for it to require an eye test for all recruits (Allason-Jones 1999, 137). If the shrine did not specialise only in problems of the eye, then it is possible the re-used statue finger might also have been used as a votive offering. An altar to Aesculapius from the site could have come from a healing shrine, since Aesculapius was one of the most important healing gods in the Roman world, although it was found on the other side of the fort, re-used in a wall near the north-east gate (*CSIR 1.1*, no. 181). An altar found somewhere near the fort's north-west corner is suggestive of a religious site closer to the find-spot of the votive items, but unfortunately it has an illegible inscription (*CSIR 1.1*, no. 301).

Military equipment and horse harness (Fig. 6.5)

5. *Copper alloy scabbard runner* (W: 5 mm B: 2 mm). Road surface or levelling, late Roman, 15018, BR405.

Heart-shaped terminal of scabbard-runner of rectangular cross-section and bevelled edges. There are files marks on the under surface. Late second to third century.

6. *Copper alloy buckle* (W (attachment loop): 17 mm B: 1 mm surviving L: 21 mm). Patching within road metalling, mid-fourth century, 15179, BR305.

Incomplete buckle with T-shaped attachment loop, poor quality casting. Late second to third century.

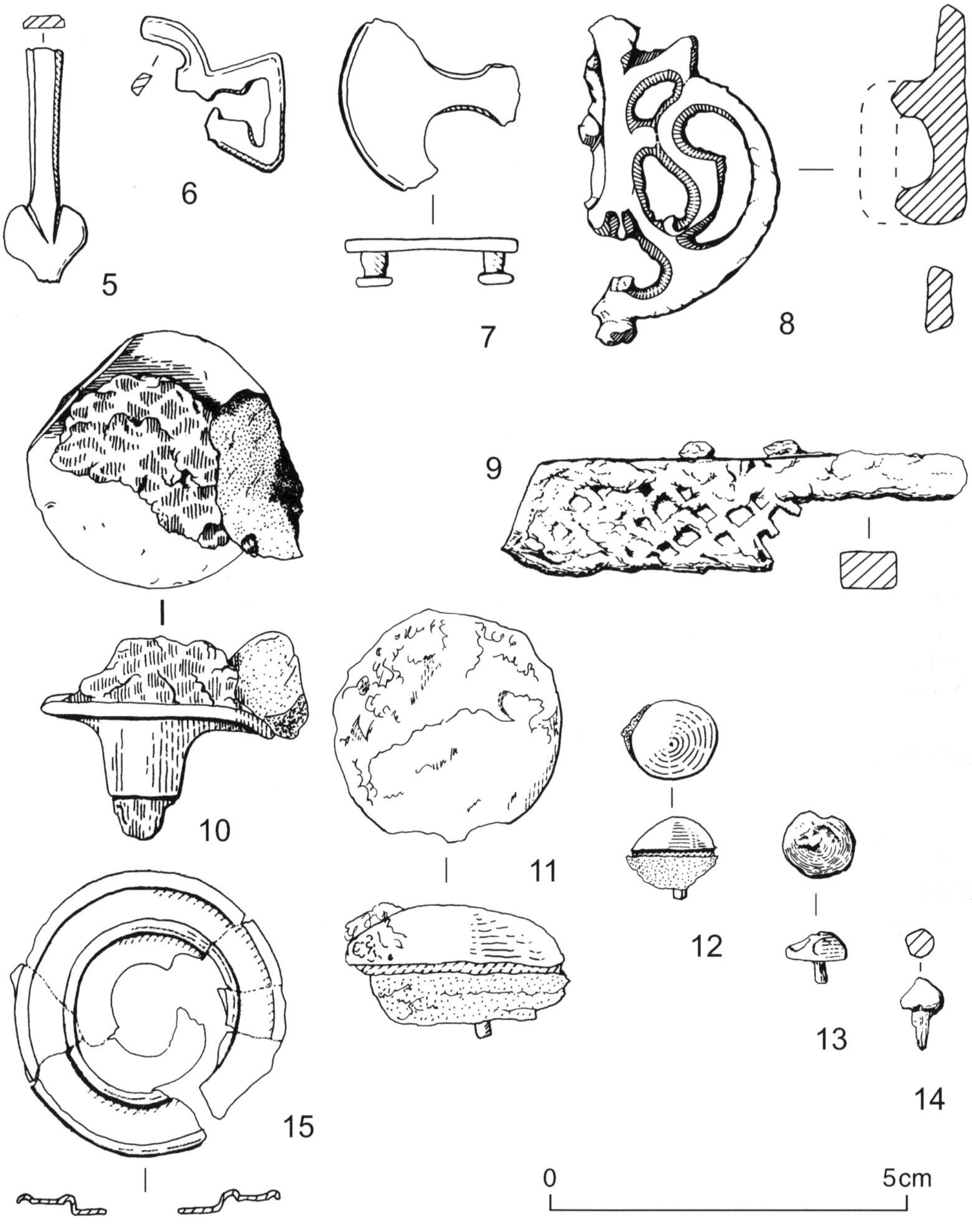

Fig. 6.5 Military equipment: 5–8; box fittings: 9–15. Scale 1:1

7. *Copper alloy mount* (L: 25 mm W: 23 mm+ B: 2 mm B (overall): 8 mm D (shank head): 6 mm). Fill of plough marks, probably second century, 15213, BR312.

Incomplete pelta-shaped mount, possibly originally silvered, with two disc-headed shanks for attaching to leather *c*.4 mm thick.

8. *Copper alloy harness slider* (L: 45 mm W: 26 mm+ B: 4 mm). Dump layer, late second century?, 15332, BR434.

Incomplete, openwork mount, with central bar with foliate terminal. The bar divides and curls back on itself. When excavated, it had a rectangular attachment loop projecting from the lower surface.

The harness mount and one of the possible harness fittings (no. 7) come from early layers; the other pieces are residual in later contexts. The buckle with T-shaped attachment loop is the most common type of buckle found on the site; 14 examples are known from the fort and vicus. Pelta-shaped studs have been found used on soldiers' belts in

Spain, but this appears to be a late Roman fashion, and it is possible pelta-shaped mounts of the late second and third century were only used on horse harness (Aurrecoechea Fernández 1996, 109).

Box fittings and studs

9. *Copper alloy lock bolt* (L: 61 mm W: 16 mm B: 8 mm). Natural silting at base of slope, late second century, 15341, BR436.

Lock bolt with lattice pattern.

10. *Copper alloy bell-shaped stud* (D: 36 mm shank W: 5 mm). Modern, 15003, BR262.

Undecorated skirt, distorted and covered in iron corrosion.

11. *Copper alloy stud with lead solder* (D: 32 mm shank W: 3 mm). Dump layer, late second or third century, 15315, BR426.

Large, slightly domed circular head filled with lead solder, with an iron shank.

12. *Copper alloy stud* (D: 12 mm W (shank): 2 mm). Silt layer under road surface, third century?, 15300, BR429.

Small stud with a lead-solder filled domed head and square-sectioned shank.

13. *Copper alloy stud* (D: 12 mm W (shank): 2 mm). Tumble from late second century road, 15348, BR439.

Small, circular stud, slightly hollow, with short, square-sectioned shank.

14. *Copper alloy tack* (head W: 3 mm shank W: 1 mm). Late/post Roman silting, 15164, BR291.

Small, conical-headed tack with incomplete square-sectioned shank.

15. *Copper alloy fitting* (D: 35 mm B (overall): 3 mm D (hole): 11 mm). Modern, 15003, BR206.

Large, hollowcast fitting with a slightly raised rib round the outer edge and a more prominent ridge half-way between the edge and the large central hole. The size of the central hole is unusual, but the piece is in too poor a condition to be sure this was original.

Box fittings are common site finds both inside the fort and in the *vicus*. Unsurprisingly the most common elements are the studs used in some numbers to decorate and attach panels to the wood. Bell-shaped studs used as box-fittings are known from Germany and Hungary, where up to 18 were used on a single box (Allason-Jones 1985, pl. 1; Alföldi *et al.* 1957, Abb 84, no. 105; 345; cf. Abb. 85, no. 188). A total of 73 bell-shaped studs are known from South Shields, few of which match in design. Most are unstratified, but the earliest stratified examples come from contexts dating to the very early third century.

The use of composite studs filled with lead solder on boxes is demonstrated by examples on a casket from Colchester, which was also found with a lock mechanism and a ring-key in place (Crummy 1983, 85, nos 2178–90). Excavations at South Shields from 1983 to 2012 have produced 37 composite studs of all sizes, nearly a third of all the studs recovered during that period. The site has also produced six lock bolts and nine ring-keys. The number of ring-keys found show small caskets were common, and it is likely most of the studs and fittings come from small boxes that held individuals' private possessions rather than larger storage chests.

Household (Fig. 6.6)

16. *Copper alloy escutcheon and bucket fragment* (Escutcheon L: 73 mm W: 40 mm) B (max): 8 mm Vessel B: 1 mm). Infilling in area of subsidence over quarry pit, late third to mid fourth century, 15040, BR311, BR314.

A split-tail escutcheon with a badly worn attachment loop, found associated with a fragment of the vessel with a plain lip and the remains of two irregular-headed rivets from a repair. There are remains of lead solder on the back of the escutcheon and on the vessel. This type of escutcheon is found on vessels with a flat base and a flared mouth or ones with a bulbous body above a narrow footring (Sedlmayer 1999, Abb. 24; Taf. 47.2; den Boesterd 1956, pl. vi, no. 153), and dates from the late second to the early third century (Corder 1990, 230–1, Sedlmayer 1999, 108). The vessels may have been used to hold the water used for mixing with the wine during formal dining, as they have been found associated with wine jugs and strainers in grave assemblages (*ibid.*, 108; Abb. 24).

One other example of a similar escutcheon has been found at South Shields (Allason-Jones and Miket 1984, no. 3.765). Other evidence for the use of bronze wine services at the site are two strainer or dipper handles, a jug handle and a small fragment of a strainer bowl (ibid., 3.373; SF nos BR568 and BR656 (unpublished); Croom 2010, fig. 34, no. 59) and probably a bucket handle (Allason-Jones and Miket 1984, 3.408).

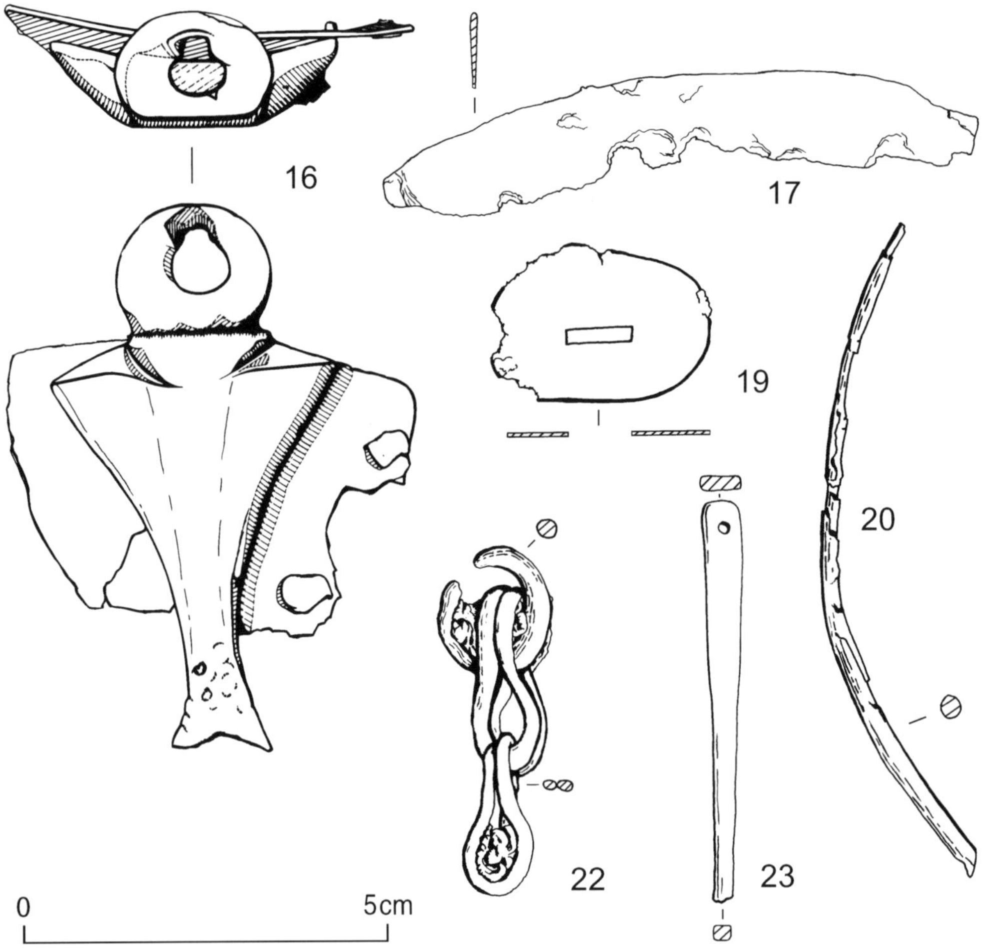

Fig. 6.6 Household items. Scale 1:1

17. *Copper alloy vessel* (L: 92 mm W: 13 mm B (max): 1.5 mm). Packing in south-east terminal of ditch B (Snape 1994, 135), late third or early fourth century, 15058, BR298.

Possible rim fragment from vessel, with a thickened, plain rim.

18. *Iron escutcheon* (L: 100 mm W: 24 mm D (hole): 9 mm). Infilling in area of subsidence over quarry pit, late third to mid fourth century, 15040, I667.

Strip pierced with hole, probably from a wooden bucket.

19. *Copper alloy hilt-guard*? (L: 29 mm W: 21 mm B: 1 mm slot L: 9 mm W: 2 mm). Road surface or levelling, late Roman, 15018, BR403.

Oval sheet pierced by slot, possibly a hilt-guard from the handle of a knife, although these are generally not very common in the Roman period.

20. *Copper alloy cosmetic implement* (L: 94 mm D: 3 mm). Possible silting at base of slope, late second century, 15322, BR431.

Incomplete cosmetic implement, with the remains of an angled head, in poor condition.

21. *Copper alloy cosmetic spoon* (W: 5 mm). Layer cut by roadside gully, third century,15289, BR423.

Very fragmentary remains of a long bowl from a cosmetic implement, with projection at the junction between shank and bowl.

22. *Copper alloy chain* (Loop D: 16 mm B:3 mm; link L: 14 mm W: 11 mm B: 10 mm; B (of wire): 2 mm). Tumble from the late second-century road, 15348, BR440.

Short length of chain consisting of a circular attachment loop and two links formed by annular loops folded and twisted over so that the loops of double wire are at right-angles to each other.

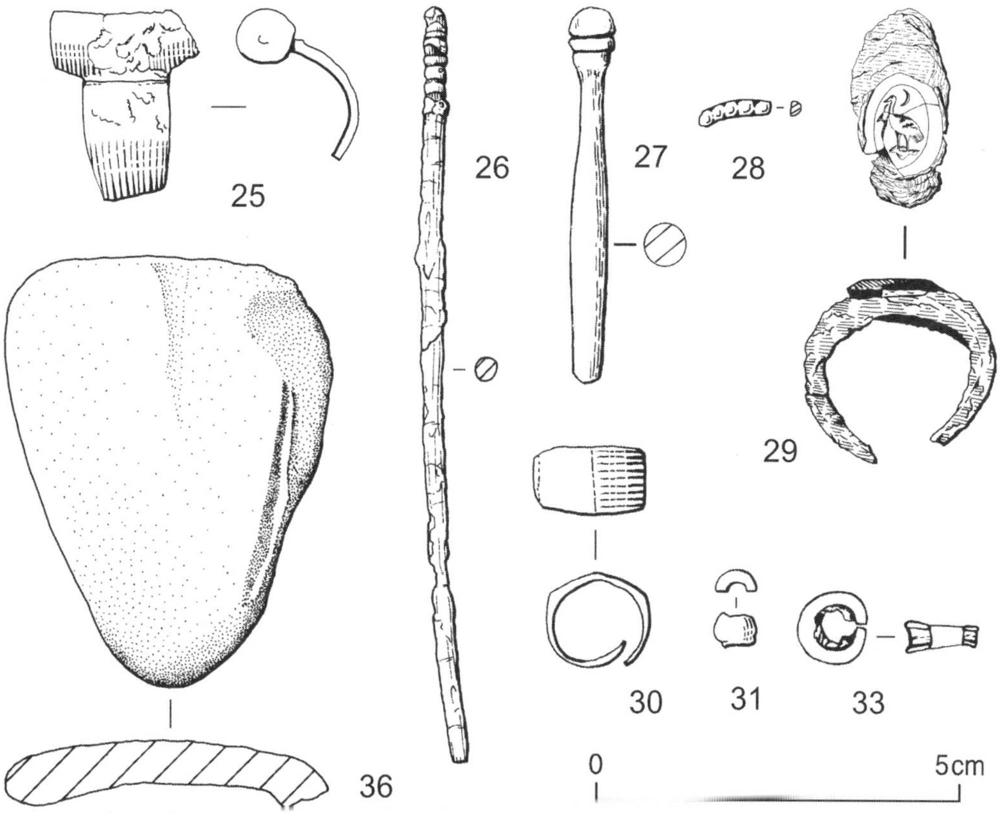

Fig. 6.7 Personal equipment: 25–33; pottery: 36. Scale 1:1

23. *Bone needle* (L: 53 mm W (head): 5 mm B (shank): 3 mm). Possible natural silting, late second century, 15478, B174.

Incomplete roughly finished needle with flattened head pierced by 1.5 mm hole and a square-sectioned shank.

24. *Iron hook* (L: 235 mm D: 12 mm). Layer in area of subsidence over quarry pit, fifth century, 15019, I202.

Gently curved circular-section bar, curving back on itself at either end. One end is curved into a hook.

There was also a pierced disc cut from a body sherd of a samian bowl just under the rim from the fill of a robber trench (SF no. P246) and a 45 mm diameter disc in burnt red sandstone (SF no. S181, fifth-century layer).

Personal equipment (Fig. 6.7)

25. *Copper alloy brooch* (W: 19 mm L: 22 mm B (bow): 2 mm). Layer cut by roadside gully, third century, 15289, BR422.

Incomplete knee-brooch with wide, flat bow and open cylinder with a spring on an iron axis bar. Parallels in the north include Corbridge, Vindolanda, Kirkby Thore, Brough, and Piercebridge (Bayley and Butcher 2004, 256, Hull T175A). Late second or third century in date.

26. *Copper alloy pin* (L: 101 mm D: 3 mm). Fill above area of subsidence over quarry pit, late Roman, 15151, BR415.

Incomplete pin with ridge and groove decorated head. Circular cross-section, facetted shank.

27. *Bone pin* (L: 50 mm D (shank): 4 mm). Fill of robber trench cut by outer ditch, fourth century, 15110, B137.

Incomplete pin with a roughly spherical head with a groove creating a collar.

28. *Copper alloy bangle* (W: 1 mm B: 1 mm). Layer, late third or fourth century, 15257, BR407.

Minute fragment of bangle with a semi-circular cross-section, decorated with incisions on upper surface to create a cable pattern. Fourth century.

Fig. 6.8 Iron ring with intaglio

29. *Iron finger ring with intaglio* (L: 26 mm W: 22 mm B: 13 mm Intaglio: L: 13 mm W: 10 mm B: 2 mm). Possible floor surface containing fuel ash, late second century or later, 15321, INT4.

M. Henig writes: Nicolo glass intaglio, light blue on the flat upper surface and 'black' below (Fig. 6.8). The gem is oval in form and has a flat upper face and sides which are bevelled outwards (shape F2). The gem is unfortunately broken, with the pieces held in place by the ring's corrosion. The gem seems to have been set in a copper alloy box setting within the bezel of an iron ring with simple flattish hoop expanding towards the bezel (Henig 1978, type III, fig. 1). This feature has not, to my knowledge, been observed in the case of iron rings but silver rings sometimes have a gold box-setting. A silver ring with a gold collet, dated to the later second century, found near Wotton-under-Edge is in Gloucester Museum (Henig 1981, 130–1; pl. 8.1, no. 2) and similar examples are recorded from the Rhineland (Hnekel 1913, 58, nos 421–2; Taf. xxi). The visual effect here would have been very similar. Iron is silvery in colour and the copper alloy could, indeed, have been brassy (*orichalcum*) looking like gold.

The device, which is cast in a mould and not cut, portrays an eagle standing to the left upon a thunderbolt (*fulmen*) resting atop a globe. The head of the eagle is turned right and it holds a wreath in its beak. The allusion is, of course, to Jupiter, whose attributes were the eagle and the thunderbolt. The wreath stands for Roman victory and the globe for world rule. All in all this would have been a highly appropriate device for a Roman soldier.

The intaglio is paralleled by another nicolo-glass intaglio from Caerleon, which was excavated from a drain deposit dated *c.*230–96 (Henig 1978, 270, no. 697; pl. xxi). A much finer, and clearer example of the same type is an intaglio cut on an agate from Aldborough, Yorkshire (*ibid.,* 293, no. app. 69; pl. xxvi). A black jasper ring-stone from Saint-Marcel (Indre) should also be noted (Guiraud 1988, 172, no. 732; pl. xlix).

30. *Copper alloy finger-ring* (W (overall): 15 mm B: 9 mm). Layer over road surface (Snape 1994, 141), late fourth or fifth century, 15075, BR244.

Small ring with slight thickening at the shoulders and a plain bezel sloping towards the centre. The band, now broken, tapers in width towards the back (min. W: 3 mm). The majority of Roman rings have a flat bezel, rather than a peaked bezel such as this; there is one cast type with thickening at the shoulder, but it has a narrower band and a small circular bezel (Alföldi *et al.*1957, Taf lxxviii, no. 7; cf. P. A. S. LIN-47D233). A sheet metal example from Intercisa also has a peaked bezel, but has openwork decoration (Alföldi *et al.* 1957, Taf. lxxx, no. 11). Third century.

31. *Glass bead* (D: 5 mm). Fill of quarry pit, fourth century, 15192, G233.

Incomplete globular bead in opaque turquoise glass, with a narrow streak of green in the metal. This type of bead is very long-lived and cannot be closely dated.

32. *Hobnails*

An item of footwear, represented by a group of 56 hobnails, was found in an early third-century make-up layer (15282, SF no. I299) and another (*c.*24 hobnails) from the fill of a late second-century pit (15336, SF no. I304).

33. *Copper alloy loop* (D: 9 mm W: 3 mm B: 2 mm). Spread of soil, possibly from road-robbing, 15527, BR445.

Rectangular cross-section, with concave surface on the outer edge. Pennanular.

Crafts

34. *Bronze-working*

Three pieces of copper alloy waste were recovered, all of them of molten, including a piece weighing 61 g from a late third/early fourth-century road surface (15021, SF no. BR281). There was a droplet piece from the filling above subsidence over a quarry pit (15040, SF no. BR315), and a slightly larger piece from a late second-century road surface (15450, SF no. BR432). A stone bar-mould for producing ingots was recovered from the late fourth-century road surface (Croom 1994, fig. 7.14, no. 117).

35. *Antler-working*

A possible pin blank was recovered from the fill of the north-west terminal of ditch B (Snape 1994, 135; late third or early fourth century, 15239, SF no. B149). Other pieces of antler-working come from late fourth or late fourth/early fifth century contexts, and cover the range of stages found in antler-working, from a sawn tine to wedges and trimmed pieces (B128, B130, B142, B148, B150).

Evidence for antler-working is often found in late Roman layers on the site, so the quantity of pieces recovered here is not unexpected, although it is noticeable almost all come from the area of the ditches rather than the *vicus*. Of greater interest are the three pieces of molten copper alloy and the bar-mould. Although they were not found in close proximity, they may be evidence of a metal-working workshop in the area. Even the statue finger (no. 4), if not an amulet or votive offering brought in from elsewhere, could have come from the workshop where the statue was cut up, or been intended for the workshop for recycling. Evidence for non-ferrous metalworking has also recently been discovered in the *vicus* equally close to the defences at the south corner of the fort (Fig. 6.1; trench labelled 2009).

Other

36. *Triangle* (L: 56 mm W: 45 mm B: 6 mm). Fill of gully or quarry pit, fourth century, 15176, P270.

Carefully shaped triangle cut from body sherd of a samian bowl, including part of the junction between wall and base or footring, although this edge of the triangle is broken. It has carefully smoothed edges, and the whole surface slip has been removed, apart from traces in the remains of the carination. While discs of re-used pottery in a range of sizes are common, other shapes are extremely rare, so it is of note that there is another similar-sized triangle from the site cut from an amphora sherd (SF. no. P468, fourth century, courtyard house), although the use of such pieces is unknown.

Discussion

The assemblage from the possible market area can be compared both with a similarly sized group recovered from the nearby ditches and road, and with a larger group recovered from excavations in the *vicus* on the other side of Baring Street (Fig. 6.1). In some respects all three areas are similar; all have approximately the same proportion of items relating to household use, personal adornment and pieces associated with women. The market area assemblage is similar to that from the *vicus* area in having a higher proportion of military and horse harness items than the ditches (10% and 9% compared to 4%), and at least three times as many items relating to box fittings (10% and 7% compared to 2%). In contrast, it is closer to the ditches assemblage when considering religious items. In the market area and ditches items with possible religious connections make up approximately 10% of each assemblage, while in the *vicus* the figure is only 1% (a single pipe-clay figurine). The items from the ditches, however, are mainly from ritual depositions in ditch terminals (Snape 1994, 137) rather than possible evidence for a temple or shrine. The market area is unusual in the low number of discs and pierced discs it produced, considering both are common site finds; there was a single pierced pottery disc and one stone disc. This makes up 5% of the site assemblage, compared to 16% in the ditches and 15% in the *vicus*. The market area also stands out for having more evidence for non-ferrous metalworking in its assemblage.

The most important pieces from the assemblage are the items relating to religion. The stone bowl is elaborate in form and unusual in having been set on a column or stand of some type, whilst the presence of the plaster eyes raises the possibility of a nearby healing shrine or temple. Both hint at a building or buildings of interest in the vicinity.

Acknowledgements

With thanks to all those who provided the illustrations, principally David Nelson and Roger Oram.

Bibliography

Alföldi, M. R., Barkóczi, L., Fitz, J., Sz. Póczy, K., Radnóti, A., Salamon, Á., Sági, K., Szilágyi, J., Vágó, E. B. (1957) *Intercisa II (Dunapentele). Geschichte der Stadt in der Römerzeit*, Budapest.

Allason-Jones, L. (1985) 'Bell-shaped studs'? In M. C. Bishop (ed.) *The Production and Distribution of Roman Military Equipment,* 95–108. BAR, International Series 275. Oxford.

Allason-Jones, L. (1999) Health care in the Roman North. *Britannia* 30, 133–146.

Allason-Jones, L. and Miket, R. (1984) *The Catalogue of Small Finds from South Shields Roman Fort.* Society of Antiquaries of Newcastle upon Tyne Monograph 2.

Aurrecoechea Fernández, J. (1996) Bronze studs from Roman Spain. *JRMES* 7, 97–146.

Barker, P., White, R., Pretty, K., Bird, H. and Corbishley, M. (1997) *The Baths Basilica, Wroxeter: Excavations 1966–90,* English Heritage Archaeological Report 8. London.

Bayley, J. and Butcher, S. (2004) *Roman Brooches in Britain: a Technological and Typological Study based on the Richborough Collection.* Report of the Research Committee of the Society of Antiquaries of London 68. London.

Bayley, J., Croxford, B., Henig, M. and Watson, B. (2009) A gilt-bronze arm from London. *Britannia* 40, 151–162.

Bidwell, P. and Speak, S. (1994) *Excavations at South Shields Roman Fort, Volume 1,* Newcastle upon Tyne.

Clauss, M. (2000) *The Roman Cult of Mithras: the God and his Mysteries.* Edinburgh.

Corder, S. (1990) Two escutcheons from Rochester, Northumberland. *AA,* 5th series, 18, 230–231.

CSIR 1.1 = Phillips, E. (1977) *Corpus Signorum Imperii Romani: Great Britain, Volume 1, Fascicule 1: Corbridge , Hadrian's Wall East of the North Tyne.* Oxford.

CSIR 1.5 = Brewer, R. (1986) *Corpus Signorum Imperii Romani Volume 1, Fascicule 5: Great Britain, Wales.* Oxford.

Croom, A. T. (1994) Small finds. In P. Bidwell and S. Speak (eds.) *Excavations at South Shields Roman Fort, Volume 1,* 177–206. Newcastle upon Tyne.

Croom, A. T. (2010) The small finds. In M. Snape, P. Bidwell and G. Stobbs (eds) Excavations in the military *vicus* south-west of the Roman Fort at South Shields in 1973, 1988 and 2002. *Arbeia Journal* 9, 43–132, 75–87.

Croxford, B. (2003) Iconoclasm in Roman Britain? *Britannia* 34, 81–95.

Crummy, N. (1983) *The Roman Small Finds from Excavations in Colchester 1971–9.* Colchester Archaeological Report 2. Colchester.

den Boesterd, M. H. P. (1956) *The Bronze Vessels in the Rijksmuseum G. M. Kam at Nijmegen*. Nijmegen.

Guiraud, H. (1988) *Intailles et Camées de l'Epoque Romaine en Gaule*, Gallia supplement 48. Paris.

Henig, M. (1978) *A Corpus of Roman Engraved Gemstones from British Sites,* BAR British Series 8, 2nd edition. Oxford.

Henig, M. (1981) Continuity and change in the design of Roman jewellery. In A. King and M. Henig (eds) *The Roman West in the Third Century. Contributions from Archaeology and History,* BAR International Series 109, 127–143. Oxford.

Henkel, F. (1913) *Die roemischen fingerringe der Rheinlande.* Berlin.

Sedlmayer, H. (1999) *Die römischen Bronzefäße in Noricum,* Monographies *Instrumentum* 10.

Snape, M. (1994) The southwest gate, *intervallum* street and fort ditches. In P. Bidwell and S. Speak (eds) *Excavations at South Shields Roman Fort, Volume 1,* 107–144. Newcastle upon Tyne.

Snape, M., Bidwell, P. and Stobbs, G. (2010) Excavations in the military *vicus* south-west of the Roman Fort at South Shields in 1973, 1988 and 2002. *Arbeia Journal* 9, 43–132.

Stern, B. (2011) *Analysis of sample S209 for organic residues by gas chromatography-mass spectrometry.* Unpublished report, University of Bradford.

Wardle, A. (1998) The small objects. In J. D. Shepherd (ed.) *The Temple of Mithras, London. Excavations by W. F. Grimes and A. Williams at the Walbrook.* English Heritage Archaeological Report 12, 110–207. London.

7

THE ROMAN NAMES OF THE FORT AT SOUTH SHIELDS AND AN ALTAR TO THE *DI CONSERVATORES*

Paul Bidwell

Lindsay Allason-Jones' first major publication, written with Roger Miket, was *The Catalogue of Small Finds from South Shields Roman Fort* (1984). As thanks for this work, indispensable for the study of material culture in Roman Britain, the following essay is offered to Lindsay. It explores the possibility that the fort at South Shields had the name *Arbeia* only in the late Roman period. A new reading of the inscription on an altar published by Martin Lister in 1683, the first record of a Roman object from South Shields, seems to give the original name of the fort, which also appears in the Ravenna Cosmography.

There is no other fort-name on Hadrian's Wall which has generated so much recent debate as *Arbeia*. It appears only in the *Notitia Dignitatum* (*ND Oc* XL.7 *pictura*, and XL.22) where it is given as the location of the *praefectus numeri Barcariorum Tigrisiensium* (prefect of the unit of Tigris Boatmen). The original attribution of the name to the fort at South Shields was made by Cadwallader Bates (1898, 152, n. 21), principally because of the eastern associations of the recently-discovered tombstone of Regina, with its Palmyran style and dedicator and its inscription in Latin and Aramaic (*RIB* 1064). The tombstone is now known to date approximately to the later part of the second century (Colledge 1976, 231–3) and has nothing to do with the Tigris Boatmen, who arrived at South Shields towards the end of the third century if not later. More to the point, Bates also noted the position of the fort at South Shields at the mouth of the River Tyne, implying that it was a suitable location for the unit. His identification, made incidentally in an article on the Anglo-Saxon geography of Northumbria, seems to have been overlooked. Eric Birley's equation of *Arbeia* with South Shields some forty years later was probably made independently (Birley 1939, 221–2). He gave no reason for his identification of the name, but it might well have been the same as that given by Rivet and Smith (1979, 256), which was that South Shields 'is the only suitable base for a *Numerus Barcariorum*'. Richmond (1952, 1–2) repeated this identification, adding that *Arbeia* was 'transmuted by the post-Roman Britons into *Caer Urfe*, which the sixteenth-century antiquary John Leland found still known [by the monks of Tynemouth]'.

Rivet and Smith (1979, 256) regarded the derivation of the name *Arbeia* as unknown. A few years later, Kennedy (1986) noted the similarity of the name to the Aramaic ^{c}*Arbāyā* and *Bet*^{c}*Arbāyē*, meaning 'the Arabs' and 'the home of the Arabs', referring to northern Mesopotamia (Arabia in classical literature) and the largest group in its population. He saw this as 'surely more than mere coincidence', because the Boatmen would originally have been raised in northern Mesopotamia, through which the Tigris flows. *Arbeia* was thus likely, according to Kennedy, either to have been an ethnic element in the full name of the unit which became attached to the fort at South Shields or to have been a re-naming of the fort by the unit to commemorate their homeland. An entirely different explanation for the name was proposed by Andrew Breeze (2001): despite Rivet and Smith's judgement that its derivation was unknown (confirmed by Smith in a personal communication cited in Kennedy's note), 'the laws of Celtic philology' in fact allowed the name to be understood as 'stream of wild turnips' (or perhaps 'of rape', or even 'of black mustard'). Nothing was said by Breeze of Kennedy's explanation of the name, and in the same article Breeze also analysed the names of Corbridge (*Corstopitum* in the Antonine Itinerary and *Corie Lopocarium* in the Ravenna Cosmography) without reference to the Vindolanda writing-tablets which make it clear that in the pre-Hadrianic period Corbridge was *Coria*. These omissions were listed in a brisk rejoinder by Hodgson (2002), replied to by Breeze (2004), and again countered by Hodgson (2005). To some extent, these differences resulted from a collision of disciplines, and Hodgson (2002, 174) was surely right to demand in this sort of enquiry a synthesis of all the possible strands of evidence – topographical, archaeological and historical, as well as philological.

This essay explores one of the implications of the hypothesis put forward by Kennedy, that South Shields was re-named *Arbeia* in the late-Roman period. The original name of such an important fort, controlling the main landfall in northern Britain for east-coast shipping, might be expected to appear in the Ravenna Cosmography; Kennedy suggested the name **Orea clasis* (i.e. *Horrea Classis*: 107.46 (188)). The Cosmography was compiled shortly after AD 700 by a cleric in Ravenna, who seems to have used three separate sources for the British section (Rivet and Smith 1979, 185, 190–200). The two that concern us here are a map of southern Britain, excluding the south-western peninsula but ending at, and apparently including, Hadrian's Wall, and a second map covering northern Britain beyond the Wall. It was from this second map, considered by Rivet and Smith to have been a Flavian military map updated for the Severan campaigns of AD 208–11, that the name *Horrea Classis* was copied; it appears in the manuscripts as *Oleiclavis*, *Olea Clavis* and *Oleclavis*. The name also appears later in this section, in a similarly corrupt form, but seems to refer to a separate site, of Flavian date, north of the line of the Antonine Wall. Its first appearance is as part of a group of names in the Scottish lowlands and Northumberland north of the Wall but with a few interpolations from regions to the north and south. Rivet and Smith (1979, 373) considered that it was possibly a gloss attached to the missing name of South Shields, which they took to be *Arbeia*; this possible gloss might have been another interpolation amongst the group of names north of the Wall. Kennedy regarded *Horrea Classis* not as a gloss on the missing name of South Shields but rather as its full name which had been replaced by *Arbeia* in the *Notitia Dignitatum*, accepted by him as a later source than the one used in the Ravenna Cosmography.

Another possibility is that the name of South Shields can be found amongst the unidentified sites in northern England in the part of the Ravenna Cosmography which was based on the map of southern Britain. Because of their position in relation to other groups of names, two of these unidentified names – **Lugudunum* and **Dictum* – appear

Ravenna Cosmography 107	*Notitia Dignitatum Occidentis XL*
16 (140) *Dixio* (**Dictum*)	22. *Arbeia*
17 (140) *Lugunduno* (**Lugudunum*)	23. *Dicti* (**Dictum*)
17 (141) *Coganges* (**Concangis*)	24. *Concangios* (**Concangis*)
18 (142) *Corie Lopocarium* (**Coria*)	

Table 7.1 Fort and settlement names in north-east England appearing in the Ravenna Cosmography and Notitia Dignitatum

to be in north-east England south of Hadrian's Wall (Table 7.1). They are followed by two other names *Coganges* (**Concangis*, Chester-le-Street) and *Corie Lopocarium* (**Coria*, Corbridge), which are in that locality and immediately precede the list of forts (called *civitates* in the Cosmography) on the Wall. These four names are preceded by another group of seven names, which, starting at Lanchester, follows Dere Street southwards, with a diversion westwards to Bowes, and then goes across to York and down to Brough-on-Humber. The seventh site, *Devovicia* (107.16 (139), if it is the *Delgovicia* of the Antonine Itinerary (*AI* 466.3, Iter I), as seems probable, is in East Yorkshire and was identified by Rivet and Smith (1979, 331–2) as the settlement at Wetwang. These two groups of names represent places east of the Pennines between the lower Tyne valley and the Humber, though there are omissions, for example Ebchester and Malton.

In the *Notitia Dignitatum*, **Dictum* and **Concangis* appear together, omitting **Lugudunum* which separated them in the Ravenna Cosmography. **Dictum* is preceded by a new name, *Arbeia*. These three forts, occupied by *numeri*, are near the beginning of the chapter (XL) listing the units under the command of the *dux Britanniarum*. They are preceded by *legio VI* and then three units of *equites*, placed first in the list because of their higher status (Hodgson 1991, 89–90), and are followed by seven further *numeri* and then the section '*item per lineam valli*'. The locations of the first four, or possibly five, of the seven *numeri*, are on an east–west arc which follows on from Chester-le-Street, across to Dere Street and then branching off to Bowes, Brough and Kirkby Thore on the road across Stainmore down into the Eden Valley, then across to Papcastle, presumably via the road passing by the much earlier fort at Troutbeck and then running south of Blencathra and Skiddaw and up the west side of Bassenthwaite Lake or across the Whinlatter Pass. If *Magis* is Burrow Walls, the route ended on the west coast.

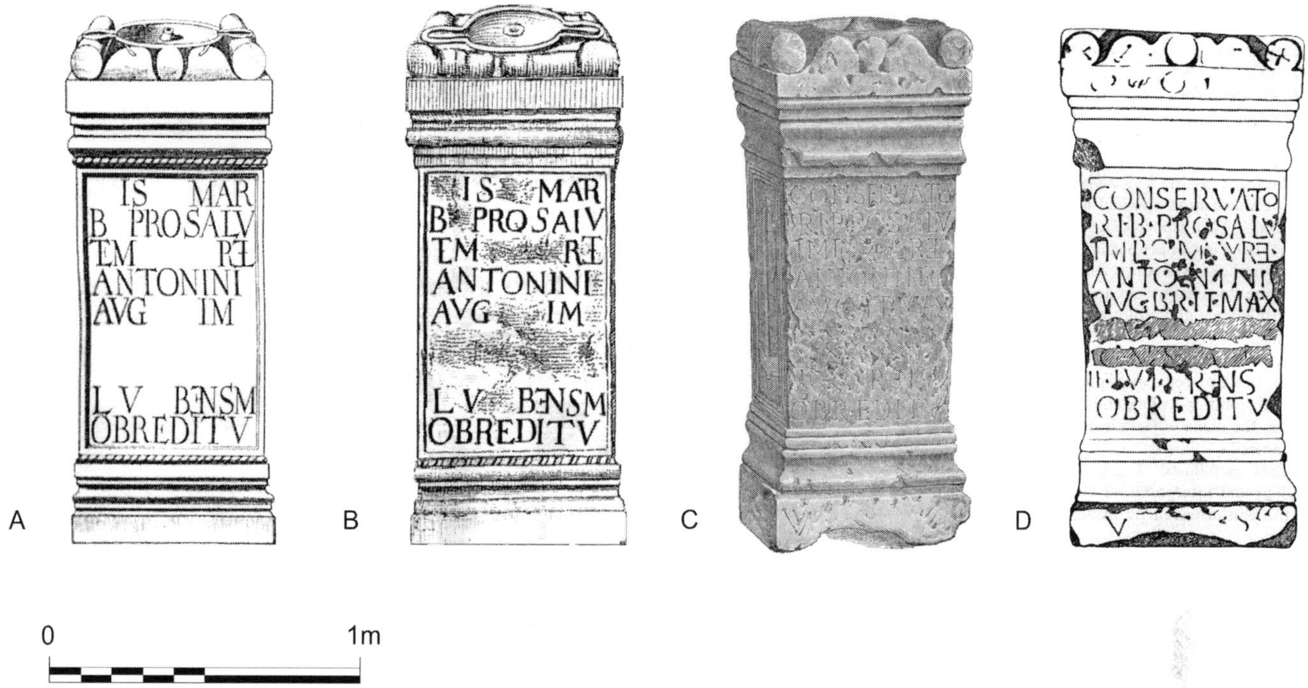

Figure 7.1 Drawings of the altar to the Di Conservatores *from South Shields. A. After Lister 1683. B. After Chandler 1763, pars III, tab. I.III. C. After Bruce 1875, no. 537. D. After Collingwood 1923, fig. 3. Only Collingwood's drawing was published to scale; the other three drawings have been scanned so that the die bearing the inscription is shown at about the same height as in Collingwood's drawing*

Both the Ravenna Cosmography and the *Notitia Dignitatum* have some sequences of names in geographical order. Other passages are jumbled, but the close association in both documents of **Dictum* and **Concangis* and their position in relation to adjacent lists of names in geographical order are surely meaningful. In the *Notitia Dignitatum*, the small group to which they belong can be taken to begin the sequence that runs from east to west, and in the Ravenna Cosmography, they preface the Wall-list, which begins in the east. All the names in this small group should be in the area south of the Wall, and fairly close to its eastern end where the adjacent sequences begin. In the Ravenna Cosmography, the area extends as far west as Corbridge (**Coria*), which, because it is not a late-Roman fort, is omitted from the *Notitia*. **Dictum*, appearing in both documents, is perhaps at Wearmouth or at the mouth of the Tees (Frere 1967, 232–3). In the Cosmography, that leaves **Lugudunum*, omitted from the *Notitia*, where instead we find *Arbeia*. Could this, quite simply, represent a change in the name of the fort at South Shields?

With this question, the matter might perhaps have rested, but a well-known altar to the *Di Conservatores* from South Shields could supply an answer. According to Collingwood (1923, 60), line 9 would have given the name of the dedicator (Fig. 7.1, D). Wright was more specific: 'the termination *-ens* may well conceal the adjectival form of the group which made the dedication' (*RIB* 1054). Early readings of the text by Lister and others gave this line as 'L V BENSM', containing at least a hint of the adjectival name *Lugudunenses*. Unfortunately, the inscription was very weathered when it was found more than three centuries ago, and much of the text is difficult to read (Fig. 7.1A). Its discovery was described by Martin Lister (1683, 70):

> 'I have with much trouble got into my hands a Piece of Roman Antiquity, which was but a very few years ago discovered upon the South Bank of the River Tine, near the Sheilds in Bishoprick. It is a very large and fair Roman Altar of one entire Stone. But after all my cost and pains, I am very sorry to find the Inscription very ill defaced, that much of it is not legible. And I believe it hath been also mis-handled by those who have endeavoured to read it; whereas if the remainder of the Letters had been exactly measured, and the face blackt and lightly washt off again, as in Prints, some things more might have been spelled'.

It had been sent to Lister at York and then, according to Horsley (1732, 287), was passed on to a Mr Giles at Norwich. This was presumably a staging post on its journey to Oxford, for an 'advertisement' at the end of the volume of

Figure 7.2. The altar to the Di Conservatores *at South Shields. The height of the altar is 1.26 m, and its width is 0.60 m*

the *Philosophical Transactions* (p. 112) in which Lister described the altar states that it:

> 'together with another ancient Roman one ... are safely arrived at Oxford, where they will speedily be set up, together with some others of the Worshipful Elias Ashmole Esquire, in the Court before the Musaeum by Him lately furnished'.

Chandler (1763, pars 3, tab. I, III) included it in his Marmora Oxoniensia (Fig. 7.1B). By 1923, when the altar was drawn by Collingwood (Fig. 7.1D), it had been placed in the entrance hall of the Ashmolean Museum, presumably having been moved to the new building when it was erected in the mid-19th century (Collingwood 1923, 55). The altar was placed on permanent loan to the Arbeia Roman Fort Museum in the early 1980s. The drawing and transcription published by Collingwood in 1923 are reproduced in *RIB* (1054), with the addition of a line on the capital reading '*Dis*' and a fuller version of Geta's erased titles, as follows:

Dis (on capital)
Conservato
rib(us) pro salu(te)
imp(eratoris) C(aesaris) M(arci) Aurel(i)
Antonini
Aug(usti) Brit(annici) Max(imi)
[et imp(eratoris) C(aesaris) P(ubli) Sep(timi)
Getae Aug(usti) Brit(annici)
.... *]rens*
ob reditu(m)
v(otum) s(olvit) (on base)

> 'To the gods the Preservers for the welfare of the Emperor Caesar Marcus Aurelius Antoninus Augustus, Most Great Conqueror of Britain, [and of the Emperor Caesar Publius Septimius Geta Augustus, conqueror of Britain], ... for their return fulfilled the vow'.

The altar was dedicated during the joint reign of Caracalla and Geta, which followed the death of Severus at York on 4 February AD 211 and ended after little more than a year with Geta's murder by the hand of Caracalla. It is the only inscription of this brief reign from Britain. Collingwood (1923, 61–2) suggested that it marked the departure from the Tyne of the new emperors and their expeditionary army.

In its various journeyings and locations since the early 1680s, it is possible that the altar was damaged either by rough handling or further weathering. Comparison of the original reading by Lister with what still remains (Figs 7.1A, 7.1D, 7.2) will show not only what has been lost but also allows the accuracy of his transcription to be assessed:

line 2: Lister read this as '*Disdeabusq; Matr*', but, remarkably, he also offered an alternative and nearly correct reading of lines 2 and 3 as '*Conservato / ri. b. pros* &c', proposed by '... that excellent Antiquarie Dr. *Johnson* of *Pomfret* [Pontefract]' (Lister 1683, 72). Of the letters in line 2 – 'CONSERVATO' – Lister's 'IS' is the second down-stroke of the 'N' followed by 'S'; 'MAR' is a misreading of 'VATO', the 'MA' standing for 'VA' and the 'R' an amalgamation of the 'T' and the small 'O'.

line 3: 'RIB PRO SALV': Lister mis-read the 'R' as a 'B' and the following two letters were not read, but 'PRO SALV' is shown correctly (these are still some of the most easily legible letters).

line 4: 'IMP C M AVREL': 'IM' was read as 'TEM', the first two letters ligatured (perfectly understandable, as it would have provided the correct ending of 'SALV' at the end of the previous line, though in fact the word was abbreviated); the last three letters were given correctly as 'REL', the last two ligatured. The intervening five letters, omitted by Lister, are not easily readable.

line 5: 'ANTONINI': read correctly by Lister.

line 6: 'AVG BRIT MAX': 'AVG', correctly read by Lister, is now far from clear; the 'I' of Lister's 'IM' is probably the 'T' of 'BRIT'. The 'M' of 'MAX' is still clear.

lines 7–8: erased in antiquity, following the murder of Geta.

line 9: see below.

line 10: 'OB REDITV': the clearest line in the inscription, read in full by Lister.

Lister's reading, as far as it went, was reliable. He correctly recorded lines 5 and 10 in their entirety, and much of line 3. When his readings went astray in lines 2, 5 and 6, this was either because he saw only fragments of letters, or because he reconstructed fragments wrongly. Three eighteenth-century illustrations of the altar add nothing of importance: Thomas Gale (1709, 9) omitted line 6; Horsley (1732, 192, n. 54, II, 287), as he stated explicitly, did not see the altar and copied the other drawings; Chandler (1763, tab. I, II) seems to have made a new drawing but showed the same letters as Lister (Fig. 7.1B). Fuller readings were published by Hübner in 1873 (*CIL* VII, no. 496) and by Bruce (Fig. 7.1C; 1875, no. 537), and the definitive version, apart from line 9, by Collingwood and Wright (*RIB* 1054).

It is line 9, containing the name of the dedicator or dedicators with which we are mainly concerned here (Fig. 7.3). Lister has the letters as 'L V BENSM', with a wide space

Figure 7.3. A. Line 9, photograph. B. Line 9, digital scan. The drawing of the letters shows the fragments now visible in a solid line. Note that the final letter 'M', though no longer visible, was included in Lister's drawing

between the 'L' and 'V' and a larger gap between the 'V' and 'B'; the 'E' and 'N' were ligatured with the 'E' reversed. All subsequent readings show the letters 'ENS', which are still clear. The preceding 'B' was taken for an 'R' by Bruce and Collingwood; it was omitted by Hübner who read 'P' farther to the left. Of Lister's final 'M', there are now no traces, and it is not shown by Hübner, Bruce or Collingwood. The main difficulty concerns Lister's first two letters, 'L' and 'V'. Bruce shows a vertical stroke at the beginning of the line, then nothing more until the 'R' (Lister's 'B'). Collingwood shows two vertical strokes, then a 'V', and then a further upright and a fragment curving to the left, these two last elements resembling a rather irregular 'D' (perhaps this is Hübner's 'P'). However, he did not include these in his transcription, adding that 'I cannot at present either read or confidently restore the dedicator's name' (Collingwood 1923, 60).

The only published photograph of the altar was taken by E. J. Phillips (1977, pl. 44, no. 182). The inscription, lit obliquely from the right, shows up as well as in any of the subsequent attempts to record it. These attempts consisted of the making of a papier-mâché squeeze, which showed very little, and then of more sophisticated techniques. Further photography was carried out using raking light from several directions, and then it proved possible to secure the assistance of two postgraduate students from the University of Applied Science at Mainz who were developing new techniques of studying carved and inscribed stonework using high-resolution digital cameras. The first method adopted was to film the inscription under lights moving from left to right at a constant speed, so that the full range of light and shade on the minute contours of the inscribed face was recorded. All the marks already visible on the photographs showed up well, but no additional letters or fragments of letters were discernible. The second method was to scan the face to produce a reverse image of its contours. The result resembled the picture of a squeeze, the difference being that the scan was much sharper and minutely detailed. Contrasts in the depths of the features on the inscribed face, whether letters or later marks, were represented by varying tones: the deeper the feature, the paler its tone (Fig. 7.3B).

If a photograph and the scan are examined together, and if the previous drawings are referred to, a clearer reading of line 9 emerges, but first it is necessary to analyse the processes obscuring the text which were highlighted by the scan. Weathering probably occurred in antiquity and perhaps at Oxford 'in the court before the *Musaeum*' if the altar was kept there until it was moved into the new Ashmolean Museum in the mid-nineteenth century. The erosion of the inscribed surface is not uniform; it is particularly weathered on the left-hand side. There is damage to the two sides of the frame. The left-hand side has almost entirely disappeared; the weathering of the break shows that this happened before the altar was taken indoors. There are also a series of deep marks on the face. Some seem random, but most belong to two groups: the main group runs vertically down the centre of the face, starting at the top with a large mark in the middle of the deep moulding immediately above the frame and continuing with marks cutting the bottom of line 2, lines 3–6, the top and middle of line 9, and the bifid moulding below the frame; there is also a group of smaller marks running down diagonally to the left from the mark in the main group at the top of line 9. If at some stage the altar was buried face upwards, the marks might have been made by spades or picks when the soil above was cultivated or worked over to remove rubble.

When attempting a reading of line 9, this damage must be borne in mind. Starting from the left, where the surface is more weathered, two vertical lines appear. They are also on Collingwood's drawing. The left-hand line might well represent part of the marking-out of the frame that surrounds the inscription: it is in line with the fragment preserved at the upper left-hand corner of the frame. There is then a third vertical line, its lower part cut out by a deeper mark which belongs to the diagonal group described above. Collingwood then has a 'V', faintly visible on the photograph but not on the scan. Which of the vertical lines represents Lister's 'L' is alas uncertain. If the first vertical line is part of the margin, the upright of the 'L' ought to be the second line from the left, given the space between it and the 'V' shown by Lister. However, there are no traces of the horizontal part of an 'L'. The third of these lines, as noted above, is obscured at the bottom by a deeper mark; there is a smaller mark to its right. These marks might have been taken by Lister to represent the horizontal part of the 'L'. If so, the space between the supposed 'L' and the 'V' in the drawing is too wide.

In the photograph, immediately to the right of the 'V', there appears a 'G'. Its vertical part and the lower part of its curve are faint but clear; even fainter is the upper part of its curve, removed at the top by a deeper mark which is part of the diagonal group. This letter, not seen before, was only discovered when the inscription was viewed under raking light. Following the 'G', there are a series of deeper marks which include the feature taken for a 'B' by Lister and for an 'R' by Bruce and Collingwood but ignored by Hübner. There is a large mark just beyond the top left of this feature, which is represented by smaller and slightly elongated marks. They all belong to the main group of marks which run down the centre of the inscribed face. In the scan, the upper, right-facing part of the feature taken as a 'B' or 'R' is a deep, worm-shaped mark; the lower part is a small mark which might have been made by a single blow from a pick. What was taken for the upright to the left is more regular than the other marks but is deeper than the letters. It is therefore doubtful whether these marks actually represent a letter. The ligatured 'EN' and the 'S' are clear. Of Lister's final 'M', there is no trace, as noted above. It has not been obscured by later marks, and the face of the stone is fairly smooth. Perhaps the traces of the letter observed by Lister were very faint and later weathering was sufficient to remove them entirely.

The reading of the line that emerges from this analysis consists of the following letters: 'V, G, E, N, S'. Two of Lister's letters, 'L' and 'R' are rejected; his 'M' is no longer visible. At the beginning of the line, there is space for two letters which included vertical lines. Between the 'G' and ligatured 'EN' is space probably for four letters. Line 9 would thus contain eleven letters, counting the ligatured 'EN' as one letter; lines 2, 3 and 6 have ten letters, line 4 nine letters, and lines 5 and 10 eight letters. '*[L]ug[udun]ens(es)*' would certainly fit (and the upright to the left of the 'V' could be accepted as the top of the 'L''), but the letters 'VG' might suggest another possibility: *cohors V Gallorum*, which was certainly at South Shields by AD 213 (*RIB* 3272); at least part of the unit probably occupied the accommodation in the supply-base during the Severan campaigns (Hodgson 2001, 34–5). There is just about enough space for the letters 'VG' to have been preceded at the beginning of line 9 by '*coh(ors)*', if the 'O' was smaller than the other letters, as at the end of line 2. The vertical line immediately preceding the 'V ' could be the end of an 'H', but the second vertical line is where the '*c*' should have been. The space for three letters following the 'G' could have been occupied by 'ALL', giving '*Gall(orum)*, but the following three letters, 'ENS', about which there is no doubt, make this reading implausible.

Returning to '*[L]ug[udun]ens(es)*', in the context of a military site, a group defining itself by its geographical location, suggested by the ending '*-ens(es)*'(or '*-ens(is)*'), is likely to have been the *vicani* (or *vicus*), inhabitants of the settlement outside the fort – the military *vicus*– as in the dedication to Vulcan by the *vicani Vindolandesses* (*RIB* 1700, where it is noted that *Vindolandenses* has been assimiliated to *Vindolandesses*). The ending does not occur with the national or tribal names used for most auxiliary units. Parallels to the final abbreviation can be found, for example, in dedications to Mercury and Rosmerta by the '*vicani [vici N]ediens(is)*' (HD036510, from a civilian *vicus* between Ladenburg and Bad Wimpfen) and to Jupiter for the welfare of the emperor by the *vic(ani) Trullens(es)* (HD031986, Lower Moesia). However, these inscriptions raise the question of how the dedicators on the South Shields inscription described themselves. If they were *vicani*, we would expect the abbreviations '*vic(ani)*' or 'v*ik(ani)*', or some version of '*vicani vici*', which many examples in the Heidelberg Epigraphic Database indicate was the most common term used in dedications made by the community of the *vicus*. There is scarcely space for more than two letters in line 9 before '*[L]ug[udun]en(ses)*', and the first letter begins with an upright: 'VIC' or 'VIK' seem impossible. There are no other reasons for rejecting this upright, so we might suppose that the word '*vicani*' began at the end of line 8, and that the end of the word, the letters 'NI', were carried over to the beginning of line 9, which would fit the upright at the beginning of this line. A decisive objection to this reconstruction is that in Wright's reconstruction of the erased lines 7–8 – '*et imp(eratoris) C(aesaris) P(ubli) Sep(timi) / Getae Aug(usti) Brit(annici)*' – there are 10 and 12 letters. The latter line is longer than any other in the inscription, so there can hardly have been four more letters – 'VICA'. A more abbreviated form of Geta's titles is also improbable: Caracalla's have three lines.

Vicani, however, were not the only group which identified themselves by their geographic location. *Numeri, vexillationes* and *cunei*, irregular formations which are well attested in third-century Britain, often used place-names to identify themselves alongside their ethnic origins. An example from Hadrian's Wall is the *cuneus Frisionum Aballavensium*, their name known on an altar of AD 241 at Papcastle, where they had been transferred from Burgh-by-Sands or *Aballava* (*RIB* 883). In the *Notitia Dignitatum*, some units were identified solely by the names of forts to which they were, or had previously been, attached: for example, the *numerus Longovicanorum*, *milites Anderetiani*, and *numerus Turnacensium*. An earlier example is possibly an inscription of the '*numeri Magn<c>e(n)s(ium)*' from Carvoran, which was *Magnis* (*RIB* 1825). On the South Shields inscription, the first letter of line 9 could have been 'N', incorporating the upright at the beginning of the line. If there was then an ethnic name (say *Maurorum*, *Frisionum* or *Palmyrenorum*), it must have been abbreviated to the initial letter. Equally, a *numerus* could be defined by its function rather than its ethnic origin, as with the *numerus Exploratorum Bremeniensium* at High Rochester (*RIB* 1262, 1270) or the *n(umerus) Barc(ariorum)* at Lancaster (*RIB* 601). Accordingly, line 9 could be restored as '*n(umerus) (?) [L]ug(u)[dun]ens(iu)m*', the question mark standing for a letter representing the function or ethnic origin of the unit. An advantage of this version is that it incorporates Lister's final letter in line 9 – 'M' – which, though no longer preserved, we should accept, given the general reliability of his reading.

One other problem remains: the date of the source used in the Ravenna Cosmography for southern Britain extending as far north as Hadrian's Wall. It possibly relied on a mid-4th-century map, perhaps that sent by Alypius, while *vicarius* of Britain, to the emperor Julian in AD 360–63, though the subject of the map is not specified (Rivet and Smith 1979, 192). If this were so, the Ravenna Cosmography should have named the fort as *Arbeia* rather than *Lugudunum*: the *numerus barcariorum Tigrisiensium* is thought to have arrived at South Shields in the late third century at the beginning of Period 7, when the fort was rebuilt with a new plan of late-Roman type. One solution would be to accept that the *numerus* arrived after the date of the Cosmography, perhaps in the years following AD 367 when drafts of the continental field army were sent to Britain (Hoffmann 1969, 339; cf. Hodgson 1991, 88–9). The only reason to link the *numerus* with the fort in Period 7 (first proposed in Bidwell 1989, 87; cf. Bidwell and Speak 1994, 42) was that the rebuilding was so radical that it suggested the presence of a new garrison, and replacement of *cohors V Gallorum* by the *numerus* seemed the most straightforward solution. The later arrival of the *numerus,* and the presence of an unknown unit at South Shields from the late third century to the AD 360s, are perfectly possible. Alternatively, perhaps the source, if it was a mid-fourth-century map, contained out-of-date information. Rivet and Smith (1979, 192, 260) were only able to pick out one 'piece of information which we know to be late', the addition, apparently in the fourth century, of the honorific title of *Augusta* to the name of *Londinium* (cf. Birley 2005, 398, n. 4). Research during the subsequent thirty years or so since the publication of *The Place-Names of Roman Britain* has shown that two omissions are inconsistent with a mid-fourth-century date for the main British source, at least as far as the Hadrian's

Wall zone is concerned. The list of Wall-forts does not include Newcastle (*Pons Aelius* or *Aelii*) and Drumburgh (*Concavata*). The first of these forts is now known to have been established in the late second or early third century, probably under Severus (Bidwell and Snape 2002); Drumburgh was probably a Hadrianic fort but had perhaps been abandoned in the later second century, though it was eventually rebuilt (Hodgson 2009, 20–22). If we take the Ravenna list of Wall-forts to be reliable, these omissions would indicate that it actually dated to no later than the final decade or so of the second century. Of course, it might be objected that many other omissions in the document mean that no part of it can be trusted at this level of detail, but the fact remains that the two missing forts are the only ones on the Wall which were not Hadrianic foundations continuously occupied (apart from the period of the Antonine Wall) down to the end of the Roman period.

Single written sources which are partly defective and fragmentary readings of inscriptions cannot be the basis for definite statements. What can be judged probable is that the original name of South Shields was *Lugudunum*, as in the Ravenna Cosmography; the name would fit the surviving letters on the part of the altar to the *Di Conservatores* which contains the name of the *vicani* or an irregular unit that made the dedication. The most likely reading of line 9 is: '*n(umerus) (?) [L]ug(u)[dun]ens(iu)m*' ('the unit of the (?) of *Lugudunum*'), the question mark standing for a letter representing the function or ethnic origin of the unit.

Equally probable is Kennedy's hypothesis that *Arbeia* was an Aramaic word and represented a re-naming of the fort of *Lugudunum* by its late Roman garrison. His suggestion that its previous name was actually *Horrea Classis* could still be near the mark. Rivet and Smith thought that it might have been a gloss, misplaced north of the Wall, on the name of the fort at South Shields, the latter being omitted from the Ravenna Cosmography. The words could equally be a gloss on the name *Lugudunum*. It has to be admitted that few changes of place-names in the Roman period are known, and some probable instances are contested (see Bidwell 2005 for background to the controversy over *Cilurnum* – Chesters). The case for *Lugudunum* and *Arbeia*, however, is strong. *Lugudunum* was almost certainly in north-east England, the name fits the surviving letters in the appropriate line on the altar from South Shields, and there is no reason to doubt that the name *Arbeia* in the *Notitia Dignitatum* also referred to South Shields. Finally, it can be proposed that the section of the Ravenna Cosmography which deals with places in northern England and includes *Lugudunum*, regarded here as the original name of the fort at South Shields, was based on information much earlier than the mid-fourth century. This is supported by the omission from the document of the forts at Newcastle, now known to have been a late second- or early third-century foundation, and at Drumburgh, probably abandoned by the end of the second century though later rebuilt.

Acknowledgements

The scanning of the altar was carried out by Bjorn Brecht and Bruno Kessler of the University of Applied Sciences, Mainz, as part of the research for a small exhibition on Lister's discovery of the altar. Lister was an early Fellow of the Royal Society, and the exhibition, accommodated in the Arbeia Roman Fort Museum in 2009–10, was kindly funded by the Society's 'Local Heroes' programme, marking its 350th anniversary. I am grateful to Susanne Geck and Alex Croom for arranging the programme of scanning, and to Nick Hodgson for commenting on a draft of this paper.

Bibliography

Allason-Jones, L. and Miket, R. (1984) *The Catalogue of Small Finds from South Shields Roman Fort*. Newcastle upon Tyne.

Bates, C. J. (1898) The Beornicas and the Deras, *AA* 5th series 19, 147–59.

Bidwell, P. (1989) South Shields – *Arbeia*. In C. Daniels (ed.) *The Eleventh Pilgrimage of Hadrian's Wall*, 83–9. Newcastle upon Tyne.

Bidwell, P. T. (2005) Connections between the military units of Spanish origin in Britannia and their homelands'. In C. Fernández Ochoa and P. García Díaz (eds) *Unidad y diversidad en el Arco Atlántico en época romana*. BAR International Series 1371, 35–8. Oxford.

Bidwell, P. T. and Snape, M. E. (2002) The history and setting of the Roman fort at Newcastle upon Tyne, *AA* 5th series 31, 251–81.

Bidwell, P. and Speak, S. (1994) *Excavations at South Shields Roman Fort, Vol. 1*. Society of Antiquaries of Newcastle upon Tyne Monograph Series 4. Newcastle-Upon-Tyne.

Birley, A. R. (2005) *The Roman Government of Britain*. Oxford.

Birley, E. (1939) The Beaumont inscription, the *Notitia Dignitatum*, and the garrison of Hadrian's Wall. *TCWAAS* new series 39, 190–226.

Breeze, A. (2001) The British-Latin place–names *Arbeia,*

Corstopitum, Dictim and *Morbium. Durham Archaeological Journal*, 16, 21–5.

Breeze, A. (2004) The Roman place-names *Arbeia* and *Corstopitum*: a reply. *AA* 5th series 33, 49–51.

Bruce, J. C. (1875) *Lapidarium Septentrionale*. Newcastle upon Tyne.

Chandler, R. (1763) *Marmora Oxoniensia, Pars 3*. Oxford.

Hübner, E. (1873) *Corpus Inscriptionum Latinarum, vol. vii. Inscriptiones Britanniae Latinae.* Berlin.

Colledge, M. A. R. (1976) *The Art of Palmyra*. London.

Collingwood, R. G. (1923) An altar from South Shields, now at Oxford. *AA* 3rd series 20, 55–62.

Collingwood, R. G. and Wright, R. P. (1965) *The Roman Inscriptions of Britain. I, Inscriptions on Stone*, 1–2400. Oxford.

Frere, S. S. (1967) *Britannia. A History of Roman Britain.* London.

Gale, T. (revd. Gale, R.) (1709) *Antonini Iter Britanniarum Commentarius Illustratum*. London.

HD *Epigraphische Datenbank Heidelberg* (http://edh-www.adw.uni-heidelberg.de/)

Hodgson, N. (1991) The *Notitia Dignitatum* and the later garrison of Britain. In V. A. Maxfield and M. J. Dobson (eds) *Roman Frontier Studies 1989: Proceedings of the XVth International Congress of Roman Frontier Studies,* 84–92. Exeter.

Hodgson, N. (2001) The origins and development of the Roman military supply-base at South Shields: an interim report on the results of excavations in the eastern quadrant and central area, 1990–2000. *Arbeia Journal* 6–7, 25–36.

Hodgson, N. (2002) The Roman place-names *Arbeia* and *Corstopitum*: a rejection of recently suggested meanings. *AA* 5th series 30, 173–4.

Hodgson, N. (2005) The Roman place-names *Arbeia* and *Corstopitum*: a response to the response. *AA* 5th series 34, 151–2.

Hodgson, N. (2009) *Hadrian's Wall 1999–2009. A Summary of Excavation and Research Prepared for the 13th Pilgrimage of Hadrian's Wall*, Kendal.

Hoffmann, D. (1969) *Das spätrömische Bewegungsheer und die* Notitia Dignitatum, Epigraphische Studien 7. Düsseldorf.

Horsley, J. (1732) *Britannia Romana.* London.

Kennedy, D. L. (1986) The place-name *Arbeia. Britannia* 17, 332–3.

Lister, M. (1683) An account of a Roman monument found in the Bishoprick of Durham, and of some Roman antiquities at York, sent in a letter from Martin Lister, Esq. *Philosophical Transactions*, 13 (no. 145), 70–4.

Phillips, E. J. (1977) *Corpus Signorum Imperii Romani, Vol. 1, Fasc. 1*: *Corbridge, Hadrian's Wall East of the River North Tyne*. Oxford.

Richmond, I. A. (1952) *The Roman Fort at South Shields. A Guide*. Newcastle upon Tyne.

Rivet, A. L. F. and Smith, C. (1979) *The Place-Names of Roman Britain.* London.

Tomlin, R. S. O. Wright, R. P. and Hassall, M. W. C. (2009) *The Roman Inscriptions of Britain. III, Inscriptions on Stone*, 3001–550. Oxford.

8

COMMEMORATING THE WALL: ROMAN SCULPTURE AND INSCRIPTIONS FROM HADRIAN'S WALL

David J. Breeze

The Roman army tended to erect simple inscriptions to mark their building work on Roman frontiers. The centurial stones on Hadrian's Wall are peculiarly crude and are unusual in that respect. At the other end of the spectrum are the ornate 'distance slabs' from the Antonine Wall in Scotland, some of which bear sculptural scenes representing the events associated with the invasion and conquest of southern Scotland at the beginning of the reign of Antoninus Pius (138–61). As a group, these are unparalleled on any Roman frontier (Ferris 2000, 110–3). Yet Hadrian's Wall has one stone which has received insufficient attention.

Past accounts

In 1807, Dr. John Lingard, vice-president of Crook Hall College in the parish of Lanchester, undertook a tour of Hadrian's Wall. He started out from Wallsend on 24 August. In the entry under the heading GLENWHELT, he recorded: 'Near the bridge over the Irthing, a sugarloaf hill 200 yds [*c.* 183 m] from the wall called Rose hill; a platform on top – 12 yds [*c.*11 m] diameter; ditch round it; figure of flying victory' (Bosanquet 1929, 155). Rose Hill was destroyed in order to build Rose Hill railway station in 1836; the station was subsequently re-named Gilsland. It has been suggested that Rose Hill had been a medieval motte.

A few years later, Hodgson mentioned the 'diluvial' hills of the area between the Tipalt and the Irthing, noting that

> 'One of these, a little north of the Wall, was called ROSS-HILL, and before it was levelled to form the Ross-hill station on the railway, it had on its crown a platform of about 12 yards diameter, surrounded by a ditch, within which was found a stone 43 inches by 23, bearing in high relief a flying Victory, and an eagle with extended wings and statant on the earth in one corner, and on the other a rock with a tree growing out of it, and some other device, but so much injured that I could not guess for what it had been intended.' (Hodgson 1840, 295)

Bruce was equally puzzled:

> 'the latter object the late Mr. Fairholt conceived to be a circular hut, such as he has shown in the woodcut [Fig. 8.1]. In the sculptures on the Antonine column in Rome [now known as the Column of Marcus], the ancient Germans are represented as occupying similar huts. The remains of circular dwellings are frequently to be met with in the hill forts of the North of England. The only other instance of a flying Victory met with in the mural region is the figure found at HUNNUM.' (Bruce 1875, no. 422)

In the third edition of *The Roman Wall*, Bruce cites Fairholt slightly differently:

> 'It is very graceful in design. I make the object on the right to be a domed building, shaded by a tree, and situated on a rock. It may probably represent a British house, after the fashion of the Gaulish ones on the Antonine column in Rome.' (Bruce 1867, 252)

Fairholt's drawing remained in successive editions of the *Handbook to the Roman Wall*, but otherwise the stone (Fig. 8.2) seems to have slipped from general view, though it is referenced in appropriate publications.

In the late 1940s, Stuart Piggott, while preparing a book on the antiquarian William Stukeley, sought the advice of

Fig. 8.1 The woodcut by F. W. Fairholt

Ian Richmond on Arthur's O'on which lay north of the Antonine Wall in Scotland (Fig. 8.3). Stukeley had described this structure but not visited it, basing his description on the drawings of the architect Andrew Jelfe (Piggott 1950, 60–1). Richmond suggested that it might have been the shrine of a water goddess, but, fresh from writing his first edition of the *Handbook to the Roman Wall*, more significantly pointed out the similarity between Arthur's O'on and the building on the Rose Hill sculpture (Richmond 1947).

In 1960 Kenneth Steer published a detailed account of Arthur's O'on (1960). This circular, domed stone building was destroyed in 1743 but several earlier records of it survive. The earliest may date to about 800. In his *Select Documents of Early British History*, written shortly before 800, Nennius stated that on the banks of the river Carron, the Emperor Carausius erected a 'Round House of polished stone … he erected a triumphal arch to commemorate his victory' (Nennius, ch. 23 = Morris 1980, 24). Steer's interest stemmed from the preparation of the inventory of Stirlingshire by the Royal Commission on the Ancient and Historical Monuments of Scotland, which extended to the cutting of some trenches across the site of the building in 1950, though unfortunately nothing was found. Steer's later paper also contains useful information on the structure (Steer 1976).

Arthur's O'on lies 3 km north of the fort at Falkirk on the Antonine Wall. It sits on a flat topped spur, a little below the crest with restricted outlook to the north and north-west, but wide views in other directions. Although antiquarian accounts differ in details, it is clear that Arthur's O'on ('Oven') was a circular, domed structure 6.705 m high and with an internal diameter of 5.806 m, erected on a foundation platform 1.325 m deep. The wall was of dressed freestone, two stones thick, each stone being about 1.220 m long, 305 mm wide and 600 mm broad, with a lewis-hole on the upper surface. The masonry was neatly coursed with no straight joints and mortared. The wall narrowed in thickness towards the top and the roof was corbelled with both the inner and outer surfaces subsequently dressed smoothly. The entrance, to the east, was an arched opening 2.743 m high and 1.524 m wide. There was a gap in the upper stonework, first recorded in the twelfth century, but which had grown larger since. It is not clear whether this was an original feature, though the statement by Stukeley (1720, 12–27) that the jambs were splayed internally may suggest that it was indeed a window. Internally, there were two string courses, 1.220 and 1.830 m above the floor. Sibbald, writing at the beginning of the eighteenth century, detected on the outside of the structure some letters which may have been erased, an eagle's head, 'a figure much worn out, or partly deleted, which resembles Wings, and seems to have been the Figure of *Victory*', perhaps the head of a spear, and the letters I.A.M.P.M.P.T. (Sibbald 1707, 42–6). The only object recorded having been found inside the building was a finger of brass discovered in a crevice about 1700.

Fig. 8.2 Photograph of the sculpture (the author)

Steer firmly stated that Arthur's O'on was Roman in date and, noting its unusual form of construction, concluded that it was a shrine or temple, the finger being derived from a cult statue, while the east facing door would be appropriate for a temple. Sibbald recorded that the horns of great cows had been found around the building as if ritual sacrifices had been made there. Steer noted the coincidence of Victory on both Arthur's O'on and the Rose Hill stone and suggested that the former was a 'war-memorial, or *tropaeum*, erected to commemorate a victory – and presumably the victory that was crowned by the completion of the Wall' (Steer 1960, 109). He also noted the existence of a possible war-memorial at Jarrow beyond the eastern end of Hadrian's Wall.

Jocelyn Toynbee discussed the Rose Hill sculpture in 1964, offering the following interpretation:

> 'This badly weathered piece shows a half-draped Victory flying towards the left, with her arms outstretched before her, as though she had supported some object in her hands. That object, which would have come just beyond the point at which the left-hand portion of the frieze is broken off, may well have been a shield supported on the other side by a corresponding Victory, flying towards the right. The now headless bird (eagle?, or owl?) which stands with outspread wings below the surviving Victory, and the little domed shrine set amid rocks and trees to the spectator's right of her, might have reference to a deity portrayed upon the hypothetical shield. That this was a temple frieze is very likely; if so, we have no means of knowing whether the god or goddess who owned it was local or Graeco-Roman. But at any rate the style and the content of the sculpture are both fully classical.' (Toynbee 1964, 138–9, n. 6, which includes a reference to Arthur's O'on and to the Bath pediment which Toynbee saw as a parallel)

Lewis in his *Temples in Roman Britain* (1965, 79) drew attention to a second possible parallel to the Rose Hill building. The monk, William of Malmesbury, in his *Deeds of the English Bishops* published in 1125 (Winterbottom 2007, III, 99, 3), recorded the existence of a Roman vaulted stone building in Carlisle (*est in Lugubalia civitate triclinium lapideis fornicibus concameratum)* bearing on the façade the inscription, *Marii Victoriae* (*scripturaque ligitus in fronte triclinie* '*Marii victoriae*'). This has been variously restored as *Marti Victori* or *Marti Victoria ae(dem)...*, that is, 'a temple to Mars Victor' (*RIB* 950). Lewis suggested that this may have been a domed rather than a vaulted building. It had disappeared by the end of the sixteenth century.

The authors of the relevant volume of the *Corpus of Sculpture of the Roman World* also acknowledged the similarity between the Rose Hill sculpture and Arthur's O'on (Coulston and Phillips 1988, no. 265). They went so far as

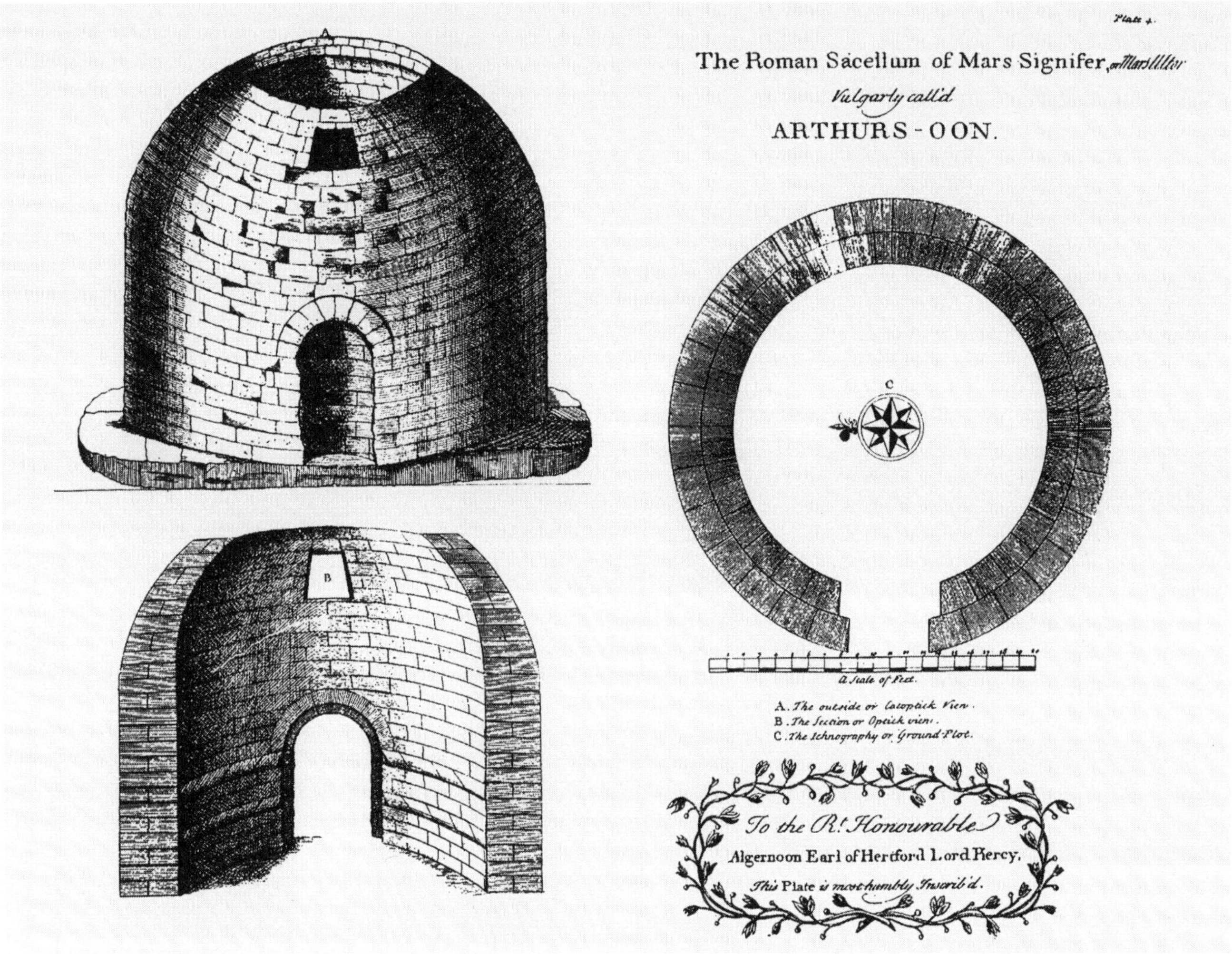

Fig. 8.3 The drawing of Arthur's O'on by A. Gordon published in 1726

to consider that the building depicted on the Rose Hill stone was Arthur's O'on. They noted the discrepancies – the landscape, the lintel to the door and the opening in the dome – but suggested that these were not conclusive.

Discussion

There is, as Richmond pointed out, a superficial similarity between Arthur's O'on and the building depicted on the Rose Hill sculpture. The two structures are domed with a tall entrance and possibly no other aperture, though the door on Arthur's O'on is rounded while that on the Rose Hill sculpture a flat lintel. Both stood beside a frontier, both a little to the north of it. Both appear to have a link to Victory. We can do no better than Kenneth Steer and agree that it is likely that both were victory monuments linked to the construction of the Walls. Even so, a note of caution should be interjected for Hölscher (1967) has reminded us that some images of Victory were used to symbolise universal Roman rule rather than always necessarily to celebrate specific, real victories. Nevertheless, the proximity of both victory monuments to their respective frontiers is suggestive.

The similarities between the two monuments are certainly provocative, but it remains the case that there are no parallels on Roman frontiers (though see Lewis 1965, 78–83 for round temples on the northern frontier of Britain). Steer pointed out the closest analogies to the corbelled dome:

> 'are not to be found in Roman architecture, but in the tholoi, or vaulted tombs, of Mycenae, and especially the more sophisticated examples such as the so-called "Treasury of Atreus"... The latter, built around 1,250 BC, was still visible in the nineteenth century. In Rome itself corbelled vaulting was only employed for a few early subterranean structures such as the lower chamber of the Tullianum and some cisterns on the Palatine.' (Steer 1960, 107)

All these possible parallels are either in Rome or in the eastern part of the Empire. Could the link be Hadrian himself, who we have come to accept played a distinctive role in the planning of Hadrian's Wall (Stevens 1955; Breeze 2009)? It is likely that Hadrian visited Mycenae in 124. Tony Birley has made out a case for Hadrian visiting Troezen and Hermione, the latter just 3 km from Mycenae during his visit to Greece that year (Birley 1997, 178–9). Such an association would be particularly appropriate bearing in mind Hadrian's positive attitude to Greece.

Arthur's O'on was erected in a location with wide views to the south and east, but also in a place where it could be seen from ships sailing up the Firth of Forth and probably also up its tributary, the River Carron, to a harbour at Camelon (Tatton-Brown 1980, 341). Tatton-Brown pointed out that in the second century Arthur's O'on would have stood closer to the edge of the raised beach; he also proposed that this was the *Victoria* of Ptolemy and the Ravenna Cosmographer.

In its general location, Arthur's O'on is closer to the Roman monument at Jarrow than that at Rose Hill. Whatever the form of the monument at Jarrow, or wherever it was in that area, the text of the inscriptions indicate that it had imperial associations and, we may presume, had been erected close to the River Tyne (Richmond and Wright 1943; *RIB* 1051). In such a position, it could be seen from ships proceeding upstream. But, this begs a question: why were there two, or even three if the Carlisle building is brought into play, possible Victory, or at least commemorative, monuments on Hadrian's Wall?

It is possible that the Jarrow inscription and the Rose Hill temple commemorate different events. The former was related to the construction of the Wall. The later may be related to an entirely separate event, a victory. Here a distinction must be drawn between the events leading up to the building of Hadrian's Wall and the Antonine Wall. The latter was constructed following an authentic Roman victory in which the bounds of the empire were extended and for which the emperor received the appellation *Imperator*, that is Conqueror, and a special Victory coin was issued. At the beginning of Hadrian's reign, 117, 'the Britons could not be kept under Roman control'. A coin issue of 119/20 presumably refers to the same event. There followed the construction of Hadrian's Wall. But this did not follow a triumphal acquisition of new territory. Would it have warranted the erection of a temple? It may, however, have commemorated the cost of victory. Two generations after the troubles of 117, Cornelius Fronto, a senator and former consul, noted the great losses in Britain during the reign of Hadrian. They were serious enough to have led to 3,000 reinforcements being sent to the island. There has been considerable debate about the date of this warfare within Hadrian's reign, but a recent discussion favours Fronto's comment as referring to the warfare at the beginning of the reign (Breeze *et al.* 2012). The fighting, clearly serious, perhaps resulted in a victory worth celebrating through the construction of a temple.

There are other possible explanations. The Rose Hill stone was found close to the western end of the Stone Wall of Hadrian, which led the editors of the *Corpus of Sculpture of the Roman World* to suggest that it marked the end 'of the entire stone Wall as intended in the original scheme' (Coulston and Phillips 1988, no. 265). This stretch of the Wall is also interesting in other ways. The Wall ditch here is unusually wide at 15.200 m while the milecastles and turrets in the mile to the west have distinctive plans and may have been amongst the first to be built on the Wall (Symonds 2005). This may have been because the valley of the River Irthing was a natural route for travelers and needed controlling; if this was the case a line of communication might have been thought to be an appropriate location for a special monument. Graafstal, noting the early building of this section of Wall, has commented that it 'is a tempting thought that the Gilsland relief belongs to an early-Hadrianic monument that commemorated the delivery of the western terminus of the Wall, part of which seems to have been carefully prepared in anticipation of the emperor's visit in 122' (Graafstal 2012, 151). Yet, we should be careful in offering hypotheses; the structure may have been erected in this position simply because it stood on the watershed between the Tyne and the Irthing basins (Breeze 2006, 284).

If there was a monument at the east end of the Wall, then we might expect another at the western end of the Wall. Although no such monument is known here, the vaulted/domed building with the inscription to Mars and Victory recorded at Carlisle, may have served a similar purpose. We may also note that there are other unusual features on Hadrian's Wall. Excavations in 1924 at Rudchester 3 m west of the fort revealed that the north face was erected on a foundation course of coarse white stone, the lowest course being topped by an elaborately moulded plinth (Brewis 1924, 103). Of note too are the exceptionally well dressed stones in the outer face of the fort wall beside the west gate of Birdoswald (Wilmott 1997, 104–9). All we can do is note the existence of these unusual features.

Conclusions

It seems almost certain that both Arthur's O'on and the domed building on the Rose Hill sculpture are Victory monuments, and they should probably be joined by the building in Carlisle. As Lewis remarked, 'it is remarkable that all three cases refer to Victory, and two represent eagles' (Lewis 1965, 79). While Arthur's O'on presumably commemorated a Victory and the construction of a frontier, the Rose Hill stone may not have marked the construction of Hadrian's Wall but another military event of that emperor's reign, or indeed may have simply commemorated Roman dominance: certainty is impossible on present evidence. The Rose Hill sculpture, in classical style, itself presumably sat within a temple. This presumed temple lay towards the west end of the stone section of Hadrian's Wall, but also on the watershed between the two great river systems of the frontier. The existence of some form of monument near the eastern end of Hadrian's Wall together with one towards the middle suggests that one should be sought towards the western end of the Wall. The possibility that the Rose Hill monument was the inspiration of Hadrian, who appears to have directed some aspects of the building of Hadrian's Wall, must be borne in mind. If that was the case, Arthur's O'on may have been a copy of its southern predecessor. It remains interesting that no such monument has been found on any other frontier of the Roman Empire.

Acknowledgements

I am grateful to Iain Ferris for commenting on an earlier version of this paper.

Bibliography

Birley, A. R. (1997) *Hadrian, the Restless Emperor.* London.

Bosanquet, R. C. (1929) Dr. John Lingard's Notes on the Roman Wall. *AA* 4th series, 6, 130–62.

Breeze, D. J. (2006) *J. Collingwood Bruce's Handbook to the Roman Wall.* 14th edition. Newcastle upon Tyne.

Breeze, D. J. (2009) Did Hadrian design Hadrian's Wall? *AA* 5th series, 38, 87–103.

Breeze, D. J., Dobson, B. and Maxfield, V. (2012) Maenius Agrippa, A Chronological Conundrum. *Acta Classica* 55, 17–30.

Brewis, P. (1924) Roman Rudchester. Report on Excavations, 1924. *AA* 4th series 1, 93–120.

Bruce, J. C. (1867) *The Roman Wall.* 3rd edition. Newcastle upon Tyne.

Bruce, J. C. (1875) *Lapidarium Septentrionale.* Newcastle upon Tyne.

Coulston, J. C. and Phillips, E. J. (1988) *Corpus Signorum Imperii Romani, Corpus of Sculpture of the Roman World, Great Britain I, 6, Hadrian's Wall West of the North Tyne, and Carlisle.* Oxford.

Ferris, I. (2000) *Enemies of Rome, Barbarians through Roman Eyes*, Stroud.

Graafstal, E. P. (2012) Hadrian's haste; a priority programme for the Wall. *AA* 5th series 41, 123–84.

Hodgson, J. (1840) *History of Northumberland*, Newcastle upon Tyne.

Hölscher, T. (1967) *Victoria Romana, Archaeological research on the history and nature of the Roman goddess of victory from the beginning to the end of the 3rd century A.D.* Mainz.

Lewis, M. J. T. (1965) *Temples in Roman Britain.* Cambridge.

Morris, J. (1980) *Nennius. British History and Welsh Annals.* London and Chichester.

Piggott, S. (1950) *William Stukeley.* Oxford.

Richmond, I. A. (1947) *Handbook to the Roman Wall.* 10th edition. Newcastle upon Tyne.

Richmond, I. A. and Wright, R. P. (1943) Stones from a Hadrianic war memorial on Tyneside. *AA* 4th series 21, 93–120.

Sibbald, R. (1707) *Historical Enquiries.*

Steer, K. A. (1960) Arthur's O'on: A Lost Shrine of Roman Britain. *Archaeological Journal* 115, 99–110.

Steer, K. A. (1976) More light on Arthurs O'on. *Glasgow Archaeological Journal* 4, 90–2.

Stevens, C. E. (1955) Hadrian and Hadrian's Wall. *Latomus* 14, 384–403.

Stukeley, W. (1720) *An Account of a Roman Temple and other Antiquities near Graham's Dike in Scotland.* London

Symonds, M. (2005) The construction order of the milecastles on Hadrian's Wall. *AA* 5th series 34, 67–81.

Tatton-Brown, T. (1980) Camelon, Arthur's O'on and the main supply base for the Antonine Wall. *Britannia* 11, 340–3.

Toynbee, J. (1964) *Art in Roman Britain.* London.

William of Malmesbury (1125) *Gesta pontificum Anglorum.*

Wilmott, T. (1997) *Birdoswald. Excavations of a Roman fort on Hadrian's Wall and its successor settlements: 1987–92.* London.

Winterbottom, M. (ed.) (2007) *William of Malmesbury, Gesta Pontificum Anglorum, The History of the English Bishops.* Oxford.

9

MONUMENTALISING MILITARY SERVICE: SOLDIERS IN ROMANO-BRITISH SCULPTURE

Jon Coulston

Introduction

Soldiers occur in the figurative arts of the Roman imperial period through three principal mechanisms. They appear in their thousands in state art, mainly stone sculpture on triumphal display monuments erected in Rome and other centres, such as Constantinople and Thessaloniki. Some 750 figural gravestones and other funerary monuments survive from across the empire with representations of deceased soldiers, sometimes with friends and family (Anderson 1984; Busch 2001; Hope 2003; Coulston 2007; Feucht 2011). Soldiers and other military subjects also figure in a great range of small artworks, such as coins, figurines, paintings, mosaics, ivories, glass and metalwork (Bishop and Coulston 2006, 1–22). These three modes of representation vary with time and place, responding to political, cultural and religious imperatives. In some regions a particular genre predominates, as with the figural *stelae* in the first-century AD Rhineland, or the painted mummy portraits in the Egyptian Fayyum (Walker and Bierbrier 1997). Other areas, such as the Iberian Peninsula and the lower Danube, exhibit only a handful of figural funerary monuments for the whole Roman period. In Britain the vast majority of stone sculpture, as with stone inscriptions, was created by the army to fulfil both its public and private needs. Indeed, Julio-Claudian soldiers seem to have hit the beaches sculpting, and right through to the Tetrarchic period in the British provinces they continued to depict themselves in stone, even when such practices fell away in nearby provinces. This continuous 'insular' tradition is the subject of the present paper, involving a corpus of material which the writer has studied over a number of decades with the invaluable help and companionship of Lindsey Allason-Jones.

The usual criteria of site context, epigraphy, and sculptural style may be employed in dating the representation of soldiers in British sculpture, but with the added facility of diagnostic forms of dress and equipment. The rectangular cloak (*sagum*), fastened by a brooch at the wearer's right shoulder, was unhelpfully ubiquitous during the first to fourth centuries (Bishop and Coulston 2006, 111, 144, 184.). Thus a *sagum* alone, without a military inscription, unlike the *paenula*, does not help with date, or indeed necessitate identification as a soldier, and some gravestones remain problematic (*e.g.*Brewer 1986, nos 19, 27). However, the circular cloak (*paenula*) was worn primarily by infantrymen and not after the later second century (Fig. 9.1). The latest surviving depictions in Britain are sculptures from Antonine Wall sites (Fig. 9.3; Keppie and Arnold 1984, nos 90, 111, 135e). It fastened down the upper front and opened up to form the characteristic frontal 'W' when hitched up over the shoulders to free the arms. A tunic with short sleeves gave way to long sleeves around the turn of the second and third centuries. Similarly, long, tight trousers came into use by soldiers at about the same time under the influence of northern European and Levantine clothing fashions (Bishop and Coulston 2006, 144, 184). Short swords worn on the right side by soldiers below the rank of standard-bearer also denote a first- to second-century depiction, succeeded in the Antonine period and thereafter by long swords (*spathae*) on the left. Waist-belts with a circular belt-buckle, and *spathae* carried on a broad baldric are indicative of figures dating from the Severan period to before the Tetrarchy (Figs 9.4–9.6; *ibid.*, 154–63, 182–4). There are virtually no pieces of sculpture, or inscriptions, found along the northern frontier of Britain after the Tetrarchic period, though note the possible exception of the late fort gate keystone sculpture

Fig. 9.1 Full-figure gravestone of a soldier in a paenula*, Castlesteads, Cumbria. Photograph: J. C. N. Coulston*

Fig. 9.2 Full-figure sculpture of an archer, Housesteads, Northumberland. Photograph: J. C. N. Coulston

from Vindolanda (Coulston and Phillips 1988, no. 448). Inscriptions along the Wall end with *RIB* 1613 and 1912.

Two principal types of funerary relief will be reviewed: the standing soldier; and the triumphant rider, with or without ancillary groom (*calo*) or defeated barbarian. These grooms represent the substantial numbers of male grooms and servants accompanying Roman troops in garrisons and in the field (Speidel 1989; Phang, 2005; 2008, 234–7). Each type will be examined in turn, progressing chronologically forward, and moving generally from south to north in Britain. An interesting related phenomenon which will also be examined is the leakage of contemporary military equipment detail into other sculptural genres, particularly the representation of deities. All these works may be assumed to have originally been painted to aid visibility and comprehension of detail (Coulston and Phillips 1988, xvii; Bull 2007, 11, 20. See *RIB* 141).

Standing soldier gravestones

In AD 43 Roman soldiers seem to have virtually hit the beach sculpting, to judge from the early appearance of Julio-Claudian funerary *stelae*. The gravestone of M. Favonius Facilis at Colchester (Essex) is comparable with the finest continental representations of armoured *centuriones* (*RIB* 200; Huskisson 1994, no. 47; Phillips 1975). This gravestone, with its niched figure, sculpting style and other decorative elements, indicates the importation of Rhenish funerary practices with the Claudian invasion army, Facilis' *legio XX* having come over from Novaesium, modern Neuß, Germany (Manning 2000, 69). The Colchester gravestone may have been damaged during, and thus would predate, the Boudican Revolt (Phillips 1975, 102; Huskisson 1994, 23).

A number of unarmoured, standing soldier gravestones exhibiting *paenulae* are found at first-century sites such as Gloucester (Gloucestershire) (Henig 1993, no. 142). At Londinium, the status of the city as provincial capital, succeeding Camulodunum some time after the Boudican Revolt, plus the presence of a series of forts, ensured that some soldiers died there while on service. Several fragmentary figural gravestones represent soldiers, and while not all are closely datable, the Camomile Street soldier's gravestone is most likely Flavian or Trajanic. This dating is based on general execution and ornament, and by carefully detailed equipment (Marsden 1980, 82–3; Bishop 1983). It has one of the best representations of

Fig. 9.3 Full-figure funerary sculpture of three legionaries with paenulae, Croy Hill, Strathclyde. Photograph: J. C. N. Coulston

Fig. 9.4 Ring-buckle gravestone, Bath, Avon. Photograph: J. C. N. Coulston

a *paenula* with its fastenings to survive from the western provinces. The cloak was specifically posed to reveal a sword on the man's right side, and one studded strip with lunate terminal of his apron. At Bath (Avon) a number of soldiers who died, presumably while taking the waters, were commemorated with figural *stelae*, one exhibiting a *paenula* (Cunliffe and Fulford 1982, no. 48). A number of *legio XIV* gravestones from Wroxeter (Shropshire) were erected in association with the legionary fortress there, occupied *c.*AD 67–84 (Manning 2000, 70–1, 75–6). Most bear a rosette in a gable, without figural sculpture (*RIB* 293–5; Henig 2004, nos 148–50), but one represents T. Flaminius, standing full length and wearing *caligae* with a shafted-weapon by his side (*RIB* 292; Henig 1993, no. 147).

Predictably, the legionary fortresses at York (Yorkshire) and Chester (Cheshire) provide examples of *paenula*-clad figures, and some fragmentary representations which may be contemporary (Tufi 1983, no. 99; Henig 2004, nos 34, 45, 50, 53, 78). A fine full-figure representation of the *optio* Caecilius Avitus with a staff and *tabulae* was found at Chester, comparable with such insignia depicted on *stelae* from other provinces (*RIB* 492; Henig 1993, no. 32. *Cf.* Schober 1923, no. 157; Balty and Van Rengen pl. 19). Also at Chester, the *stela* of the *imaginifer* M. Aurelius Diogenes shows an *imago* with carrying handle near the butt, topped by an imperial portrait bust (*RIB* 521; Henig 2004, no. 53; cf. Éspérandieu 1907–81, no. 5850; for the standard type see Töpfer 2011, 26–8, 132). At York, L. Duccius Rufinus, *signifer* of *legio VIIII*, exhibits his standard with *phalerae* up its shaft (*RIB* 673; Tufi 1983, no. 44. See Töpfer 2011, 32–3, 132–7). Templeborough (Yorkshire) has produced two auxiliary soldiers, a simple *miles* and an *emeritus* of *cohors IIII Gallorum*, who emulated legionary practice by having full-figure gravestones erected (*RIB* 619–20; Tufi 1983, no. 102–3). This transfer of practice may be seen elsewhere, as with the group of very fine Rhenish auxiliary gravestones from Bad Kreuznach (Éspérandieu 1907–81, no. 6125, 6136–37; Coulston 2007, 546).

Once Hadrian's Wall was established a number of standing soldier gravestones were erected displaying *paenulae*, notably at Castlesteads (Cumbria, Fig. 9.1; Coulston and Phillips 1988, no. 227) and High Rochester (Northumberland; Phillips 1977, no. 272). Less easily categorised because it has no inscription, is the well-known *stela* depicting an archer found at Housesteads (Northumberland, Fig. 9.2; Smith 1968; Coulston and Phillips 1988, no. 200). This might be interpreted as a funerary work based on the devolved rosettes which appear in the spandrels of the arched niche. The man's bow is very accurately rendered and he may have belonged to the only known formation of archers in Britain, *cohors I Hamiorum* (Coulston 1985, 237, 279, 282–3). However, the man also holds an object across his lower body which has the blade profile of a billhook, rather than that of a military axe. Billhooks appear mainly as the attribute of provincial woodland deities (*e.g.* Éspérandieu 1907–81, no. 3001; Coulston 1985, 279),

Fig. 9.5 Ring-buckle gravestone, Brougham, Cumbria. Photograph: J. C. N. Coulston

Fig. 9.6 Ring-buckle gravestone of an imaginifer, Carrawbugh, Northumberland. Photograph: J. C. N. Coulston

whereas axes very rarely appear in the iconography of Roman soldiers (Bishop and Coulston 2006, fig. 133.4).

Alongside the rich iconography of Antonine Wall distance slabs and other monumental sculptures (see below), a small number of funerary representations of soldiers survive displaying *paenulae*. A small stone from Shirva (Dunbartonshire) represents a man holding a shafted weapon and *tabulae* (Keppie and Arnold 1984, no. 111). A block from Croy Hill (Strathclyde) depicts three soldiers, one older, bearded man standing between two clean-shaven ones (Fig. 9.3; *ibid*., no. 90; Coulston 1988). This may be a representation of a father and two sons. They each carry a curved, rectangular shield, with a correctly rendered rectangular boss plate, and a carefully delineated *pilum*. Their helmets are off and slung from shoulder or shield in the manner of soldiers seen on Trajan's Column in Rome (Cichorius 1896–1900, Scenes IV, XII, XLVIII–IX, LVI, LXIX, LXXXVI–II, XCVIII, CI–II, CXXVI–III). Each man also wears a *paenula*, the latest dateable occurrence of this cloak form in Romano-British iconography. The dress and equipment identifies the soldiers as *legionarii*, members of one of the many legionary *vexillationes* building and garrisoning installations throughout the province and along the northern frontiers (Coulston 1988, 13–5; see now Davies 2009).

Moving solidly forward into the third century, the figural gravestone found in London of the *legio II Augusta* soldier, Vivius Marcianus, depicts the deceased full-length, in a niche, holding a scroll and a staff (*RIB* 17; Wacher 1995, 85, fig. 36). The latter is long and dome-headed in the third-century style (Bishop and Coulston 2006, 185). A broad waist-belt is fastened with a small ring-buckle. The fragmentary *stela* of the *speculator* Lucius Celsus, also of *II Augusta* and from London, has only the head of a figure surviving, but similarity to the Marcianus stone, and the legionary title '*Antoniniana*', also securely date this piece to the third century (*RIB* 19;

Wacher 1995, 85, fig. 35). Rather more enigmatic is another London gravestone depicting a soldier in a *sagum* and a long-sleeved tunic, who carries a ribbed, oval shield (Marsden 1980, 83). The clothing suggests Antonine or later date, while the shield might be earlier.

A fragmentary gravestone with a standing, niched figure, from Bath, has lost its inscription and the head and feet of the deceased (Fig. 9.4; Cunliffe and Fulford 1982, no. 47). However, the remaining detail is well preserved and shows a soldier in a long-sleeved tunic and *sagum*, holding a scroll and a shafted object. The latter has also lost its top, but may be a weapon with a spirally wrapped shaft (*hasta* or, less likely, *pilum*), or a standard. If the latter, the lack of attached medallions on the upper shaft might suggest an *aquila*, an *imago* or a *vexillum*. A waist-belt is depicted with the lower part of a ring-buckle appearing out from under the tunic folds. At the soldier's left hip is a scabbarded sword with a prominent peltaform chape (Bishop and Coulston 2006, figs 78.4–6, 99.8).

The gravestone of Marcus Aurelius Nepos at Chester is remarkable for the crudity of execution, especially in the bodily proportions of the deceased and his wife (*RIB* 491; Henig 2004, no. 33). Nevertheless, the sculptor was concerned to make two features arrest the viewer's attention: Nepos' *vitis*, which is disproportionally long, and his ring-buckle, which is prominently exaggerated in size. The presence of the man's wife was also a more common inclusion after soldiers were allowed to legally marry, and sometimes whole families appeared to emphasise community and continuity (Phang 2001; for earlier 'wives' see Hofmann 1905, fig. 49; Éspérandieu 1907–81, no. 5798; 1931, no. 9; Ferri 1933, fig. 275; Tufi 1983, no. 99).

Further north again, a fragmentary and badly mutilated gravestone from Brougham (Cumbria) has been misinterpreted as showing a funerary banquet scene (Fig. 9.5; Wright and Phillips 1975, no. 226). However, close examination reveals that two full-figure standing men are depicted, the less damaged on the right wearing tunic, *sagum*, and a waist-belt with a central ring-buckle flanked by certainly one, possibly a pair, of domed studs (Coulston 1993, 2–3). Despite the severe damage, this is the most detailed rendition of a third-century ring-buckle belt yet found in Britain.

Other gravestones of men wearing tunic and *sagum* may also have commemorated third-century soldiers, such as one from York figuring a man holding a staff and scroll, and standing alongside a child (*RIB* 699; Tufi 1983, no. 55). Three damaged *stelae* from Chester all seem to exhibit *saga*. One is of a standard-bearer who held a scroll and perhaps has a sword on his left side (Henig 2004, no. 80). The standard has a handle above its butt, but the top is broken away in such a way as to preclude a *signum* or a *vexillum*, but could have been either an *aquila* or an *imago*. A second stone has lost all detail beyond the outline of the *veteranus* figure (*RIB* 517; Henig 2004, no. 39). The third is lost from the waist down, but the man's right arm is extended in the pose of holding the strap-ends of his waist-belt, so characteristic of third-century soldiers (*ibid.*, no. 79; Hofmann 1905, fig. 51; Éspérandieu 1907–81, no. 5507; Wagner 1973, nos 31, 34, 371).

The gravestone of an unknown soldier from Carrawburgh (Northumberland) is the most enigmatic of the group (Fig. 9.6; Coulston and Phillips 1988, no. 193). Bodily proportions and modelling of detail are only slightly less crude than on the Nepos stone. However, within these limitations, the attention to military equipment is striking. The man is clothed in tunic and *sagum*, and his waist belt exhibits both the ring-buckle and the pendent strap-end which are so characteristic of third-century military iconography. In his right hand he carries a standard which has a lower, curved handle and is topped by a bull statuette. In his left is a small, bossed shield, rectilinear with four curving sides. The board is anomalous because standard-bearers of the first to third centuries invariably appear with small round shields, largely because they required both hands to carry and manoeuvre the standard (Bishop and Coulston 2006, 91, 182). Although the curved, rectangular form of legionary shield did continue in use at least to the mid-third century (James 2004, nos 629–32; Bishop and Coulston 2006, 180–82), this would have been inappropriately large for a standard-bearer, so it is unlikely that the shield on the Carrawburgh stone was one of these, scaled down by the sculptor. The bull *imago* might represent a totemic legionary insignia of a type seen on Trajan's Column, and the *legio VI victrix* would seem a likely candidate (Cichorius 1896–1900, Scene XLVIII; see Keppie 1984, 206–9 and Töpfer 2011, 131–2, 143–4). However, auxiliary regiments may also have carried such animal *imagines*, although their insignia are less well attested than those in legionary usage (Tufi 1983, no. 106; Töpfer 2011, 143–4). Thus it seems most likely that the deceased soldier belonged to *cohors I Batavorum*, the principal third-century formation at Carrawburgh (*RIB*1534–36, 1544–5, 1553, 1559–60, 1562).

Fig. 9.7 Unfinished rider gravestone, Maryport, Cumbria. Photograph: J. C. N. Coulston

Fig. 9.8 Rider gravestone, Stanwix, Cumbria. Photograph: J. C. N. Coulston

Triumphal rider gravestones

The depiction of Longinus Sdapezematycus, a *duplicarius* of *ala I Thracum*, at Colchester, is the earliest insular example of the 'rider' (*Reitertypus*) form of gravestone (*RIB* 201; Schleiermacher 1984, no. 76; Huskisson 1994, no. 48). It includes both the relatively unusual modelling of the deceased's cuirass as scale armour, and the earliest representation of a vanquished Briton in Romano-British art.

Rider type gravestones for legionary and auxiliary cavalry which occur through the period from Augustus to Trajan in the Rhineland, appear in a number of early instances in southern Britain, following on from the Colchester example already mentioned. At Cirencester, Sextus Valerius Genialis of the *ala Thracum* (*RIB* 109; Schleiermacher 1984, no. 75; Henig 1993, no. 137) and Dannicus of the *ala Indiana* (*RIB* 108; Schleiermacher 1984, no. 74; Henig 1993, no. 138) exhibit widely different competence of execution. The former is a fine representation of a standard-bearer with a well-detailed cavalry helmet and standard (Robinson 1975, fig. 300; see also Webster 1986; Töpfer 2011, 148–52). The latter has a niched figure which is very cramped and ill-proportioned. The *stela* of Rufus Sita, *eques cohortis* of *VI Thracum* at Gloucester, is not quite so crudely executed, but the horse seems to be galloping out of the niche (*RIB* 121; Schleiermacher 1984, no. 79; Henig 1993, no. 140). Genialis and Sita wear *spathae* which the sculptors have exaggerated in prominence, in the manner of some continental representations, and which has been linked to the dominant convention of depicting the horseman from his right side, not obscured by his shield (Schleiermacher 1984, nos 5–6, 8, 17, 20, 27). All three stones figure vanquished Britons. Further examples of rider *stelae* have been found at Bath (*RIB* 159; Schleiermacher 1984, no. 69; Cunliffe and Fulford 1982, nos 44–5) and Wroxeter (*RIB* 291; Schleiermacher 1984, no. 81; Henig 2004, no. 146), some fragmentary and some with a barbarian below the horse. A group of five, of first- to second-century date, at Chester includes two with barbarians, one with a *calo*, and at least one of these stones certainly belonged to an *eques legionis XX* (*ibid.*, nos 36, 48, 54, 57–8 (*RIB* 499, 538, 550–51); Schleiermacher 1984, nos 70–2). Unusually the sculpture with the *calo* has the groom preceding the horse in the continental, largely Danubian manner (cf. *ibid.*, nos 90, 117, 130).

Further north, the rider *stela* of Insus, an *eques* of the *ala Augusta*, was discovered at Lancaster (Lancashire) in 2005 (Bull 2007). Red paint was still evident in the letters of the inscription. It is an extraordinary piece which represents the deceased riding over a crouching and decapitated barbarian. Insus holds both his *spatha* and the severed head by its hair in his right hand. Although the figural execution is quite basic, there are many small details of clothing and equipment which indicate good knowledge and close attention by the sculptor. Other less dramatic rider stones without inscriptions have been found in the North West at Ribchester (Lancashire) and Kirkby Thore (Cumbria) (Schleiermacher 1984, no. 82; Edwards 2000, fig. 23; Bull 2007, 31, 48). Two more such stones are known, but without clear findspots (Collingwood Bruce 1875, nos 754–5; Schleiermacher 1984, no. 83; Bull 2007, 48).

The earliest representation of a soldier in the Hadrian's Wall region is the rider gravestone of Flavinus, an *eques* of the *ala Petriana*, reused in Hexham Abbey (Northumberland). It is presumed to have been originally erected outside the Flavian fort at Corbridge (*RIB* 1172; Schleiermacher 1984, no. 77; Phillips 1977, no. 68). It is extraordinary both for its size (2.64 m high) and its sculpted detail. The deceased's helmet has a large horsehair crest and extravagant side-plumes, but it is impossible to be more specific about the form of helmet and whether or not it may be categorised as a 'sports' type (Robinson 1975, 89–139, fig. 306; 1976, 3–6).

A number of rider gravestones also appear along Hadrian's Wall. These are more difficult to date closely, but the *stela* of Marcus Aurelius Victor from Chesters (Northumberland) may, based on the name, belong to the third rather than second century (*RIB* 1481; Coulston and Phillips 1988, no. 191). They also tend to be rather crudely executed, although one from Maryport (Cumbria) is very valuable because it is unfinished, and thus informative on sculptural processes (Fig. 9.7; Coulston 1997, 123, fig. 8.16. See Phillips 1976; Coulston and Phillips 1988, xvii–viii, nos 170, 477, 534). Others occur at Stanwix (Cumbria, Fig. 9.8; *RIB* 2030; Schleiermacher 1984, no. 80; Coulston and Phillips 1988, no. 231) and Halton Chesters (Phillips 1977, no. 259). The latter is so damaged that only parts of the horse and the fallen barbarian survive, but the man has a small, bossed, rectangular shield (Fig. 9.9). Whereas all the defeated adversaries on previously discussed rider gravestones carried oval or sub-oval boards, this is the first to show the rectangular type. This shield seems to have been characteristic of northern Britain, appearing as it does on Antonine Wall distance slabs (Keppie and Arnold 1984, nos 68, 137; cf. Tacitus, *Agricola* 36), and on reliefs depicting native war gods from Maryport and possibly Birdoswald (Cumbria) (Coulston 1997, 119–20, fig. 8.13; Coulston and Phillips 1988, no. 162). An actual shield of this type made of leather has been found at Clonoura (Co. Tipperary) in Ireland (Coulston 2008, 313, fig. 4). The rectangular form continued to be used in northern Britain into the early medieval era, represented on Pictish sculptures (Henderson and Henderson 2004, figs 51, 78, 100, 179, 183, 186).

Two further sculptures have been identified as rider gravestones, both without inscriptions. The first is a rider carrying a spear and shield from Whitecombe, near Dorchester (Dorset) (Cunliffe and Fulford 1982, no. 144; Schliermacher 1984, no. 78). He may be armoured. If the piece is early, then it might belong to the conquest period; if second or third century in date then it is a real geographical outlier for military gravestones. On the other hand there are southern rider god reliefs, executed on a smaller scale, and there is the possibility that the piece is cultic not funerary (Henig 1993, no. 123, 125; Huskisson 1994, nos 29–30). The well-known 'Sarmatian' relief found at Chester depicts a rider wearing a tunic and *sagum*, a short bladed weapon along his right thigh, and a conical helmet (Henig 2004, no. 59). He appears to carry a *draco* standard (Coulston 1991, 102, fig. 7; Töpfer 2011, 153). These features are paralleled by representations of Sarmatian cavalry in continental sculpture and the link has been made with the undoubted presence of Sarmatian troops in the North West of England in the later second and third centuries (Richmond 1945; Edwards 2000, 49). However, while there is definite 'Sarmatian' influence exerted on the Chester piece, the possibility may be entertained that this sculpture represents a Danubian rider-god with military features. Such deities are sometimes shown carrying a *draco* (Coulston 1991, 109, fig. 15).

Two other gravestones of cavalrymen which depict the deceased may date to the third-century, both from Chester. Amongst a group of banquet *stelae*, that of Aurelius Lucius includes a crested helmet and a sword (*RIB* 522; Henig 2004, no. 43; see also *ibid.*, nos 24, 35, 44, 61, 64–5, 67–70). Occasionally weapons appear in funerary dining scenes on military gravestones elsewhere (Éspérandieu 1931, no. 24). A rider gravestone depicts the deceased with an almost knee-length mail cuirass (*RIB* 550; Henig 2004, no. 56). This has been seen as a diagnostic dating feature but it is actually inconclusive, due not least to the crudeness of overall execution (Dixon and Southern 1992, 38, repeated by Henig 2004, 20).

Other military sculptures

Soldiers and military equipment did not only appear in Romano-British funerary sculpture, but also on monumental

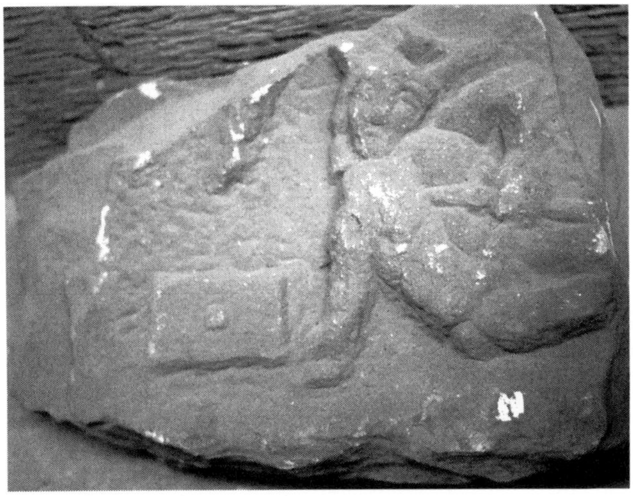

Fig. 9.9 Rider gravestone with fallen barbarian, Halton Chesters (Northumberland). Photograph: J. C. N. Coulston

reliefs associated with military buildings. Cavalrymen ride triumphantly over vanquished Caledones on the two Antonine Wall distance slabs from Bridgeness (West Lothian) and Summerston Farm (Lanarkshire), very much in the style of rider tombstone figures (Keppie and Arnold 1984, no. 68, 137). On the Bridgeness slab a *suovetaurilia* is carefully depicted, the ceremony traditionally initiating military campaigns, as seen on Trajan's Column and other metropolitan monuments (Cichorius 1896–1900, Scenes VIII, LIII, CIII; Ryberg 1955). A *vexillarius* of *legio II Augusta* stands in the background of this scene. A number of standard-bearers also appear on other distance slabs, one with a finely rendered *aquila*, and several with *vexilla* (Keppie and Arnold 1984, nos 52, 68, 135). Stones from Chesters and Housesteads also represent *vexillarii*, the former wearing a crested helmet with finely rendered details of ear-flanges and 'nasal' point (Coulston and Phillips 1988, nos 239, 400; cf. Robinson 1975, figs 257, 261, 274, 278, 281). A relief of a pointing, half-figure man, now at Vindolanda (Northumberland), presumably represents a soldier (Fig. 9.10; *RIB* 1394; Phillips 1977, no. 290). Although not a stone sculpture, but a mould carving of funerary significance, a cavalryman (0.08 m high) appears on a lead coffin found at Cefn On (Glamorgan). Unlike on most rider *stelae*, the rider is seen from his left side (Murray Threipland 1953, 73, fig. 1). He wears a crested helmet and carries a sub-oval shield and a *vexillum*.

There are numerous carvings of standards without bearers, often in association with an inscription, and both legionary *vexilla* and centurial *signa* are well represented (Phillips 1977, nos 86, 177–8, 281, 287; Keppie and Arnold 1984, nos 44, 67; Coulston and Phillips 1988, nos

Fig. 9.10 Relief of a soldier, Chesterholm, Northumberland. Photograph: J. C. N. Coulston

249, 252; Hassall and Tomlin 1995, 379–80, pl. x). Eagles alone without a shaft may reference legionary *aquila* (Phillips 1977, nos 87, 103, 170, 287; Keppie and Arnold 1984, nos 67, 137; Coulston and Phillips 1988, no. 388). These all served in a similar manner to legionary animal insignia, as did the two stones with Dacian *falces* carved for *cohors I Aelia Dacorum* at Birdoswald (Cumbria) (Coulston 1981; Coulston and Phillips 1988, no. 266–7). These third-century sculptures may be seen as a feature for the strong continuing cultural identity of Dacian auxiliaries (*RIB* 1920; Oltean 2009).

There is also a phenomenon of 'spillage' of contemporary military equipment details into the representation of deities. Such features stand out from the mainstream of Hellenising attributes. For example, deities with shields, such as Mars, Minerva and native war gods, have an oval board with a central, circular boss when seen from the front, and often a central, horizontal handgrip across the boss opening when seen from behind (*e.g. ibid.*, nos 67, 161; Keppie and Arnold 1984, no. 12; Coulston and Phillips 1988, nos 67–8, 161). Mars figures might appear with helmet crest and side plumes in the manner of Roman cavalrymen (*e.g.* Coulston and Phillips 1988, no. 67). Third-century belts and sword furniture are particularly noticeable when they are worn by deities, as with the ring-buckle belts on a figure on the side of an altar to Jupiter from Wallsend (Tyne and Wear) (Phillips 1977, no. 194; Coulston 1983), and on a Mars plaque from Custom Scrubs (Gloucestershire) (*RIB* 132; Henig 1993, no. 60; cf. *ibid.*, nos 48–59 for similar warrior gods without ring-buckles). A Mars statue from Old Carlisle (Cumbria) has a *spatha* with an eagle-headed pommel, suspended from a broad baldric (Wright and Phillips 1975, no. 238, pl. xii; Coulston 1993, 2–3; for eagle-pommels see Piccottini 1968, no. 21; Bishop and Coulston 2006, fig. 129; for other

Mars figures with broad baldrics see Filtzinger 1971, fig. 5; Tufi 1983, no. 10). A small statue of Attis from London has a bow which is very accurately rendered in the features of its limbs, ears and nocks, quite different from the usual, stylised 'Cupid's bow' of Greco-Roman art (Coulston 1985, 238, fig. 35).

Discussion

The *agency* behind sculptural creation is often indicated, in terms of patronage, political and religious will, and economic support, by dedicatory and votive inscriptions. Commanding officers caused monuments to be set up through their own patronage on their own behalf, or on behalf of their regiment. Military formations celebrated the achievements of architecture and building by dedicating their works to emperors, under the administration of provincial governors and unit commanders. They also made collective religious votive dedications. Individual soldiers made religious offerings according to their status and means, and people made provision for funerary monuments in their own lifetimes, in wills and through the conscientiousness of their heirs. Some of these works can be characterized as institutional and 'official', most dealt with in this present paper can be seen as initiatives for 'private' purposes (Phillips 1977, xiii–xix; Coulston and Phillips 1988, xv–xix; Henig 1999; 2009).

It is much more difficult to determine who physically created the sculptures. Ancient artists and artisans very rarely signed their works. One exception, from Housesteads, involved the carver named Aurelius, a name which does little to narrow down a second- to third-century date (*RIB* 1625). There is no evidence of 'artists' coming from the continent, or from the towns of southern Britain, to produce sculpture in the north. Traditional views of the Roman army, based on the experience of more modern periods, were reluctant to credit soldiers with the skills, training, and even cultural flair for 'art'. However, the almost complete lack of indication of any intrusive personnel, taken in conjunction with the style, repertoire, working methods and limitations of sculpture created at military installations in Roman Britain, make it abundantly clear that the vast majority of work was executed by soldiers within the army, or, possibly (based on no specific evidence), by veterans trained within the army and continuing to work after military discharge.

All of the sculptures in Northern Britain, with very few exceptions, were carved in the locally available sandstones. Apart from millstones, the little stone which came into Britain from the continent was confined mainly to south-east England. That is not to say that personnel did not move, but the evidence again suggests that such movement was lateral, along the frontiers through the army, not core-to-periphery, as may have been more significantly the case for works in southern British towns, villas and shrines. Occasionally, ideas of continental forms of gravestone or sculptural decoration came across to Hadrian's Wall from the Danubian and Rhenish frontiers (*e.g.* Coulston and Phillips 1988, no. 192). Most exotically, a sculptor working at South Shields produced two gravestones of a form and decorative detail most akin to works at Palmyra (Syria), and even carved a Palmyrene inscription on one of them (Phillips 1977, nos 247–8). However, he was in one case definitely working for a soldier client, in the other quite likely was doing so, and he himself may have been moving around the empire as a soldier (*ibid.*, no. 67). Put bluntly, there was no other workforce available outside the army to provide inscriptions and figural sculpture in their various forms for military installations (Keppie and Arnold 1984, xvii–viii; Coulston and Phillips 1988, xviii). This is not to deny that there were any continental and/or civilian sculptors operating in Britain (*e.g. RIB* 149), just not ones significantly active in areas dominated by military installations. Soldiers were trained in a great range of constructional and artistic skills as part of their career development, and the military iconography of Roman Britain was a direct product of this training (*Digest* 50.6.7; Watson 1969, 76, 181).

The normal model entertained by scholars for ancient artistic production is the 'workshop' in which lifetimes were spent gaining and refining skills. Young apprentices joined and were trained up by older masters, eventually becoming masters themselves. This allows the workshop's products to be defined and traced if the output is sufficient. Within this, attempts might be made to identify individuals' 'hands', as for example in studies of major projects employing substantial numbers of sculptors, such as Trajan's Column (Rockwell 1981–83; Coulston 1990; Conti 2001). Unfortunately, for military sites along the frontiers there is seldom enough surviving material to work with (but compare Coulston and Phillips 1988, nos 200 and 201, 202 and 203). In a sense, the individual military formation, legion or auxiliary regiment, was the 'workshop' in which skills were learnt, spread and developed, some of which were perhaps brought into the army by new recruits, but over time styles and methods became something of a formation signature. The differing plans of milecastles on Hadrian's Wall, for example, are an illustration of this specificity in the field of architecture (Breeze and Dobson 2000, 66–72).

At the lowest level, features displayed by more than one sculpture from a given site might be linked in such a way as to suggest that the pieces were the products of one period, working group, or even of one hand. The large number of second-century altars recovered at Maryport provides just such a situation (*RIB* 809–31, 833–43; Breeze 1997; Coulston 1997; forthcoming). The proportions, mouldings and other decoration can be analysed together with the names of dedicants, titles of regiments and styles of epigraphy. Thus it seems that at this fort a variety of men carved inscriptions with varying competence. In some cases altars which appear to be the work of one sculptor exhibit differing letter forms, demonstrating that epigraphic carving could be a separate process from shaping and ornamenting the altar. To judge from the decorative repertoire, at least two sculptors worked for two or three different commanders, and more than one sculptor worked for an individual officer as patron.

The scatter of funerary iconography across Britain reflects the fluid troop movements of the conquest period. Stabilisation of the northern frontier of Britannia in the Trajanic period initiated a long period of occupation along the two Walls. That being true, the small number of gravestones from Antonine Wall sites speaks to the short occupation of that line (Hodgson 1995; 2009). This coincided with increasing use of stone in architecture and fortifications across the province, and thus a greater incidence of surviving inscriptions and stone sculptures. This also meant that the concomitant stoneworking skills were more uniformly practiced throughout the army on a local level, with decreasing emphasis on legionary work.

Overall, the corpus of military iconography from Roman Britain includes some 88 pieces: 31 standing soldiers and 24 rider gravestones. Of these, some 12 can be attributed to the third century, including five which provide definite examples of the ring-buckle type (Figs 9.4–9.6). As has been observed of other similar *corpora*, there is a predictably disproportionate element of higher ranks as compared with *milites gregarii*. Britain provides a useful body of standard-bearers, particularly amongst the cavalry.

The gravestones form part of an empire-wide presentation of identity, status and career achievement by soldiers who belonged to a self-regarding community of professional service (Pegler 1997; Goldsworthy and Haynes 1999; James 1999; Coulston 2004; 2007; Roymans 2004; Gardner 2007; Swan 2009; Galestin 2009; van Driel-Murray 2009; Saddington 2009). By far the most important feature of this iconography was the use of military equipment as a visual identifier. Staffs of various types, standards, shafted weapons and *tabulae* could be employed to distinguish rank. Interestingly there are no representations from Britain of soldiers as musicians, and no displays of *dona militaria*, as seen in other provinces. However, this was principally achieved by emphasising the armed state of soldiers and their signature military belts (*baltei* or *cingula*, depending upon period). The Camomile Street soldier is a fine manifestation of this, comparable in its posing of the *paenula* to reveal equipment with the half-figure gravestone at Strasbourg (France) which has an apron, richly laden with metallic fittings, spilling out from the niche, down over the inscription (Éspérandieu 1907–81, no. 5495). The high relief of the apron straps makes it clear that this was the plan all along, and that the mouldings of the inscription below were of secondary importance. Similarly, third-century gravestones paid great attention to belts and baldrics, often over-emphasising the size and prominence of the ring-buckle. This was particularly true of the military gravestones in Rome where the soldiery formed a community distinct and separate from the rest of the metropolis' mass population (Coulston 2000, 94–7, fig. 5.3, 5, 17, 21; Busch 2001; 2007; 2011, 121–25, figs 59–60, 65, 75–6). The belt on the gravestone from Brougham may be regarded in this light (Fig. 9.5). Soldier-sculptors' knowledge of contemporary equipment facilitated the transference of such details to depictions of deities.

Some rider stones, such as those from Ribchester and Kirkby Thore, make a vivid play with shafted weapons which pin fallen barbarians to the ground. However, swords received much greater attention from sculptors of rider *stelae* with their over-large pommels and guards. Although swords had a special cultural significance to the tribal aristocracies of Iron Age Europe, and this undoubtedly fed into the ethos of elite cavalry service amongst northern Europeans, the iconographic prominence may be viewed as a feature of the developing imperial army culture. Similarly, the Insus stone commemorated a particular Roman military action, the taking of an enemy head. This is paralleled in funerary sculpture from the continent (Éspérandieu 1907–81, no. 5784; Schleiermacher 1984, no. 22), and on such triumphal works as Trajan's Column and the Great Trajanic Frieze in Rome (Cichorius 1896–1900, Scenes XXIV, LVI, LXXII, CXIII, CXLVII; Leander Touati 1987, pls 3–4, 13–14, 32), one of the metopes of the Tropaeum Traiani at Adamclisi (Romania) (Florescu 1965, fig. 183), and on one Antonine Wall distance slab (Keppie and Arnold 1984, no. 68). It was practiced within the context of the army and should not be linked with some 'Celtic' ritual (*contra* Goldsworthy 1996, 271–3; see now Armit 2012). All types of Roman soldiers took heads, but there may have been a particular cavalry emphasis because the *spatha*, rather than the *gladius Hispaniensis*, lent itself ideally to a decapitating cut delivered from the saddle. The Insus stone may even have commemorated an actual achievement, as did other *stelae* of cavalrymen who wished to be remembered for feats of particular skill (cf. *ILS* 2558; Krüger 1974, no. 9; Schleiermacher 1984, nos 22, 98; Farkas and Gabler 1994, no. 83; James 2011).

The British corpus is also interesting for its regional-chronological spread. The closest provinces with troop concentrations and strong cultural links with Britain were the two Germanies, yet there the pattern was different. The greatest concentration of both standing soldier and rider gravestones was in the Julio-Claudian and Flavian period, but they both tailed off with very few second-century pieces. In contrast with Britain and the Upper Danubian region, the Germanies have remarkably few third-century figural gravestones (as evidenced by Éspérandieu 1907–81; 1931; Schleiermacher 1984; Stoll 1992). This was a reflection of funerary practice rather than currency of equipment types. After all the ring-buckle belt was ubiquitous, and the German provinces have seen the most detailed artefactual study of the form (Oldenstein 1976). Thus the continuity of the erection of figural gravestones in Britain may be considered as something of an 'insular' tradition, maintaining rider *stelae* through the second century, and joining the renaissance of standing soldier depiction seen during the third.

Bibliography

Anderson, A. S. (1984) *Roman Military Tombstones*. Princes Risborough.

Armit, I. (2012) *Headhunting and the Body in Iron Age Europe*. Cambridge.

Balty, J. C. and Van Rengen, W. (1993) *Apamea in Syria. The winter quarters of legio II Parthica*. Bruxelles.

Bishop, M. C. (1983) The Camomile Street soldier reconsidered. *Transactions of the London and Middlesex Archaeological Society* 34, 31–48.

Bishop, M. C. and Coulston, J. C. N. (2006) *Roman Military Equipment from the Punic Wars to the Fall of Rome*, 2nd edition. Oxford.

Breeze, D. J. (1997) The regiments stationed at Maryport and their commanders. In R. J. A. Wilson (ed.) *Roman Maryport and Its Setting*, Cumberland and Westmorland Antiquarian and Archaeological Society, extra series 28, 67–89.

Breeze, D. J. and Dobson, B. (2000) *Hadrian's Wall*, 4th edition. London.

Brewer, R. J. (1986) *Corpus Signorum Imperii Romani, Great Britain I.5, Wales*. Oxford.

Bull, S. (2007) *Triumphant Rider. The Lancaster Roman Cavalry Tombstone*. Lancaster.

Busch, A. W. (2001) Von der Provinz zum Zentrum – Bilder auf den Grabdenkmälern einer Elite-Einheitt. In P. Noelke (ed.), *Romanisierung versus Resistenz und Wiederaufleben einheimischer Elemente. Kolloquium Köln 2001*, Mainz, 679–94.

Busch, A. W. (2007) '*Militia in urbe*': the military presence in Rome. In L. de Blois and E. lo Cascio (eds) *The Impact of the Roman Army (200 BC–AD 476). Economic, Social, Political, Religious and Cultural Aspects*. Impact of Empire 6, Leiden. 315–41.

Busch, A. W. (2011) *Militär in Rom. Militärische und paramilitärische Einheiten im kaiserzeitlichen Stadtbild*. Wiesbaden.

Cichorius, C. (1896–1900) *Die Reliefs der Traianssäule*, II–III. Berlin.

Collingwood Bruce, J. (1875) *Lapidarium Septentrionale. A Description of the Monuments of Roman Rule in the North of England*. London.

Conti, C. (2001) Gli scultori della Colonna Traiana. In F. F. Farina, G. Calcani, C. Meucci, M. L. Conforto and A. N. Al Azm (eds) *Tra Damasco e Roma. L'Architettura di Apollodoro nella Cultura Classica*, Roma, 199–215.

Coulston, J. C. (1981) A sculpted Dacian *falx* from Birdoswald (*RIB*1914). *AA* 5th Series, 9, 348–51.

Coulston, J. C. (1983) A fragmentary altar to Jupiter from Wallsend. *AA* 5th Series, 11, 309–13.

Coulston, J. C. (1985) Roman Archery Equipment. In M. C. Bishop (ed.) *The Production and Distribution of Roman Military Equipment. Proceedings of the Second Roman Military Equipment Seminar*, BAR International Series 275, Oxford, 220–366.

Coulston, J. C. (1988) Three legionaries from Croy Hill. In J. C. Coulston (ed.) *Military Equipment and the Identity of Roman Soldiers: Proceedings of the Fourth Roman Military Equipment Conference*, British Archaeological Reports Supplementary Series 394, Oxford, 1–29.

Coulston, J. C. N. (1990) Three new books on Trajan's Column. *JRA* 3, 290–309.

Coulston, J. C. (1991) The '*draco*' standard, *JRMES* 2, 101–14.

Coulston, J. C. (1993) Two representations of 3rd century equipment from Cumbria. *Arma* 3.1, 2–4.

Coulston, J. C. N. (1997) The stone sculptures. In R. J. A. Wilson (ed.) *Roman Maryport and Its Setting*, Cumberland

and Westmorland Antiquarian and Archaeological Society, extra series 28, Kendal, 112–31.

Coulston, J. C. N. (2000) 'Armed and belted men': the soldiery in imperial Rome. In J. Coulston and H. Dodge (eds), *Ancient Rome. The Archaeology of the Eternal City*, Oxford, 76–118.

Coulston, J. C. N. (2004) Military identity and personal self-identity in the Roman army. In L. de Ligt, E. L. Hemelrijk, and H. W. Sengor (eds), *Impact of Empire* IV. *The Empire at the Lower Level: Effects of Roman Rule on Life in Italy and the Provinces*, Amsterdam, 135–52.

Coulston, J. C. N. (2007) Art, culture and service: the depiction of soldiers on funerary monuments of the 3rd century AD. In L. de Blois and E. lo Cascio (eds) *The Impact of the Roman Army (200 BC–AD 476). Economic, Social, Political, Religious and Cultural Aspects.* Impact of Empire 6, Leiden, 529–61.

Coulston, J. C. N. (2008) Immortalising victory: votive weapons depositions in northern Europe and the Roman empire. In A. Abegg-Wegg and A. Rau (eds) *Aktuelle Forschungen zu Kriegsbeuteopfern und Fürstengräbern im Barbaricum*, Neumünster, 307–30.

Coulston, J. C. N. (forthcoming) The Maryport altars revisited. In A. W. Busch and A. Schäfer (eds), *Weihealtäre in Tempeln und Heiligtümern*, Köln.

Coulston, J. C. and Phillips, E. J. (1988) *Corpus Signorum Imperii Romani, Great Britain I.6. Hadrian's Wall West of the North Tyne, and Carlisle*. Oxford.

Cunliffe, B. W. and Fulford, M. G. (1982) *Corpus Signorum Imperii Romani, Great Britain I.2. Bath and the Rest of Wessex*. Oxford.

Davies, J. L. (2009) Size matters: campaign forts in Britain. In W.S. Hanson (ed.) (2009), *The Army and Frontiers of Rome. Papers Offered to David J. Breeze on the Occasion of His Sixty-Fifth Birthday and His Retirement from Historic Scotland*, Journal of Roman Archaeology Supplementary Series 74, Portsmouth RI, 44–54.

Dixon, K. R. and Southern, P. (1992) *Roman Cavalry from the First to the Third Century AD*. London.

Edwards, B. J. N. (2000) *The Romans at Ribchester. Discovery and Excavations.* Lancaster.

Éspérandieu, E. (1907–81) *Recueil général des bas-reliefs, statues et bustes de le Gaule romaine.* Paris.

Éspérandieu, E. (1931) *Recueil général des bas-reliefs, statues et bustes de le Germanie romaine*. Paris.

Farkas, Z. and Gabler, D. (1994) *Corpus Signorum Imperii Romani, Ungarn II. Die Skulpturen des Stadtgebietes von Scarbantia und der Limesstrecke ad Flexum-Arrabona.* Budapest.

Ferri, S. (1933) *Arte romana sul Danubio.* Milano.

Feucht, B. (2011) Uniformity up to the grave? Funerary inscriptions of Roman legionaries in Western Europe. *Ancient Society* 41, 147–83.

Filtzinger, P. (1971) *Limesmuseum Aalen.* Stuttgart.

Florescu, F. B. (1965) *Das Siegesdenkmal von Adamklissi. Tropaeum Traiani*, ed. 3. Bucaresti.

Galestin, M. C. (2009) Frisian soldiers in the Roman army. In A. Morillo, N. Hanel, and E. Martín (eds) *Limes XX. Roman Frontier Studies*, Madrid, 833–46.

Gardner, A. (2007) *An Archaeology of Identity. Soldiers and Society in Late Roman Britain.* Walnut Creek CA.

Goldsworthy, A. (1996) *The Roman Army at War, 100 BC–AD 200.* Oxford.

Goldsworthy, A. and Haynes, I. (eds) (1999) *The Roman Army as a Community*, Journal of Roman Archaeology Supplementary Series 34, Portsmouth RI.

Hassall, M. W. C. and Tomlin, R. S. O. (1995) Inscriptions. *Britannia* 26, 371–90.

Henderson, G. and Henderson, I. (2004) *The Art of the Picts. Sculpture and Metalwork in Early Medieval Scotland.* London.

Henig, M. (1993) *Corpus Signorum Imperii Romani, Great Britain I.7. Roman Sculpture from the Cotswold Region, with Devon and Cornwall.* Oxford.

Henig, M. (1999) Artistic patronage and the Roman military community in Britain. In I. Haynes and A. Goldsworthy (eds) *The Roman Army as a Community.* Portsmouth RI, 151–64.

Henig, M. (2004) *Corpus Signorum Imperii Romani, Great Britain I.9. Roman Sculpture from the North West Midlands*. Oxford.

Henig, M. (2009) Roman sculpture from the Hadrian's Wall region. In M. F. A. Symonds and D. J. P. Mason (eds), *Frontiers of Knowledge. A Research Framework for Hadrian's Wall, Part of the Frontiers of the Roman Empire World Heritage Site*, 1, Durham, 155–60.

Hodgson, N. (1995) Were there two Antonine occupations of Scotland? *Britannia* 26, 29–49.

Hodgson, N. (2009) The abandonment of Antonine Scotland: its date and causes. In W. S. Hanson (ed.) *The Army and Frontiers of Rome. Papers Offered to David J. Breeze on the Occasion of His Sixty-Fifth Birthday and His Retirement from Historic Scotland*, Journal of Roman Archaeology Supplementary Series 74, Portsmouth RI, 185–93.

Hofmann, H. (1905) *Römische Militärgrabsteine der Donauländer.* Wien.

Hope, V. M. (2003) Trophies and tombstones: commemorating the Roman soldier. *World Archaeology* 35.1, 79–97.

Huskinson, J. (1994) *Corpus Signorum Imperii Romani, Great Britain I.8. Roman Sculpture from Eastern England*. Oxford.

James, S. (1999) The community of the soldiers: a major identity and centre of power in the Roman empire. In P. Baker, S. Jundi and R. Witcher (eds), *TRAC 98. Proceedings of the Eighth Annual Theoretical Roman Archaeology Conference, Leicester, 1998*, Oxford, 14–25.

James, S. (2004) *The Excavations at Dura-Europos Conducted by Yale University and the French Academy of Inscriptions and Letters, 1928–1937. Final Report VII. The Arms and Armour and other Military Equipment.* London.

James, S. (2011) *Rome and the Sword. How Warriors and Weapons Shaped Roman History.* London.

Keppie, L. J. F. (1984) *The Making of the Roman Army from Republic to Empire.* London.

Keppie, L. J. F. and Arnold, B. J. (1984) *Corpus Signorum Imperii Romani, Great Britain I.4, Scotland.* Oxford.

Krüger, M. L. (1974) *Corpus Signorum Imperii Romani, Österreich I.5. Die Reliefs der Stadtgebiete von Scarbantia und Savaria.* Wien.

Leander Touati, A. M. (1987) *The Great Trajanic Frieze. The Study of a Monument and of the Mechanisms of Message Transmission in Roman Art.* Stockholm.

Manning, W. H. (2000) The fortresses of *legio XX*. In R. J. Brewer (ed.), *Roman Fortresses and Their Legions*, London, 69–81.

Marsden, P. (1980) *Roman London.*London.

Murray-Threipland, L. (1953) Part of a Roman lead coffin lid from Glamorgan. *Antiquaries Journal* 33, 72–4.

Oldenstein, J. (1976) Zur Ausrüstung römischer Auxiliareinheiten. *Bericht der Römisch-Germanischen Kommission* 57, 49–284.

Oltean, I. A. (2009) Dacian ethnic identity and the Roman army. In W. S. Hanson (ed.) *The Army and Frontiers of Rome. Papers Offered to David J. Breeze on the Occasion of His Sixty-Fifth Birthday and His Retirement from Historic Scotland*, Journal of Roman Archaeology Supplementary Series 74, Portsmouth RI, 90–101.

Pegler, A. (1997) Social organisations within the Roman army. In K. Meadows, C. Lemke and J. Heron (eds), *TRAC 1996. Proceedings of the Sixth Theoretical Roman Archaeology Conference*, Oxford, 37–43.

Phang, S. E. (2001), *The Marriage of Roman Soldiers, 31 BC–AD 235. Law and Family in the Imperial Army.* Leiden.

Phang, S. E. (2005) Soldiers' slaves, 'dirty work', and the social status of Roman soldiers. In J. J. Aubert and Z. Váhelyi (eds), *A Tall Order: Writing the Social History of the Ancient World.* München.

Phang, S. E. (2008) *Roman Military Service. Ideologies of Discipline in the Late Republic and Early Principate.* Cambridge.

Phillips, E. J. (1975) The gravestone of M. Favonius Facilis. *Britannia* 6, 102–5.

Phillips, E. J. (1976) Unfinished Roman sculptures in North Britain. *Archaeological Journal* 133, 50–6.

Phillips, E. J. (1977) *Corpus Signorum Imperii Romani, Great Britain I.1,Corbridge, Hadrian's Wall East of the River North Tyne*. Oxford.

Piccottini, G. (1968) *Corpus Signorum Imperii Romani, Österreich II.1. Die Rundskulpturen des Stadtgebietes von Virunum*. Wien.

Richmond, I.A. (1945) The *Sarmatae*, *Bremetennacum Veteranorum* and the *regio Bremetennacensis*. *JRS* 45, 15–29.

Robinson, H. R. (1975) *The Armour of Imperial Rome.* London.

Robinson, H. R. (1976) *What the Soldiers Wore on Hadrian's Wall.* Newcastle upon Tyne.

Rockwell, P. (1981–83) Preliminary study of the carving techniques on the Column of Trajan. *Marmi Antichi*, Studi Miscellanei 26, Roma, 101–11.

Roymans, N. (2004) *Ethnic Identity and Imperial Power. The Batavians in the Early Roman Empire*. Amsterdam.

Ryberg, S. (1955) *Rites of the State Religion in Roman Art*. Memoirs of the American Academy in Rome 22, Rome.

Saddington, D. B. (2009) How Roman did auxiliaries become? In A. Morillo, N. Hanel, and E. Martín (eds) *Limes XX. Roman Frontier Studies*, Madrid, 1017–24.

Schleiermacher, M. (1984) *Römische Reitergrabsteine. Die kaiserzeitlichen Reliefs des triumphierenden Reiters*. Bonn.

Schober, A. (1923) *Die römische Grabsteine von Noricum und Pannonien*. Sonderschriften des österreichischen archäologischen Institutes in Wien 10, Wien.

Smith, D. J. (1968) The archer's tombstone from Housesteads. *AA* 4th Series, 46, 184–91.

Speidel, M. P. (1989) The soldiers' servants. *Ancient Society* 20, 239–47.

Stoll, O. (1992) *Die Skulpturenausstattung römischer Militäranlagen an Rhein und Donau. Der Obergermanisch-Rätische Limes*. Pharos. Studien zur griechisch-römischen Antike 1.2, St Katherinen.

Swan, V. G. (2009) *Ethnicity, Conquest, and Recruitment: two case studies from the northern military provinces*. Portsmouth RI.

Töpfer, K. M. (2011) *Signa Militaria. Die römischen Feldzeichen in der Republik und im Prinzipat*. Mainz.

Tufi, S. R. (1983) *Corpus Signorum Imperii Romani, Great Britain I.3. Yorkshire*. Oxford.

Van Driel-Murray, C. (2009) Ethnic recruitment and military

mobility. In A. Morillo, N. Hanel, and E. Martín (eds) (2009) *Limes XX. Roman Frontier Studies*, Madrid, 813–22.

Wacher, J. (1995) *The Towns of Roman Britain*. London.

Wagner, F. (1973) *Corpus Signorum Imperii Romani, Deutschland I.1. Raetia und Norucum*. Bonn.

Walker, S. and Bierbrier, M. (1997) *Ancient Faces. Mummy Portraits from Ancient Egypt*. London.

Watson, G. R. (1969) *The Roman Soldier*. London.

Webster, G. (1986) Standards and standard bearers in the *alae*. *Bonner Jahrbücher* 186, 105–15.

Wright, R. P. and Phillips, E. J. (1975) *Roman Inscribed and Sculptured Stones in Carlisle Museum*. Carlisle.

10

THE CORBRIDGE HOARD REVISITED

M. C. Bishop

Introduction

In 2013, it will be 25 years since the publication of the Corbridge Hoard final report and nearly half a century after the original find (Allason-Jones and Bishop 1988), so the present volume, together with those milestones, may seem like a good opportunity for some reflection upon the whole project. Amongst the many difficulties of working on the publication of the English Heritage backlog excavation report for the training excavations at Corbridge (Bishop and Dore 1989), one of the many joys available to me as light relief was studying the Hoard with Lindsay, whose sense of humour and down-to-earth approach to the somewhat sparse documentary sources available to us was as refreshing as it was amusing.

Excavated in 1964, with an interim report published in *Archaeologia Aeliana* (Daniels 1968), the Hoard had then rested on the proverbial back-burner for nearly two decades with the sole exception of the famed segmental armour, which H. Russell Robinson had reconstructed in time for display at the 1969 Roman Frontier Congress in Cardiff (Robinson 1974). Robinson's magnum opus, *The Armour of Imperial Rome* (1975), not only brought the armour to the attention of a wider public, but also introduced the illustrations of Peter Connolly, even if (to his mild chagrin, as he reminded me later) Peter's signature was not readily apparent on the colour plate that was also used on the dust jacket. However, the meme that persisted, and one which *was* credited, was supplied by his three reconstruction drawings of the main types of segmental armour (the Corbridge A, B/C and Newstead types). It remains impossible to think of a better way of explaining how the armour worked in a diagrammatic form. Peter Connolly's reconstruction drawings also appeared (slightly modified by Peter) in Allason-Jones and Bishop 1988.

Publication of reconstructions of the armour in Robinson's book, and the comparatively high profile of just that one aspect of the Hoard, meant there was a clear need to supply some balance by publishing the context of the armour within the Hoard and of the Hoard itself within the wider archaeological record, as well as detailed records of the armour fragments that informed Robinson's reconstructions. This was underlined by the discussion of the Hoard that was occurring in the literature, based only on the limited (and, as it turned out, not wholly correct) information supplied in the interim report: this ranged from the informed (Manning 1972) to the highly speculative (Davies 1970), although thankfully the dreaded word 'ritual' had yet to be introduced into the mix. The present writer is regularly asked if he has considered a ritual context for the deposition of the Corbridge Hoard; he has: there is no evidence to support the notion.

The original brief for the backlog publication did not include the Hoard, so – given the present writer's interest in Roman military equipment – it was natural that an attempt should be made to remedy this. Enlisting the help of Lindsay, and with the support of Stephen Johnson – who, in his role of Inspector of Ancient Monuments responsible for that particular backlog project, was a vital ally – we set about the work that would ultimately lead to the monograph (which, ironically, ended up being published the year before the main report).

A number of areas invite reconsideration in the light of subsequent discoveries, but one area that remains unchanged is that of the accuracy of Robinson's interpretation of the armour.

Figure 10.1 The internal leathers on a reconstruction Corbridge-type lorica segmentata shoulder guard, showing the use of roves

Subsequent finds

For the purposes of comparison with the Corbridge Hoard, the finds from the putative armoury next to the headquarters building at the Carlisle Millennium site are the most relevant, despite the fact that it did not constitute a hoard. The armour included some scale armour, some pieces of '*lorica segmentata*' (which, incidentally, proved the contemporaneous use of Newstead and Corbridge types in the Hadrianic period), but a lot more segmental armguards. These last comprised elements of three armguards, still articulated when deposited, and supplied a vital missing detail concerning the functioning of segmental armour, whether it be body or limb armour. Although there was no surviving organic material in the Corbridge Hoard, mineralisation preserved the internal leathers and these provided Robinson with the vital clue to understanding how '*lorica segmentata*' worked. Unlike von Groller (who thought the metal plates were riveted to a leather jacket; Bishop 2002, 2), Robinson realised the Hoard armour proved they were attached to leather straps, a far more practical solution (and one familiar from his knowledge of Renaissance armour). However, no subsequent finds provided information on the nature of the internal leathers, specifically whether they were tanned or oiled (Fig. 10.1). The Carlisle Millennium material supplied the missing information (Bishop 2009, 687–705). Since it contained considerable amounts of organics, including tanned leather, and the armguards were articulated, their internal leathers should have been in place. The fact that nothing survived to be found is the clearest indication yet that tanned leather was not used for them. The best working hypothesis is that some form of oiled leather was employed (Raab 2011). Moreover, it throws an interesting light on the different processes involved in the preservation of the Carlisle materials by comparison with the mineralisation of the Hoard. If the deduction about the use of oiled leather on the armguards is correct, then the Carlisle organics had had time for the internal leathers to decay but also for the associated pieces of tanned leather to be preserved. The process that preserved the Corbridge Hoard would seem to have been quicker, assuming the same sort of leather was used for both types of armour, since the internal leathers did not have time to rot before mineralisation.

Two mismatched half sets of girth hoops were excavated at Stillfried in Austria in 2000 and were interpreted as booty (Eibner 2000; Keil 2001). Although they are still awaiting full publication, the present writer was able to examine the armour whilst it was undergoing conservation at the Römisch-Germanisches Zentralmuseum in Mainz and it was evident that whilst one half had eight bands, the other had seven. The implication that Roman soldiers might use non-matching halves to their armour obviously has a bearing on the half sets of '*lorica segmentata*' in the Hoard.

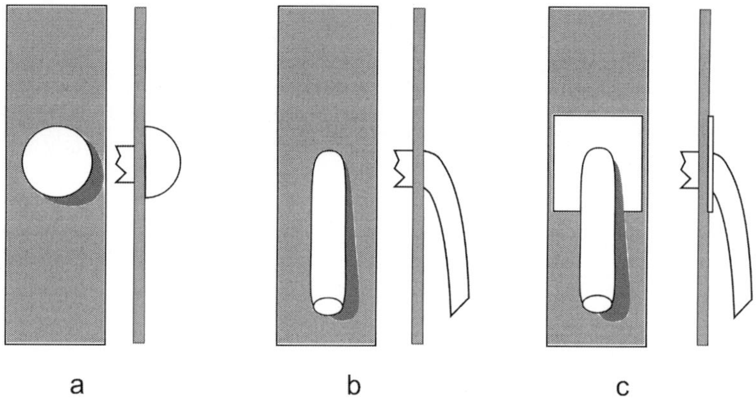

Figure 10.2 Types of rivetting on Corbridge Hoard armour internal leathers: a) peening; b) hammering over; c) hammering over through a rove. Not to scale

Whilst modern sensibilities may find it difficult to believe, the Roman army may not always have been as well turned out as had previously been thought.

The legionary fortress at León has provided another interesting insight into the armour. A discovery from a building adjacent to the rampart produced a considerable amount of armour. As well as confirming the use of both Corbridge and Newstead types of '*lorica segmentata*' together, it unambiguously demonstrated their use into the fourth century AD (Aurrecoechea 2007). Whether this was peculiar to Spain, or was in fact a wider phenomenon, is unclear, but a fourth-century fragment of the Newstead type from Carlisle hints that this may not have been an isolated instance (Caruana 1993).

Detail

It is inevitable that details sometimes seem insignificant at the time, but later prove to be of importance. In the case of the armour, one question that has sometimes been asked – was a central plate between the two breastplate halves missing? – is easy to answer, once it is realised that it is based upon a misunderstanding. Reconstructions of the Corbridge breastplates can often be seen to gape, leading to the accusation that they could not have been effective and that an additional plate must have sat between them. Quite apart from the fact that the breastplates were very obviously paired – one with a hinged strap and the other with a hinged buckle to receive the strap – there is a simple explanation for the difficulties experienced by re-enactors: fit. Few modern men have the physique required of a Roman soldier and too many wear armour that is too small for them. Indeed, with correctly sized armour, the gape can be effectively negated by the simple measure of wearing a padded undergarment that levels the shoulder units and provides additional padding against blows to the shoulder (where the armour is clearly designed to offer maximum protection). Such a garment, similar to a medieval arming doublet, has been equated by the present writer with the *thoracomachus* of the anonymous writer of the *De Rebus Bellicis* (16–17) and – perhaps – with the enigmatic *subarmale* (or *subarmalis*) of the *Historia Augusta* (*Aurelian* 13.3; *Claudius* 14.8, Bishop 1995). It was customary, rather than unusual, in the ancient and medieval world to wear some form of energy-absorbing undergarment with body armour, so the fact that '*lorica segmentata*' was also designed to be used with it is unsurprising. Segmental armour from the Antonine period is shown worn with *pteryges*, which seems to have been a development of this padded undergarment more often seen with other forms of armour (Bishop 2002, 80). Thus there is little reason to question Robinson's interpretation of the armour finds and, there are no missing components that were not included in the original report.

What does stand out upon reflection are the details of the fixtures and fittings on the armour. Beginning with the internal leathering, it is apparent that a wide range of styles – perhaps derived from different craftsmen – went into making the cuirasses in the Hoard work. Internal leathers were secured to the ferrous plates of the armour by means of copper-alloy rivets. A rivet was passed through the plate from outside, through the strap, and 'peened over' (the protruding end was hammered to broaden it, often in the form of a neat dome, and thus secure the strap; Fig. 10.2a). An alternative to peening was simply to hammer the terminal down to lie parallel with the surface of the strap (Fig. 10.2b). A third method was to use a washer, known as a 'rove', on top of the strap (so the rivet passed through plate, strap, and then rove before being peened or hammered over; Fig. 10.2c). In terms of technical competence, peening is the most sophisticated, hammering over the least, and the last may well be indicative of repairs performed by the owners, rather than by skilled or semi-skilled armourers (who were presumably responsible for peened rivets). Examples of all these techniques are to be found amongst the Corbridge Hoard armour (Allason-Jones and Bishop 1988, 23–51 with figs 26–71). Peening can be seen on Cuirasses 1–5 and (exclusively) on all of the girth-hoop sets (Cuirasses 1–6). Hammering over is apparent on Cuirasses 5 and 6. Finally, rectangular roves can be seen on Cuirasses 1, 3 and 6.

The lack of consistency in the techniques of securing the internal leathers is probably a strong argument for repairs having been carried out. Equally persuasive is the evidence of the internal leathering on the backplates of Cuirass 5. Instead of two parallel vertical straps, one large sheet of leather had been used and this is not found anywhere else amongst the Hoard armour.

Repair/damage

If there was a theme to the Corbridge Hoard, then, it was damage and repair. This was perhaps best characterised by the bundles of spearheads with their broken shafts, since these demonstrated the most obvious defects. Breaking of spear shafts in action must have been a common problem and possibly one reason why shafted weapons were equipped with a conical metal ferrule, which not only protected a weapon if it was grounded but also provided a secondary head in the event of damage to the main blade. One of the documents recovered from the excavations at Carlisle was a report from a *decurio* to his commanding officer, detailing the items that some of his troopers were lacking (Tomlin 1999). These included *gladia instituta* (rather quaintly being given the 'wrong' gender, but possibly meaning 'regular' or 'standard issue' swords); *lanciae pugnatoriae* (combat javelins, presumably to distinguish them from those used in the *Hippika Gymnasia*); and *subarmales* (thought by Tomlin to be a type of weapon but equally likely the arming doublet discussed above), and the inevitable question begged is why the troopers came to be missing these items. Were they perhaps excessively careless? It seems unlikely. These were all rather large items to 'lose', particularly with so many men in one *turma* being affected. The answer, then, may lie in damage or loss in action: after all, a spearhead awaiting re-shafting was effectively 'lost' to its owner.

The pieces of armour in the Hoard, on the other hand, have their own particular interest, since they were not matching pairs. The pieces in the chest had been separated from their companion pieces, implying that the pieces retained in service were mismatched with other pieces. This is unsurprising in the light of the two mismatched sets of girth hoops found at Stillfried (Bishop 2002, 47). So why were the separated halves in the box? It seems they were being cannibalised. One upper shoulderguard had already been taken off a type C and transplanted to a type A and a similar fate presumably awaited the other pieces, had they not been buried (Allason-Jones and Bishop 1988, 23–7). The Carlisle Millennium finds illustrated this 'cut'n'shut' process dramatically with segmental armguards that had been put together using components from different parent sets (Bishop 2009, 704). The damage and repair to those speak directly of combat and the same reason may lie behind the presence of the armour (and the spears) in the Hoard. Cannibalisation was widely used by the Royal Air Force during the Second World War (Smallwood 1994, 100–3) and, more recently, in order to keep sorties flying over Libya, the RAF was forced to cannibalise three of its Typhoon aircraft to supply spares for those in the front line (Anon. 2011). Combat generates a heterodox demand for components with which supply can seldom keep pace; this leads to cannibalisation. Far from being an abnormal state of affairs, it was (and is) the norm.

Warfare

The implication of the synchronised dating of the Carlisle Millennium and Corbridge Hoard finds, together with the indications of damage and repair in both assemblages, is clear: the army in northern Britain was engaged in combat. Moreover, the finds suggest that the Roman army was accustomed to being in action in this province in the early years of the Hadrianic period and had adapted to dealing with its demands upon their equipment. It is possible, but by no means certain, that some significance should be attached to the presence of articulated armguards amongst the Carlisle assemblage. In a military context, this technology had only comparatively recently been used in the Dacian Wars, although its origin lay in gladiatorial equipment. Armguards, together with helmet bowl reinforces, were part of a package of measures providing greater emphasis on personal defence resulting from encountering a new and dangerous threat. Its deployment in Northern Britain suggests a similar perception of risk.

All of this lends added weight to references in the numismatic and literary sources to trouble with the Britons under Hadrian (such as the *Historia Augusta* and Fronto; Breeze and Dobson 2000, 25; 2012, 19–20) and reminds us of the Vindolanda Tablets' testimony to earlier skirmishing with British cavalry, in the Trajanic period (Bowman and Thomas 1994, 106–8). Here, then, is the context for the repaired and in-need-of-repair armour, the broken shafted weapons, and the careful management of resources of which the Corbridge Hoard speaks so eloquently. The system was under stress, but it was working.

Legionary/auxiliary

The contents of the Hoard throw up so many questions and answer so few that it sometimes seems like a hopeless task attempting to hear what it is saying. One area which has to be tackled, however, is that of the nature of the garrison. The question of differentiation of legionary and auxiliary equipment has continued to be discussed since the publication of the Hoard report, yet there is still no convincing proof that auxiliary troops used *lorica segmentata* (Coulston 1988; Bishop and Coulston 1993, 206–9; 2006, 254–9).

Some relevant information has emerged from amongst the Vindolanda writing tablets. First, a possible Roman name, Coria, has been revealed for Roman Corbridge (Bowman and Thomas 1994, 96–7). Associated with this was the information that troops of *cohors I Tungrorum* from Vindolanda were outposted to Coria; in fact, more were at Corbridge (if the identification is correct) than remained at their home base (*loc. cit.*). The principle this demonstrates, the fragmentation of garrisons, is attested elsewhere, and it is important for understanding how the Roman army operated (Bishop 1999; Davies 2009, 47–51; Hopewell and Hodgson 2012, 41–2). Whilst auxiliaries from Vindolanda were at Coria, the tablets also show that legionaries were present at the former site (Bowman and Thomas 1994, 126). The size of this presence at Vindolanda is unclear, and the deployment of legionaries within auxiliary units for training purposes is recorded by Tacitus (*Agricola* 28), but it only serves to further weaken the old binary notion of legionaries in fortresses and auxiliaries in forts. Clearly mixing did occur.

Excavations at Alchester were at one time thought to provide evidence of the use of *lorica segmentata* by auxiliaries (Sauer 2001, 22–8), although in truth this was only based on the same arguments as those used first by Ulbert (1970) and subsequently by Maxfield (1986). However, the narrative evolved with further work and the site was posited as an early British legionary base, albeit an abnormally small one, at which point the case for auxiliaries using segmental armour evaporated (Sauer 2005, 122; Bishop 2012, 140). The practice of brigading auxiliaries and legionaries together has most recently been used to explain the layout of the fort at Llanfor (Hopewell and Hodgson 2012, 40–2).

Thus our understanding of Roman garrisoning policies, far from making the suggestion of a legionary presence at Corbridge less likely, has if anything enhanced that view. This can also be viewed with the benefit of hindsight from the later second and third centuries, when legionary detachments are attested at Corbridge within the military compounds. Indeed, Corbridge and Carlisle both had legionary components in garrison then, recalling the pairing of the two sites in the Hadrianic period (Breeze 2006, 421 and 463). Did Carlisle and Corbridge share some strategic significance? Of course they did: both lay on the Stanegate and on one of the major roads north into Caledonia (Margary 1973, 455 and 476, Margary [roads] 7 and 8). Therefore, the reasons for there being legionaries at the two sites in the early second century were probably the same as they were later.

What was it for?

After many years, the Hoard has recently benefited from a new display in the site museum at Corbridge (Fig. 10.3), together with the inevitable interactive component. Whilst it is difficult to view the latter without the *daemon* of Peter Connolly muttering over one's shoulder about computer reconstructions, it provides a welcome presentation of the finds in an appealing form. It is, of course, informed by the Hoard report, differing in only one major aspect, mischievously suggesting that – like countless coin hoards and Samuel Pepys' 'Parmazan' cheese (Latham 1985, 664) – the Hoard chest may have been buried with the intention of recovery. This idea deserves testing in the light of the available evidence.

There is no denying that the chest was very carefully packed. The sets of armour had been collapsed (abnormally so) and at least in part stacked one within the other. Moreover, there seems to be ample evidence of it having been wrapped in cloth, presumably as a protective measure. However, the question one inevitably asks is whether this was done with the intention of recovery after burial or if instead there never was an intention to bury the material. So how might this be determined?

If the chest was concealed with the intention of recovering it at a later date it would seem logical that it would not be

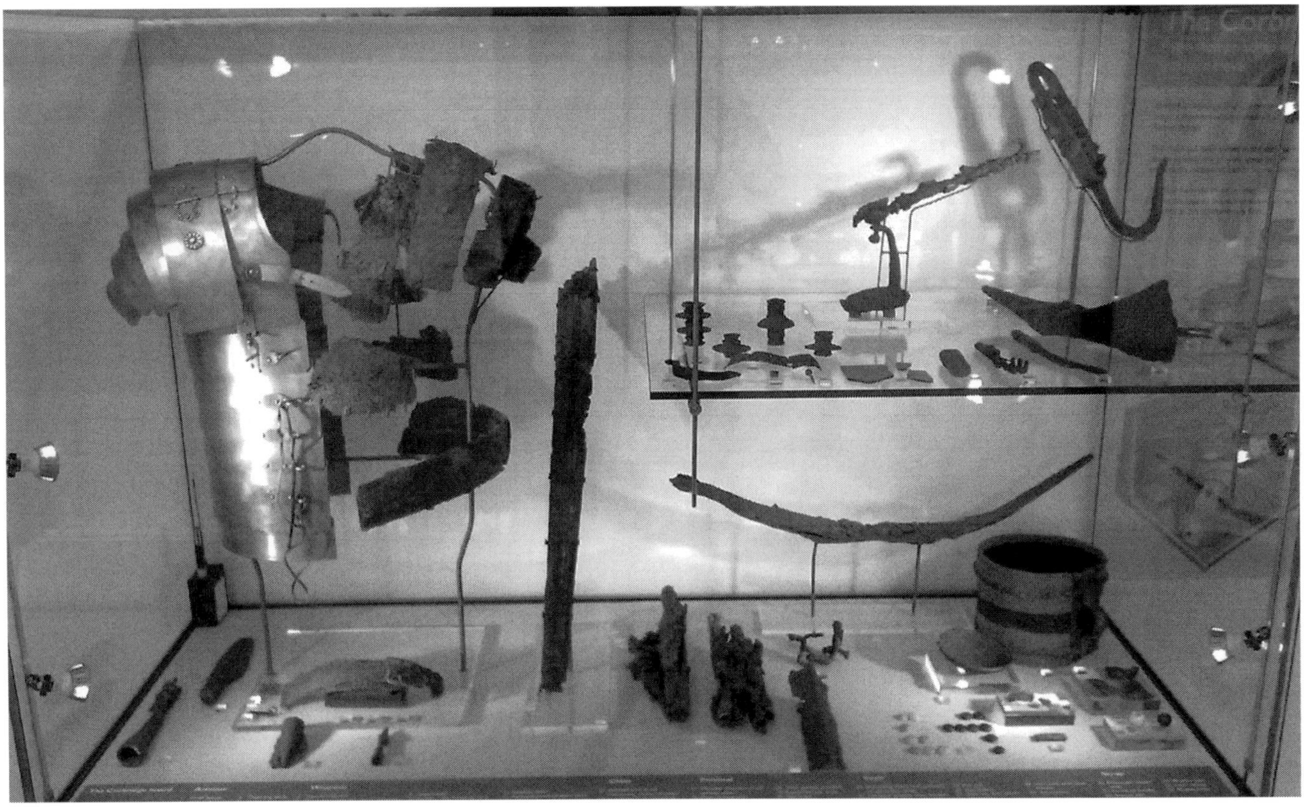

Figure 10.3 Intended for recovery? The new Hoard display at Corbridge Roman site museum

buried at any great depth, since all that would be required would be effective concealment and this could be achieved in a shallow pit with only enough covering it to mask its location (although, at the same time, its exact position would have to be noted in some way). If this were the case, it follows that the chest should have been found when the next phase of the fort began to be constructed. However, the pit in which the chest was buried was in fact quite deep. So deep, in fact, that the excavators initially interpreted the box as belonging to the first phase of occupation, rather than the second or third which was favoured in the Hoard report on stratigraphical grounds. Indeed, examination of the crucial section drawing (Allason-Jones and Bishop 1988, fig. 6) shows that the pit was cut through a destruction level and well into the underlying parent material. Sealed beneath the Phase III destruction level, and cutting through the Phase I destruction horizon, the pit was a minimum of 0.5 m deep. The chest was probably in the region of 0.3m high (scaling up the contents in the excavation photograph suggests a minimum depth for them, which had presumably settled, of 10 inches (0.25 m) whilst the longest unbroken piece of corner reinforcement was 0.22 m (*ibid.*, fig. 3)). The trench X5/6 was excavated to a depth of 5 ft 1 in (1.55 m) and the base of the chest lay just above that (*ibid.*, figs 2–5). Given that the putative lid was found at 3 ft 9 in (1.14 m), then 0.3 m as a minimum height for the chest is not unreasonable, since it had to be sufficient to justify the excavators misinterpreting the Phase I destruction layer as a timber floor with a section sawn out (cf. Daniels 1968, 16). The level above the primary destruction, 1067, was around 0.1 m deep here and this is the highest point of the deposits overlying the natural and underlying the Phase III destruction. Thus the pit dug for the Hoard chest must have been at least 0.5 m deep (and up to 0.7 m to judge from the section drawing), the chest being covered with at least 0.1 m of backfill as well as an additional 0.1 m of destruction debris. Not only would the Hoard's location have been hidden from the subsequent garrison, but those burying it would have known this, since they would have been aware of the processes involved in, and inevitable results of, razing the interior of a fort (the ramparts were left standing (Bishop and Dore 1989, 133–5)). Thus, buried in a pit and with the surrounding buildings burned and pulled down on top of it, the location of the chest was effectively lost and there would have been no practicable way of marking it without also giving away its presence to a resource-hungry enemy.

Conclusions

Any report of the nature of the Corbridge Hoard volume is bound to be 'of its time'. It is, nevertheless, incumbent upon the reporters to maintain an interest in, and perhaps even continue to question, the nature of a find and their conclusions about it. Appropriately, as this paper was being written, another important find of armour – this time from Caerleon – was being excavated in the laboratory at the National Museum of Wales (Anon. 2010; Tubman 2011) and will doubtless bring with it more important information about the nature of deposition, loss, damage, and warfare that is every bit as enlightening as that provided by the Corbridge Hoard.

Acknowledgements

I should like to thank my friend and colleague, Dr Jon Coulston, for taking the time to read and comment upon an early draft of this paper. As ever, any faults, terminological infelicities, and serial commas that may remain are solely my responsibility.

Bibliography

Allason-Jones, L. and Bishop, M. C. (1988) *Excavations at Roman Corbridge: the Hoard,* HBMCE Archaeological Report 7, London.

Anon. (2010) 'Rare Roman suit of armour found at Caerleon dig' <http://www.bbc.co.uk/news/uk-wales-11288684> accessed 9.2.13

Anon. (2011) 'RAF Typhoon jets "grounded owing to spares shortages"', <http://www.bbc.co.uk/news/uk-13081691> accessed 14.10.12

Aurrecoechea Fernandez, J. (2007) Las armaduras segmentadas (*loricae segmentatae*) en los yacimientos Romanos de la provincia de León: un estudio de conjunto. *Archivo Espanol de Arqueologia* 80, 153–82.

Bishop, M. C. (1995) Aketon, *thoracomachus*, and *lorica segmentata. Exercitus*, 3.1, 1–3.

Bishop, M. C. (1999) *Praesidium*: social, military, and logistical aspects of the Roman army's provincial distribution during the early principate. In A. Goldsworthy and I. Haynes (eds) *The Roman Army as a Community*, 111–18. Portsmouth, Rhode Island.

Bishop, M. C. (2002) *Lorica Segmentata vol.I: A Handbook of Articulated Roman Plate Armour, JRMES* Monograph 1, Chirnside.

Bishop, M. C. (2009) The body armour. In C. Howard-Davis (ed.) *The Carlisle Millennium Project: Excavations in Carlisle, 1998–2001, Volume 2: The Finds*, 687–705. Oxford.

Bishop, M. C. (2012) *A Handbook of Roman Legionary Fortresses*. Barnsley.

Bishop, M. C. and Coulston, J. C. N. (1993) *Roman Military Equipment from the Punic Wars to the Fall of Rome.* London.

Bishop, M. C. and Coulston, J. C. N. (2006) *Roman Military Equipment from the Punic Wars to the Fall of Rome*, 2nd edition. Oxford.

Bishop, M. C. and Dore, J. N. (1989) *Corbridge: Excavations of the Roman Fort and Town, 1947–80*, HBMCE Archaeological Report 8. London.

Bowman, A. K. and Thomas, J. D. (1994) *The Vindolanda Writing-Tablets, Tabulae Vindolandenses II*. London.

Breeze, D. J. (2006) *J. Collingwood Bruce's Handbook to the Roman Wall*, 14th edition. Newcastle upon Tyne.

Breeze, D. J. and Dobson, B. (2000) *Hadrian's Wall*, 4th edition. Harmondsworth.

Breeze, D. J. and Dobson, B. (2012) Maenius Agrippa, a chronological conundrum. *Acta Classica* 55, 17–30.

Caruana, I. 1(993) A third century lorica segmentata backplate from Carlisle. *Arma* 5, 15–18.

Coulston, J. C. (1988) Three legionaries at Croy Hill. In J. C. Coulston (ed.) *Military Equipment and the Identity of Roman Soldiers. Proceedings of the Fourth Roman Military Equipment Conference*, BAR International Series 394, 1–29. Oxford.

Daniels, C. M. (1968) A hoard of iron and other materials from Corbridge. *AA* 4th Series, 46, 115–26.

Davies, R. W. (1970) Note on the hoard of Roman equipment buried at Corbridge. *Durham University Journal* new series 31.3, 177–80.

Davies, J. L. (2009) Size matters: campaign forts in Britain. In W. S. Hanson (ed.) *The Army and Frontiers of Rome. Papers Offered to David J. Breeze on the Occasion of his Sixty-Fifth Birthday and his Retirement from Historic Scotland, JRA* Supplementary series 74, 44–54. Portsmouth Rhode Island.

Eibner, C. (2000) Ein römischer Spangenpanzer aus Stillfried an der March. *Archäologie Österreichs* 11.2, 32–4.

Hopewell, D. and Hodgson, N. (2012) Further work at Llanfor Roman military complex. *Britannia* 43, 29–44.

Keil, S. (2001) *Die Werkstattausgrabung, Restaurierung und Rekonstruktion von zwei Elementen römischer Schienenpanzer.* Unpublished RGZM report.

Latham, R. (ed.) (1985) *The Shorter Pepys.* London.

Manning, W. H. (1972) Ironwork hoards in Iron Age and Roman Britain. *Britannia* 3, 224–50.

Margary, I. D. (1973) *Roman Roads in Britain*, 3rd edition. London.

Maxfield, V. A. (1986) Pre-Flavian forts and their garrisons. *Britannia* 17, 59–72.

Raab, A. (2011) Die Lederung einer Lorica Segmentata. In C. Koepfer, F. W. Himmler, and J. Löffl (eds) *Die römische Armee im Experiment*, 105–12. Berlin.

Robinson, H. R. (1974) Problems in reconstructing Roman armour. In E. Birley, B. Dobson, M. G. Jarrett (eds.) *Roman Frontier Studies 1969*, 24–35. Cardiff.

Robinson, H. R. (1975) *The Armour of Imperial Rome.* London.

Sauer, E. W. (2001) Alchester, a Claudian "vexillation fortress" near the western boundary of the Catuvellauni: new light on the Roman invasion of Britain. *Archaeological Journal* 157, 1–78.

Sauer, E. W. (2005) Inscriptions from Alchester: Vespasian's base of the Second Augustan Legion(?). *Britannia* 36, 101–33.

Smallwood, H. R. (1994) *2nd TAF Spitfire: Story of Spitfire ML 407*, 2nd edition. Hallstead.

Tomlin, R. (1999) The missing lances, or Making the machine work. In A. Goldsworthy and I. Haynes (eds) *The Roman Army as a Community*, 127–38. Portsmouth, Rhode Island.

Tubman, J. (2011) 'Micro-excavation of Caerleon armour: overlapping plates and curved corners' <http://tinyurl.com/armourblog> accessed 9.2.13.

Ulbert, G. (1970) *Das römische Donau-Kastell Rißtissen, 1: Die Funde aus Metall, Horn und Knochen.* Stuttgart.

11

CHARACTERISING CULT COMMUNITIES IN THE ROMAN PROVINCES: SOME OBSERVATIONS ON SMALL FINDS EVIDENCE FROM THE SANCTUARY OF LIBER PATER, APULUM

Ian Haynes

Soldier-civilian interaction in provincial society has long fascinated students of the Roman Empire. Relations between these groups have been characterised in strikingly different ways in case studies drawn from diverse regions (e.g. Alston 1999; Pollard 2000; Shaw 1983). The aim here is not to weigh the merits of these explanatory models, something the author has attempted elsewhere (Haynes 2013) but to examine new small finds evidence from one very specific setting, the Liber Pater sanctuary located within *Colonia Aurelia Apulensis* in Dacia. While the picture that emerges from this site is not claimed to be wholly representative of soldier-civilian interaction, something which clearly varied significantly in time and place, it is hoped that the analysis advanced may encourage further artefact-based approaches to this subject. Despite the path-breaking work of Lindsay Allason-Jones and a select band of specialists, it is clear that such approaches are often neglected in comparison to those that draw primarily upon written sources.

Distinguishing the presence of military and civilian groups on the basis of small finds evidence is a bigger challenge than is sometimes appreciated. Allason-Jones (2001), Cool (2010, 1–4) and Gardner (2007, 262–3) have all noted the dangers of assuming that there is such a thing as a one size fits all 'military assemblage'. Furthermore, neither the soldiery nor the civilian population constituted monolithic or unchanging entities. Attempts to trace the presence of civilians/non-combatants within forts have usefully highlighted some of these complexities (Allison 2005; 2006; Allison, Fairbairn, Ellis and Blackall 2004; Driel-Murray 1995; 1997; 1998; James 2001; 2004), while discussion of the distribution of ostensibly military artefacts beyond the fort walls, in extra mural settlements (Birley 2010; 2013) and still further afield (Bishop 1991; 1999; Nicolay 2008) has raised important questions about both the agents involved and the role of the sites concerned.

The issue of soldier-civilian interaction at temples and shrines has also emerged latterly. This is a theme of some interest as it has particular ramifications for our understanding of cultural change in provincial society. While it must be acknowledged that the military community represented a small proportion of the overall provincial population, the soldier's role as bringer of cults is often stressed by those who understand his social importance in broader terms, as an agent of cultural transformation. But the story of ritual and religion in the Roman Empire goes beyond plotting the importing of cults by soldiers and indeed other groups; it is not limited to the staccato introduction of rigidly defined practices into isolated enclaves, it is a story of interaction and evolution. Across the Empire cults and devotees moved and mingled. Soldiers of all ranks were actively involved in these broader processes; they were not fettered to a notional 'Roman military religion' and in several instances soldiers and civilians worshipped alongside one another.

To appreciate this better archaeologically, we need to look again at the small finds evidence. Historically, many analyses have sought to identify the presence of different groups on the basis of structural archaeology, assuming that the presence of certain building types must necessarily indicate, for example, a military presence. But the evidence of small finds, ceramics and faunal evidence all offer different perspectives, which can challenge presuppositions about architectural types and their uses. At the level of the individual, ascribing the discard of an artefact, however distinctive, to the presence of a soldier is also problematic. Even the most diagnostic pieces of Roman military equipment would have been susceptible to re-appropriation and complex processes of secondary discard, quite aside from the fact that civil use of soldiers' arms and dress was probably more widespread than is often acknowledged (James 2001, 83).

The use of indicators other than military equipment as evidence of soldierly identity is still more complex and there remains a lively debate as to the degree to which other artefacts can be attributed to military users, as noted below. Conversely, the claim that an artefact was necessarily the possession of a civilian is also problematic. Soldiers did not spend all their time in full battle array, they required a range of artefacts that were commonly found in domestic settings – and indeed, they may have made more extensive use of objects that have been attributed to female users than their civilian peers. Simon James and others have recalled the modern parallel of the 'housewife' carried by modern soldiers who are frequently dependent on themselves alone for basic needlework tasks (James 2006). As Lindsay Allason-Jones (1995) has noted it is much harder to 'sex' a small find than many studies assume.

But the problem that lies ahead of us is not simply one of determining the presence of different groups. The presence of artefacts that may be characterised as belonging to both military and civilian groups is one thing – but the claim that this indicates shared participation in an activity, say for example a cult ritual, is quite another. Even where the presence of both civilians and soldiers can be demonstrated within a given location, more is required. Evidence is needed to show shared participation in cult practice. How might this be revealed by the evidence of artefacts?

Due consideration of context is, of course, an essential prerequisite for any meaningful archaeological analysis. Accordingly this paper will scrutinize specific archaeological contexts within which finds that may be deemed diagnostic of military and non-combatant identity have been found. In so doing, it will deal not simply with isolated finds, but with finds which appear in sufficient quantity to demonstrate a discernible pattern of activity. The finds chosen to illustrate the dynamic are not especially elaborate finds, but they offer a strong indication of the presence of three broad groups. The presence of users of military equipment is indicated by a range of military belt plates, the presence of women by a large number of hair pins and the possible presence of children by what appear to toys. All these elements can be found within cult pits excavated at the sanctuary of Liber Pater in Apulum.

The site and its setting

Colonia Aurelia Apulensis emerged within the wider conurbation of Apulum, the largest Roman settlement north of the Danube. Major Roman activity at this site, strategically located by the River Mureş in Western Transylvania, began with the construction of a *castra* of *Legio XIII Gemina* under Trajan. The legion remained here until Rome withdrew from the region in the second half of the third century AD. Over time the Apulum conurbation grew in importance, ultimately becoming the headquarters of the governor of the Three Dacian provinces, and boasting not one but two neighbouring cities (Diaconescu and Piso 1993; Piso 1995). *Colonia Aurelia Apulensis* was the southernmost of these two cities, and was raised to colonial status under Commodus. It spread over some 300 hectares and was adorned with multiple substantial buildings and a fine colonnaded *cardo*.

Though over the centuries many inscriptions had been recovered from the area of the *colonia*, remarkably little was known about it prior to Alexandru Diaconescu's attempts to confirm the limits of the ancient city in 1989. At that time Romania was still a communist dictatorship with strict restrictions on flying, thus ruling out aerial photographic analysis, and on the use of detailed mapping. Archaeological geophysics had not yet been employed in the region. Accordingly, Diaconescu set about his task by digging a series of evaluation trenches. It was in one of these, located 900 m south of the legionary fortress and now known to lie within the north western corner of the *colonia* that he came across a cache of sculptures and inscriptions relating to the Liber Pater cult. The range and character of these finds made it clear that Diaconescu had discovered a sanctuary dedicated to the god. Further limited excavation on tight resources then followed in 1990–1992, before the site was temporarily abandoned (Schäfer and Diaconescu 1997). Investigations at the site recommenced under the umbrella of the new tri-national Apulum Project began in 1999, under the co-direction of Diaconescu, the present author and Alfred Schäfer. The small finds and ceramic evidence discussed here was recovered by the project-team between 1999 and 2003.

Extensive geophysical survey and aerial photography work undertaken as part of the Apulum Project has since illuminated the nature of the part of the town within which the sanctuary lay (Fig. 11.1). This work was undertaken by Kris Lockyear of UCL, Ioana Oltean and Bill Hanson, both then of Glasgow University and by GSB Prospection Ltd (2003). To the north of the site, just within the walls of the city, stood a theatre, close to which stood what appears,

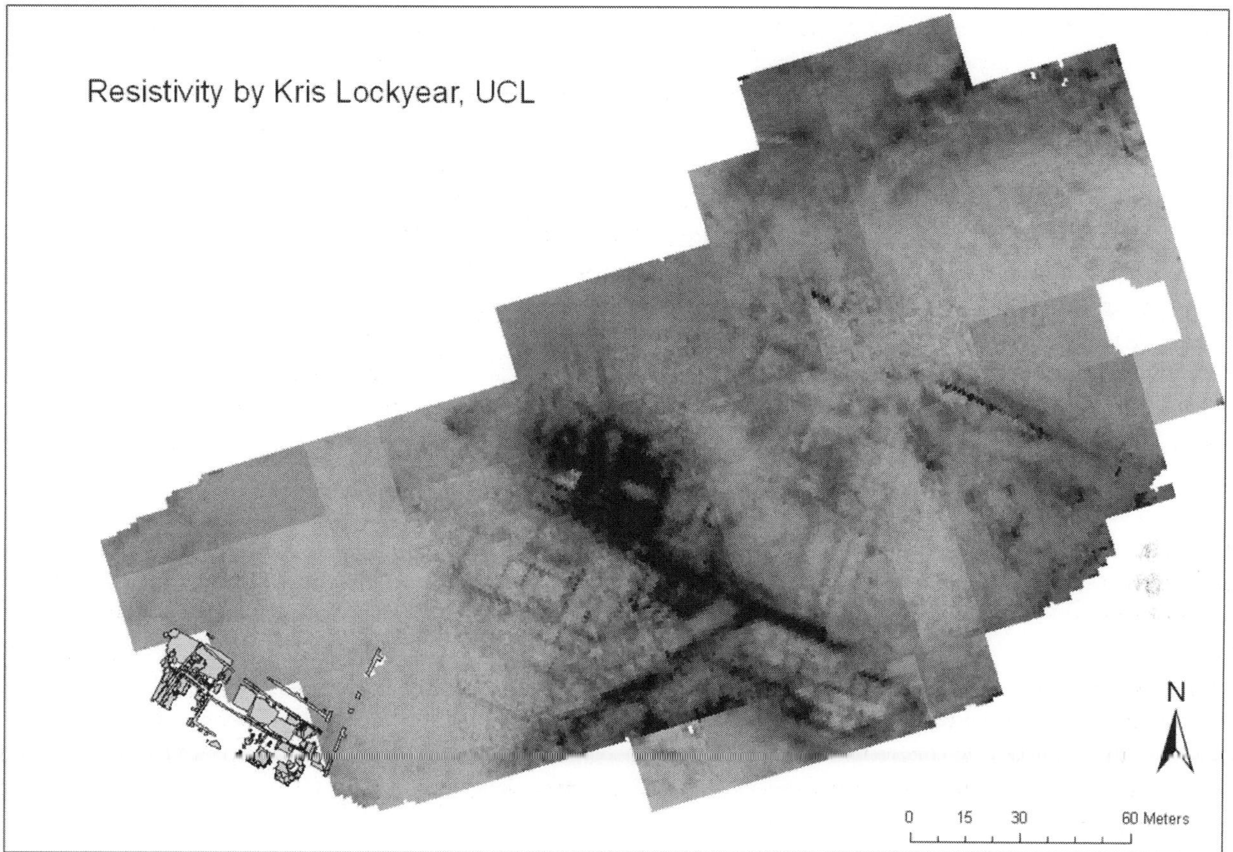

Figure 11.1 Plot of resistivity survey with excavated area in pink. The semi-circular anomaly representing the probable theatre lies in the centre of the image. This structure appears to be built up against the city's northern wall. To the south the strong anomaly appears to represent the location of a bath complex. Stephen Bell/Kris Lockyear/Apulum Project

from the geophysical evidence, to be a bath house, while substantial houses lay to the north-west and west of the site. Conversely the land to the east appears markedly less built up. The cult area itself is partially truncated by a railway embankment to the south, obscuring much of the archaeology. Limited magnetometry survey immediately south of the embankment, however, suggests that part of this area may have been given over to pottery production, a characteristic of the area around the sanctuary both prior to its construction and once it was in full use (GSB Prospection Ltd 2003).

By the conclusion of excavations in 2003 an area of 1006 m^2 had been investigated. This area includes those parts explored in work between 1989 and 1992. Excavation allowed the team to investigate all phases of the site's history, from its origins as a green field site, via its use as an industrial area, through the construction, development and abandonment of the sanctuary (the latter marking the latest phase of ancient activity), stone robbing in the early modern period and the subsequent truncation of archaeological deposits through ploughing in the twentieth century.

The fuller story of the site is discussed in the site monograph (Haynes, Diaconescu and Schäfer forthcoming), but the evidence discussed in this paper concerns Phase IV of the site, the period between the late second and mid-third century AD, during which the sanctuary operated (Plate 4). The evidence for the site's layout during this phase may be understood as follows. Cult statues and related material uncovered by Diaconescu appear to have stood in a garden space. Apulum Project excavations unearthed more of this space together with a porch leading into it and a passageway to the north. Within this passageway Apulum Project team members located pits, several of which contained material associated with cult practice at the site. While it is common to use the term *favissa* in archaeological accounts of such pits, the term is avoided here, as it was used in a very specific context in its ancient definition; *De Significatione Verborum* (78.10, 78.11) makes it clear that the term is explicitly linked to Rome's own Capitolinum. Accordingly the looser modern formulation 'cult pits' is preferred. We will return to these features and their interpretation below.

A separate building (B6) in which large altars were displayed was also located at the north-western edge of the excavated area. Immediately to the north of B6 lay an alleyway and a mithraeum, the southern end of which was exposed during the final days of the Apulum Project. The mithraeum is now the target of a separate field project and will not be discussed further here. To the south and west of the garden court the project team discovered kilns indicating that pottery production was taking place in the immediate vicinity of the cult centre while it was in use.

The four largest and most clearly defined cult pits (henceforth CP) are of particular importance to the analysis offered here. It must be appreciated that the sanctuary suffered considerable damage in the centuries following its abandonment. The walls were extensively robbed and ancient ground surfaces were severely disturbed. A large number of artefacts were found within these disturbed contexts. While it is reasonable to suggest that most, perhaps all, of them originally came from the sanctuary site, the original circumstances of their deposition are hard to reconstruct. The cult pits were, however, sufficiently deep to avoid extensive disturbance and it is possible to say a great deal about their formation. For the purposes of this paper it is sufficient to note that the cult pits were dug within the sanctuary complex in the first half of the third century. A coin in the fill of CP1 dated from the reign of Elagabalus (issued AD 218–219; Gazdac 2005) while the latest four of the 10 coins found in CP2 were issued by Severus Alexander (AD 222–235, Gazdac 2005). In keeping with what is known of cult practice elsewhere in the empire, these pits were dug within the complex so that objects associated with the sanctuary's rituals could be interred on sacred ground. The fact that CP2 clearly cuts the edge of CP1 points to a sequence of pit cutting, something that is itself suggestive of ritualised practice. The pits were all substantial, with the largest measuring over 6 m long and 1 m deep, and all contained a rich range of materials – including animal bones, general coarsewares, cult pottery, ceramic 'incense burners', glass vessels, terracottas, worked bone, bronze and iron finds.

Precisely what triggered the decision to dig a pit is open to question. It is likely that new pits were prepared in anticipation of, or in response to, a major event in the sacred year. While this may have been linked to a desire to regularly clear the area of accumulating offerings and perhaps to replace objects on a cyclical basis, it may also have been linked to major feasts. Certainly the well-preserved lower fills of CP1 show that pottery vessels (Fiedler 2005; Höpken and Fiedler 2008) were laid out on the floor of the pit and then covered with animal bone, much of which showed signs of having been cooked (Carnell 2007). Whatever the trigger, however, it is clear that once opened the pits were used to inter other rubbish that had gathered within the sanctuary. While it is important to remain mindful of the mixture of deposits within the pits, the essential point is that all the material here seems to have come from within the cult site, and from the same period of the sanctuary's use.

Finds evidence from the Liber Pater site

In addition to the sculptural and epigraphic evidence summarised below, and those other finds unearthed during Diaconescu's work between 1989 and 1992, the Liber Pater site yielded 4,175 small finds, 1,200 fragments of glass and 357,667 sherds of pottery, much of which was produced in kilns in the immediate vicinity. To these finds should be added considerable quantities of ceramic building material, mainly tile, which were also the focus of extensive research. The major categories of small find included: 1300 iron objects (887 nails, 34 objects with clearly determinable functionality, 379 unidentifiable fragments), 347 lamp fragments, 179 terracotta figurines, 253 pieces of worked bone (113 examples of which were hair pins), 91 coins (of which 11 were illegible) and 14 brooches (13 of which were of copper-alloy and one of which was of iron). There were also 66 copper-alloy objects of other types discovered, many of which are directly relevant to our enquiry here. Detailed analysis of this rich assemblage (including EVE calculations), and the extensive animal bone evidence (including MNI data), will be included in the final project reports, but it is already possible to consider evidence germane to the question of military/civilian interaction here.

The presence of weapons, helmets and body armour at cult sites has been widely noted and the votive deposition of such artefacts much discussed (see for example Flügel and Obmann 1992; Driel-Murray 1996), but these items are almost entirely absent from this assemblage. Indeed, the only such artefact discovered by the team was a small spearhead (SF 4103) (Mustaţa 2007) discovered in a context post-dating the sanctuary's use. Even here there is a small possibility that the spearhead was not a weapon, but that it could have been carried on a cult standard, though the piece is too

Figure 11.2 Copper-alloy decorative mount of Utere Felix type in the form of the letter L. SF 1145. Found in abandonment contexts above the sanctuary. (max. l. 46 mm, max. w. 40 mm). Alexandru Diaconescu/Apulum Project

Figure 11.3 Copper-alloy belt plate with openwork decoration. SF 3636. Found in pit adjacent to the Altar Room (B6). Phase IV. (max. l. 29 mm, max w. 20 mm). Alexandru Diaconescu/Apulum Project

Figure 11.4 Copper-alloy belt plate with pierced work decoration. SF 4220. Found in Cult Pit 2. Phase IV. (max. l. 39 mm, max. w. 26 mm). Alexandru Diaconescu/Apulum Project

Figure 11.5 Copper-alloy belt plate with lunullae *apertures. SF 2507. Found in Cult Pit. Phase IV (max. l. 53 mm, max w. 50 mm). Alexandru Diaconescu/Apulum Project*

fragmentary to support further comment. The presence of military worshippers is, however, strongly suggested by the copper-alloy fittings recovered at the sanctuary.

Altogether 11 fittings from military belts can be identified in the assemblage along with a pendant and 14 studs of types familiar from military settings. While many of these artefacts, such as an L-shaped mount (SF 1145) which once formed part of the *Utere Felix* lettering attached to a *cingulum* (Fig. 11.2) – a mount type well known in Dacia (Petculescu 1991) – were discovered in disturbed contexts associated with the abandonment of the sanctuary, several clearly came from spaces with altars (Fig. 11.3; SF 3636, 3970), or from the cult pits (Figs 11.4 and 11.5; SF 1274, 1316, 2507, 3232, 4220, 4451, 5043). The implication is clear; these objects were being used in the sanctuary area. As explained above, it is not necessary to assume from this that they were necessarily offerings themselves, as once the cult pits had been dug they were used not only to dispose of primary refuse from feasting events, but also secondary refuse that had built up in the sanctuary space and left to wait until an appropriate pit was available. Belt fittings and studs may often have detached themselves from the dress of visiting soldiers and ended up amongst the routine sweepings of the sanctuary floor.

Discussion of these fittings and their military significance invites consideration of the brooch finds from the site. Of these five are knee brooches, two are late versions of the so-called Aucissa type and one is a skeumorphic brooch with the bow in the shape of an axe (Bogdan and Cociş 2006). The majority of these were found in disturbed contexts formed after the abandonment of the sanctuary, but of the three that were clearly deposited during Phase IV, two (a knee brooch, SF 2670 and a late Aucissa brooch, SF 2571) were discovered in CP4, while the third (another knee brooch, SF 1238) was discovered in the altar room B6 (Bogdan and Cociş 2006). Students of Roman brooches will be familiar with the common appellation of knee brooches as *Soldatenfibeln*. This link has been advanced on account of the relative frequency with which such brooches are found at fort sites on the German limes. It is, however, very clear that they cannot be linked exclusively with soldiers. Not only is their distribution in some provincial areas consistent with a far wider range of identity groups (Bayler and Butcher 2004, 179) and surprisingly limited in some others where soldiers were concentrated (McIntosh 2011, 166), tombstones on the Danube frontier show them worn by women. Similarly, though the early types of Aucissa brooch have been associated with military users in some

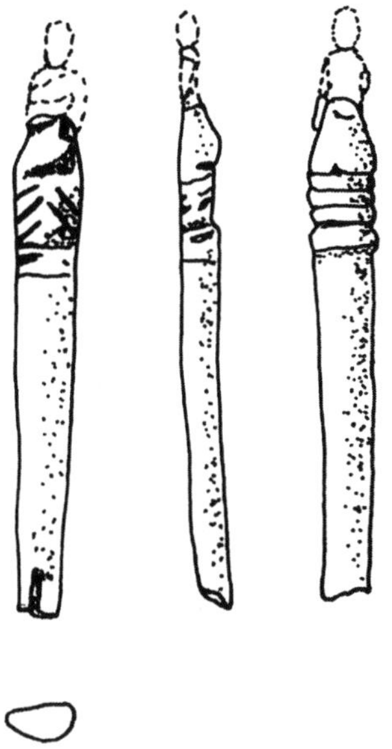

Figure 11.6 Hair pin in the form of Venus Pudica. SF 4237. Found in Cult Pit 2. Phase IV. (47 mm). Szilamer Panczel/Apulum Project

provinces, notably Britain, there is no need to assume that their use was confined to soldiers. I leave open here the question of the whether the axehead brooch has a military significance, though I am very impressed by the pioneering work of Stephanie Hoss (pers. comm.) which raises the possibility that some plate brooches were so understood. This brooch was found in a context formed after the abandonment of the sanctuary, so a link between its wearer and the rituals of the sanctuary is anyway harder to demonstrate.

Having looked at the possible evidence for military dress, and thus military involvement in the Liber Pater sanctuary, we may now turn to the epigraphic material unearthed by Diaconescu in 1989. Three inscriptions leave no doubt at all that soldiers worshiped the god at this site. These were a dedicatory plaque honouring the god set up by a *miles* of *Legio XIII Gemina,* a plaque depicting Pan offered by a *beneficiarius consularis* and a metal votive to the Danubian riders which was stamped with COH(ORS) I S(AGITTARIORUM) TIBISC(ENSIUM) (Schäfer and Diaconescu 1997). This combination is interesting in itself, for it reflects three different military constituencies, legionaries, special duties soldiers attached to the governor's staff and auxiliaries. We may identify their respective headquarters with some confidence. *Legio XIII Gemina* lay about a kilometre north of the sanctuary; the governor's residence also lay in Apulum, but the auxiliary unit was, as its title indicates, at Tibiscum, one hundred kilometres to the south-west.

Crucially for our investigation though, the evidence from the Liber Pater sanctuary makes it equally clear that civilians worshiped the god here too. Leaving aside the epigraphic evidence, to which I shall return, two categories of finds strongly suggest a broader demographic; these are hair pins and children's dolls.

Hair pins and what is believed to be a cosmetic pallet were found within the sanctuary area (Panczel 2007). The association with female users can be debated, and it may be argued that it is only contemporary prejudice that leads to the simple assumption that cosmetic pallets and hair pins indicate female presence, but this does appear the most likely explanation, seen for example with a pin depicting Venus (Fig. 11.6). While we cannot claim to know the full range of hairstyles worn by Rome's soldiers, and there were perhaps a variety of styles adopted by irregulars, there are good reasons for believing that legionaries and auxiliaries wore their hair relatively short, if at times somewhat shaggy. None of the styles depicted on soldiers' funerary monuments would have been long enough to support the wearing of a pin. Furthermore the literary evidence may suggest the existence of restrictions to the length soldiers could grow their hair (Claudian *Eutrop.* 1, 383).

However we read this evidence, it seems that the large number of hair pins found at the sanctuary is, at the very least, indicative of the presence of non-soldiers. While many of the hair pins recovered were residual, 53 were found in Phase IV and of these 39 were found within cult pits (Panczel 2007).

The second broad category of material concerns terracotta figures. It is abundantly clear that terracotta figurines of deities were used in a broad array of contexts. They appear to have served as objects of devotion, souvenirs of shrine visits and sometimes as offerings. All of these uses are suggested by the finds contexts at the Liber Pater shrine. Yet by no means all the terracotta figures found in the shrine are of deities. In an excellent evaluation of the terracotta finds from the Apulum excavation Mariana Egri (Egri 2010) has noted the presence of 16 fragmentary busts with smiling faces, big eyes and big ears (Plate 5). Though there is no garment depicted, each bust wears a necklace with a crescent-like pendant, a *lunula*. Egri argues convincingly that these busts are in fact toys. She notes that one such was discovered in a child's grave at Sucidava in Lower Dacia, and that the excavator (Tudor 1978, 105, fig. 32/4) interpreted it as a puppet. Thus understood, she notes, the busts should be understood as clay heads for dolls or puppets; the rest of the body was made from cloth, sometimes with clay balls inside (Gramatopol 1991, 424, fig. 433). The lunula necklace is the *crepundia* worn by every Roman child until the end of childhood (*RE* IV.2, s.v. *crepundia*; Egri 2010).

The puppet figures do not seem to have been the only toys to have been discarded in the sanctuary. Egri (2010) notes that two fragments of wheeled toys were recovered in CP1 and a further five were interred in CP2. The most reasonable explanation for the presence of so many toys in the sanctuary, Egri attractively argues, is that they were offered to the god during the coming of age ceremonies known to have been enacted at the *Liberalia* on the 17 March. It was at this time that boys received the *toga virilis*; what better way to dispose of the trappings of childhood?

If Egri is correct, and I strongly believe that she is, we have here a strong indication of another group of non-soldiers within the complex at the same time as it is being used by soldiers. In addition to the four fragmentary puppets found in B6, an area associated with cult activity, four further puppets were found within the cult pits themselves.

If the evidence of small finds appears to indicate the presence of both women and children in the Liber Pater site, what of the epigraphic evidence? The short answer is that no inscriptions from the sanctuary mention women. The longer answer is that women are underrepresented in the epigraphy of the Roman world generally and that there are only two further inscriptions from this site that have not been discussed. Importantly these two do, at least, point explicitly to the presence of civilians. The first, discovered by Alexandru Diaconescu in his original excavations, was a marble votive commemorating the Thracian Hero (Schäfer and Diaconescu 1997). An inscription reveals that the votive was offered by Aurelius Taciturnus and his son Aurelius Tacitus. The fact that neither dedicant specifies a military rank and the fact that the text is in Greek in this Latin-speaking environment, strongly suggest that both are civilians. Unfortunately the age of Aurelius Tacitus cannot be adduced; it is possible, but not certain, that he was a child.

The final inscription to be recovered from the Apulum sanctuary attests the presence of another civilian, a freedman priest (Sicoe 2005). The dedication: CAUTOPATI / DEO / LOC CRATUS AUG COL is open to different readings, but two points are clear, the first is that the principal focus of the dedication is to Cautopates, the second is that the dedicant was one of the *Augustales* of the *colonia*. As noted above, the reference to the city's status indicates a date during or after the reign of Commodus and thus a date broadly contemporary with the cult pits. The discovery of a dedication to Cautopates within the Liber Pater sanctuary might surprise some readers, who would prefer perhaps to believe that it came from the neighbouring mithraeum, but as Sicoe has pointed out, dedications to Cautopates are known from temples to other gods, too (Sicoe 2005; Vermaseren 1956, no. 639; 1960, no.1728).

Conclusion

There are many temple sites in the Roman Empire where the presence of both soldiers and civilians has been implied or assumed. Only at a relatively small proportion of these, however, is there clear epigraphic evidence for both. When such evidence is available, it is often deemed sufficient to carry the discussion of soldier/civilian interaction. Yet as Pollard (2000, 142–7) demonstrated in his attempt to map soldier/civilan interaction at Dura-Europos, cult buildings which provide inscriptional evidence for the presence of both groups may, in fact, be being used by soldiers and civlians at different periods. By no means all inscriptional evidence can be tightly dated.

As the data from the Liber Pater sanctuary shows, small finds offer particularly important insights into the problem. They can suggest the presence of groups that are underrepresented in the archaeological record. Furthermore, when the finds themselves are unearthed in controlled conditions, they can make it easier to determine whether or not the presence of distinct groups was concurrent or sequential. The series of pits in the Liber Pater sanctuary, all dug during the first half of the third century, make it clear that soldiers and civilians were using the cult buildings there at the same time over a sustained period.

Acknowledgements

The author would like to take this appreciation to thank Lindsay Allason-Jones for being such an outstanding teacher and colleague. Special thanks also go to Dr Rob Collins and Frances McIntosh for their work on this volume. Work on this paper would not have been possible without the ground work undertaken by the Apulum Team. It is a pleasure here to record my debt to my co-directors, Dr Alexandru Diaconescu and Dr Alfred Schäfer, and to the fields and finds supervisors who made all the difference to the Project's success.

Bibliography

Allason-Jones, L. (1995) 'Sexing' small finds. In P. Rush (ed.) *Theoretical Roman Archaeology: Second Conference proceedings*, 22–32, Avebury

Allason-Jones, L. (2001) Material culture and identity. In S. James and M. Millett (eds) *Britons and Romans: Advancing an Archaeological Agenda,* CBA Research Report 125, 19–25, York.

Allison, P. M. (2005) Mapping artefacts and activities within Roman military forts. In Z. Visy, (ed.) *Limes XIX: Proceedings of the XIXth International Congress of Roman Frontier Studies,* 833–46. Pécs 2003.

Allison P. M. (2006) Mapping for gender: interpreting artefact distribution in Roman military forts in Germany. *Archaeological Dialogues* 13.1, 1–20.

Allison P. M., Fairbairn, A. S., Ellis, S. J. R. and Blackall, C. W. (2004) Extracting the social relevance of artefact distribution in Roman military forts. *Internet Archaeology* 17.

Alston, R. (1999) The ties that bind: soldiers and societies. In A. Goldsworthy and I. P. Haynes, (eds) *The Roman Army as a Community, JRA* supplementary series 34, 175–96. Rhode Island.

Bayley, J. and Butcher, S. (2004) *Roman Brooches in Britain: A Technological and Typological Study based on the Richborough Collection*, Report of the Research Committee of the Society of Antiquaries of London 68, London.

Birley, A. (2010) *The nature and significance of extramural settlement at Vindolanda and other selected sites on the Northern Frontier of Roman Britain.* Unpublished PhD thesis, University of Leicester.

Birley, A. (2013) The fort wall: A great divide? In R. Collins and M. Symonds (eds) *Breaking Down Boundaries: Hadrian's Wall in the 21st Century. JRA* Supp. ser. 93, 85–104. Portsmouth, Rhode Island.

Bishop, M. C. (1991) Soldiers and military equipment in the towns of Roman Britain. In V. Maxfield and M. J. Dobson (eds) *Roman Frontier Studies 1989,* 21–27. Exeter.

Bishop, M. C. (1999) *Praesidium:* social, military, and logistical aspects of the Roman army's provincial distribution during the early principate. In A. Goldsworthy and I. P. Haynes (eds) *The Roman Army as a Community, JRA* Supp. ser. 34, 111–18. Portsmouth, Rhode Island.

Bogdan, D. and Cociş, S. (2006) The Brooches. Unpublished interim report, Apulum Project.

Carnell, A. (2007) The Animal Bones from the Cult Pits. Unpublished interim report, Apulum Project.

Cool, H. E. M., (2010) A different life. In R. Collins and L. Allason-Jones (eds) *Finds from the Frontier: Material Culture in the 4th–5th Centuries,* 1–9. CBA Research Report 162, York.

Diaconescu, A. and Piso, I. (1993) Apulum. In D. Alicu and H. Boegli (eds) *La politique édilitaire dans les provinces de l'Empire romain*, 67–82. Actes du Ier Colloque Roumano-Suisse Deva 1991.

Driel-Murray, C. van (1995) 'Gender in question' in P. Rush (ed.) *Theoretical Roman Archaeology 2nd Conference Proceedings* 3–21. Aldershot.

Driel-Murray, C. van (ed.) (1996) *Military Equipment in Context,* (Proceedings of the Ninth International Roman Military Equipment Conference, Leiden, 1994), *JRMES* 5.

Driel-Murray, C. van (1997) Women in forts? *Geselleschaft Pro Vindonissa, Jahresbericht 1997*, 55–61, Brugg.

Driel-Murray, C. van (1998) A question of gender in a military context. *Helinium* 34, 342–62.

Egri, M. (2010) Terracotta figurines from Apulum. Unpublished interim report, Apulum Project.

Fiedler, M. (2005) Kultgruben eines Liber Pater-Heiligtums im römischen *Apulum* (Dakien), *Germania* 83, 95–125.

Flügel, C. and Obmann, J. (1992) Waffen in Heiligtumern des Mithras. *JRMES* 3, 67–71

Gardner, A. (2007) *An Archaeology of Social Identity. Soldiers and Society in Late Roman Britain*, Walnut Creek Ca

Gazdac, C. (2005) The Coins. Unpublished interim report, Apulum Project.

Gramatopol, M. (1991) *Artele miniaturale în antichitate*. Bucharest.

GSB Prospection Ltd (2003) Apulum Project Geophysical Survey. Unpublished interim report, Apulum Project.

Haynes, I. P. (2013) *Blood of the Provinces: The Roman Auxilia and the Making of Provincial Society from Augustus to the Severans.* Oxford.

Haynes, I. P., Diaconescu, A. and Schäfer, A. (forthcoming) *Excavations in the Sanctuary of Liber Pater, Apulum.*

Höpken, C. and Fiedler, M. (2008) Votive pottery. Unpublished interim report, Apulum Project.

James, S. T. (2001) Soldiers and civilians: identity and interaction in Roman Britain. In S. James and M. Millett (eds) *Britons and Romans: Advancing an archaeological agenda,* CBA Research Report 125, 77–89. York.

James, S. (2006) Engendering change in our understanding of the structure of Roman military communities, *Archaeological Dialogues,* 13.1, 31–6.

McIntosh, F. (2011) Regional Brooch Types in Roman Britain– evidence from Northern England. *AA* 5th Series 40, 155–82.

Mustaţa, S. (2007) *The Iron Material*. Unpublished interim report, Apulum Project.

Nicolay, J. A. W. (2008) *Armed Batavians: Use and Significance of Weaponry and Horse Gear from Non-military Contexts in the Rhine Delta (50 BC to AD 450)*. Amsterdam.

Oltean, I. A. and Hanson, W. S. (2006) Alba Iulia, Partoş: The Aerial Evidence. Unpublished interim report, Apulum Project.

Panczel, S. (2007) *Artefacte Din Os (Bone Small Finds)*. Unpublished interim report, Apulum Project.

Petculescu, L. (1991) *Utere felix* and *optime con(serva)* mounts from Dacia. In V. A. Maxfield and M. J. Dobson (eds) *Roman Frontier Studies 1989*, 392–6. Exeter.

Piso, I. (1995) Eine Parallele zwischen den Praetoria der Statthalter in Carnuntum und in Apulum. *Carnuntum Jahrbuch* 1993/94, 203–9.

Pollard, N. (2000) *Soldiers, Cities and Civilians in Roman Syria*, Ann Arbor.

Schäfer, A. and Diaconescu, A. (1997) Das Liber Pater Heligtum von Apulum (Dakien). In H. Cancik and J. Rüpke (eds) *Römische Reichsreligion und Provinzialreligion*, 195–218, Tübingen.

Shaw, B. D. (1983) Soldiers and society: the army in Numidia. *Opus* 2, 133–59.

Sicoe, G. (2005) *The Marble Base of Kautopates*. Unpublished interim report, Apulum Project.

Tudor, D. (1978) *Oltenia romană*. Bucharest.

Vermaseren M. J., (1956) *Corpus Inscriptionum et Monumentorum Religionis Mithriacae, Vol I*. The Hague.

Vermaseren M. J., (1960) *Corpus Inscriptionum et Monumentorum Religionis Mithriacae, Vol II*. The Hague.

12

THE BOSTON HELMET: A PRELIMINARY ACCOUNT OF A PARTHIAN/ROMAN-ERA ARTEFACT AT THE MUSEUM OF FINE ARTS

Simon James

The helmet in the MFA

This helmet, or more accurately helmet bowl or skull (parallels indicate that it is only half of a head defence), has long been on public display in room 110 of the Museum of Fine Arts, Boston, where first I saw it during a visit in February 2011 (Fig. 12.1). Although the piece has previously appeared in print, this was a very brief account and photograph in a little-known volume. Because it is of considerable academic importance yet has hitherto escaped the attention of wider scholarship, I requested permission from the MFA to study and publish the helmet more fully. Further scientific examination is currently continuing, and so the following is a preliminary note on this important artefact, in anticipation of a fuller future publication.

The artefact, which hereafter I call the Boston helmet, is also highly relevant to the theme of the present volume, celebrating the work of Lindsay Allason-Jones who has contributed so much to our understanding of Roman metalwork and other material culture, particularly from Britain. The Boston helmet has important things to tell us about martial cultural interactions in another important but far less well-understood zone of the imperial *limites*: the lands where in the early centuries AD Rome faced Parthia, the only other empire surviving on her borders. More specifically, it manifests interactions between Rome and those peoples who found themselves living in the zone of contact, uneasy coexistence and sometimes violent confrontation between the two empires, a great swathe of territory running from the Black Sea to the Arabian Desert.

The MFA holds very little information about the helmet, which lacks an exact provenance, although available information suggests it was found in eastern Turkey or Iran. When I first saw it in 2011, it was displayed on a mount as though a complete head defence, with its long curled apex projecting forwards, the case label identifying it as 'Parthian'. However, especially to scholars of Roman military equipment, which archaeologically is attested in exceptional detail, the general design and construction of the artefact as a piece of armour is immediately familiar. This was never more true than when I first saw it, while the furore in Britain surrounding discovery of a Roman helmet with a strikingly similar 'Phrygian cap' form, at Crosby Garrett, Cumbria, England, was still continuing following its sale at auction in October 2010, and its subsequent disappearance from public view (Fig. 12.2; Worrell and Pearce 2011, 402–7; Worrell *et al.* 2011; Breeze and Bishop 2013).

Archaeological parallels, both general and specific, confirm what inspection of the MFA piece itself suggests, namely that it is actually only part of a more elaborate head defence: it protected the crown, neck and ears only; the wearer's face and forehead had originally been defended by a separate enveloping facemask, now lost, but evidently of a form similar to that which survived on the new Crosby Garrett find. Encountering the Boston piece was doubly timely from my point of view, as I was also working on a publication discussing a decorated copper alloy cheekpiece from Hatra, Iraq, on which is depicted a male bust sporting a similar Phrygian cap (Fig. 12.4, no. 8; James 2013). Additionally, I had recently become aware of another more broadly related piece, with a lofty forward-projecting apex terminating in an eagle face, in a museum in the South of France (below).

Provenance, acquisition, records and publication

Museum documentation records that the MFA was offered the helmet for purchase by an Iranian dealer, Mohammad Yeganeh in 1978, and preserves a short report of work conducted on the helmet to authenticate it prior to acquisition (Examination no. 78.95). This recorded receipt of the object by the Museum laboratory on 19 October 1978, and its examination using X-rays (which are also preserved), metallographic sampling and UV inspection. The helmet had already been 'restored' when it reached the laboratory, although the Museum also acquired a photo of the fairly intact right side of the helmet in its unrestored state, probably taken by or for the dealer (print numbered T76/1749), showing the find crumpled and still quite extensively encrusted with corrosion products. The report noted and described the extensive recent repairs to the piece (indeed partial reconstruction of its left side and cosmetic treatment) using epoxy and fibreglass. The X-rays showed little not already apparent to the naked eye. A small squarish sample was cut from the edge of the piece for energy dispersive X-ray fluorescence (the unfilled site clearly visible in 2012). This analysis showed the metal to be a copper alloy with 14–16% zinc, i.e. a brass. A photomicrograph of a section showed corrosion products over a 'dezincified' surviving metal surface and a brass core, which was noted to be consistent with corrosion processes of a genuinely antique brass artefact.

Satisfied that it was a genuine antiquity, the MFA purchased the piece via the Morris and Louise Rosenthal Fund on 14 February, 1979, and gave it the accession number 1979.41. The only previous publication of the object was a single page of text and a photograph in a little-known illustrated volume of acquisitions published by the Museum in the decade following its acquisition (Boston Museum of Fine Arts 1987, 100–1). The brief text discussed the distribution of the fabric Phrygian cap (*kidaris*) it was evidently imitating, and noted that it was the only known example of this kind of helmet.

In the publication, again, no exact provenance is given; it was assessed to be 'Probably from Iran or Eastern Turkey', and described as 'Parthian, first century BC to fourth century AD' [*sic*] (Boston Museum of Fine Arts 1987 100–1). Nothing further has subsequently come to light about the circumstances of discovery of this artefact, nor is it now very likely to. The general provenance given is plausible on stylistic details (below). Its elaborate surface decoration is certainly consistent with ornament depicted on headgear in the wider Parthian milieu, while its 'Phrygian cap' form also fits such a regional context. Its state of preservation suggests deliberate burial, most likely in a grave (broadly contemporaneous helmets were found in a tomb at Tell Oum Hauran, near Nawa, Syria (Abdul-Hak 1955; Robinson 1975, 121, pls 345–8, 133, pls 397–8; Garbsch 1978, nos N1 and N2). Alternatively, it may have been a votive offering, perhaps from a shrine. It must be presumed to have been recovered during an illicit excavation, after which it was smuggled to the West. Soon after the helmet was purchased, Mohammad Yeganeh's name occurred in association with other near-certainly looted items coming illicitly from, or via, Turkey (Gill 2007). The probable damage and loss of precious contextual data this implies are of course strongly to be deplored; however, the artefact has now been publicly displayed for many years, and especially given other, clearly related recent discoveries it is timely to publish it, to seek to salvage something of its scholarly value.

Description

I examined the object at the MFA on 17 April 2012, photographing and drawing it, and discussing it with current curators Rita Freed and Lawrence Berman, and conservator Pamela Hatchfield. The helmet bowl is made of thin brass plate (see *supra*). Although this exceeds 1 mm in thickness at points around the edge, overall the metal was generally considerably thinner, as was directly visible at cracks and holes (especially at weaknesses created by punching and chasing), and generally indicated by the way impressed surface decoration shows as dimples and ridges on better-preserved areas of the interior. The piece is correspondingly very light: currently it weighs 832 g, after loss of some original metal and addition of unquantified amounts of restoration material.

No traces of specific use wear or pre-depositional damage (such as weapon impacts) have been observed, although some such evidence could have been obscured by burial damage, corrosion, and heavy restoration. Overall dimensions of the piece today (likely close to the originals) are: max. height *c.*400 mm; width *c.* 220 mm; front to back *c.*240 mm.

In its current state the helmet surface generally comprises greenish copper salts, with some areas of dull reddish metal ('dezincified' alloy now overwhelmingly copper) and a few small patches of gold-coloured metal (intact brass, apparently exposed during the heavy-handed 'restoration' process which prioritised cosmetic appearance). Originally, then, the helmet would have been a bright gold colour, unless there was any secondary treat-

Figure 12.1 The Boston helmet (photograph courtesy of the Museum of Fine Arts, Boston: original image rotated to the correct orientation)

ment of the surface, e.g. through silvering or tinning. No indications of this were observed, but the possibility has yet to be investigated scientifically.

The method of manufacture now seems fairly clear, as a result of close inspection, and discussion of the piece with MFA staff. I owe particular thanks to Rita Freed for a crit-

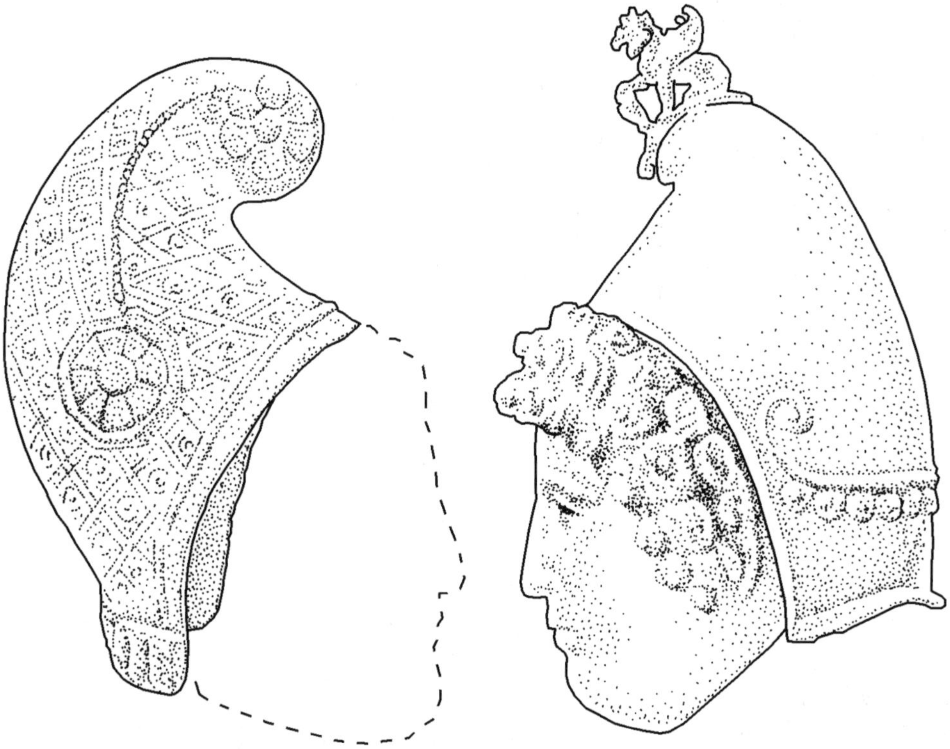

Figure 12.2 The Boston helmet and the similar piece, complete with face mask, from Crosby Garrett, Cumbria UK (not to common scale: drawings by Simon James)

ical conversation while inspecting the helmet, which helped elucidate how it was made. The bowl appears to have been formed from a single sheet of brass plate: there are no indications of any join in the thin metal across the brow area, or down either side. However, the extreme overhanging apex cannot plausibly have been formed by raising the bowl over a stake, from a flat plate to a rough hemisphere to the elongated 'Phrygian' form. Most conclusively, as Rita Freed pointed out, even if the basic helmet shape could somehow had been formed by raising, it would seem to be impossible to create the back-to-back repoussé flowers which adorn the apex: these had been hammered out from the inside.

The proposed interpretation is that the piece was indeed formed of a single piece of plate, continuous across the brow and down the sides, in a process of hammer-forming and repeated annealing requiring great skill. The plate was worked from the rear to form the repoussé rosettes on the overhanging apex (see below); the lateral rosettes and the chain of 'pearls' linking the flowers were likely executed at the same time. Then the sheet was folded to position the flowers back to back. The emergent bowl was then closed by a seam which ran from the front root of the overhanging apex, running around it, over the top and down the back of the bowl. This long join was skilfully disguised in the form of the narrow axial ridge, for strength the plate edges probably overlapped and soldered/brazed, rather than butted edge to edge. Near the lower edge, the join area is only discernible now in the décor of the central 'ringlet' by a narrow band visible as subtly different texture/colour in the metal.

The outer surface of the helmet was almost entirely covered with decoration executed in two related ways: larger, localised, raised motifs and decorative elements created by hammering from the back of the plate (repoussé work, more correctly *repoussage*), and finer depressed detail, dots and lines across almost the entire surface created by hammering with a narrow-pointed instrument (chasing), from the outside. Both techniques displaced metal without removing any. The smaller repoussé elements are raised 1–2 mm out of the plane of the surrounding plate. The major flower motifs are elevated as much as 6–8 mm. As we have seen, at least some of the repoussé work must have been executed before the plate was closed into the bowl form. It is likely that all the chased decoration was undertaken afterwards: the bowl could simply have been filled with pitch for this work, which was then all melted out afterwards.

The main elements of the decoration comprise:

- A plain, narrow, chase-defined ridge over the top and down the back of the helmet to an intersection with:
- a border, repoussé with chased cabling, across the nape of the neck, below which is:
- a series of 11 repoussé elements covered with slightly sinuous chased lines, representing the wearer's hair in 'ringlets';
- a repoussé/chased cable border parallel with, but 10–15 mm back from, the edge of the face aperture;
- a large, six-petalled repoussé/chased flower (or perhaps star or sun: see below), *c.*55 mm diameter, occupying the whole of each side of the overhanging apex. The repoussé centre was punched to simulate stamens, the petals ornamented with chased lines.
- Another large, eight-petalled repoussé flower, also *c.*55 mm across, chased in the same way, within an octagonal repoussé/chased border, in the middle of each side of the helmet,
- On each side, a curving row of domed repoussé 'beads' or 'pearls' connecting the two flower motifs, and continued from the eight-petal motif to the face-framing cable border,

The intermediate surface fields not subjected to *repoussage* were filled with repeating chased ornament. This comprised a grid, in places almost orthogonal but in others strongly rhomboidal, defined by 'cables' comprising a pair of lines with short angled 'dashes' between. The resulting pattern of quadrilaterals was not entirely symmetrical about the roughly axial 'cable' down the brow of the piece. Each quadrilateral contained a circle, within which was a cross and four 'dashes' aligned on its points. Lines of punched decoration, surrounding the circles and bordering the quadrilateral fields, filled much of the remaining space.

Little of the surface, then, was left undecorated, except around the underside of the overhanging apex and along the upper/rear axial ridge, perhaps because it was difficult to add chased detail to these areas without denting the helmet, although they could be artefacts of heavy-handed restoration. The main area without chased or repoussé ornament were around the edges of the aperture. A strip of plain metal 6–8 mm deep was left all the way around, including the lower edge of the neck guard below the repoussé 'ringlets'. This was entirely featureless, except for apparent traces of a very slight secondary ridge in front of the repoussé cabling around the face aperture. However, this might represent the remains of solder or brazing used to apply the only observed addition to the bowl: some kind of edging-strip, fragments of which remain *in situ* at several points. These fragments, extensively distorted by corrosion, were observed on the outer surface only. Most of this applied edging is lost, but it apparently originally ran all the way around the aperture, perhaps in the form of another cabled border. It was evidently of different composition, today with surfaces of greyish/whitish corrosion products, perhaps indicating high lead or tin content. It may originally have been of a colour contrasting with the gold of the main brass construction.

Four small holes *c.*1.5 mm in diameter were also punched through the plate across the brow area, two pairs, either side of the centre-line, punched from the outside. These holes are likely to have been used to attach the face mask. There is no trace of any riveted hinge-plate attachment, so it is likely that the face-mask simply had a leather-strip 'clam-shell' hinge laced on via the four holes, opening forwards and upwards like a medieval helmet visor, perhaps only far enough to allow donning and doffing. There is no indication of how the helmet was held shut either; perhaps it was simply by laces attached to the lower rear corners of the mask, tied around the nape of the neck above the 'ringlets', as was clearly the method used on the Crosby Garrett parallel.

There are no indications of any other attachments, e.g. for crest-holders, although it should be noted that the Crosby Garrett helmet appears to have been surmounted by a small cast gryphon figurine apparently simply soldered on, an addition which could easily have been lost. The British helmet also had loop attachments, perhaps for coloured streamers.

Discussion

The basis of the MFA's original identification of this helmet as Parthian appears to have been based on its supposed area of discovery, its 'Oriental' Phrygian cap form, and its manufacture in brass, a known feature of metalworking in pre-Roman Anatolia, and used in some Hellenistic coinages of the region (Ponting 2002). At the time of its discovery, no very close archaeological parallels to the Boston helmet were known. Indeed, no helmet has yet been identified from the Parthian empire itself, although several later Sasanian examples are attested (James, 1986). Neither are there very clear iconographical representations of Parthian helmets. On the other hand, there was a widespread tradition across the later Classical and Hellenistic Greek world of making 'Phrygian' or 'Thracian' helmets with overhanging apices, their modern names reflecting recognition that their overhanging apices were inspired by the Phrygian

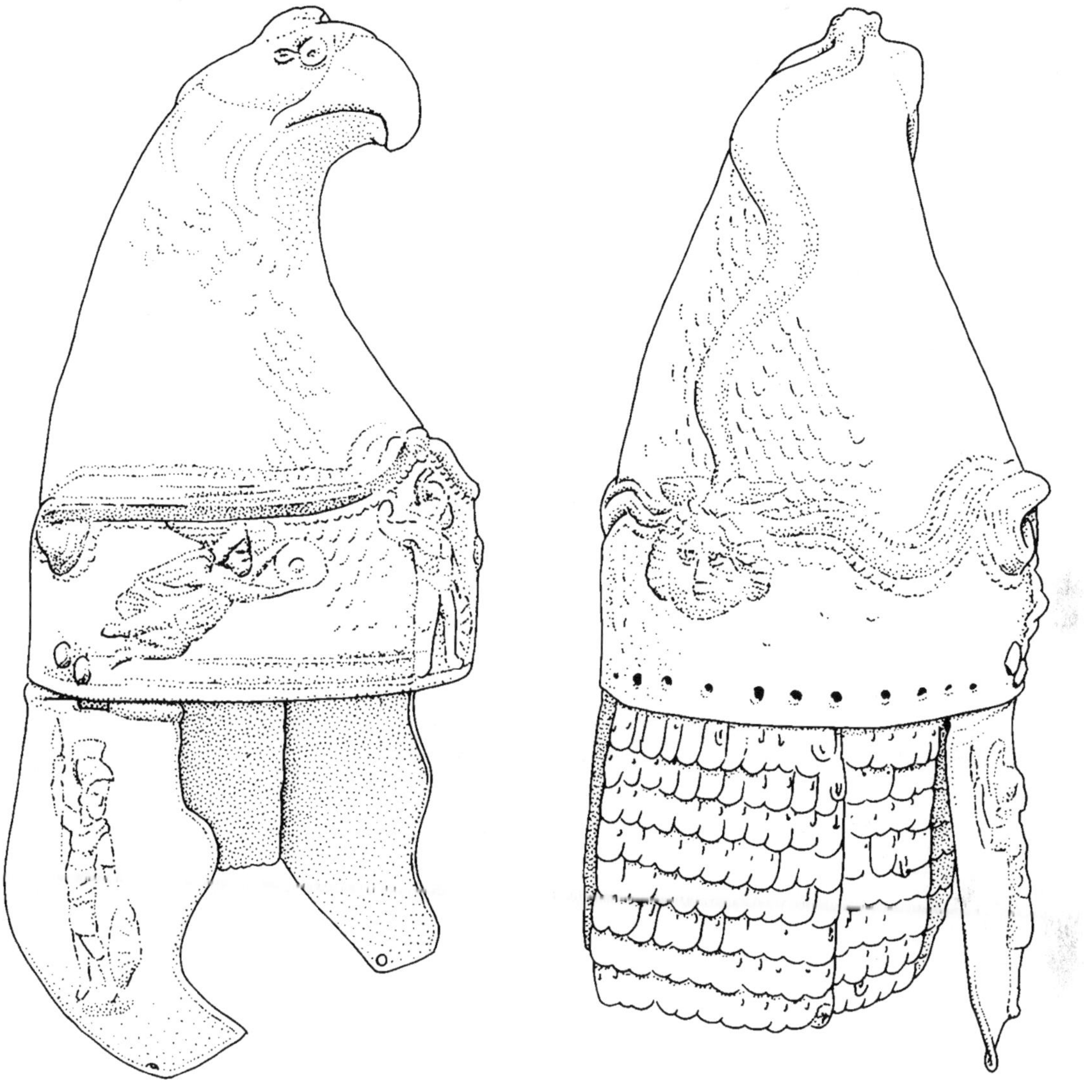

Figure 12.3 Eagle-topped helmet of unknown provenance, now in Mougins Museum of Classical Art, France (drawings by Simon James)

cap. Yet in their general form, especially with regard to facial and neck protection, they were much more inspired by Greek armour traditions than the textile headdress, which primarily offered a model for an apex which served just as a crest to exaggerate the height of the wearer; they are nowhere near such direct reproductions of the form of the cloth headdress as the Boston helmet. If the Greek helmets and the Boston piece express processes of imitation of the same textile artefact in metal, they represent distinct and parallel traditions of armour-making.

However, as was observed above, a number of key characteristics of the Boston helmet – its general conformation, brass construction, and elaborate repoussé and chased decoration – show that it is clearly intimately related to Roman helmet designs, specifically imperial forms current from the later first to third centuries AD. This would already have been apparent had knowledge of the helmet spread through the Roman archaeological community previously, even before discovery of the particularly close comparator from Crosby Garrett.

Substantial numbers of copper alloy bipartite 'face helmets' are known from the Roman Empire, from Britain to Syria (Robinson 1975, 107–27; Garbsch 1978, 62–71). These form part of an even wider population of helmets and other armour boasting rich repoussé and chased decoration, commonly exhibiting *horror vacui* like the Boston piece. And many of these Roman examples are made of brass rather than tin bronzes.

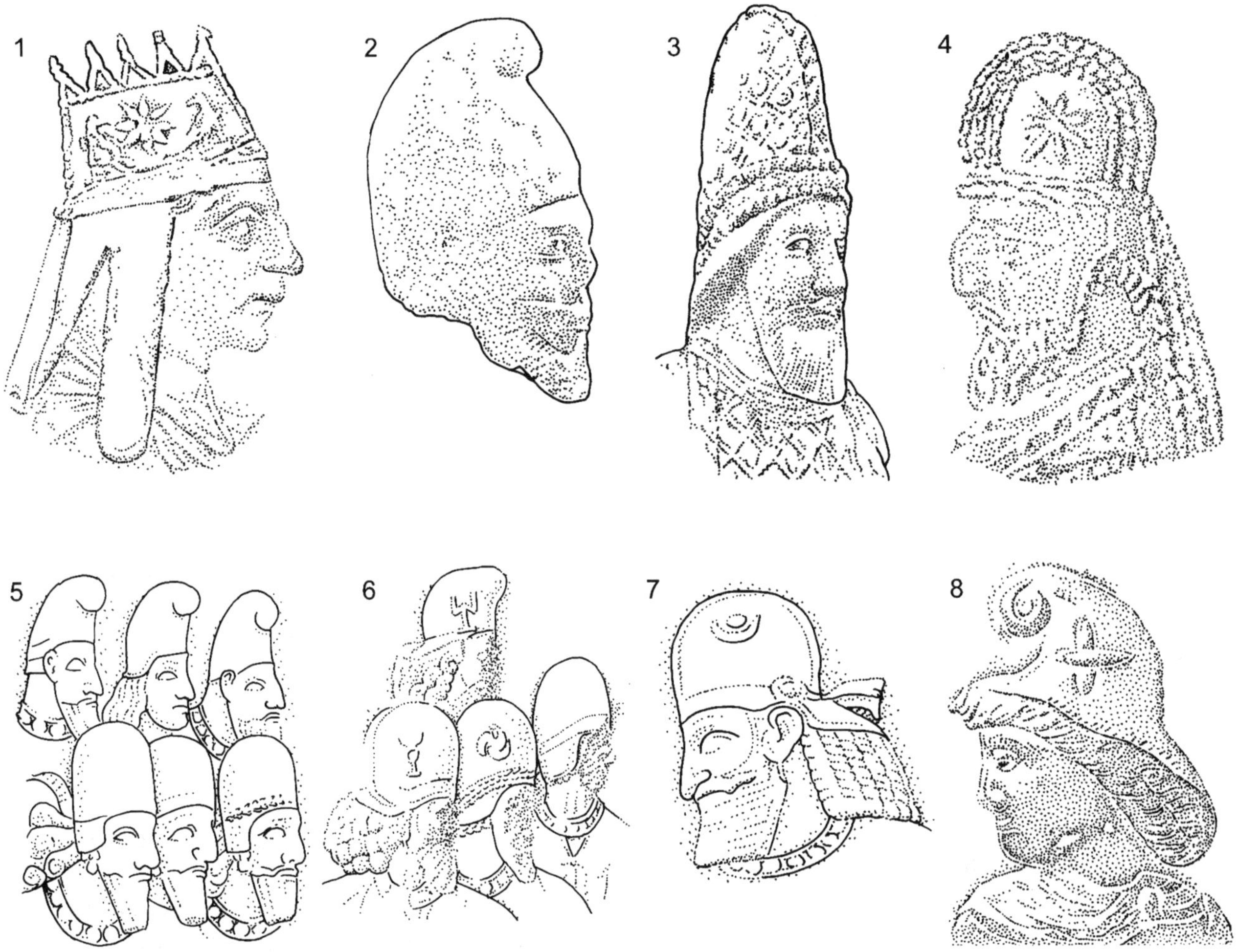

Figure 12.4 Near Eastern headgear from iconographic sources: 1. On coin of Tigranes II of Armenia (first century BC); 2. Statue head with Phrygian cap, Hatra (probably second–third century AD); 3. Statue of King Sanatruq, Hatra (third century AD); 4. On coin of Orodes I of Parthia (first century BC); 5. Relief of Shapur I at Darab (third century AD); 6. Relief of Shapur I, Naqsh-e Rajab (third century AD); 7. Relief of Bahram II and his court, Naqsh-e Rustam (third century AD); 8. Bust in Phrgian cap with astral symbols on a Roman-style copper alloy cheekpiece from Hatra (third century AD). (Drawings by Simon James)

New Roman helmets continue to come to light, of which the Crosby Garrett helmet is but one example. A further relevant recent appearance (like the MFA piece, of uncertain origin) is a tall, 'quasi-Phrygian' eagle-headed helmet now in the Mougins Museum of Classical Art, France (Fig. 12.3; Fischer 2012, 112 and Abb. 307; citing Junkelmann 2011). This piece clearly relates to a much older and more fragmentary find from Ostrov, Rumania (Robinson 1975, 135, pls 407–10; Garbsch 1978, no. O58). These helmets, while diverse in appearance, all nevertheless belong in terms of technique, style and iconography to a well-understood Roman imperial tradition of armour-making. To be sure, they are 'orientalising': many, although probably not all, Roman helmets with face masks were designed for the ritualised equestrian performances described by Arrian in his treatise *Techne Taktika* (De Voto 1993), in which exotic stereotypes (Amazons, Trojans) may have been pitted against 'Greeks'. One wooden shield from Dura-Europos, perhaps intended for such quasi-theatrical displays of cavalry skills, is painted with scenes of the Trojan War; another shows Greeks fighting Amazons (James, 2004, nos 616 and 617).

What, then, of the Boston helmet? Could this simply be a 'stray' Roman piece which ended up in the territory of Parthia or an Arsacid satellite like Armenia? An item of Roman armour has even been found in a Partho-Sasanian sanctuary at Masjid-i-Solaiman, Iran, likely a votive offering of spoils of war (Ghirshman 1971, 174, pl. iiia). In fact, details of the decoration of the MFA piece actually suggest something more complex.

If the general design, construction and embellishment techniques featured in the Boston helmet indicate strong links to the Roman armies – and incidentally help narrow down its dating to the first three centuries AD, most likely between 100 and the mid-third century – the details of its decoration would be clearly anomalous in a Roman milieu. Besides simulating (and often idealising) facial features and hair of the wearer, embellishment of Roman pieces draws on a repertoire concentrating on distinctly Classical figures (gods and heroes), symbolic animals (e.g. lions, snakes, especially eagles) and motifs (e.g. eagle's wings and feathers, shields, battle trophies). The Boston helmet stands out strongly from this background, in that such motifs are absent. Decoration is primarily geometric, with the exception of the stylised 'flowers' and 'ringlets of hair' at the neck. Further, the ensemble of *repoussé* and chased elements is clearly intended to be 'read' in conjunction with the overall shape of the piece to constitute a skeuomorph in metal of a quilted fabric headdress, apparently encrusted with rows of pearls, something unparalleled in Roman helmets, at least before the fourth century.

However, by comparison with the relative archaeological riches of Europe, we still know so little about the archaeology of Rome's major eastern armies that it remains just possible that the Boston helmet represents a regional Roman military fashion. Yet, while the eastern finds we do have, such as the pair of helmets from a grave near Nawa in Syria (above) do indeed indicate that some distinctly eastern traits can be identified in local armour, such pieces seem overall to remain much closer to the wider imperial decorative tradition than the Boston helmet does.

We should probably take the Boston piece much more at face value, and place weight on the combination of its apparent general provenance in Turkey or Iran, with the detail of its skeuomorphism. The precise combination of 'quilting' and 'Phrygian' shape is hard to parallel. However, sculptural and numismatic iconography dating to the last century BC and the first few centuries AD reveals that Phrygian caps were actually worn by prominent individuals in many parts of South-west Asia, including Armenia and Commagene (Young 1964) and, in Northern Mesopotamia, at Edessa and Hatra (James 2013; Fig. 12.4, no. 2). In this region such caps were used alongside other aristocratic or royal headgear, notably a form of 'mitre' with a fore-and-aft ridge and parabolic profile. Both hat types are depicted on nobles in early Sasanian royal reliefs (Fig. 12.4, nos 5–7). And notably a statue of King Sanatruq of Hatra depicts the king in a 'mitre', the surface of which is covered with 'quilting' in a pattern closely similar to that on the Boston helmet (Fig. 12.4, no. 3). It is also at least an interesting coincidence that a 'Roman-style' cheekpiece from Hatra bears a depiction of a male in a Phrygian cap with a flower, or more likely star or sun, on the side (Fig. 12.4, no. 8; James 2013), echoing that on the MFA piece. Star or sun symbols on the sides of hats also feature on first-century BC coins of Orodes I of Parthia (Fig. 12.4, no. 4) and Tigranes II of Armenia (Fig. 12.4, no. 1). The Hatra cheekpiece additionally sports a crescent and disk on the apex, which, with the star/sun, forms a pair of astral symbols in the same locations as the flowers (if such they are) on the Boston helmet. These examples converge to suggest that the cultural context of the Boston helmet is to be sought within the western fringes of the Arsacid world, and the zone of contention with the Roman Empire.

Is the Boston helmet perhaps, then, a western Parthian imitation and adaptation of a Roman cavalry helmet? It could be: there is certainly other evidence for apparent eastward transmission of Roman traits to Partho-Sasanian helmet design from Dura-Europos, where an iron helmet belonging to one of the Sasanian attackers sported a 'Roman-style' crown reinforcement and probably Roman-inspired mail neck-defence (James, 1986). However, I would question the assumptions underlying such a hypothesis, especially of any simple binary opposition between distinct and well-defined 'Roman' and 'Parthian' martial cultures across which borrowings could occur. While Roman military culture may have been quite strongly homogenising, it is not clear that the Arsacid world was so uniform in these regards. As we learn more from archaeological finds – we hope, from properly sanctioned excavations – I suspect that we will rather find growing evidence for multi-directional exchanges of military practice, technology, styles and fashions across this vast zone, without any single sharp boundary, with the Roman military and the Arsacid court as just two foci with a number of others between and around them, from the Eurasian steppe to the north, via polities like Armenia and Commagene to Hatra and the peoples of the dry steppe to the south.

If we then consider the longer temporal context alongside the wider geocultural picture, I anticipate we will be able to see how multiple regional military traditions evolving in interaction in alliance and conflict around the boundary zone between Rome and Parthia, all themselves descended from roots in the Hellenistic era, and before that from earlier traditions of the Classical Greek world and the sprawling

Achaemenid empire – in which Phrygian headdresses were already widely worn. The manufacture of the Boston piece and many contemporary Roman helmets from brass may itself reflect this common descent from earlier Southwest Asian traditions of metalworking, representing a cultural network into which Rome became integrated in the last century BC, contributing to widespread Roman use of brass in Augustan times and beyond, for a range of artefacts from armour to imperial '*orichalcum*' coinages. Rather than imitating Roman armour, then, the Boston helmet may rather attest Near Eastern models of the last century BC and the first two centuries AD, from which Roman examples like the Crosby Garrett piece were derived. Perhaps they were adapted from eastern helmets brought into the empire as spoils of war – or by copying examples owned by 'Parthian' and 'Arab' auxiliary recruits, such as those already stationed at Mainz in the first century AD (Selzer 1988, nos 90 and 91).

Acknowledgements

I am extremely grateful to current and past staff of the Boston Museum of Fine Arts for their generosity in facilitating and supporting the present study: curators Rita Freed, Lawrence Berman, and conservator Pamela Hatchfield. Former curator Tim Kendall kindly supplied information on the acquisition of the Boston helmet. Dr Matthew Ponting also generously provided valuable information on early brass. Finally, I would also like to thank the editors of the present volume, Rob Collins and Frances McIntosh, for giving me the opportunity to contribute to the celebration of Lindsay's work.

Bibliography

Abdul-Hak, S. (1955) Rapport préliminaire sur des objets provenant de la nécropole romaine situeé a proximité de Nawa (Hauran). *Annales Archéologiques de Syrie* 4/5, 163–88.

Boston Museum of Fine Arts (1987) *A Table of Offerings: 17 Years of Acquisitions of Egyptian and Ancient Near Eastern Art by William Kelly Simpson for the Museum of Fine Arts, Boston*. Boston, Museum of Fine Arts.

Breeze, D. J. and Bishop, M. C. (2013), *The Crosby Garrett Helmet*. Pewsey, Armatura Press

De Voto, J. G. (1993) *Flavius Arrianus, Techne Taktika (Technical handbook), and Ektasis kata Alanon (Expedition against the Alans)*. Chicago, Ares.

Fischer, T. (2012) *Die Armee der Caesaren – Archäologie und Geschichte*. Regensburg, Verlag Friedrich Pustet.

Garbsch, J. (1978) *Römische Paraderüstungen*. München, Beck.

Ghirshman, R. (1971) La terrasse sacrée de Masjid-i-Solaiman. *Iran* 9, 173–4.

Gill, D. (2007) Legless in Boston: reunited in Antalya? *Looting Matters: Discussion of the archaeological ethics surrounding the collecting of antiquities*. http://tinyurl.com/Limes-James1 (accessed 20 September 2012).

James, S. T. (1986) Evidence from Dura-Europos for the origins of late Roman helmets. *Syria* LXIII, 107–34.

James, S. T. (2004) *Excavations at Dura-Europos, Final Report Volume VII, The Arms and Armour, and other Military Equipment*. London, British Museum Press.

James, S. T. (2013) Roman: Partho-Sasanian martial interactions: Testimony of a cheekpiece from Hatra and its parallels. In L. Dirven (ed.) *Hatra. Politics, Culture and Religion between Parthia and Rome*, Leiden, E. J. Brill, 217–34, 347–51.

Junkelmann, M. (2011) Roman militaria. In M. Merrony (ed.) *Mougins Museum of Classical Art*, 235–66. Mougins Mougins Museum of Classical Art.

Ponting, M. J. (2002) Roman military copper–alloy artefacts from Israel: questions of organization and ethnicity. *Archaeometry* 44.4, 555–71.

Robinson, H. R. (1975) *The Armour of Imperial Rome*. London, Arms and Armour Press.

Selzer, W. (1988) *Römische Steindenkmäler: Mainz in Römischer Zeit Landesmuseum Mainz, katalogreihe zu den Abteilungen und Sammlungem Begründet und herausgegeben von Berthold Roland, Band 1*. Mainz, Von Zabern.

Worrell, S., Jackson, R., Mackay, A., Bland, R. and Pitts, M. (2011) The Crosby Garrett Roman Helmet. *British Archaeology* 116, 20–7.

Worrell, S. and Pearce, J. (2011) Roman Britain in 2010, II. Finds reported under the Portable Antiquities Scheme. *Britannia* 42, 399–437.

Young, J. H. (1964) Commagenian Tiaras: Royal and Divine. *American Journal of Archaeology* 68.1, 29–34.

13

A PIPECLAY PSEUDO-VENUS FIGURINE FROM BINCHESTER ROMAN FORT, COUNTY DURHAM

Iain Ferris

Introduction

While conducting background research for the preparation of the final report on the excavations in and around the fourth-century commandant's house or *praetorium* at Binchester Roman Fort (*Vinovium*), near Bishop Auckland, County Durham (Ferris 2010), it came to my attention that there were three highly-interesting but unpublished small finds from earlier campaigns of work at the site. It was therefore decided to prepare three notes on these pre-1976 finds for publication, of which this is the third (for the others see Ferris in press and forthcoming).

The fragmentary pipeclay Pseudo-Venus figurine which forms the subject of this note was recovered during salvage excavation of a number of pits on the edge of the scarp at Binchester in 1929 by J. McIntyre outside the fort to the south of the *vicus* buildings excavated by Proud and Hooppell in the nineteenth century (Ferris 2010, 540). McIntyre's excavations were never fully published, though some of the finds from the site were eventually deposited in the Bowes Museum, Barnard Castle where I examined them in the late 1970s.

In this note the Binchester Pseudo-Venus figurine will first be described and discussed in terms of parallels for the object from elsewhere in Britain, and then a brief discussion of the possible significance of the find will be presented.

The Binchester Pseudo-Venus figurine

The Binchester find, in white pipeclay, is a central fragment of a Venus or Pseudo-Venus figurine, with just the lower torso and upper legs of the female figure present (Fig. 13.1). The figurine appears to have been cleanly and deliberately cut off at both top and bottom. This is a well-known type, classified by Jenkins as a Type 2 Pseudo-Venus (Jenkins 1959, 60). Generally around 160 mm in height, complete figures of this type consist of the naked goddess posed in a somewhat insouciant manner, standing upright and relaxed, facing forwards, with her left arm held down by her side where she holds a garment or drape of some kind, and with her right arm raised to allow her to arrange a strand of her elaborately-braided hair. Another, more complete Pseudo-Venus figurine was found in a residual context at Binchester during excavations in 2009.

These items were produced in some quantity in central Gaul and the Cologne region, particularly in the first and second centuries AD, and were widely traded and sold across the western Empire (Green 1976, 20; Henig 1984, 200; Camuset-Le Porzou 1985; Bémont *et al.* 1993), along with a range of other common types of pipeclay figures, including the so-called *Dea Nutrix* or nursing mother figure and more specialised items such as the models of animals and other figures which accompanied the Colchester 'child's burial' (Eckardt 1999), the Arrington, Cambridgeshire child burial (Taylor 1993), and others at Godmanchester, Cambridgeshire (Taylor 1997).

There is a considerable academic literature on the production and distribution of pipeclay figurines in the western provinces of the Roman Empire (for a bibliographic survey see Wallace 1995) but little detailed study of the Romano-British examples since the work of Frank Jenkins (Jenkins 1959 and, on Kent in particular, Jenkins 1977).

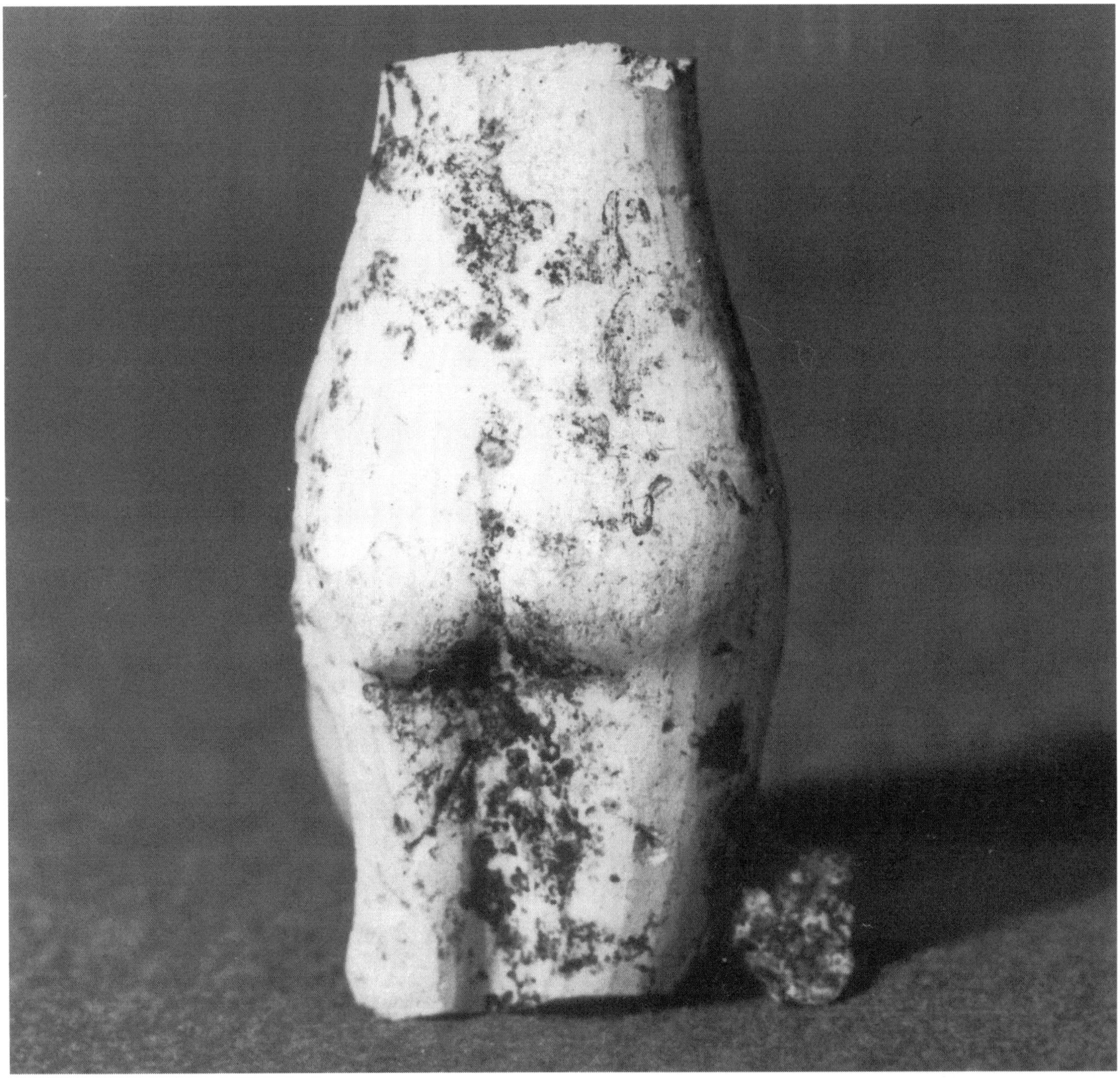

Figure 13.1 The pipeclay Pseudo-Venus figurine from Binchester, Roman fort, County Durham

Discussion

There appears to be considerable significance in the fact that the Binchester Pseudo-Venus figurine under discussion here was evidently deliberately but carefully broken before its disposal by burial in a pit in the *vicus*. Unfortunately we do not know the details of any other finds from the same pit.

Such pre-depositional damaging of Venus or Pseudo-Venus figurines might have been part of a wider trend in the treatment of such items in certain specific contexts. Both the examples of Venus pipeclay figurines from Colchester published by Crummy (Crummy 1983, 141, nos. 4262 and 4263) are also partial. Given that one of these (no. 4262) was residual in a modern context this might not be thought to be due to anything other than post-depositional damage. However, the other partial Venus figurine (no. 4263), consisting simply of the torso and lower body, with part of one arm only, the other being broken off at the shoulder, was excavated from a grave in the Butt Road cemetery. I have noted elsewhere a trend for the customisation of certain types of objects in Roman Britain to transform them into anatomical *ex votos* (Ferris 2012, 62, 64, 65) and in this context have cited the appearance of cut or neatly-broken Venus figurines represented by three or four sets of feet, torsos, and separate heads from the Mill Street site, Caerleon (Evans 2000, 300–2; Ferris 2012, 65, 121) and at St Dunstan's Terrace, Canterbury where a broken Pseudo-Venus figurine was placed in a cremation burial (Lynne Bevan pers. comm.).

However, if one looks at the case of the Bronze Age figurines from Keros, an island in the Cyclades of Greece, a study from outside the Roman world and from an earlier period, then further complexities of interpretation could perhaps be inherent in studying broken objects such as the Romano-British Pseudo-Venus figurines. On Keros a number of special deposits were found of quite carefully broken figurine fragments buried in small pits; none of the hundreds of fragments conjoined, nor were there chippings or smaller fragments present that would suggest that the breaking of the figurines had taken place here (www.arch.cam.ac.uk/keros). The excavators have suggested that the figurine fragments were already broken when brought to the site for ritual burial and that the act of burial here was the final stage of an extended process of creation and use of whole figurines, breaking of those figurines after some time and for some unknown reason, and pilgrimage to Keros bearing the retained and curated figurine fragments. A possible guesthouse for the accommodation of pilgrims was found on an islet nearby. Could similar complex motives have been behind what appears to have been the ritual breaking of pipeclay Venus figurines at the Mill Street, Caerleon site and at Binchester and other sites, as discussed above?

The Binchester Pseudo-Venus figurine would perhaps have originally been used at the site as an *ex voto* either in a household shrine or perhaps in a more formal religious context related to the well-attested cult of the *Matres Ollototae* at the site (Ferris 2011, 25, 35–36, 152). Its subsequent deliberate but careful mutilation and fragmentation marks another possible symbolic or ritual role for the object, as does its final disposal by burial in a pit or perhaps *favissa*.

The pipeclay Pseudo-Venus figurine from Binchester Roman fort is without doubt an interesting find which throws a little light on religious activity at the site. The publication here of this artefact makes a singular contribution to the elucidation of the archaeology of Binchester and to some extent to the study of the material culture of northern Roman Britain more widely. It is now relatively common to use archaeological evidence in the form of material culture and its contexts to discuss ritual in Roman Britain, to a great extent due to the work of Lindsay Allason-Jones and other pioneering small finds specialists like her, and it is therefore curiously apposite and timely that the previously-unpublished Binchester figurine from the 1929 excavations should now enter the formal archaeological record in the form of a note in this dedicatory volume.

Acknowledgements
The figurine is in the archaeological collections at the Bowes Museum, Barnard Castle. I would like to thank the museum's photography department of the 1970s for providing the black and white print of the object reproduced here.

Bibliography

Bémont, C., Jeanlin, M. and Labanier, C. (eds) (1993) *Les Figures en Terre Cuite Gallo-Romaines*, Documents d'Archéologie Francaise 38. Paris.

Camuset-Le Porzou, F. (1985) *Figurines Gallo-Romains en Terre Cuite*. Paris.

Crummy, N. (1983) *The Roman Small Finds from Excavations in Colchester 1971–9*, Colchester Archaeological Report 2. Colchester.

Eckardt, H. (1999) The Colchester 'child's grave', *Britannia* 30, 57–89.

Evans, E. (2000) *The Caerleon Canabae: Excavations in the Civil Settlement 1984–1990*, *Britannia* Monograph Series 16, Society for the Promotion of Roman Studies, London.

Ferris, I. M. (2010) *The Beautiful Rooms Are Empty. Excavations at Binchester Roman Fort, County Durham 1976–1981 and 1986–1991*, Durham County Council Excavation Monograph.

Ferris, I. M. (2011) *Vinovia. The Buried Roman City of Binchester in Northern England,* Amberley, Stroud.

Ferris, I. M. (2012) *Roman Britain Through Its Objects*. Amberley, Stroud.

Ferris, I. M. (forthcoming) A note on a seventeenth-century model firearm from Binchester Roman Fort, County Durham, *Durham Archaeological Journal*.

Ferris, I. M. (in press) A Roman carved jet dog from Binchester Roman Fort, County Durham, *Durham Archaeological Journal*.

Green, M. J. (1976) *The Religions of Civilian Roman Britain,* BAR British Series 52. Oxford.

Henig, M. (1984) *Religion in Roman Britain*. Batsford, London.

Jenkins, F. (1959) The cult of the 'Pseudo-Venus' in Kent, *Archaeologia Cantiana* 72, 60–76.

Jenkins, F. (1977) Clay Statuettes of the Roman Western Provinces. Unpublished PhD thesis, University of Kent, Canterbury.

Taylor, A. (1993) A Roman lead coffin with pipeclay figurines from Arrington, Cambridgeshire, *Britannia* 24, 191–227.

Taylor, A. (1997) A Roman child burial with animal figurines and pottery, from Godmanchester, Cambridgeshire, *Britannia* 28, 386–93.

Wallace, C. (1995) Gallo-Roman Clay Figurines, *Roman Finds Group Newsletter* X, 2–5.

www.arch.cam.ac.uk/keros The Cambridge Keros Project website. Accessed November 2011.

14

NOTES ON THE VINDOLANDA 'CALENDAR': RELATED ARTEFACTS AND THE PURPOSE OF THE VINDOLANDA FRAGMENT

Alexander Meyer

Excavations within the confines of the third century stone fort at Vindolanda in 2008 produced an 83 × 21 mm fragment of copper alloy (Fig. 14.1), which seems to be a small portion of a circular band approximately 350 mm in diameter (Tomlin 2010). The flat 'upper' or 'front' surface of this strip is labeled SEPTEMBER and includes 15 holes spaced evenly along its length. Furthermore, the second, fourth and eighth holes are subscribed with K, N and ID, respectively. These final three labels are clearly abbreviations for *kalendae, nonae,* and *idus*, and have led to the very sensible assumption, since moments after its discovery, that this fragment is part of a perpetual calendar (Birley 2009). As such, the holes were presumably intended to receive a peg, pegs or some other type of marker. In this interpretation each hole represents two days. Thus the hole labelled *kalendae* corresponds to the 1 September, the *nones* marks the 5th, and the *ides* denotes the 13th, keeping in mind that the first hole represents the final days of August. This artefact is reminiscent of the personal *parapegma* mentioned by Cicero (*Att.* 5.14.1, 15.1). It is clear from Cicero's letters that he assumed his friend Atticus had a device upon which he marked the date with a pin or *clavus* (Lehoux 2007, 200–1). One might imagine that this device looked much like the Vindolanda fragment. Nevertheless, subsequent to the initial publication of the Vindolanda fragment, Michael Lewis argued that the fragment belonged to an anaphoric water clock (*horologium hibernum*) rather than to a calendar (Lewis 2009).

Lewis presents a compelling argument based on the similarities between the Vindolanda fragment, similar artefacts discovered at Grand in northeastern France (Fig. 14.2; CIL XIII.2.1 5955) and Salzburg, Austria (Fig. 14.3; Benndorf *et al.* 1903), and Vitruvius' description of an anaphoric water clock (*De arch.* IX 8.8–15). However, close scrutiny of these fragments and this passage of Vitruvius reveals that each of the three artefacts was part of a unique device whose nature is not entirely clear and that each of those devices had some similarities to the clock described by Vitruvius but was not identical to it. Nevertheless, the Vindolanda fragment provides an intriguing insight into the nature of timekeeping on the edges of the Roman Empire and indicates a true desire to unite the vast territory of the empire in one chronological framework.

Like the Vindolanda fragment, the Grand and Salzburg fragments seem to have had 182 or 183 holes to mark days (i.e. one for every two days) and the Grand fragment has very similar labels to the Vindolanda fragment. Thus they are, on a fundamental level, quite similar to the Vindolanda fragments. The use of these fragments as calendars would have been simple. Either one marker with its two ends or sides differentiated by colored paint or a mark of some sort would have been inserted into a hole to mark the first day represented by the hole and turned the following day to mark the second day, or two markers may have been used simultaneously to straddle the locations that represented the days between those represented by holes. Thus, the first of the two markers would be removed on odd numbered days, to be placed in the subsequent hole on the following even-numbered day (according to the modern method of dating).

A simple calendrical interpretation of the Vindolanda fragment is complicated, however, by the appearance of the letters AE written perpendicularly to the line of date holes and straddling the space between the twelfth and thirteenth holes. The AE is undoubtedly an abbreviation of *aequinoctium*. The holes between which it is placed represent the 21 and 23 September. Indeed the letters seem to be slightly

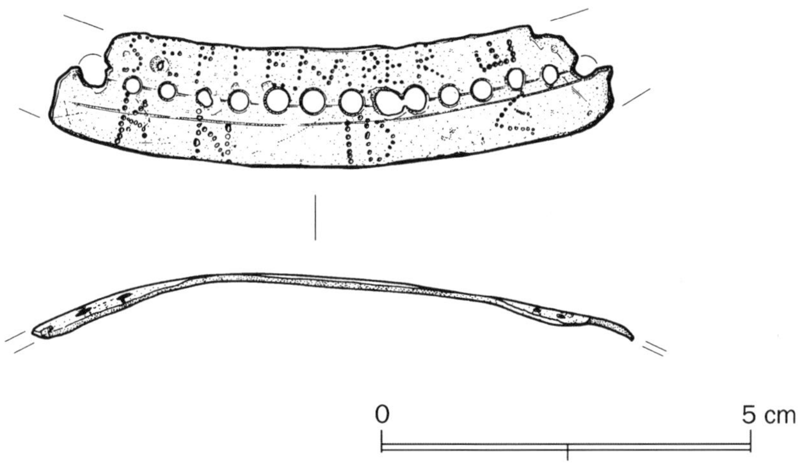

Figure 14.1 The 'calendar' fragment from Vindolanda, reproduced by permission of the Vindolanda Trust. Drawing by Mark Hoyle

closer to the latter hole, suggesting that the equinox should be associated with the 22nd or 23rd of the month. The inclusion of the equinox on this fragment is significant because it adds an astronomical aspect to what appears otherwise to be a simple calendar. In this way it associates the Vindolanda fragment with astrologically and astronomically inclined *parapegmata* rather than *fasti* that tracked civil cycles and public religion (Birth forthcoming; Lehoux 2007).

Indeed, there are some puzzling details about each of these three fragments, especially when compared to Vitruvius' description of the anaphoric clock. First, while the Grand and Salzburg fragments were evidently parts of complete discs that may correspond to the *tympana* of anaphoric water clocks as described by Vitruvius (IX 8.8; cf. Evans 1998, 155–6), the Vindolanda fragment is only a narrow band. This has led Lewis to concede that the Vindolanda device was 'more down-market', while maintaining that it was nonetheless part of an anaphoric clock. Furthermore, Lewis supports this argument by suggesting that the Vindolanda fragment was 'nailed to a wooden backing' in order to create an ecliptic disc (Lewis 2009, 228). This solution would require that holes be drilled in the wood in order to maintain the functionality of the holes in the bronze ring or that the bronze ring was raised from its wooden mounting. Indeed there is evidence of solder on the back of the Vindolanda fragment that suggests it was attached to a fixed base or some sort of metal framework. While this is by no means impossible, it is not an entirely satisfactory solution.

Second, the Salzburg fragment, unlike the Grand and Vindolanda fragments, was decorated and labelled with depictions of constellations and astrological signs. In this regard it is the only one of the three that conforms to Vitruvius' description of the anaphoric clock (IX 8.8). The inclusion of these depictions and notations suggests that the Salzburg fragment was intended to predict or mimic the progression of the astrological year rather than the Julian calendar. On the other hand, the Grand and Vindolanda fragments include labels for the holes corresponding to the *kalends*, *nones* and *ides* of each month. Thus the Grand and Vindolanda fragments seem to have served primarily as a means by which to track calendar dates.

This distinction is not, however, absolute. The Salzburg fragment includes labels for months as well as astrological phases, the autumnal equinox is labeled on the Vindolanda fragment, and the eighth day before the *kalends* of each month (i.e. the beginning of astrological phases) is labelled on the Grand fragment. In this way, all three fragments display elements of astrological tools and calendars, although their primary purpose may not have been as calendars.

Indeed, the form of the Grand and Salzburg fragments is remarkably like that of the *tympana* of the anaphoric waterclock described by Vitruvius. In particular, one may note the variable spacing between holes in these fragments. This is reminiscent of Vitruvius' description of the spacing of the 12 celestial signs *(xii caelestium signorum)* on the *tympanum* of an anaphoric clock, which are spaced at greater or smaller distances apart according to their distance from the rotational centre of the disc (IX 8.8). Furthermore, the focus of the Grand fragment seems to have been off-centre, thereby allowing extra space to be included between the holes corresponding to winter (i.e. shorter) days, with the winter solstice placed furthest from the 'centre'. Similarly, a large hole corresponding to the equatorial north pole is visible beside the head of the charioteer portrayed on the Salzburg fragment. Variation in the distance between holes

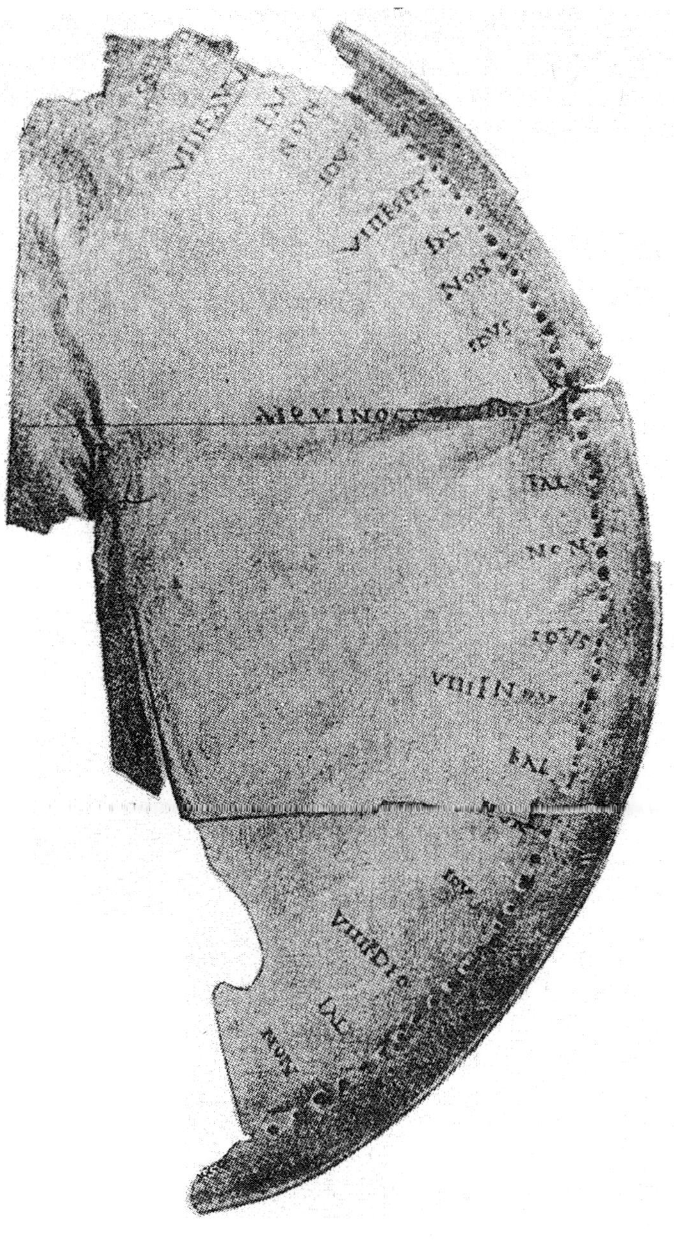

Figure 14.2 The 'calendar' fragment from Grande, from Maxe-Werley (1887)

is not, however, apparent in the Vindolanda fragment. Although one cannot discount the possibility that similar variations would be more apparent if more of the Vindolanda artefact had survived and been recovered, Birth notes that the even spacing of the holes in the Vindolanda fragment causes the line of the equinox to bisect the ring of the original artefact evenly (Birth forthcoming). Therefore, the Vindolanda fragment is unlikely to have been part of a device intended to measure hours of varying lengths.

The writing preserved on the three fragments also shows remarkable variation and suggests that each was part of a distinct mechanism. The majority of text on the Vindolanda fragment is oriented toward the outside of the ring formed by the band on which it is written. However, the label AE(*quinoctium*) is oriented so as to be read while on the left side of the ring. Meanwhile, the text on the reverse of the Salzburg fragment is meant to be read from the inside (i.e. while at the top of the disc) and the majority of the text on the Grand fragment is meant to be read on the right side of the disc. Furthermore, the marker used to mark the date on the Grand fragment was moved clockwise one hole every other day, while the marker on the Vindolanda tablet was moved anti-clockwise one hole. The direction of the marker's movement on the Salzburg fragment is more dif-

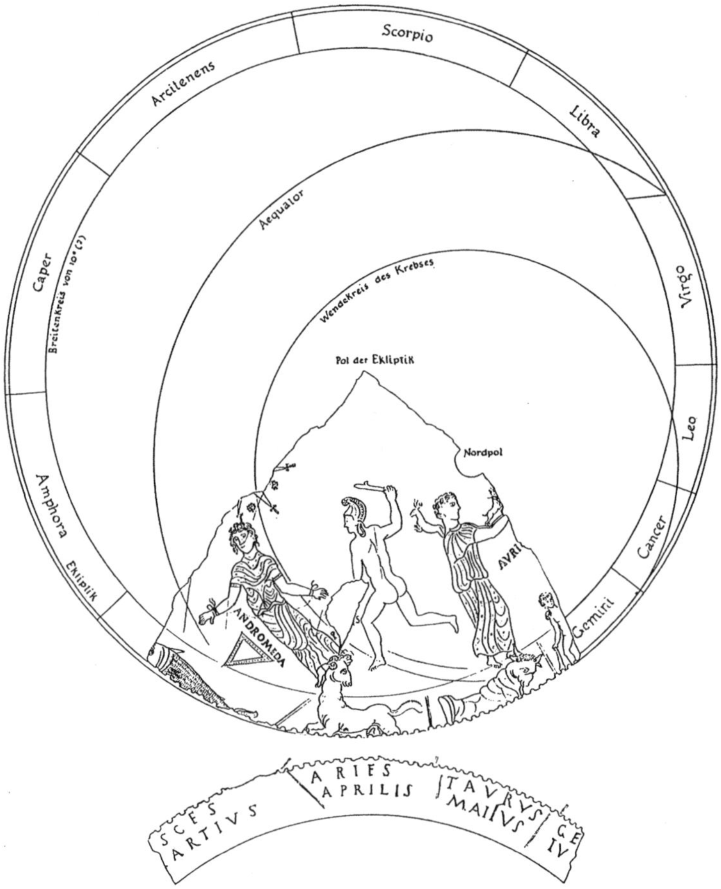

Figure 14.3 The 'calendar' fragment from Salzburg (Benndorf et al. *1903)*

ficult to determine, since it was inscribed on both sides, but it would seem that the front of the disc, which was decorated with astrological signs and constellations, was rotated anti-clockwise, or the marker was moved clockwise. Thus each of these fragments was oriented differently from the others and followed a different design.

The text on the Grand fragment also complicates its association with Vitruvius' anaphoric clock. Indeed, close examination suggests that this disc was not intended to rotate as Vitruvius recommends. All the text on this disc, except the label corresponding to the ides of August, reads from the inside of the disc to the outside. The label for the *ides* of August, however, reads from the outside in. Thus, if the disc were rotated as the marker advanced in accordance with the date, the writing for this label would be upside down as it approached the marker, or, perhaps more accurately, the surviving labels for all dates except the *ides* of August would have been upside down, depending on where in the circle the marker was placed. This complication could be mitigated if one were to assume that the date was to be marked on the disc when it was in the same position every day. However, this solution would suggest that the ides of July, or some date between it and eight days before the *kalends* of August, was at the top of the calendar when it was calibrated each year. It is more reasonable to expect the first of January, the first of July, a solstice, or an equinox to be in this place of prominence on the circle. Thus neither a rotating, nor a static solution is ideal. However, a stationary solution in which the disc of the Grand fragment remained in a fixed position while the marker was moved around it is preferable.

This does not preclude the hypothesis that the Grand fragment was part of an anaphoric water clock. One need only to shift one's frame of reference and imagine a version of Vitruvius' clock in which the frame marking hours is rotated, rather than the *tympanum*. This might involve a slightly more complicated mechanism than that described by Vitruvius but could certainly perform the same function and describe the varying lengths of diurnal and nocturnal hours throughout the year.

On the other hand, the Salzburg and Vindolanda fragments seem to have been intended to rotate. Indeed the fact that the Salzburg fragment belonged to a disc with a diameter of about 170 cm suggests that it was meant to be circled by the observe and the shallow grooves on the face of the Vindolanda fragment may be the result of abrasion between the rotating disc and a fixed element of the device. The text of these fragments is oriented in a way that indicates that the date was meant to be tracked at the top and bottom of the disc and band, respectively. However, this suggestion fails to account for the orientation of AE(*quinoctium*) on the Vindolanda fragment which, according to this interpretation, would have been upside down while approaching the bottom of the circle and the marker. Moreover, the text on the reverse of the Salzburg fragment is oriented differently to the vignettes of the signs of the Zodiac as depicted on the obverse. The design of the Salzburg fragment may be explained by the supposition that the disc and whatever apparatus it was attached to were meant to be flipped in order to read the marker's position on the back. The two-sided nature of this fragment makes it unlikely that it was attached to an apparatus such as that described by Vitruvius. It is difficult to believe that a piece of machinery as complicated as Vitruvius' anaphoric water clock would be flipped or spun in order to facilitate reading the reverse of its primary *tympanum*, especially considering its size.

It is not enough, however, to point out the discrepancies between Vitruvius' anaphoric clock and these three fragments. One must attempt to identify what purpose each of the artefacts may have served, if they were not, in fact, part of anaphoric clocks. It seems clear that the Grand fragment was, in all likelihood, part of a very similar apparatus. While the writing on the artefact suggests that it did not rotate in the manner described by Vitruvius, the spacing between the holes around its rim and the asymmetrical layout of the fragment suggest that it could be used to measure hours of varying length throughout the year. Furthermore, some aspects of the fragment's layout suggest that it was not ideally suited to be a simple calendar.

Indeed, the labels that accompany the date holes on the Grand fragment are not as closely associated with the holes themselves as one would expect. This is most pronounced in the cases such as the ides of September and the *kalends* of December where the labels are removed from the holes by about a centimeter. Furthermore, the labels do not line up precisely with their associated holes. If one bases the relationship between the holes and labels on the label for the equinox and *viii kal oct* it would seem that the labels ought to be above (or just anti-clockwise from) their corresponding holes. However, if one follows this scheme, the labels become noticeably misaligned by the time one reaches the *kalends* of September or the *ides* of October. In this way the labels seem to be more approximations of dates than demonstrative indications of them. Ultimately, holding the makers of this artefact to such high standards may be unfair. This imprecision may also be an indication of the craftsman's ignorance of the science behind his product and, thereby, suggest that he was mimicking another device, without detailed knowledge of its function or that the correspondence of the holes and labels was of secondary importance. Similarly the holes may have been added to the artefact by an apprentice or by a craftsman less-skilled than the designer of the object. The suggestion that the labels were intended only as approximations of the date is, perhaps, the more attractive hypothesis. If one accepts the interpretation of the Grand fragment as a piece of an anaphoric clock, rather than a simple calendar such as the one mentioned by Cicero, the absolute correspondence between the date and the hole in which the marker was placed would be of little practical value. The difference between the measurement taken from one hole and the next would have made little practical difference to the reader. Furthermore, consultation of another calendar, astronomical observation or other forms of time measurement would have allowed the caretaker of the clock to correct the position of the marker periodically. Indeed, after examination of an 'excellent photograph' supplied to him by the Musée des Antiquités Nationales, O. Neugebauer observed that the disc 'has a lip around the edge, obviously in order to hold a disk [*sic*] on which the constellations were painted' (Neugebauer 1975, vol. II, 870 n. 6). Neugebauer is apparently describing the reverse side from that on which the dates are labeled, but his observations may support the association of this fragment with an anaphoric clock and strengthen its similarity to the Salzburg fragment.

The Salzburg fragment is similarly imprecise regarding dates. The months labelled on the back of the fragment are differentiated from each other by rough lines. However, the association of these calendrical months with astrological signs on the back of the fragment makes it unclear whether the lines themselves are meant to indicate the start and end of months or the passage of the sun into different phases of its transit through the Zodiac (Benndorf *et al.* 1903). Indeed, traces of an etched circle on the face of the fragment that seems to represent the line of the equator divides *Pisces* from *Aries* and *Martius* from *Aprilis* on the reverse of the disc, marking the date of the spring equinox. This and the absence of more precise calendrical dating suggest that the makers of this device were more concerned with astrological matters than they were with producing a precise calendar. Furthermore, the remnants of a hole much larger than the marker holes around the rim of the fragment, has long been recognized as marking the axis around which the mechanism of the Salzburg device rotated. This hole and the enormous size of the Salzburg fragment suggest that the fragment itself remained stationary, while other parts of the apparatus moved.

There are also calendrical oddities on the three artefacts. For instance, the Vindolanda fragment includes 13 complete holes and traces of two more. The left most of the holes ought to correspond to the last days of August. However, since August had 31 days it is unclear how one ought to have navigated the 'calendar' during this period. Presumably one was meant simply to place the marker in the final hole before the *kalends* of September for just one day before moving it forward.

Thirty-one day months seem to have been treated the same on the Grand fragment. In this case the problem is even more pronounced. The entire month of October is preserved on the Grand tablet and includes 16 holes, including one for the thirty-first day of the month. This may then be contrasted to the representations of September and November, which each include just 15 holes. Of course, this is perfectly logical and only represents a small logistical complication; one must remember which month had 30 days and which had 31.

The treatment of 31 day months on the Salzburg fragments is problematic because of the imprecision of the dividing lines between months. The etched lines that divide astrological phases and calendar months on the front and the back of the artefact do not align properly; they are offset by one hole. This may introduce an error of up to four days. This discrepancy was noted by Rehm, who investigated the possibility that it may be the result of the migration of the zodiac over 300 years, but he reached no clear conclusion (Benndorf *et al.* 1903, 40–1). Furthermore, the marks on the front and back are not offset in a uniform direction. While the dividing lines between *Martius* and *Aprilis* and between *Aprilis* and *Maiius* are shifted forward of their corresponding marks on the front of the fragment, the dividing line between *Maiius* and *Iunius* on the back is shifted backwards. This results in a month which only appears to contain 28 days.

These imperfections in the layouts of the Grand, Salzburg, and Vindolanda fragments suggest that they were not ideally suited to be used simply as calendars. Nor, however, are these fragments identical to Vitruvius' description of the anaphoric water clock. Indeed, the differences between the fragments indicate that they were parts of distinct apparatuses that may have been used in different contexts and for different purposes. Timekeeping is, of course, among these purposes, but so is datekeeping. In fact, it is unclear whether these devices, especially that from Vindolanda, were intended to predict astronomical events such as solstices and equinoxes or if one was expected to observe such phenomenon by other means and calibrate these devices accordingly, thereby correcting the calendrical ambiguities of the devices themselves.

Nevertheless, the discovery of the Vindolanda fragment has intriguing implications. First, is suggests that devices like these were widespread. Vindolanda is positioned on the very northern extreme of the empire, yet someone, perhaps the commander of the garrison, had reason to be concerned with the date. This in turn drove him to acquire a device to track dates and the means to know when the equinoxes and solstices occurred. His reasons for needing to know the date include practical concerns such as the need to date official documents such as strength reports but these dates need not have been entirely accurate. Events at Vindolanda had no immediate or direct influence on Rome, nor did events in Rome affect life at Vindolanda for days, if not weeks, after their occurrence.

Indeed, one may imagine that the date could be confused by a relatively isolated population like that at Vindolanda. Nevertheless, the Vindolanda fragment could have been used to determine when fixed astronomical events occurred and to act as a check on the actual date. If the fragment was part of a water clock, that clock could be used to measure the length of day and night in order to identify the equinoxes and solstices. If it was not part of a clock, one may infer that such a device was available to confirm or correct the calendar by identifying the solstices and equinoxes.

More significantly, however, this concern with the date and its accuracy as demonstrated by the Vindolanda fragment suggests a preoccupation with preserving at least notional synchronization and therefore unity of chronology between Rome and distant parts of the empire. The population of Vindolanda could only ensure that it celebrated festivals and performed rituals on the proper days by having a reliable means by which to determine the date. The Vindolanda fragment represents a crucial means by which this was achieved, even if its exact role and the nature of the device of which it was part are obscure. Through this artefact we may see not only the ubiquity of an impressive ancient technology but also an expression of the commitment shown by some in the Roman Empire to unite the empire, at least metaphorically, through a shared chronological framework. This widespread commitment to timekeeping would ensure that observances, such as annual dedications for the well-being of the emperor, could be performed at the correct time and, more broadly, that events around the empire could be placed within a single, unified chronological framework. This in turn has implications about the practice and maintenance of bureaucratic and ritual behaviours in the Roman military that affected soldiers and officers alike. Thus, while it is not possible to say with certainty what type of device the Vindolanda fragment was a piece of, the fragment remains significant and can inform our understanding of Roman imperial ideology.

Bibliography

Benndorf, O., Rehm, A. and Weiss, E. (1903) Zur Salzburger Bronzescheibe mis Sternbilden, *Jahreshefte des österreichischen archäologischen Institutes in Wien* 6, 35–49.

Birley, A. R. (2009) Artifact: perpetual calendar, *Archaeology* 62.1, 72.

Birth, K. (forthcoming) The Vindolanda Timepiece: Time and Calendar Reckoning in Roman Britain, *Oxford Journal of Anthropology*

Evans, J. (1998) *History and Practice of Ancient Astronomy*. Oxford University Press. Oxford.

Lehoux, D. (2007) *Astronomy, Weather, and Calendars in the Ancient World: Parapegmata and Related Texts in Classical and Near Eastern Societies*. Cambridge University Press, Cambridge.

Lewis, M. (2009) A Roman clock at Vindolanda, *Current Archaeology* 228, 12–17.

Maxe-Werly, L. (1887) notes sur des objets antiques découverts à Gondrecourt (Meuse) et à Grand (Vosges), *Mémoirs de la Société Nationale des Antiquaires de France,* ser. 5, 48, 170–8.

Neugebauer, O. (1975) *A History of Ancient Mathematical Astronomy*, 3 vols. Springer. Berlin.

Tomlin, R. S. O. (2010) Inscriptions, *Britannia* 41, 441–69.

15

A BEAD FROM HOUSESTEADS REVISITED

H. E. M. Cool

In every specialist's life there are items that which you look at and think, 'That's interesting – but I've not come across one before, and it is going to be difficult to say anything useful about it'. For these there is a need to publish with an illustration, and hope that somewhere, in the future, new data will emerge to put it into context. I suspect that one of the beads that Lindsay published from the 1971–84 excavations at Housesteads fell into this category. By chance over the past year or two, information has accumulated that allows a little more of its story to be told. It is a tale of serendipity and sod's law of the sort every finds specialist will be familiar with, and I hope she will enjoy it.

The bead came from the dereliction layers overlying Building XIII in the north-east quarter of the fort (Rushworth 2009, 178–9). It was described as a 'globular bead of black opaque glass, decorated with blue trails and three horns of yellow, each with a central natural glass blob'. It has a diameter of 13 mm and a length of 9 mm, and it was suggested that it belonged to Guido's Group 3 (Allason-Jones 2009, 471 no. 431, fig. 14.23). This is a miscellaneous group of beads with horns which Guido herself seems to have regarded as something of a ragbag, covering a long time span from later prehistory and through the Roman period (Guido 1978, 60–1). Unfortunately the drawing of the Housesteads bead occurred on a figure that was very poorly reproduced in the volume, or at least it was in my copy. It was unlikely that anyone would have got a good impression what any of the glass objects illustrated actually looked like from it.

So the bead would probably have languished there unrecognised, had not a colour picture of it been included amongst a batch of items Georgina Plowright asked me to comment on, in advance of the redisplay of the Housesteads site museum (Plate 6). From that it was possible to see that the blue trails are a distinctive pale blue/turquoise shade and that there are two of them in a zig-zag pattern which cross over each other to form frames, which enclose the opaque yellow 'horns'. Their centres appear to be black. From the description they must be translucent blue/green or green, as that is what 'natural' glass is. It is worth noting that in any photograph the centre will thus look black, as what will be visible is the black ground through the translucent glass. The trails are marvered smooth. The horns are almost flush with the black ground of the bead.

It was here that serendipity struck, for eighteen months previously, Ed McSloy of Cotswold Archaeology had sent me a photograph of a bead from an excavation they had recently conducted. This, I recalled, looked very like the Housesteads bead. It was globular and made of very dark glass appearing black. An opaque white trail forming a zig-zag pattern ran from the top to the bottom. An opaque pale turquoise blue trail had been applied over the white trail in a similar zig-zag to form the frames. There were six eyes apparently formed of slices of cane consisting of an opaque yellow ring around what appeared to be, from the photograph, a black centre. These were arranged with one in each frame formed by the crossing trails. The trails were marvered smooth and the canes stood slightly proud of the surface. This bead was larger than the Housesteads one, with a diameter of 30 mm and a length of 25 mm. It was this larger size that allowed the larger number of eyes than the Housesteads bead had. Other than that though, the two were very similar, each having the same colour scheme including the distinctive shade of pale turquoise blue.

The Cotswolds Archaeology bead came from near Hawling in Gloucestershire (Site 12.05), which lies about

20 km north of the Roman villa at Barnsley Park. There, a note in my files alerted me to the presence of a possible parallel from this site. This was described as a globular black bead with white and sky-blue swags, and opaque yellow eyes with brown centres (Webster and Smith 1982, 109 no. 64, fig. 28). The drawing made it a little difficult to see how these were arranged, but did indicate that it had a diameter of 20 mm and a length of 15 mm.

Once this parallel was pointed out to Ed, he found two colour pictures of it on the Corinium Museum website.[1] From that it was possible to see that the Barnsley Park and the Hawling beads were very similar. On the Barnsley Park bead the opaque white trail was again crossed by the zigzags, in the now familiar pale turquoise blue shade, forming the frames for the yellow canes. The trails were marvered and the eyes stand very slightly proud of the body of the bead.

On the principle that one unusual bead is just that, but three is a group, we now have the core of a type which I propose to call LBB (Lindsay's Birthday Bead) for the rest of this note. When were LBBs in use? The Barnsley Park bead came from a context assigned to Phase 9, which was dated to after AD 400. The Hawling bead came from a pit that contained several coins, the latest of which was of 364–78, and pottery of a type expected to date to after AD 350. This indicates we are dealing with a very late Roman form. The Housestead bead itself came from a context that would happily fit this date, or later.

I have suggested that beads on Roman sites which are not easily 'Guidoised' are likely to belong to the end of the fourth century and into the fifth century (Cool 2000, 50), and LBBs fall into this category. The liminal position of the Barnsley Park bead can be seen in Guido's bead books. She published it as an exotic Roman form in *Glass Beads of the Prehistoric and Roman Periods in Britain and Ireland* (1978, 233). It was also used as the type example of her black bead 2viii category in her posthumously published *The Glass Beads of Anglo-Saxon England AD 400–700* (1999, 25, 183). It is interesting to note that on the figure there (pl. 2) the pattern of trails appears to be impressionistic rather than accurate, judged from the Corinium Museum photographs. Our lives as specialists would be made much easier if we could always have colour photographs, and line drawings depicting an accurate unrolling of the pattern.

Guido's Group 2viii is listed with only five members. For three of these, including the Barnsley Park bead, the colour combinations are stated, and it is clear that the other two do not match it exactly. The fourth is without description there, but is likely to be the one published on p. 232 of her 1978 Roman volume. If so, the trails are white and it does not have the distinctive pale turquoise blue glass. The fifth is described as 'similar to Barnsley Park bead'. It came from the late sixth–seventh century Grave 15, Black Patch, Pewsey in Wiltshire. It seemed to be a good candidate for being another LBB and, if so, started to hint of a cluster in the West Country.

It seemed appropriate at this stage of the search to consult Brugmann's (2004) corpus of early Anglo-Saxon beads where over 32,000 beads from 106 sites are summarised. She had a type called *Overlying Crossing Waves Common* (Brugmann 2004, 77, fig. 112). The ones illustrated (by colour photograph) as the type example both come from Mill Hill, Deal with the upper one clearly being an example of an LBB following the Barnsley Park fashion of having the white and turquoise trails crossing to form frames for the central yellow and black eyes. Brugmann, however, places the bead from Black Patch in her *Overlying Crossing Waves Insular* form, which have a different colour combination. In both cases the same grave number was cited so it had to be assumed they were talking of the same bead. An inspection of the Devizes Museum excellent online database (www.wiltshireheritage.org.uk) produced two beads with the wave-like zig-zag trails and eye from the site. Clearly neither could be our possible LBB, as their grounds were white and red. Both authors cited the cemetery from which the bead had come as unpublished, but some intensive 'Googling' revealed that an Anglo-Saxon cemetery under one of the alternative names for the site that Brugmann, but not Guido, gave, had been published subsequently (Annable and Eagles 2010). Inspection of this publication revealed the grave had two polychrome beads. One was a simple white wavy trail on a dark background, and so not the bead in question. The other was described as 'opaque red wide crossing trails on yellow dots and white wide crossing trails'. The figure (*ibid.*, fig. 42.4g) was not colour-coded and the omission of the word 'body' leaves us wondering whether we are dealing with a yellow-bodied bead. Table 5 (*ibid.*, 46) notes the ground as 'dark'. This is presumably the bead the Guido was referring to, though it may be noted that though the catalogue entry mentions dots, none are shown on the illustration. Sadly we have to conclude that the grave does not contain another LBB. A specialist's life is full of occurrences like this where promising leads are struck by the sod's law of a dead end.

So what are LBBs? Should they be seen as 'Roman' or 'Anglo-Saxon' or are these very unhelpful labels? Within an end of Roman Britain milieu, black beads are normally seen as exotic imports into Britain from more Barbarian parts of Europe (e.g. Guido 1978, 15; 1999, 17). When discussing her Group 2viii Anglo-Saxon beads, Guido (1999, 25) noted that several including the Barnsley Park bead occurred in late Roman contexts, and that they did not appear to be common on the Continent. Brugmann considered her *Overlying Crossing Waves Common* beads to be 'widely distributed on the continent, Scandinavia and England'. It should be noted here that widely distributed is certainly not a synonym for common as only seven beads out of the large Brugmann corpus belonged to the type, i.e. 0.02%. Another large corpus including 13,000 beads is that amassed by Swift as part of her study of regionality in the late Roman west. She had a category amongst the polychrome beads of annular/globular with double swags and eyes, into which LBBs could fall. Again they were widespread but not common (Swift 2000, 107, 298, fig. 133). She found 16 occurrences in comparison to the common types where 60 or more were not unusual. Interestingly too, her distribution of cylindrical black beads is again widespread but not common within the north-western provinces (*ibid.*, 293 fig. 112).

With Brugmann and Swift we see the perennial problem that a Roman specialist will look for *comparanda* within the Empire, and an Anglo-Saxon one will look for the same sort of information further north, beyond the frontiers. Put the two together, however, and it can be seen that the traits that came together to form LBBs do not appear ever to have been common, but were widespread. They certainly need not have any ethnic overtones. Is it worth asking at this point whether LBBs *need* to have been imported?

We know that black jewellery generally became increasingly popular in the late Roman period in Britain. This was frequently made in jet and shale and the suggestion that this might have been linked with Mystery religions has been made (Allason-Jones 1996, 17). Black glass, or to be precise very dark glass appearing black, is also noted amongst the jewellery. Black glass finger rings, whilst never common, were made in styles that have resemblances to the contemporary third to fourth century metal rings, such as the shouldered glass finger ring from Caister-on-Sea (Darling and Gurney 1993, 87 no. 249). Black glass is also used on specifically British types of third century artefacts, most notably on the gilded disc brooches which often have 'black' central glass settings (Mackreth 2011, 160; see for example one from Richborough in Bayley and Butcher 2004, 134 no. 388). It was also occasionally used to make the moulded 'intaglios' with crude standing figures, as on one from Silchester (Henig 1978, 255 no. 543). During the later fourth century there was a revival in the use of glass counters. These normally had either white or black grounds with coloured dots centrally. The growing numbers of site finds with dated contexts suggest that these were in use from the mid fourth century at the earliest, and are increasingly looking as if they might be more typical of the end of the century (Cool 2011, 23–5; see also Viner 116 no. 251 not noted there). They are another insular form. A complete set was found in a grave at Lankhills and illustrated by a coloured figure (Clarke 1979, pl. Ib) where the dots on the white counters can be seen to be an opaque pale blue turquoise shade. On another set from a grave at Lullingstone, Jenny Price and I had fortunately noted the shades of the coloured spots in some detail and again an opaque blue-tinged turquoise was noted as one of the colours used (Cool and Price 1987, 139 no. 391).

There was therefore a tradition of working with black glass for objects in the later Roman period in Britain. Furthermore, at the time when the LBBs appear to have been made, one insular type was combining a black ground with the distinctive shade of turquoise blue seen on them. When taste moved to wanting black jewellery, including beads, there is no reason why the Romano-British bead makers could not have started to make new forms to satisfy the demand.

Within Britain, if one wanted to bet on where this was most likely to happen, it would be the West Country where two of the LBBs were found. It was an area whose people embraced the concept of being consumers of material culture with open arms. Most West Country sites have prolific finds assemblages and regional variants of types can frequently be identified. We can note the phenomenon in the developed T-shaped brooches, both as far as the designs and the metal used are concerned (Bayley and Butcher 2004 167, figs 138–9). It can also be seen in material like hair pins (Cool 1991, figs 15–17) and toilet sets (Eckardt and Crummy 2008, figs 29–31). Within the very late Roman milieu it surfaces in the form of distinctly regional forms of late Roman belt equipment (Swift 2000, 2). Glass working in at least one colour appropriate for these beads was being carried out in the region, as shown by the evidence for the melting of an opaque yellow glass at Catsgore in the later third to earlier fourth century (Biek and Kay 1982).

To return to the Housesteads bead itself. What information can it provide about the occupation there? At the very least it is one of the few items in the Housesteads assemblage that can unequivocally be dated to the end of the fourth century. This is useful given that hard evidence for occupation extending that far is scant. Rushworth argued for a formal military presence continuing until the end of the fourth century (2009, 318). He had to do it by a careful marshalling of the patterns in the data, to show that absence of evidence could not be equated with evidence of absence. This bead nibbles away at that absence of evidence.

Rushworth then made a case for continuing occupation reverting to more local patterns of life, and possibly being an aspect of the military bands model advanced relationship to the continuing occupation at Birdoswald (Wilmott 1997, 408–9). It is, perhaps, worth reflecting that this bead indicates material was still reaching the site from some distance. If the West Country origin for LBBs is correct, this could even provide a small strand of evidence that Housesteads was still incorporated into the military organisation of the Diocese of *Britannia* at the beginning of the fifth century. The West County certainly shows signs of militarisation at this period. White (2007, 57) has gone as far as postulating that we are missing a section of the *Notitia Dignitatum* which would have covered the command of the western shores of Britain. If correct, it would have probably gone some way to explain the militarisation we see from other sources. Against a background of movement between different, but still functioning commands, the travels of the little bead from Housesteads would become intelligible. Without it, the question of how the bead arrived must remain a great puzzle.

Note

1 In the Corinium Museum website go to the collections section, and then in the search facility select advanced search. Object name = bead, Material = glass, Object number = A320 section (http://coriniummuseum.cotswold.gov.uk/)

Acknowledgements

Firstly I must thank Ed McSloy and Cotswold Archaeology for drawing the Hawling bead to my attention and allowing me to consider it here. Even greater thanks are due to Ed who has done the legwork for locating the Barnsley Park bead images, and more recently for checking the context details for the Hawling bead.

Secondly my thanks to Georgina Plowright for inviting me to look at the Housesteads material, and so alerting me to this interesting piece. Kevin Booth kindly gave me permission to use the work I did for English Heritage as the basis of this note, and Nicky Westgate of English Heritage took the photo of the bead.

And thirdly, thanks to Lindsay for all her help, scholarship and friendship over a great many years. Where would we all have been without her work!

Bibliography

Allason-Jones, L. (1996) *Roman Jet in the Yorkshire Museum*. York.

Allason-Jones, L. (2009) The small finds. In A, Rushworth (ed.) *Housesteads Roman Fort – the Grandest Station,* 430–87, English Heritage. Swindon.

Annable, F. K. and Eagles, B. N. (2010) *The Anglo-Saxon Cemetery at Blacknall Field, Pewsey, Wiltshire,* Wiltshire Archaeological and Natural History Society Monograph 4. Devizes.

Bayley, J. and Butcher, S. (2004) *Roman Brooches in Britain: a technological and typological study based on the Richborough collection,* Report of the Research Committee of the Society of Antiquaries of London 68. London.

Biek, L. and Kay, P. J. (1982) Evidence of glass meltings. In R. Leech (ed.) *Excavations at Catsgore 1970–1973,* Western Archaeology Trust Excavation Monograph 2, 132–3. Bristol.

Brugmann, B. (2004) *Glass Beads from Early Anglo-Saxon Graves.* Oxford.

Clarke, G. (1979) *The Roman Cemetery at Lankhills,* Winchester Studies 3: Pre-Roman and Roman Winchester Part II. Oxford.

Cool, H. E. M. (1991) Roman metal hair pins from southern Britain, *Archaeological Journal* 147, 148–82.

Cool, H. E. M. (2000) The parts left over; material culture into the 5th century. In T. Wilmott and P. Wilson (eds) *The Late Roman Transition in the North,* BAR British Series 299, 47–65. Oxford.

Cool, H. E. M. (2011) The small finds. In S. Ford Teague, E. Biddulph, A. Hardy and L. Brown (eds) *Winchester – a City in the Making,* Oxford Archaeological Monograph 12, Digital Contents Part 3 section 3, 1–104. Oxford.

Cool, H. E. M. and Price, J. (1987) The glass. In G. W. Meates (ed.) *The Roman Villa at Lullingstone, Kent. Volume II the wall paintings and finds,* Kent Archaeological Society Monograph 3, 110–41. Maidstone.

Darling, M. J. and Gurney, D. (1993) *Caister-on-Sea. Excavations by Charles Green, 1951–55,* East Anglian Archaeology 60. East Dereham.

Eckardt, H. and Crummy, N. (2008) *Styling the body in Late Iron Age and Roman Britain,* Monographies Instrumentum 36. Montagnac.

Guido, M. (1978) *The Glass Beads of the Prehistoric and Roman Periods in Britain and Ireland*, Report of the Research Committee of the Society of Antiquaries of London 35. London.

Guido, M. (1999) *The Glass Beads of Anglo-Saxon England* c.*AD 400 – 700*, Report of the Research Committee of the Society of Antiquaries of London 56. London.

Henig, M. (1978) *A Corpus of Roman Engraved Gemstones from British Sites*, 2nd edition, BAR British Series 8 . Oxford.

Leech, R. (1982) *Excavations at Catsgore 1970–1973*, Western Archaeology Trust Excavation Monograph 2. Bristol.

Mackreth, D.F. (2011) *Brooches in Late Iron Age and Roman Britain.* Oxford.

Rushworth, A. (2009) *Housesteads Roman Fort – the Grandest Station.* Swindon.

Swift, E. (2000) *Regionality in Dress Accessories in the late Roman West,* Monographies Instrumentum 11. Millau.

Viner, L. (1986) Glass objects. In A. McWhirr (ed.) *Houses in Roman Cirencester*. Cirencester Excavations III, 116–7. Cirencester.

Webster, G. and Smith, L. (1982) The excavation of a Romano-British rural establishment at Barnsley Park, Gloucestershire, 1961–1979. Part II *c*.AD 360–400 +, *Transactions of the Bristol and Gloucestershire Archaeological Society* 100, 65–189.

White, R. (2007) *Britannia Prima*. Stroud.

Wilmott, T. (1997) *Birdoswald. Excavations of a Roman Fort on Hadrian's Wall and its successor Settlements*, English Heritage Archaeological Report 14. London.

16

KEEPING WATCH: A KEY HANDLE FROM FONT-Y-GARY, VALE OF GLAMORGAN

Nina Crummy and Mark Lodwick

Lindsay has always enjoyed teasing the meaning from an object and its context, and we hope that this small contribution for her birthday volume will amuse and entertain her.

The hollow terminal of an unusual leaded bronze key handle (Fig. 16.1) was found by Mr J. Lambert while metal-detecting at Font-y-Gary, Rhoose, Vale of Glamorgan, in 2011 and reported to the Portable Antiquities Scheme (PAS) Finds Co-ordinator, Mark Lodwick, at Amgueddfa Cymru – National Museums Wales (PAS NMGW-C14CE7). Font-y-Gary lies not far from the shore of the Bristol Channel and a number of Roman period finds are listed on the Heritage Environment Records from the surrounding area. More recently the PAS has recorded an assemblage of metal detector finds there, perhaps suggesting a domestic site in the vicinity. A few miles to the east a third century courtyard building at Cold Knap may have been a *mansio* serving a port or a ferry crossing to the north Devon coast (PRN 93263; Burnham and Davies 2010, 311–2).

Cast using the lost-wax method, with additional details added cold, the terminal shows the conjoined and addorsed heads of two deities topped by a boar's head, which sits above them like a shared helmet (Fig. 16.2). Raised areas beneath the deities are almost certainly the upper edges of a calyx, making its length of 62 mm a minimum for the complete handle. Unlike the usually matching faces on classical depictions of the god Janus, those on the terminal differ considerably. One is smooth-cheeked and undoubtedly young. As with many objects meant to be viewed in profile, it is asymmetrical seen full-face. From the side the nose seems very small but face-on it has excessively wide nostrils. A curved line below the dot for the pupil represents the iris in the wide-open oval right eye, while the left is plain apart from a dot at the top that is probably the misplaced pupil. In profile the face is so bland that its gender is ambiguous, yet in its implacable blankness it is reminiscent of the face masks of cavalry parade helmets. Full-face it can be identified as Mercury, although this is not the classical god with a winged traveller's hat, but one whose wings rise and curve back like horns, or perhaps like the paired snake heads at the top of a caduceus, so that they double up as the boar's ears and eyes. The other head is of a mature male with a wrinkled forehead, beard and drooping moustache. His eyes are closed, the lids smooth. On his neck the beard is shown by angled grooves. Rudimentary animal ears and horns identify him as Faunus-Pan. The boar's face is plain, with no attempt to represent the pelt. Its crest is small, as are its oval eyes, and short tusks rise from its lower jaw to flank its snout. The jaws were modelled as closed, but are pierced by a suspension hole set behind the tusks.

The same triple-headed motif appears on two keys from excavations in Rheinland-Pfalz, Germany and on three others found in the Rhineland. The three latter are of vague or unknown provenance. One is probably from Nida (Frankfurt-am Main, Hesse), another is from the Eifel region and so lies within the same general area as the two from Rheinland-Pfalz, and one was recorded in an antiquarian collection in Bonn *c.* 1900 (Lehner 1911, Taf. 20, 2; Swinkels 2011). A fourth unprovenanced piece was recorded in an antiquarian collection in Berlin (*ibid.*), but there is little reason to suppose that it came from eastern Germany and it may be yet another Rhineland piece. For a seventh handle of this form from the *limes* see the Appendix.

Only the two excavated pieces from Rheinland-Pfalz are discussed in any detail here. One is from Niederbieber, Kr. Neuwied, on the east bank of the Rhine, the other from Ochtendung, Kr. Mayen, which lies only about 10 km away

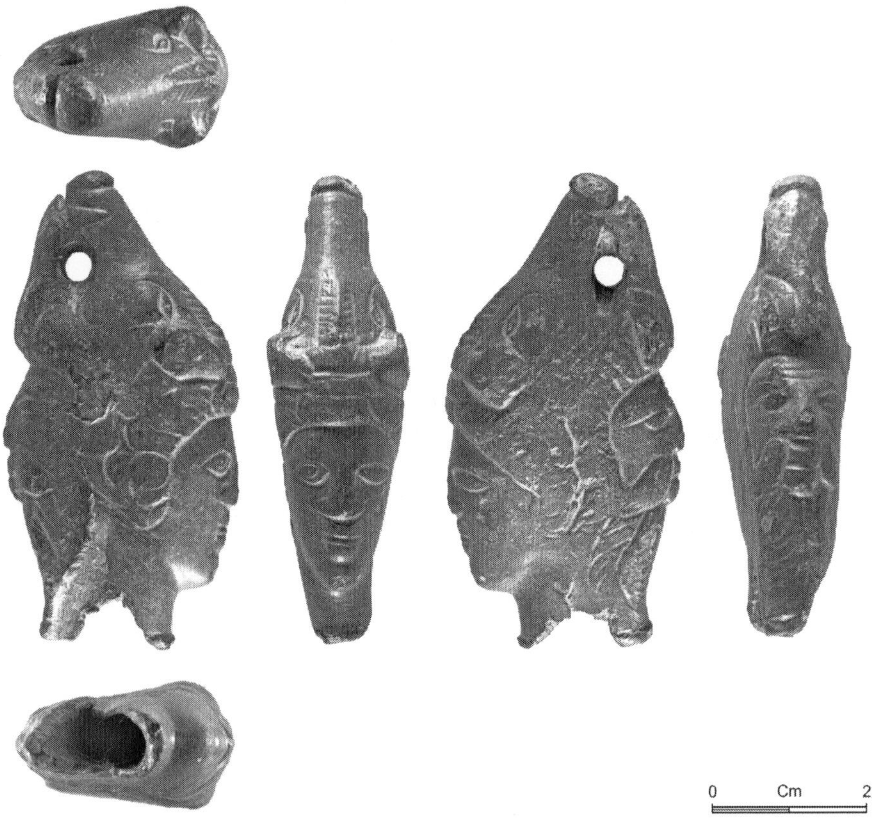

Figure 16.1 Key handle fragment from Font-y-Gary, Rhoose, Vale of Glamorgan. © Portable Antiquities Scheme. Scale 1:1

to the SSW, towards Mayen and the Eifel Hills. The Ochtendung key was found during the excavation of a Roman building. Its handle (length 78 mm), is very worn, but the three heads can still be identified and are set in the same arrangement, again with a suspension hole through the boar's jaw (Menzel 1986, 115, Taf. 118, 273). The shaft of the handle below the heads is worn smooth. The key bit is missing but the long iron shank and total surviving length of the piece (199 mm) suggest that it was an L- or T-shaped lift-key. The Niederbieber key was found in the *vicus* adjacent to the Roman fort built *c.*AD 185 (*ibid.*, 115–6, Taf. 119, 274; Lehner 1991, 284, abb. 3–4, Taf. 20, 1; Cüppers 1990, 501–3). Its damaged bit was probably of lever-lock type (length 144 mm). On the handle (length 91 mm), the heads of the gods rise from a short round calyx set above decorated bead and reel mouldings. The heads are more accomplished than those on the Font-y-Gary fragment, with little, if any, additional detailing added after casting. Mercury's wings are more like short pointed horns rising from his hair, the eyes of Faunus-Pan are clearly closed, and his long beard is thick and flowing. The boar's pelt is defined by short incised grooves. Its snout is more prominent, and there is no suspension hole through the jaws. The quality of this piece suggests that the Font-y-Gary and Ochtendung handles are devolved versions.

The substantial number of figurative key handles found in the region of the upper Rhine and spreading outwards into northern Gaul and along the Rhine to Britain suggests that many of them, like figurative knife handles, were made in workshops in that area, while variants found in other regions may be local products (Kaufmann-Heinimann 1998, 35). With so few examples of the triple-headed key handle design recovered so far, two from within a few miles of each other, another three almost certainly from within the wider region (those from Bonn, the Eifel and Nida), it is highly likely that all were made in the Rheinland-Pfalz, perhaps even in the Niederbieber-Ochtendung area. Alternatively, the more accomplished Niederbieber piece may be an upper Rhine product from which the other handles were copied. Although Niederbieber is on the German *limes*, the recovery of the key from the *vicus* rather than from within the fort, coupled with the lack of any military associations for the Ochtendung key, would seem to rule out a direct link to the Roman military in south Wales for the Font-y-Gary fragment.

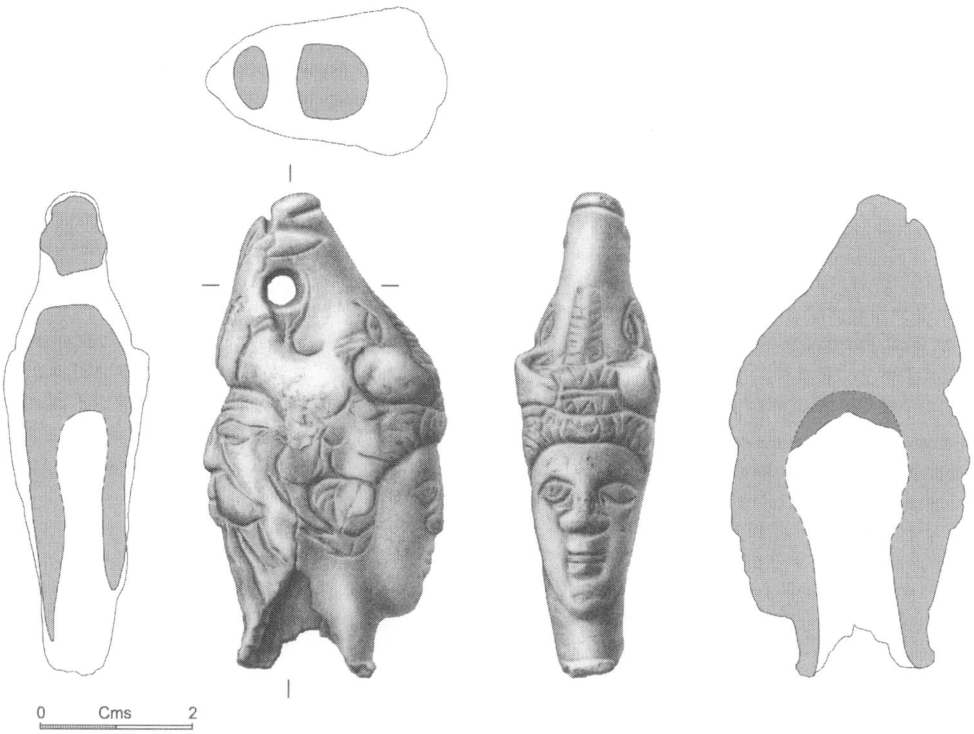

Figure 16.2 Key handle fragment from Font-y-Gary, Rhoose, Vale of Glamorgan. © Amgueddfa Cymru – National Museum Wales; illustrator J. Chadwick. Scale 1:1

The context of the Niederbieber handle points to a third century date for the Font-y-Gary piece. This is confirmed by a lever-lock key with strong stylistic associations to both that was found in a late third century cremation at Krefeld-Gellep (Nordrhein-Westfalen). Its handle is in the shape of a horse's head rising from a round calyx above decorated bead and reel mouldings, and through the animal's jaws is a perforation that matches the one through the jaws of the Font-y-Gary boar. The key was among a group of fittings from a large box and is unlikely to have been new when deposited (Pirling 1989; Pirling and Siepen 2000, 155–6, grave 5393, Taf. 117, 6). Zoomorphic keys in Britain are of similar date, such as a more or less complete lift-key with lion handle from third century or later ditch fill at Baldock (Hertfordshire), a lever-lock key with lion handle from second to third century occupation at Fishbourne (W. Sussex), and a lion handle from Brampton (Norfolk) found with a coin of Faustina I and a repaired samian bowl in a pit dated to the late second or early third century (Stead and Rigby 1986, 136, fig. 59, 370; Cunliffe 1971, 118, fig. 50, 144; Henig 1984a, 407).

Many figurative key and knife handles show an animal emerging from a calyx, a motif that had long been part of the metalworker's repertoire (*e.g.* Kaufmann-Heinimann 1994, Tafn 88–9; Tassinari 1993, form P2210), but the arrangement of calyx and decorated bead and reel mouldings seen on the Niederbieber and Krefeld-Gellep key handles is quite distinctive. It also occurs on an unpierced horse-head key handle from Bavay (Nord) and on a closely similar unprovenanced example in the Getty Museum (Faider-Feytmans 1957, pl. 42, 258; Getty Museum, online art object 35629). The Bavay and Getty Museum horse-head handles stand in the same relationship to that from Krefeld-Gellep as the Niederbieber triple-headed handle does to those from Font-y-Gary and Ochtendung – the modelling is more accomplished and they lack the suspension hole – suggesting that two workshops producing designs within the same tradition are involved here, or one workshop with a gradually devolving series of designs.

The watchers

Zoomorphic key handles are well-represented along the Rhine and in northern Gaul, but depictions of humans usually show them only as victims of wild beasts. The exception is a key handle from Augst in the form of a head of Dionysus-Bacchus, the saviour god who promised rebirth

(Kaufmann-Heinimann 1977, 136, Tafn 145–6, 228; Henig 1984b, 103–6, 110). The animals shown on key handles are part of the same tradition of otherworldly protection as Dionysus-Bacchus, being strong aggressive creatures with chthonic power. Keys bearing such images provided security above and beyond the practical and also implied that what they guarded was particularly important and valuable (Henig 1984a; Kaufmann-Heinimann 1998, 32–7).

Dogs and lions are depicted most frequently, sometimes just as a head, but sometimes with part or almost all of the body as well. The latter are the most striking. A key with a handle in the form of a wakeful hound resting its head on its paws invokes not only fierce household guard dogs – *cave canem* – but also dogs as the ushers of souls to the underworld and Cerberus on watch before the gates of Hades (Henderson 1949, 129, pl. 36, 117; Wilson 1968, 103, pl. 59, 191; Menzel 1960, Tafn 38–9; 1966, Taf. 66; Faider-Feytmans 1957, pl. 42, 262–3; Kaufmann-Heinimann 1994, Taf. 82, 204). The image implies that if earth-bound guard dogs were roused to attack someone illicitly tampering with the key and its lock, then death would follow fast. Like the dog, lions combine the promise of powerful protection with the threat of vicious retaliation and explicit funerary symbolism, as the beast represents the power of all-conquering death. On some key handles the lion is alone, but on others they are shown with prey animals (often just the head), and lions from Brampton in Norfolk and Venthône in Switzerland are depicted savaging humans (Faider-Feytmans 1957, pls 41–2; 1979, pl. 104; Espérandieu and Rolland 1959, 76–7, pl. 51; Henig 1984a; Leibundgut 1976, Taf. 57; 1980, 125–9, pls 154–9; Kaufmann-Heinimann 1977, Tafn 137–45; 1994, Taf. 82; Menzel 1960, Taf. 39; 1966, Taf. 66, 215; 1986, Tafn 119–20). Similar images were used on funerary monuments and as apotropaic images on small personalia (Toynbee 1973, 65–7; Henig and Wickenden 1988, 107; Crummy 2010, 79–81). A key handle that shows a human being mauled by a lion carries the added threat of the fate awaiting a condemned criminal in the arena. It promises not just death, but a legalised, public, and horrific death.

Although not as well-represented as lions, panthers on key handles were also shown either alone or with their prey, and one example from Sierre, Switzerland, lies over a naked youth while savaging an animal head in its jaws (Boon 1974, fig. 32, 6; Faider-Feytmans 1957, pl. 42, 256–7; Leibundgut 1976, 99–100, Tafn 57–8; 1980, 126–7, Tafn 156–8, 165–7). Like the lion, the panther hints at death in the arena, but it is chiefly associated with Dionysus-Bacchus, whose image appears on the key from Augst mentioned above. An openwork key or knife handle from Godmanchester (Cambridgeshire) topped by the head of a Nilotic animal falls into this same group, as in the northern provinces African creatures symbolised both fertility and the dangers of the afterlife (Henig 1984c, 245; Crummy and Philips 2008, 85).

Horses also occur on key handles, although some of those detached from their iron bits may have been classed as knife handles (Faider-Feytmans 1957, pl. 42; Boucher 1973, 150, no. 242; Pirling and Siepen 2000, Taf. 117, 6; Menzel 1986, Taf. 117, 264, Taf. 118, 266, 269, 272). The horse is associated with warfare and the underworld through its links to mother goddesses such as Epona (Green 1992a, 204–7), and on keys it too promises retribution and death to thieves. Stallions are aggressive, as are all horses trained for battle, and the keys show the animals in attack stance, with heads straining forward and ears laid back. When used on the keys of luggage boxes they may represent not just the protection of the contents but travel in general. This is best demonstrated by the chest from Krefeld-Gellep mentioned above. Its horse-head key and four dolphin drop-handles convey an image of travel by sea and land, matching the dolphin and bridled horse on the Wallsend lead shrine of Mercury, patron of travellers, published by Lindsay in 1984 (Pirling and Siepen 2000, 155–6, grave 5393, Taf. 117, 1–4, 6; Allason-Jones 1984).

Within this general context of protective imagery, the form of the triple-headed key handles can be seen as particularly complex, not only because it links three guardians, but also because it unites Gaulish/Germanic imagery with that of Rome. Head symbolism and triple images occur frequently in the iconography of pre-Roman and Roman Germany, Gaul and Britain, with multiplication reinforcing the symbolic power of an individual deity (Green 1992b, 169–205; 1997a, 208–11, 216–20; 1997b, 114–16, 214–16). Often a single image was replicated three times, sometimes each image was varied slightly, sometimes two matching images flank a different third, or sometimes one feature is tripled. One of the most important characteristics of these key handles is that their heads face in three different directions, emphasising their role as vigilant guardians. In this they can be compared to triple-faced deities from Britain, Gaul and Germany (Ross 1958, 13–14 (though see Amit 2012, 34–6); Green 1997a, 214–16).

Another major characteristic of these triple-headed key handles is the merging of human with animal, a feature of imagery in Iron Age and Roman north-west Europe that hints at shamanic dream-states (Creighton 2000, 40–54; Aldhouse-Green and Aldhouse-Green 2005, 128–30). In La Tène art humans may have animal features, such as horns, antlers or wings, and horses may have human heads or appear to pass through human heads (*ibid.*, 128–9; Creighton 2000, 44–5). A mount of Late Iron Age date, probably from the river Ribble near Ribchester, combines the heads of a hawk, a bull and a human (Hildyard 1954; Ross 1958, 33).

Unlike the other protective animals used on key handles, boars could be prey animals, and they appear as such on key handles from Trier and Augst that respectively show a hound with a small boar's head and a lion mauling a boar; a suspension hole like those in the Font-y-Gary and Ochtendung boars passes through the jaws of the Augst boar (Menzel 1966, 88, Taf. 66, 215; Kaufmann-Heinimann 1977, 134, Taf. 144, 222). There is, however, little evidence for the consumption of wild boar meat in Iron Age Gaul, where domesticated pig meat was preferred for feasts and was sometimes deposited in burials (Meniel 1987, 89–100; Green 1992a, 46–7). Strabo noted that Gaulish pigs were exceptionally tall, fierce and fast, and that it was unwise for the inexperienced to approach them (Strabo, *Geographia*, IV.4, 3). Wild boars were sure to be even larger and more aggressive, and they were cult animals, associated with a variety of gods, hence the use of boar images on amulets, helmets, war trumpets and weapons (Thevenot 1968, 156; Foster 1977, 1, 5; Green 1992a, 46, 87–91, 218; 1992b, 139–41). In the north-west provinces the image of a boar as a watchful guardian on a key handle would therefore be as appropriate as that of a hound, lion, panther or stallion, conveying exactly the same message of sudden attack and death.

Mercury and Faunus-Pan had some shared roles in Roman religious belief and more complex cult associations in the north-west provinces. Mercury was patron not only of travellers and eloquence, but also of flocks, commerce and wealth – making him an appropriate deity to appear on keys securing cash or other valuables – and in Gaul, Germany and Britain he was conflated with many local deities, including a boar god and a triple-faced god, while Faunus-Pan, deity of the forest and the natural world in general, is matched by the Celtic antlered god, Cernunnos, who is himself sometimes associated with Mercury and may be shown with stubby horn-like antlers rather than a full rack (Henig 1984b, 18–9; Green 1997a, 120; 1997b, 197–8; *LIMC* VI.1, 552, nos 531–4). Although Johns has pointed out that there are no certain images of Faunus from the ancient world, Ovid clearly identifies him with Pan and describes him as similarly naked, horned and hoofed (Johns 1986, 95–6; Ovid, *Fasti* II, 268–88; IV, 649–64). His horns echo those of the ram/goat who is one of Mercury's companion animals, and there are yet stronger links between the two. Faunus originated as a local pre-Roman rural deity in Latium, but he gained far wider popularity with the spread of the Empire and he acquired Celtic by-names, such as those inscribed on the spoons in the late Roman Thetford treasure (Ovid, *Fasti* II, 193; Johns 1986). Like Mercury he was a protector of flocks and their fertility, and, again most pertinently in the case of key handles, he was regarded as a guardian of treasure (Smits 1946, 56; Johns 1986, 94, 98).

To add to this rich plurality of associations and meanings, in Gaul and Germany there are further links between Mercury and Faunus-Pan-Cernunnos and between Mercury and the unnamed boar-god. In the territory of the Lingones in northern Gaul a stone image dated to *c.*100 BC to *c.*AD 100 from Euffigneix (Haute-Marne) shows a boar with massive crest set vertically on the chest of a deity with a torc around his neck and large eyes carved into his sides, perhaps an example of a trance-state (*CIL* XIII, 223–4; Thevenot 1968, 156–7; Green 1997b, 94–5; Maier 1997, 112). A votive inscription referring to Mercury Moccus was found not far away at Langres (Haute-Marne), and, as Moccus is probably cognate with Welsh *mochyn* (pig), this local deity may be the Romanised form of the god depicted at Euffigneix (*CIL* XIII, no. 5676; Thevenot 1968, 157; Green 1997a, 149; Maier 1997, 112–3, 196). Inscriptions from Bonn point to the Ubii, the Germanic people in the Niederbieber region, worshipping Gebrinius, a local deity whose origins and early cult symbols are obscure but who is shown on an altar as a fully classical Mercury accompanied by his ram and carrying his snake-headed caduceus (Green 1997a, 149; Maier 1997, 126).

Among the Remi, to the north of the Lingones, representations of a triple-faced god occur in some numbers both before and after the Roman conquest of Gaul; in both Reims and Paris he is linked to Mercury, while at Langres the central head of the three bears horns or antlers (*LIMC* VI.1, 553, nos 535–8; Green 1992b, 173–8; 1997a, 115). Two reliefs from Reims show Cernunnos flanked by Mercury and Apollo, and the three gods appear together on an altar from central Gaul, all arguably showing the triple-faced god in separated, Romanised forms (*LIMC* VI.1, 552, nos 531–2, 534).

The triple-faced god of the Remi sometimes united youth and old age, the older face bearded, the younger one smooth-cheeked (Green 1992b, 174), and the same combination of old and young human heads appears on artefacts from Iron Age Germany. When viewed one way up, fragments of gold foil from a grave at Bad Dürkheim (Rheinland-Pfalz) show a youthful beardless face with a vegetal crown, but when reversed an older bearded face appears, while a brooch from Niederschönhausen (Berlin) has a mature male head above the pin mechanism, a naked human body with the disproportionately large head of a youth on the bow, and a returned foot in the form of a ram's head (Amit 2012, 114, illus. 4.19–4.20). The conventional terms used for the various parts of brooches has led to their being illustrated upside down, and when worn foot upmost, as it would have been, this brooch is even more obviously a cult object. The ram's head on the curved foot no doubt represents the indigenous ram-headed snake god, here shown looming over the naked youth, who is suspended upside down with his arms held or tied behind his back like a sacrificial victim, while the older disembodied head sits upright beneath him. Associated with fertility, healing and death, in Gaul the ram-headed snake was associated with both Cernunnos and Mercury (Green 1997a, 195–6).

Amit has noted other Iron Age head pairings apart from youth and age, such as wakefulness and sleep, body and soul, the living world and the underworld, the embodied and the disembodied (as on the Niederschönhausen brooch); open and closed eyes may represent watchfulness and sleep in some contexts but life and death in others (Amit 2012, table 4.2). That at least two such pairings occur on the triple-headed key handles underlines the strong Gaulish/Germanic element used in the depiction and interpretation of Mercury and Faunus-Pan.

The finely nuanced and interlinked imagery used on the key handles cannot avoid – no doubt never intended to avoid – referencing Janus, the Roman two-faced god who looked to both the future and the past, who as *Chaos* was there before the world was formed, who presided over time, beginnings and endings, transitions such as planting, harvest, birth, marriage and death, and liminal structures such as boundaries and bridges, passages and gates, doors and thresholds (Varro, *de lingua latina* VII, 26–7; Ovid *Fasti* I, 63–294; Cicero, *de natura deorum* II, 67). Ovid named him *caelestis ianitor aulae*, gatekeeper of the celestial hall, whose double head could watch over the gates of heaven without losing time by moving (*Fasti* I, 133–40). His cult epithets included *Patulcius* and *Clusius*, Opener and Closer, and his symbols were a staff and a key (*ibid.*, 99, 129–30, 254).

The triple images on these key handles provide explicit and powerful symbols of protection for whatever lay behind their locks. Keys control the threshold, the *limes*, between closed and open, the point of weakness in the transition from exclusion to access. The watchful boar represents aggressive guardianship on behalf of the legitimate owner, and vicious retaliation, perhaps death, to any thief. The Janiform human heads promise to keep watch throughout the ages of life, from youth to old age, awake and asleep, in this world and the next. That they are Mercury and Faunus-Pan-Cernunnos, gods of commerce, treasure, travel, flocks, fertility and the natural world, implies protection in all spheres of existence – urban, rural and wild, human and animal, commercial and domestic, at home and abroad. Their power was recognised and acknowledged by both the fully Romanised and not so Romanised peoples of central and southern Germany and north-east Gaul. All possible areas of weakness were secured.

Conclusion

The interconnected imagery of the three heads on the key handles is a sophisticated union of gods and cult symbols that contrives to combine the iconography of north-east Gaul, the middle Rhine region and Rome into a single unit of watchful protection. Until the Font-y-Gary fragment was found, this complex design seemed to have been pertinent to only a few inhabitants of the middle Rhineland, especially when set against the greater spread of the commercially successful hound, horse and lion key handles with their easily understood zoomorphic representations of protection. With the distribution opened up by the British find, it seems that the unusual and complex triple-headed imagery on these handles was more widely understood and appreciated. No longer localised but still rare, keys bearing the three heads may have had some special association, perhaps being used to lock buildings, rooms or boxes with a particular cultic significance.

Within the context of the German handles, the find from Font-y-Gary is an intriguing *tabula rasa* that raises more questions than it can answer. How did it travel from the continent to South Wales – as a trade item or set within the lock of a box? Is it a stray outlier of a type with a very narrow distribution, or did a cult in the middle Rhine region have followers at a small settlement at Font-y-Gary? Detached from its iron bit – perhaps by decay or perhaps deliberately – was the handle used as a votive offering of some kind? Its full history will probably never be told.

Appendix

As is so often the way in archaeology, after this paper had been submitted to the editors, we learned about another example from Tiel-Passewaaij in the Netherlands. Thanks to the patience of the editors and the generosity of colleagues, there was just time to incorporate it here.

The Tiel-Passewaaij key was a metal-detector find after excavations had finished and roadworks had begun on a

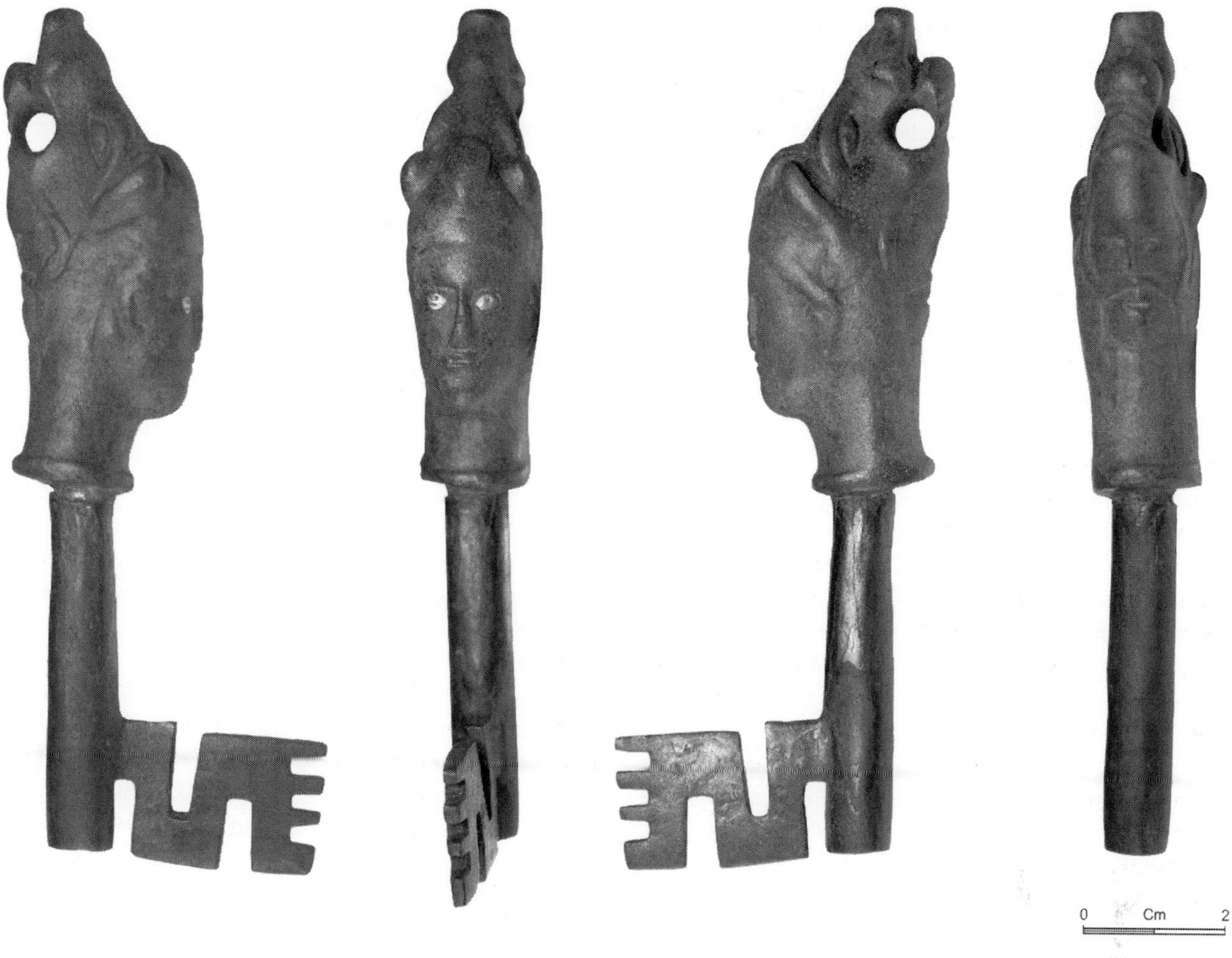

Figure 16.3 Key from Tiel-Passewaaij, Netherlands. © K. Abens. Scale 1:1

major site, where excavations over eight years had uncovered a large cemetery set between by two Batavian rural settlements (Aarts and Heeren 2011, fig. 3.4). The site is about ten kilometres south of the German *limes*. The key came from the area of grave 227, which was surrounded by a ditch that contained a bell-shaped stud from a lock-plate. Ditch-deposition was a regular part of the burial rite at the cemetery, and there is a strong possibility that both stud and key came from the same box. The phased development of the cemetery and the pottery from the area in which it was found suggest the key dates to the late second to third century. The position of the site close to the *limes* matches that of the German sites, while its generally rural nature is similar to that of Ochtendung, and the quantity of military equipment it has produced links it to Niederbieber and is a reminder that many Batavians joined auxiliary units of the Roman army (Aarts and Heeren 2011, 183–5). As with the Rhineland keys, there are hints of a military connection for the example from Tiel, but no proof.

The key is 120 mm long and has an elaborate bit of lever-lock type. The handle is worn, but is clearly devolved while remaining visually stunning (Fig. 16.3). Faunus-Pan has closed eyes, but the features of the head are so reduced that the profile is almost flat, and the moustache and beard are smooth, slightly raised areas, with the moustache resembling a strap rather than hair. The boar's head is rather more detailed, with hints of the pelt on the cheeks; its jaws are pierced. Mercury's features are as usual quite bland, but he has a far more prominent profile than Faunus-Pan, and his eyes are nielloed so that they shine to stress that he is awake and watching (Aarts and Heeren 2011, 187, 189; Swinkels 2011). The heads are set on a short plain base with a projecting tang slotted into the hollow shank of the key.

The plain base of the handle, the method of fixing the handle to the shank and the devolved nature of Pan's face all suggest that this is a late example, probably made in the

Batavian *civitas*, perhaps at Nijmegen, towards the end of the third century. That its provenance closes the gap between Font-y-Gary and the middle Rhineland suggests a route by which the key found in South Wales may have travelled to Britain, but it is probably the latest in date and provides no evidence for an evolutionary transmission of this unusual triple-headed design, with Niederbieber the earliest at one end of the route and Font-y-Gary the latest at the other. Instead it supports the idea that the Font-y-Gary key is a middle Rhineland product.

Acknowledgements

We are grateful to Richard Brewer, Amgueddfa Cymru – National Museums Wales, for suggesting the Font-y-Gary fragment as an appropriate subject for this paper and for providing the illustration, and to Sally Worrell, Portable Antiquities Scheme, who first drew Mark Lodwick's attention to the Niederbieber key. For information about the Tiel key and permission to add it to our paper we would like to thank Alexandra van Steen, Director of the Flipje en Streekmuseum in Tiel, the key's owner, K. Aben, who also generously provided the images, and Stijn Heeren of VU University, Amsterdam, who most kindly provided details of its context and associations.

Bibliography

Aarts, J. G. and Heeren, S. (2011) *Opgravingen bij Tiel-Passewaaij 2. Het grafveld aan de Passewaaijse Hogeweg*, Zuidnederlandse Archeologische Rapporten 41, Archeologisch Centrum Vrije Universiteit. Amsterdam.

Aldhouse-Green, M. and Aldhouse-Green, S. (2005) *The Quest for the Shaman*, Thames & Hudson. London.

Allason-Jones, L. (1984) A lead shrine from Wallsend, *Britannia* 15, 231–2.

Amit, I. (2012) *Headhunting and the Body in Iron Age Europe*, Cambridge University Press. Cambridge.

Boon, G. C. (1974) *Silchester: the Roman Town of Calleva,* David & Charles. Newton Abbot.

Boucher, S. (1973) *Bronzes romains figurés du Musée des Beaux-Arts de Lyon*, de Boccard. Lyon.

Burnham, B. C. and Davies, J. L. (2010) *Roman Frontiers in Wales and the Marches*, Royal Commission on the Ancient and Historical Monuments of Wales. Aberystwyth.

Cicero: Marcus Tullius Cicero, *de Natura Deorum.* Loeb Classical Library edition, trans. H. Rackham (1933), Harvard University Press Cambridge. Mass./London.

Creighton, J. (2000) *Coins and Power in Late Iron Age Britain*, Cambridge University Press. Cambridge.

Crummy, N. (2010) Bears and coins: the iconography of protection in late Roman infant burials, *Britannia* 41, 37–93.

Crummy, N. and Philips, T. (2008) A zoomorphic Roman handle from New Street, Godmanchester. *Proceedings of the Cambridge Antiquarian Society* 97, 83–7.

Cunliffe, B. (1971) *Excavations at Fishbourne, 1961–9*, Report of the Research Committee of the Society of Antiquaries of London 26, 26–7. London.

Cüppers, H. (ed.) (1990) *Die Römer in Rheinland-Pfalz*, Theiss. Stuttgart.

Espérandieu, E. and Rolland, H. (1959) *Bronzes antiques de la Seine-Maritime*, Gallia Supplément 13. Paris.

Faider-Feytmans, G. (1957) *Recueil des Bronzes de Bavai*, Gallia Supplément 8. Paris.

Faider-Feytmans, G. (1979) *Les Bronzes romains de Belgique*, von Zabern, Mainz.

Foster, J. (1977) *Bronze Boar Figurines in Iron Age and Roman Britain*, BAR British Series 39. Oxford.

Getty Museum, online art object 35629: http://tinyurl.com/Limes-Crummy1 accessed 22.6.12

Green, M. (1992a) *Animals in Celtic Life and Myth*, Routledge. London.

Green, M. (1992b) *Symbol and Image in Celtic Religious Art*, Routledge. London.

Green, M. (1997a) *Dictionary of Celtic Myth and Legend*, Thames & Hudson. London.

Green, M. (1997b) *The Gods of the Celts*, Sutton. Stroud.

Henderson, A. M. (1949) Small objects in metal, bone, glass, etc. In J. P. Bushe-Fox *Fourth Report on the Excavations of the Roman Fort at Richborough, Kent*, Report of the Research Committee of the Society of Antiquaries of London 16, 106–60. London.

Henig, M. (1984a) A bronze key handle from Brampton, Norfolk, *Antiquaries Journal* 64, 407–8.

Henig, M. (1984b) *Religion in Roman Britain*, Batsford. London.

Henig, M. (1984c) Amber amulets, *Britannia* 15, 244–6.

Henig, M. and Wickenden, N. P. (1988) A hoard of jet and shale. In P. J. Drury *The Mansio and Other Sites in the Eouth-eastern Sector of Caesaromagus*, Council for British Archaeology Research Report 66, 107–10. London.

Hildyard, E. J. W. (1954) A triple-headed bucket mount, *Antiquaries Journal* 34, 225–9.

Johns, C. (1986) Faunus at Thetford: an early Latian deity in Late Roman Britain. In M. Henig and A. King (eds)

Pagan Gods and Shrines of the Roman Empire, Oxford University Committee for Archaeology Monograph 8, 93–103. Oxford.

Kaufmann-Heinimann, A. (1977) *Die römischen Bronzen der Schweiz I: Augst und das Gebiet der Colonia Augusta Raurica*, von Zabern. Mainz.

Kaufmann-Heinimann, A. (1994) *Die römischen Bronzen der Schweiz V: Neufunde und Nachträge*, von Zabern. Mainz.

Kaufmann-Heinimann, A. (1998) *Götter und Lararien aus Augusta Raurica*, Forschungen in Augst 26, Römermuseum. *Augst.*

Leibundgut, A. (1976) *Die römischen Bronzen der Schweiz II: Avenches*, von Zabern. Mainz.

Leibundgut, A. (1980) *Die römischen Bronzen der Schweiz III: Westschweiz, Bern und Wallis*, von Zabern. Mainz.

Lehner, H. (1911) Ausgewählte Einzelfunde aus Niederbieber, *Bonner Jahrbücher* 120, 279–85.

Maier, B. (1997) *Dictionary of Celtic Religion and Culture*, trans. C. Edwards, Boydell Press. Woodbridge.

Meniel, P. (1987) *Chasse et élevage chez les Gaulois (450–52 av. J. C.)*, Errance. Paris.

Menzel, H. (1960) *Die römischen Bronzen aus Deutschland I: Speyer*, von Zabern. Mainz.

Menzel, H. (1966) *Die römischen Bronzen aus Deutschland II: Trier*, von Zabern. Mainz.

Menzel, H. (1986) *Die römischen Bronzen aus Deutschland III: Bonn*, von Zabern. Mainz.

Ovid: Publius Ovidius Naso, *Fasti*. Loeb Classical Library edition, trans. J. G. Frazer, revd. G. P. Goold (1931), Harvard University Press. Cambridge, Mass./London.

Pirling, R. (1989) Einige ungewöhnliche Grabfunde des 3. Jahrhunderts aus Krefeld-Gellep, *Archäologie im Rheinland 1988*, 86–7

Pirling, R. and Siepen, M. (2000) *Das römisch-fränkische Gräberfeld von Krefeld-Gellep 1983–88*, Germanische Denkmäler der Völkerwanderungszeit 19, Steiner. Stuttgart.

Ross, A. (1958) The human head in insular pagan Celtic religion, *PSAS* 91, 10–43.

Smits, E. C. H. (1946) *Faunus*, Leidsche Uitgeversmaatschappij. Leiden.

Stead, I. and Rigby, V. (1986) *Baldock: the excavation of a Roman and pre-Roman settlement, 1968–72*, Britannia Monograph 7, Society for the Promotion of Roman Studies. London.

Strabo, *Geographia*. Loeb Classical Library vol. 2, trans. H. L. Jones (1923), Harvard University Press. Cambridge, Mass./London.

Swinkels, L. (2011) Note on the Tiel key. In J. G. Aarts and S. Heeren. *Opgravingen bij Tiel-Passewaaij 2. Het grafveld aan de Passewaaijse Hogeweg*, Zuidnederlandse Archeologische Rapporten 41, 189. Amsterdam.

Tassinari, S. (1993) *Il vasellame bronzeo di Pompei*. L'Erma di Bretschneider. Rome.

Thevenot, E. (1968) *Divinités et sanctuaires de la Gaule*, Fayard. Paris.

Toynbee, J. M. C. (1973) *Animals in Roman Life and Art* Thames & Hudson. London.

Varro: Marcus Terentius Varro, *de Lingua Latina*. Loeb Classical Library edition, trans. R. G. Kent (1951), Harvard University Press. Cambridge, Mass./London.

Wilson, M. G. (1968) Other objects of bronze, iron, silver, lead, bone and stone. In B. Cunliffe (ed.) *Fifth Report on the Excavations of the Roman Fort at Richborough, Kent*, Report of the Research Committee of the Society of Antiquaries of London 23, 93–110. London.

17

ART AND SOCIETY: GEMS FROM NORTHERN BRITAIN

Martin Henig

When Lindsay and I began our studies of the art and culture of Roman Britain, the subject was almost hermetically sealed from the archaeological study of the wider Empire. Roman Britain, 'RB' for short, was, as a subject, virtually an island by itself, obeying its own rules which were not those of Classical Archaeology, which concerned itself with the art of the Mediterranean in Greek and Roman times. This was partly the result of the subject being created by Francis Haverfield, R. G. Collingwood and others in the wake of topographers going back to Camden, in which Classical art was scarcely considered seriously. RB sculpture was dismissed for the most part as barbarous, native work; apart from a few pieces from southern England, notably Bath. Most of it was from the north of the province, and was simply of interest because, like the distance slabs from the Antonine Wall, it provided incidental evidence about the Roman army alongside the inscriptions. Small objects, such as gems, earrings, jet pendants and the like, were even more incidental to the great task of reconstructing a historical narrative and establishing the locations of the varied military units. Coins were a partial exception to this derision of the study of small objects because they provided documentary and dating material for that history, alongside inscriptions on stone, while brooches were also (for some reason) regarded as reliable for close dating.

Would-be 'Classical archaeologists' without access to funds found themselves in a real quandary, for there seemed to be no way of pursuing the study of Roman art in Italy, Greece or the East. When one suggested to those who were in charge of Romano-British studies here that one's ambition was to work on Roman minor art in Britain, more than one eyebrow would be raised in disbelief. However, already in the early 1960s, half a century ago, the very first signs of a changing attitude had been observed. Jocelyn Toynbee provided immense encouragement in her monumental works on the art of Roman Britain (1962; 1964). In addition the Royal Commission on Historic Monuments, in its volume devoted to Roman York (RCHM 1962) provided a section on jet, a subject which, much further refined, Lindsay has made her own, revealing the range of materials which were used in this industry (Allason-Jones 1996).

However as far as my particular contribution to this celebration is concerned, Dorothy Charlesworth's paper on 'Roman jewellery found in Northumberland and Durham' published the year before Toynbee's catalogue and the York volume appeared (Charlesworth 1961) has to be my real starting point. It was the first paper to attempt to survey gems and other jewellery from Britain in a regional context and was to form the basis of my own study of gems from British sites, many of which came from the Northern (military) areas of Roman Britain. Naturally, the number of gems has been greatly augmented across the whole province since she wrote, though in this article I will concentrate on England north of the city of York. Several military stations, amongst them Carlisle, Birdoswald, Housesteads, Wallsend, Vindolanda, South Shields and the fort of Newstead in southern Scotland, which have been excavated or, in the case of Newstead, field-walked systematically, to yield an impressive number of gems in the process. Alongside gems, of course, other items of jewellery have been found: for example Charlesworth noted only a few earrings, while others have been found since; this is another important category of *kleinfund* studied by Lindsay (Allason-Jones 1989a).

Such studies, both individual categories of objects and corpora of artefacts from sites such as South Shields (Allason-Jones and Miket 1984) throw a considerable light on social history, and correct some very evident biases, notably that of gender. Earrings, pendants and at least a proportion of the gems assembled in this paper were worn by women, whom students of the *macho* world of Romano-British scholarship have tended to ignore in favour of the army, its forts and weapons, until Lindsay wrote her epoch making book, *Women in Roman Britain* (1989b).

The mainstay of Classical art-historical studies lies in the major arts of sculpture, wall-painting and mosaics. There is plenty of sculpture from the frontier compared to the rest of Britain, much of it from Scotland and Hadrian's Wall assembled in three fascicules of CSIR. A final fascicule on Northern Britain, which will be co-authored and edited by Lindsay, deals with a large area south of the Wall. Most of this material is carved on sandstone and although there are many individual pieces of attractive quality, and all of it reflects the lives of soldiers and their families as well as civilians in the frontier zones, the majority does not reflect the highest standards of *Romanitas*. Nevertheless, the fact that so much of it was commissioned by members of the officer class, some of equestrian or even senatorial rank, renders it important and significant for the study of Roman civilization. I am an enthusiastic advocate for the qualities of the best Romano-British art, but the almost total lack of marble, and the absence of the fine grained limestones of middle and southern England means that Northern sculptors faced a real challenge, which on occasion they triumphantly overcame. As for remains of interior decoration, these are virtually completely lacking.

Notwithstanding, the so-called minor arts remain, and not only reveal the aspirations of their owners but augment evidence from sculpture and epigraphy. While, as is normally the case with site-finds, there are few engraved gems of the very first order as art, the intaglios from these northern forts and their *vici* are of the same standard as the majority of those from the Roman Empire and attest the *Romanitas* of their wearers both in their artistic style and as indicators of literacy amongst them, both because of their use to seal letters and other documents, and because of their varied subject matter.

What follows is, inevitably, a selective survey of Roman art in the north reflected in gems, picking out certain themes, and, where possible, sometimes comparing them with contemporary sculpture from the region in order to indicate how significant they are as a medium for expressing the ethos of the owner.

War and peace: seals for the Roman military community

Some gems have a particularly military resonance like the very fine Eagle and Standards gem from Birdoswald (Henig in Wilmott 1997, 283–4 no. 86) found in association with the Turf Wall and so presumably the prized possession of a centurion or some other legionary officer of the Hadrianic period. Gems such as this reflect the sacred insignia in the shrine of the standards. A small part of a slab depicting an eagle standing on a thunderbolt comes from Corbridge (Phillips 1977, 53 no. 170), bringing to mind an agate intaglio found just south of our study area at Aldborough (*Isurium Brigantium*) portraying an eagle standing on a thunderbolt, below which is a globe (Henig 2007a, no. app. 69). However, a nicolo intaglio from the fort at Binchester, Co. Durham, set in a late first- or early second-century iron ring, depicting an eagle eviscerating a hare upon an altar (Henig in Ferris 2010, 404, pls 89 and 90) surely also alludes to Jupiter and the triumph of Imperial Rome as does a similar gem from Vindolanda (Birley and Greene 2006, 109–10, no. 50). Of course Jupiter is also represented in his usual guise of Capitoline Jupiter on gems from Vindolanda (Birley and Greene 2006, 66, no. 1) and Newstead (Elliot and Henig 1982, 297 no. 1) which depict him seated or standing (Elliot and Henig 1982, 297 no. 13) with his eagle at his feet. Actual images of the god in stone or bronze were assuredly to be found in military headquarters buildings.

It is not surprising that images of warriors are frequently encountered, many of them in the aspect of Mars, in his various guises, or as heroes who might have been recognised for what they were or else could have been interpreted as the god. The Mars Ultor type, in which the god stands on guard to the front, spear in one hand and supporting a shield with his other, is represented by an intaglio from Corbridge (Henig 2007a, no. 79) well matched by representations of Mars on sculptured reliefs from Housesteads (Coulston and Phillips 1988, 26 no. 67) and Risingham (Phillips 1977, 72–4 no. 215).

Individual soldiers might have preferred to see themselves more actively engaged in heroic endeavour, like the hero who is shown on a nicolo gem from the fort at Vindolanda, putting on a greave (Birley and Greene 2006, 68 no. 4). Whether its owner recognised it as Achilles or as his own heroic self is unknown. Other Achilles figures holding the armour of Thetis are the subject of a Corbridge gem (Henig 2007a, no. 457) and another from Watercrook in Cumbria (Henig 2007a, app. 154). In addition to these, another heroic soldier, possibly intended for Achilles or Alexander the Great is attested on gems from Chesters

(Henig 2007a, no. 468), Vindolanda (Birley and Greene 2006, 76 no. 13) and Housesteads (Henig in Rushworth 2009, 468–70 no. 422). A head and torso of this youthful heroic type is the subject of a first century sardonyx found on Arthur's Seat, Edinburgh which it is tempting to associate with Flavian military activity (Henig 2007a, no. 467) and we might note a later example in red jasper from the amphitheatre or *ludus* at Caerleon (*ibid.*, no. 466). All of these could of course have been 'read' by their owners as Mars, though the youth holding a sword on a nicolo intaglio from Corbridge was surely recognisable by even a moderately well-educated army officer as Theseus with the sword of his father Aegeus (*ibid.*, no. 456).

The heroic persona of Hercules, god and hero, is often found on gems, though surprisingly only a few are known from our region. A sardonyx mounted in a silver ring from Corbridge depicts him standing, easily recognisable from the club he is holding (Henig 2007a, no. 428). A rather more accomplished intaglio, a cornelian of Hadrianic date from Vindolanda, depicts the head of a youthful Hercules, with lion-skin draped around the neck (Birley and Greene 2006, 72 no. 9); there is a similar representation of about a century later, on a cameo from South Shields, which, as we shall see, has relevance to political and military events at that time. Hercules of course appears on several sculptures from the Wall region, including the vigorous relief of Hercules fighting the Lernian hydra from Corbridge (Phillips 1977, 3–4 no. 6). We might expect to find gems depicting his labours, especially the ever popular fight between Hercules and the Nemean lion (note the altar from Housesteads; Coulston and Phillips 1988, 13 no. 30).

To return to Mars, one of the most popular types on gems but not on sculpture, shows him nude apart from a loin-cloth, striding purposefully along and shouldering a trophy; there are examples of the *Mars Gradivus* type from Corbridge (Henig in Bishop and Dore 1988, 217–8 no. 14), Vindolanda (Birley and Greene 2006, 113 no. 55) and Housesteads (Henig in Rushworth 2009, 469–70 no. 425). A striking variant is a chalcedony intaglio from Red House near Corbridge in which a similar trophy-bearing figure wears a military tunic and may be intended to show not Mars but rather his son Romulus, founder of Rome, and thus alluding to historic myth (Henig 2007a, no. app. 156).

These intaglios all evoke victory and the goddess or personification of Victoria is common in glyptic art. A typical example is the cornelian intaglio from Hardknott, Cumbria depicting Victory in her typical pose holding out a wreath and shouldering a trophy (Henig in Bidwell *et al.* 1999, 119–20 no.55). A red jasper intaglio from an early Antonine context at the Tofts site, Piercebridge, Co. Durham depicts Victory signing a shield proclaiming the success of Roman arms (Henig 1988, 46, pl. 2). An even finer intaglio, a cornelian from Newstead (Elliot and Henig 1982, 298 no. 24), figures Victory crowning a trophy and may have been given to the owner for services in war, possibly the wars of Marcus Aurelius, like the well-known cornelian intaglio depicting Victory not only signing a shield but standing before a trophy on a gem which may have belonged to the later emperor Pertinax found at Lullingstone, Kent (Henig 2007b, 4 and col. pl. I). Alternatively, as Adrian Marsden has proposed, it may date to the British campaigns of the Severans (Marsden 2011, 432 and see below). In sculpture the striking reliefs of Victory from Housesteads, perhaps surmounting gateways in front of or within the fort (Coulston and Phillips 1988, 36–8 nos 99 and 100) and the superb inscribed plaque in Durham from Lanchester, depicting a pair of victories standing on armillary globes holding up a *corona civica* which contains the name of *Legio XX* (RIB I no. 1063), emphasise the importance of Victory to the army.

Other deities popular with soldiers included Minerva. Like Mars, she is portrayed with spear and shield, for example on intaglios from Carlisle (Henig in Padley 1991, 158 no. 589), Vindolanda (Birley and Greene 2007, 94–5 no. 32), Bearsden on the Antonine Wall (Henig 2007a, no. app. 125), and at Newstead (Henig 2007a, no. 243). However, while on this subject, it is important not to develop too deterministic an attitude to the devices which people chose for their signet rings. We should remember that Minerva was widely evoked by civilians, including women, as a protective deity (see below).

Figures of Minerva were sometimes conflated with Victory and Fortuna as on intaglios from Housesteads (Henig in Rushworth 2009, 468–70 no. 422) and Vindolanda (Birley and Greene 2006, 108 no. 49). Such a highly syncretised figure is carved on a relief from Birrens, though here she wears the mural crown of a territorial goddess and is equated with Dea Brigantia, while an *omphalos* by her side is an attribute of Juno Caelestis (Keppie and Arnold 1984, 7–8 no. 12).

Fortuna was, indeed, a significant power in nature, steering the fate of the individual with her rudder and she is a common signet device, represented on gems for example from Poltross Burn milecastle (Henig 2007a, no. 318) and Chesters (*ibid.*, no. 325). The goddess was frequently evoked upon inscriptions and there is a splendid statue of the goddess from the commandant's bath house at Birdoswald – men were especially vulnerable when naked – (Coulston and

Phillips 1988, 7–8 no. 15) and another from Castlesteads (Coulston and Phillips 1988, 8 no. 16). A darker deity was Nemesis, whose shrine was often in an amphitheatre, as at Chester (Henig 2004, 6 no. 13) but she appears on intaglios in our region from the annexe of the fort at Mumrills (Henig in Keppie *et al.* 1995, 661–2 illus. 37) and Newstead (Elliot and Henig 1982, 297 no. 10) and at the latter site an amphitheatre has tentatively been identified.

Some devices on gems, while not attested on local sculpture, would have been familiar to soldiers from the coins they handled every day. Aequitas with her scales appears on a red jasper from Vindolanda (Birley and Greene 2006, 85–6 no. 23), and is also recorded on an intaglio from the fortress at York (Henig 2007a, no. app. 80). She is evoked on another intaglio from Vindolanda depicting a *modius* (corn-measure) containing the traditional crops of Rome, wheat and poppy; over the *modius* are the scales of equity (Henig 2007a, no. app. 201; Birley and Greene 2006, 73 no. 10). Fair-dealing was a premier military quality; so was *Fides Publica*, associated with the corn-supply, the soldier's 'daily bread' and identified with the goddess Ceres, who is figured on gems from Vindolanda (Birley and Greene 2006, 74 no. 11 and 86–7 no. 24), Corbridge (Henig 2007a, no. 266) and Bearsden (*ibid.*, no. 271). She has a male equivalent, *Bonus Eventus*, who is likewise concerned with successful harvests and success in general, with examples from Vindolanda (Birley and Greene 2006, 84–5 no. 22; 115 no. 61), Poltross Burn milecastle (Henig 2007a, no. 207), and Chesters (*ibid.*, no. 211). One representation from Ravenglass in Cumbria depicts *Bonus Eventus* with his usual ears of corn but has a wreath of Victory substituted for his offering dish (*ibid.*, no. app. 110).

Romanitas: living in a sacred landscape

One remarkable gem, a nicolo evidently from an early third-century context at Vindolanda, depicts the shepherd Faustulus discovering Romulus and Remus being suckled by the *Lupa Romana* (Birley and Greene 2006, 106–7 no. 47, scene not identified). This is paralleled by the relief in the pediment of a shrine evidently dedicated to Roma Aeterna at Corbridge (Phillips 1977, 12 no. 37). The side of that shrine depicted a faun playing *auloi* (double pipes) flanked by two craters from which vines are springing in luxuriant growth (Phillips 1977, 12–13 no. 38). The scene, as Phillips points out, is evocative of Virgil's description of the site of Rome inhabited by fauns and nymphs (*Aeneid* 8,314), and indeed fauns and nymphs are often to be seen on gems, strongly suggesting that the wearers were sophisticated and educated enough to understand the mythological contexts of their chosen seal-devices.

Many other gems evoke this sacro-idyllic landscape, amongst them an intaglio from Newstead which figures a satyr playing *auloi* (Henig 2007a, no. 179). In the same category and also from Newstead is the nicolo intaglio figuring a dancing maenad, likewise playing *auloi* (Elliot and Henig 1999, 394–6 no. 34 illus. 2). The other rustic musical instrument which would have evoked the origins of Rome was the pan-pipes and an intaglio from Carlisle portrays a satyr with this instrument which he plays as his hound runs alongside him (Henig in Caruana 1992, 98 no. 1). Another intaglio, from Vindolanda depicts Pan, probably also holding pan pipes although details are not very clear (Birley and Greene 2006, 95–6 no. 34). There are intaglios from Corbridge (Henig 2007a, no. 493), Mumrills (*ibid.*, no. 494) and Vindolanda (Birley and Greene 2006, 98–9 no. 36 and 105–6 no. 46) which figure offerings being made at small shrines in the countryside. Although these little structures are doubtless envisaged as being in the Italian countryside, they would pass muster for the very many little shrines dedicated, often, to native gods around the forts. One such deity was Cocidius, variously equated with Silvanus and Mars, who had a major sanctuary at Bewcastle. One intaglio depicting a huntsman holding up a dead hare before his hound, from South Shields (Henig 2007a, no. 184) has indeed received attention from amongst others Professor I. A. Richmond and Dr David Smith, and I would concur that Silvanus Cocidius was very probably intended. A more conventional image of Silvanus holding a falx and accompanied by a hound has been found at Vindolanda (Birley and Greene 2006, 80 no. 18).

The non-appearance of obviously native deities, whose names are recorded on altars, may be put down to the fact that the tradition of seal cutting remained rather more conventionally classical than did sculpture, at least in the Latin West. But figures of Mars on seals could readily have been taken by their owners as representations of Mars Thincsus for example (see Coulston and Phillips 1988, 65 no. 161), while mother goddesses (Coulston and Phillips 1988, 67–73 nos 164–73) might have been recognised in gems depicting Fortuna or Ceres. The largest gold ring in the Backworth hoard (Charlesworth 1961, 24 no. 1) bears, simply inscribed in the gold of the bezel, the name of the *Matres Cocoae* to whom the cache was evidently dedicated, and thus the ring was not intended for further use by a mortal.

On the other hand, it has been noted that Bacchus and his entourage are rare in official art, on sculpture and in inscriptions but frequently encountered on mosaics and frescoes and in the minor arts of metalwork and especially gems which are relevant here (Hutchinson 1986). A beautiful red jasper from Carlisle evidently depicts a satyr holding the infant Bacchus (McCarthy, Padley and Henig 1982, 84) while from Vindolanda an intaglio with a related subject, portrays a satyr dangling its own baby (Birley and Greene 2006, 79 no. 17). There is a superb intaglio from Corbridge (Plate 7; Henig 2007a, no. 153; CO22962), depicting a satyr, or perhaps Bacchus himself, contemplating a theatre mask. A spirited study of the head of a maenad, or perhaps Ariadne, from Vindolanda (Birley and Greene 2006, 81–2 no. 19; Henig 2007a, no. 287) is also a striking example of glyptic art. There are also many gems depicting satyrs (Henig 2007a, nos 167, 171–4, 176, app. 41) from Carlisle, Newstead, Castlesteads, South Shields, Chesters, Cappuck and Vindolanda. As such figures were often included on gems depicting rural sacrifices, even when a satyr is shown by himself, he may indicate the wearer's awe of wild nature, whether he or she was a soldier stationed in a fort or a civilian dwelling in the *vicus*.

Sacrifice was central to Roman religion. A small but important intaglio from Old Penrith depicts a sow wearing a sacrificial belt around her waist (Henig in Austen 1991, 178–9 no. 614). Pigs were important creatures in cult and Aeneas of course sacrificed a white sow with her piglets when he landed in Italy at Lanuvium as is shown on the *Ara Pacis* (Zanker 1988, 203–4, fig. 157), while of course the Bridgeness distance slab from the Antonine Wall portrays a *suovetaurilia* (Keppie and Arnold 1984, 27–8 no. 68). This was the ritual sacrifice to Jupiter of a boar, ram and bull carried out by the legate of *Legio II Augusta*, presumably at the completion of their work. Female animals would have been offered for a major goddess such as Ceres (see Ovid, *Fasti* I, 349). Gems depicting a bull, as in the case of a black jasper intaglio from Vindolanda (Henig 2007a, app. 176; Birley and Greene 2006, 75 no. 12), or a ram in that of a cornelian from Newstead (Henig 2007a, no. 604) very probably possessed the same sacrificial allusion.

A major concern for soldiers and civilians in the forts and civil settlements was food supply. An intaglio depicting a corn-measure has already been mentioned. Another intaglio, this time from Carlisle shows a countryman hand-reaping (Henig in McCarthy 1990, 144–5 no. 287). Two grains of corn on a woman's ring in the Backworth Hoard (Henig 2007a, no. 722) likewise express this concern and inevitably invoke Ceres and Bonus Eventus.

The pleasures of life

There was a fair social mixture amongst the military community of northern Britain and we need to remember that the commanders of units, those of equestrian rank, and some others, were amongst the elite of the Empire. A garnet intaglio set in a gold ring and lost by a Hadrianic prefect at Housesteads depicted a theatre mask (Charlesworth 1969; Henig 2007a, no. 525). Another intaglio, in red jasper depicting a pair of confronted theatre masks is known from South Shields (Henig 2007a, no. 526). A third intaglio, from the fort at Kirkbride in Cumbria actually figures a dramatist (*ibid.*, no. app. 7). There cannot have been many opportunities to indulge in thespian tastes in northern Britain, so maybe we can infer an element of nostalgia here. Equally, as far as is known, there were no hippodromes in Britain apart from one recently located at Colchester, one suspected in London and perhaps one or two other major cities, but a cornelian intaglio from Chesters, now lost, depicted four chariot teams in the Circus Maximus at Rome (*ibid.*, no. 513) and thereby revealed the sporting enthusiasm of a senior officer, if it does not merely symbolise the changing fortunes of life, 'all the world is a circus!'. Another intaglio, from Housesteads figured a racing chariot drawn by two horses, a *biga*, being driven by Victory (Henig in Rushworth 2009, 469–70 no. 427). The obvious context is the circus, though it may simply have symbolised the owner's own (victorious) career. We may note in passing that Pliny the Younger employed the device of a *quadriga* as a signet device (Pliny, *Ep.* X, lxxiv).

Much better attested, at least on inscriptions, is hunting, sometimes associated with the god Silvanus; who can forget Gaius Micianus's altar from Bollihope Common in County Durham (RIB I no. 1041) giving thanks to the god for allowing him to bag a remarkably fine boar which had eluded previous prefects of the *Ala Sebosiana*? Silvanus is depicted upon an intaglio from Vindolanda (Birley and Greene 2006, 80 no. 18). The goddess Diana was of course especially concerned with the chase, and is represented by a gem set in a silver ring found at Chollerford (Henig 2007a, no. 255) and in a somewhat similar guise on a relief found between Vindolanda and Housesteads (Coulston and Phillips 1988, 4 no. 6). The Silvanus-Cocidius gem from South Shields has already been mentioned, but other gems depict men carrying huntsman's staves from which hares or other kills would be suspended, including fine examples from Castlesteads and Housesteads (Henig 2007a, nos 185 and 186). An intaglio from Newstead is cut with a spirited representation of a running hound (*ibid.*, no. 625).

One of the best known palaeographic discoveries of recent decades from northern Britain, is the letter from Claudia Severa to her friend Sulpicia Lepidina inviting her to a birthday party (*Tab. Vindol.* II. 291: Bowman 1994, 127 no. 21). As in military circles today the social round of entertaining and partying would have filled much of the spare time of the officer class and its dependents. Perhaps the black jasper intaglio from Vindolanda depicting Methe (Birley and Greene 2006, 68 no. 4) who protected one from intoxication actually belonged to Sulpicia Lepidina. The other three examples of intaglios depicting Methe come from Bath and Sea Mills in Somerset and Caerwent in Monmouthshire (Henig 2007a, nos 343–5) all in southern Britain and are likewise of late first or early second century date.

Of course women would have been prominent in the North as elsewhere as Lindsay has shown in her magisterial survey, and the jewellery of well-off women would undoubtedly have included gems. The only amber ring yet found in Britain, a piece of delicate and beautiful jewellery surely designed to be worn by a rich lady, was found at Carlisle and bears a head of Minerva in relief on its bezel (McCarthy *et al.* 1982, 88–9, pl. iva). This was an object of the highest luxury, probably carved in a specialist workshop in Aquileia, though a rarity even in Italy. It was not designed for hard wear but for show at a party. Another very expensive and large gem is the famous cameo from South Shields, carved in Indian sardonyx and depicting a bear with its prey (Henig 2007a, no. 735). In style it is suggestive of a Severan date and in all probability was set in a brooch, worn by a woman in the suite of the empress Julia Domna. I know of only one other cameo depicting a bear, from Caesarea Maritima in Israel (unpublished, and not so fine), so even the subject appears rare. In any case, cameos of this quality are excessively uncommon as site finds and that has meant that the gem has hardly been appreciated in context. In quality it is comparable to so-called *staatskameen* of the time, and it too was surely carved in a studio in southern Europe. It may have had a protective aspect, driving away evil forces, but that would have been secondary to its artistic value. A more normal cameo, but certainly highly valued as it was set in a third-century gold ring, is the Medusa mask from Vindolanda (Henig 2007a, no. 730; Birley and Greene 2006, 123 no. 30, SF 18), and of course this device also well-known on jet pendants from York and elsewhere (e.g. Allason-Jones 1996, 24 nos 1–3) and was certainly apotropaic.

Several items are clearly love tokens and these include the only jet cameo from the Wall region, a double-sided pendant depicting facing male and female heads on the obverse and the *dextrarum iunctio*, conjoined male and female right hands (Henig 2007a, no. 759). It must have been a marriage or betrothal gift carved in the late third century, probably in York. The clasped hands are a common device, especially in cameo where they often carry messages wishing the couple harmony and good fortune (cf. *ibid.*, no. app. 30).

A red jasper intaglio from Bewcastle depicting a female portrait in the style of Faustina the younger or Lucilla (Henig in Austen 1991, 33–4 no. 153) may have served the same purpose. It is more likely that it is the portrait of a girl wearing the current late second century coiffure than an empress and the same goes for a similar gem from Chesters, displaying the portrait of a young woman with a slightly more mature visage (Henig 2007a, no. 483). Such fairly conventional female portraits are common elsewhere, both in intaglio and in cameo: an intaglio in Oxford bears a portrait inscribed *έκγρια* ('the lady') (Henig and MacGregor 2004, 71 no. 5.51) and a cameo in a private collection bears the legend *τέ καλέ* ('for the beautiful girl') (Henig 1990, 25 no. 45), both suggestive that we are dealing with the Roman equivalent of portrait miniatures rather than images of ladies of the Imperial court, except that the custom seems to have been to present these little works of art to the betrothed. A gold ring from Vindolanda containing a six sided cornelian intaglio, deliberately leached and inscribed on the sides, ANIMA MEA ('my soul') is another charming love token given by a man to his beloved (Birley and Greene 2006, 123 no. 32; Henig 2007a, no. 746).

Space must be found for symbolism, for seals almost more than other types of object were personal, expressing the identity of the owner. Indeed even with the gems discussed above there may have been truly personal choices exercised. Was the raven depicted on a lovely agate intaglio set in a silver ring from Vindolanda (Birley and Greene 2006, 67 no. 3) selected as a thereomorphic image of Apollo, and thus a symbol of prophecy, the *avatar* of a non-Roman deity like the Teutonic Odin (bearing in mind the fact that the fort was garrisoned by a Batavian regiment), or was it simply the image of the owner's favourite pet? A fine study of two confronted long legged, and fairly long necked birds, possibly ostriches, set in a second century gold ring and found near Carlisle (Henig 2007a, no. 667) is also a highly individual choice. The Roman passion for sea-food is well known but were the two shrimps on a red jasper from Birdoswald (Henig in Wilmott 1997, 285 no. 88) and the single shrimp on an intaglio from Bearsden (Henig 2007a, no. app. 193) more than mere pleasing conceits?

Concerns about the Evil Eye resulted in the wearing of Medusa heads, as we have seen, though only one example in cameo is recorded. Another common specific against baleful forces was the combination of animal and human elements such as the *hippalectryon* from Castlesteads, Cumbria (Henig 2007a, no. 382). Other examples include the combination of Silenus head with elephant mask from Corbridge (Plate 8; Henig 2007a, no. 379, CO22827) and another from the same site in which an eagle head is combined with masks of Silenus and a maenad (*ibid.*, no. 378).

In a society where death was common, including death of the young, much more often from disease or in the case of women in childbirth, as can be attested in numerous inscriptions, it is not surprising to find on a small nicolo intaglio set in a gold ring from the Backworth hoard a mourning figure leaning on an inverted torch (Henig 2007a, no. 523). Such figures are often equated with Cupid and there is another example in which the mourning figure is winged from Vindolanda (Birley and Greene 2006, 112 no. 53). The device is common on cameos though none of these has yet been found in North Britain, and is essentially borrowed from funerary art (see Tufi 1983, 48 no. 77).

Natives and strangers

We know from inscriptions of a unit of Hamian archers from Syria at Carvoran and of individual traders such as the Palmyrene Barathes who buried his Catuvellaunian wife at South Shields (Phillips 1977, 90–1 no. 247). A few intaglios from the North suggest the presence of foreigners from as far away as the East Mediterranean. For example, a sardonyx intaglio from Corbridge depicts Zeus Heliopolitanos, the great god or *baal* of Baalbek (Henig 2007a, no. 351), an important outlier of such gems so common in the Levant. Iao, a deity who is mainly to be found on magical amulets which frequently bear this name or the magical word 'Abraxas', another possible name for the god, is the subject of a gem set in a silver ring from a cache of jewellery secreted in the strong room in the headquarters of Great Chesters (Aesica) fort (*ibid.*, no. 367). Several Mithraea are known on the Wall, and Mithraic gems are attested but to date none has been recorded here or elsewhere in Britain. The Egyptian gods were more widely disseminated, and there is very probably a representation of Jupiter Sarapis from Vindolanda (Birley and Greene 2006, 82–3 no. 20; Henig 2007a, no. 355). Unfortunately there is a chip above the god's head just where his distinctive corn-measure would have been. There is no doubt about the bust of a youthful Heliosarapis likewise from Vindolanda combing the solar rays of the sun-god, the corn-measure of Sarapis, the horns of Ammon and the serpent staff of Asklepios (Birley and Greene 2006, 101–2 no. 41; Henig 2007a, no. app. 148). A glass intaglio from Vindolanda displays a head of the Libyan deity Jupiter Ammon (Birley and Greene 2006, 110 no. 51). The sun god, himself, was venerated quite early in Rome but certainly became more widely venerated under oriental influence, though it is a matter for dispute whether the fine head on a cornelian from Carzield (Henig 2007a, no. 27) or even the gem found by Curle at Newstead depicting a figure of the sun god saluting the dawn (Elliot and Henig 1982, 298 no. 16; Henig 2007a, no. 30) are strictly to be classed as oriental.

No early Christian gem has yet been identified so far north. I have deliberately excluded York and Yorkshire from the survey, but it is worth mentioning that a cornelian intaglio depicting two fish hanging from an anchor has recently been identified in the York *colonia* (Henig 2011, 9), showing that Christianity was almost certainly present in our region by the late third century.

Gems and politics

This paper has treated gems, as they most usually were viewed in antiquity, as belonging to the personal sphere, but they were displayed publicly and intaglios were employed for sealing. A starting point has to be another intaglio apparently depicting a bust of Serapis flanked by busts of the Dioscuri found at Castlesteads, Cumbria (Henig 2007a, no. 358). The inscription of three Greek letters E Z C standing for *εις Ζεγc Cαραπιc* 'one Zeus Sarapis' alludes to the cult, but as the head of the bearded figure is so like that of the Emperor Septimius Severus who assumed a strong identity with the Egyptian god, and the date of the gem as judged by style is early third century, it probably shows Severus and his sons who campaigned in North Britain and Scotland from 208–211 when Severus died in York. Indeed the gem is close to the appearance and style of lead sealings employed by the expedition at this time. It was, incidentally, very probably during this period when the bear cameo from South Shields was lost. From South Shields there is an intaglio depicting the young Caracalla as Mercury and a sardonyx cameo of Hercules whose features again recall Caracalla, who seems to have modelled himself on this saviour god (Henig 1986). Two important additions to this evidence comprise what seems to be a portrait of the young Geta, on a red jasper from Birdoswald (Henig in Wilmott 1997, 284–5 no. 87) and, even more significant, a red jasper depicting Caracalla at about the time he became a colleague of his father from Newstead

(Elliot and Henig 1999, 395 and 397 no. 36, illus. 3). This lends credence to the probability that the fort at Newstead was recommissioned for the campaign.

One other portrait gem, a bearded Antonine head on a nicolo from Vindolanda (Birley and Greene 2006, 112–3 no. 54), seems to depict Commodus and was surely worn by someone with connections with one of his governors Ulpius Marcellus, Pertinax or Clodius Albinus. Such a seal which implies support for the regime is very likely to have been bestowed on the soldier or official who subsequently wore it as a mark of favour, and may, indeed, have been employed to seal official correspondence and packages sent out from the fort. In this connection we might note a deed for the sale of a slave from Dura Europos on the Euphrates, and dated to AD 243, which bears the authenticating sealing of an official, the portrait of the reigning emperor Gordian III (Welles *et al.* 1959, 142–9 no. 28, pl. lxxi.2).

Manufacture

Lindsay has been a pioneer in her work on one glyptic craft that was practiced in Britain, jet-carving, and the Vindolanda pendant was most probably carved in a workshop in York in the later third century; although there is a little evidence for jet working elsewhere in the north, for instance at Binchester (Ferris 2010, 89, 564), such a refined object is most likely to have been crafted in a major centre. As has been plain from the above survey most gems follow a standardised pattern, and display common types whether they have been cut in the Levant, the Balkans, Italy or elsewhere. We can on occasion isolate workshops, and show how widespread the manufacture of seals was through the provinces, including Britain, while at the same time admitting that many gems were imported either commercially or on the fingers of their wearers. Aquileia has long been recognised as a major centre of production not just of intaglios but of amber objects. A number of workshops have been tentatively suggested for Roman Britain (Henig 2009), including one in Bath of the later first century. The Snettisham Roman jeweller's hoard is suggestive of another in Norfolk in the mid-second century.

However for the purposes of this paper, the one identifiable purely local workshop is one which specialised in the cutting of red jasper intaglios in a highly decorative and patterned manner. The putative Silvanus-Cocidius gem (Henig 2007a, no. 184) is perhaps the finest gem ascribed to the workshop, others are a *Bonus Eventus* gem from Castlesteads (*ibid.*, no. 185), a satyr holding an infant Bacchus from Carlisle (McCarthy *et al.* 1982, 84) and Bacchus contemplating a mask (Henig 2007a, no. 153), a figure making an offering (*ibid.*, no. 493) and probably a Mars Ultor (*ibid.*, no. 79) all from Corbridge (cf. Henig 2009, 145–6). I have tended to locate the workshop in the bustling city of Carlisle, although on the model of the jeweller's hoard from Snettisham, it was very possibly peripatetic, and there is suggestive evidence for a jeweller from the vallum, near Halton Chesters in the form of a shale mould in which gold leaf could be impressed (Charlesworth 1961, 7–8).

In addition it is tempting to suggest that seal cutters formed part of the entourage of Septimius Severus and that the portraits of the young Geta from Birdoswald, Caracalla from Newstead and possibly other gems were cut here including some from further south in Britain which could have been cut for distribution in York, or even further north (Henig 2009, 146–7). Marsden, studying both numismatic and glyptic evidence, has recently strongly supported the theory that there were gem-cutters, and probably more than one at work in Britain producing gems associated with the Severan campaigns (Marsden 2011). Even though key gems he cites from Stainfield near Lincoln and Caistor St Edmund outside Norwich were found much further south that does not mean the work was not done much further north, at York or even South Shields.

What conclusions can be drawn for this very far from complete review of the evidence of gems from Britain north of York? Certainly it reveals a significant repository of art and reveals refined tastes at least amongst the literate and the educated serving in, or connected in some way with the army, the Roman military community as we should call it. This paper has indeed given me the opportunity to expand on an earlier exploration of art in that community of men and women, soldiers and civilians, natives and foreigners (Henig 1999) concentrating on one group of material, surely as important as any for really understanding the culture. I have always been delighted by the range of evidence produced at Vindolanda which should be seen alongside with the now famous tablets as evidence for a highly literate culture. Quite a number of these gems were discussed by me long ago, but others have turned up since I last had regular contact with the site. But tireless field walkers at Newstead and excavations at forts throughout the region have been and are considerably expanding our information.

Many, perhaps most, catalogues of gems are of non-provenanced, or ill-provenanced stones. A great deal of information can be obtained by meticulous study of such material, but one of the key aims of any archaeological study is lost, that is to tie artistic and archaeological material in with the lives of the people who owned and used them. This has of course always been central to Lindsay Allason-Jones' own work and this paper salutes her achievements in the area to which she has devoted so many years of study.

Bibliography

Allason-Jones, L. (1989a) *Ear-rings in Roman Britain,* BAR British Series 201. Oxford.

Allason-Jones, L. (1989b) *Women in Roman Britain.* London.

Allason-Jones, L. (1996) *Roman Jet in the Yorkshire Museum.* York.

Allason-Jones, L. and Miket, R. (1984) *The Catalogue of Small Finds from South Shields Roman Fort.* Newcastle upon Tyne

Austen, P.S. (1991) *Bewcastle and Old Penrith. A Roman Outpost Fort and a Frontier Vicus. Excavations 1977–78.* Cumberland and Westmorland Research Series 6.

Bidwell, P., Snape, M. and Croom, A. (1998) *Hardknott Roman Fort, Cumbria.* Cumberland and Westmorland Research Series 9.

Birley, B. and Greene, E. (2006) *The Roman Jewellery from Vindolanda (Research Report N.S.IV, fasc. V. Beads, intaglios, finger-rings, ear-rings and bracelets).* Greenhead.

Bowman, A.K. (1994) *Life and Letters on the Roman Frontier.* London.

Caruana, I. D. (1992) Carlisle: Excavation of a section of the annexe ditch of the first Flavian fort, 1990. *Britannia* 22, 45–109.

Charlesworth, D. (1961) Roman jewellery found in Northumberland and Durham, *AA* 4th series 39, 1–6.

Charlesworth, D. (1969) A gold signet ring from Housesteads, *AA* 4th series 47, 39–43.

Collingwood, R. G. and Wright, R. P. (1965) *The Roman Inscriptions of Britain. I Inscriptions on Stone.* Oxford.

Coulston, J. C. and Phillips, E. J. (1988) *Corpus Signorum Imperii Romani Great Britain I.6. Hadrian's Wall west of the North Tyne and Carlisle.* Oxford.

Elliot, J. Walter and Henig, M. (1982) Engraved gemstones from the Roman frontier post at Newstead, Roxburghshire, *PSAS* 112, 295–9.

Elliot, J. Walter and Henig, M. (1999) Further engraved gemstones from Newstead (Trimontium), Roxburghshire, *PSAS* 129, 393–8.

Ferris, I. (2010) *The Beautiful Rooms are Empty. Excavations at Binchester Roman Fort, County Durham 1976–1981 and 1986–1991.* Durham.

Henig, M. (1986) Caracalla as Hercules? A new cameo from South Shields, *Antiquaries Journal* 66, 378–80.

Henig, M. (1988) The chronology of Roman engraved gemstones, *JRA* 1, 142–52.

Henig, M. (1990) *The Content Family Collection of Ancient Cameos.* Houlton Maine and Oxford.

Henig, M. (1999) Artistic patronage and the Roman military community in Britain. In A. Goldsworthy and I. Haynes (eds) *The Roman Army as a Community.* JRA Supplementary Series 34, 150–64. Portsmouth, Rhode Island.

Henig, M. (2004) *Corpus Signorum Imperii Romani Great Britain I.9. Roman sculpture from the North West Midlands.* Oxford.

Henig, M. (2007a) *A Corpus of Roman Engraved Gemstones from British Sites* (3rd edition). BAR British Series 8. Oxford.

Henig, M. (2007b) The Victory gem from Lullingstone Roman villa, *Journal of the British Archaeological Association* 160, 1–7.

Henig, M. (2009) Gem workshops in the provinces: Roman Britain. In G. Sena Chiesa and E. Gagetti (eds) *Aquileia e la glittica di età ellenistica e romana,* 141–8. Trieste.

Henig, M. (2011) Sealed in stone. Roman gem stones excavated in York by YAT, *Yorkshire Archaeology Today* 20, 7–9. York.

Henig, M. and MacGregor, A. (2004) *Catalogue of the Engraved Gems and Finger-rings in the Ashmolean Museum,* BAR International Series 1332. Oxford.

Hutchinson, V. J. (1986) *Bacchus in Roman Britain: The evidence for his cult,* BAR British Series 151. Oxford.

Keppie, L. J. F. and Arnold, B. J. (1984). *Corpus Signorum Imperii Romani Great Britain I.4. Scotland.* Oxford.

Keppie, L. J. F., Bailey, G. B., Dunwell, A. J., McBrien, J. H. and Speller, K. (1995) Some excavations on the line of the Antonine Wall, 1985–93. *PSAS* 125, 601–71.

Marsden, A. (2011) An intaglio featuring Victory and Fortuna from Caistor St Edmund, Norfolk an a putative glyptic workshop connected to the Severan campaigns in Britain, *Oxford Journal of Archaeology* 30, 427–34.

McCarthy, M. R. (1990) *A Roman, Anglian and Medieval site at Blackfriars Street, Carlisle.* Cumberland and Westmorland Research Series 5.

McCarthy, M. R., Padley. T. G. and Henig, M. (1982) Excavations and finds from the Lanes, Carlisle, *Britannia* 13, 79–89.

Padley, T. G (1991) *The Metalwork, Glass and Stone objects from Castle Street, Carlisle Fascicule 2.* Cumberland and Westmorland Research Series 4.

Phillips, E. J. (1977) *Corpus Signorum Imperii Romani Great Britain I.1. Corbridge. Hadrian's Wall east of the North Tyne.* Oxford.

Royal Commission on Historical Monuments (1962) *England. City of York. I. Eburacum. Roman York.* London.

Rushworth, A. (2009) *Housesteads Roman Fort – The Grandest Station. Excavation and Survey at Housesteads by Charles Daniels, John Gillam, James Crow and others*. London.

Toynbee, J. M. C. (1962) *Art in Roman Britain.* London.

Toynbee, J. M. C. (1964) *Art in Britain under the Romans.* Oxford.

Tufi, S. R. (1983) *Corpus Signorum Imperii Romani Great Britain I.3. Yorkshire.* Oxford.

Welles, C. B., Fink, R. O. and Gilliam, J. F. (1959) *The Excavations at Dura Europos. Final Report V part 1. The Parchments and Papyri.* New Haven.

Wilmott, T. (1997) *Birdoswald. Excavations of a Roman Fort on Hadrian's Wall and its successor settlements 1987–92.* London.

Zanker, P. (1988) *The Power of Images in the Age of Augustus.* Ann Arbor, Michigan.

18

PERSONAL POSSESSIONS OR TRADED GOODS? FINDS OF DECORATED MOULD-BLOWN GLASS VESSELS ON FLAVIAN SITES IN NORTHERN BRITAIN

Jennifer Price

Introduction

This exploration of the decorated mould-blown tablewares in northern Britain is an interim study, but I hope that it will entertain Lindsay and also provide a plausible background for the handsome African-head vessel that she wrote about long ago (Allason-Jones and Miket 1984, 284–5).

Vessels with designs in relief formed by blowing glass into decorated moulds first appeared in the Roman world in the early first century AD. The moulds were made in two or more pieces for lifting away from the inflated vessel, and the form and decoration of the vessel followed the contours of the mould, introducing a novel and easily recognisable element to early Imperial assemblages of glass tablewares. Multiple copies of identical glass vessels with surfaces quite distinct from those on contemporary free-blown or moulded glass were produced and the vessels became a significant, though minor, part of the glass tablewares in circulation for about half a century thereafter. This glass has attracted scholarly attention since the nineteenth century because of the potential to recognise the products of moulds derived from the same archetype or the links between the design elements of groups of vessels and through these, the periods of production and patterns of distribution of different forms and decorative schemes. Many studies of single vessels, groups of vessels and regional and more general surveys have been published (e.g. Harden 1935; Israeli 1964; Lehrer 1979; Rütti *et al.* 1988; Price 1991; Scatozza Höricht 1991; Stern 1995; Sennequier *et al.* 1998; Fontaine-Hodiamont 2010; Buljević 2012).

The exact date of the invention of mould-blowing is uncertain. A find of decorated tableware in an Augustan context has been claimed at Magdalensberg in Austria (Czurda-Ruth 1998, no. 782 pl. 2, cf. Stern 2000, 165) but other finds of tablewares do not appear until the Tiberian–early Claudian periods. Early groups have been recognised in Italy and adjacent regions, and many more dated finds are known in different areas of the Roman world, including the north western provinces, in the Claudian and Neronian periods (see discussion of production and dating in Price 1991, 57–71).

Britain became a Roman province too late to contribute to discussion about the initial phases of production of decorated mould-blown vessels, but developments within the province and changes to the frontiers provide a series of chronological horizons for examining the changing patterns of glass use in the decades following AD 43. No mould-blown tablewares have been recognised in pre-Conquest or early Claudian contexts, but they occur, usually in small numbers, in military and proto-urban settlements in late Claudian, Neronian and early Flavian deposits. The majority of the forms were probably used for drinking, though a few fragmentary pieces of larger size may have been serving vessels, such as bowls or jugs (Price 1991, 68, 70; Cool and Price 1995, 42–55; Price and Cottam 1998, 60–6). In the Claudian and Neronian periods, the two most common forms are bluish green and coloured cylindrical cups with scenes showing named gladiators, charioteers or wrestlers, which are found only in the western provinces, and small convex bowls with vertical close-set ribs on the body in the same range of colours, which are found in many parts of the Roman world. Versions of both forms, blown into a variety of moulds, are found quite widely in Britain (see lists in Price and Cottam 1998, 60–1, 63–4). Other forms, such as ovoid beakers, which have a range of designs including gladiators and chariot racing, triangular bosses or close-set vertical ribs (*ibid.*, 61–3), are broadly contemporary but less common and not so closely dated.

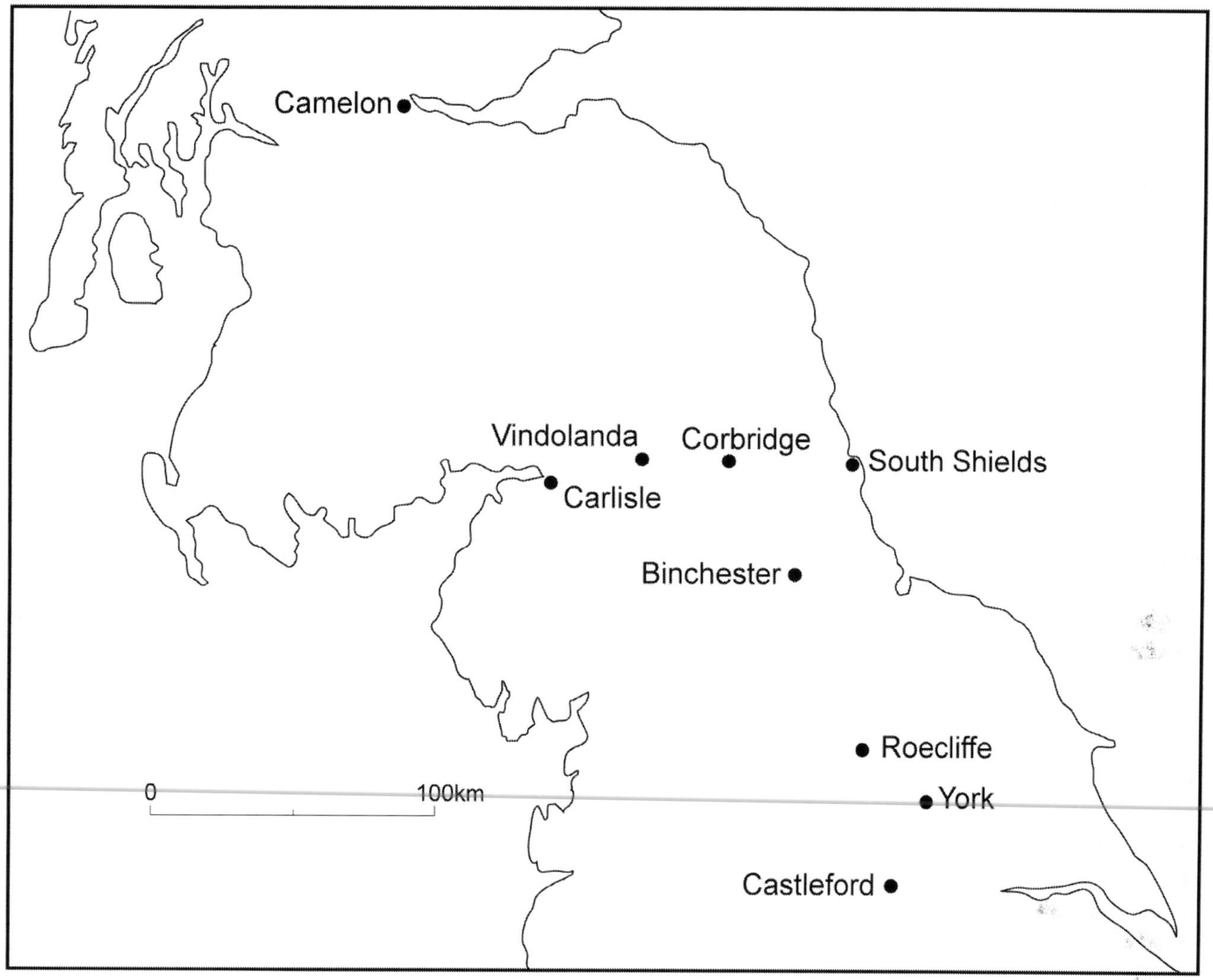

Figure 18.1 Map of sites with mould-blown fragments in Yorkshire and the northern frontier

Two other forms, tall conical beakers and head-shaped beakers, are rarely visible in the archaeological record before the late Neronian period. The conical beaker was a new shape among glass vessels at this time and the mould-blown versions became well-known in the early Flavian period. They were decorated with designs, often in high relief, such as almond-shaped bosses, geometric patterns including rings, meanders, shells, spirals and vegetal motifs (Price and Cottam 1998, 65–6; cf. Price 1991, pls 18b–c, 19, for some of the designs). The beakers with almond-shaped bosses occur in many parts of the Roman world, while others have more limited patterns of distribution. Many were made in bluish green or coloured glass, although beakers with geometric and foliage designs were often produced in colourless or nearly colourless glass, a new kind of glass becoming popular for tablewares in the late Neronian–early Flavian period.

The vessels finished as beakers in the form of an African head are much less common. Several variants have been identified, some with a name in Greek or Latin letters included in the design (e.g. Price 1974; 1991, 70–1, pl. 17d; Stern 1995, 204–6) but few have come from closely dated deposits and many are without provenance.

Finds in the northern frontier region

All of the drinking vessel forms outlined above have been recorded in the northern frontier region. The military occupation commenced at around AD 70–71 and many forts were established in the early and middle Flavian periods (Bidwell and Hodgson 2009, 8–13, Hanson 2007, 21–9). The majority have not produced any decorated mould-blown glass, but aproximately 30

Site	Cylindrical cups	Convex bowls	Ovoid beakers	Conical beakers	Head Beakers	
Castleford	–	3	–	2	–	5
York	1	1	1	4	–	7
Roecliffe	–	–	–	1	–	1
Binchester	–	–	1	2	–	3
South Shields	–	–	–	–	1?	1?
Corbridge	–	–	–	1	–	1
Vindolanda	–	1	–	–	–	1
Carlisle	2	2	–	5	–	9
Camelon	–	–	–	1	1?	2?
Totals	3	7	2	16	2?	30?

Table 18.1 Finds of decorated mould-blown vessels in northern Britain

vessels are known from nine of the forts or their *vici* (Fig. 18.1, Table 18.1)

Cylindrical cups with chariot-racing scenes

Three finds from York and Carlisle come from cups recording at least two different chariot races (Fig. 18.2, A–C). Each of the complete vessels had an inscription zone above the main decorative frieze showing four charioteers (*aurigae*) belonging to the four circus factions, the Reds, Whites, Blues and Greens, racing four-horse chariots (*quadrigae*), but they vary in their dimensions, the names of the competitors, and the quality and detail of the overall designs. The distribution of chariot racing cups with one decorative frieze is confined to the north western provinces with concentrations at military sites in the Rhine provinces and Britain and also in central and northern France. Numerous different moulds have been identified (Rütti *et al.* 1988, nos 1–22, pls 1–4; Sennequier *et al.* 1998, nos 1–11, pl. 1, nos 94–100, pl. 6; Follmann-Schulz 1998, nos 1–33) although some of these have not been recognised in Britain.

Figure 18.2, A, a blue–green body fragment in York without known findspot (Harden 1962, 136, fig. 88a) is from a well-known, carefully modelled group of cups which has the names Pyramus, Eutycus, Ierax, and Olympus above the four teams of horses, and a frieze of running animals on the lower body (Rütti *et al.* 1988, type A1, nos 1–10; Follmann-Schulz 1998, nos 1–7; Sennequier *et al.* 1998, nos 1–4). At least seven other cups from this mould are known in Britain, five from London (RIB II.2 nos 2419.14–15; Shepherd 1996, 107 nos 93–96 fig. 64, and unpublished), and one each from Colchester (RIB II.2 no. 2419.13; Cool and Price 1995, 45, 48, no. 232, fig. 3.1) and Lincoln (unpublished).

Figure 18.2, B shows the profile and design of the cup represented by 21 streaky dark blue rim and body fragments found in four Period 3B contexts (*c.*AD 85–*c.*105?) in excavations at Annetwell Street in the Flavian fort at Carlisle (partly published in RIB II.2 no. 2419.6). This group of cups is shorter and not as carefully modelled as the previous one, the names of the charioteers – Eutychus, Musclos, Olympus and Foenix – are different, and there is a zone of lattice on the lower body. A nearly complete example was found in Mainz (Whitehouse 2001, 59–62, 324, no. 530) and others are listed by Rütti *et al.* (1988, type A3/4, nos 17–20), Follmann-Schulz (1998, nos 20–3), Sennequier *et al.* (1998, nos 7–8) and Foy and Fontaine (2010, nos 107–9). Three other examples are known in Britain, from Caistor by Norwich (RIB II.2 no 2419.5) and London and Lincoln (both unpublished). The presence of so many pieces of the Annetwell Street cup suggests that it may have survived as a complete vessel until at least the middle of the ninth decade of the first century.

Figure 18.2, C shows the form probably represented by two tiny bluish–green body fragments with the heads and foreparts of two horses found in residual contexts in the Northern Lanes, Carlisle (Price and Worrell forthcoming nos 23–4). Despite differences in the spelling of the names of the charioteers – Eutychus, Mussculosus, Olympus and Poenix – the vessels blown into this mould appear to record the same contest as the one seen in Figure 18.2, B, but other details, such as the height of the main frieze and the design on the lower body, are different. Fragments from this group of cups are widely known (Rütti *et al.* 1988, type A2, nos 11–16; Follmann-Schulz 1998, nos 8–19; Sennequier *et al.* 1998, nos 5–6; Foy and Fontaine 2010, nos 102–4), and more examples have been found in Britain than any of the other groups of chariot cups. At least 14 are known from Richborough, Canterbury, Colchester, Brickett Wood near Verulamium and

Figure 18.2 Cylindrical cups with circus scenes: A. fragment from York (after Harden 1962); B. fragments and roll-out of design from Annetwell Street, Carlisle; C. part of design of fragments from Northern Lanes, Carlisle

London (RIB II.2 nos 2419.7–12; Price 1995a; Cool and Price 1995, 46, and unpublished).

Convex ribbed bowls

The small convex bowls with vertical ribs found very widely in the Roman world are a long-lived form in the western provinces, since they occur in Tiberian/Claudian as well as early Flavian contexts (see Price 1991, 67–70 for some examples in dated contexts). They were blown into many different moulds, and the dimensions of the vessels and the length, width and setting of the ribs vary considerably. In Britain, they have come from Neronian–early Flavian contexts (see lists in Price and Cottam 1998, 60–1 and discussion in Cool and Price 1995, 51–3; Price 1995b, 152)

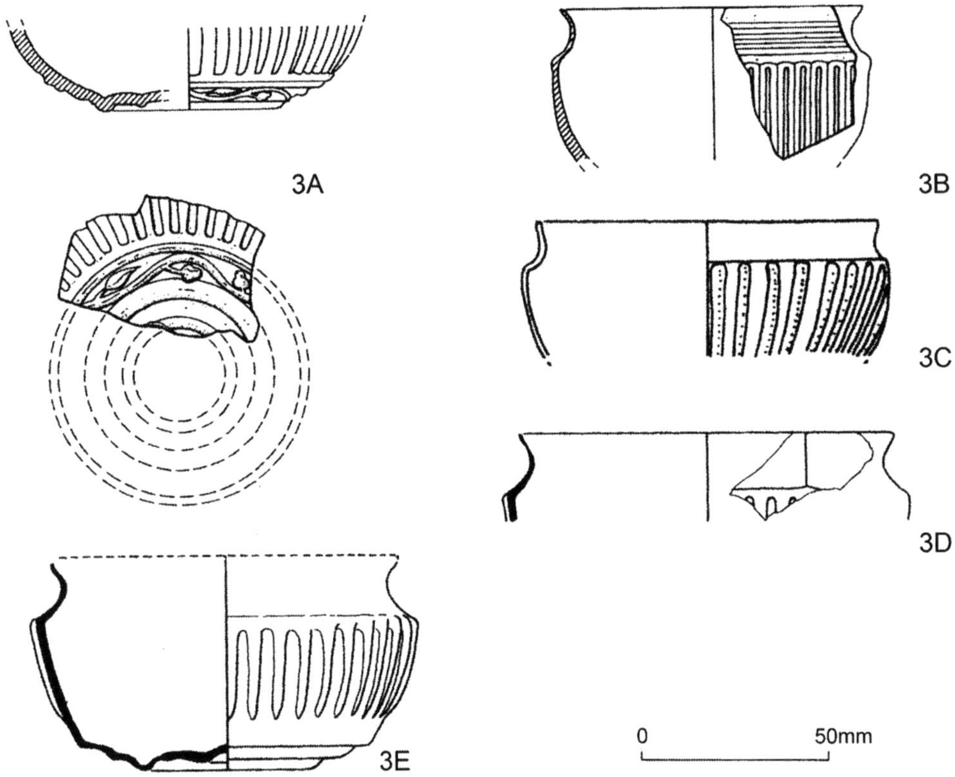

Figure 18.3 Convex cups with vertical ribs: A. Castleford (after Cool and Price 1998); B. Castleford (after Price and Cool 1998); C. St Mary's Abbey, York (after Cool 1988); D. Blackfriars Street, Carlisle (after Price 1991); E. Blackfriars Street, Carlisle (after Price 1991)

At least seven examples have been noted in northern Britain, at Castleford, York, Vindolanda and Carlisle (Fig. 18.3, Plate 9). The Vindolanda piece, from an unstratified context in the north-east corner of Stone Fort 2 (Price 1985a, 206 no. 1), is tiny and undiagnostic, and very little survives of one of the three bowls from phase 1 contexts (*c*.AD 71–*c*.AD 86) in the fort at Castleford, but a little more can be said about the other finds. The most complete is a dark blue bowl found in phase 3 contexts (*c*.AD 79–end first century) at Blackfriars Street, Carlisle (Price 1990, 166 no. 6, fig. 159) which preserves the complete profile (Fig. 18.3, E, Plate 9), and the others show parts of the rim and body, or of the body and base (Fig. 18.3, A–D). Three pieces, one from Castleford (Cool and Price 1998, 142–3, 154 no. 40, fig. 52), St Mary's Abbey, York (Cool 1998, 303–4 no. 4, fig. 2) and Blackfriars Street, Carlisle (Price 1990, 166 no. 7, fig. 159) come from small bowls with a concave zone and sharp angle below the everted rim and closely set ribs on the body, which are comparable with many finds from elsewhere in Flavian or later contexts in Britain, as at Colchester, Caersws and Wroxeter (Cool and Price 1995, 52–3 nos 243–5, fig. 3.3; Cool and Price 1989, 32 no. 12, fig. 20; Cool and Price 2002, 229 nos 59–60, fig. 6.4). The body and base fragment (Fig. 18.3, A) from Castleford (Cool and Price 1998, no. 39, fig. 52) is more unusual, as there is a band of stylised foliage on the lower body, a feature noted occasionally on other ribbed bowls, as at Vindonissa, Switzerland (Berger 1960, 55 no. 141, pl. 9; Fünfschilling 2010, 131 fig. 2.3) and in a funerary context in the Auvergne (information from Sally Cottam). It has been argued (Cool 1998, 304) that the presence of a ribbed bowl in a small group of early glass may hint at pre-Flavian occupation at St Mary's Abbey in York, but this is not necessarily the case as similar vessels are known in early–mid Flavian contexts at Castleford and Carlisle as well as at Caersws and Wroxeter in western Britain.

Ovoid beakers

Two ovoid beakers have been noted in the region. One (Fig. 18.4, Plate 10), a pale bluish–green fragment found in a phase 1 context (*c.* AD 80) in the fort at Binchester, County Durham (Price and Worrell 2010, 273, 298 no. 1,

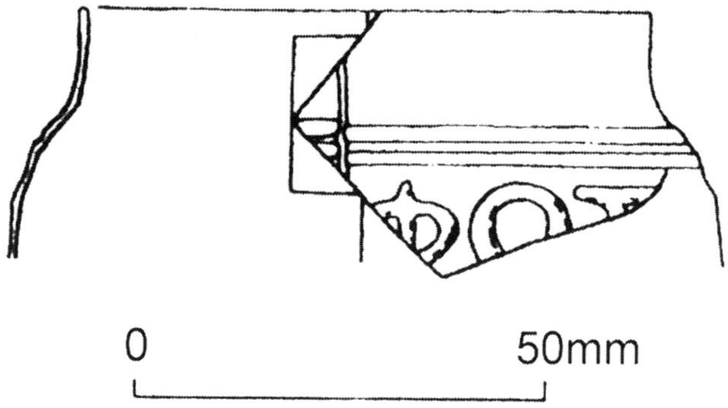

4A

Figure 18.4 Ovoid beaker with Greek inscription from Binchester (after Price and Worrell 2010)

fig. 79; RIB II.2 no. 2419.38), is most unusual. The surviving part of the rim and upper body shows a vertical mould seam to the left and two narrow horizontal ribs above the letters .ΦΟΠ.., part of an inscription in Greek letters reading ΕΥΦΡΑΙΝΟΥ ΕΦΟΠΑΡΕΙ ('Enjoy yourself as long as you are here'). Mould-blown drinking vessels with mottoes in Greek letters have been recorded in the eastern and western Mediterranean regions (e.g. Harden 1935, groups F–L), but no other examples are known in Britain, and only a few have come from the Rhine provinces. These include pieces of two bulbous bowls with inscriptions similar to the Binchester beaker at Tongres, Belgium (Cosyns *et al.* 2005), and fragments of cylindrical beakers with ΚΑΤΑΧΑΙΡΕ ΚΑΙ ΕΥΦΡΑΝΟΥ ('be happy and rejoice') and other mottoes in the western *canabae legionis* at Nijmegen, Netherlands (van Lith 2006, 153 nos 411–12, fig. 7), at Krefeld-Gellep (information from Renate Pirling) and Rottweil (Hoffmann 2002, 25–6, 304 R174, pl. 12), Germany, and at Oberwinterthur and Vindonissa, Switzerland (Fünfschilling 2010, 132 fig. 4).

The complete beaker almost certainly had three decorative zones separated by narrow horizontal ribs – the inscription below the shoulder, a band of stylised foliage in the middle of the body and gadroons on the lower body. A very close parallel in colourless glass was found near Marseilles (Morin-Jean 1913, fig. 248; Harden 1935, 175 group G.I.iii; Foy and Nenna 2001, 178 no. 283; Fontaine and Roussel-Ode 2010, 178, fig. 3, 1–2), and another in yellowish–brown glass, from Kerch, Crimea (Harden 1935, 175, group G.I.iva; Price 1991, pl. xviib) has identical decorative zones but the stylised foliage is in the top register and the inscription is in the middle of the body. The second ovoid beaker, from a contexts dated to AD71/79–100 or later, at Blake Street, York (Cool 1995, 1564–5 fig. 736 no. 5894), has closely set ribs on the body similar to those on the convex cups already discussed. Ovoid ribbed beakers are not very common, although some are known in the Rhine provinces, in the *canabae legionis* at Nijmegen (van Lith 2006, fig. 7.435) and at Baden, Oberwinterthur and Lausanne-Vidy in Switzerland (Fünfschilling 2010, fig. 2.4,7,7). In Britain there is one in a Flavian deposit at Caerleon (Price and Cottam 1998, fig. 15b) and another in the early civil settlement at Wroxeter (Cool and Price 2002, 229 no. 61).

Conical beakers

This is by far the most common mould-blown vessel form recorded in northern Britain. Sixteen examples with two principal groups of designs have been recognised, accounting for more than 50% of the total number of vessels. Eight, made in blue–green, pale greenish or coloured glass, have patterns with almond-shaped bosses, and five, all made in greenish colourless or colourless glass, have geometric or vegetal patterns. The remaining three, dark blue and colourless body fragments and a colourless base, are more difficult to classify, but the blue piece is likely to be from a beaker similar to the ones with almond-shaped bosses, and the colourless base may come from a beaker with geometric or vegetal designs.

Several patterns occur on the eight examples with almond-shaped bosses. Figure 18.5, B–D illustrates fragments of two pale green and yellow–green beakers with 3-stepped bosses and circular pellets from phase 2 (AD 85/90–135/40) and unstratified contexts in the *vicus* at Castleford (Cool and Price 1998, nos 36–7, fig. 52) and a pale green piece without provenance from York with 2-stepped bosses and pellets (Harden 1962, 136, fig. 88 H.G.273). Two others in pale blue–green glass with 2-stepped bosses (not illustrated) were found in a Flavian deposit of scrap glass for recycling at Fisher Street, Carlisle (information from Ingemark *et al.* 2008). Another blue–green piece (not illustrated) comes from the defences of the legionary fortress in York (St

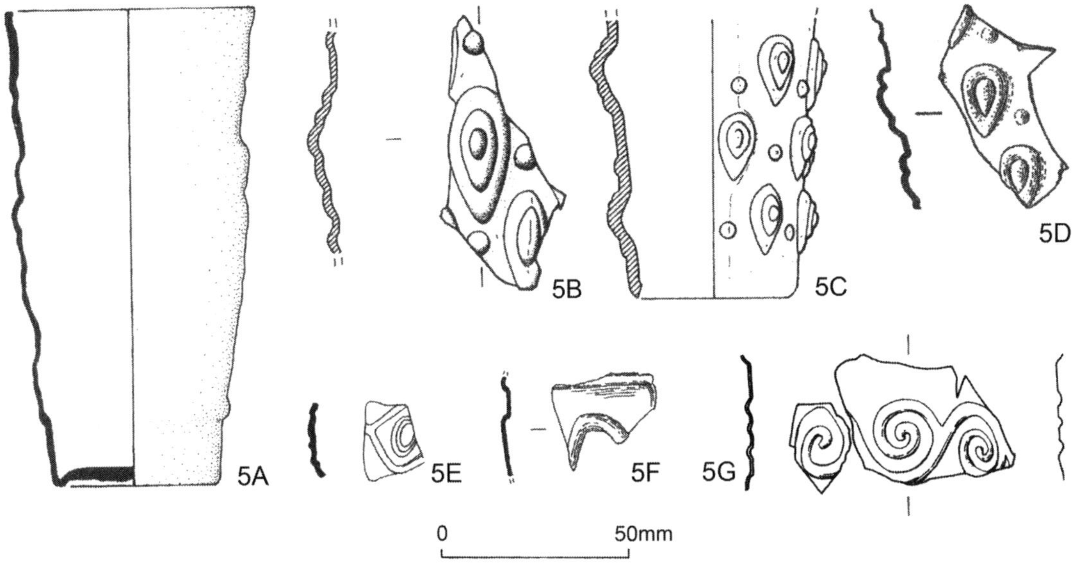

Figure 18.5 Conical beakers: A. Profile; B.–C. Castleford (after Cool and Price 1998); D. York (after Harden 1962); E. Corbridge (after Allen 1988); F. York (after Price 1995c); G. Binchester (after Price and Worrell 2010).

Leonard's – information from H. E. M. Cool), and the remaining two are a blue–green body fragment with simple bosses (not illustrated) from the fort occupied *c.*AD 71–*c.*AD 85 at Roecliffe, north Yorkshire, (Allen 2005, 202, 204, fig. 36.3) and a yellowish–brown body fragment (Fig. 18.5, E) with diamond lattice enclosing a 3-stepped boss from an unknown context at Corbridge (Allen 1988, 287 no. 2, fig. 131). Some of these patterns are widely distributed in the Roman world, while others, particularly the bosses enclosed in diamond lattice, appear to be concentrated in the north-west provinces (see lists of Romano-British examples in Price and Cottam 1998, 65–6) though they are not prevalent in northern Britain. Only the Corbridge fragment and an unidentified dark blue fragment also from St Leonards, York (information from H. E. M. Cool) were made in strongly coloured glass, but other coloured beakers are known in Flavian contexts in western Britain, at Caersws, Powys (Cool and Price 1989, 38 nos 16–17 fig. 20) and Chester (unpublished).

Two pieces from colourless beakers with geometric motifs are known in the region, one (Fig. 18.5, F) from a residual context in Barrack 2 in the legionary fortress at York (Price 1995c, 347, 335 no. 13, fig. 142) and the other (not illustrated) in a deposit dated to *c.* AD 84–5 in the annexe ditch of the first Flavian fort at Carlisle (Cool 1992, 64, 67 no. 4, fig. 10). Similar geometric motifs occur on a beaker said to come from Syria (Harden *et al.* 1987, 157 no. 79) and on a group of beakers found in Italy and the western provinces (Scatozza Höricht 1991, fig. 16d). Fragments in the Rhine frontier region are known in the *canabae legionis* at Nijmegen, Netherlands (Isings 1980, 293 find 1/67 no. 7, figs 6–7; van Lith 2006, 155–7 no. 433, fig. 7), at Ladenburg, Germany (Hoffmann 2002, pl. 84.37) and at Augst and Oberwinterthur, Switzerland (Fünfshilling 2010, 131, fig. 3.4–5). In Britain, finds with geometric motifs are not very common, although some have come from London (unpublished), and others are known in Caerleon (information from Denise Allen) and Wroxeter (Cool and Price 2002, 232, nos 76–8 fig. 6.4).

Three others have spiral and leaf-like designs. The best preserved of these is from Binchester (Fig. 18.5, G), from a context dated to AD 95/100–110/120, which has a horizontal band with wavy stems and tightly twisted tendrils with a horizontal rib below (Price and Worrell 2010, 273, 298 nos 12/13, fig. 79). Vertical spiral motifs occur among beakers found in Pompeii and Herculaneum, where one was found with other glass vessels in a packing case in a shop (Scatozza Höricht 1986, 40 no. 66; 1991, 83, fig. 15). They are also known in southern France (Foy and Nenna 2001, 181 no. 302; Fontaine and Roussel-Ode 2010, 183 no. 23, fig. 4) and Normandy (Arveiller and Vanpeene 2010, 161 fig. 6.1), but the only close parallel for the Binchester design appears to be a horizontal spiral frieze on a beaker also decorated with pan-pipes, meanders and other motifs from Charleville, Ardennes (Arveiller and Vanpeene 2010,161, fig. 6.2). The remaining pieces (not illustrated), from the northern Lanes in Carlisle and Site A at Camelon, are very small although both were probably conical beakers with floral or vegetal decoration. The one from Carlisle (Price and Worrell forthcoming no. 25) is from near the base of a beaker with a horizontal cordon and probably a three-lobed leaf, while the minute body fragment from an Antonine deposit of glass probably collected for recycling at Camelon (Price forthcoming no. 6) has a sharply defined motif in high relief, perhaps a bud or leaf. Comparable decoration has been recorded among the fragments collected for recycling at around the end of the first century in pits in the *canabae legionis* at Nijmegen (Isings 1980, 293 Find 1/67 no. 8, fig. 5.7; Hanut 2010, 142 fig. 10) and at Augst (Fünfschilling 2010, fig. 3.9), and also on a few colourless beaker fragments in Britain, including one from a late Neronian/early Flavian context in the legionary fortress at Usk (Price 1995b, 152–3, 155 no. 27, fig. 43). The colourless base fragment already mentioned, from period 3A (AD 72/73–83/84) in the first Flavian fort at Carlisle (Howard-Davis 2009, appendix 8, 1334, vessel 67) is also likely to come from a beaker with either geometric or vegetal motifs (Fig. 18.5, F–G). Identification of the final colourless body fragment, from an unstratified context at Binchester (Price and Worrell 2010, 273 no. 14, fig. 79) as a conical beaker with horizontal or slightly diagonal ribs in low relief is more tentative, and parallels are difficult to find.

African-head beakers

African-Head beakers may be represented by two dark blue examples in northern Britain, although there is some doubt about each of them. The first, a fragment of a thick-walled, dark blue vessel blown in a two-part body mould with a separate base, formerly in the Museum of Antiquities and now in the Great North Museum in Newcastle upon Tyne, preserves part of a head with African features (Plate 11). No information about its provenance has survived, and at one time it was thought to come from Pompeii (Anon. 1914, xxi), though it has been accepted more recently as a find from South Shields (Charlesworth 1959a, 54–6, pl. v, 4; Allason-Jones and Miket 1984, 284–5) and so has been included in this survey. The surviving piece (present height 71 mm, base diameter *c*.48 mm) shows the hair-line above the forehead on the right side of the face, the eyes, broad nose, open mouth and teeth, chin with dimple, lower parts of the ears with vertical mould-seams behind them, and parts of two rows of raised ovals representing curled hair on the lower part of the back of the head above the cylindrical neck. As the rim and top of the head are missing it is unclear whether this was originally a drinking vessel or a flask, but it is noticeably more robust than most head-flasks. Three other blue–green and coloured examples of head beakers have been recognised in Britain. Substantial parts of two from a mould with the name C. CAESI below the hair-line on the back of the head are known from a Flavian–early second century rubbish deposit outside the legionary fortress at Caerleon and an unknown context in King William Street, London (Boon 1969, 95–7, fig. 2; Price 1974; RIB II, 2 no. 2419.36–37; Price 2011, 15, 35 nos GB-GOB.001–2, pl. 1), and several small dark blue fragments were found in Flavian contexts in the *vicus* at Caersws, Powys (Cool & Price 1989, 32, 36 no. 11). The dimensions of the South Shields vessel are broadly comparable with those of the beakers from Caerleon and London, although the glass is thicker and the mould is different. It is also similar in size to a fragmentary purplish–brown example found in the same packing case in Herculaneum as the beaker with vertical spirals mentioned above (Scatozza-Höricht 1986, 52 no. 103, form 33, pls xii, xxiii).

The four body and base fragments from Flavian and Antonine contexts at Site A at Camelon have curving and asymmetrical features which are distinctly different from the regular patterns and sharply defined motifs of most mould-blown vessels. They are comparable with the features on fragments from Caersws, as well as the Caerleon and London African-head beakers, and have been interpreted as another African-head beaker, although they are too small for the form or design to be identified securely.

Discussion

The decorated mould-blown drinking vessels often found in settlements occupied in the late Neronian–early Flavian period disappear rapidly after this time, so the development of the northern frontier from around AD 70/71 onwards is a valuable fixed point for examining the latest phases of their production and use. The quantity recorded in the region is not very large, but the 30 cups, bowls and beakers contribute to our knowledge of the forms in circulation during the eighth decade of the first century. Military sites established in the early 70s, such as Castleford, York, Roecliffe and Carlisle have produced the majority of the finds, the greatest quantity coming from York and Carlisle. The foundation dates of Binchester, South Shields, Corbridge, Vindolanda and Camelon are less clear, but it is noteworthy that mould-blown fragments are absent at many of the forts established towards the end of the decade, such as Red House Corbridge (Charlesworth 1959b; 1979) Elginhaugh (Price and Worrell

2007), Strageath (Price 1989) or Inchtuthil (Price 1985b). The virtual absence of finds in Scotland, apart from the two at Camelon, might perhaps be explained by the later foundation dates of the forts, although the patterns of supply and the organisation of collection of broken glass for recycling may be factors of equal importance.

Two main chronological groups are visible among the northern finds, the cups and bowls already known in the early Neronian period and the two kinds of beakers which do not appear until the late 60s. It is unclear when production of the earlier group of vessels ended but the small numbers found at sites first occupied in the early Flavian period suggest that this may have occurred before the beginning of this period. Cylindrical cups with chariot-racing scenes, which were presumably made as momentos of memorable events and therefore valued by their owners, are uncommon in northern Britain. The three pieces from York and Carlisle may well have arrived as personal possessions and been carefully curated, the cup from Annetwell Street apparently surviving as a complete vessel until at least *c*.AD 85. Ribbed bowls are more frequent finds and may still have been made in the early years of the eighth decade. The seven examples known from Castleford, York and Carlisle may thus have reached the region through trade and been purchased locally, although the dark blue bowl found at Blackfriars Street, Carlisle survived for some years as it was deposited after *c*.AD 79. Another vessel that was perhaps a personal possession rather than a local purchase is the motto beaker found at Binchester.

The vessels in the second chronological group very probably arrived in the region as currently traded goods. Some forms of tall conical beakers seem to have been produced until nearly the end of the eighth decade, and examples are known in deposits dated to AD 79 at Pompeii and Herculaneum (Scatozza Höricht 1986, 40 no. 66, 52 no. 103, pls vii, xii). The 16 beakers have been noted widely in northern Britain, they account for more than 50% of the total number of finds of decorated mould-blown vessels and they show more variation in their designs and colours than any of the other forms. The presence of beakers in colourless glass at York, Binchester, Carlisle and Camelon is particularly interesting, as mould-blown glass in this colour was not common. It was used for a limited group of Flavian mould-blown vessels with designs in high relief imitating the relief carving of more costly tablewares which may have been some of the last mould-blown beakers in production. African-head beakers were also probably made in the early Flavian period since they have also come from the Vesuvian towns, but they are rare objects and may perhaps have been produced as novelties.

The mould-blown vessels found in northern Britain are very similar in their forms and designs to contemporary finds elsewhere in the north-west provinces, but nothing is currently known about the organisation of production and distribution. It is possible that the vessels were made in a few workshops and traded widely, and equally possible that they were blown in many different places by itinerant glassworkers with sets of moulds who travelled to their markets in the forts and towns of different provinces, but neither hypothesis is provable.

Cool and Baxter (1999, 89–91) have argued that regional differences in the proportions of finds of seven types of Flavian drinking vessels, including three mould-blown forms, cylindrical cups, convex bowls and conical beakers, may indicate regional preferences, with consumers in southern Britain favouring the new forms such as tall beakers and those in the Midlands and northern Britain the older forms of low cups. This is an intriguing suggestion but it was based on small numbers of finds and is not supported by the current information about the mould-blown forms in northern Britain. As is shown in Table 18.1, tall conical beakers now outnumber the low cylindrical cups and convex bowls by a considerable margin, and they were reaching forts and *vici* in the region in some quantity in the eighth decade of the first century.

Acknowledgments

I am very grateful to Denise Allen, Yvonne Beadnell, Rob Collins, Hilary Cool, Sally Cottam, David Hill, Dominic Ingemark, Val Maxfield, Tim Padley, Renate Pirling, Mark Taylor and Jeff Vietch for sharing information with me and for helping with the preparation of this paper.

Bibliography

Allason-Jones, L. and Miket, R. (1984) *The Catalogue of Small Finds from South Shields Roman Fort.*. Society of Antiquaries of Newcastle upon Tyne Monograph Series 2. Newcastle upon Tyne.

Allen, D. (1988) Roman glass from Corbridge. In M. C. Bishop and J. N. Dore (eds) *Corbridge, Excavations of the Roman Fort and Town, 1947–1980*. English Heritage Archaeological Report 8, 287–93. London.

Allen, D. (2005) Glass, 202–4 in M. Bishop, A new Flavian

military site at Roecliffe, North Yorkshire. *Britannia* 36, 135–223.

Anonymous (1914) Photograph 'Portion of blue glass vase of Roman date, representing a human face, from Pompeii'. *AA* 3rd series 11, xxi.

Arveiller, V. and Vanpeene, N. (2010) Verres romains soufflés dans un moule: le Nord de la France. In C. Fontaine-Hodiamont (ed.) *D'Ennion au Val Saint-Lambert. Le verre soufflé-moulé.* Actes des 23e Rencontres de l'Association française pour l'Archéologie du Verre. 158–68. Brussels.

Bidwell, P. and Hodgson, N. (2009) *The Roman Army in Northern England.* Arbeia Society, Newcastle upon Tyne.

Berger, L. (1960) *Römische Gläser aus Vindonissa.* Basel.

Boon, G. C. (1969) Roman glass in Wales. *Annales du 4e Congres des "Journees Internationales du Verre"* (Ravenne-Venise 1967), 93–102.

Buljevic, Z. (2012) *Traces of Ennion and Aristeas in the Roman province of Dalmatia*, Arheološki Muzej. Split.

Charlesworth, D. (1959) Roman glass in northern Britain. *AA* 4th series 37, 33–58.

Charlesworth, D. (1959b) The glass, 164–6 in C.M. Daniels. The Roman Bath-house at Red House, Beaufront, nr. Corbridge. *AA* 4th series 37, 85–176.

Charlesworth, D. (1979) Glass, 58–61 in W. S. Hanson, C. M. Daniels, J. N. Dore, and J. P. Gillam. The Agricolan supply-base at Red House, Corbridge. *AA* 5th series 7, 1–98.

Cool, H. E. M. (1992) The vessel glass, 63–8 in I. Caruana. Carlisle, Excavation of a Section of the Annexe Ditch of the First Flavian Fort. *Britannia* 23, 45–109.

Cool, H. E. M. (1995) Glass vessels from 9 Blake Street. In H. E. M. Cool, G. Lloyd-Morgan and A. D. Hooley. *Finds from the Fortress. The Archaeology of York. The Small Finds*, 1559–88. Archaeology of York fasc.17 vol 10. York.

Cool, H. E. M. (1998) Early occupation at St Mary's Abbey, York: the evidence of the glass. In J. Bird (ed.) *Form and Fabric. Studies in Rome's Material Past in Honour of B. R. Hartley.* 301–5, Oxbow Books. Oxford.

Cool, H. E. M. and Baxter, M. J. (1999) Peeling the onion: an approach to comparing vessel glass assemblages. *Journal of Roman Archaeology* 12, 72–100.

Cool, H. E. M. and Price, J. (1989) The glass vessels. In J. Britnell. *Caersws Vicus, Powys, Excavations at the Old Primary School, 1985–86.* BAR British Series 205, 31–43. Oxford.

Cool, H. E. M. and Price, J. (1995) *Roman Vessel Glass from Excavations in Colchester, 1971–85.* Colchester Archaeological Report 8. Colchester.

Cool, H. E. M. and Price, J. (1998) The vessels and objects of glass. In H. E. M. Cool and C. Philo. *Roman Castleford volume I. The Small Finds. Yorkshire Archaeology 4.* West Yorkshire Archaeology Service, 141–93. Wakefield.

Cool, H. E. M. and Price, J. (2002) Vessel glass associated with the military occupation. In J. Chatterton. (ed.) *The Legionary Fortress at Wroxeter. Excavations by Graham Webster, 1955–85.* English Heritage Archaeological Report 19, 225–53. London.

Cosyns, P., Vanderhoeven, A., Vynckier, G., Janssens, K. and Schalm, O. (2005) Two fragments of mold-blown glass beakers with Greek inscriptions from Tongeren (Belgium). *Journal of Glass Studies* 47, 179–83.

Czurda-Ruth, B. (1998) Die römischen Gläser vom Magdalensberg 2. *Die Ausgrabungen auf dem Magdalensberg 1980–1986. Magdalensberg Grabungsbericht* 16, 459–507.

Follmann-Schulz, A. B. (1998) Annexe. Les verres à scenes de spectacles retrouvés a Benelux, das le Vorarlberg (Autriche), et en Allemagne: un aperçu preliminaire. In G. Sennequier *et al. Les verres romains à scènes de spectacle trouvés en France.* 154–64. Association Française pour l'Archéologie du Verre. Rouen.

Fontaine-Hodiamont, C. (ed.) (2010) *D'Ennion au Val Saint-Lambert. Le verre soufflé-moulé.* Actes des 23e Rencontres de l'Association française pour l'Archéologie du Verre. Brussels.

Fontaine, S. and Roussel-Ode, .J (2010) Vases soufflés-moulés du Haut-Empire trouvés en Narbonnaise. In C. Fontaine-Hodiamont (ed.) *D'Ennion au Val Saint-Lambert. Le verre soufflé-moulé.* 177–203. Actes des 23e Rencontres de l'Association française pour l'Archéologie du Verre. Brussels.

Foy, D. and Fontaine, S. (2010) Verres soufflés dans un moule à décor de scenes de spectacles. In C. Fontaine-Hodiamont (ed.) *D'Ennion au Val Saint-Lambert. Le verre soufflé-moulé.* 85–112. Actes des 23e Rencontres de l'Association française pour l'Archéologie du Verre. Brussels.

Foy, D. and Nenna, M-D. (2001) *Tout Feu, Tout Sable.* Édisud. Aix-en-Provence.

Fünfschilling, S. (2010) Le verre soufflé dans un moule en Suisse romaine. In C. Fontaine-Hodiamont (ed.) *D'Ennion au Val Saint-Lambert. Le verre soufflé-moulé.* 129–35. Actes des 23e Rencontres de l'Association française pour l'Archéologie du Verre. Brussels.

Hanson, W. S. (2007) *A Roman Frontier Fort in Scotland. Elginhaugh.* Tempus. Stroud.

Hanut, F. (2010) Le verrerie romaine soufflé dans un moule en Gaule septentrinale: le Benelux. In C. Fontaine-

Hodiamont (ed.) *D'Ennion au Val Saint-Lambert. Le verre soufflé-moulé.* 137–58. Actes des 23e Rencontres de l'Association française pour l'Archéologie du Verre. Brussels.

Harden, D. B. (1935) Romano-Syrian glasses with mould-blown inscriptions. *JRS* 25, 163–86.

Harden, D. B. (1962) Glass in Roman York. In *Eburacum. An Inventory of the Historical Monuments in the City of York, 1.* Royal Commission on the Historical Monuments of England, 136–41, HMSO. London.

Harden, D. B., Hellenkemper, H., Painter, K. and Whitehouse, D. (1987) *Glass of the Caesars,* Olivetti. Milan.

Hoffmann, B. (2002) *Römisches Glas aus Baden-Württemberg.* Jan Thorbecke Verlag. Stuttgart.

Howard-Davis, C. (2009) *The Carlisle Millennium Project. Excavations in Carlisle, 1998–2001. Volume 2: the Finds.* Lancaster Imprints 15. Lancaster.

Ingemark, D. Johnson, M. and Anderson, S. (2008) Excavation of two Romano-British pottery kilns and associated structures, Fisher Street, Carlisle. *Transactions of the Cumberland and Westmorland Antiquarian and Archaeological Society* 3rd series 8, 19–35.

Isings, C. (1980) Glass from the *canabae legionis* at Nijmegen. *Berichten van de Rijksdienst voor het Oudheidkundig Bodemonderzoek* 30, 281–346.

Israeli, Y. (1964) Sidonian mould-blown glass vessels in the Museum Ha'Aretz. *Journal of Glass Studies* 6, 34–41.

Lehrer, G. (1979) *Ennion – a first century glassmaker.* Ramat Aviv.

van Lith, S. M. E. (2006) Römische Glasgefässe aus den westlichen *canabae legionis* in Nijmegen. *Kölner Jahrbuch* 39, 111–202.

Morin-Jean (1913) *Le verrerie en Gaule sous l'Empire romain.* Paris.

Price, J. (1974) A Roman mould-blown negro-head glass beaker from London. *Antiquaries Journal* 54, 291–2.

Price, J. (1985a) The glass. In P. T. Bidwell. *The Roman Fort of Vindolanda.* English Heritage Archaeological Report 1, 206–14. London.

Price, J. (1985b) The Roman glass. In L. F. Pitts and J. K. St. Joseph. *Inchtuthil the Roman Legionary Fortress. Britannia* Monograph Series 6, 303–12. London.

Price, J. (1989) The Roman glass. In S. S. Frere and J. J. Wilkes. *Strageath. Excavations within the Roman Fort 1973–86. Britannia* Monograph Series 9, 192–203. London.

Price, J. (1990) Roman vessel and window glass. In M. R. McCarthy. *A Roman, Anglian and Medieval Site at Blackfriars Street, Carlisle.* Cumberland and Westmorland Antiquarian and Archaeological Society Research Series 4, 163–79.

Price, J. (1991) Decorated mould-blown glass tablewares in the first century A.D. In M. Newby and K. Painter (eds) *Roman Glass: Two Centuries of Art and Invention.* Society of Antiquaries of London Occasional Paper 13, 56–75.

Price, J. (1995a) The Canterbury-London Group of Chariot-Race Cups. In K. Blockley, M. Blockley, P. Blockley, S. Frere and S. Stow. *Excavations in the Marlowe Car Park and Surrounding Areas. The Archaeology of Canterbury, 5.* Canterbury Archaeological Trust, 1220–7. Canterbury.

Price, J. (1995b) Glass vessels. In W. H. Manning, J. Price and J. Webster. *Report on the Excavations at Usk 1965–1976. The Roman Small Finds,* University of Wales Press, 139–91. Cardiff.

Price, J. (1995c) Roman flass. In D. Phillips and B. Heywood. *Excavations at York Minster, Volume 1: From Roman Fortress to Norman Cathedral,* RCHME, 346–71. London.

Price, J. (2011) Mould-blown and impressed designs and names on vessels in Britain. In D. Foy and M-D. Nenna (eds) *Corpus des Signatures et Marques sur Verres Antiques, Volume 3,* Association Française pour l'Archéologie du Verre, 15–82. Aix en Provence-Lyon.

Price, J. (forthcoming) The Roman glass from Camelon. In V. Maxfield *Excavations at Camelon,* Society of Roman Studies. London.

Price, J. and Cottam, S. (1998) *Romano-British Glass Vessels: a Handbook.* Council for British Archaeology Practical Handbook in Archaeology 14. York.

Price, J. and Worrell, S. (2007) Glass. In W. S. Hanson. *Elginhaugh: a Flavian fort and its annexe. Britannia* Monograph Series 23, 445–70. London.

Price, J. and Worrell, S. (2010) Roman glass. In I. Ferris. *The Beautiful Rooms are Empty. Excavations at Binchester Roman Fort, County Durham 1976–1981 and 1991.* English Heritage/Durham County Council, 268–332. Durham.

Price, J. and Worrell S (forthcoming) *Catalogue of Glass from the Northern Lanes, Carlisle.*

RIB II, 2: Frere, S. S. and Tomlin, R. S. O. (eds) (1991) *Collingwood R. G. & Wright R. P. The Roman Inscriptions of Britain. Volume II: Instrumentum Domesticum. Fascicule 2: weights, gold vessel, silver vessesl, bronze vessels, lead vessels, pewter vessels, shale vessels, glass vessels, spoons,* Alan Sutton. Stroud.

Rütti, B., Berger, L., Fünfschilling, S., Stern, W. B and Spichtig, N. (1988) Die Zirkusbecher der Schweiz. *Gesellschaft Pro Vindonissa Jahresbericht 1987,* 27–104.

Scatozza Höricht, L. A. (1986) *I Vetri Romani di Erculano.* "L'Erma" di Bretschneider. Rome.

Scatozza Höricht, L. A. (1991) Syrian elements among the glass from Pompeii and Herculaneum. In M. Newby and K. Painter (eds) *Roman Glass: Two Centuries of Art and Invention*. Society of Antiquaries of London Occasional Paper 13, 76–85. London.

Sennequier, G., Hochuli-Gysel, A., Rütti, B., Fünfschilling, S., Berger, L., Nelis-Clément, J. and Landes, C. (1998) *Les verres romains à scènes de spectacle trouvés en France,* Association Française pour l'Archéologie du Verre. Rouen.

Shepherd, J. (1996) The glass, 99–114 in G. Milne and A. Wardle. Early development at Leadenhall Court, London and related research. *London and Middlesex Archaeological Society Transactions* 44, 23–169.

Stern, E. M. (1995) *The Toledo Museum of Glass. Roman Mold-Blown Glass; the First through Sixth centuries*, "L'Erma" di Bretschneider /Toledo Museum of Art. Rome.

Stern, E. M. (2000) Three notes on early mold-blown glass. *Journal of Glass Studies* 42, 165–7.

Whitehouse, D. (2001) *Roman Glass in the Corning Museum of Glass. Volume II*. Corning Museum of Glass. Corning, New York

19

STORIES FROM BLACK BANGLES: JEWELLERY AND OTHER FINDS OF JET-LIKE MATERIALS IN ROMAN SCOTLAND

Fraser Hunter

Introduction

One of Lindsay's long-running interests has been black jewellery of jet and related organic-rich stones, ranging from innovative work on its provenancing to important artefactual studies (e.g. 1996; 2002; 2005; 2011; Allason-Jones and Jones 1994; 2001). It is an interest we have shared over the years, and this paper examines what the small but informative corpus of material from Roman Scotland can add to the picture. An advantage of working on Scottish material is the episodic nature of the Roman occupation; even if a find is not well-stratified, the site generally provides a date bracket, in contrast to the problems on long-lived sites elsewhere in the province. It gives the Scottish material a typochronological value over and above the social interpretations which it can provide. This paper will review the nuts and bolts of distribution, date and type before turning to what these finds can tell us about life and connections on the frontier, and considering the origins of this ornamental habit in the Roman period.

Time and place

Jewellery and other items made from black, shiny stones are known from 14 Roman sites in Scotland, totalling 52 objects or rough-outs and 28 pieces of certain or possible working debris (Fig. 19.1; Table 19.1; see Appendix for references to individual finds). They are a small and occasional presence in assemblages: only around 30% of excavated sites have produced examples, mostly fewer than five finds. Only Camelon (Plate 13), Cramond, Mumrills, Newstead and Bothwellhaugh have larger numbers, the latter two inflated by working debris. To put this in context, this is much less common than brooches (some 275 from 27 Roman military sites in Scotland), but about equivalent to glass bangles (over 40 fragments from 12 sites). The latter have received far more academic treatment (e.g. Kilbride-Jones 1938; Stevenson 1956; 1976; Price 1988; Hoffmann 2003); their black equivalents merit more attention, for they can tell us interesting things.

Finds come from Flavian, Antonine, and perhaps Severan sites. Most are from Antonine sites, with only Elginhaugh and Doune producing securely Flavian material, but a number of older finds come from sites with multiple occupations and cannot be closely dated. Unstratified finds could date to earlier or later occupation, as there was a long-running tradition of such black jewellery in Scotland (e.g. Callander 1916). All such strays are recorded here, but some must come with caveats. In the case of Bar Hill, for instance, two Iron Age-style ring-pendants came from the enigmatic structure underlying the fort which may either be Iron Age or a Roman temporary structure, while one Bothwellhaugh find came from turf used to build the rampart and was presumably dug up in Roman-period building works.

Object types

The restricted range of object types is dominated by bangles, which are found on 11 of the 14 sites (Table 19.1). Ring-pendants are reasonably common, with examples from three sites and manufacturing debris from one or two more, but other types are represented by only one or two examples.

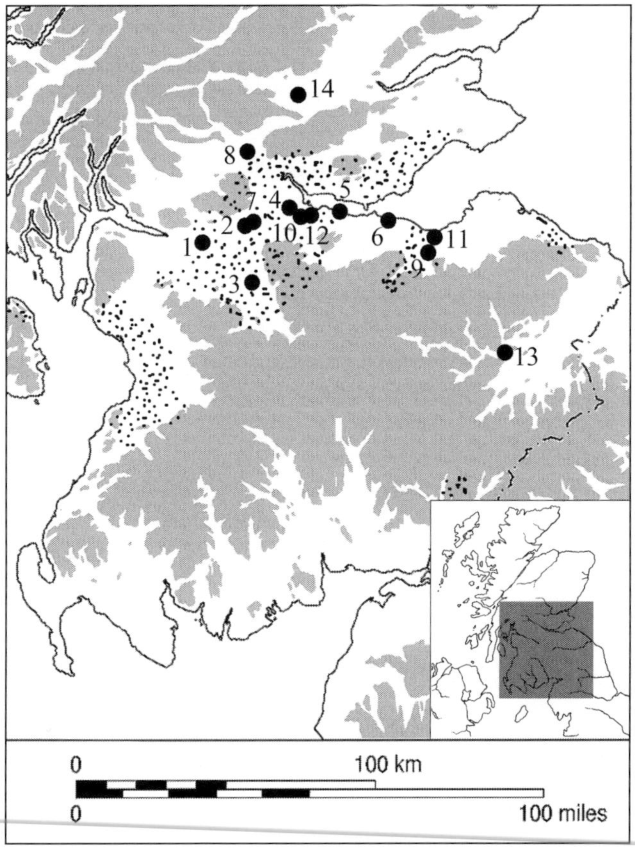

Figure 19.1 Roman sites in Scotland producing black organic-rich stone finds. Stippling marks areas where the raw material is known to occur. 1, Balmuildy; 2, Bar Hill; 3, Bothwellhaugh; 4, Camelon; 5, Carriden; 6, Cramond; 7, Croy Hill; 8, Doune; 9, Elginhaugh; 10, Falkirk; 11, Inveresk; 12, Mumrills; 13, Newstead; 14, Strageath

Bangles

Most of the Scottish bangles find ready parallel in other major assemblages (Fig. 19.2; cf. Lawson 1975; Mills and Woodward 1993, 140, fig. 7). Two are decorated with circumferential grooves, a common type. The Elginhaugh single-grooved example is hand-carved while the Newstead one, lathe-turned with three grooves, is probably a Kimmeridge product, with close parallels from Silchester (Lawson 1975, fig. 5 no. 40a) and Dorchester (Mills and Woodward 1993, fig. 76.1). Features such as distinctive asymmetrical kinks on the inner surface from detaching a core or residual turning marks show that between a fifth and a third of the bangles were lathe-turned (the traces are not always clear); where the material has been analysed these were shale, probably Kimmeridge Shale. Dating evidence is not good, but the datable examples are Antonine and may be connected with the second-century distribution of black-burnished ware from Dorset.

Cramond has produced a more unusual bangle with a tall-oval or lentoid section (Fig. 19.3, no. 33). In Scotland this would normally be seen as an early Medieval type (Hunter 2008, 104–6); however, this example seems to be well-stratified in Roman-period (Severan?) levels. Parallels have proved rather elusive, but a similar form from Alcester suggests the type was known in the Roman period (Lloyd-Morgan 2001, 249, fig. 162 no. 198).

Only one bangle, from Newstead, is intact (Plate 12); it was probably deposited in one of the pits on the site which produced so many well-preserved items. Most bangles were discarded after they had broken, but two from Newstead had been reworked into tusk-shaped pendants (e.g. Fig. 19.3, no. 47), while the ends of a fragment from Balmuildy were reshaped, probably with the intention of fitting them into collars to repair the bangle, indicating they were valued items.

The range of shapes is quite typical; more unusual is the range of sizes. They show a clear bias towards larger armlets (internal diameters 70–90 mm) in contrast to other published datasets from Roman Britain which mostly show a strong peak around 55–65 mm with a smaller spread or secondary peak at 75–85 mm (Figure 19.2; see also Lawson 1975, fig. 3). The size of armlet an individual can wear is constrained by the size of their hand, and the size range suggests both male and female use, the latter generally dominant in Roman Britain. One of the southern samples, Caister-on-Sea, lacks the larger sizes, suggesting users here were female. By contrast, the strong emphasis on the larger end of the spectrum in Roman Scotland implies that these items were mostly worn by men; interestingly, a similar pattern is seen in the predominantly first-century material from the Caerleon legionary baths (Zienkiewicz 1986, 212).

Ring-pendants

Ring-pendants come from three sites, with manufacturing evidence from another (Fig. 19.4, top row). Such rings, normally with a circular or oval section, are too small for bangles, generally too large for beads, and some show a deliberate constriction or wear facet where a thong has fastened to them. Those with grooves are likely to be pendants, but others could have been hair rings (e.g. Allason-Jones 1996, 46, no. 283; a more ornamental example). The type has not seen detailed synthesis, but seems to have a long date range and broad distribution (see Hunter 2004, 107 for a summary). Its origins are Iron Age – indeed, the examples from Bar Hill may relate to underlying Iron Age activity – but an unfinished example from Camelon confirms manufacture in Roman Scotland (Fig.

Site	*number*	*date*	*bangle*	*pendant*	*bead*	*vessel*	*other*	*rough-outs/ working debris*	*Notes*
Balmuildy	2	A	2	–	–	–	–	–	1 reworked
Bar Hill	4	A	*	1	–	–	coin mould	2/–	1 post-medieval pencil; pendants perhaps Iron Age; rough-outs for bangle & ring-pendant
Bothwellhaugh	14	A	*	–	–	–	–	7/7	1 IA; rough-outs include bangle
Camelon	7	F/A	4	*	–	–	–	2/1	rough-outs probably ring-pendants
Carriden	1	A	1	–	–	–	–		
Cramond	6	A/S	4	1	–	–	–	1/–	bangle rough-out
Croy Hill	1	A	–	*	–	–	–	1/–	pendant or bead rough-out
Doune	1	F	–	–	–	1	–	–	
Elginhaugh	2	F	1	–	–	1	–	–	
Falkirk, Kemper Ave	1	A	1	–	–	–	–	–	
Inveresk	2	A	2	–	–	–	–	–	
Mumrills	5	A	–	–	–	1	finger ring, whorl	2/–	
Newstead	31	F/A	4	1	2	–	whorl	3/20	2 bangles reworked; pendant, beads, working debris and some bangles from field-walking
Strageath	3	A	2	–	–	–	–	1/–	bangle rough-out
no of sites	14	–	9(+2)	3(+2)	1	3	3	8	
no of objects	80	–	21	3	2	3	4	47	

F, Flavian; A, Antonine; S, Severan; IA, Iron Age; * denotes the artefact type is represented at the site by a rough-out; these are included in the site tallies at the bottom as '(+x)'.

Table 19.1 Summary of black stone finds from Roman Scotland

19.3, no. 25 and Plate 13), while Croy Hill has a related type, a disc pendant (Fig. 19.3, no. 35).

Such pendants are known from military contexts elsewhere in the northern frontier and further afield: from the military zone, South Shields, Carrawburgh and Watercrook (Allason-Jones and Miket 1984, 319–20, no. 7.171; Allason-Jones and Mackay 1985, 34–5, no. 101; Potter 1979, 218, fig. 87 no. 88); from southern Britain, London (Newgate), Canterbury, Rope Lake Hole (Dorset), Caerleon, Tort Hill West (Cambridgeshire) and Silchester (Murdoch 1991, 177, no. 505; Leveson-Gower 1995, 1188, fig. 526, no. 1269; Cox and Woodward 1987, fig. 93 no. 135; Zienkiewicz 1986, 214, fig. 78 no. 24; Bevan 1998, 83, fig. 50.1; Lawson 1975, 256, fig. 7 no. 59). Lindsay's work showed that an example from South Shields was an import from central Scotland, while ring-pendants also occur in lithomarge, an exotic mottled stone, at Housesteads and Carlisle (Allason-Jones and Jones 1994, 270–1; Stevenson and Collins 1976, pl. 1; Padley 1991, 158, fig. 144); these too are likely to be imports from north of Hadrian's Wall (Goldberg in prep.). I have not yet found a Continental example, and it seems likely that the type was adopted from British Iron Age habits – most likely in the northern frontier, as they are markedly more common in northern than southern Britain in the Iron Age.

Other finds

Other jewellery is rare. Two beads are known, both field-walking finds from around the fort at Newstead (Fig. 19.4, nos 52–3). They could be Iron Age rather than

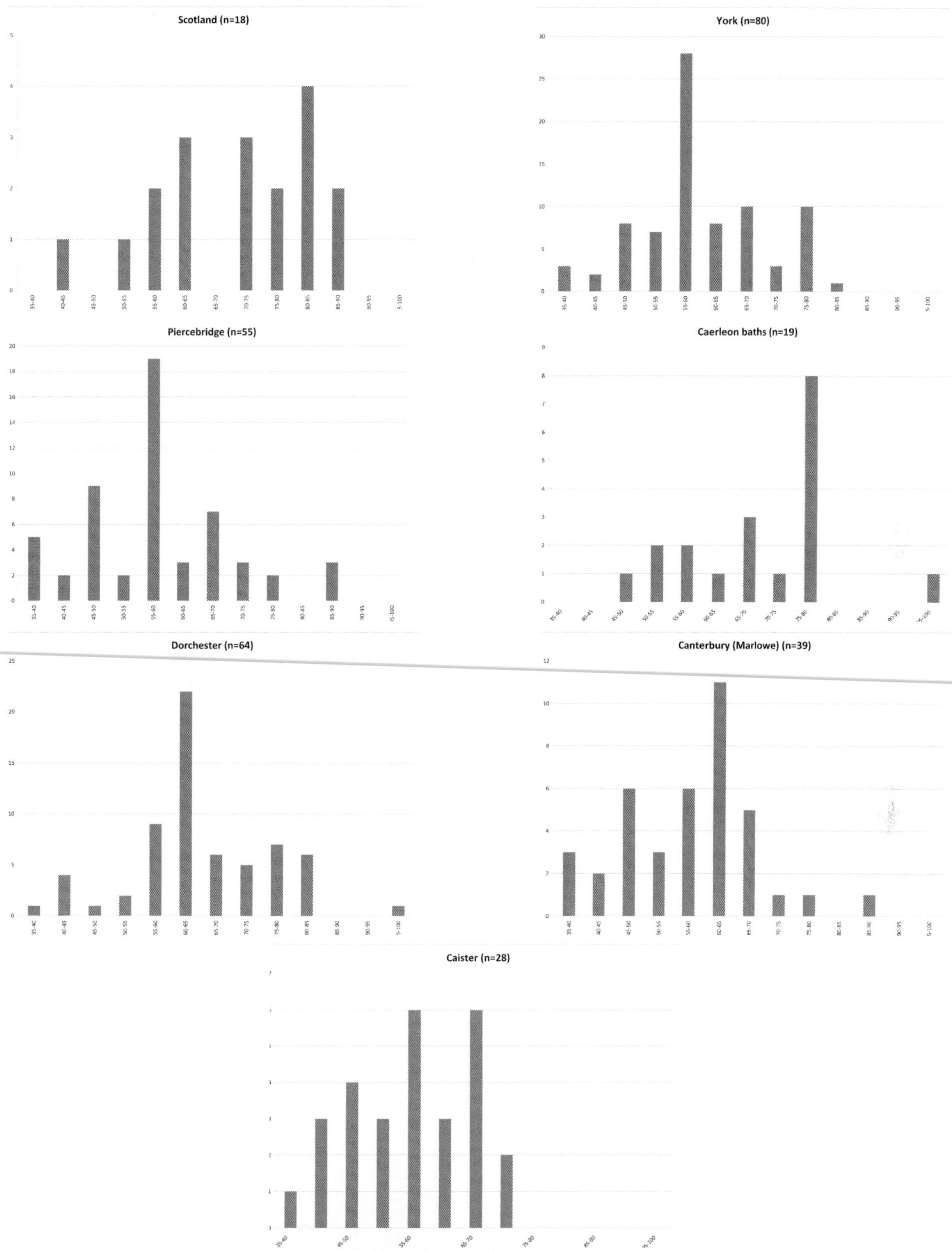

Figure 19.2 internal diameter range of the Scottish bangles compared to those from York (Allason-Jones 1996), Piercebridge (Fairless 2008), Caerleon baths (Zienkiewicz 1986, 212–4), Dorchester (Mills and Woodward 1993), Marlowe car park, Canterbury (Leveson-Gower 1995), and Caister-on-Sea (Darling and Gurner 1993, 84–95)

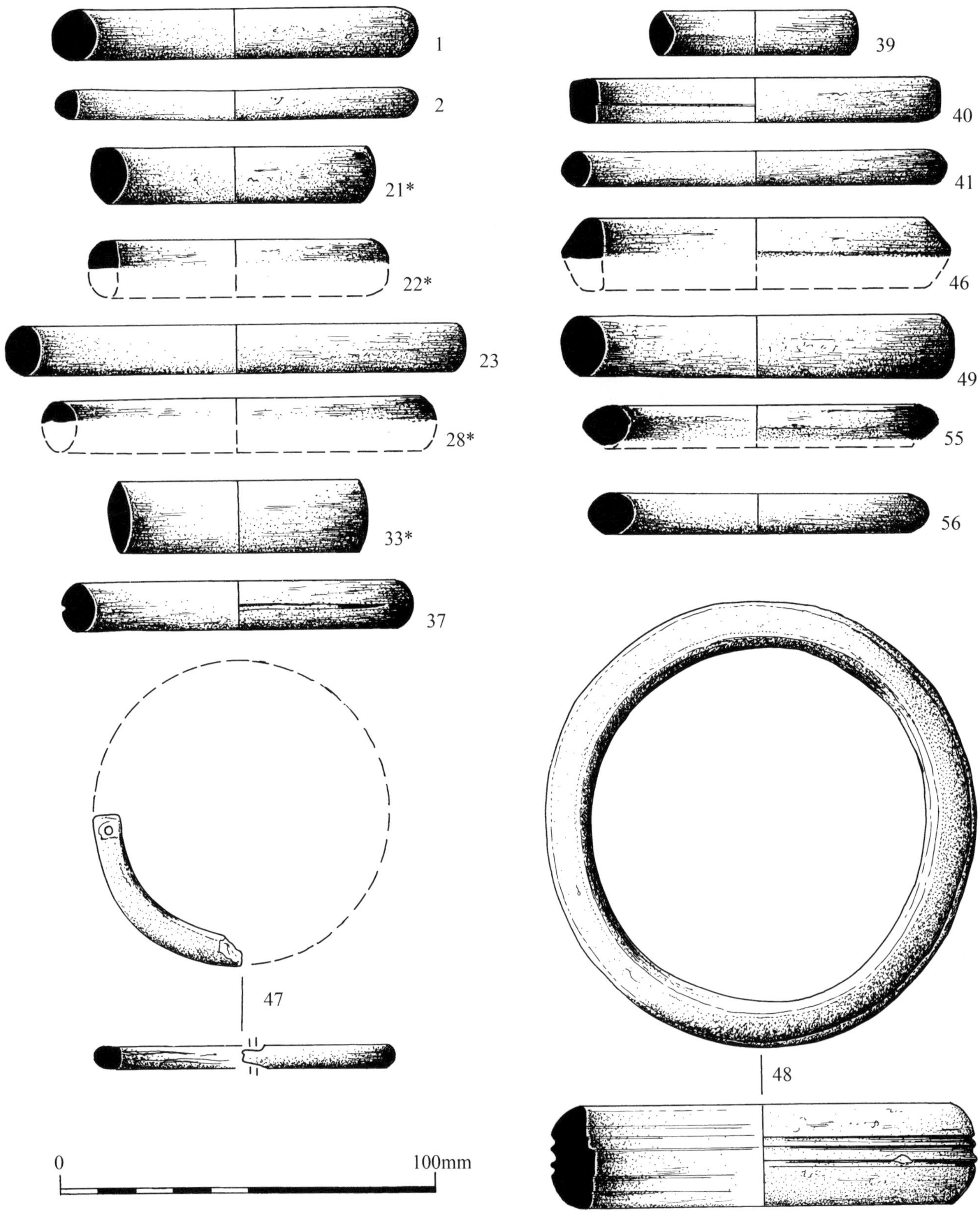

*Figure 19.3 Selection of bangles. Numbers refer to Appendix; those marked * are redrawn from publications. Drawn by Alan Braby*

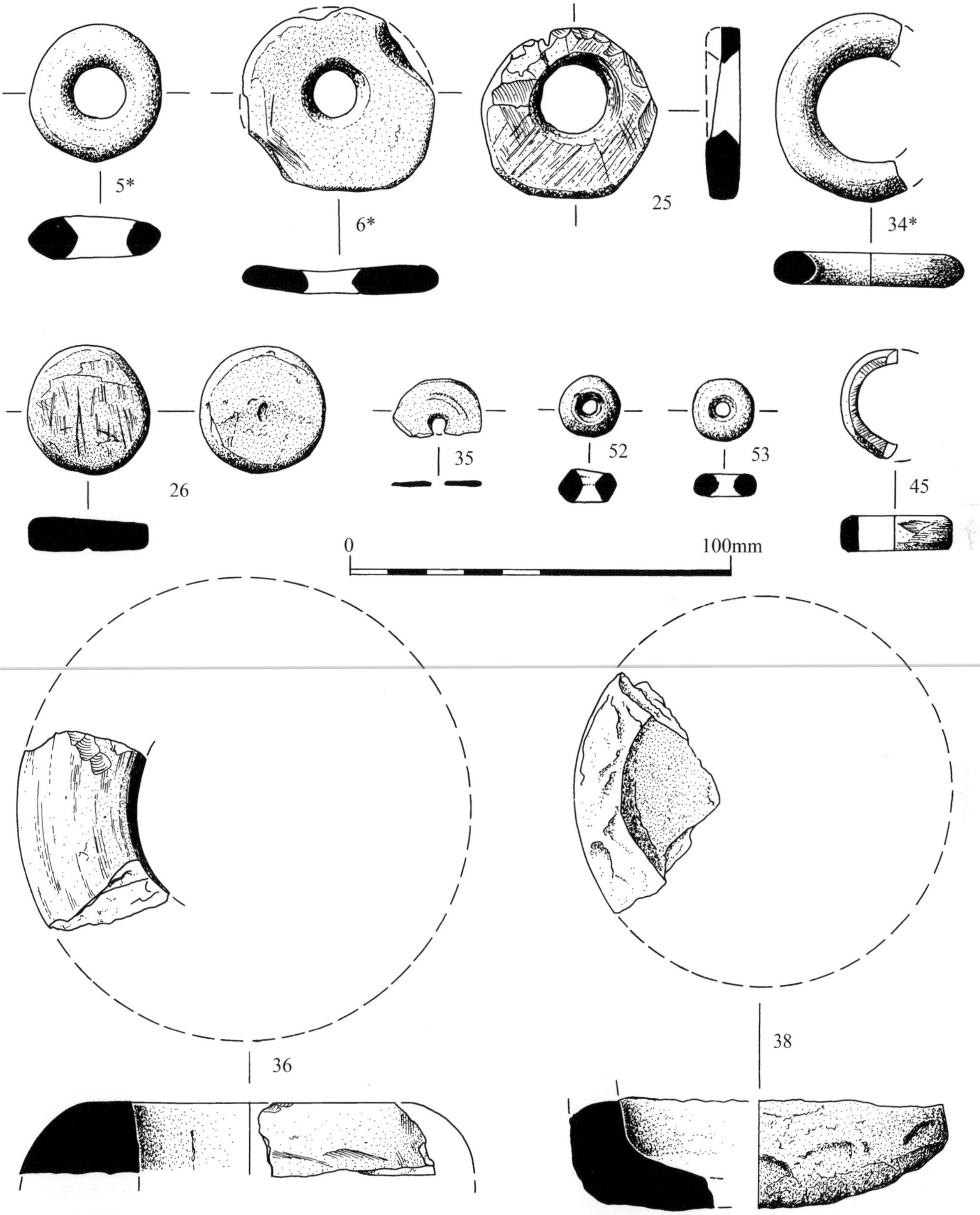

*Figure 19.4 Ring-pendants, beads, finger rings and vessels from various sites. Numbers refer to Appendix; those marked * are redrawn from publications. Drawn by Alan Braby*

Roman, although the biconical bead with a pronounced hourglass perforation finds occasional Roman parallels (e.g. South Shields; Allason-Jones 1983, 133, no. 6), as does the irregular disc bead (e.g. Allason-Jones and Miket 1984, no. 7.73–74). Only a single finger ring is known, from Mumrills; it seems to be a plain band, a relatively rare form in the Roman period with a few parallels (Fig. 19.4, no. 45; Allason-Jones 1996, 37, no. 175; Allason-Jones and Miket 1984, 311–2, no. 7.103, with a more circular section; Bevan 2010, 396; Crummy 1983, 45, fig. 49 no. 1739).

There are only a few non-jewellery items. A coin mould from Bar Hill is a unique find, plausibly connected with manufacturing the tin denarii used for ritual deposits in the principia well (Holmes and Hunter 2001, 173). Spindle whorls are known from Newstead and Mumrills. Vessel fragments are attested in the Flavian period, from Elginhaugh and Doune, and in the Antonine period at Mumrills (Fig. 19.4, nos 36, 38). Initially the Doune fragment was thought to be a very substantial D-sectioned bangle, 23 mm wide and 20 mm tall as it survives (as a bangle it would have been at least 40 mm high), but comparably large Roman-period bangles are elusive; the largest I can find, from Caerleon canabae, is only 16 × 21mm (Greep 2000, 445, fig. 116 no. 1), while one from Neath, now split, was around the same size (Marvell and Heywood 1992, 285, fig. 42 no. 2). Doune is unlikely to be an Iron Age survival, since large Iron Age bangles are tall but thin and firmly pre-Roman (e.g. Stead 1991, 90). It is more likely that this was the rim of a vessel, presumably a narrow-diameter thick-walled vase or beaker; fragments of similar form and size are known (e.g. Ilchester; Leach 1982, 217, fig. 103 no. 9a; Alcester; Lloyd-Morgan 2001, 249, fig. 162 no. 205).

Implications and origins

Overall, the range of finds is notably restricted and dominated by bangles. This is not particularly surprising: the more ornate products of the jet industry, such as pins, bead necklaces and figurines, are primarily a later Roman phenomenon, from the late second/early third century onwards (Allason-Jones 2002). Early military finds elsewhere in Britain are also bangle-focussed: this is hard to assess on sites which saw extended occupation as the late Roman material swamps the picture, but a number of first-century sites have produced only, or primarily, bangles, such as the fortresses at Usk and Caerleon (bath-house assemblage) or the forts at Hayton (Yorkshire) and Tiverton (Devon) (Manning 1995, 99–100; Zienkiewicz 1986, 213; Johnson 1978, fig. 16 no. 4; Maxfield 1991, 79). This geographical spread indicates that the habit was not restricted to one area.

The question of how 'jet' bangles were adopted in the Roman world is an interesting one. Such bangles are known in the Iron Age across Europe, but intermittently in time and space (Venclová 1998); by the late La Tène period, they are only attested to any extent in Britain and the northern French coast, where outcrops of Kimmeridge shale were extensively worked (Lefort and Marcigny 2009). The use of such black stone jewellery on the Continent in the Roman period is restricted and predominantly late Roman (Hagen 1937; Todd 1992; Allason-Jones and Jones 2001; Allason-Jones 2005). It is hard to see this as a habit introduced with the conquest, and much easier to see it as an adoption from local tradition. But where and how did this happen? There was a flourishing late Iron Age production in Dorset, based on the Kimmeridge sources, and this must have played a key part (Cunliffe 2005, 506–8), but this has rather dominated our picture of black jewellery in the British Iron Age. There was also an extensive Scottish tradition, focussed in areas near the sources in central, western and northern Scotland (Callander 1916; Hunter 2004; 2007; forthcoming a), while hints of further Iron Age regional traditions where raw material was available can be found in site reports (e.g. Staple Howe, E Yorkshire; Brewster 1963, 118–22; Murton High Crags, Northumberland; Jobey and Jobey 1987, 188–90; more generally, Challis and Harding 1975, 24–5). The habit among the army clearly predates the Flavian arrival in Scotland (as the examples above indicate) and may have been acquired in Dorset, but could the use of this material in Scotland relate to local availability of sources and skills? The technology would support this, as far as the evidence goes, since it is consistent with Scotland rather than Dorset (see below), while the range of products includes ring-pendants, more a northern rather than a southern type. Whatever the scenario, the range of material is essentially an Iron Age one in its bangles and pendants – this was acquired on these shores, not brought from the Continent.

Raw material and production

Lindsay's work with the late Mick Jones showed how the petrological techniques of oil geochemistry could be applied to tiny samples of archaeological objects in order to provide detailed provenance information (Allason-Jones and Jones 1994, 2001; see also Teichmüller 1992). This is a powerful but specialist technique. Work on the Scottish material has so far used a simpler, blunter set of techniques, with the combination of visual inspection, surface X-ray fluorescence analysis and X-radiography to provide broad categorisations of material type (Hunter *et al.* 1993; Davis 1993). It cannot provide specific provenance information, but allows broad-level differentiation of the material. The majority of the Scottish finds (41 of 80) have been subject to analysis. The most striking feature is that jet is unknown on Roman sites (there is one late Roman jet import on an indigenous site, discussed below): most of the finds are shale or cannel coal.

This can be correlated with evidence of production. Manufacturing debris is known from eight sites in the form of unfinished material or, more rarely, flakes and chips of working debris. The quantities from any one site are small and mostly undiagnostic; many are simply gathered slabs with only initial test-working to assess quality. Only at Bothwellhaugh can the process be reconstructed. This represents the typical Scottish Iron Age method of manufacture, with the rounding-off of a block and its bifacial hourglass perforation followed by expanding this out to the desired diameter and rounding off the exterior. One of the rough-outs was residual and must relate to Iron Age working, but other finds seem secure: a quantity of working debris was recorded from the base of the fort ditch, and nothing in its condition suggests that it was redeposited material. This puts the manufacturing contemporary with the fort. Other working debris is less diagnostic, but two aspects are clear: there is no evidence of lathe-turning (all the lathe-turned objects are finished imports), nor of manufacture by removing a central core. This is important, as core-removal was the dominant technique for bangles in the southern British Iron Age (Callander 1916; Hunter 2004; 2007; forthcoming a; Cunliffe 2005, 506–9; Cox and Woodward 1987; Mills and Woodward 1993).

This raises the question of who the suppliers were. Was this material made locally by local craft-workers? The analytical techniques employed so far do not allow us to specify exact sources, but the technology is consistent with this, at least at Bothwellhaugh. Most of the sites with working debris are from central Scotland, where the raw materials were available (Gibson 1922; Hunter 2008, fig. 1). Local craftworkers would have local knowledge of sources, although the ability of the army to locate other resources such as clay and stone locally indicates that they rapidly established a good understanding of what was available. Lindsay has noted the complexity of supply arrangements for black stones in Roman Britain, with working debris in areas far from their geological homeland and the careful selection of non-local material in areas close to apparently usable sources (Allason-Jones 2002, 130–1). This can be seen in the Scottish data in a rough-out from Strageath and (less securely) working debris from Newstead, distant from raw material sources. This raises intriguing questions about the identity of the manufacturer and their market – and also demands that excavators take care to recover the production waste, too readily discarded in the field.

Exports beyond the frontier

Lindsay's work has shown that black stone jewellery from north of Hadrian's Wall made its way onto Roman sites (Allason-Jones and Jones 1994, 271–2). The reverse process can also be traced occasionally. Roman black shiny stone jewellery was not generally sought after on indigenous settlements, as they had their own products, but a small group from the hillfort of Traprain Law is distinctive in their use of the lathe and their decoration (Hunter 2009, 234, fig. 21.6). Decorated bangles were exceedingly unusual in local tradition, which may have made these desirable items. The Traprain examples are typically late Roman: two shale bangles with notched decoration and one of cannel coal with ring and dot decoration, a jet quadrangular pyramidal bead, and an unusual cannel coal decorated cylinder, perhaps a knife handle. Another piece can now be added to the puzzle: a ring-pendant from Traprain Law decorated with a cable-twist pattern is paralleled at Haltonchesters on Hadrian's Wall (Cree 1924, 271, fig. 15.37; Allason-Jones 2010, fig. 11.4 no. 186). These are hybrids, as the form is ultimately an Iron Age one but the decoration is a Roman style found on bangles and finger rings. It seems most likely that the Traprain find, not the Haltonchesters one, was the imported piece, as decoration is exceedingly rare in the northern Iron Age.

No other site in Scotland has produced such Roman 'jet' imports with one potential exception: a lathe-turned finger ring from the Lochspouts crannog (Munro 1882, 174, fig. 170). The style is simple, just a plain circular section, but the technology is unparalleled locally; there are other Roman finds from the site (*ibid.*, figs 178–80).

There is another strand to this story. While jet pins are unknown from Roman sites in Scotland, there is an intriguing group of Iron Age bone pins (and one needle) stained black, presumably to mimic jet (Hunter 2005, updated in Hunter *et al.* 2013, 261). They have a broad distribution in southern and western Scotland; those which can be dated come from Roman Iron Age contexts, though the dating is rarely tight. Most are shank fragments, but the only one with a surviving head (from Kilellan, Islay) seems to be a copy of a late Roman facetted-head pin (Hunter

2005; Ritchie 2005, fig. 92.6, from a late pre-Roman/Roman Iron Age midden; cf. Allason-Jones 1996, 40–2). There are broader Romano-British parallels for blackening bone to emulate jet (e.g. Allason-Jones 2002, 125). Not all were intended as copies: Broxmouth hillfort has produced a stained bone needle, a type not found in jet in the Roman world (there is a similar bone needle stained black from Carlisle; Padley 1991, 190). Decoration rather than emulation was probably the aim here. This is true also of two hemispherical gaming pieces from Broxmouth (East Lothian), again Roman Iron Age in date, also stained black (Hunter *et al.* 2013, 271–3).

Conclusion

This small group of material casts some fresh insights into life in the frontier zone. Such black shiny jewellery was an uncommon but persistent element among military communities. Bangles predominate, and the sizes of many indicate they were male ornaments. Some are lathe-turned shale imports, probably from Kimmeridge, coming in most plausibly with the black-burnished ware trade, but others were made locally, and the agents behind this are tantalising. Does this represent an initiative of soldiers or vicus inhabitants? Some seem likely to stem from the local population as the production technology matches theirs. There is a wider question of the origins of the Romano-British habit; material from first–second century sites predominantly comprises types of Iron Age character, and it seems that this habit was adopted in Roman Britain from local traditions; it is unclear if there was one source or several for this. Lindsay has shown that ornaments made in central Scotland made their way to Hadrian's Wall in the later Roman period, showing a desire for this unusual material among frontier communities, while some late Roman decorative material made the return journey to a high-status indigenous site, Traprain Law. The black stone jewellery and other finds from Scotland offer a small glimpse into this world of connections and craft skills.

Acknowledgements

This paper is some small measure of repayment for the good advice, excellent publications, interesting debates and intriguing gossip which Lindsay has provided over the years. For access to material and information on unpublished finds I am grateful to Sue Anderson, Geoff Bailey, David Breeze, Julie Franklin, Bill Hanson, Lawrence Keppie, Val Maxfield and Dawn McLaren.

Bibliography

Allason-Jones, L. (1983) Jet and shale. In R. Miket. *The Roman Fort at South Shields: excavation of the defences 1977–1981*, 133. Gateshead: Tyne & Wear County Council.

Allason-Jones, L. (1996) *Roman Jet in the Yorkshire Museum*. York: Yorkshire Museum.

Allason-Jones, L (2002) The jet industry and allied trades in Roman Britain. In P. Wilson and J. Price (eds). *Aspects of Industry in Roman Yorkshire and the North*, 125–32. Oxford: Oxbow Books.

Allason-Jones, L. (2005) Coals from Newcastle. In N. Crummy (ed.) *Image, Craft and the Classical World: essays in honour of Donald Bailey and Catherine Johns*, 181–6. Montagnac: Editions Monique Mergoil.

Allason-Jones, L. (2007) Small objects. In W. S. Hanson. *Elginhaugh: a Flavian fort and its annexe*, 396–443. London: Society for the Promotion of Roman Studies.

Allason-Jones, L. (2010) The small finds. In J. N. Dore. *Haltonchesters: excavations Directed by J. P. Gillam at the Roman fort, 1960–61*, 143–59. Oxford: Oxbow Books.

Allason-Jones, L. (2011) *Jet, Shale and Other Allied Materials*. Roman Finds Group datasheet 2.

Allason-Jones, L. and Jones, D. M. (1994) Jet and other materials in Roman artefact studies. *AA* 5th Series 22, 265–72.

Allason-Jones, L. and Jones, J. M. (2001) Identification of 'jet' artifacts by reflected light microscopy. *European Journal of Archaeology* 4.2, 233–51.

Allason-Jones, L. and Mackay, B. (1985) *Coventina's Well: a shrine on Hadrian's Wall*. Chesters: Trustees of the Clayton Collection.

Allason-Jones, L. and Miket, R. (1984) *The Catalogue of Small Finds from South Shields Roman Fort*. Newcastle upon Tyne: Society of Antiquaries of Newcastle upon Tyne.

Bevan, L. (1998) Jet, shale, copper alloy, iron and lead objects. In P. Ellis, G. Hughes, P. Leach, C. Mould and J. Sterenberg. *Excavations Alongside Roman Ermine Street, Cambridgeshire, 1996*, 82–85, BAR British Series 276. Oxford.

Bevan, L. (2010) Jet and shale objects. In I. Ferris. *The Beautiful Rooms are Empty: excavations at Binchester Roman fort, County Durham, 1976–1981 and 1986–1991*, 395–403. Durham: Durham County Council.

Brewster, T. C. M. (1963) *The Excavation of Staple Howe*. Malton: East Riding Archaeological Research Committee.

Callander, J. G. (1916) Notice of a jet necklace found in a cist in a Bronze Age cemetery, discovered on Burgie Lodge Farm, Morayshire, with notes on Scottish prehistoric jet ornaments. *PSAS* 50, 201–40.

Challis, A. J. and Harding, D. W. (1975) *Later Prehistory from the Trent to the Tyne*. BAR British Series 20. Oxford.

Christison, D., Buchanan, M. and Anderson, J. (1901) Account of the excavation of the Roman station of Camelon, near Falkirk, Stirlingshire, undertaken by the Society in 1900. *PSAS* 35, 329–417.

Cox, P. and Woodward, P. (1987) The Kimmeridge shale. In N. Sunter and P. J. Woodward (eds) *Romano-British Industries in Purbeck*, 165–72. Dorchester: Dorset Natural History and Archaeological Society.

Cree, J. E. (1924) Account of the excavations on Traprain Law during the summer of 1923. *PSAS* 58, 241–84.

Crummy, N. (1983) *The Roman Small Finds from Excavations in Colchester 1971–9*. Colchester: Colchester Archaeological Trust.

Cunliffe, B. (2005) *Iron Age Communities in Britain* (4th edition). London: Routledge.

Darling, M. J. and Gurney, D. (1993) *Caister-on-Sea: excavations by Charles Green, 1951–55*. East Anglian Archaeology 60. Norwich: Norfolk Museums Service.

Davidson, J. M. (1952) Bothwellhaugh. In S. N. Miller (ed.) *The Roman Occupation of South-western Scotland*, 172–87. Glasgow: Robert Maclehose & Co.

Davis, M. (1993) The identification of various jet and jet-like materials used in the Early Bronze Age in Scotland. *The Conservator* 17, 11–18.

Fairless, K. J. (2008) Objects of jet, shale and similar materials. In H. E. M. Cool and D. J. P. Mason (eds) *Roman Piercebridge: excavations by D W Harding and Peter Scott 1969–1981*, digital chapter 11, part 6. Durham: Architectural and Archaeological Society of Durham and Northumberland.

Gibson, W. (1922) *Cannel Coals, Lignite and Mineral Oil in Scotland*. London: Memoirs of the Geological Survey of Scotland, Special Reports on the Mineral Resources of Great Britain 24.

Greep, S. (2000) Objects of shale. In E. Evans. *The Caerleon Canabae: excavations in the civil settlement 1984–90*, 444–8. London: Society for the Promotion of Roman Studies.

Hagen, W. (1937) Kaiserzeitliche Gagatarbeiten aus dem rheinischen Germanien. *Bonner Jahrbucher* 142, 77–144.

Hoffmann, B. (2003) Roman glass from Newstead and Vindolanda. *Annales du 15e Congrès de l'Association Internationale pour l'Histoire du Verre, New York 2001*, 41–4. Nottingham.

Holmes, N. (2003) *Excavation of Roman sites at Cramond, Edinburgh*. Edinburgh: Society of Antiquaries of Scotland.

Holmes, N. and Hunter, F. (2001) Roman counterfeiters' moulds from Scotland. *PSAS* 131, 167–76.

Hunter, F. (2004) Objects of stone, slate, oil shale and related material. In G. Ewart and D. Pringle (eds) Dundonald Castle Excavations 1986–93, 104–7. *Scottish Archaeological Journal* 26.

Hunter, F. (2005) Analysis of unusual bone pins from Kilellan Farm, Islay, and MacArthur Cave, Oban. In Ritchie (2005), 183.

Hunter, F. (2006) Recent finds from Strageath Roman fort. *Tayside & Fife Archaeological Journal* 12, 81–8.

Hunter, F. (2007) The cannel coal. In C. Ellis. Total excavation of a later prehistoric enclosure at Braehead, Glasgow, *PSAS* 137, 179–264 (204–19)

Hunter, F. (2008) Jet and related materials in Viking Scotland. *Medieval Archaeology* 52, 103–18.

Hunter, F. (2009) Traprain Law and the Roman world. In W. S. Hanson (ed.) *The Army and Frontiers of Rome*, 225–40. Journal of Roman Archaeology (Supplementary Series): Portsmouth, Rhode Island.

Hunter, F. (forthcoming a) Craft in context: artefact production in later prehistoric Scotland. In I. Ralston and F. Hunter (eds). *Scotland in Later Prehistoric Europe*. Edinburgh: Society of Antiquaries of Scotland.

Hunter, F. (forthcoming b) Shale and amber. In M. Kirby. *Excavations at Musselburgh Primary Health Care Centre: Iron Age and Roman discoveries to the north of Inveresk fort, East Lothian*. Edinburgh: SAIR.

Hunter, F., Gibson, A. M. and Gerken, J. (2013) The worked bone and antler. In I. Armit and J. Mackenzie (eds). *An Inherited Place: Broxmouth hillfort and the south-east Scottish Iron Age*, 251–309. Edinburgh: Society of Antiquaries of Scotland.

Hunter, F. J., McDonnell, J. G., Pollard, A. M., Morris, C. R. and Rowlands, C. C. (1993) The scientific identification of archaeological jet-like artefacts. *Archaeometry* 35, 69–89.

Jobey, I. and Jobey, G. (1987) Prehistoric, Romano-British and later remains on Murton High Crags, Northumberland. *AA* 5th Series 15, 151–98.

Johnson, S. (1978) Excavations at Hayton Roman fort, 1975. *Britannia* 9, 57–114.

Keppie, L. J. F. (1981) Excavation of a Roman bathhouse at Bothwellhaugh, 1975–76. *Glasgow Archaeological Journal* 8, 46–94.

Keppie, L. J. F. and Mearns, J. (1985) Small finds. In L. J. F. Keppie. Excavations at the Roman fort of Bar Hill, 1978–82, *Glasgow Archaeological Journal* 12, 49–81 (microfiche 1).

Keppie, L. J. F. and Murray, J. F. (1981) A Roman hypocausted building at Falkirk, *PSAS* 111, 248–62.

Kilbride-Jones, H. E. (1938) Glass armlets in Britain. *PSAS* 72, 366–95.

Lawson, A. J. (1975) Shale and jet objects from Silchester. *Archaeologia* 105, 241–75.

Leach, P. (1982) *Ilchester volume 1: excavations 1974–1975*. Bristol: Western Archaeological Trust.

Lefort, A. and Marcigny, C. (2009) L'artisanat du lignite: Naqueville (Manche). In P. Giraud (ed.). *Gaulois sous les pommiers: découvertes de l'âge du Fer en Basse-Normandie IXe–Ier siècle av. J.-C.*, 75–6. Cabourg: Cahiers du Temps.

Leveson-Gower, J. (1995) Objects of shale and jet: the C.A.T. objects. In K. Blockley, M. Blockley, P. Blockley, S. S. Frere & S. Stow (eds) *The Archaeology of Canterbury V: excavations in the Marlowe Car Park and surrounding areas*, 1184–93. Canterbury: Canterbury Archaeological Trust.

Lloyd-Morgan, G. (2001) Jet and shale. In P. Booth and J. Evans (eds) *Roman Alcester: Northern Extramural Area. 1969–1988 Excavations*, 247–9. York: CBA Research Report 127/Roman Alcester 3

MacDonald, G. and Park, A. (1906) *The Roman Forts on the Bar Hill, Dumbartonshire*. Glasgow: Maclehose & Sons.

Manning, W. H. (1995) *Report on the Excavations at Usk 1965–1976: the Roman small finds*. Cardiff: University of Wales Press.

Marvell, A. G. and Heywood, B. (1992) Excavations at Neath. *Bulletin of the Board of Celtic Studies* 39, 170–298.

Maxfield, V. A. (1991) Tiverton Roman fort (Bolham): excavations 1981–1986. *Devon Archaeological Society Proceedings* 49, 25–98.

Maxwell, G. S. (1975) Excavation at the Roman fort of Bothwellhaugh, Lanarkshire, 1967–8. *Britannia* 6, 20–35.

Miller, S. N. (1922) *The Roman Fort at Balmuildy (Summerston, near Glasgow) on the Antonine Wall*. Glasgow: Maclehose, Jackson & Co.

Mills, J. M. and Woodward, P. J. (1993) Shale and jet. In P. J. Woodward, S. M. Davies and A. H. Graham (eds) *Excavations at the Old Methodist Chapel and Greyhound Yard, Dorchester, 1981–1984*, 139–45. Dorchester: Dorset Natural History & Archaeological Society.

Munro, R. (1882) *Ancient Scottish Lake-Dwellings or Crannogs*. Edinburgh: David Douglas.

Murdoch, T. (1991) *Treasures & Trinkets: jewellery in London from pre-Roman times to the 1930s*. London: Museum of London.

Padley, T. G. (1991) *The Metalwork, Glass and Stone Objects from Castle Street, Carlisle: excavations 1981–2*. Kendal: Cumberland and Westmorland Antiquarian and Archaeological Society.

Potter, T. W. (1979) *Romans in North-West England: excavations at the Roman forts of Ravenglass, Watercrook and Bowness on Solway*. Kendal: Cumberland and Westmorland Antiquarian and Archaeological Society.

Price, J. (1988) Romano-British glass bangles from East Yorkshire. In J. Price, P. R. Wilson, C. S. Briggs and S. J. Hardman (eds) *Recent Research in Roman Yorkshire*, 339–66. BAR British Series 193. Oxford.

Rae, A. and Rae, V. (1974) The Roman fort at Cramond, Edinburgh. Excavations 1954–1966, *Britannia* 5, 163–224.

Ritchie, A. (ed.) (2005) *Kilellan Farm, Ardnave, Islay: excavations of a prehistoric to early Medieval site by Colin Burgess and others 1965–76*. Edinburgh: Society of Antiquaries of Scotland.

Robertson, A., Scott, M. and Keppie, L. (1975) *Bar Hill: a Roman fort and its finds*. BAR British Series 16. Oxford.

Stead, I. M. (1991) *Iron Age Cemeteries in East Yorkshire*. London: English Heritage.

Stevenson, R. B. K. (1956) Native bangles and Roman glass. *PSAS* 88, 208–21.

Stevenson, R. B. K. (1976) Romano-British glass bangles. *Glasgow Archaeological Journal* 4, 45–54.

Stevenson, R. B. K. and Collins, G. H. (1976) Beads of reddish marbled stone (lithomarge). *Glasgow Archaeological Journal* 4, 55–6.

Teichmüller, M. (1992) Organic petrology in the service of archaeology. *International Journal of Coal Geology* 20, 1–21.

Todd, M. (1992) Jet in northern Gaul. *Britannia* 23, 246–8.

Venclová, N. (1998) Black materials in the Iron Age of Central Europe. In F. Müller (ed.), *Münsingen-Rain, ein Markstein der keltischen Archäologie: Funde, Befunde und Methoden im Vergleich*, 287–98. Bern: Verlag Bernisches Historisches Museum.

Zienkiewicz, J. D. (1986) *The Legionary Fortress Baths at Caerleon II. The Finds*. Cardiff: National Museumof Wales/CADW.

Appendix: finds of jet-like material from Roman sites in Scotland

Abbreviations: Length, Width, Thickness, internal, external, Diameter, perforation. All dimensions in millimetres. % = surviving % of original bangle. * = incomplete dimension. + = illustrated

Balmuildy (Antonine)

1+ Bangle fragment, rounded D section, internally rounded; reworked after breakage by grooving around ends, perhaps to repair with collars. L 102, W 12, T 13.5; int D 80–85 (41%). Shale. Annexe E ditch. Hunterian F.1922.49 (Miller 1922, 95)

2+ D-sectioned bangle fragment. L 55, W 7, T 7.5, int D 80–85 (20%). Shale. Annexe E ditch. Hunterian F.1922.50 (Miller 1922, 95)

Bar Hill (Antonine)

3 Unfinished broad D-sectioned bangle, split horizontally and broken. Perforation virtually finished, with near-vertical face and smoothed knife-cuts at top edge. Outer edge shows abraded knife-cut facets; face uneven, with abrasion scars. L 111, W 24, T 12*, int. D 70–75 (48%). Cannel coal. Hunterian F.1936.83 (MacDonald and Park 1906, 91; Robertson et al. 1975, 48, fig. 13.59)

4 Badly-damaged coin mould with one original rounded edge surviving; dished circular feature with standing figure. Reverse heavily abraded to shape. 38 × 27 × 7.5. Shale/cannel. Hunterian F.1936.84 (MacDonald and Park 1906, 91; Robertson et al. 1975, 48, fig. 13.60)

5+ Ring-pendant with hour-glass perforation; surface worn. Pre-fort; burning associated with feature linked to proposed Antonine labour camp, but could be Iron Age. D 34.5, T 9, perf. D 15. Shale. Hunterian F.1985.1 (Keppie and Mearns 1985, no. 1)

6+ Roughout with central hourglass perforation (D 12 mm). Faces uneven, one with some abrasion; edges cut and slightly abraded to round off corners; subsequent edge-flaking probably to shape it rather than representing later damage. From turf build-up at earliest levels in NE corner of courtyard; Iron Age? 52 × 47 × 9. Shale. Hunterian F.1985.2 (Keppie and Mearns 1985, no. 2)

Bothwellhaugh (Antonine)

7 Part-shaped roughout. Modified natural slab, triangular, one edge cut, others roughly snapped and flaked with some knife-trimming. 186 × 89 × 15. Shale/cannel. Trench 3. Hunterian F.1939.325 (Davidson 1952, 182; 'a few pieces of shale')

8 Much-broken fragment with no original edges, preserving a flaked partial perforation near one surviving edge. 45 × 31 × 8.5. Shale. Bottom of ditch, trench 2. Hunterian F.1939.326/1

9 Broken flake from squared block. One edge cut square, part of one corner surviving. Flake scars and groove on surface, perhaps marking-out line. 38.5 × 28.5 × 7. Shale/cannel. Bottom of ditch, trench 2. Hunterian F.1939.326/2

10 Broken squared roughout; two surviving edges and part of angled third cut square. 36 × 30 × 8.5. Shale. Trench 3. Hunterian F.1939.326/3

11 Squared roughout fragment, one edge cut square, others broken; faces flaked to thin them. 37 × 18.5 × 9.5. Shale/cannel. Trench 3. Hunterian F.1939.326/5

12 Roughout, part-perforated; block part-rounded by flaking; faces uneven. Pecked hollow on each face, not quite opposed. From body of NE rampart; residual Iron Age. 81 × 80 × 18.5. Shale/cannel. Hunterian F.1981.33 (Maxwell 1975, 33, fig. 5a)

13 Rounded bangle roughout, abandoned after bifacial perforation was completed. Edge rounded by cutting and flaking; surfaces flaked and chiselled. Over-thinning led it to snap. 92 × 62 × 22. Cannel. On phase 3 slabbing N of bathhouse. Hunterian F.1982.22 (Keppie 1981, 73 no. 22)

14 Working debris; flake from irregular corner of part-squared block. 35 × 26.5 × 12.5. Shale/cannel. Hunterian F.1939.326/4

15 Working debris. 31 × 15 × 9.5. Material uncertain. Hunterian F.1939.326/7

16 Working debris. 10 × 8 × 6. Material uncertain. Hunterian F.1939.326/8

17 Working debris. 17.5 × 14 × 8.5. Material uncertain. Hunterian F.1939.326/9

18 Part-worked block? Naturally smooth triangular slab with concavity cut into one side. Purpose unclear. 69 × 40.5 × 7. Shale. Hunterian F.1940.6 (Davidson 1952, 184)

19 Working debris. Flake from corner of squared block. 30 × 21.5 × 13.5. Shale/cannel. Hunterian F.1940.7 (Davidson 1952, 184)

20 Working debris; flake removed from corner of block. 54.5 × 25 × 19. Cannel. On phase 3 slabbing N of bathhouse. Hunterian F.1982.22

Camelon

21+ Bangle fragment, asymmetrical oval section; fracture surfaces worn. L 57, W 10, T 16, int D 50–55 (33%). Shale. Antonine. Falkirk Museum, CAM 76.289 (context info from V Maxfield)

22+ D-sectioned bangle fragment, split horizontally, probably lathe-turned. L 64.5, W 7.5, T 9*, int. D 60–65 (33%). Shale. Antonine. Falkirk Museum, CAM 76.45 (context info from V Maxfield)

23+ Bangle fragment with asymmetrical oval section, exterior more rounded. Well polished, almost no toolmarks. Some exterior use-wear. L 55, W 9, T 13, int. D 75–80 (20%). ?Shale. NMS FX 175 (Christison et al. 1901, 397)

24 Bangle fragment, faces lost and section uncertain. L 27, W 8, int. D 70–75. Not seen, not analysed. From AOC excavations in southern area of fort complex (sf.179; information from D McLaren).

25+ Roughout, probably for a ring-pendant. Perforated disc, one face abraded (filed?), one flaked and abraded; edges cut and rounded by abrasion. Off-centre biconical perforation (D 18mm) in course of abrasion. Abandoned due to flaking of one side. 45 × 44 × 8. Cannel. NMS FX 224 (Christison et al. 1901, 412)

26+ Roughout for bead or ring-pendant. Faces abraded; edges cut and then abraded to shape; rectangular section with rounded edges; incipient central perforation on one side. 32 × 33 × 9. Shale. NMS FX 225 (Christison et al. 1901, 412)

27 Working debris; broken flake. 40 x 40 mm. Not seen, not analysed. From AOC excavations in southern area of fort complex (sf. 90; information from D McLaren)

Carriden (Antonine)

28+ D-sectioned bangle fragment. L 27, W 8, T 5*, int. D ?. Not seen. Latrine drain fill in bathhouse. Falkirk 2006-11-74 (G. Bailey, pers. comm.)

Cramond

29 Bangle of triangular section. Not seen, not illustrated; dimensions not given. Antonine level in building in retentura. Edinburgh Museum (Rae and Rae 1974, 197 no. 4)

30+ D-sectioned bangle fragment. L 76, W 8, T 12, int. D 85–90. Not seen. Unstratified, bathhouse. Edinburgh Museum (Holmes 2003, 120, illus. 118.1)

31 Bangle, oval section; interior angle suggests lathe-turned. L 42, W 5.5, T 6, int. D 50–55 mm. Not seen, not analysed, but photo indicates splitting typical of shale. From C Hoy's unpublished excavations at Cramond Road, 1984 (information from D. McLaren)

32 Bangle, section unclear due to spalling. L 24, W 5, int. D 70–75? Not seen, not analysed. From C Hoy's unpublished excavations at Cramond Road, 1990 (information from D. McLaren)

33+ Unfinished bangle, narrow lentoid section. L 62, W 5, T 19, int. D 55–60. Not seen. Blocking material between two buildings. Edinburgh Museum (Rae and Rae 1974, 197 no. 6)

34+ Ring-pendant, oval section. L 48, W 12, T 8, int. D 27. Not seen. Residual in post-medieval layers, bathhouse. Edinburgh Museum (Holmes 2003, 120, illus. 118.2)

The archive from Charlie Hoy's unpublished excavations around Cramond indicates that seven further 'jet' items were found, including two more bangles, but these cannot currently be located. They are not included in the tallies in this paper.

Croy Hill (Antonine)

35+ Bead or pendant roughout. Thin flat irregular disc with near-central biconical perforation. Crudely rounded, with edges and faces abraded; marking-out line on one face defines part of a circle 5 mm from the edge, giving an intended perforation some 10 mm D. L 23, W 2.5, T 5. Shale? With excavator (W. S. Hanson, pers. comm.)

Doune (Flavian)

36+ Vessel. Large, heavy rounded rim fragment, split horizontally; well-finished, with abrasion on the outer edge probably from repair. L 49, W 22.5, T 19.5*, int D 60–65 (20%). Not analysed; visually resembles canneloid shale. From fort ditch. With excavator, Headland Archaeology (J. Franklin, pers. comm.)

Elginhaugh (Flavian)

37+ Oval-sectioned bangle, decorated with irregular circumferential groove in centre of outer face, petering out to one end. Post-depositional wear. L 46.5, W 8, T 11.5, int D 70–75 (18%). Cannel. Layer sealed by road in E gate. NMS unreg. (Allason-Jones 2007, 441, fig. 10.42 no. 239)

38+ Fragment of flat base of vessel c.110 mm in diameter, with straight sides and thick walls. Hand-made, not lathe-turned. L 62, W 42, T 28. Shale. Demolition spread over barrack 12. NMS unreg (Allason-Jones 2007, 441, fig. 10.42, no. 240)

Falkirk, Kemper Avenue (Antonine)

39+ Small bangle; lentoid section with angled interior; production technology unclear. L 30, W 6, T 12, int D 40–45 (25%). Cannel. E of bath building. Falkirk 1981.16.15 (Keppie and Murray, 257 fig. 6.1)

Inveresk (Antonine)

40+ D-sectioned bangle fragment, lathe-turned. L 61, W 8, T 10.5, int. D 70–75 (25%). Seen, not analysed; visually identified as shale. Inveresk Gate, phase 2 midden. NMS unreg. (Bishop 2004, 149, fig. 99.127)

41+ D-sectioned bangle fragment, lathe-turned. L 37, W 7, T 8, int. D 80–85 (14%). Seen, not analysed; visually identified as shale. PPCM site, unstratified, N of fort (sf.18) (Hunter forthcoming b)

Mumrills (Antonine)

42 Flat base fragment from circular lathe-turned vessel; rounded rib at step into lost wall; two rectangular fragments of raised decoration partially preserved. Probably a dish. Base diameter *c.*90 mm. L 36, W 30, T 5. Seen, not analysed; visually identified as shale. Fieldwalking. Falkirk unreg. (G. Bailey, pers. comm.)

43 Whorl, low hemispherical section, cylindrical perforation (D 14 mm). D 39, T 12. Shale. Falkirk 1972-69-648 (G. Bailey, pers. comm.)

44 Two triangular shale fragments, non-joining but from the same block, with a slice removed from between them. Some vertical abrasion on some edges, while others are notably angled, suggesting this was a part-prepared roughout either deliberately or accidentally split. 92 × 57.5 × 12.5; 94 × 60 × 10. Shale. NMS FRB 600 and 601

45+ D-sectioned finger ring fragment with narrow facets on the faces. Polished, but residual facets and abrasion scars visible. L 28.5, W 4, T 10, int. D 20 (50%). Cannel. NMS FRB 616

Newstead

46+ Reworked bangle fragment, split horizontally; probably D-sectioned; broken hourglass perforation at one end and marking-out lines on other from attempts to reuse as pendant. L 31.5, W 11, T 9*, int. D 80–85 (10%). Material uncertain. Fieldwalking (W. Elliot, pers. comm.)

47+ Bangle, reused as pendant by perforating one end and shaping the other (now broken). Relatively narrow but broad D-section; asymmetrical angle on inner surface implies lathe-turned; angled abrasion scars from smoothing interior. Drilled perforation (D 2mm) at one squared end, other end tapered; discarded after further breakage. L 53, W 7.5, T 6.5, int D 55–60 (27%). Shale. NMS FRA 1176 (Curle 1911, pl. xciii no. 19)

48+ Intact bangle; tall D-section with lathe-ridging on interior. Decorated with band of three circumferential lathe-cut grooves, the central slightly deeper. Well-finished. Ext D 114.5, W 12, T 26, int. D 90 (100%). Shale. NMS FRA 1177 (Curle excavations)

49+ Bangle, near-oval section with asymmetric interior suggesting lathe-turned; surface worn, laminated and cracked. L 86.5, W 12, T 16, int. D 75–80 (34%). Shale? NMS FRA 1178 (Curle excavations)

50 Ring-pendant fragment, well-finished. L 32, W 9.5, T 5*, int. D 20–25 (34%). Cannel. Fieldwalking (W. Elliot, pers. comm.)

51 Fragmentary whorl, one face lost; barrel-shaped with flat ends; biconical perforation, D 3.5–7.5 mm. D 34.5, T 10. Shale. NMS FRA 465 (Curle excavations)

52+ Biconical bead with well-smoothed hourglass perforation (3–9.5 mm); tapers in section, surface worn. D 14.5, T 9. Material uncertain. Fieldwalking; from knoll SE of fort, in the same area as the working debris. NMS FRA 5326

53+ Disc bead, slightly irregular, with hourglass perforation. D 16, T 6. Not analysed. Fieldwalking SW of fort (W. Elliot, pers. comm.)

54 Working debris? Blocks and flakes of a dark material with a strong conchoidal fracture have been recovered by a number of field-walkers in the area around NT 5722 3433, immediately SE of the fort. Most show no clear signs of working, but the material is not local to the area, so they are likely to be broken-up working debris. There are three flaked blocks which may be rough-outs; six clear pieces of flaked working debris; and 14 fragmentary blocks showing no clear sign of working (NMS 5245, 5606 and X.2009.12). Not analysed

Strageath

55+ D-sectioned bangle fragment, ridge on interior from lathe-turning. L 46.5, W 11.5, T 11, int. D 60–65 (23%). Cannel. Antonine street. NMS FRG 1594 (Frere and Wilkes 1989, no. 103)

56+ Bangle fragment, well-rounded in section; hand-cut. L 34, W 12, T 11, int. D 60–65 (15%). Cannel. Antonine demolition layer. NMS FRG 1595 (Frere and Wilkes 1989, no. 104)

57 Working debris; flake broken from surface of part-finished bangle. 39.5 x 21.5 x 10.5. Cannel. Antonine demolition layer. NMS FRG 1609 (Hunter 2006, 85, illus. 4)

Notes

Bar Hill: Keppie and Mearns (1985), cat. 21 'shale disc' is omitted as it is a slate pendant.

Camelon: Christison *et al.* (1901, 412) mention three shale whorls/discs, but one is ceramic.

Elginhaugh: sf 241 'rectangular block of tapered section' is a natural block, as are other shale items in the archive.

Cramond: see note after entry for possible additional material.

20

LOST AND FOUND: CASUAL LOSS AND (RE)DISCOVERY OF ROMAN OBJECTS FROM THE NORTHERN FRONTIER

Rob Collins

Introduction

The 'native' farmsteads and settlements of Northumberland are infamous for the dearth of evidence of contact with the Roman army that occupied Hadrian's Wall. Indeed, these sites are clichéd for the almost ubiquitous assemblage of a (broken) quernstone, a small handful of recognisably Roman sherds of pottery and a fragmentary glass bangle. However, over the years more members of the public have found and reported objects of Roman provenance from a number of locations across Northumberland. In the past decade, these discoveries have been recorded almost exclusively through the local Portable Antiquities Scheme (PAS) officer; prior to the advent of the Scheme, many such discoveries were reported to Lindsay Allason-Jones at the Museum of Antiquities. These newly discovered objects provide new avenues into the study of the interaction between the Roman military and the population of the frontier zone, a theme that Lindsay has devoted much of her career exploring and this paper is humbly offered for years of mentorship and collegiality.

Romans and natives, soldiers and civilians

The archaeology of the Roman frontier of northern Britain is often dominated by the monumental complex of Hadrian's Wall, though active campaigning through northern England began in the AD 70s and continued north into Scotland in the following decades. The thousands of Roman soldiers that marched and rode across the middle of Britain in those years introduced a new range of objects along with the violence of military occupation. Marching camps and forts provide testament to the rapidity of campaigning, but within this era of initial occupation, it is uncertain what the impact was on the overall pattern of native settlement. By AD 122, the emperor Hadrian famously visited Britain and was initiating or inspecting works for his new mural-frontier, which created a clearer border for the empire. Antoninus Pius imitated Hadrian's work with his own Wall during a brief northern advance into southern Scotland, but Hadrian's Wall was once again the primary defended line in the AD 160s, with outpost forts occupied north of the Wall. Large-scale long-term occupation never again advanced north of Hadrian's Wall, though there were certainly military campaigns and probably relatively frequent raids. The outpost forts appear to have been occupied up to the early fourth century, and Hadrian's Wall was held until at least the early fifth century.

Over these three centuries of military occupation of northern England and occasionally southern Scotland, there was considerable opportunity for Roman–native interaction in both hostile and peaceful (or at least non-hostile) situations. However, with notable exceptions such as the prominent hillfort of Traprain Law, relatively little Roman material culture has been found outside of the forts and their associated extramural settlements north of Hadrian's Wall (Hunter 2007). Archaeological excavation has demonstrated this repeatedly. A number of rural sites in Northumberland were excavated by George Jobey in the 1960s and '70s, and these rarely produced more than ten small objects of Roman provenance – the clichéd handful of sherds and fragmentary glass bangle being the most common assemblage (e.g. Jobey 1970; 1971; 1973).

Two observations can be made, however, that could be said to impact on how much Roman material would be found on the sites excavated by Jobey. First, many of these sites were in upland locations, and consisted of a single building complex – that is to say a single farmstead. The argument here is that the occupants of farmsteads in upland locations may not be as likely to be recipients or users of Roman objects or to import such objects to upland sites as opposed to lowland settlements. The second observation is that Jobey often used trenches that were well-placed for determining an overall sequence of occupation of a site rather than a complete open-area excavation. The argument in this instance is that an open-area excavation method would be more likely to produce more objects. While both observations are reasonable, they can be proven as unrelated to the amount of Roman material found on rural sites. Jobey attempted to excavate lowland sites to provide a balanced account of rural settlement in Roman Northumberland, though such sites were often difficult to identify and were still typically only a single farmstead. Recent excavations, however, have been able to explore lowland sites far larger than Jobey's sites in advance of development, as well as making use of open-area excavation (e.g. Proctor 2009). In such cases, the paucity of Roman material is still striking, despite the methods employed and the presumably larger populations of such sites.

On top of this paucity of Roman material, dating the occupation of such settlements is often difficult unless radiocarbon dating can be employed. In the absence of the latter, it is often the Roman objects that provide a starting- or ending-date for a sequence. What is notable, however, is that most of the Roman material culture is of an early date, having been produced in the late first or second century typically, with third and fourth century material even more rare. When considered against the backdrop of Roman military movements, it then can become uncertain as to what was happening when the Roman goods were brought to the site. Is it material from initial contact during the conquest phase, or did the goods only arrive on site following consolidation of the frontier with the construction of Hadrian's Wall? Are the Roman objects from rural settlements evidence of peaceful trade and contacts? Or are such objects the booty of successful raiders displayed in their home communities? Were there considerable restrictions in the range of Roman objects available, or was there an active rejection of Roman material culture?

The North-East and the PAS

More than 2,500 objects of Roman date have been recorded from the North-East. As seen in Plate 16, Roman objects have been found fairly extensively throughout the region, though there is a notable decline in objects found in the west of the region, in the Pennines and Cheviots, or north of the River Aln. Another conspicuous gap in distribution can be found in the greater metropolitan areas of Newcastle and Sunderland. The Wall corridor appears to be significant in the distribution of objects, but this distribution is exaggerated by the apparent gap in discoveries between the Tyne and Wear. Furthermore, the southern half of Northumberland has a fairly reasonable distribution and is comparable to the distribution of objects in County Durham and Teesside. However, it must be remembered that these distributions reflect search patterns as much as the positive indication of Roman activity. For example most of the Roman objects from southern Northumberland have been found and recorded through the efforts of individual searchers using metal detectors; the lack of Roman objects from north Northumberland can be seen in objects of other periods, reflecting where people search more than where the objects may or may not be found. Therefore, it is better to place weight on the positive evidence – that is to say the objects themselves and where they are found.

The objects represent a large range of object types and categories, with coins being the most numerous (1,500 records), and ceramic and metal vessels being the second most numerous category (240 records). Following these is a mix of dress accessories including brooches, finger rings, and pins, *militaria* including evidence for weaponry, armour, and other fittings and accessories, and the more ubiquitous range of fixtures and fittings, along with occasional examples of religious and domestic objects. In comparison with other regions of England, for example Yorkshire and East Anglia, the North-East does not have as diverse an assemblage of object types, and certainly in far lower quantities. However, Roman evidence is more frequently encountered in the North-East than in the south-west of England and most of Wales, proportionally. The north also has more evidence of a military presence identifiable through PAS data than some regions. This highlights the importance of regional diversity in Roman Britain, and differences in the quantities and diversities of object types are probably a material correlation to regional differences in various aspects of rural settlement, including cultural choices and preferences.

In most cases, the largest concentrations of objects can be associated with a known Roman settlement, usually a fort or town. This is the case for the large assemblage from Piercebridge and also Corbridge. These assemblages are both riverine deposits recovered by divers. In the case of Corbridge, the objects were deposited along the river bed after eroding from the river bank. At Piercebridge, there may have been some riverside erosion of archaeological deposits, but the evidence to date suggests intentional deposition, probably of ritual or religious significance. The Piercebridge assemblage is very large, consisting of more than 5,000 objects, and contains of number of unusual objects as well as more everyday items, including 1,297 coins, 111 brooches, 155 items of military equipment, and 60 kg of pottery and animal bone. Its very size distorts regional statistics, and it forms the basis of its own study (Walton 2008). These two groups do, however, demonstrate that the largest concentrations of Roman objects are still associated with military and urban communities rather than the people of the countryside. This explains, at a general level, the assemblages from Piercebridge, Binchester, Corbridge, the Wall corridor, and High Rochester, and the less numerous objects from Bowes and Lanchester. That said, a number of clusters of material remain, and a few of these are worth considering more closely, with particular reference to the Roman material found in Northumberland and to the north of Hadrian's Wall.

Felton

The area of Felton, Northumberland, has produced a number of objects of Roman date that have been reported singly over the past decade. The individual finds are rarely important in and of themselves, but this steady accumulation of data points to settlement in the area. The most significant discovery was that of a third century hoard (NCL-C39B46) consisting of 99 coins dominated by issues of the Severan dynasty and deposited sometime after 227. Twelve other objects have been found with a 2 km distance; eight of these are first- and second-century coins, such as the denarius of Antoninus Pius (NCL-E6B7C6). But there is a petal-shaped mount (NCL-740961) that is typical of Romano-British art and could have belonged to a vessel or harness fitting and an incomplete and worn dragonesque brooch (NCL-D8DCE6), still retaining yellow and turquoise enamel in the cells of the body.

Warkworth

The area of Warkworth has produced a number of objects (ten), scattered outside of the village, but again indicating a settlement somewhere in the locality. As with Felton, nearly half of the scattered assemblage consists of coins of early Roman date (four in total). But other objects include a trumpet brooch (NCL-D132A1), a lock bolt (NCL-7F9275), a harness fitting (NCL-344F84), and an incomplete chatelaine (NCL-B79326). This latter is missing the toilet implements that would have suspended from it, but the body is complete, and its decorative cellwork retains traces of white enamel. Further enamel arranged in a swirling motif of symmetrically opposed cells infilled with blue and white can be seen on the discoidal top of a stud (NCL-AE5DB4).

Portgate, Great Whittington, & Ryal

In addition to the assemblage of objects found in the River Tyne, probably eroded out of the riverbank and associated with the town of Corbridge, there is a very significant cluster of objects from the greater Corbridge area, covering Dere Street as it approached the Portgate and the areas surrounding the present villages of Great Whittington and Ryal, both of which are located adjacent to the Devil's Causeway. Within this area more than 75 objects of Roman date have been recorded. More than half of these discoveries have been coins, mostly of early Roman date, but there are also considerable numbers of other objects.

Objects and coins have been found in small numbers along the road linking Corbridge to the Portgate through Hadrian's Wall, including a phallic pendant (NCL-D89384) and a vessel escutcheon in the shape of a leaf (NCL-D48E04). At the northern extreme of this belt, only five objects of Roman date have been recorded from the village of Ryal, but this includes two bells (NCL-377033 and NCL-625A82). Two trumpet brooches (NCL-6311B6; NCL-6EE4C2) and a large pin, probably belonging to a late penannular brooch (NCL-1D6807) have also been found. What is intriguing about Ryal is that so far, no Roman coins have been found.

In contrast, the fields around the village of Great Whittington have produced a very large and significant assemblage of Roman material from a rural context. A total of 27 Roman coins have been recorded, with the earliest issue a Republican denarius of Marc Antony dating 32–31 BC and the latest a nummus of the House of Valentinian dating 364–378. Twenty-two of these coins could be identified sufficiently to enable coin loss analysis to be completed (Plate 17), one of the few PAS sites in the North-East with enough coins to complete such as analysis. Relative to most sites in Roman Britain (Walton 2012), coin loss around Great Whittington is rather irregular. There is a clear peak of activity in the late first and early second century, followed by a drop in activity in the Antonine period, and a slight increase in the late second and early third centuries. Significantly, there is relatively little activity associated with the later third and fourth centuries, when Roman coinage is most prolific in Britain. However, when one considers the denominations represented, the majority of coins are denarii of the early Roman currency system, suggesting that perhaps there was not as much exchange of the smaller denomination base-metal coins. In addition to these individual coins, a small group of eight nummi was recovered, and this group was lost at some point in the first half of the fifth century (Collins 2008).

Twenty-one other objects of Roman date have been recorded from Great Whittington, and include a number of dress accessories, military equipment, harness equipment, and objects with a possible religious significance. Amongst the brooches are a Nauheim type (NCL-BC1EE6), a trefoil-cup brooch (NCL-34AD01), a T-shaped bow brooch (NCL-1B2CB5), and a Fowler A3 penannular brooch (NCL-BBB6E2). There have also been a dragonesque brooch (NCL-2B2544), headstud brooch (NCL-7FB222), trumpet brooch (NCL-802ED7), and variant of a trumpet brooch (NCL-7FD5A4) recorded, as well as a knee brooch (NCL-1B5052). The condition of the brooches is variable; the dragonesque brooch is largely complete and retains a good patina, though this was found in a field retained as pasture. Those brooches and other objects found in arable fields are often more fragmentary and poorly preserved. This assemblage represents the most diverse brooch assemblage recorded by the PAS in the region (excluding Piercebridge). Other dress accessories include a finger ring (NCL-C88983) and a copper-alloy pinhead (NCL-34C688).

A tentative suggestion can be made for an area of ritual or votive significance outside of the village of Great Whittington. A fairly discrete area has produced a copper-alloy miniature socketed axe (NCL-346DE5) that is best paralleled by Iron Age and Roman examples from votive or religious contexts (Kiernan 2009). In the same area, a pair of copper-alloy *paterae* were found (NCL-335745 and NCL-33CC76). These were found together, NCL-33CC76 considerably more fragmentary and resting inside NCL-335745, which was more complete and bore evidence for repair of the handle fitting. While the vessels clearly were used and repaired through their life, the practice of burying them may have religious significance (Allason-Jones 2010).

The high number of coins and objects from the fields around the village of Great Whittington indicates a site of some significance, contrasting with the evidence from Warkworth and Felton noted above, both of which were notable clusters of Roman objects. The fact that there may even be a religious or votive zone within the greater area of the settlement is also significant. Artefact distributions to the north and south of the village, notably along the Devil's Causeway, Dere Street, and Hadrian's Wall, further link the site at Great Whittington into the road network and Wall corridor.

These three areas, Felton, Warkworth, and Great Whittington – all of which are north of the Wall – indicate that there are more rural sites of Roman date to be identified, many of which may have a more diverse material culture than rural sites previously excavated. These areas are only three of many examples of Roman clusters that can be examined in more detail. Unfortunately, there is rarely any archaeological information that can be associated with PAS-recorded objects. However, a consideration of distinct classes of artefacts can more easily indicate differences in the region that have some bearing on our understanding of the people of the frontier.

Militaria and harness equipment

Military equipment and items related to harness have been found throughout the North-East region, but in relatively limited numbers north of Hadrian's Wall. Great Whittington offers a notable cluster of military objects, including an openwork buckle (NCL-9F54E2), a sword scabbard chape (NCL-31E084), a conical stud probably from a helmet (NCL-CDEC6), and the crossguard of a sword (NCL-1CABE7). These fittings and objects can all be dated to the second–third centuries, and a button-and-loop fastener of second century date (NCL-34B047) was also found in the area.

Two other small clusters of material can also be noted. A hooked strap fitting (NCL-96F745) for harness and a spearhead of probable Roman date (NCL953034) were found in the Ulgham area. In the Harbottle parish a knobbed terret (PUBLIC-878F35), two knobs from another terret (NCL-6270B1) and harness hook (NCL-637BE0) were found. Of further interest are two individual objects, both of which are large and conspicuous harness fittings (Plate 18). The copper-alloy mount inlaid with enamel and millefiori (NCL-A38DF3) was found in the Glanton parish, one of a small handful of examples found in Britain that can probably be associated with the harness of a cavalry officer. An equally conspicuous strap fitting, but one more firmly in the Romano-British tradition was found in the Whittingham parish (NCL-74DE87). All other military equipment and harness fittings can be associated with Roman forts, and are thus not unexpected findings.

Vessels

The evidence for vessel use in Northumberland, including glass, metal, and ceramic very starkly contrasts with other types of objects. While there are only 38 records of vessels, nearly all of these are from the Wall corridor or related to the fort at High Rochesther. The exceptions are a mortaria rim found outside of Warkworth (NCL-AF22224) and the pair of *paterae* found at Great Whittington (NCL-335745 and NCL-33CC76). It is striking that so few ceramic vessel sherds or those of other materials have been found relative to other types of metalwork. While the data from the PAS is biased toward metal objects because of the dominance of metal detectorists contributing data, excavated rural settlement sites in Northumberland also have small quantities of Roman ceramics compared to rural settlements in Yorkshire.

Coins

Only the fields around Great Whittington have provided enough coins from a rural settlement to enable a coin loss analysis, already discussed above. What is striking, however, is the very distinct geographical and chronological distribution of the coins. For the county of Northumberland, there are 172 records of coins. Of the 49 records of fourth-century nummi and 18 records of third-century radiates and a further five records of radiates-or-nummi, nearly all these late Roman coins are found along the Wall corridor or south of it, the exceptions being two nummi found near Norham and those examples found around Great Whittington. This means that the remaining 100 or so records of other denominations are of early Roman coins, with 48 of these representing silver denarii and 23 records of the large sestertii coins. More than 35 of these first- and second-century coins are found north of the Wall, dominated by silver denarii and primarily issued by Antoninus Pius, Trajan, and less frequently Hadrian. Proportionally, the majority of coins, even those of the first and second century are found along the Wall or south of it, with Great Whittington being the notable exception just north of the Wall. The coins that do penetrate into rural areas north of the Wall are largely silver denarii, which may have had a bullion value as much as a monetary value.

Brooches

For the county of Northumberland, there are 40 Roman brooches recorded, with approximately 30 of these from the area to the north of Hadrian's Wall. Of these latter, almost all the brooches are of early Roman date, with only a pin probably belonging to a late penannular brooch (NCL-1D6807) and three knee brooches offering any exceptions. The most commonly occurring form is the trumpet brooch, and in general most of the forms are part of the bow-family of brooches though four dragonesque brooches have been recorded between the Wall and the Scottish border. Perhaps unsurprisingly, all the brooch forms found in Northumberland to date are those also commonly found on military sites (McIntosh 2011). The exceptions are a trefoil-cupped plate brooch (NCL-BBB6E2) and a variation on the trumpet brooch (NCL-7FD5A4) that seem to deviate starkly from the more standard brooch types, and both of which were found outside Great Whittington (Plate 19).

Discussion

The distribution of military and harness equipment and ceramic, glass, and metal vessels is extremely limited to the north of Hadrian's Wall. This is to perhaps be expected with military equipment, as the Roman army would probably have liked to keep arms out of the hands of potential enemies. But ceramic vessels are more often a symptom of trade and exchange, and the general paucity of this evidence is telling. The few pottery sherds of Roman or Romano-British manufacture recovered from excavated sites are often very abraded, suggesting a long use life for any Roman vessels that found their way to native farmsteads.

In contrast, coins and brooches are more widespread in distribution and much more common, though still found in relatively low numbers. Coins and brooches tend to date to the later first and second centuries, with material of the third and fourth centuries almost entirely lacking from north of the Wall, with the exception of Great Whittington. The more regular occurrence of Roman coins and brooches suggests a selectivity of material on the part of the residents of farmsteads. Coins have a limited use away from urban and military sites and the majority of these are still found along the Wall and to its south, but these still found their way to native sites north of the Wall. Brooches have a greater aesthetic appeal, and their occurrence is not as surprising. However, the fact that the brooch forms found are generally those found on military sites is revealing of the source of such material (if unsurprising). The question becomes how is such material exchanged? Is it done under peaceful conditions, with such objects purchased by natives, or given to them by soldiers? Or were such trinkets acquired through plunder? To that extent, Roman material from north of Hadrian's Wall can be considered in a similar manner to the Roman material found in Scotland (e.g. Hunter 2007).

Roman objects may have been acquired through violent acts of raiding and warfare as much as through peaceful exchange. The presence of clusters of Roman material, often of only a small range of objects and dispersed across a small patch of the countryside may be further indicative of the distribution of booty acquired through raiding by small groups of raiders. What is notable, however, is that such clusters of material are not always perceived or immediately recognizable. It is only through the steady accumulation of data, discovered and recorded through repeated searches over many years that enable such areas of interest to be identified. Furthermore, the objects found around Great Whittington are exceptionally concentrated; most of the clusters of Roman material are diffuse, with single objects spread out across an area with a 3.5–5 km diameter. The diffusiveness of these clusters in Northumberland contrast with counties with denser patterns of settlement, for example parts of Yorkshire and Lincolnshire. In these latter areas, tens and even hundreds of Roman objects are likely to be found in a single field. The higher incidence of Roman material in such areas is indicative of the successful integration of the countryside into the Romano-British package of material culture in contrast to the areas north of Hadrian's Wall.

The date of the material from north of the Wall, primarily brooches and coins dating to the later first and second century, can be tied to a period when the forward line of Roman military occupation in the frontier vacillated. Therefore the occurrence of such material north of the Wall could also indicate the first tentative steps of accepting Romano-British material culture in the countryside, perhaps specifically during the occupation of the Antonine Wall when the Roman governor and his soldiers would have been attempting to consolidate their control of the intervallum landscape.

In summary, we cannot be certain to what extent Roman objects made their way into the countryside of the frontier (under peaceful or violent circumstances). There are indications of a selection of material, and this needs to be explored more fully in reference to excavated sites, also including data from Scotland for further comparison. However, more Roman objects are found and recorded each year, slowly increasing the amount of Roman-native interaction observable through the archaeological record. Lindsay has been crucial to the gathering of this information throughout her career, establishing not only a precedent for the recovery of such data, but also leading the way in its interpretation.

Bibliography

Allason-Jones, L. (2010) A tale of four *paterae*. *AA*, 5th series 39, 427–32.

Collins, R. (2008) The latest Roman coin from Hadrian's Wall: A small 5th C purse group. *Britannia* 39, 256–61.

Hunter, F. (2007) *Beyond the Edge of the Empire – Caledonians, Picts and Romans*. Rosemarkie, Groam House Museum.

Jobey, G. (1970) An Iron Age settlement and homestead at Burradon, Northumberland. *AA*, 4th series 48, 58–96.

Jobey, G. (1971) Excavations at Brough Law and Ingram Hill. *AA*, 4th series 49, 71–93.

Jobey, G. (1973) A native settlement at Hartburn and the Devil's Causeway, Northumberland. *AA*, 5th series 1, 11–53.

Kiernan, P. (2009) *Miniature Votive Offerings in the Roman North-West*. Mainz and Ruhpolding.

McIntosh, F. (2011) Regional brooch-types in Roman Britain: evidence from northern England. *AA*, 5th series 40, 155–82.

Proctor, J. (2009) *Pegswood Moor, Morpeth: A later Iron Age and Romano-British farmstead settlement*. London.

Walton, P. (2008) Finds from the River Tees at Piercebridge, in H. Cool and D. Mason (eds), *Roman Piercebridge: Excavations by D. W. Harding and Peter Scott 1969–1981*, Newcastle: Architectural and Archaeological Society of Durham and Northumberland, 286–93.

Walton, P. (2012) *Rethinking Roman Britain: An applied numismatic analysis of the Roman coin data recorded by the Portable Antiquities Scheme*. Wetteren, Moneta Monograph 137.

21

KNOWN UNKNOWNS: 'INVISIBLE' PEOPLE IN TEMPORARY CAMPS

Rebecca H. Jones

> '…there are known knowns; there are things we know we know. We also know there are known unknowns; that is to say we know there are some things we do not know. But there are also unknown unknowns – the ones we don't know we don't know.'
>
> United States Secretary of Defense, Donald Rumsfield, February 2002

When Donald Rumsfield made this statement at a press conference about the war in Iraq in February 2002, he would have been unaware of the extent to which they would be quoted and the ridicule which followed. Yet the statement is clear, and very applicable to a festschrift dedicated to a friend and colleague who did much to advance our knowledge of the people beyond the soldiers on the frontiers of the Roman Empire. Lindsay has helped us to search for the known unknowns, and no doubt moved some previously unknown unknowns into that category.

Lindsay's research on the human and social aspects of frontier studies, gleaned through meticulous study of artefacts, has provided thought provoking stimulus and entertaining discussions on numerous occasions. But one area where these humans remain largely invisible is that of Roman camp studies. Temporary camps have seen a resurgence of interest in recent years, thanks to overarching syntheses of their archaeology (Welfare and Swan 1995; Davies and Jones 2006; Jones 2011; 2012) and detailed large scale excavations at the site of Kintore in Aberdeenshire (Cook and Dunbar 2008). Although four primary functional classifications have been identified (marching, practice, siege, construction), the majority of camps in Britain were probably constructed for the purpose of housing soldiers engaged in the broad category of 'marching': undertaking land reconnaissance, policing, campaigns and manoeuvres. As the name suggests, camps were occupied temporarily, perhaps any time from a single night to a few weeks, and it is therefore unsurprising that they leave limited archaeological trace. Indeed, our knowledge of the majority of the camps in Britain is restricted to their perimeter traces: either an upstanding earthen rampart and external ditch, or, more often, the ditch revealed through differential cropmarkings from aerial survey and photography (Fig. 21.1). These ghost traces bely the hive of activity that must have been present in their interiors, which frequently appear to be barren. Yet many of the larger camps housed thousands of men in leather tents, potentially accompanied by pack animals, wagons, horses and possibly civilians. We get a glimpse of this from the classical sources who tell us, for example, that the Roman Consul Metellus in the late second century BC expelled camp followers who had 'mingled with the soldiers and roamed about with them by day and night' (Valerius Maximus *Facta et dicta memorabilia* II. 7.1–2) and that Scipio Africanus the Younger expelled, 'traders, prostitutes, clairvoyants and diviners' on arrival at a camp close to Numantia during the Celtiberian Wars of the second century BC (Appian *Iberica* 85). In the mid-first century BC, Caesar reports that Cicero confined his troops to their camp, allowing not a single camp follower to pass beyond the entrenchment, implying that their inclusion within the camp was not out of the ordinary, although elsewhere he refers to traders camped outside but close to the rampart of the camp (*de Bello Gallico* VI. 36–7). This perhaps suggests that they could enter and roam the camp but not actually stay there overnight. Both Polybius, writing in the second century BC and Hyginus, writing probably in the second century AD,

Figure 21.1 Aerial view of the camp at Dalginross in Perthshire, taken from the south-west in 1996. Rows of pits can be seen in the interior. © Crown Copyright: RCAHMS. SC1164173. Licensor www.rcahms.gov.uk

describe the layout of Roman camps and make no space allocation for camp followers, despite the remarks in other authors suggesting such personnel were relatively commonplace. This may be because their inclusion in the camp was seen as bad practice, therefore having no place in military manuals, rather than reflecting actuality. Vegetius, writing much later (late fourth–early fifth century AD), does make reference to servants, baggage, pack-horses and vehicles (*Epitome Rei Militaris* III, 6), as one would expect for the Roman army on the move.

Probably the most valuable source for helping us to assess internal space within camps is the *de munitionibus castrorum* by the writer referred to as Hyginus. Although it may have been a theoretical treatise for a hypothetical army, it might also relate to the campaigns of the Emperor Marcus Aurelius on the Danube (Birley 1966; 1982). A

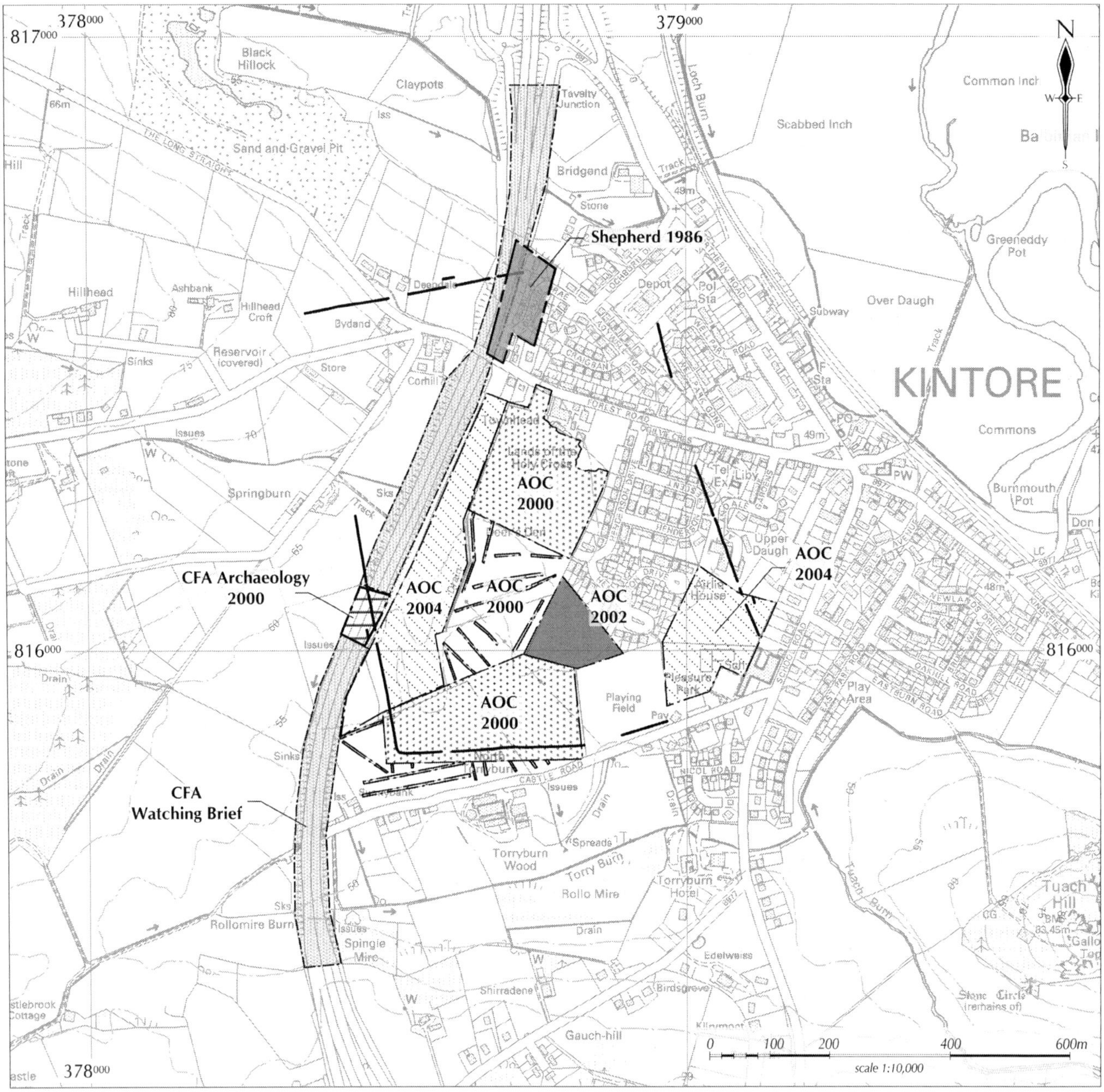

Figure 21.2 Plan of the extent of the excavations at Kintore in recent years (scale 1:7,500)

fascinating military manual, Hyginus supplied detailed dimensions for the actual amount of space allocated to each component of the camp (*de munitionibus castrorum* 1–2, 8–19). For example, a century of 80 men occupies a space of 120 Roman feet by 30 Roman feet and, although only eight tents are pitched (with eight men (a *contubernia*) occupying each tent and 16 men on guard duty), the remaining space is taken by the centurion. This means that the space for a complete cohort (480 men) is 120 by 180 Roman feet (or 720 by 30 Roman feet if lengthways), totalling 21,600 sq Roman feet. This equates to about 35.5 by 53.2 m, an area of some 1890 m² (0.19 ha).

Kintore

When it comes to the archaeological evidence, our understanding of marching camps and their interiors has been revolutionised by a series of excavations in advance of housing developments at the village of Kintore, not far

Figure 21.3 View of an Oven (O087) from the excavations at Forest Road, Kintore. © AOC Archaeology Group

from Aberdeen (Cook and Dunbar 2008; Cook *et al.* forthcoming) (Fig. 21.2). Although the camp was first recorded as an earthwork in the nineteenth century, ploughing has levelled the remains so that only the cropmark of the perimeter ditch has been visible from the air. None of the aerial photographs of the site gave a hint of the wealth of evidence that was subsequently yielded by the excavations in the interior, with some 180 Roman ovens and numerous pits now recorded (Fig. 21.3). One of the fascinating pieces of evidence to be gleaned from the excavations of the pits and ovens is just how little material culture has been left behind. Only a scatter of artefacts has been found, the majority of evidence representing scraps: metalworking and waste, perhaps resulting from routine camp repairs, and fragments of material from the ovens which may have been attached to wooden materials which had been burnt for fuel. But the ovens themselves were not as uniform as might have been expected. A wide variety of different styles of construction were revealed, ranging from unlined cooking pits to those with stone and cobble lining, from simple single ovens to double ovens with two cooking ends sharing a single ash pit, and evidence from the fills indicating potentially different roofing structures. The ovens appeared to be scattered irregularly throughout the camp, with possible lines identified close to the south-eastern corner, although this is by no means certain (Cook and Dunbar 2004). But the differing styles employed in the ovens and even the differing fuel used gives us a rare hint of the dietary preferences and predilections of the soldiers inhabiting the camp – perhaps indicative of differing backgrounds and ethnicity.

When it comes to estimating the numbers of soldiers housed within a camp, this is highly speculative and fraught with difficulty (see Jones 2012, 47–58). Assessments have been made which have put forward suggestions of the number of men housed per hectare or acre, but these rarely take account of the space that would have been given over to the headquarters tents, commanding officers accommodation, space for baggage animals, horses, wagons *et cetera*. Even the extensive excavations at Kintore cannot provide much assistance here because of the irregularity of the ovens. We do not know the size of the army bivouacked within, but radiocarbon dates suggest that the primary occupation of this camp was in the Flavian period. Assessments of the army that marched with Agricola in the early AD 80s have ranged from 18,000–25,000 (Mann 1985, 23; Breeze 1988, 9–10; Hanson 1991, 137); from this we can infer that Kintore, a camp measuring some 44 hectares/110 acres, may have housed somewhere in the region of 480 men per hectare/200 men per acre (Jones 2012, 58). It is interesting to note that this is not too dissimilar to the estimates of camp density made by General William Roy in the eighteenth century (Roy 1793, 52) and he, at least, had direct experience of housing troops under canvas. The figures that calculate for extremely small areas to be given over to troops (e.g. Gilliver 1999, 84–5) surely would have represented cramped, overcrowded, difficult living spaces, particularly when one considers the presence of animals, the need for latrines, all of which would have made the camps extremely unpleasant places in which to stay. Furthermore, the highest figures, when multiplied up to the largest camps in Britain such as Logie Durno in Aberdeenshire (57 hectares/144 acres) and St Leonards in the Scottish Borders (70 hectares/170 acres), would propose the movements of armies far larger than those which are known to have operated. Even if the huge camp at St Leonards represents the travels of the Emperor Septimius Severus and his sons in the early third century AD, as has been suggested (St Joseph 1969; Jones 2011, 111–12), which would then include elements of the Praetorian Guard, the Emperor's household and the staff required to administer the running of the Roman empire, the higher density figures are unreasonable. Given the vast spaces which were potentially occupied by marching camps, there was no reason for the soldiers to be cramped in even more uncomfortable living conditions than must have already been the case. The numbers game can potentially be played *ad nauseum*, but by attempting to calculate the numbers of men and size of armies, we can start to consider what life might have been like for soldiers within these camps.

Evidence from remote sensing

Alongside the excavated evidence from Kintore, several camps have displayed internal features from aerial and geophysical survey.

Inchtuthil

Outside the legionary fortress at Inchtuthil in Perthshire lie three temporary camps, two representing two phases of use of the same space on the plateau to the west of the fortress. Within these, distinct pairs of lines of pits can be seen, together with numerous others scattered about the interior (Fig. 21.4). Those running around the perimeter are assumed to be ovens, replicating usual practice in Roman forts, although the experience of Kintore tells us that ovens can be found throughout the interior, not restricted to the perimeter. Nine of the pits in the interior have been excavated and found to contain a small amount of pottery and probable sheep-ribs, thereby indicating that they were routine rubbish pits (Frere 1985). The double lines of these pits probably indicates streets between groups of tents and the longest 'street' in the south-west part of camp II, some 220 m long, is close to the 720 Roman feet (213 m) that Hyginus allocated to a cohort (*de munitionibus castrorum* 2; Maxwell 1982). If two cohorts camped back to back, then the distance between these double rows, some 3.5–4.5 m wide, is insufficient to represent space for tents but must represent the roadway between such cohorts (Frere 1985, 232).

Dalginross

One of the camps for which the clearest evidence for internal features can be identified is at Dalginross in Perthshire (Fig. 21.1), outside a Flavian fort. The camp has a particular type of gateway ('Stracathro') which is assumed to date to the Flavian period in Scotland (Jones 2009). Within the camp, two clear parallel lines of pits can be identified in its northern half, but these are significantly different to the parallel lines at Inchtuthil, being some 20–22 m apart and 78–84 m long. This internal gap, some 67–74 Roman feet wide, is only a little wider than the 60

Figure 21.4 Aerial view of the camps at Inchtuthil in Perthshire, taken from the south-east in 1977. The pairs of rows of pits can be clearly seen along with numerous other pits in the interior and exterior of the camps. © Crown Copyright: RCAHMS. SC359708. Licensor www.rcahms.gov.uk [1]

Roman feet allocated by Hyginus to the strip (*striga*) for two centuries camped opposite each other. The length, some 264–284 Roman feet, is a little longer than the 240 Roman feet that would have been allocated to two centuries camped lengthways. However, if all ten tents of a century plus that of their centurion were erected, rather than the eight advocated by Hyginus plus centurion (due to 16 men always being on guard duty – *de munitionibus castrorum* 1), then this could take the length up to 264 Roman feet, equivalent to the 78 m clearly visible on the south side of the two lines. It is, therefore, possible that the remains of four centuries camped close together are being indicated at this point within the camp, raising the question as to the location of the other two centuries within the cohort, unless this

Fig. 21.5. Transcription of the cropmarks of the camps at Moss Side in Cumbria by English Heritage, showing the lines of pits. © English Heritage. NMR.

is being generous with space and a full cohort is what is indicated here. This position is also on the north side of the *Praetorium*. According to Hyginus, this space could be allocated to a Praetorian cohort (*de munitionibus castrorum* 6), but it is unlikely that the Praetorian Guard was encamped in a 9.2 ha camp in Perthshire, and more likely that a legionary or quingenary cohort is detectable here.

Further south within the Dalginross camp, a further line some 78 m or 264 Roman feet in length can be detected. Again, this possibly represents two full centuries camped side by side in a line rather than facing each other. Other pits within the camp occur in small groups, presumably indicating clusters of activity, whether representing areas where troops were stationed or rubbish pits for other disposal activity, perhaps relating to the quartering of animals.

Glenlochar

At Glenlochar in Dumfriesshire, a Roman fort with evidence for Flavian and Antonine occupation is known on the east bank of the River Dee, together with at least five temporary camps and other cropmarks. One of these camps (V) displays numerous pits in its interior on aerial photographs, although it is interesting to note that it has an attached annexe, a relatively rare feature on camps (Jones 2011, 76–9; 2012, 101–5) and this annexe is relatively barren, suggesting different activities were conducted here that did not require the excavation of significant sub-surface features. Unlike Inchtuthil and Dalginross, regular lines cannot be ascertained although short lines and groups of pits can be discerned. Close to the south side of the camp, three almost oval clusters of pits can be discerned, all potentially delimiting areas of activity presumably relating to troop housing. All three are some 50 m to 53 m in length (169–179 Roman feet), close to Hyginus' 180 Roman feet measurement for a cohort (180 × 120 Roman feet). It is possible that these represent the camping area for legionary cohorts, as these were apparently stationed close to the perimeter (*de munitionibus castrorum* 2). However, this numbers game can go on indefinitely and the fact remains that, although there are clusters within Glenlochar, the pits do not display the regularity and rows visible at Inchtuthil and Dalginross.

Dalswinton

On the east bank of the River Nith in Dumfriesshire lie a number of Roman sites including a two-phase Flavian fort, a possible further fort, several camps and other cropmarks. Known from aerial survey and excavations on the fort (Richmond and St Joseph 1957), large-scale magnetometry survey in 2009 suggested numerous internal features within a large camp on the haughland at Dalswinton Bankfoot. A line of larger pits is visible close to the north-west perimeter ditch, which may be the remnants of cooking ovens as noted earlier (Hanson *et al* in prep). But others elsewhere within the camp may be ovens or pits, and again hint at activities rarely seen from scrutiny of aerial photographs.

Moss Side/White Moss

The Roman camps at Moss Side (Fig. 21.5) lie just to the south of Hadrian's Wall, near Crosby-on-Eden to the east of Carlisle. Previously recorded and published (Welfare and Swan 1995, 41–2), new information from cropmarkings came to light in August 1995 after that publication had gone to press (Small 2008). As well as a level of complexity in the numbers of camps recorded here, the new photographs revealed regular rows of pits aligned on some of the visible entrances. These are perhaps clearest in the larger camp of the group (Moss Side 2: Welfare and Swan 1995, 41–2) and the small annexe or attached camp on its north side. A line of pits can be seen running from just west of the centre of camp 2 eastwards towards the entrance in the centre of the east side. This line measures around 135 m and does not obviously equate to a Roman measurement, but running perpendicular to this line and aligned on an entrance in the north side is a double row of pits flanking the routeway into the camp. These rows, measuring some 81 m long, are similar in length to those observed at Dalginross, possibly representing two centuries of 10 tents camped lengthways. Furthermore, in the attached camp or annexe, a very clear double row of pits flanks the road bisecting the camp from east to west, with the southern half further divided into three fairly equal segments separated by double rows of pits. Each of these segments measures around 33 m by about 35 m, therefore approximately 120 Roman feet by 120 Roman feet, space for four centuries according to Hyginus. This could therefore indicate some 12 centuries or two cohorts camped on the south side of the line, or slightly fewer if ten tents were pitched rather than eight. Either way, the regularity of the lines of pits and their seeming correlation with measurements given by Hyginus does indicate one working hypothesis for calculating space requirements for soldiers within temporary camps.

Conclusions

The annexe or attached camp at Moss Side measures around 1.2 hectares or nearly 3 acres in size. We noted at Kintore that some 480 men might have been housed per hectare (200 men per acre) which could therefore be extrapolated to assume that around seven or eight centuries occupied this small camp/annexe at Moss Side. Yet, looking at the lines of pits, it is also possible that two cohorts could have been housed purely in the southern half of the camp. This therefore demonstrates not only the difficulties in trying to assess troop numbers, even when using a combination of archaeological evidence and ancient military manuals, but also that we could be dealing with differing functions of these camps. Welfare has argued that Moss Side could be a construction camp for Hadrian's Wall (forthcoming), but in which case, one would perhaps expect a less dense occupation because it would have been inhabited for a prolonged period of time. The northern half of the annexe revealed far fewer pits; this may reflect actual usage of the camp rather than cropmark bias and perhaps we should consider that the northern segment housed administration tents, equipment, perhaps for constructing the Wall, and animals, although one could consider the latter needing waste pits just as much as the humans. In contrast, Kintore probably housed a battle group campaigning in north-eastern Scotland in the first century AD. Although the function of the camps at Moss Side is less clear, some could relate to initial campaigns in the area but they could equally have functioned for training and manoeuvres as well as housing soldiers involved in the construction of Hadrian's Wall.

Another way of calculating camp density has concentrated on the use of an *actus* when laying out the camp. The *actus* is a unit of length measuring 120 Roman feet and was used by Roman land surveyors when dividing up the landscape (Dilke 1971, 82–4). Maxwell has suggested that many camps were laid out utilising the square *actus* and has used the evidence from the small camps of around 1 hectare in size near Chester and York to suggest that a quingenary legionary cohort of 480 men would have required 8 square *actus* (which equals 1 hectare), each century requiring about 1 square *actus* with additional space for the rampart and *intervallum* (Maxwell 2004, 82–5). This gives a density of over 620 men per hectare (240+ men per acre) or 480 per hectare (194 per acre) if strictly using the one cohort per hectare method. Further arguments for the use of the *actus* by the Roman army have been made, including the suggestion that a cohort required 2 square *actus* ('*actus quadrati*') and that cavalry troops had four times the space allocation of infantry (Richardson

2000, 431–2). This equates to around 480 men per acre (1,186 per hectare), a rather too high density figure suggesting extremely cramped conditions.

Whilst the densities proposed by these two methodologies differ considerably, the use of the *actus* by the Roman army has much to commend it. Across Britain, there are a number of camps at around two hectares in size. This equates to 16 square *actus*, possibly two cohorts according to the lower density calculations, or between five and eight using the higher density figures. But eight cohorts in a 2 hectare (5 acre) camp seems very high, and would indicate a gigantic army if scaled up to some of the larger camps found in Britain. Many of the camps on the Antonine Wall are around 2 hectares in size and if the troops quartered in these camps were engaged in construction duties on the Antonine Wall, the reality might well lie in the lower figures which could reflect a more accurate estimation of the likely numbers of men available to be deployed (Hanson and Maxwell 1986, 133–4; Breeze 2006, 63–4). This could also be extrapolated to the possible 'construction' camp at Moss Side suggesting just over a cohort was housed here. A further argument for the use of the *actus* is was made by Breeze following his excavations of the Roman fort of Bearsden on the Antonine Wall. Much of the internal layout of this fort is now known and he has suggested it was laid out using the *actus* (Breeze 1984a, 41).

That Roman camps were laid out using *actus* is very plausible, and certainly some form of calculation based on the Roman foot must have been used. It is interesting to note that the argument that approximately one *actus* was given to each century would produce an army of approximately the size suggested by historical sources for the camp at Kintore relating to the campaigns of Agricola in the first century AD (Maxwell 2004).

Yet, none of the exercises noted here fully take account of the space that would have been required for the baggage animals who usually accompanied the army on campaign and the space required for the horses with cavalry units. That is because these are not quantified in sufficient detail in the available sources and difficult to detect archaeologically. The actual number of men stationed within the perimeter of the camps cited here must lie somewhere between the extremes given, and almost certainly are at the lower end of the spectrum if the assessments relating to the number of men available to occupy camps such as Kintore are correct. Even if the tents were pitched relatively close together, there would usually need to be space for wagons, mules, and other activity in the camp. Estimations have been made regarding the number of mules that would have been required for an army on campaign (e.g. Peddie 1987, 27–32; Breeze 1988; Fulford 2000), and archaeology can furnish a little additional evidence. For example, excavations at the battlefield site of Kalkriese in Germany, where Germanic tribes destroyed three legions under their commander Varus in AD 9, have so far revealed finds relating to animal harnessing as well as the skeletal remains of eight horses and 30 mules, no doubt a fraction of that which accompanied the army on campaign (Schlüter 1999; Wells 2003, 54–5).

It is worth commenting that, despite far greater evidence of the internal arrangements within forts and considerably more extensive excavation over several decades, the density and composition of fort garrisons is also often unknown. Although several attempts have been made to correlate fort types with particular garrisons, there is still disagreement and any direct correlation between internal fort area and the size of the garrison difficult to sustain. For example, at the later first century AD (Flavian) fort at Elginhaugh in Midlothian, despite significant large area excavation revealing 11 barracks of which at least six were interpreted as stable barracks, it was not possible to be fully confident about the nature of the occupying garrison (Hanson 2007). Whilst excavations on fort barracks have led to the identification of stabling areas, no such level of confidence is currently possible within the interior of temporary camps, and the ratio of cavalry to infantry for a campaigning army remains an unknown quantity which can only be estimated. Although some of the historical sources can indicate the make up of specific armies at particular points in time, such as the troops at Agricola's disposal in his final season and at the battle of Mons Graupius, even these do not give us precise figures because not all the legions and auxiliary units may have been at full strength, and the number of mules required remains an unknown factor. Evidence from the bronze military diplomas and Vindolanda writing tablets indicate that detachments of troops were regularly stationed away from their bases (Roxan 1978; Bowman and Thomas 1991; 1994); additional evidence from Dura-Europos suggests that units may have been under strength at various points in time (Breeze 1984b) and we cannot always assume standard figures for legionary and auxiliary regiments.

Despite the various valiant attempts that have been made to assess the numbers of troops quartered within a camp, they are subject to numerous variables: topography; the ratio of legionaries to auxiliary troops; the ratio of infantry to cavalry; the number of mules and size of baggage train; the possible availability of space for camp followers; the space allocated to the *principia*; and the potential presence of the emperor and his large household in some circumstances.

Yet, that there were standard ways of laying out a camp are clear from the surviving texts and the archaeological evidence. This paper might not have brought us significantly closer to understanding the activities or numbers of soldiers housed within temporary camps but I hope that I have identified the known unknowns – the things that we know that we do not know.

Acknowledgements

I am grateful to the editors, Rob and Frances, for allowing me to submit a paper on a subject area where our knowledge of people and objects is so sparse. This paper had its inspiration from the new transcription of the camps at Moss Side/White Moss by Cathy Stoertz at English Heritage and I am grateful to Fiona Small and Helen Winton for providing access to the material. I would also like to thank Andy Smythe at BBC Newcastle who invited me to interpret and discuss the mapping of this camp. I also thank AOC for Figure 21.3, English Heritage for Figure 21.5 and RCAHMS for Figures 21.1 and 21.4.

Bibliography

Classical sources

Appian: *Iberica* (*History of Rome: The Spanish Wars*) (Loeb Classical Library)

Caesar: *de Bello Gallico* (*The Gallic War*) (Penguin Classics)

Hyginus: *de munitionibus castrorum* (*The Fortification of the Camp*) (Gilliver 1993)

Valerius Maximus: *Facta et dicta memorabilia* (*Memorable Sayings and Doings*) (Oxford University Press)

Vegetius: *Epitome Rei Militaris* (*Epitome of Military Science*) (Milner 1996)

Modern works

Birley, E. (1966) 'Alae' and 'Cohortes Milliariae'. In *Corolla Memoriae Erich Swoboda Dedicata. Romische Forschungen in Niederosterreich V.* Cologne, 54–67.

Birley, E. (1982) The dating andcharacter of the tract 'de munitionibus castrorum'. In G. Wirth, (ed.) *Romanitas-Christianitas. Untersuchungen zu Geschichte und Literatur der römischen Kaiserzeit,* 277–81. Berlin and New York.

Bowman, A. K. and Thomas, J. D. (1991) A military strength report from Vindolanda. *JRS* LXXXI, 62–73.

Bowman, A. K. and Thomas, J. D. (1994) *The Vindolanda Writing Tablets. Tabulae Vindolandenses* II. London, British Museum Press.

Breeze, D. J. (1984a) The Roman fort on the Antonine Wall at Bearsden. In D. J. Breeze (ed.) *Studies in Scottish Antiquity Presented to Stewart Cruden,* 32–68. John Donald, Edinburgh.

Breeze, D. J. (1984b) Demand and supply on the northern frontier. In R. Miket and C. Burgess (eds) *Between and Beyond the Walls: Essays on the Prehistory and History of North Britain in Honour of George Jobey*, 264– 86. John Donald, Edinburgh.

Breeze, D. J. (1988) The logistics of Agricola's final campaign. *Talanta, Dutch Archaeological and Historical Journal* 18/19, 7–22.

Breeze, D. J. (2006) *The Antonine Wall*. Birlinn, Edinburgh.

Cook, M. and Dunbar, L. (2004) Kintore. *Current Archaeology* 194, 84–9.

Cook, M. and Dunbar, L. (2008) *Rituals, Roundhouses and Romans: Excavations at Kintore, Aberdeenshire 2000–2006. Volume 1. Forest Road*, Scottish Trust for Archaeological Research Monograph 8. Edinburgh.

Cook, M. J., Dunbar, L. & Heawood, R. (forthcoming) *Rituals, Roundhouses and Romans: Excavations at Kintore, Aberdeenshire 2000–2006. Volume 2, Other Sites*, Scottish Trust for Archaeological Research Monograph. Edinburgh.

Davies, J. L. and Jones, R. H. (2006) *Roman Camps in Wales and the Marches*. University of Wales Press, Cardiff.

Dilke, O.A.W. (1971) *The Roman Land Surveyors*. Newton Abbot, David & Charles.

Frere, S. S. (1985) B. The pits: discussion. In L. F. Pitts and J. K. St Joseph (eds) *Inchtuthil. The Roman Legionary Fortress. Britannia* Monograph Series 6, 229–39. London.

Fulford, M. (2000) The organization of legionary supply: the Claudian invasion of Britain. In R. J. Brewer (ed.) *Roman Fortresses and their Legions*, 41–50. Society of Antiquaries and National Museums and Galleries of Wales, London & Cardiff.

Gilliver, C. M. (1993) The *de munitionibus castrorum*: Text and translation. *Journal of Roman Military Equipment Studies* 4, 33–48.

Gilliver, C. M. (1999) *The Roman Art of War.* Tempus, Stroud.

Hanson, W. S. (1991) *Agricola and the Conquest of the North* (2nd edition). London, Batsford.

Hanson, W. S. (2007) *Elginhaugh: a Flavian fort and its annexe. Britannia* Monograph Series 23, London.

Hanson, W. S. and Maxwell, G. S. (1986) *Rome's north-west frontier: The Antonine Wall*. Edinburgh, Edinburgh University Press.

Jones, R. H. (2009) "Lager mit *claviculae*" in *Britannia.* In

W. S. Hanson (ed.) *The Army and Frontiers of Rome*. JRA Supplementary series 74, 11–24. Portsmouth, Rhode Island.

Jones, R. H. (2011) *Roman Camps in Scotland*. Society of Antiquaries of Scotland, Edinburgh.

Jones, R. H. (2012) *Roman Camps in Britain*. Amberley, Stroud.

Mann, J. C. (1985) Two 'Topoi' in the Agricola. *Britannia* XVI, 21–4.

Maxwell, G. S. (1982) Roman temporary camps at Inchtuthill: an examination of the aerial photographic evidence. *Scottish Archaeological Review* 1.2, 105–13.

Maxwell, G. S. (2004) The Roman penetration of the North in the late first century AD. In M. Todd (ed.) *A Companion to Roman Britain*: 75–90. Oxford, Blackwell.

Milner, N. P. (1996) *Vegetius: Epitome of Military Science* (2nd edition). Liverpool, Liverpool University Press.

Peddie, J. (1987) *Conquest. The Roman Invasion of Britain*. Stroud, Sutton.

Richardson, A. (2000) The numerical basis of Roman camps. *Oxford Journal of Archaeology* 19.4, 425–37.

Richmond, I. A. and St Joseph, J. K. (1957) The Roman Fort at Dalswinton in Nithsdale. *Transactions of the Dumfrieshire and Galloway Naturural History & Antiquaries Society* (3rd series) XXXIV, 9–21.

Roxan, M. (1978) *Roman Military Diplomas 1954–1977*, Institute of Archaeology, London Occasional Publication 2. London.

Roy, W. (1793) *The Military Antiquities of the Romans in North Britain*. Society of Antiquaries, London.

St Joseph, J. K. (1969) Air reconnaissance in Britain, 1965–8. *JRS* LIX, 104–28.

Schlüter, W. (1999) The Battle of the Teutoburg Forest: archaeological research at Kalkriese near Osnabruck. In J. D. Creighton and R. J. A. Wilson (eds) *Roman Germany. Studies in Cultural Interaction*. JRA Supplementary series 32: 125–159. Portsmouth, Rhode Island.

Small, F. (2008) National Mapping Programme: Brampton to Birdoswald. Unpublished English Heritage Research Department Report 69/2008.

Welfare, H. (forthcoming) The function of temporary camps along Hadrian's Wall. In P. Bidwell and N. Hodgson (eds) *Limes XXI: Proceedings of the 21st Congress of Roman Frontiers Studies. Held in Newcastle-upon-Tyne in 2009*. Oxford, British Archaeological Reports.

Welfare, H. and Swan, V. (1995) *Roman Camps in England: The field archaeology*. London, HMSO.

Wells, P. S. (2003) The Battle that Stopped Rome. Emperor Augustus, Arminius, and the slaughter of the legions in the Teutoburger forest. New York, W.W. Norton.

22

THE RISE AND FALL OF THE HOUSESTEADS AMPHITHEATRE

Tony Wilmott

While working on the excavation of the legionary amphitheatre in Chester (Ainsworth and Wilmott 2005; Wilmott *et al.* 2006) and on a general book concerning the amphitheatres of Roman Britain (Wilmott 2007), a number of puzzling references to an amphitheatre at Housesteads were noted. This paper examines the brief history of the idea of the existence of this amphitheatre, its demise, and its importance. It is offered to Lindsay in the knowledge of her enthusiasm for the more obscure by-ways of archaeological lore, and with thanks for many years of friendship.

John Collingwood Bruce's first, 1851, edition of the *Roman Wall* contained no general account of the appearance and function of milecastles, but only the comment that the excavation of the milecastle at Cawfields in 1848 (Clayton 1855a) had solved the question as to whether there were any places at all where the Wall could have been crossed. This led him to speculate 'that the passages at Busy Gap, Rapishaw Gap and other places are of Roman formation' (Bruce 1851, 249), but there was certainly no idea of a system of crossings. The concept of gates northwards at every milecastle was expressed for the first time in Bruce's third edition, by which time the excavations of Milecastles 42 (Cawfields) in 1848, 39 (Castle Nick) in 1854, and 37 (Housesteads) in 1853 had 'safely … put … us in possession of the plan for the whole' (Bruce 1867, 73). The correct conclusion – that Wall crossings existed, and were located at the forts and milecastles along the frontier – was established. This being the case, the discovery of the Knag Burn Gate by John Clayton in 1856 (Clayton 1855b; 1856) created an unwelcome complication in the anatomy of the Hadrian's Wall frontier with regard to the crossings through the curtain as they were then understood. It was a surprise and an exception (which, of course, it remains). The new gateway needed a particular explanation. The identification of an apparent amphitheatre very close to the gate provided it.

The feature once interpreted as an amphitheatre at Housesteads is a large oval depression lying to the north of Hadrian's Wall, north-east of the Knag Burn Gate. It is up to 4.6m deep, measuring 33 × 28.5m (Welfare 2009, 247–8, fig. 10.7 feature 39). It was first observed by Henry MacLauchlan during his celebrated 1852–4 survey of the Wall. His plan of the site labels the feature 'Amphitheatre', though in his *Memoir* (MacLaughlan 1858, 39), he states the matter cautiously, noting only that

> 'it is circular and, although north of the Wall [it] was, perhaps, an amphitheatre',

John Hodgson (1840, 192) was similarly cautious, saying that the feature was

> 'apparently made by human labour; but whether it was used as an amphitheatre, or is merely the alveus of an ancient quarry, it is vain to conjecture'.

Clayton reported the discovery of the Knag Burn gate in 1855, describing its excavation the following year (Clayton, 1855b; 1856). At the time of the discovery of the gate there was already an idea of linking it with the putative amphitheatre

> '[the gate] might be found on further examination to have some connection with what were conjectured to be the remains of an amphitheatre.' (Clayton 1855b, 58)

Clayton (1856, 202) was clearly dubious about the interpretation of the site as an amphitheatre:

Figure 22.1 A woodcut illustration of the Housesteads amphitheatre that appeared in early editions of The Handbook to the Roman Wall

'The excavation which attracted the attention of Mr MacLauchlan is scarcely of sufficient dimensions to justify the title of amphitheatre, but a learned commentator observes "that the little *ampheatrum castrense* of the Romans was probably only intended for the soldiers of the guard who amused themselves there with gladiators"'

There can be little doubt of the identity of the 'learned commentator', and the slightly sarcastic tone of what follows suggests disagreement – Clayton's comment continues:

> 'The conjecture of Mr MacLauchlan has received countenance from the highest authority on matters relating to the Roman Wall (Dr Bruce) .... the passage in question leads to no other place, and it is possible that through it the Roman soldiers found an easier access to their place of entertainment than through the massive portals of the northern outlet of the neighbouring fortress of Borcovicus'

Others supported the identification. Albert Way (1858) added an appendix to MacLauchlan's *Memoir*, entitled a '*Supplementary notice of the discovery, in 1856, of a gateway at the Knag Burn, found, subsequently to the survey by Mr MacLauchlan in excavation made by John Clayton Esq. Near Housesteads*'. In this appendix, which re-printed Clayton's account of the excavation, Way concluded that the function of the Knag Burn Gate was precisely to communicate with the amphitheatre. The complication that the amphitheatre lay north of the Wall was solved by reference to the extra-mural position of the amphitheatres of Cirencester and Silchester, which for Way (1858, 95) confirmed:

> 'in a certain measure … the conjecture that the excavation adjacent to Housesteads had likewise been destined for those disports for which we find provision made in the most remote parts of the empire, on sites of any extensive or permanent occupation by the Romans'.

Amphitheatres were situated without the city walls, and there was therefore no inconsistency in their being extra-mural with regard to Hadrian's Wall.

As Clayton intimated, Bruce had seized enthusiastically upon MacLauchlan's speculative identification and Way's interpretation of the Knag Burn gate. On 20 July 1860, Bruce was invited to speak at a meeting of the Archaeological Institute at Gloucester following the Institute's visit to Cirencester. His address was enthusiastic:

> 'One interesting feature of Corinium is its extramural amphitheatre. We find the amphitheatrum castrense outside the walls at Dorchester, Silchester, Caerleon, Richborough and several other places. We also have one in the north of England adjacent to the mural station of Borcovicus. It is however, small in comparison with that of Cirencester, but large enough for the garrison, which consisted only of one cohort. In the sculptures of Trajan's column we perceive two amphitheatres erected during the Dacian campaigns. It was necessary to give the soldiers amusement. When the tribune of the Tungrian cohort at Borcovicus, on the great Northern Barrier, found that his men were suffering from the sameness of their daily toil, all he had to do was to catch a couple of Caledonians, and off with them to the amphitheatre'. (Archaeological Journal 1860, 345–6)

The relish of Bruce's last sentence is irresistible.

It was perhaps ironic that in the self-same edition of his great work in which he celebrated the discovery of the regular system of milecastle gates Bruce had to account for the exception, and in the 1867 third edition of *The Roman Wall* he reiterated that the Knag Burn Gate was intended purely as an access to the amphitheatre:

> 'the object of the gateway has been to give access to a place of entertainment – an amphitheatre on a small scale – which is on the north side of the Wall. It is one hundred feet across and about ten deep, and has doubtless been furnished with wooden seats. The path leading from the gateway to the entrance into the amphitheatre may be traced. Amphitheatres similar in construction to this, though larger, have been found at Silchester, Dorchester, Cirencester, Banbury and Caerleon among other places … These amphitheatres, like the one before us, were all outside the walls of the encampments. The Roman soldiers on the northern frontiers would often be in need of amusement. It cannot be supposed that their mode of seeking it would be more refined than that of the inhabitants of Rome itself.' (Bruce 1867, 191)

The woodcut illustration (Fig. 22.1) exaggerates the size and scale of the feature, and is clearly very much influenced by the interpretation. This illustration was reproduced in successive editions of the *Handbook to the Roman Wall*. By the third edition (Bruce 1885), the prose had empurpled:

> 'Nettles may usually be seen growing in the bottom of it, a sure sign of human presence. Has the arena been soaked in human blood?'

And this was repeated ten years later in the fourth edition, edited after Bruce's death by Robert Blair (1895).

Bruce (1867, 157–8) further suggested that the Housesteads amphitheatre might indicate the existence of similar structures elsewhere on the line of the Wall, particularly at Chesters, where a relief seemed to him to depict the scene of a man being savaged by a lion in the presence of an amphitheatre official carrying a flag. In the *Lapidarium Septentrionale* Bruce (1875, 77) followed up his interpretation of this relief by stating that

> 'It is not probable that so important a Roman station as CILURNUM would be destitute of an amphitheatre for the entertainment of the military. On the banks of the river, between the station and the 'Oxclose' there are some semi-circular recesses well adapted for the formation of an amphitheatre. The stone before us was found in the locality; when entire it would be a fitting head-stone for the principal entrance.'

Bruce acknowledges the fact that this interpretation derived from his conversations with 'Sig. Montiroli of Rome'. This was an Italian architect Giovanni Montiroli, who was working on the design of the ceiling trophies for the library at Alnwick Castle (Montiroli 1870), and who had published observations on the Roman Forum (Montiroli 1859). Unfortunately for this theory, there is in fact no parallel for a presiding official with a flag in the contemporary iconography of the arena. For various reasons this relief is now interpreted as pertaining to the cult of Cybele (Coulston and Phillips 1988, 43, no. 115), an interpretation that had been advanced in the first account of the object, by John Horsley (1732, 215–6), and dismissed by Bruce.

When the Housesteads amphitheatre began its appearance on the archaeological stage, very little indeed was known of the amphitheatres of Britain, and the existence and identifications of even those now best established were debated. William Stukeley (1723; 1776) had identified the sites of amphitheatres at Silchester, Richborough and (especially) Dorchester, and in the years following other suggestions had been made, including Cirencester. In the same year as the Knag Burn Gate was discovered, H. M. Scarth (1858) claimed to have identified one, and possibly two, small amphitheatres at Charterhouse-on-Mendip. Smaller sites were identified on very flimsy evidence indeed, to the disapproval of A. Hadrian Allcroft (1908, 587–9), who, in his *Earthwork of England* grumbled that:

> 'The fact is that amphitheatres, with their implication of butchery, are as much an obsession with the multitude as are the Druids with their supposed unholy rites. Antiquaries of repute have gone out of their way to voice the totally unwarranted assertion that "every Roman town in Britain had its amphitheatre". As well expect every petty town in India to boast an English-built theatre.'

And

> '... the determination to find amphitheatres all over the map has led to their being claimed for places as far apart as ... Fifeshire and ... Cornwall, although both these counties were regions which the Romans never occupied ... In plain truth any convenient hole in the ground has been fixed on by irresponsible visionaries as an amphitheatre.'

He disbelieved the Housesteads amphitheatre saying that 'it might have been a quarry', and

> '... It is of course quite possible that a quarry hole of convenient character may have actually been used by the Romans or Romano-Britons for purposes of sport, but even so to call such holes by the name of amphitheatres is misleading.'

One of Allcroft's main issues was with the definition of an amphitheatre – that the term meant something far grander than some of the very small structures that had been proposed.

Practical research on amphitheatres in the form of excavation was a remarkably late field of study in comparison with other areas of Romano-British archaeology. In 1847 the discovery of the theatre at Verulamium led to large-scale excavation disinterring the whole building. Two years later, in 1849, the Richborough amphitheatre was the first to be partially excavated and the identification confirmed, even if the details of the structure were misinterpreted (Wilmott *et al.* 2009). This was a major step forward in the study of British amphitheatres. However Charles Roach Smith's (1850, 167) expressed hope that the

> 'researches [at Richborough] which, under the personal guidance of Mr Rolfe, have so successfully terminated will, it is trusted, create a desire in individuals who may command the means, to institute an examination of analogous works in other parts of the country, with a view to decide their mode of construction'

was not immediately realised. In fact it was half a century until the second excavation designed to examine a British amphitheatre scientifically took place. This excavation was at Housesteads in 1898, when R. C. Bosanquet (1904, 252–3), who trenched the feature 'at the request of some members of the Society's council': clearly doubt remained. The report on his work appeared under the sub-heading 'The so-called amphitheatre'. Two trenches excavated showed thick beds of freestone chippings, no level floor to an arena, and 'nothing that could be construed as seats or supports for seats'. It was clear that the feature was, in fact, a quarry, exploiting one of the few limestone outcrops lying within a few yards of the Wall and fort (Welfare 2009, 248, fig. 10.1). The Knag Burn Gate is now understood to have replaced the north gate of the fort in the later second century as the main route northwards (Crow 1995, 26).

In the years since Bosanquet's work, the existence of small amphitheatres at auxiliary fort sites has become established. The first to be suggested in Britain was, an earthwork at Tomen-y-Mur, Gwynedd (Allen 1888), and in Germany at the forts of Dambach, on the Raetian *limes* (ORL *abt* A, *band* vi, 42–3), and Zugmantel, on the *limes* of Upper Germany (ORL *abt* A *band* ii, 73; *abt* B, *band* ii, *taf* 1). Collingwood and Richmond (1969) were the first to take up the 1888 suggestion that the earthwork at Tomen-y-Mur was an auxiliary amphitheatre, the counterpart to the structures known at the legionary forts of Chester and Caerleon, in their attempt to distinguish between civil amphitheatres and military *ludi*. The subsequent discovery of an apparent amphitheatre near the forts of Newstead (*Trimontium*), Roxburghshire (Clarke *et al.* 1996) further demonstrated that such structures existed. However, the most dramatic discovery of an auxiliary amphitheatre was as recently as 2003, when the totally unexpected discovery and complete excavation of a small, timber built, auxiliary amphitheatre took place at Künzing in Bavaria (Schmotz 2006).

This apparently simple case of a hypothesis that lasted for a brief period before being disproved is important because of its context both in the exploration of Hadrian's Wall and in the history of amphitheatre studies in Britain. The Housesteads 'amphitheatre' was interpreted in the light of current understanding of the passages through Hadrian's Wall, and within the context of knowledge and speculation on amphitheatres in the nineteenth century. It was only the second proposed amphitheatre to be examined, and the first to be disproved by proper archaeological means. Since it was disproved, it has become clear that amphitheatres were provided at some auxiliary forts, though as yet no such structure has been confirmed on Hadrian's Wall.

Bibliography

Ainsworth, S. and Wilmott, T. (2005) *Chester Amphitheatre– from Gladiators to Gardens*. Chester.

Allcroft, A .H. (1908) *Earthwork of England.* London.

Allen, J. R. (1860) 'Proceedings' *Archaeological Journal* 27, 345–6.

Allen, J. R. (1895) Amphitheatre at Tomen y Mur, Merionethshire. *Archaeologia Cambrensis* 5, 267–8.

Blair, R. (ed.) (1885) *J Collingwood Bruce Handbook to the Roman Wall,* 4th edition. Newcastle upon Tyne.

Bosanquet, R. C. (1904) Excavations on the line of the Roman Wall in Northumberland; The Roman Camp at Housesteads. *AA* 2nd series 25, 192–300.

Bruce, J. C. (1851) *The Roman Wall.* London.

Bruce, J. C. (1867) *The Roman Wall.* 3rd edition. London.

Bruce J. C. (1875) *Lapidarium Septetrionale, or a descrpition of the Monuments of Roman Rule in North Britain.* Newcastle upon Tyne.

Bruce, J. C. (1885) *Handbook to the Roman Wall.* 3rd edition. Newcastle upon Tyne.

Clarke, S., Tebbs, A. and Wise, A. (1996) *Newstead 1996; the northern vicus and the amphitheatre, excavation and survey.* University of Bradford interim report. http://www.trimontium.freeserve.co.uk/bradford1.html

Clayton, J. (1855a) Account of excavations of the milecastle of Cawfields. *AA* 1st series 4, 54.

Clayton, J. (1855b) The Roman Wall. *Proceedings of the Society of Antiquaries of Newcastle-upon-Tyne*, O series 1, 56–8.

Clayton, J. (1856) Borcovicus. *Proceedings of the Society of Antiquaries Newcastle-upon-Tyne*, O series 1, 201–3.

Collingwood, R. G. and Richmond, I. A. (1969). *The Archaeology of Roman Britain.* 2nd, revised edition. London.

Coulston, J. C. N. and Phillips, E. J. (1988) *CSIR Great Britain, vol I, Fasc 6, Hadrian's Wall west of the North Tyne and Carlisle*. Oxford.

Crow, J. (1995) *Housesteads.* London.

Hodgson, J. (1840) *A History of Northumberland Part 2, Vol III.* Newcastle-upon-Tyne.

Horsley, J. (1732) *Britannia Romana.* London.

Maclauchlan, H. (1858) *Memoir Written During a Survey of the Roman Wall*. Newcastle upon Tyne.

Montiroli, G. (1859) *Osservazioni sulla topografia della parte meridionale del Foro Romano: e de' suoi piu' celebri monument; dimostrata in quattro tavole ed illustata da una veduta generale / dell' architetto Giovanni Montiroli.* Rome.

Montiroli, G. (1870) *Alnwick Castle: decorazioni interne eseguite per ordine di Sua Eccellenza Algernon Percy quarto duca di Northumberland K. G. negli anni 1855 al 1866 dall'architetto cavaliere Giovanni Montiroli.* Rome.

Scarth, Rev. H. M. (1858) Some account of the investigation of barrows on the line of the Roman road between Old Sarum and the port at the mouth of the river Axe, supposed to be the *Ad Axum* of Ravennas. *Archaeological Journal* 16, 143–54.

Schmotz, K. (2006) Das hölzerne Amphitheater von Künzing, Lkr. Degendorf. Kenntnisstand und erste rekonstruktionnsätze nach abschliss de gelädearbeiten im Jahr 2004. In K Schmotz (ed.) *Vorträge des 24. Niederbayerischen Archäologentages*, 95–118. Deggendorf.

Smith, C. R. (1850) *The Antiquities of Richborough, Reculver and Lympne.* London.

Stukeley, W. (1723) *Of the Roman amphitheatre at Dorchester.* London.

Stukeley, W. (1776) *Itinerarium Curiosum.* 2nd edition, 163. London.

Way, A. (1858) Supplementary notice of the discovery, in 1856, of a gateway at the Knag Burn, found, subsequently to the survey by Mr MacLauchlan in excavation made by John Clayton Esq. Near Housesteads. In H. Maclauchlan, *Memoir Written During a Survey of the Roman Wall.* 92–6. Newcastle upon Tyne.

Welfare, H. (2009) Survey of Housesteads environs. In A. Rushworth (ed.) *Housesteads Roman Fort; The Grandest Station.* Swindon.

Wilmott, T. (2007) *The Roman Amphitheatre in Britain.* Stroud.

Wilmott, T., Garner, D. and Ainsworth, S. (2006) The Chester Amphitheatre Project 2003–5; an Interim Report. *English Heritage Historical Review* 1, 6–23.

Wilmott, T., Linford, N. and Martin, L. (2007) The Roman Amphitheatre at Richborough (*Rutupiae*), Kent; non-invasive research. In T. Wilmott (ed.) *Roman Amphitheatres and Spectacula: a 21st Century Perspective*, BAR International Series 1946, 85–94. Oxford.

23

THE WALL'S FIRST GREAT COLLECTION: THE CLAYTON COLLECTION

Frances McIntosh

John Clayton has been hailed as the saviour of Hadrian's Wall (Woodside and Crow 1999, 85) and the material he collected during his lifetime will be the subject of this paper. He was born in Newcastle 10 June 1792 and died 14 July 1890, aged 98. He was the fourth of 11 children of Nathaniel and Dorothy Clayton (Welford 1895, 577). His father Nathaniel Clayton bought the Chesters estate in 1796 (Hodgson 1840, 418) and this estate included the Roman fort of *Cilurnum* and the bridge crossing the North Tyne. John trained as a lawyer and worked in Newcastle in the family firm. He was also his father's successor as Newcastle's Town Clerk (1822–1867). In this role he was an extremely important member of civic life in the city, being heavily involved in the Dobson and Grainger redevelopment of the city centre and the construction of the railway between Newcastle and Carlisle (Anon. 1890, 10).

Although his father was not a particularly keen antiquarian (levelling parts of the fort to landscape his grounds; Bidwell and Snape 1993, 7), Clayton's grandmother, Bridget Atkinson, was the first honorary female member of the Society of Antiquaries of Newcastle upon Tyne in 1813, and this may well have influenced John. He himself was a member from 1832 until his death in 1890. He was also a member of the Literary and Philosophical Society for 65 years, 57 of which he was the Vice-President (Watson 1897, 255–6), and a Fellow of the Society of Antiquaries of London from 22 February 1866 until his death.

Having succeeded to the Chesters estate in 1832, Clayton wasted little time in beginning to investigate the site he now owned. From the early 1840s, when he first began to excavate at Chesters, Clayton conducted an excavation somewhere along Hadrian's Wall nearly every year until his death. These excavations were led firstly by William Tailford Sr. (*c.*1803–*c.*1855), and then by his son, William Tailford Jr. (1831–1912). In Clayton's memorial it was said 'Whenever an estate came into the market having on it some portion of the Wall, he strove to become its possessor' (*Daily Journal* 1890, 33). By the time John Clayton died in 1890 he owned all of Hadrian's Wall from Acomb to Cawfields (Woodside and Crow 1999, 85). As well as excavating, Clayton had an active interest in preserving Hadrian's Wall for future generations. By purchasing these sites he saved them from damage and stone robbing, sometimes even moving the farmhouse off the line of the Wall. Soon after 1860, the farm at Housesteads was moved from below the fort to its present day site, with Shield-on-the Wall, Peel Cottage and Steel Rigg Farm also being moved or demolished (*ibid.*, 86–7).

Clayton kept the finds from the excavations in the pagoda in his garden (which became known as the Antiquity House), on the veranda fronting his house and in the house itself (Budge 1903, v). Certain items did go to the British Museum, such as the military diploma found in 1879 and the coins from Coventina's Well, but by and large he kept most of the material within his collection together. This is not to say that he and his workmen collected every item from site, as is the practice today. The collection is lacking any quantities of animal bone, body-sherds of pottery, and any coarse-ware (despite regularly finding deposits of this type of material, for example Clayton 1876, 173 notes the presence of 'large quantities of horns and bones of deer and cattle, oyster shells'). The practice in the nineteenth century was often to 'cherry-pick' what was deemed interesting and important, and many of the finds we would describe as bulk-finds today were ignored. Despite this less than perfect recovery method, the collection contains upwards of

Site	*Excavated/not*	*No. items*
Carrawburgh	1871, 1873 and 1876	171
Carvoran	1886 he bought the site	26
Central Sector	Unknown (probably from Central Sector)	2288
Chesters	From 1840s onwards	4374
Coventina's Well	1875 and 1876	153
Haltwhistle (various sites)	Unclear as to exact dates	83
Housesteads	1850 onwards	140
Turret 26b (Brunton)	1873, 1878 and 1880	2
Turret 29a (Blackcarts)	1873	2
Turret 45a (Walltown)	1885 or 1883?	?
Turret 45b (Walltown West)	1883	?
Milecastle 29 (Tower Tye)	1857	?
Milecastle 37 (Housesteads)	1852 and 1853	4
Milecastle 39 (Castle Nick)	1854	2
Milecastle 42 (Cawfields)	1847, 1848, 1849	14
Vindolanda	Inscriptions from Crindledykes plus material inherited when he bought the site from A. Hedley in 1863	23

Table 23.1 List of sites where Clayton excavated and the number of items known to come from each site

11,000 items including 53 centurial stones, 95 altars, a whole range of dress accessories, tools, militaria and ceramics (Tables 23.1 and 23.2).

Although Clayton was well versed in Latin and Greek, and was competent enough to analyse the material from his excavations, he often consulted many experts in various fields for opinions, identifications and advice. His closest and longest-running acquaintance in this form was John Collingwood Bruce. Bruce published the majority of Clayton's excavations, ensuring that we can now construct a timetable of his work. The two men's main platform for publicising the work was at the monthly meetings of the Society of Antiquaries of Newcastle upon Tyne (printed in the society's Proceedings) and in the Society's annual journal *Archaeologia Aeliana.* Clayton also invited other scholars to his house to view various parts of the collection and wrote to them for advice on identification. For example, Charles Roach Smith (20 August 1807–2 August 1890) worked with Clayton and Bruce on the identification and cataloguing of the coins from Coventina's Well, and Clayton corresponded regularly with the German scholar Emil Hübner regarding the reading of inscriptions found during his excavations.

After Clayton

After John Clayton's death his estate passed to his nephew Nathaniel George Clayton (1833–1895). In his will he asks his executors to catalogue within a calendar month:

> 'the pictures and framed prints and the statues marbles Bronzes Shells Mineral Specimens and other Articles of virtue and all the Altars Vases Sculptures and all and every the Roman remains which shall be in or about or belonging to my Mansion house of Chesters or the gardens or pleasure grounds'. (John Clayton proved 1886)

There is no proof as to whether this cataloguing was attempted within the time frame laid out by John Clayton, but we do know that Nathaniel contracted the architect FW Rich to build the museum. On 6 August 1890 (less than a month after John Clayton's death), Nathaniel wrote to Mr Blair saying: 'I am going to see Mr Rich's plan of the Museum tomorrow' (Nathaniel Clayton). As the building was in the planning stage so soon after John Clayton's death, it is possible the idea for the museum was conceived before he died, but there is no evidence. In a letter from Rich to the Society of Antiquaries of Newcastle upon Tyne in 1928, he states that the erection of the museum was completed within Nathaniel's lifetime (248). Nathaniel's son, John Bertram (1861–1900), who inherited the estate at his father's death, oversaw the moving of the items to the museum, and presumably the opening. Both William Tailford Jr. and J. P. Gibson were involved with this stage of preparation. John Clayton took care over the provenance of his finds and it was said that: 'when several small objects were found they were either tied together by a string or placed in a box, and in this way they were kept until they were arranged … in the Museum' (Budge 1903, 31). This suggests that we may be cautiously confident in assigning provenance to items using the two early catalogues discussed below.

Site	*Source*	*No. items*
Corbridge	2 Late Medieval copper alloy skillets/ewers, donated by Collingwood Bruce	2
Birdoswald and Barcombe (Thorngrafton)	Clayton purchased the Barcombe purse, whilst Collingwood Bruce gave him the Birdoswald purse	2 arm purses and 63 coins
Nether Denton	Material found when building vicarage in 1868, Clayton did not excavate	184
Great Chesters	Purchased 1886, exc. 1894-7	135
Kirkby Thore	Discovered in 1838- Clayton received the material from his grandmother Bridget Atkinson	124
Pompeii	Some tesserae – presumably a souvenir	>10
Multiple Milecastles and turrets, including Haltwhistle Burn	F.G. Simpson excavated 1907 – 1914	1500 records
Housesteads	R. C. Bosanquet excavated here in 1898	142 coins, numerous iron arrowheads and three pieces of stonework

Table 23.2 Material in the collection not excavated by Clayton

In 1900, R. H. Hall (an Egyptologist from the British Museum) was asked by John Bertram to create a hand-list for visitors to the museum. It is not clear exactly when this was started, and John Bertram died before it was completed (there are items in the collection which have been marked by Hall, but do not appear in his catalogue). When John Bertram died in 1900, his mother, Mrs Nathaniel Clayton (Isabel) was allowed to continue to live there by the heir; firstly her son Edward Francis (1865–1922) and then her great-nephew John Maurice (1902–1979). In the summer of 1900 Isabel asked E.A. Wallis Budge to carry out 'numbering, mounting, labelling and exhibition of the antiquities', as well as to create a catalogue (Budge 1903, vi). Budge was actually Hall's superior in the department of Egyptian and Assyrian antiquities but was no better qualified than Hall to identify and catalogue Roman material. Isabel seems to have chosen him as he was known to the family (he had met John when visiting Chesters in 1887), and worked for the British Museum, which gave him status in her eyes. As well as a catalogue of the collection on display, Budge arranged for mounts for the large stones, and re-arranged the order of the items in the table-cases (which had been there when Hall carried out his catalogue).

The 1896 Pilgrimage along Hadrian's Wall visited 'the new museum next [to] the entrance lodge where all the inscriptions and other objects have been collected and displayed to the best advantage' (*Proceedings* vol. 7, 230). Here Gibson and Mr Blair showed them round, apologising for the incomplete nature of the displays, explaining they were still in the process of setting up, and that 'three weeks before there was not a single object in the room' (*ibid.*). The first visitor book for the museum starts on 24 March 1896, so in fact before the Pilgrimage of June 1896, meaning that Gibson and Blair's claim of a three week preparation cannot be entirely true.

After Clayton's death some archaeological work on the sites within the Clayton estate did take place, and the material from this work became part of the collection. All of the material from these excavations is distinguishable from the Clayton-era material (Table 23.2). Maintenance of the Wall within the Clayton estate, as well as further archaeological investigation, was carried out under the supervision of F. G. Simpson (Woodside and Crow 1999, 92). R. C. Bosanquet excavated at Housesteads in 1898, under the aegis of the Society of Antiquaries of Newcastle (Bosanquet 1904, 204). Unusually, for work supported by that society, the material did not go into their museum. The finds went to the Clayton Collection, for reasons not clear, and this was the start of Bosanquet's association with the collection which continued for many years. From 1907 Simpson and J. P. Gibson excavated at Haltwhistle Burn, the Vallum at Cawfields, and elsewhere, again this material became part of the Clayton Collection.

The Clayton Trustees

When Isabel Clayton died in 1928, John Maurice Clayton (her great-nephew) decided to sell the Chesters estate, however the collections were listed as a separate lot in the auction. When local archaeologists and other interested parties discovered this, they pressured John Maurice into keeping the collection together somehow, preferably in the museum. Bosanquet played a key role in this effort, corresponding with others to ask for their support, and contacting John Maurice. Captain A. M. Keith bought the land and house at the auction in 1929, but not the collection. The action group persuaded John Maurice to sign a Deed of Trust in which 'the Settlor has handed over to the Trustees the collection of Roman Antiquities' and they persuaded Captain Keith to take on the museum and its collection.

This deed was signed on 21 November 1930 and very quickly the Clayton Trustees were set up. The original Trustees were: Captain Keith (the owner of the land and museum); George MacDonald (numismatist and archaeologist); B. M. Holland Martin (occupation unknown); R. G. Collingwood (archaeologist); William Parker Brewis (archaeologist); and R. C. Bosanquet (archaeologist). At the first meeting Captain Keith agreed to take on the upkeep of the museum building, and to pay for a caretaker. Fairly soon after forming, the Trustees made an appeal for an endowment fund, and some of the pamphlets from this remain in the Clayton Trustees Paperwork. The Trustees were hoping to raise £500 by this appeal, to put towards the care of the collection. The members changed over time, and there was a hiatus in meetings between 1936 and 1949, but the museum remained open to visitors throughout. Within the archive of the Clayton Collection are the visitor books which run from 1896–1954 (with an unexplained gap from 1912–1924). Capt. Keith died on 14 Mary 1955 whilst the museum and its collection have remained in the care of the Trustees with a member of the family on the board of the Trustees, maintaining the link with the current owners of the estate.

The Ministry of Works were approached, and agreed to take Guardianship of Chesters Fort in June 1953. Prior to this the site had been managed by the Keith family. The site then came under the Department of Environment (which absorbed the Ministry of Works in 1970), who retained responsibility until 1983 when the site came under the care of English Heritage. The museum and finds were still under the care of the Trustees. Until 1950 it seems there was no curator of the Clayton collection, only a caretaker who looked after the museum, and was paid by Capt. Keith. Between 1950 and 1972, Grace Simpson was the Honorary Curator of the collection, and spent a great deal of time working on it, in particular the material excavated by her father, F. G. Simpson. When she left the position Dr David Smith, who at the time was the curator at the Museum of Antiquities, University of Newcastle, took over until 1987. Lindsay Allason-Jones has been a Trustee since 2 August 1987, at which time she became the Honorary Curator.

The role of William Tailford Jr after the death of John Clayton is unclear, but he appears to have continued in employment on the estate, as he was still there when Budge worked on the catalogue in 1903. From census records we can see that Tailford Jr was living in the lodge next to the museum by 1901. It may be that he was the caretaker or custodian, as someone had to be present to open the museum to visitors. There are no records remaining which give us information as to what happened after his death in 1912. Despite there being records of caretakers or custodians of the museum from 1930, the names of most of them are not known. This may be due to missing paperwork; the names of a few can be gleaned from minutes of the Trustees meetings. However credit must be given to them for their work in caring for the collection, and maintaining the museum building. For example, we know that in the 1980s Mr and Mrs Rutherford worked as Custodians of the museum and were well respected for their work.

Since the first Guardianship agreement at Chesters there was a separation between the care of the Museum and care of the fort. The creation of the post of Curator of Hadrian's Wall Museums by English Heritage in 1983 ended this, as both were now under English Heritage care. This was also the first time that there had been a paid curator for the Clayton Collection and so was an important step forward. The post was filled by John Dore (1983–1986), Sally Dumner and Bill Hubbard (both temporary), before Georgina Plowright took up the position in 1987, retiring in 2012. It was under Georgina's tenure that an electronic catalogue of the collection was begun, and she oversaw a complete refurbishment and re-display of the museum at Chesters in 2008.

The collection, almost fully catalogued as of September 2012, contains *c.*13,500 items (including 2,000 archive items). Unfortunately, due to the lack of documentation from the time of the excavations, some items are difficult to provenance. There is so little paperwork of John Clayton's at all that it is thought that the Clayton family destroyed much of his paperwork after he died. This lack of documentation means nearly 2,000 items have only a provenance of the 'central sector of Hadrian's Wall'.

The significance of collection

As mentioned above, there are some limitations within the Clayton Collection, namely the provenance information, and the highly selective manner in which finds were collected. Nevertheless it still has huge potential for informing us on many aspects of life on the Wall. There are other broad themes to which the collection can contribute, here two will be highlighted; religion and the construction of Hadrian's Wall.

Coventina's Well, just west of Carrawburgh fort, was discovered by lead miners in 1876, and John Clayton as landowner was informed (Allason-Jones and McKay 1985, 2). He began excavation there in October discovering the now famous altars and ceramic thuribles/incense burners, as well as high numbers of coins. Coventina is unknown elsewhere in Britain, with only two altars in Spain and one from southern France known about. As such it is a highly significant votive deposit from Hadrian's Wall, with much of the material being on display at Chesters Museum.

The inscriptions and sculpture, which were among Clayton's favourite items, have been studied from their first discovery, and are mostly catalogued *in The Roman Inscriptions of Britain*, *Corpus Inscriptionum Latinarum* or *Corpus Signorum Imperii Romani*. Their wider significance as a collection however has not been fully discussed. The impact they have on our understanding of the varied religious practices occurring on the Wall, is just one aspect that would warrant further attention.

In terms of the construction of the Wall, the large number of centurial stones within the collection; 53 in total, are extremely important. They are invaluable in understanding the method of constructing Hadrian's Wall. In Clayton's day the argument over who built Hadrian's Wall was still raging, with Clayton and Collingwood Bruce firmly on the side of Hadrian. What was needed was more evidence, and Clayton's excavations provided this in terms of some specific inscriptions. In 1926, R.G. Collingwood wrote *A Guide to the Chesters Museum* which mainly focussed on the inscriptions, and picked out three which he thought proved 'without any possibility of doubt that the great Wall was built not by Severus but by Hadrian' (13). These three are CH 245, CH 270 and CH 436, all dedication slabs:

> RIB 1666, CIL vii 663. Museum reference number CH245. Milecastle 42. Commemorative stone to Hadrian.
>
> 'Im[p(eratori) Caes(ari) Train(o)] | H[adriano Aug(usto) | le[g(io) II Aug (usta) | A(ulo) Pla[torio neopte leg(ato) pr(o) pr(aetore)]'
>
> 'For the Emperor Caesar Trajan Hadrian Augustus the Second Legion Augusta (built this) under Aulus Platorius Nepos, propraetorian legate'
>
> RIB 1736, CIL vii 730, Museum reference number CH270. Great Chesters. Commemorative stone to Hadrian.
>
> 'Imp(eratori) Caes(ari) Trai(a)n(o) Had[ri]a | no Aug(usto) p(atri) p(atriae)'
>
> 'For the Emperor Caesar Trajan Hadrian Augustus, father of his country'
>
> RIB 1634, CIL vii 662. Museum reference number CH436. Milecastle 37. Dedication slab from, set up by the 2nd Legion under Aulus Platorius Nepos, Governor of Britain c. 121–124.
>
> '...] | leg(io) II [Aug(usa)] | A(ulo) Platorio N[epote ...'
>
> '...the Second Legion Augusta under Aulus Platorius Neops ...'

As well as the collection as a whole there are finds which are individually important, not least the Carvoran modius, found in 1915 (RIB 2415.56), which is the only example of a modius known from Roman Britain, and one of only a handful known from the entire empire (Haverfield 1916). Or the military diploma dating to AD 146 found at the South Gate of Chesters in 1879 (RIB 2401.10 and 2401.13, RMDii no. 97). The original is now in the British Museum, but an electrotype is displayed in the museum.

The PhD currently being carried out by the author on the Clayton Collection is highlighting areas of future research on the collection. One such area is the pottery, with over 5,000 sherds there is much work to be done. John Dore in the 1980s and 1990s carried out work on the Corbridge pottery to put it into a typological series, and Alex Croom of Tyne and Wear Archives and Museums has been working on cataloguing this material for inclusion into the Hadrian's Wall pottery database. It would be a great achievement to get the Clayton material included in this. Some of the case studies in the PhD (being undertaken at Newcastle University) will focus on object groups not previously studied in the collection, for example the brooches and the militaria.

Currently the collection is on long-term loan to English Heritage, and under the remit of the Curator of Roman Collections and displayed at Chesters Roman fort (Plate 21). The material not on display is stored at Corbridge Roman Site, and work is in progress to include the catalogue in English Heritage's Collections Online Programme. The fact we still have this collection today is testament to the many people who have been involved in keeping it together

and safe since John Clayton's death in 1890, of whom Lindsay is but one.

I would like to offer this paper in thanks to all the help, guidance and support Lindsay has given me over the years, without which I would not be in the position to write this paper at all.

Acknowledgements

David Breeze and Georgina Plowright kindly sent me their work on the Clayton family tree. The current Clayton Trustees allowed me to look through their paper archives and are generously funding my PhD.

Bibliography

Allason-Jones, L. and Mckay, B. (1985) *Coventina's Well. A Shrine on Hadrian's Wall.* The Clayton Trustees, Gloucester.

Anonymous. (1890) *In Memoriam. Mr. John Clayton of Chesters.* Printed at the *Daily Journal* office, Clayton St. Newcastle-Upon-Tyne.

Anonymous. (1896) *Proceedings of Society of Antiquaries*, vol. 2. Newcastle upon Tyne.

Bosanquet, R.C. (1904) Excavations on the line of the Roman Wall in Northumberland. The Roman Camp at Housesteads. *AA* 2nd series 25, 193–300.

Proceedings of the Society of Antiquaries of Newcastle Upon Tyne. 1928. 4th series 3.21.

Bidwell, P. and Snape, M. (1993) *The Roman Fort of Chesters and its Environs. A survey of the extent and preservation of the archaeological deposits.* Tyne and Wear Museums.

Budge, E. A. W. (1903) *An Account of the Roman Antiquities preserved in the Museum at Chesters Northumberland.* Gilbert and Rivington, London.

Collingwood, R. G. (1926) *A Guide to the Chesters Museum.* Newcastle upon Tyne.

Grenville, J., Gourley, H., Harrap, A., Rawson, D. and Roskams, S. (2002) *2001 Conservation Plan. Chesters Roman Fort.* York University for English Heritage.

Haverfield, F. (1916) Modius Claytonensis: the Roman bronze measure from Carvoran. *AA* 3rd series 13, 85– 102.

Hodgson, J. (1840) *History of Northumberland* Part 2, vol.3. Newcastle upon Tyne.

Watson, R. S. (1897) *The History of the Literary and Philosophical Society of Newcastle-Upon-Tyne (1793–1896).* Walter Scott, London.

Welford, R. (1895) *Men of Mark 'twixt Tyne and Tweed.* Walter Scott, London.

Woodside, R. and Crow, J. (1999) *Hadrian's Wall. An Historic Landscape.* National Trust, London.

Archival sources

John Clayton (Proved 30 April 1886) NPR/1/33. Northumberland Record Office.

Nathaniel Clayton. 6 August 1890. L728 C527. Newcastle upon Tyne City Library.

F. W. Rich. 1894. NRO 3165/P/1936. Northumberland Record Office.

24

AN ETRUSCAN MIRROR FROM THE COLLECTION OF THE SOCIETY OF ANTIQUARIES OF NEWCASTLE UPON TYNE

Andrew Parkin

The Society of Antiquaries of Newcastle upon Tyne is well known for its extensive collections of archaeological material from the North-East of England, but the Society also possesses objects from further afield. One of the most striking of these is a fragmentary Etruscan mirror (no. 1923.30) from the end of the fourth century BC (Plate 22). This mirror was published by Brian Shefton in *Archaeological Reports* (1969–70, 56–7). Nevertheless it is worth revisiting as it raises a number of interesting questions of interpretation.

The fragment is of cast bronze and represents nearly half of the original mirror. The handle is missing, but the remains of a hole perhaps for one of the rivets that would have attached it are visible. On the front there is a floral ornament in the area of transition (talon) between the disc of the mirror and the handle, while the rim is decorated with a tongue pattern. On the back is an engraving that represents the rape of the Trojan princess Kassandra by the Greek hero Aias, son of Oileus, who is also known as the Lesser Aias. Most of Aias is missing but Kassandra is clearly depicted clinging desperately to a column as Aias tries to drag her away; one of his hands can be seen pulling at her hair, while the other is visible grasping her right arm. An inscription is situated directly above Kassandra's head evidently identifying her, although its authenticity has been questioned (Touchefeu 1981, 346, no. 81). The edge of the engraved scene is decorated with a border of ivy leaves. Borders of a similar type have been associated with mirrors produced in the Etruscan city of Vulci (Fischer-Graf 1980), and there is a possibility that this is where the mirror was manufactured. It should be noted, however, that none of the examples cited in Fischer-Graf's extensive study have the distinctive dots present on the ivy leaves of the Newcastle mirror.

According to myth, during the sack of Troy, Kassandra sought refuge in the Temple of Athena. She held onto the goddesses' statue, the palladion, in the hope of gaining Athena's protection. However Aias burst into the temple and dragged her away from the statue, an exploit which disgraced the Greeks and antagonised the goddess. This act of impiety is an iconographic theme that is frequently reproduced in antiquity (Touchefeu, 1981, 339*ff.*), although once it had become an established subject, artists varied it to suit their own ends (Woodford 1993, 110). It occurs with some regularity on Attic red-figure vases, including many found in Italian contexts, and would have been familiar to an Etruscan audience. One of the most well-known examples is from a representation of the sack of Troy on the shoulder of a red-figure hydria from Nola, attributed to the Kleophrades painter (Beazley 1974, 6–7; Woodford 1993, 114*ff.*). In addition the scene is found in Etruscan art, for example on a mural dating to 320–310 BC, from the François tomb at Vulci (Andreae 2004, 188). There are also several mirrors which depict this scene. Examples from Paris and Milan represent Aias dragging Kassandra by the hair from the cult statue of Athena (Oleson 1975, pl. 37, fig. 5; Touchefeu 1981, 346, no. 82).

The Newcastle mirror differs significantly from all of these examples. Instead of holding on to the palladion, Kassandra grasps a column, which, as far as I am aware, is unparalleled in representations of this episode (Plate 23). Brian Shefton (1970, 57) thought that the column was surmounted by a Phrygian cap and that this represented the statue of Athena. Certainly Phrygian caps are frequently associated with Easterners and on many occasions specifically with Trojans. A Paestan amphora in Vienna (no. 724) represents Kassandra clinging on to a statue of Athena

wearing what appears to be a Phyrgian cap (Davreux 1942, 166). This might be seen as supporting a case for understanding the Newcastle mirror as showing the statue of Athena in some kind of artistic short-hand, with the fact that she is worshipped in the Eastern city of Troy implied by the presence of the Phrygian cap on top of a column. However there are problems with this reading of the scene. Representations of Athena in a Phrygian cap are unusual. In addition I have found no other examples of columns surmounted by Phrygian caps. Trendall (1987, 261) observes that on the Vienna amphora 'almost the entire picture has been repainted, thus obscuring much of the original drawing'. Therefore this image cannot be relied on to support an interpretation of the column on the Newcastle mirror.

An alternative reading would see the column surmounted by an Ionic or Aeolic capital. It has not been rendered particularly well but this is a far more straightforward explanation than attempting to create a connection to Athena by means of a Phrygian cap. One of the capital's volutes is visible, while the other is partially obscured by an ivy leaf. There are several instances where Ionic columns have been associated with images of the rape of Kassandra. On an Etruscan amphora in the British Museum, for example, Kassandra is shown grasping an Ionic column on top of which is a statue of Athena (Touchefeu 1981, 345–6, no. 79). Furthermore Ionic and Aeolic columns are often connected with the East Greek world, especially the cities of Asia Minor, and it is not inconceivable to see such a column as imparting an Eastern, or Trojan, ambience to this scene. Certainly there are several representations on South Italian red-figure pots that depict Kassandra in religious structures with Ionic columns (Trendall and Cambitoglou 1983, 151, no. 21a, Touchefeu 1981, 343, no. 56). There is also a representation of Kassandra being pursued by Aias on an Attic red-figure cup from Orvieto, which is noteworthy for the lack of a statue of Athena (Touchefeu 1981, 344, no. 64). Instead Aias chases Kassandra, who runs past an Aeolic column. Probably the Newcastle mirror's artist was familiar with images of the rape of Kassandra that included Ionic or Aeolic columns and chose one for her to cling to as she vainly attempted to fend off Aias.

It seems fairly certain that Etruscan mirrors were predominantly used by women (de Grummond 1982, 168*ff.*; Barker and Rasmussen, 1998, 105) and this makes the choice of subject matter surprising. An act of impiety and the threat of sexual violence seems odd to our eyes on an object associated with female adornment. We do know that the Etruscan elite were avid consumers of images of Greek mythology and had a predilection for the Trojan War, so it is perhaps here that an explanation for the mirror's subject matter can be sought (Barker and Rasmussen, 1998, 105–7).

The first account of the mirror dates to 1852 (*Bulletino dell'Instituto di Corrspondenza Archeologica*, 1852, 41) and states that it was found in Orbetello in Tuscany. It was subsequently published by Gerhard (1867, 56, pl. 400, 2) in his survey of Etruscan mirrors, where he describes it as belonging to R. de Wit. The illustration in Gerhard shows that the mirror was complete with the left-hand side, displaying Aias still preserved. This section is now lost. At some stage the mirror passed into the hands of Robert Blair of South Shields who showed it to the Society of Antiquaries of Newcastle upon Tyne on the 25 March 1891 (Anon. 1891). Blair was a collector of antiquities, as well as being the joint secretary of the Society of Antiquaries and editor of *Archaelogia Aeliana* (Oxberry 1923, 202).

Unfortunately the description of the mirror in the Society's proceedings suggests that the left portion representing Aias was no longer joined to the right when he displayed it at the Society's meeting. It also does not shed any light on how the mirror came into Robert Blair's possession. The remaining fragment of the mirror is now on display in the Shefton Gallery of Greek and Etruscan Art and Archaeology at the Great North Museum in Newcastle upon Tyne.

Bibliography

Andreae, B. (2004) Die Tomba François. Anspruch und historische Wirklichkeit eines etruskischen Familiengrabes. In B. Andreae, A. Hoffman and C. Weber-Lehmann (eds) *Die Etrusker: Luxus für Jenseits, Bilder vom Diesseits – Bilder vom Tod,* 176–207. Hirmer, München.

Anonymous. (1891) *Proceedings of the Society of Antiquaries Newcastle upon Tyne.* New Series 5, 15.

Barker, G. and Rasmussen, T. (1998) *The Etruscans.* Blackwell, Oxford.

Beazley, J. D. (1974) *The Kleophrades Painter.* Philip von Zabern, Mainz.

Beazley, J. D. (1852) *Bulletino dell'Instituto di Corrspondenza Archeologica.* Roma.

Davreux, J. (1942) *La Légende de la prophétesse Cassandre.* E. Droz, Paris.

de Grummond, N. T. (ed.) (1982) *A Guide to Etruscan Mirrors.* Archaeological News Inc., Tallahassee, Florida.

Fischer-Graf, U. (1980) *Spiegelwerkstätten in Vulci.* Gebr. Mann, Berlin.

Gerhard, E. (1867) *Etruskische Spiegel. IV.* Georg Reimer, Berlin.

Oleson, J. P. (1975) Greek Myth and Etruscan Imagery in the Tomb of the Bulls at Tarquinia. *American Journal of Archaeology* 79, 189–200.

Oxberry, J. (1923) Robert Blair, M.A. F.S.A. An Obituary Notice. *AA* 3rd series 20, 187–204.

Shefton, B. B. (1969–1970) The Greek Museum, University of Newcastle upon Tyne. *Archaeological Reports* 16, 52–62.

Touchefeu, O. (1981) Aias II. *Lexicon Iconographicum Mythologiae Classicae (L.I.M.C.)* 1, 336–51.

Trendall, A. D. (1987) *The Red-Figured Vases of Paestum.* British School at Rome, Rome.

Trendall, A. D. and Cambitoglou, A. (1983) *First Supplement to the Red-Figured Vases of Apulia.* BICS Supplement 42.

Woodford, S. (1993) *The Trojan War in Ancient Art.* Duckworth, London.

25

'DRIVE AWAY THE CLOUD OF PLAGUE': A GREEK AMULET FROM ROMAN LONDON

R. S. O. Tomlin

Roman protective charms or spells, inscribed on thin tablets (lamellae) made of gold and other metals, are often called 'phylacteries' or 'amulets' since they were rolled up and worn in cylindrical amulet-cases for magical protection. They have been known in Britain ever since the Caernarvon gold amulet was found in 1827 (*GMA* 2; *RIB* 436), but they are not common (Tomlin 2011), and one found in London raises interesting questions. It is pewter, not gold, and the metrical text is in Greek, including a verse which originated on the south coast of the Black Sea, but it may nonetheless have been inscribed in the Roman West. The scribe also made mistakes, not all of which can be resolved. Still more intriguing is the historical context, which seems to be that of the Antonine Plague, the 'great plague' of Galen (Duncan-Jones 1996; Jones 2005, 299, n. 30; Eck 2012). It is a remarkable text, and a pleasure to publish it here to honour a friend and colleague of many years standing.

This amulet was found in 1989 at Vintry in the City of London, where the Walbrook meets the Thames, during controlled metal-detecting after the Roman foreshore was exposed in Upper Thames Street at TQ 3236 8080 (Fig. 25.1). The amulet is now displayed in the Museum of London (Inv. No. 941). It is a narrow rectangular strip, 48 × 130 mm, cut from a sheet of pewter (tin alloyed with lead, in this instance approximately Sn 45%:Pb 55%), and it is complete and in good condition, except for superficial corrosion, some minor damage to the edges, and a split at one end. Four other pewter tablets were also found, but they were not found together, and their texts are not related to one another. These are unpublished except for *Britannia* 30, 375, no. 1, and their contents, inscribed in magical 'characters' or in Latin, are unrelated to the amulet discussed here.

Ancient 'curse tablets' were traditionally written on lead, and protective charms or amulets on gold and silver, but the Greek Magical Papyri sometimes specify tin (*PGM* 3, 297). Greek and Latin do not distinguish between pure tin and tin-alloy, which would be pewter used as an economical substitute for silver, whether tin was alloyed with a small proportion of copper to give it hardness, or with a larger proportion of lead to make for easier casting and to economise on the more expensive metal. Where and to what extent the Romans manufactured pewter vessels is not clear. The elder Pliny, in his confusing account of tin and lead, says that they were alloyed in equal proportions to make plumber's solder, and in two parts of tin to one of lead to make 'silvery' (*argentarium*), which was used in fraudulent silver-plating; this cannot have been much different from the Gallic practice he also mentions of washing bronze vessels with tin. But he makes no explicit reference to the manufacture of pewter vessels (*Natural History* 34, 160–2). The archaeological evidence comes largely from Britain, but this may be due to the weight of study and analysis; it has also been possible to list about a hundred vessels from France, Belgium and the Netherlands. In Roman Britain, where lead was abundant (as Pliny notes), and tin was available, there was undoubtedly an extensive pewter industry (Beagrie 1989, esp. 179–81). A 'curse tablet' from Uley was even prompted by the theft of two pewter dishes (Tomlin 1993, 130, no. 84). Most of the Bath 'curse tablets', as it happens, were not made of lead alone, but of tin alloyed with lead. They can be seen as by-products of the local pewter industry, and one is actually inscribed on a pewter plate which was then folded up and thrown into the Sacred Spring (*Tab Sulis*, 81–4; 146, no. 30). Some tablets are almost as thin as paper and could have been made by

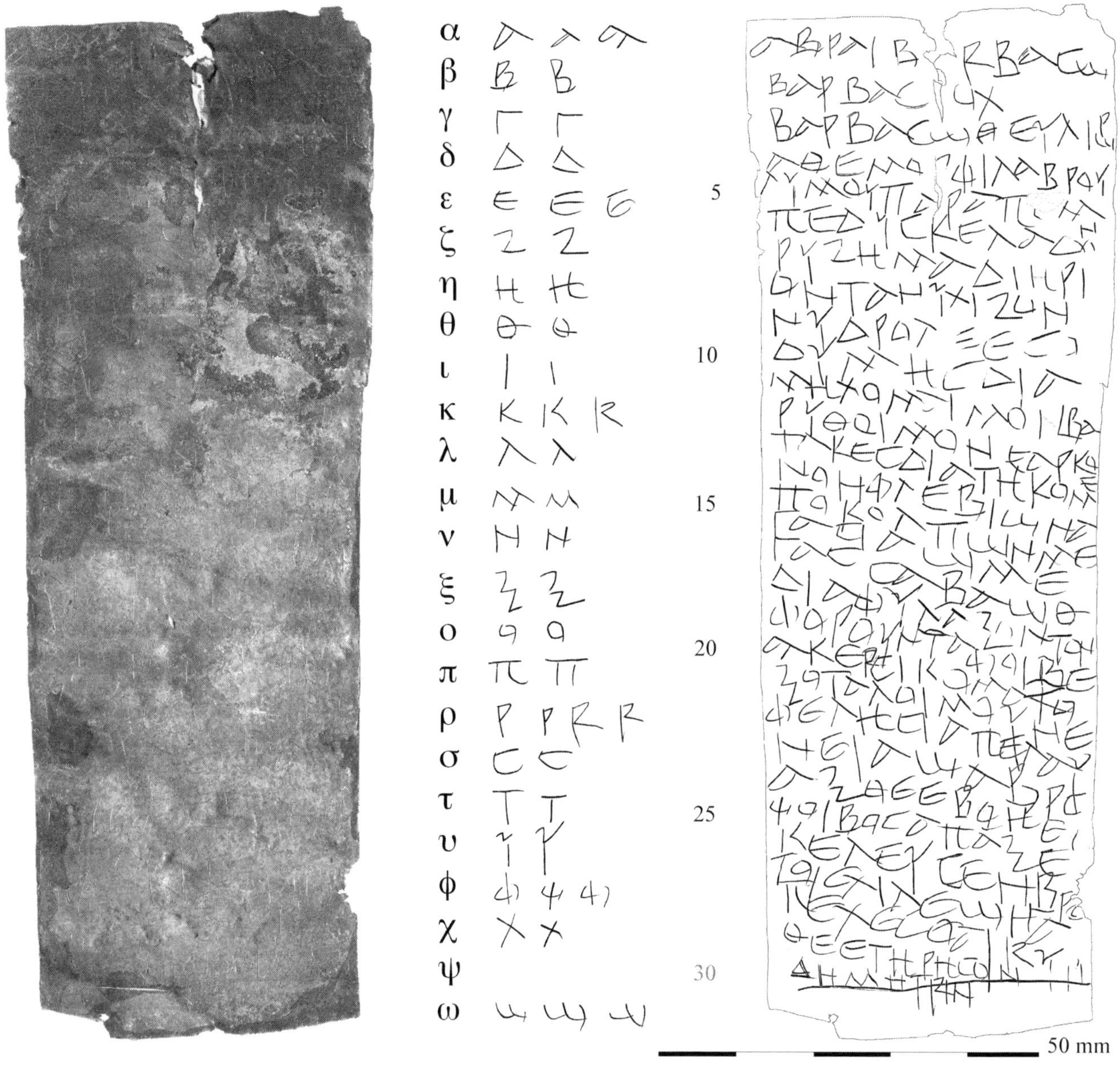

Figure 25.1 The Vintry amulet, accompanied by a drawing of the inscription and examples of individually inscribed Greek letters. The photograph is by courtesy of the Museum of London; the drawing is by the author

'slush moulding'; melting scrap pewter and pouring it onto a smooth surface, then drawing a wooden squeegee across it. This would have produced a smooth, resilient surface, ideal for inscribing with a sharp-pointed iron *stilus*.

The Vintry amulet carries 30 lines of Greek letters, and was written for a man with the Greek name *Demetri(o)s*. At first sight it looks as if it was imported into Britain from a Greek-speaking province, suspended from the neck of Demetrios presumably, but the association of pewter with Britain and the Gallic provinces raises the question of whether the amulet was produced more locally. After all, it was found quite near other pewter tablets, two of which were inscribed in Latin. There is also a broad hint in the letter-forms that the scribe was familiar with Latin: three times he wrote Latin R for Greek ρ (in lines 1, 20 and 30) and corrected it once (in 20); evidently it was a mistake, and he recognised it as such. Also, in writing Greek κ with a flourish in 28, he produced a letter indistinguishable from Latin R. So it might be safer to conclude that he was bilingual, with Latin as his first language, which would imply that he was writing in the Latin-speaking West, perhaps even in Britain.[1]

This scribe wrote a legible 'book hand', not in 'cursive', partly because of his medium, which would have made it difficult for him to describe a full circle with his stilus. He constructed his letters from short, straight strokes, or from simple hooked strokes: he always wrote ο, for example, with two hooked strokes; ω with two hooked strokes and a short vertical; β with a long vertical, two hooked strokes and a horizontal. Sometimes he repeated a stroke.[2] He made only the simplest letters (γ, ζ, ι, χ) without lifting his stilus at least once. Nothing in the letter-forms prevents the dating of this amulet to the last third of the second century, a conclusion which follows from its emphasis on 'plague' and in particular from its use of a verse (19–23) current during the Antonine Plague which began in 165/6. The scribe never ligatured one letter to the next, but his misreading of -ην as -ηcι in writing νεφέληcι (21–22) suggests that he was familiar with ligatures, or that they were present in the text he was copying. As usual in ancient manuscripts he did not separate words; but, although his lines were quite short, he took trouble to complete a word within the line. Thus in 2 he postponed the third βαρβα- until 3, despite leaving a space, and sometimes he interlineated a letter or two at the end of the line to complete a word.[3] But if the word was too long for this, he divided it correctly between syllables by making the break after the vowel.[4]

The scribe's mistakes should also be noted. They will be discussed individually in the line-by-line commentary, but they fall into two classes. Some are lapses from the Classical norm, even though he was affecting an archaic style and vocabulary, but they should not be seen as mistakes, only as 'Vulgarisms' due to the spoken Greek of his time and place.[5] Others are slips of the pen, and are often due to visual confusion of one letter with another. They are copying-errors, either because he was careless, or because he did not altogether understand what he was copying. The latter is more likely, since he was transcribing a literary, poetic text full of archaic, 'Epic' vocabulary far removed from contemporary spoken Greek. This is a likely explanation of the 'Vulgar' contraction of διηέριον to διῆριον (7–8), for example, since he should have realised that ε was required by the metre. Visual confusion must have accounted for his making the initial c of cαρκοτακέc (12–13) into ε by a redundant medial stroke; and in 21–22, as already noted, he wrote cι for ν at the end of νεφέληcσι, despite wrecking the metre and syntax. His omission of the second α from Ἀβραcάξ in 23 may only be a slip of the pen, but in 24 his omission of θ from βοηθεῖ suggests visual confusion between θ and ε.

Transcript

The text may now be transcribed literally: letter by letter, and line by line, but with some concessions to modern readers. Letters will be lower-case, but proper names have been capitalized. Breathings and accents have been supplied, except for magical words and words like ευλιωρ which are corrupt. Punctuation and hyphens have also been supplied, and words have been separated. A letter lost to damage in line 1 has been restored in square brackets, and two letters omitted by oversight in 23 and 24 have been supplied in round brackets, but elsewhere divergent forms have not been normalized, nor have less obvious copying-mistakes been corrected. Latin R for Greek ρ has been tacitly corrected in 1, 20 and 30.

αβραι β[α]ρβαcω,
βαρβαcωχ, vacat
βαρβαcωθ, ευλιωρ
αθεμορφι, λάβρου
λυμοῦ παράπεμ-
πε δυcκέλαδον
ῥύζημα, διῆρι-
ον, τανυχιζον,
νυδρολεεc, ὀ-
δύμηc δια-
μηχόμαιμον, βα-
ρύθοιμον, εαρκο-
τακέc, διατηκόμε-
νον, φλεβίων ἀ-
πὸ κόλπων. μέ-
γαc Ιάω, μέ-
γαc Cαβαώθ,
διαφύλαξον τὸν
φοροῦντα. Φοῖβε
ἀκερcικόμα, το-
ξότα, λοιμοῦ νε-
φέληcι ἀπέλαυ-
νε. Ιάω, Ἀβρ(α)c-
ὰξ θεέ, βοη(θ)εῖ.
Φοῖβοc ἅπαξ ἐ-
κέλευcεν βρο-
τοῖc χιλεων ἀ-
πέχεcθαι. κύρι
θεὲ, τηρῆcον
Δημῆτριν

Translation[6]

'*Abrai Barbasō Barbasōch Barbasōth.* †*euliōr* †*athemorphi*, send away the discordant clatter of raging plague, air-borne, †*tanychizon*, †*nydrolees*, infiltrating pain, heavy-spiriting, flesh-wasting, melting, from the hollows of the veins. Great Iao, great Sabaoth, protect the bearer. Phoebus of the unshorn hair, archer, drive away the cloud of plague. Iao, God Abrasax, bring help. Phoebus once ordered mortals to refrain from †*chileōn*. Lord God, watch over Demetrios.'

Commentary[7]

1–3. The text begins with a threefold magical invocation, comprising a sequence of magical words which differ only in the final letter; examples of this are noted by Daniel and Maltomini (*Suppl. Mag.* II, 96, 1); sometimes the magical word is simply followed by the numeral γ´ ('three times') (Brashear 1991, 41). Like Ἰάω and Cαβαώθ below (15 and 16), these magical words are probably Hebrew in origin, not that the scribe knew this. βαρβαcω seems to be unattested, but is probably a variant of ἀρβαθιαω ('fourfold Yahweh'), which is often associated with Ἰάω and Cαβαώθ (for example *PGM* 2, 173): see Kotansky's note to *GMA* 57, 3, etc. Variants include βαρβαθιαωθ (*GMA* 39, 3) and βαρβαριαω (*PGM* 1, 122), while in the Caernarvon amulet it occurs as ἀρβατιαω.

3–15. The text continues with a sequence of four hexameters, telling a deity to 'send away' plague, the attributes of which fill most of 3–15.

3–4, ευλιωρ αθεμορφι. The metrical sequence which follows these two words (the division being marked by the interlineation of ρ at the end of 3) requires that they form the first two and a half feet of the first hexameter, even though as transmitted here they are unmetrical and meaningless. In 4, αθεμορφι is evidently an adjective compounded from –μορφοc ('formed'), and is in the vocative case, the final ι for ε being a trivial 'Vulgarism'. In this context, θεόμορφε ('of form divine') is an easy conjecture, the initial α being regarded as part of the mis-copying, since the deity can hardly have been 'not of divine form'; *ἀθεόμορφε would in any case be unmetrical. But ευλιωρ resists conjecture. The context requires the name of a deity, or (more likely) a bidding verb; just possibly εὔχομαι, ὦ θεόμορφε ('I beg (you), of form divine').

5. λυμοῦ is for λοιμοῦ (correctly in 21), the interchange of οι and υ being frequent in papyri (Gignac I, 197–8); it also occurs in ρύζημα (7) and βαρύθοιμον (11–12). λοιμός occurs only once in Homer (*Iliad* I 61), but the context is appropriate: the Greeks suffer a plague caused by Apollo's arrows, which in the context of another plague Ammianus Marcellinus (19.4.3) equates with the sun's rays. By an easy inversion, Phoebus Apollo can be invoked to drive plague away with his arrows (Faraone 1992, 59–64); see further, 19–23 below.

7. ῥύζημα is for ῥοίζημα (see previous note), meaning the sound of birds, wasps, etc. It is cognate with ῥοίζοc, which appropriately is used by Homer for the sound of an arrow (*Iliad* 16, 361).

7–8. As already noted, διῆριον is a 'Vulgar' and unmetrical contraction of διηέριον. This adjective is post-Homeric, but Oppian uses it of the 'air-borne' scent picked up by hounds (*Cyn.* 1, 506).

8. τανυχιζον is not attested, but is apparently a present participle compounded from τανυ- ('far'). The verb cχίζω ('sunder') may be suggested, but *τανυcχιζον would be unmetrical.

9. νυδρολεεc is also not attested, and resists conjecture. Can it be the mis-copying of an adjective like *ἀνδρολεεc, meaning 'man-destroying'? Further evidence of textual corruption is that it is unmetrical: the last syllable needs to be long.

9–10. ὀδύμηc is for ὀδύνηc by assimilation of ν to μ (Gignac I, 167), as in διαμηχόμαιμον (11). It is apparently a feminine noun in the genitive case, which would be out of place in this long sequence (7–14) of attributes, whether adjectives or present participles, of the neuter noun ῥύζημα. Its position suggests it is actually the object of διαμηχόμαιμον (see next note), so the apparent genitive should be an accusative, indicating visual confusion between -ην and -ηc; there is a better example of this confusion in νεφέληcι for νεφέλην in 21–22.

11. διαμηχόμαιμον is apparently for διανηχόμενον, by double assimilation of ν to μ (see previous note); confusion between αι and ε is frequent (Gignac I, 192–3). Metrically it is the counterpart of διατηκόμενον (13–14). The verb διανήχομαι (equivalent to διανέω, LSJ) means to 'infiltrate' or 'penetrate', but like διατήκομαι it must be understood here as transitive after ὀδύμηc (i.e. ὀδύνην), in the extended sense of 'causing (pain) to penetrate'; English 'infiltrate' offers the same ambiguity, which is easier than

to posit *διαμηχόμενον as the present participle of an over-contracted διαμηχανάομαι ('cause').

11–12. βαρύθοιμον is for βαρύθυμον, another instance of the interchange between υ and οι (see above, note to 5). The adjective is not Homeric, but does occur in later writers including the Scholia to the *Iliad* (A 365b), where it refers to Achilles' state of mind. It means 'heavy-spirited', in the sense of 'depressed' or 'indignant'. Since it is an attribute of 'plague' here, neither sense is appropriate; it has evidently been extended to mean causing these states: 'depressing' rather than 'depressed'; 'heavy-spiriting', so to speak.

12–13, εαρκοτακέϲ. The first letter carries a second medial stroke, making it ε rather than ϲ (which otherwise are identical in this hand). This is obviously a visual confusion of ϲαρκοτακέϲ ('flesh-wasting'), an adjective attested only in Proclus, *Hymn* 7, 44, which is fifth-century, but (as the editor E. Vogt notes) an adjective implicit long before in Plato, *Timaeus* 83b. Proclus prays to Athena to 'drive away the crowds of flesh-wasting, bitter diseases' (ϲαρκοτακῶν δ' ἀπέλαυνε πικρῶν ἀγελάϲματα νούϲων).

13–14, διατηκόμενον. Present participle Middle or Passive of διατήκω ('melt'); since it is an attribute of 'plague', it must be Middle and transitive, 'melting' in the sense of 'causing to melt'.

14–15, φλεβίων ἀπὸ κόλπων. Although the noun φλέβιον does exist (it is a rare diminutive of φλέψ, 'vein'), the syntax requires that φλεβίων be an adjective qualifying the noun κόλπων ('hollows'); it would either be an unattested variant of the adjective φλέβικοϲ ('of the veins'), or the scribe has simply omitted κ, which seems more likely. For the phrase, compare χθονίων ἀπὸ κόλπων ('from the hollows of the earth') used by Proclus (*Hymn* 7, 35) and his contemporary Nonnus (*Paraphrase of St John's Gospel* 20, 38).

15–17. The protective deities Ἰάω ('Yahweh') and Cαβαώθ ('of Hosts'), ultimately Hebrew, are often invoked together in phylacteries and amulets; and often in association with ἀρβαθιαω (etc.) (see note to 1–3) and Ἀβραϲάξ (22–3).

18–19. διαφύλαξον τὸν φοροῦντα ('protect the bearer') is understandably a cliché in phylacteries and amulets, for example *Suppl. Mag.* I, 2, 8–9.

20. The first letter is undoubtedly α (since it is guaranteed by the epithet of Phoebus), but the scribe has added a redundant diagonal stroke, perhaps by confusion with λ. In writing the fourth letter, he seems to have first written Latin R (compare 1 and 30), then to have scratched it out partly, and to have repeated the loop to make it Greek ρ.

19–23. These lines embody a fifth hexameter, despite the metrical hiatus after Φοῖβε, the metrically intrusive τοξότα, and the unmetrical (and ungrammatical) νεφέληϲι.

τοξότα ('archer') is vocative like ἀκερϲικόμα ('of the unshorn hair') and, since it is a dactyl, has surely been imported from another hexameter. A possible source is the anonymous and incomplete *Hymn to Apollo* quoted by Porphyry and Eusebius (ed. Heitsch 1961, 51), since it contains the invocation τοξότα Φοῖβε, but this is the only echo of language, and the epithet was undoubtedly formulaic. νεφέληϲι is apparently an Epic dative plural, but the syntax and metre require the accusative singular νεφέλην. It has already been suggested that the scribe mis-read -ην as -ηϲι, which would be visually similar, especially if ϲ were ligatured to ι, but this would also be quite a sophisticated error to make since it implies a knowledge of Epic declension, so he may have inherited it from an earlier copyist.

This hexameter is remarkable, since it is a variant of the metrical charm circulated by Lucian's 'false prophet' Alexander of Abonuteichos (on the Black Sea coast of Paphlagonia) against the Antonine Plague in the late 160s (*Alexander* 36). This was the hexameter Φοῖβοϲ ἀκειρεκόμηϲ λοιμοῦ νεφέλην ἀπερύκει ('Phoebus of the unshorn hair keeps away the cloud of plague').[8] According to Lucian, it was composed by Alexander himself for the oracular god he had manufactured: Glycon, the incarnation of Apollo's son Asclepius in the form of a snake. His verse was inscribed over doorways everywhere, but it proved to be ineffective against the Plague. The only corroboration of Lucian's account is a fragmentary and undated stone inscription from Syrian Antioch, not in fact a lintel, which reads [...]φέλην ἀπερύκει, followed by the seven Greek vowels, a protective formula (Perdrizet 1903; Robert 1980, 404). The verse is also quoted in the late fifth century by the encyclopaedist Martianus Capella (i.19), but he attributes it erroneously to Homer (*caeci poetae versum*).

The Vintry variant is significantly different: 'Phoebus' is vocative instead of nominative, despite the metrical hiatus this causes; he receives a second epithet (τοξότα), despite the damage this does to the metre; and the verb is not ἀπερύκει (indicative) but ἀπέλαυνε (imperative). But ἀπελαύνω (LSJ, 'drive away') is metrically identical with ἀπερύκω (LSJ, 'keep away'), and is also a synonym: it is used by Proclus in just this sense of 'driving away' disease (Hymn 7, 44, quoted in the note to lines 12–13 above). Overall, the verse has become a prayer addressed to Apollo, instead of an oracular charm which takes his power for granted.

How then to connect the Vintry amulet with Alexander's verse? If the latter was widely disseminated, as Lucian says, it would have been known to the author of the amulet, who could adapt it for his own purpose with the help of other oracular responses or prayers. To judge by the equation of ἀπελαύνω with ἀπερύκω, the verse may even have circulated in more than one version; the 'cloud of plague' seems to have been a cliché, since it occurs in an epitaph from Aezani (*MAMA* 9, 79). Lucian says that Alexander conciliated Apollo's oracle at Claros by recommending it to his own petitioners, but perhaps he was not the only writer to summarize its responses. Five consultations of this oracle have been linked with the Plague, and three of them entail a statue of Apollo as an archer (Parke 1985, 150–7; developed by Faraone 1992, 61–2, and Jones 2005, 298). Thracian Callipolis [Gallipoli], for example, was told to erect a statue of 'Phoebus bearing his bow, who drives away plague'; and at all the gates of Phrygian Hierapolis [Pamukkale] there was to be 'a holy statue of Clarian Phoebus, equipped with his bow which destroys diseases, as though shooting barren plague from afar'. This imagery is shared by Alexander's verse and the Vintry amulet, although the vocabulary is different.[9] According to Ammianus Marcellinus (23.6.24), the Plague affected 'everywhere, from the Persian frontier to the Rhine and Gaul'. That this included Britain has already been deduced from epigraphic evidence by Duncan-Jones (1996, 121, n. 118) and Jones (2005), but the Vintry amulet is now explicit.

23–4. The second α of Ἀβραcάξ was omitted by oversight. This protective deity, as already noted, is often associated with Ἰάω and Cαβαώθ in phylacteries.

24 (and again in 29), θεέ. This vocative form, of θεόc ('god'), is noted by LSJ as post-Classical. It often occurs in the Greek Magical Papyri.

24, βοη(θ)εῖ. As already noted, the scribe omitted θ by oversight, a visual confusion with ε which it somewhat resembled.

24–28. These lines embody a sixth hexameter, despite the unmetrical ν added to ἐκέλευcεν. Since the next word begins with a consonant, ν is unnecessary, but Gignac notes (I, 114) that Roman papyri are irregular in whether they add the movable -ν or not; by the Byzantine period it tends to be used in all positions. This hexameter, unlike the others which precede it, is not a prayer but a statement; it therefore seems to summarize an oracular response.

25, ἅπαξ. This adverb is metrical and would make sense as translated, meaning that Apollo issued his prohibition 'once, once only, once for all' (LSJ), but it is better seen as a scribal error for ἄναξ ('lord'). ν could be quite easily mistaken for π. This epithet is often applied to gods, including Apollo, for example in the Homeric *Hymn to Apollo*, 285.

27, χιλεων. This word is a genitive plural governed by ἀπέχεcθαι, but what is mankind to abstain from? χιλεων for χιλίων ('thousands') would be an easy 'Vulgarism', but apart from being unmetrical (the first ι is long), it would be too allusive to convey any meaning. The first letter is certainly χ (compare it with χ in ἀπέχεcθαι immediately below), but visual confusion between χ and λ would be quite easy in this hand. Perhaps therefore χιλεων is an anagram corruption of λεχέων (in the 'Vulgar' form *λεχίων), meaning 'beds', in the sense of 'sex' presumably rather than 'marriage', but it would be out of character for Apollo, unlike his twin-sister Artemis, to be insisting on celibacy.

28–9, κύρι θεέ. The contracted vocative κύρι, for κύριε ('lord'), is quite frequent, and Gignac (II, 27) sees it as a late-Greek declension in -ιc. For an example of the invocation κύρι θεέ, see *Suppl. Mag.* I, 20. It is of course not Christian.

29–30. The intersection of the stilus-strokes shows that the scribe wrote to the end of 29, τηρῆcον included, before drawing a line across the tablet. Its axis is more or less horizontal, and not quite that of the writing, which dips down to the right. The scribe then wrote Δημῆτριν (30) across this line, but kept to the axis of the writing, not of the line. This rather suggests that he only paused for a moment between writing 29 and then 30, perhaps to check the name of his client after copying out a long and elaborate text; there is a hint of this in his inscribing Δ twice, and then repeating the first stroke of η. It would be going too far to conclude that he 'stock-piled' such a long and specific text for when a client should appear, something which possibly happened with the Billingford amulet (Tomlin 2004; *Britannia* 37 (2006), 481, No. 51); but the latter is shorter and less specific, and the disjunction between text and bearer's name is much greater.

30. Δημῆτριν is for Δημήτριον, again by contraction, but Gignac (II 1981, 25–6) notes other personal names formed in this way as examples of a late-Greek declension in -ιc.

The six hexameters

In conclusion it may be helpful to quote the six hexameters, and the likely fragment of a seventh, in verse-form after revising them in accordance with the commentary. Letters omitted or mis-copied are supplied (in brackets), letters **in bold** are spellings now normalized. An obelus (†) marks words whose resolution is still uncertain.

†ευλιωρ θε(ό)μορφ**ε**, λάβρου λ**οι**μοῦ παράπεμπε
δυcκέλαδον ῥ**οί**ζημα, διη(έ)ριον, †τανυχιζον
†νυδρολεεc, ὀδύ**ν**η(ν) δια**ν**ηχόμ**ε**νον, βαρύθ**υ**μον,
(c)αρκοτακέc, διατηκόμενον, φλεβί(κ)ων ἀπὸ κόλπων.
Φοῖβε ἀκερc**ε**κόμα, λοιμοῦ νεφέλη(ν) ἀπέλαυνε.
τοξότα (Φοῖβε) …
Φοῖβοc ἄ(ν)αξ ἐκέλευcε βροτοῖc †χιλεων ἀπέχεcθαι.

'*euliōr* … of form divine, send away the discordant clatter of raging plague, air-borne, *tanychizon*, *nydrolees*, infiltrating pain, heavy-spiriting, flesh-wasting, from the hollows of the veins.'

'Phoebus of the unshorn hair, drive away the cloud of plague.'

'Phoebus, archer, …'

'Lord Phoebus ordered mortals to refrain from *chileōn*.'

These scraps of Greek verse ultimately derive from oracles of Apollo in Asia Minor, either by direct quotation or in summary form. Their exotic context needs no emphasis: it was the Thames-side mud in distant London. Demetrios, their bearer, in his humble way recalls Aulus Claudius Charax, the Greek historian and benefactor who commanded a Roman legion in the building of the Antonine Wall in Britain (Birley 2005, 253–4). This millionaire who enriched the healing sanctuary of Asclepius at Pergamum, and the man who could not afford gold or silver for a medical amulet, they both bear witness to the percolation of Greek literary culture across the Roman Empire of the Antonines.

Notes

1 British 'curse tablets' are written in Latin, with the exception of Uley Inv. no. 2161d.1 (Tomlin 1993, no. 52), which is Latin transcribed into Greek letters. But some magical texts from Britain are written in Greek, for example the Caernarvon amulet (see above, p. 197); and note especially the Billingford amulet (see above, p. 202) which, like the Vintry amulet, invokes Iao and Abrasax: its main text is Latin transliterated into Greek letters, but three letters revert accidentally to Roman, and the bearer's name and maternal lineage are added in Latin, inscribed in Roman cursive.

2 Examples can be seen in the third α in line 1; θ in 3; υ in 18; τ in 19; ο in 24; δ and η in 30. They are not significant, but other repetitions suggest visual confusion, for example the two horizontal strokes which make c into ε in 12, the redundant diagonal which combines α with λ in 20, the correction of R to ρ in 20.

3 ρ above ω (3), ν above ο (5), ο above κ (12), ε above μ (13).

4 The only exceptions are in 5–6, where there were two consonants, the first a nasal; and in 23–4, where he omitted α by oversight.

5 For example the confusion between οι and υ (5, 12), between οι and η (7), between μ and ν (10, 11), between ε and αι (11); also the contraction of διηέριον to διῆριον (7–8), κύριε to κύρι (28), and Δημήτριον to Δημῆτριν (30). See further the commentary ad loc.

6 This translates the text as transliterated (for example ἄπαξ, not ἄναξ, in 25), but takes account of some emendations. Not translated are the words transcribed in italics: the first four are magical terms, the other five are apparently corrupt and have been marked with an obelus (†). They are discussed in the commentary, where the forms prefixed with an asterisk (*) are hypothetical. A reconstruction of the metrical portion is offered at the end.

7 The lexicography is largely drawn from Liddell and Scott (LSJ), but I gratefully acknowledge subsequent help from the on-line *Thesaurus Linguae Graecae*. All dates are AD.

8 The manuscripts of Lucian divide between ἀκειρεκόμηc and ἀκερcεκόμηc, the form in which it occurs in Homer, but only once (Iliad 20, 39). The Vintry amulet now supports the latter reading, its ε for ι being a trivial variation which also occurs in Nonnus.

9 το[ξο]φόρον Φοῖβον, λοιμοῦ [ὕ]ποc[ευ]αντῆρα and Κλαρίου Φοῖβου | τόξοιc ἱρὸν ἄγαλμα κεκαcμένον ὠλεcινούcοιc | οἷον ὀιcτεύοντοc ἀναρδέα τηλόcε λοιμόν respectively. The translation is adapted from Parke 1985, 152 and 153–4.

Acknowledgements

Jenny Hall first made the amulet available for study and Caroline MacDonald subsequently provided the four high-resolution digital photographs from which the line-drawing has been made. It has been discussed at seminars in Oxford and Vienna, and I thank Revel Coles, Martin Goodman, Silke Hahn, Martin Henig, Simon Hornby, David Jordan, Herwig Maehler, Bernhard Palme, John Rea and Danuta Shanzer for their learned and helpful comments.

Abbreviations of corpora

GMA = Kotansky, R. 1994 *Greek Magical Amulets: The Inscribed Gold, Silver, Copper, and Bronze* Lamellae, Part I, *Published Texts of Known Provenance* (Opladen)

MAMA 9 = *Monumenta Asiae Minoris Antique* IX: Cox, C. W. M., Cameron, A., Cullen, J. and Levick, B. 1988 *Monuments from the Aezanitis* (London)

PGM = Preisendanz, K. *Papyri Graecae Magicae. Die griechischen Zauberpapyri* I, II (ed. Heinrechs, A. 1973–74) (Stuttgart)

RIB = Collingwood, R. G. and Wright, R. P. 1965, 1990–95 (ed. Frere, S. S. and Tomlin, R. S. O.) *The Roman Inscriptions of Britain*, I, *Inscriptions on Stone* (Oxford); II, *Instrumentum Domesticum*

Suppl. Mag. I, II = Daniel, R. and Maltomini, F. 1990, 1992 *Supplementum Magicum* (Opladen)

Tab. Sulis = Tomlin, R. S. O. 1988 *Tabellae Sulis: Roman Inscribed Tablets of Tin and Lead from the Sacred Spring at Bath* (Oxford) = Cunliffe, B. 1988 *The Temple of Sulis Minerva at Bath*, II, *The Finds from the Sacred Spring* (Oxford), 59–269

Bibliography

Inscriptions published in the annual 'Roman Britain' survey in the journal Britannia are cited by volume number and year, by page, and by number within the sequence.

Ancient authors

Ammianus Marcellinus

Eusebius of Caesarea: *Church History*

Galen

Homer: *Iliad*

Homeric *Hymn to Apollo*

Lucian: *Alexander*

Martianus Capella

Nonnus: *Paraphrase of St John's Gospel*

Oppian: *Cynegetica*

Plato: *Timaeus*

Pliny: *Natural History*

Porphyry

Proclus: *Hymns*

Modern authors

Beagrie, N. (1989) The Romano-British Pewter Industry. *Britannia* 20, 169–91.

Birley, A. R. (2005) *The Roman Government of Britain*. Oxford.

Brashear, W. M. (1991) *Magica Varia*. Brussels.

Collingwood, R. G. and Wright, R. P. (1965) *RIB* I, *Inscriptions on Stone*. Oxford.

Duncan-Jones, R. P. (1996) The impact of the Antonine plague. *JRA* 9, 108–36.

Eck, W. (2012) Die Seuche unter Mark Aurel: ihre Auswirkung auf das Heer. In E. Lo Cascio (ed.) *L'Impatto della "Peste Antonina"*, 63–78. Bari.

Faraone, C. A. (1992) Dangerous gods and powerful statues. In C. A. Faraone (ed.) *Talismans and Trojan Horses: Guardian Statues in Ancient Greek Myth and Ritual*, Ch. 4. New York, Oxford.

Frere, S. S. and Tomlin, R. S. O. (eds) (1990–5) *RIB* II, *Instrumentum Domesticum*. Oxford.

Gignac, F. T. (1977) *A Grammar of the Greek Papyri of the Roman and Byzantine Periods* I. Milan.

Gignac, F. T. (1981) *A Grammar of the Greek Papyri of the Roman and Byzantine Periods* II. Milan.

Heitsch, E. (1961) *Die griechischer Dichterfragmente der römischen Kaiserzeit*. Göttingen.

Jones, C. P. (2005) Ten dedications "To the gods and goddesses" and the Antonine Plague. *JRA* 18, 293–301 (with an addendum in 19, 368–9).

Parke, H. W. (1985) *The Oracles of Apollo in Asia Minor*. London.

Perdrizet, P. (1903) Une inscription d'Antioche qui reproduit un oracle d'Alexandre d'Abonotichos. *Compte Rendus de l'Academie des Inscriptions et belles-lettres*. 1903, 62–6.

Robert, L. (1980) *À travers l'Asie Mineure*. Paris.

Tomlin, R. S. O. (1993) The inscribed lead tablets: an interim report. In A. Woodward and P. Leach *The Uley Shrines: Excavation of a ritual complex on West Hill, Uley, Gloucestershire: 1977–9*, 113–30. London.

Tomlin, R. S. O. (1997) Sede in tuo loco: a fourth-century uterine phylactery in Latin from Roman Britain. *Zeitschrift fur Papyrologie und Epigraphik* 115, 291–4.

Tomlin, R. S. O. (2004) A bilingual Roman charm for health and victory. *ZPE* 149, 259–66.

Tomlin, R. S. O. (2008) Special delivery: a Graeco-Roman gold amulet for healthy childbirth. *Zeitschrift fur Papyrologie und Epigraphik* 167, 219–24.

Tomlin, R. S. O. (2011) Protective Spells in Roman Britain. In M. Corbier and J.-P. Guilhembet. L'Écriture dans la maison romaine, 137–44. Paris.

26

PUTTING SOME FLESH ON THE BONES: LEATHER BIKINIS AND BODY SIZE

Carol van Driel-Murray

This exploration of some intimate vital statistics is dedicated to Lindsay Allason-Jones, who has never lost sight of the real people and their daily concerns behind the fascinating and varied material legacy of the Roman past.

Amongst the more intriguing exhibits in the Roman Gallery of the Museum of London is a 'leather bikini' found in 1953 at the bottom of a well in Queen Street (Fig. 26.1). It rapidly gained fame (notoriety?) under the description of 'a Roman leather bikini', despite the fact that no matching top has ever been found for such garments. A more accurate designation might be 'briefs' – though in view of some of the scanty wisps identified more recently, 'V-string' or 'thong' may be more appropriate. But modern usage changes too, and 'bikini brief' now appears in lingerie catalogues for luxury panties remarkably similar in design to the Roman precursors; for example, www.victoriassecret.com offers a 'lace fronted bikini panty' (our nos 1–2) and 'eyelet V-string panty' (our nos 5–7).

The delight of popular publications and frequently illustrated, the Queen Street bikini was first published in detail in 1982 by Tony Wilmott (1982, 52–5). The stage for nubile female acrobats and 'entertainers' was already set, with Wilmott remarking coyly 'the trunks are worn, with deeply defined stretch marks across the front, the pattern of which would appear to preclude a male wearer' – an observation which holds good for all subsequent finds as well. There can be no doubt but that these articles are sex-specific, whatever the further significance. Meanwhile, London could lay claim a second bikini, found near to what was then considered to be a watch-tower at Shadwell (Fig. 26.2). That the fastenings were ripped led to predictable ribald speculation about soldiers and dancing girls, but alas, recent reinterpretation of the site reveals that the water tank in which the briefs were found belong to a fourth century industrial remodelling of the location (van Driel-Murray 2002, figs 12 and 27). Regrettably, the military connection will have to be abandoned.

During several periods of study, generously supported by the Museum of London, I was able to pick out previously unrecognised bikini fragments from four more locations (Cross Keys Court, Dowgate, London Wall, Swan Lane: Figs 26.3, 26.4, 26.5, 26.9). That London is so well provided with briefs may in part be due to the extensive record of all excavated finds maintained by the Museum of London Archaeological Archive, greatly simplifying the recognition of previously unidentifiable mystery items.

Nevertheless, the concentration of finds in the city cannot only be due to this accessibility. It is remarkable that these garments are entirely lacking in the extensive and well-researched military leather complexes, not only in Britain but also on the Continent, though the large town complexes of York, Lincoln, and Cologne remain to be searched. Indeed, on the Continent, I know of only two examples, one recently identified at Trier and almost identical to the single-eyelet thong panty from London Wall (Goethert 2007, Abb. 1, German: *tanga*) (Fig. 26.6). The other, from Mainz, is in fact the very first such garment to be recorded, having been found in the mid-nineteenth century. The object itself was lost to bombing in the War, but while looking through the inventory book of the Landesmuseum Mainz in the 1990s I was astounded to stumble on an exquisite acquisition drawing by the museum director, L. Lindenschmitt himself (Fig. 26.7). This specimen would have covered the abdomen, and is amongst the most lavishly decorated of all the garments. In turn, this drawing enabled the identification of a curious fragment from Swan

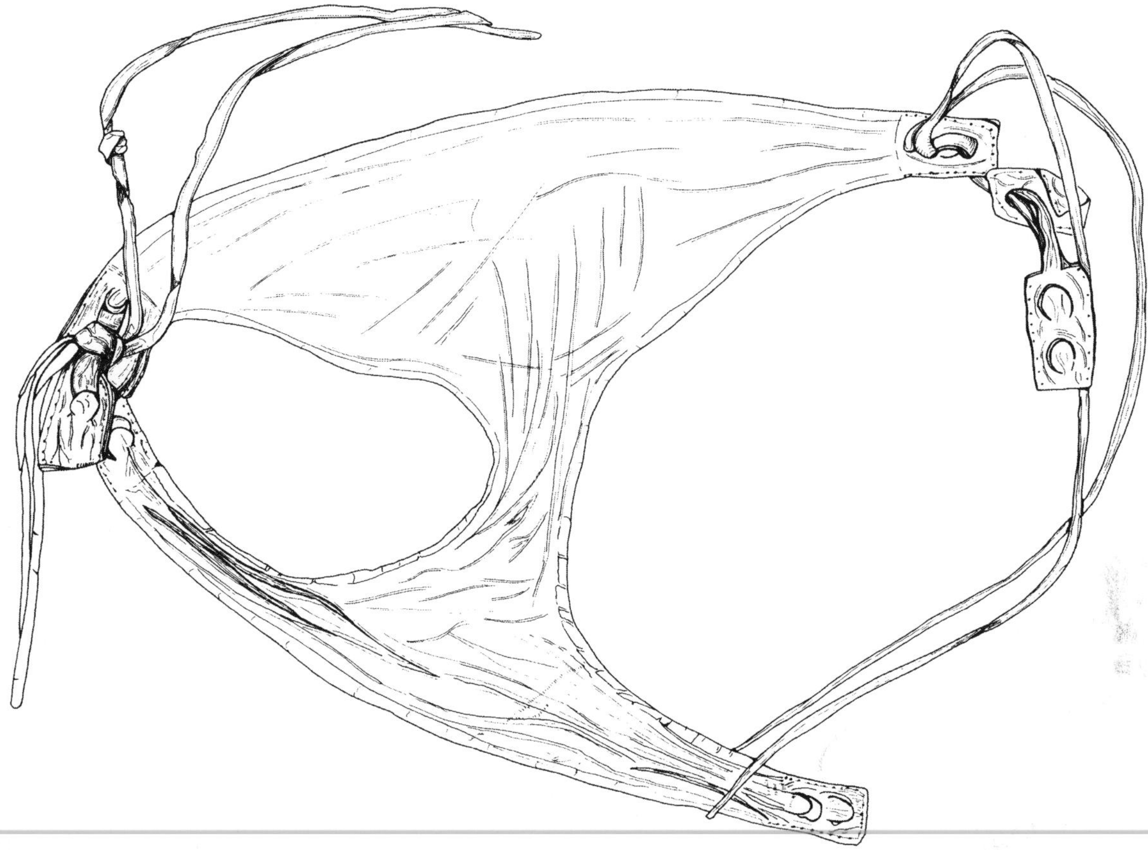

Figure 26.1 Queen Street bikini. (From Wilmott 1982, fig. 35: courtesy of Tony Wilmott and LAMAS) scale 1:3.

Lane, London as a close parallel (Fig. 26.9). The Mainz garment was found in the harbour settlement Dimesser Ort, to the north of the legionary fortress (Jung 2009, 371, nr. 416 Taf. 47, 416). The find circumstances are unknown, but despite having military roots, the settlement is regarded as being predominantly civilian in character from the mid-first century by P. Jung in his recent reassessment of the site (Jung 2009, 29–40, 225). The London bias may simply be due to the fact that this represents one of the largest collections of civilian leatherwork, but it is never the less odd that nothing comparable has appeared in other civilian complexes which I have examined, such as Voorburg (NL) or Pommeroeul (B), nor in any of the civil settlements around forts.

Only the Queen Street and the Shadwell bikinis might represent deliberate deposits of a cultic nature: the former was found on the bottom of Queen Street Well 22, and although Shadwell tank 12 was backfilled with domestic rubbish, the relatively good state of preservation suggests that the briefs had been deposited earlier, while the tank was still full of water.

Characteristic for the briefs is the hourglass shape and the fastening by means of adjustable laces, passed through an eyelet at the base of the opposite lace. The laces vary from a single pair to multiple ties woven through two rows of eyelets, rather reminiscent of early modern corsets (known as 'bodies'), though of course without stays (cf. Arnold 1985, 46 and 103). The extent of the openwork on the Mainz specimen actually prevents functional lacing and it is likely that either some sort of textile backing must have been present or that it was lined with contrasting non-vegetable tanned leather. This would have decayed as only vegetable tanned leather survives waterlogging (Fig. 26.8). There are some indications that the Shadwell example was also provided with a lining, but for the others this could not be established. Whether the skimpiest, single-lace types had a back covering is a matter of debate, as all are damaged. Goethert suggests they may resemble the modern V-string, just a little triangle over the pudenda and ties on the hip or at the back (Goethert 2007, Abb. 4). It's an interesting thought, although from the photograph the Trier example looks as though it was cut down, with re-usable leather removed, particularly as the putative 'lace' projecting from the edge is awkwardly placed for a true V-string (this is of course disputable). The shape and decoration of the London Wall and Trier briefs are almost identical, and as they are also more or less contemporary they would seem to draw on a commonly shared notion of the nature of such garments (Figs. 26.5, 26.6, and Plate 25).

Though undecorated, the Queen Street bikini is a real quality product, with multiple reinforcements, a careful fit and neatly hemmed edges for extra comfort. This example was still laced up when found (Fig. 26.1). One of the ties on the Shadwell example is also still knotted, indicating a similarly close fit, but in the case of the single-lace panties from Trier and London Wall the ties are evidently much longer (Plates 24 and 25). K.-P. Goethert experimented with several fastening methods including an arrangement incorporating a ring, a feature which seems to be indicated on some of the figurines (Wilmott 1982, fig. 35a/a). If the kink in the Cross Keys Court lace marks the position of such a ring, the circumference of the original would have been around 75–80 cm, so quite a lot bigger than the first impressions of this wispy triangle (Fig. 26.4, 26.10).

The Roman's answer to sexy lingerie?

With at least six examples in London alone, bikinis can no longer be regarded as a curiosity.

In his admirable discussion of the Queen Street briefs, Wilmott assembled a number of figurines of young female athletes wearing comparable garments (Wilmott 1982, fig. 35a). Goethert recognised another figurine in the Trier University Museum, which is particularly interesting as the woman wears a combination of what looks like a leather eyelet panty with punched decoration with a somewhat shapeless breast band, presumably of cloth, like the garments worn by the sporty ladies on the well-known Piazza Armerina mosaics (Plate 26; Goethert 2007, Abb. 3; Croom 2000, 91–2). In the latter case these are true bikinis, but they are obviously made of bands of coloured cloth, and quite unlike the figure-hugging leather briefs. The intriguing survival of gilding over the breasts and hips of a marble torso of Venus removing her sandal from the villa of Julia Felix in Pompeii (who, if scrubbed, would have been described as naked) bears a remarkable resemblance to the openwork decoration of the Mainz briefs, with breast band to match (Nat. Mus. Naples Inv. no. 152798; Kraus and von Matt 1977, pls 270 and 271). Gilded leather was quite widely used for footwear, and although such tantalising sets of underwear must inevitably be as rare in real life as in the archaeological record, the statue hints at a greater variety in form as well as a more general use of these garments over and above the chance survivals in north European archaeological complexes.

Lingerie in the twenty-first century is rather more frivolous than it was in the 1990s (let alone the 1950s) and Roman bikinis no longer look quite as risqué as they once did: it was with considerable trepidation that I took imitation-leather replicas through British customs for a presentation at the Museum of London (Fig. 26.7, Plate 24; van Driel-Murray 1999a). Even these crude copies were captivating, and Vincent van Vilsteren, curator of archaeology at the Museum of Drenthe in Assen, commissioned the late Olaf Goubitz, expert in archaeological leatherwork and its conservation, to provide functional replicas for the highly successful exhibition '10,000 Years Sex. On Love, Fertility and Lust' which toured Europe between 2003 and 2009 (Plates 24 and 25). Although the description was ambiguous, the setting again invited an association with sex and loose morals (van Driel-Murray 2003; van Vilsteren 2003).

But perhaps we need to reconsider our ideas of prostitutes and grabbing soldiers' hands, despite the popularity of the formula. There are simply too many of these garments for dancing girls and acrobats to be the only explanation, quite apart from the remarkable absence from the military contexts where one might expect such racy entertainment. Although the brief-clad girls of statues and depictions are indeed engaged in sport or gymnastics, this is in fact the only situation in which women are likely to appear in public in their undergarments. Roman authors have plenty to report on *male* bathing, but are silent on how *women* spent their leisure. In some cities there were separate baths for women, or they were restricted to special (unfashionable) times, but what sort of social activities they indulged in amongst themselves is of no interest to male writers. Thus the garments may well have been more commonly worn, but in the case of ordinary women they are consistently concealed from our view. In London, every fair-sized complex of leatherwork contained an example, rather implying that the briefs were, in reality, an infrequent, but regular, piece of female apparel. Might they be a special version of an undergarment, usually made of cloth but on occasion, perhaps for medical reasons, strengthened with leather? Naughty nighties rather than stripper's briefs?

The ample – indeed matronly – proportions of the Mainz and Swan Lane garments suggest a supportive function, perhaps after childbirth. The skimpier versions may have

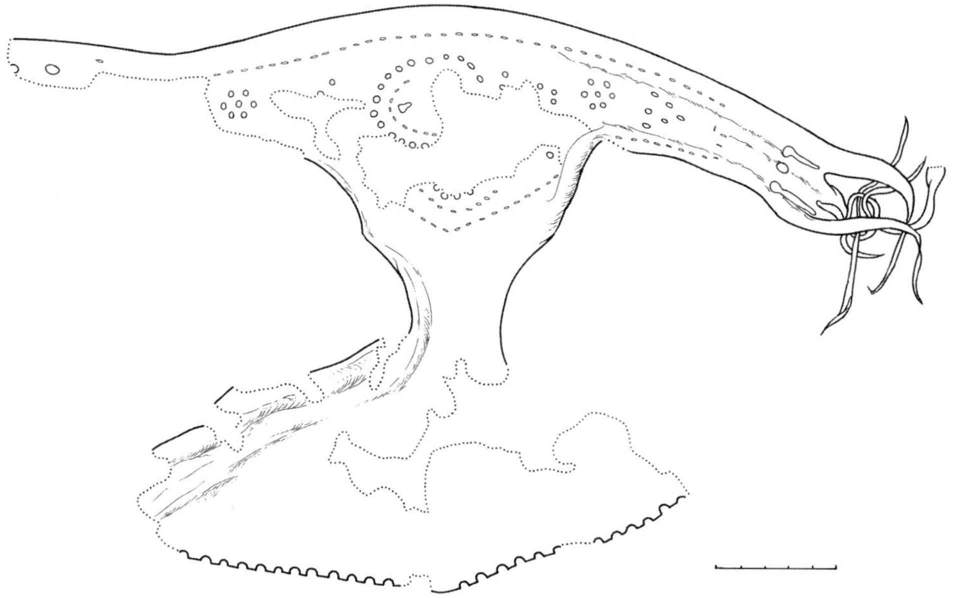

Figure 26.2 Shadwell bikini, scale 1:3

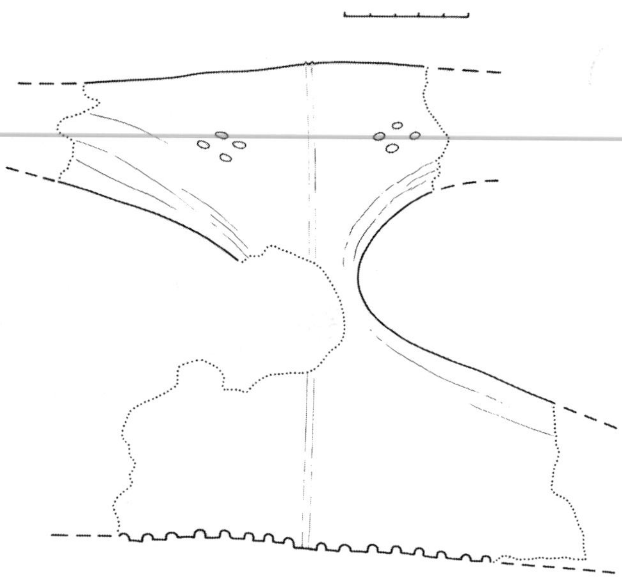

Figure 26.3 Dowgate Hill, scale 1:3

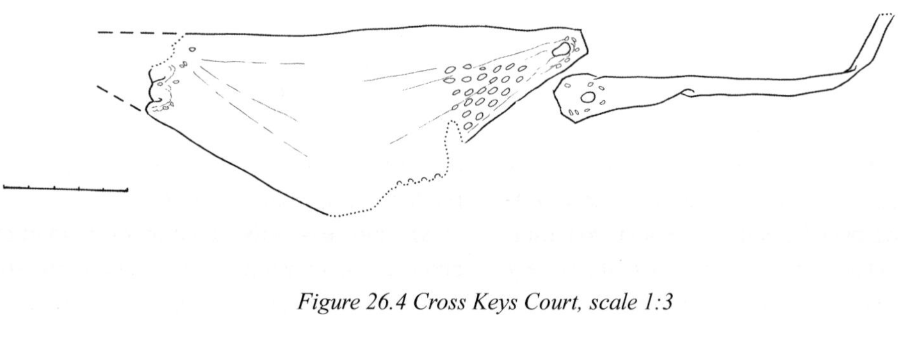

Figure 26.4 Cross Keys Court, scale 1:3

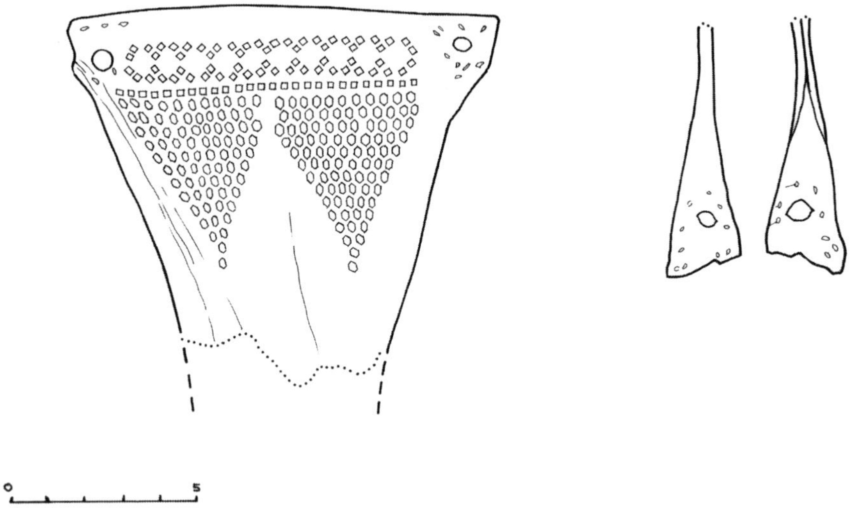

Figure 26.5 London Wall (a), (b) lace Cross Keys Court, scale 1:2

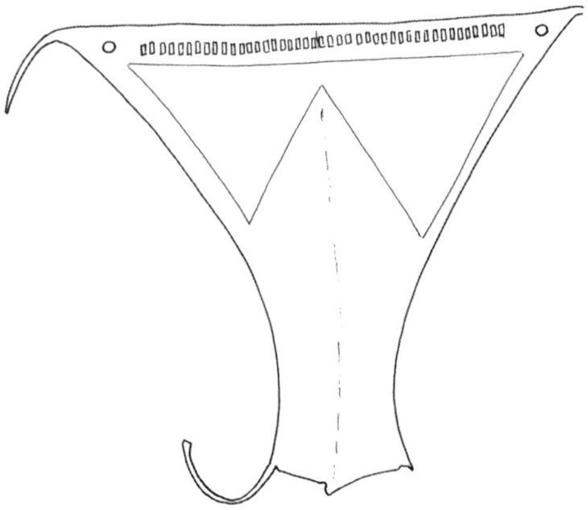

Figue 26.6 Trier, outline with indication of decorated area, scale 1:3

functioned as menstrual bands. How women coped is one of the great archaeological unmentionables (Lindsay herself being a notable exception: Allason-Jones 1989, 30), but in a curious archaeological survival experiment in the Netherlands, in which five participants attempted to live in Iron Age style for two months in winter, the female participants found rags or moss held by a leather strap to be the most comfortable solution (Boonstra 1997, 52 fig. 18). If another bikini should ever be found, the opportunity to apply DNA analysis should be seized. All the bikinis examined are made of vegetable tanned goatskin, which is waterproof, strong and relatively thin. Even so, to our standards this is not particularly inviting for intimate garments and oil-treated skin (chamois leather) would be preferable, though it is impermanent and decays under damp conditions. This was, for instance, used for close-fitting cycling shorts. Hence the leather examples may be no more than a special version of something far more common but which no longer survives in the archaeological record.

Bikinis and body size

As the only piece of Roman clothing to preserve the hip measurement, what do the bikinis tell us about the individuals who wore them?

To modern eyes, all the briefs appear to be very small, even when shrinkage of 10–15% is taken into account, fuelling suspicions as to unnatural practices. However, it is clear from surviving historical clothing that modern sizing systems are of limited use for comparative purposes, since proportions are variable and historically specific. When the

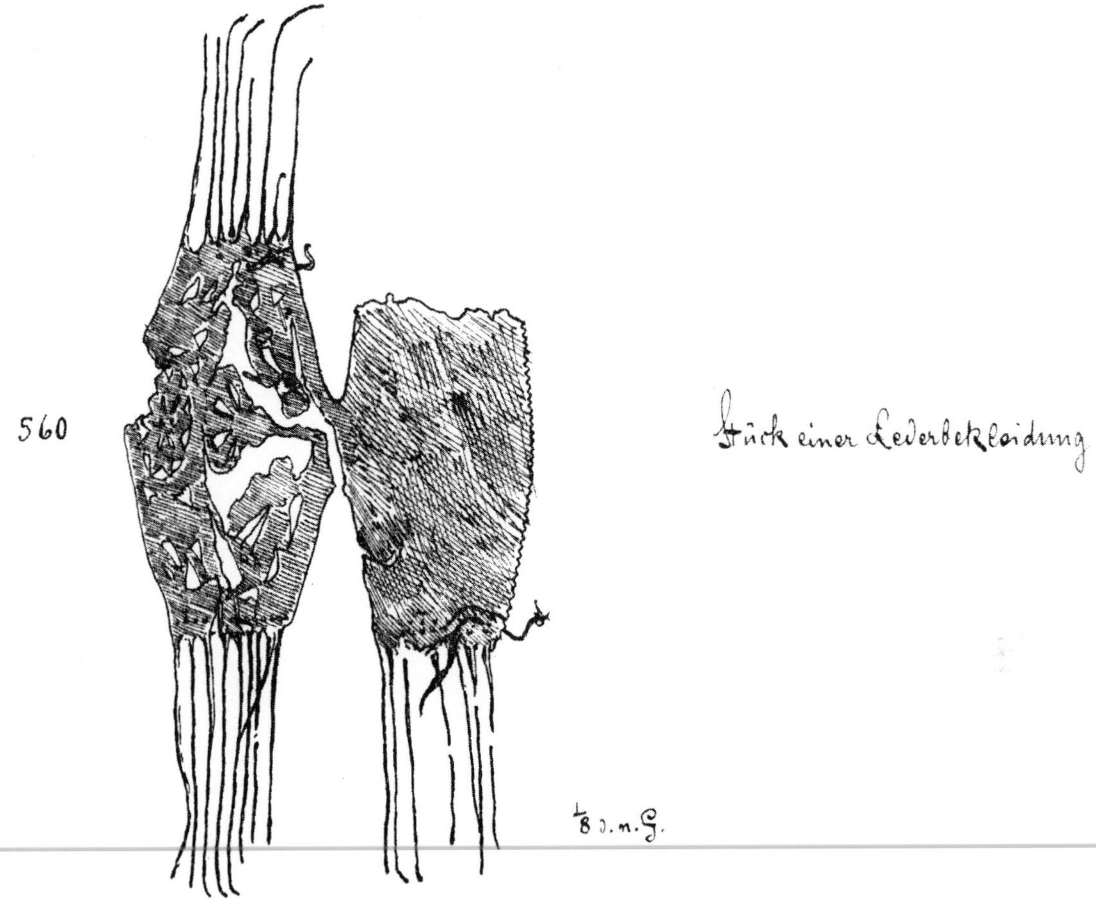

Figure 26.7 Mainz, sketch by Lindenschmitt (inventory Landesmuseum Mainz, Generaldirektion Kulturelles Erbe Rheinland-Pfalz, with permission)

Victoria & Albert Museum, London, acquired the early seventeenth century embroidered jacket which Margaret Layton wears on her portrait (V&A T767, T228-1994), there was some discussion as to whether it was possible that the mature woman shown could have worn a garment with a bust measurement of only 76.2 cm and a waist of 63.5 cm (Arnold 1985, 51). Gowns and jackets were worn over shifts as well as corsets or 'bodies' so although these come closer to the dimensions of the body, none is as close fitting as the bikinis. Nevertheless, such survivals do provide a valuable insight into changes in body mass with all the implications for diet, health and status that this entails (Komlos 1998). Surprisingly, however, there seems to be little interest in bodily dimensions in studies of surviving costume (or armour, for that matter), and only in the first volume of her series on historical patterns does Janet Arnold list some of the dimensions taken from the clothing of known individuals (Table 26.1; Arnold 1985, 127). It can readily be seen that the relationship between the bust and waist differs markedly from the modern sizing ratios.

	waist	*modern size*	*bust*	*modern size*
Eleanora	73.6	40	83.8	36
Dorothea	50.8	Child	71.1	146
Margaret	63.5	34	76.2	32

Modern sizes are not entirely consistent, varying according to country and manufacturer. Here, reference is made to Burda dressmaking patterns for Northern Europe. Continental 32 = UK 6; Continental 36 = UK 10; Continental 40 = UK 14. Pfalzgräfin Dorothea Sabina died in 1592, aged 22; Eleanora of Toledo died in 1562, aged 40, having born 11 children, Margaret Layton's jacket dates to 1610/15.

Table 26.1 Dimensions of historical clothing

The roomy garments of the Roman period give us little information on size or girth: a young woman from Martres-les-Veyre wore a wide sleeved, flowing garment, which had been shortened by sewing in a flounce, and her socks had evidently belonged to someone else, as they were several sizes bigger than her shoes (shoe size 32, socks *c.*39, normal sizes for Roman females and males respectiviely) and in view of the initials PRI sewn in the sock, they may even have belonged to a man (van Driel-Murray 1999c; Audollent

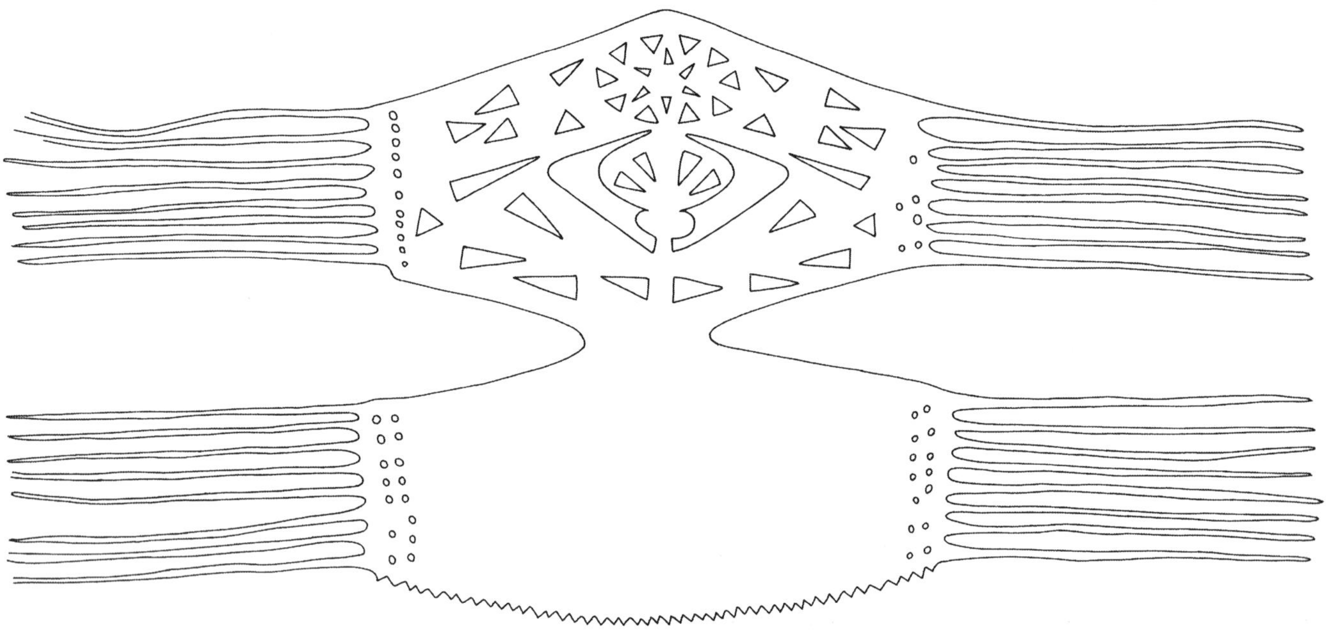

Figure 26.8 Mainz reconstructed pattern

1922). The high value of textiles and the reluctance to cut fabrics is the main reason for shortening garments by means of an external sewn flounce, as can still be seen in the traditional costume of Staphorst in the Netherlands. Since linen was not preserved in the graves of Martres-les-Veyre there is no information on underclothing, but the lady did wear a scarf with long decorative tassels to fill the rather wide neck opening of the robe (cf. Sumner 2009, fig. 117) Although fascinating in themselves, such voluminous garments tell us little about people's exact dimensions.

Roman segmented armour found in Corbridge was said to be small, but the actual girth of the soldiers concerned was not discussed (Allason-Jones and Bishop 1988). Russell Robinson commented that the plates 'dug-in even on my daughter's slender neck' (*ibid.*, 99). Roman period men's breeches preserved in the north German bogs tend to be gathered at the waist by a belt, but seem to fit more closely around the legs (Schlabow 1976). The hip measurements of the two Thorsberg trousers are between 45–50 cm, both with an inside leg of 75–80 cm and thighs only 30 cm in circumference. The Dammendorf trousers are *c.*55 cm at the hip, but the legs are even narrower than Thorsberg. These garments suggest lithe individuals in the modern male size range 46–52. Tunics had to be drawn over the head, so chest and shoulder measurements bear little relation to the body within: for what it is worth, the Thorsberg tunic has a 110 cm chest. The upper arm circumference of 29/30 cm and the 18 cm wrist – narrower than my own wrist – confirm the overall wiry impression. Rather better-preserved jackets from the graves of seventeenth century whalers buried on Spitsbergen suggest similar body mass, with narrow shoulders, spindly arms and sizes in the region of modern 44 (Comis 2005, 66).

Site	*Hip width**	*Modern size*	*Modern age*	*Pre-modern age*
Mainz	45.8 cm	38	Adult	Adult
Queen Street	36.3 cm	140	10	Adult
Shadwell	37.4 cm	146	11	Adult
Cross Keys Court	min. 24 cm with lace 42cm	child/32	juvenile	12/14
Dowgate Hill	*c.* 34 cm	134/140	9/10	14+

* indicates a measurement + 10% shrinkage allowance.

Table 26.2. Dimensions of Roman briefs

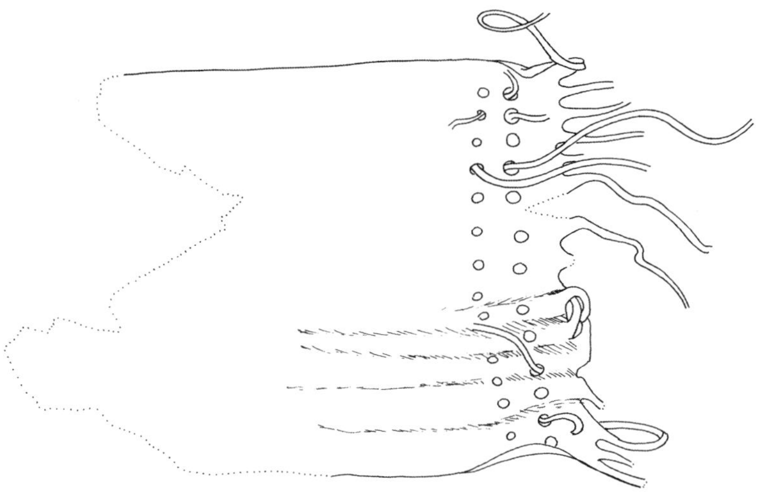

Figue 26.9 Swan Lane, scale 1:3

Particularly noticeable in surviving fitted clothing of both men and women is the narrowness of the arms and legs, the flatness of buttocks and bellies.

Overall, surviving fitted clothing suggests that people in the past had spare frames, and modern concepts of size, bodily proportions and their relationship to age and development are not easily applicable (Table 26.2). The body measurements of juveniles taken at the beginning of the twentieth century are not entirely comparable, though they do relate to children before the growth spurt of the 1950s (Martin and Saller 1959, 901). These suggest a hip measurement of *c*.30 cm for adolescent girls, which would place three of the bikinis in the adult range (Queen Street, Shadwell, Mainz), with Dowgate for a juvenile. Considering the width of the front as well as the lacing allowance of the eyelet thong briefs (Trier, London Wall, Cross Keys Court), these should also be regarded as (sub)adult. Thus besides sports wear, medicinal or sanitary purpose is quite feasible.

The only other source of information on bodily size is footwear, and here the difference between *them* and *us* is not so great, at least if we take records of shoe sizes from the earlier part of the twentieth century (Martin and Saller 1959, 973). This is hardly surprising as the foot size is more closely related to the bone structure, while the torso is shaped by muscle and fat, and can be compressed or moulded by the garments worn. Refitting the foot bones of a Roman soldier, 1.90 m tall and found stuffed into a well in the fort at Velsen (NL) together with his dagger, resulted in an estimated foot size of Continental 39 (UK size 6), which was confirmed by the surviving shoe sole (van Driel-Murray 1999b, 171). Interestingly the leather shrinkage had been minimal. Like the bikinis, shoes have the ability to reveal otherwise invisible people like women and children as specific groups. Thus in the northern provinces, we see women adopting Roman style sandals and soft shoes long before men did, alerting us to gender-specific responses to imported clothing and consumer goods (van Driel-Murray forthcoming).

Conclusion

In date the briefs span the entire Roman period, from Flavian times to the fourth century. They are infrequent, but regular finds in purely civilian contexts, suggestive of special-purpose wear, custom made and sometimes sufficiently imbued with meaning to require special deposition. They may indeed have belonged to the wardrobe of any respectable lady, serving not only as corsets, support or menstrual wear, but also as normal garments for visits to the bath house or gym. And why should women not have decorated their underclothes for their own sake? The leather briefs may give us a rare insight into women socialising, outside the gaze of men. But it is typical of the androcentric bias of authors and archaeologists alike that such garments are invariably interpreted in relation to men rather than considering how women structured their own social community through clothing, footwear and general deportment.

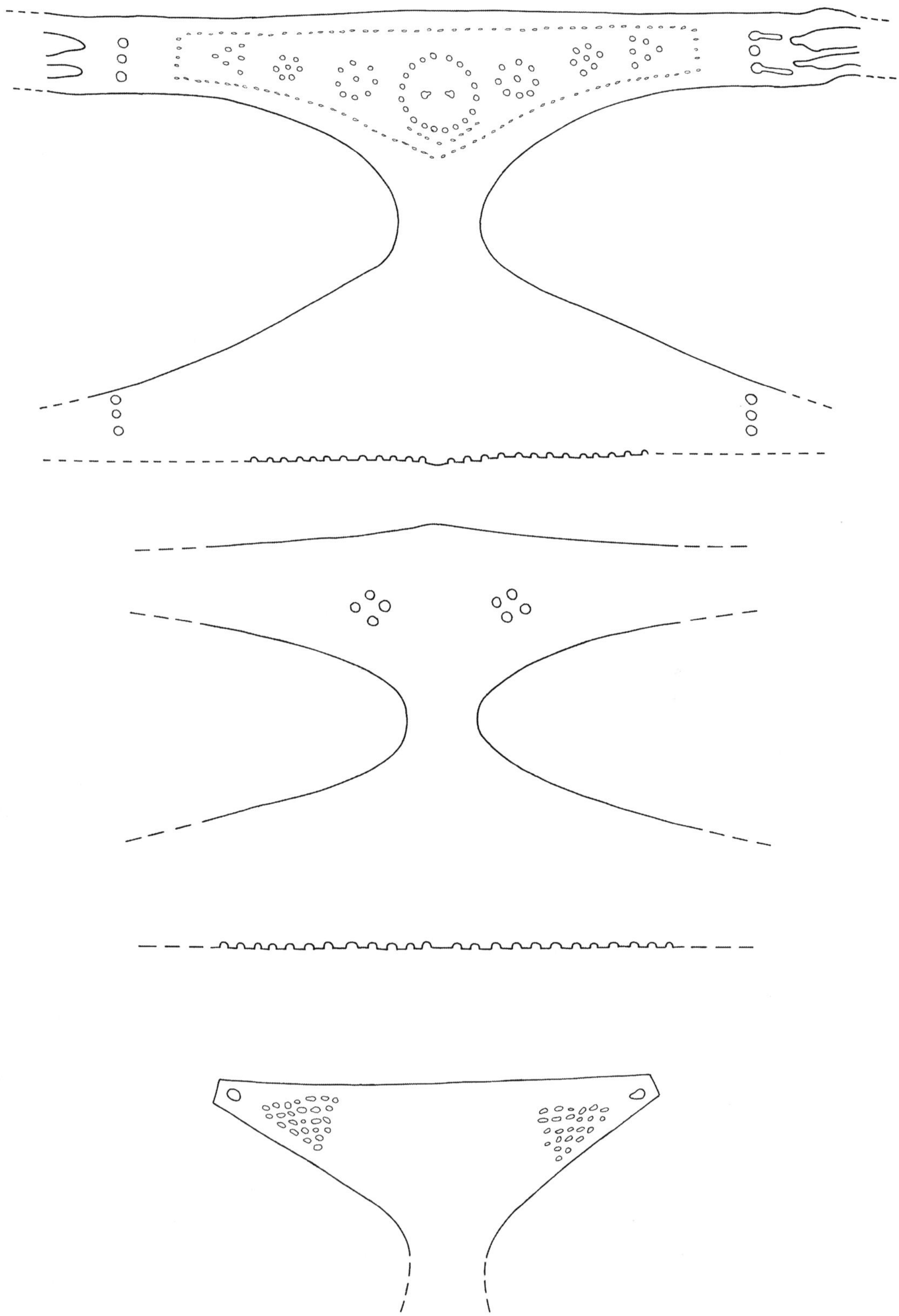

Figure 26.10 Reconstructed patterns

Acknowledgements

The recording of leatherwork in the MOL archive was generously supported by the museum, which also gave permission for the reproduction of the photos. I would particularly like to thank Jenny Hall and Nina Crummy for their assistance and encouragement. Line drawings were prepared by Bob Donker (Amsterdam Archaeological Centre) and processed digitally by Alastair Allen (Archol, Leiden). I am grateful to Tony Wilmott and the LAMAS for permission to reproduce his drawing, to Dr. K.-P. Goethert of the University of Trier for information on the Trier specimen, and to Dr. E. Riemer, Curator of the Archaeological Collection, Landesmuseum Mainz for permission to reproduce the page of the acquisition catalogue, and for additional information on the find location. Vincent van Vilsteren of the Drents Museum Assen has always enthusiastically supported research into clothing, and I am grateful for permission to reproduce some of the replicas commissioned from Olaf Goubitz for the museum.

Catalogue

1. *London Queen Street 1953*; Well 22, London, MOL Acc. no. 21233. 45 × 27.5 cm. Intact and still laced, the laces with their reinforcements stitched to the four corners, deeply creased by use. Unsmoothed goatskin. Flavian.

Ref: Wilmott 1982, no. 105, Fig. 35. (Fig. 26.1)

2. *London Shadwell 1974*; LD74 <383>, timber lined tank S12, phase 8. Excluding the laces, 34.5 × 22.5 cm. Originally, three integral laces at each corner, cusping along the back edge, and punched decoration on the front. The lace holes are distended. The garment is deeply creased and torn especially around the openwork. Smoothed goatskin. Late third/fourth century.

Ref: Van Driel-Murray 2002, figs 12 & 27. (Fig. 26.2, Plate 24)

3. *Mainz Dimesser Ort*; Landesmuseum Mainz, Inv. Nr. R.560. Under the sketch by L. Lindenschmitt the scale is noted as 1:8, with the measurement given as 940 mm on the opposite page. Almost complete pair of briefs with 8 integral fastening laces on each side, backed by paired lace holes. The back edge is cusped and an attempt to reconstruct the elaborate cut openwork of the front is given in Figure 26.8. Since the crotch area is probably deformed the exact dimensions are uncertain. Possibly found in 1858/9, circumstances unknown. Footwear from the same area ranges from the earlier first century to the later second (Inv. Nr. 489). The comparison with Pompeii, if valid, might suggest a Flavian date.

Ref: Jung 2009, 371, nr. 416, Taf. 47, 416. (Figs 26.7–26.8)

4. *London Dowgate Hill 1986*; DGH 278 <430>. 19.5 × (18.5) cm. Fragmentary briefs of unsmoothed goatskin, the back edge cusped and some decorative punch holes on the front. Strongly creased, all four corners with the ties are missing, but from the shape there would be room for 2–3 lace holes, similar to No. 2. Down the centre is a lightly impressed line, which marks the middle of a complete skin: the garment was therefore cut from the best and strongest part of the centre back. Late third century. (Figs 26.3 and Pl. 24)

5. *London Wall 1988*; LOW 358 <895> 11.5 × (10) cm. Front of an eyelet thong panty with stitching of separately attached laces at the corners (cf. No. 7) and decorated with a fine net of stamped openwork. Goatskin. Earlier second century. (Fig. 26.5, Plates 24 and 25)

6. *Trier Walramsneustrasse*; Rheinischen Landesmuseum Trier, EV 1994.161, FNr. 273. 17 × (15) cm (dimensions exclusive of lace remnants). Front of an eyelet thong panty ('tanga') with integral laces at each corner. Though it may never have had back coverage, the irregular edge finish seems to indicate that the garment was probably cut down. Fine, smoothed goatskin, with extensive net of punched openwork, almost identical to No. 5. Goatskin. Early/mid-second century.

Ref: Goethert 2007, fig 1. (Fig. 26.6)

7. *London Cross Keys Court 1981*; OPT 532 <743>. (17.5) × (7.5) cm, Triangular front of an eyelet panty with separately attached lace, decorated with stamped openwork. Crude stitching at the left edge indicates the attachment of a replacement corner, where the openwork has weakened the leather. The kink in the lace may mark the point of the hip tie on the hip, making it similar to Nos 5 and 6. Goatskin. First half of the second century. (Figs 26.4 and Pl. 24)

8. *London Swan Lane, Upper Thames Street 1981*; SWA 2187 <5014>. (290) × (16.5) cm. Creased fragment of a large garment, comparable to Mainz, with remnants of at least 15 snapped laces, backed by paired lace holes, some with laces still threaded through. The edge is plain, and as there is no sign of decorative openwork this may be the back panel. Poorly preserved goatskin. Third century. (Fig. 26.9)

9. *London Cross Keys Court 1981*; OPT 303 <689>. (6.5) × 2 cm. Perforated lace with stitching of its attachment to an eyelet thong panty like No. 5 or 7. First half of the second century. (Fig. 26.5a).

Bibliography

Allason-Jones, L. and Bishop, M. C. (1988) *Excavations at Roman Corbridge. The Hoard.* London, English Heritage.

Allason-Jones, L. (1989) *Women in Roman Britain.* London, British Museum.

Arnold, J. (1985) *Patterns of Fashion: the cut and construction of clothes for men and women c.1560–1620.* London, Macmillan (reprint 1995).

Audollent, A. (1922) Les tombes gallo-romaines à inhumation des Martres-de-Veyre (Puy-de-Dôme). *Mémoires présenté par divers savants, Académie des Inscriptions et Belles Lettres.* 13. Paris, 329–84.

Boonstra, A. (1997) *Twee Manen Lang. Zestig dagen leven als in de ijzertijd.* Walburg Pers, Zutphen.

Comis, S. Y. (2005) Onderzoek van zeventiende en achttiende-eeuwse kleding opgegraven op Spitsbergen: mogelijkheden en onmogelijkheden. *Circumpolar Studies 2.* Groningen, 61–9.

Croom, A. T. (2000) *Roman Clothing and Fashion.* Stroud, Tempus.

Driel-Murray, C. van (1999a) Roman leather bikinis. *Archeological Leather Group Newsletter* 9, 7–9.

Driel-Murray, C. van (1999b) Dead men's shoes. In W. Schlüter and R. Wiegels (Hg.) *Rom, Germanien und die Ausgrabungen von Kalkriese*/Osnabrücker Forschungen zu Altertum und Antike-Rezeption 1, 169–89.

Driel-Murray, C. van (1999c) A set of Roman clothing from Les Martres-de-Veyre, France. *Archaeological Textiles Newsletter* 28, 11–15.

Driel-Murray, C. van (2002) Leather 'bikini' or briefs. In D. Larkin (ed.) *The Roman Tower at Shadwell, London: a reappraisal.* MOLAS Archaeology Series 8, London, 57–60.

Driel-Murray, C. van (2003) Leren bikinibroekjes. In V. T. van Vilsteren. *100,000 jaar sex. Over liefde, vruchtbaarheid en wellust/ 100,000 Jahre Sex. Über Liebe, Fruchtbarkeit und Wollust.* (Catalogue Drents Museum/Helms Museum) Zwolle, 48–9.

Driel-Murray, C. van (forthcoming) Fashionable footwear: craftsmen and consumers in the N-W Provinces of the Roman Empire. In A. Wilson and M. Flohr (eds) *Beyond Marginality: craftsmen, traders and the socioeconomic history of Roman urban communities.*

Goethert, K.-P. (2007) Römische Ledertangas – zietlos modisch. Zu einem Neufunde aus Trier. *Funde und Ausgrabungen im Bezirk Trier* 39, 60–2.

Jung, P. (2009) *Die römische Nordwestsiedlung "Dimesser Ort" von Mainz. Ein Beitrag zur Siedlungsgeschichte von Mogontiacum.* Universitätsforschungen zur Prähistorischen Archäologie Bd. 175, Bonn, Habelt.

Komlos, J. (1998) Shrinking in a growing economy? The mystery of physical stature during the Industrial Revolution. *Journal of Economic History* 58, 779–802.

Kraus, T. and von Matt, L. (1977) *Lebendiges Pompeji.* Köln, Dumont.

Martin, R. and Saller, K. (1959) *Lehrbuch der Anthropologie 3rd ed. vol II.* Stuttgart. Gustav Fischer.

Schlabow, K. (1976) *Textilfunde der Eisenzeit in Norddeutschland.* Neumünster, Wachholz Verlag.

Sumner, G. (2009) *Roman Military Dress.* Stroud, History Press.

Vilsteren, V.T. van, (2003) *100,000 jaar sex. Over liefde, vruchtbaarheid en wellust/ 100,000 Jahre Sex. Über Liebe. Fruchtbarkeit und Wollust.* (Catalogue Drents Museum/Helms Museum) Zwolle.

Wilmott, T. (1982) Excavations at Queen Street and Roman wells in London. *Proceedings of the London & Middlesex Archaeological Society* 33, 1–78.

27

TAILPIECE: ROMAN MICE IN ART, ALLEGORY* AND ACTUALITY

Ralph Jackson

Arguably the most famous mouse from Roman Britain, especially for twenty-somethings, is Minimus, the engaging little rodent from Vindolanda chosen by Barbara Bell (and charmingly illustrated by Helen Forte) as the continuity creature for her introduction to the Latin language and the culture of Roman Britain (Bell 1999). Just as Minimus helped to re-energise the teaching of Latin for 7–10 year olds, so Lindsay Allason-Jones over several decades has helped to breathe new life into the study of Roman material culture. Artefacts from Roman Britain and the wider Roman world, and, in particular, those from northern Britain, have been brought out of the shadows and into the limelight through a succession of Lindsay's publications which are scrupulously researched, painstakingly assembled and often presented in novel ways. This short note on some very tiny things is humbly offered in admiration of her outstanding achievements.

In April 1995 a tiny silver figure of a mouse was brought to the British Museum for identification. It had been found with the use of a metal detector, with the landowner's permission, in a field at Stansted Mountfitchet, Essex. It was reported to the Coroner but as a single unassociated find was ruled not to be Treasure Trove and the British Museum subsequently purchased it (Plate 27; Catalogue no. 1). Semi-quantitative analysis by X-ray fluorescence disclosed a silver content of approximately 92% together with minor quantities of copper, gold, lead and zinc (British Museum Research Laboratory 52191W; File 6726). Minuscule would, perhaps, be a better description of the size of the figure since it measures just 21 mm in length and weighs a mere 7.55 g. Nevertheless, it is finely modelled and depicts a mouse in characteristic pose sitting on raised haunches, its tail folded along the ridge of its back, nibbling a convex disc-shaped object held in its forepaws. Its ears and claws are well formed, its eyes simply rendered with incised dots and its whiskers and pelt carefully depicted using short incised lines and dashes – a simple, traditional, widespread and long-standing technique for giving texture to animal pelts on miniature metal figures as, for example, on an Egyptian seventh–fourth century BC copper-alloy figure of a nursing cat (Kozloff 1981, no. 58), on the fine first century AD copper-alloy boar figure from Camerton, Somerset (Jackson 1990, 26–7, pl. 1)) and, indeed, on other mouse figures of silver and copper alloy (Cat. nos 2, 4, 6, 26, 35). On the surface beneath the rump and hind legs – an area of about 8 × 4.5 mm – are traces of the solder by which the mouse was attached to some other object. Although readily recognisable as of Roman manufacture the figure cannot be dated more closely than first–fourth century AD.

Other Roman 'nibbling' mouse figures of silver include a tiny silver-gilt creature with prominent looped tail and incised pelt, perhaps a charm or gaming-counter, attributed (probably spuriously) to the Esquiline Treasure (Cat. no. 2; Shelton 1981, 93), and two equally tiny but finely-modelled examples, one with a smooth pelt, projecting sinuous tail and square base in the British Museum collections (Cat. no. 3), the other, reputedly from the Pannonian *limes*, with a broken looped tail, incised pelt and prominent cake-like held object (Cat. no. 4). Mouse figures of copper alloy are much more numerous (Plate 28). A few are set on pedestals as miniature statuettes (Cat. no. 15; Kozloff 1981, 186, no. 172), but the

* allegory: a short moral story often with animal characters

function of others, which appear to be 'free-standing', is seldom clear. Possible exceptions are the examples from Oberstimm and Winterthur (Cat. nos 35, 36) which may have had a practical use as weights. Others are attached to lamps, form the finial of knife handles, take the form of brooches, or are even found on vessel spouts. In other media mice appear on ceramic lamps and engraved gems or are incorporated in sculpted pilasters. The majority of images are realistic and lifelike with the mouse depicted in stereotypical pose, nibbling food. The imagery accords with the habits and appearance of the house mouse (*Mus musculus/domesticus*), but it might also be taken to represent the wood mouse/field mouse (*Apodemus sylvaticus*) or even the dormouse (*Glis glis*). Certainly, while the distinctive long tail of the house mouse is sometimes conclusive, the mostly tiny mouse images are seldom sufficiently detailed to permit a clear distinction between species and there is occasionally scope, too, for confusion with rats (e.g. Babelon and Blanchet 1895, nos 1209–18). At all events, as vermin, rampant among food debris, such imagery is made explicit and given a wider context in the occasional inclusion of mice, eating or seeking food, on figured floor mosaics (Toynbee 1973, 203–4).

Whether in town or country, mice were clearly omnipresent, an integral part of daily life and a proverbial pest – Pliny noted the devastating consequences of an infestation on the Cycladic island of Gyara (*Natural History* 8, 104). At Naukratis, Egypt, it appears entirely appropriate that on the handle of a third century BC transport amphora the stamped image of a mouse was used as a control mark (Cat. no. 81). Despite their negative connotations, however, mice must generally have been accepted as an inescapable fact of life – and white mice were even regarded as creatures of joyful omen (Pliny *Natural History* 8, 223). Indeed, with their tendency to scuttle and to appear suddenly in unexpected places they must sometimes have been regarded with wry amusement, though probably not by the quartermasters at garrisons with vulnerable food stores. Mouse bones have been identified widely in Romano-British military and civilian contexts, as at Manchester, where the remains of several mice were found in an amphora embedded in the ground next to a hearth in a guard chamber of the north gate of the timber fort. It is suggested that the amphora, probably originally installed as a water butt, trapped these small animals following its disuse (Yolden 1986). Such dangers are underlined in the fable of '*The Mouse in the Wine Jar and the Cat*' (Engels 1999, 62–3). At Birdoswald bones of mice from the general sub-floor backfill of the fort's two *horrea* excavated in 1987–92, probably belong to a period when the granaries were no longer functioning as grain stores (Izard 1997, 363, 365, table 33). But at Vindolanda, in the sub-floor channels of the fort's east granary, which was in active use from the early third to the late fourth century AD, bones of mice were found in some numbers (Bennett and Timm forthcoming); while at South Shields, in a context representing the period of use of the fort's forecourt granary as a grain store in the third century, 18.3% of the small mammal bones were field mouse (MNI 36) and 30.5% house mouse (MNI 60) (Younger 1994). At Loughor it seems singularly apt that a fine idiosyncratic figure of a mouse was found in the demolition debris of the fort's second century *praetorium* which had been built on the site of an earlier granary (Cat. no. 28).

Some of the mouse imagery, then, may represent no more than genre art, a simple appreciation of co-existence with a cute, if occasionally troublesome, creature. Accordingly, the majority of metal figures are realistically depicted: the mouse crouches on all fours or sits back on its haunches, most often nibbling, or about to nibble, an object held in its forepaws. It is seldom clear exactly what is being held/nibbled but, depending on its size and form, the object is usually identified as a nut, berry, grape (or other fruit), or small cake, breadcrumb or food morsel. Only occasionally is the imagery explicit, as on a second century AD 'un-swept room' (*asarotos oikos*) mosaic from Rome, a version of the famous Hellenistic original by Sosas (Pliny *Natural History* 36.184), where a house mouse approaches a halved walnut lying on the floor (Toynbee 1973, pl. 101; Dunbabin 2003, fig. 33). The relatively large flat discoid object, held by the Loughor mouse (Cat. no. 28; Lloyd-Morgan 1997, fig. 100, no. 155), is evidently not a nut, berry or fruit, and is suggestive of a small cake. As Caylus long since observed, in describing the held object of another mouse figure (cited by Babelon 1928, 46, no. 21 and pl. xiii, 21), this recalls the imagery used to depict the cakes (*placentae*) given as offerings at temples and shrines. Even more compelling as *placentae* are the objects held by an unprovenanced copper-alloy mouse in the Leo Mildenberg collection (Zahlhaas 1996, no. 107), another from Virunum, Austria (Cat. no. 30) – significantly from the excavation of a temple – and the silver example said to have been found in the *limes* region of Pannonia (Cat. no. 4). The held objects are not only circular and convex, but have an incised segmented design – like hot-cross buns. Although they might be no more than a stylised version of the circular Roman loaf (Lloyd-Morgan 1997, 269), they correspond both to other imagery (for example the combined *phiale* and *placenta*

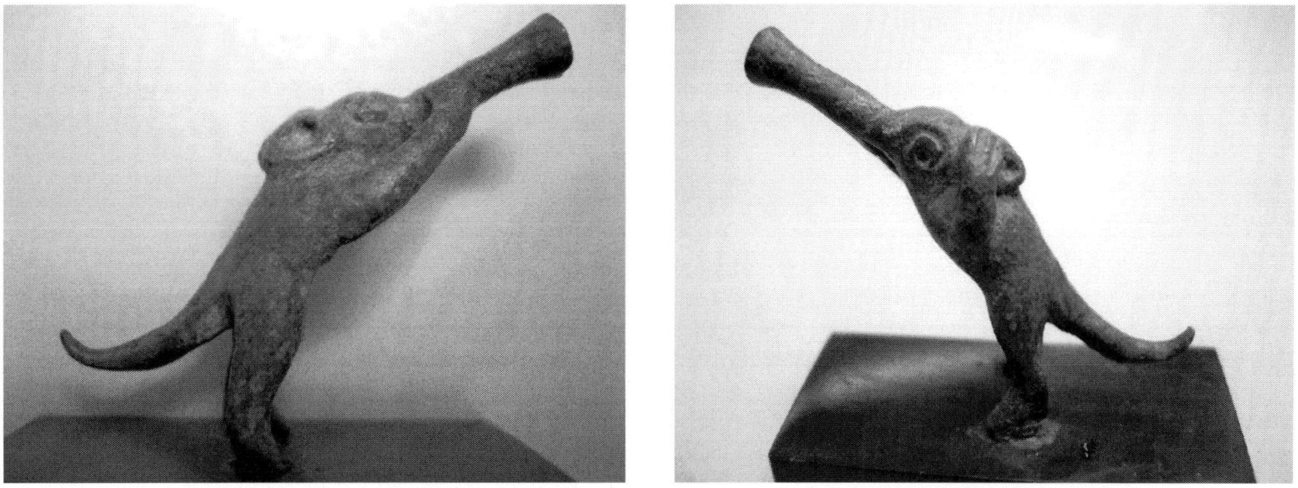

Figure 27.1 Copper-alloy 'trumpeter' mouse figure, Cat. no. 16. Photos: Ralph Jackson

held by a silver statuette dedicated to Dea Senuna at Ashwell, Hertfordshire) and to ancient references to cake-offerings, as in Martial: ' … and with incense, and new wine, and victim, there be offered to you at your fair altars many a quarter of parcelled cake (*secta plurima quadra de placenta*).' (*Epigrams* 9, 90, 16–18; also 6, 75, 1). An interesting picture is conjured up: those sacrificial cakes and other food offerings that were not whisked off the altars and scoffed by unscrupulous priests – as observed by a sceptical Asklepian incubant, Cario, in Aristophanes' *Wealth* (Act 3 scene 2) – were just as likely to be devoured by temple mice, who were well-known for hoovering up such easy pickings (e.g. *Battle of Frogs and Mice* 174–6).

But there may have been a further, deeper significance to all or some of the mouse figures, for mice, like hares, are prolific (Varro *On Agriculture* 3, 12, 4. Horace *Satires* 2, 4, 44) and both animals were sometimes used in Roman iconography as symbols of fertility. Just as the hare depicted on the tombstone of the young *medicus* Anicius Ingenuus from Housesteads might have been selected to ensure fertility in the afterlife (Rémy 2010, 116) so the presence of the mouse figure from disturbed burial debris at York hints at a grave-good with similar meaning (Catalogue no. 26). As a long-standing symbol of rebirth and fertility in the otherworld that might explain why in southern Italy in the fourth century BC it was considered appropriate both to make a distinctive type of ceramic baby-feeder in the form of a crouched mouse and to use it as a grave-good (Cat. no. 80; Künzl 1982, 113, Abb. 3b; Kozloff 1986, 45, no. 77).

Mice and hares symbolised fecundity, but they shared a further place in Roman art, namely their craving for grapes and fruit and the counterpart to the guzzling hare (Toynbee 1973, 202) was the nibbling mouse. Thus, a statuette of an Amor, once in the collection of William Hamilton (Cat. no. 25), signifies Autumn by dangling a bunch of grapes in his right hand in temptation of a mouse, which sits, tantalised, on a dish held in his left hand: Autumn, the time of harvest of wine grapes, was also a time when mice were rampant – and ravenous.

In addition to the essentially realistic, if simplified, imagery of most mouse figures some are fantasy pieces, including two which caught the attention of Jocelyn Toynbee (Toynbee 1973, pls 99–100). One (Fig. 27.1; Cat. no. 16) shows a strutting mouse blowing a trumpet, perhaps a parody of the gladiatorial and military trumpeters whose strident blasts signalled key stages in mortal combat. But there is further comic humour in this little figure, for the big blaring noise that the trumpet emits is clearly more than the tiny creature can bear and in an attempt to muffle the sound it covers its left ear with its paw. The other (Plate 29; Cat. no. 47), a copper-alloy lamp-lid from Konya, Turkey, dating to the first century AD or earlier, is a finely-modelled figure of a semi-upright mouse peeping sideways, as if to an imaginary audience, from behind a theatre mask which it holds, in place of the normal nut or morsel, in front of its face. This is clearly a parody of the actor who, in the satyr-plays, took the part of the chorus leader wearing the mask and attributes of the most aged and senior satyr, Silenus. So, we are confronted with an absurd little mouse in the guise of the immortal companion and wise teacher of Dionysus. Both these mouse figures, therefore, are intrinsically humorous and satirical, but they are also reminiscent of 'The Mountain in Labour', one of Aesop's Fables. Famously included by Horace in his epistle on *The Art of Poetry* (*Epistles* 2, 3, 136–9), where he advises against heightened rhetoric in the opening lines of a poem, the fable describes the long and

Figure 27.2 Copper-alloy lamp with hinged mouse lamp-lid, Cat. no. 39. Drawing: British Museum

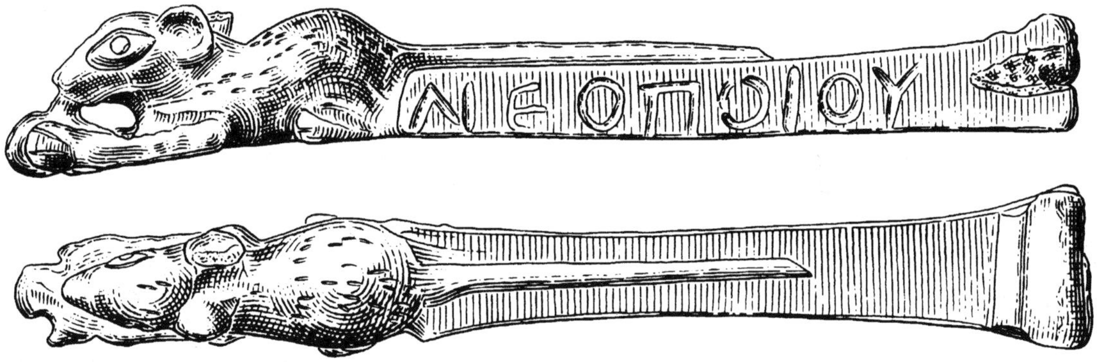

Figure 27.3 Copper-alloy inscribed mouse handle, Cat. no. 63. Drawing: British Museum

Figure 27.4 Copper-alloy mouse handle, Cat. no. 59. Photo: Ralph Jackson

thunderous groaning of a mountain 'in labour' which, after such a portent, results only in the issue of a tiny mouse, thus illustrating the popular proverb 'much ado about nothing' or, to paraphrase Horace, avoid extravagant claims that can only end in absurdity.

The use of artificial lighting for indoor illumination, above all oil lamps, which allowed some control over the length of the day, was a form of conspicuous consumption of wealth and the *sine qua non* of elegant dining. In consequence lamps and lampstands might be made to impress and there was a wide range of ornate lamps in addition to the plainer examples. Both copper-alloy and pottery lamps provided fields for decoration, principally on their upper face, which incorporated incised, moulded or relief ornament, while a few were plastic lamps modelled in the round. Mice were included in the decorative repertoire occasionally as plastic lamps (Cat. nos 38, 57) but more often as individual figures or as components of a wider scheme. The exceptional Silenus mouse figure was a lamp-lid and other hinged lids for both the circular filling-hole and ovoid wick-hole of some metal lamps also took the form of a mouse, though in the more stereotypical crouched nibbling pose (Fig. 27.2; Cat. nos 39–47). Another favoured position for mice on lamps was as a crouched figure approaching the nozzle (Fig. 27.6; Cat. nos 48–53, 56). These little mice, illuminated by the flame of the lamp, are in a location that at first sight appears un-natural for a creature that tends to avoid exposure. That may be the point, of course, that they are caught unawares. But there is another possibility, namely that far from being abnormal their presence on lamps reflected the reality of daily life – mice in search of food, and not just the detritus of a banquet lying on an unswept floor (Dunbabin 2003, 64–6) but specifically olive oil. For, in a revealing passage in the *Battle of Frogs and Mice* (*Batrachomyomachia* 174–96), a burlesque animal epic parodying the *Iliad*, Athena refuses to take the side of the mice, as Zeus wishes, stating that they have done her much mischief. That mischief, it transpires, consists not only of keeping her awake with their constant squeaking and the destruction of her sacred robes by voracious nibbling but also 'spoiling my garlands and my lamps too, to get the oil'. Whatever the case, the enduring appeal and, perhaps, reality of mouse imagery on lamps is indicated by the wide date range – from the third –second century BC to the sixth–seventh century AD (Cat. nos 39, 51, 52, 57).

Some mouse figures may have been linked to Venus, for mice were connected with the goddess through her early manifestation as a Roman garden *numen* associated with growth and fertility (Ferguson 1970, 71). A few have a more direct link to deities, including the finely-contexted, if enigmatic, find from Kaiseraugst; a nut-nibbling mouse perched at one end of an ornate copper-alloy stand (Cat. no. 37). The stand appears to have been the base for a statuette of Somnus, one of several statuettes thought to be the contents of a *lararium*, which had been stored beneath the floor of a room in a house that burnt down in the mid-third century AD. Somnus, the personification and god of sleep, brother of Death and son of Night, is shown with normal attributes, youthful and naked, with wings on his head and the remains of what was probably an inverted torch in his right hand. Darkness and poppies are common associations but the connection with a mouse is un-paralleled. Probably there was a connection to sleep, death and re-birth, though it may be, as Kaufmann-Heinimann observed (1994, 64; 1998, 133), that both the god and his accompanying creature acquired particular meaning from a regional tradition – the group of statuettes are Gallo-Roman.

Only marginally less enigmatic is the significance of the mouse on a distinctive series of second – third century AD copper-alloy handles (Fig. 27.3; Cat. nos 61–5; Jackson 1994; Künzl 2001). Three faces of the rectangular-sectioned grip are inscribed with a Greek text naming a temple official (Elpidephoros on one knife handle, Hygeinos Kanpylios on the others), while the fourth – upper – face is occupied by the extended straight or lightly sinuous tail of a crouched mouse that forms the finial of the handle. Of the five known examples three lack a provenance, but the other two are both from Asia Minor – more specifically both are probably from Ephesus, and one was found with a large set of medical and surgical instruments. Künzl (1982) argued compellingly for an association with Apollo Smintheus, a healing deity whose cult animal was a mouse, who was linked to Asklepios and who was worshipped especially in this part of western Asia Minor in the later second century AD. Though none of the handles preserve the iron 'business end' Künzl has suggested they were the handles of writing implements – probably the spatulae used for spreading and clearing the wax surface on stilus tablets – and that, like Martial's *xenia* (especially *Epigrams* 14, 3–7, 19 and 21), they were distributed as gifts by Elpidephoros and Kanpylios during or on completion of their term of office (Künzl 2002a, 12–16; 2002b, 75–6).

Mice are also to be found as finials on other copper-alloy knife handles, their posture adapted to the requirements of the terminal (Fig. 27.4; Cat. nos 58–60). Thus, to provide a comfortable grip, a handle in the Townley collection locates the nut-nibbling mouse beyond a simple

Figure 27.5 Townley drawing of mouse and cockerel gem, Cat. no. 71. Image: British Museum

moulding in a near-vertical position sat back on its haunches; while the nut-nibbler which emerges from a calyx on a handle in Bonn has a sinuous tail in order to provide a suspension loop. Similarly, on an amber knife-handle from Carlisle a small perforation was contrived, possibly for suspension, between the chin and forepaws of a crouched nibbling mouse. Henig links this mouse handle to the night, sleep, death and rebirth imagery frequently used for figured amber and which he attributes both to the intrinsic qualities of amber and to the popularity of the chthonic god Liber-Bacchus in the region of Aquileia where much amber was manufactured (McCarthy *et al.* 1983, 268–9).

Copper-alloy brooches, too, occasionally took the form of a mouse, including the examples from Monk Soham, Suffolk and Roxby cum Risby, North Lincolnshire, the latter enhanced with silver tail and eyes (Cat. nos 66, 67). Like fly brooches they may have been intended to evoke momentary surprise followed by amusement as well as, perhaps, recalling Athena's (and others') nibbled garments. More discreet are the engraved mouse images on gemstones, including two crouched nibblers on carnelian intaglios in the Snettisham jeweller's hoard (Cat. nos 75, 76), one on a red jasper gem in an iron ring from Colchester (Henig 1978, no. 623) and another seated on an ear of corn on a carnelian gem-set gold ring from Harpenden, Hertfordshire (Cat. no. 78). A more complex image on a red jasper intaglio from Corbridge (Cat. no. 77) shows a nibbling mouse emerging from a nautilus shell, a long-standing symbol of the womb (Barb 1953, 204–8). Combined with the fecund mouse, as Henig observed, the image could hardly be bettered as a symbol of the teeming life of the other-world (McCarthy *et al.* 1983, 268). On composite and magical gems (e.g. Cat. nos 72–4) mice appear with various creatures and produce – owl, serpent, lizard, lion, crane, unicorn, grapes, corn and olives – while two gems in the Townley collection show a mouse being rough-handled by a cockerel. In one case (Cat. no. 70) the cock stands on a wine-cup tugging the creature's tail which it holds in its beak while the mouse hangs onto the vessel's rim for dear life. In the other (Fig. 27.5; Cat. no.71) a cock stands in front of a cornucopia flanked by poppy-heads and an ear of corn and brandishes a mouse which it holds by its tail in its beak, while a butterfly passes overhead. The cockerel was a bird of good omen, as emphasised by the corn, poppy-heads and cornucopia, and this was perhaps underlined by its protection of such abundance from vermin.

Perhaps the finest mouse gem from Britain is the intaglio in a third century gold finger-ring found in excavations at Bow, London, where a stretch of the Roman road from London to Colchester was revealed together with roadside buildings, burials and grave goods (Cat. no. 79). The engraved image is of a pair of confronted crouched mice seemingly sharing a choice morsel, a scene which Henig convincingly identifies as an evocation of the fable of the town mouse and country mouse in which a visiting town mouse disparages the simple fare of his country cousin only to have their richer banquet on the reciprocal visit rudely and dangerously curtailed by a Molossian hound (Henig 2008, 234). This famous fable which exemplified the human dichotomy of choosing between the respective merits and hazards of town and country was included in Horace's *Satires* (2, 6, 77–117). And perhaps with this fable in mind Martial describes a country visitor to his friend Faustinus' luxury Baiae villa bringing (very aptly) sleepy dormice as his gift (Martial *Epigrams* 3, 58, 33–6).

In fact, several other fables are evoked by mouse imagery. Thus, it is probably more than coincidence that a copper-alloy lamp type with a nibbling mouse behind the nozzle (Fig. 27.6; Cat. nos 48, 49) also features two lion-heads. For this was perhaps a reminder for the viewer that mercy brings its reward and that even the weak or lowly can sometimes assist the powerful, a message conveyed by the Aesopic fable of the proverbially fierce lion caught and bound by hunters and rescued by the tiny mouse, whose life he had previously spared, who gnaws through the ropes. Similarly, the juxta-

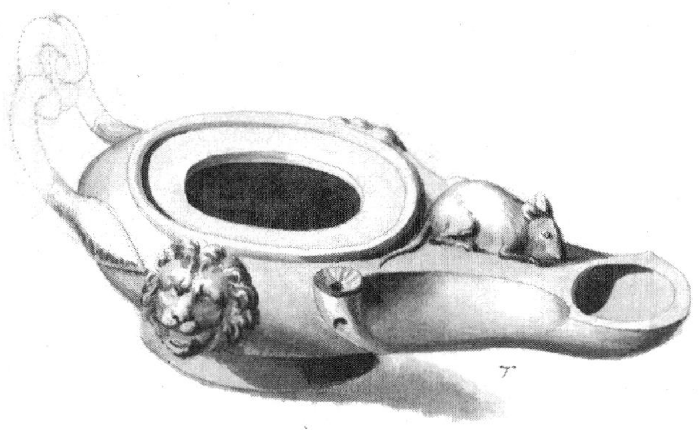

Figure 27.6 Townley drawing of copper-alloy lion and mouse lamp, Cat. no. 49. Image: British Museum

Figure 27.7 Pottery lamp with mouse outweighing an elephant, Cat. no. 54. Photo: British Museum

position of a mouse safely resting between the horns of a bull's head on a copper-alloy spout from Scawby, Lincolnshire (Cat. no. 68) might have been designed to evoke the fable of the mouse and the bull, in which a bull, angered by the bite of a mouse, is unable to rout the creature from its hole with his horns, exemplifying the adage 'the great do not always prevail'. A more explicit version of a similar sentiment is visualised on the discus of two pottery lamps from the Bay of Naples (Fig. 27.7; Cat. nos 54, 55): with its beak a stork suspends a balance, in one pan of which is an elephant in the other a mouse – counter-intuitively the diminutive mouse outweighs the proverbially large elephant, once again reminding us that size is not everything.

So, to return to our little figure from Stansted, it may have been made 'just for fun' but it might equally have embodied a particular meaning: the Roman mouse was a tiny creature of many parts and its imagery was as widespread as the animals themselves, in forts, towns, *vici*, houses, temples and burials the length and breadth of the empire.

A select catalogue of mouse figures and other mouse imagery

Silver figures

British Museum

1. *Stansted Mountfitchet, Essex* (BM 1995,0903.1); MD find, unassociated; L. 21 mm. Wt. 7.55 g.

A tiny silver mouse on raised haunches, its tail folded along the ridge of its back, nibbling a nut, berry or fruit held in its forepaws. Ears, eyes and claws are depicted and the whiskers and pelt simply rendered by means of incised lines and dashes.

2. *Rome* (BM 1866,1229.49); one of 15 pieces of jewellery associated with the Esquiline Treasure, but probably a subsequent (nineteenth century) addition; fourth cent. AD; L. 23 mm.

A tiny silver-gilt mouse on raised haunches, nibbling an ovoid nut, fruit, berry or other morsel of food, held in its forepaws. The tail is curled, its tip resting on the creature's right flank, presumably contrived to provide a loop in order to grip or suspend the object. Ears and eyes are depicted and the pelt represented by incised lines.

Dalton 1901, no. 239; Shelton 1981, 93, no. 54, pl. 47; Tait 1976, 124, no. 183.

3. *Provenance unknown* (BM 1926,0406.8); Ht. 13.9 mm. L. 31.5 mm.

A tiny silver mouse on raised haunches, its sinuous tail projecting behind, leaning forward and nibbling a nut, fruit, berry or other morsel of food which it holds in its extended forepaws. The figure, well-modelled and finely-finished, with carefully-depicted ears and eyes and a smooth pelt, sits on a tiny flat rectangular plinth.

Other

4. *Pannonia*, *limes*, reputedly (on the antiquity market); L. 25 mm.

A tiny plump silver mouse on raised haunches, nibbling a large circular object with quartered design, probably a cake, held in its forepaws. Ears and eyes are depicted and the pelt represented by chased stippling. The broken tail was originally looped, its curled tip resting on the creature's right flank.

Christie's, *Fine Antiquities* 25 April 2001, Lot 261

Copper-alloy figures

British Museum (NB Bronze 1864 etc = Walters 1899, no. 1864)

5. *Provenance unknown* (BM 1975,0301.3; *Bronze* 1864); H. 38.1 mm.

A well-modelled small plump mouse on lightly-raised haunches nibbling a morsel of food which it holds in its forepaws. Its ears, eyes and claws are depicted and its tail folded along the ridge of its back.

6. *Provenance unknown* (BM1824,0454.20; *Bronze* 1866); L. 31 mm.

A small crouched mouse nibbling a morsel of food which it holds in its forepaws. Ears, eyes and claws are depicted and the pelt represented by incised dashes.

7. *Provenance unknown* (BM 1867,0508.803; *Bronze* 1861); H. 25.4 mm; L. 50.8 mm.

A plump crouched mouse, its muzzle resting on a nut, berry, fruit or other morsel which it holds in its forepaws and nibbles. Ears and eyes are depicted and the tail, like that of No. 2, is looped, with its tip resting on the creature's right flank.

8. *Provenance unknown* (BM1975,0301.6; *Bronze* 1870); L. 42 mm.

A plump crouched mouse nibbling a morsel of food that it grips in its forepaws. The tail is curled to form a large near-circular loop.

9. *Provenance unknown* (BM 1859,0216.147; *Bronze* 1865); L. 50.8 mm.

A crouched mouse with plump body and relatively small head, its chin resting on a pear-shaped morsel of food that it grips in its forepaws. Ears, eyes and claws depicted, tail broken.

10. *Provenance unknown* (BM1975,0301.1; *Bronze* 1862); L. 54 mm.

A mouse on raised haunches nibbling a nut, fruit, berry or other morsel which it holds in its forepaws. Eyes and ears depicted, tail and hind paws broken.

11. *Provenance unknown* (BM 1975,0301.2; *Bronze* 1863); H. 33 mm.

A small mouse on raised haunches nibbling an egg-shaped morsel of food, held in its forepaws. Eyes and ears depicted, tail broken.

12. *Provenance unknown* (BM 1873,0820.257; *Bronze* 1868); L. 50 mm.

A mouse on raised haunches, nibbling a heart-shaped nut, fruit, berry or other morsel of food, held in its forepaws. Ears and eyes are depicted and the tail is looped, its curled tip resting on the creature's right flank.

13. *Provenance unknown* (BM1975,0301.4; *Bronze* 1867); L. 24 mm.

A tiny mouse on raised haunches nibbling a proportionately large cake, nut, fruit or other morsel which it holds in its forepaws. The tail is looped, its tip resting on the creature's right flank.

14. *Provenance unknown* (BM 1975,0301.5; *Bronze* 1869); H. 24 mm; L. 32 mm.

A small mouse, sat back on its haunches, nibbling a large ovoid nut, cake or other morsel of food which it clasps in its forepaws. The tail, rather un-realistic, projects from the creature's back as a D-shaped loop, probably for suspension. Ears and eyes are depicted and the claws rather rudimentarily rendered.

15 *Provenance unknown* (BM1881,1008.1; *Bronze* 1860); H. 25 mm.

A tiny mouse on raised haunches leaning forward to nibble a proportionately large cake, nut, fruit or other morsel which it holds in its forepaws. The hind legs and sinuous tail rest on a small cavetto-moulded rectangular pedestal, which gives the impression that the mouse is a 'statue'.

16. *Provenance unknown* (BM 1824,0498.59; *Bronze* 1858); H. 38.2 mm. L. 43.6 mm.

A small mouse, standing upright on its hind legs, its curved tail projecting behind, blowing with gusto on a trumpet (*tuba*) which it holds in its right forepaw. To add to the humour of the surreal image (and a small point overlooked by Toynbee) the creature covers its left ear with the other forepaw in order to muffle its own racket! The figure is simply but skilfully rendered and finished.

Toynbee 1973, 203, pl. 100

17. *Provenance unknown* (BM 1824,0454.21); H. 23.4 mm. L. 27.1 mm.

A tiny mouse on raised haunches leaning forward and nibbling a nut or other morsel held in its extended forepaws. The looped tail, now broken, ends on the left side of the creature's rump. Well-modelled, simply-finished and a little worn, the figure has a smooth pelt and its head is lightly turned to the left.

18. *Provenance unknown* (BM 1878,1019.92); Ht. 23.1 mm. L. 36.3 mm.

A tiny mouse sat back on its haunches and nibbling a nut or other morsel which it holds in its extended forepaws. The large looped tail, which ends on the right rump, forms a D-shaped handle or suspension loop. The figure is well-modelled and simply-finished, with a smooth pelt.

19. *Provenance unknown* (BM 1878,1019.93); Ht. 17.7 mm. L. 33.1 mm.

A tiny mouse leaning forward on raised haunches and nibbling a nut or other morsel which it holds in its extended forepaws. The looped tail, now broken, ends on the right side of the creature's rump. The figure is well-modelled and simply-finished, with a smooth pelt and the head lightly turned to the right.

20. *Provenance unknown* (BM1874,0805.133; *Bronze* 1871); Ht. 34 mm. L. 104.4 mm.

A large hollow-cast crouched mouse nibbling a nut or other morsel of food which it holds in its forepaws. The tail is long, straight and broken. The underside of the hind paws is in the form of a square open socket, presumably for attachment. The figure is well-modelled but heavily corroded, and damaged on one side. Although iconographically the same as the small mouse figures this object probably had a particular and different function.

21. *Provenance unknown* (BM1975,0310.16); Ht. 24.6 mm. L. 40.5 mm.

A mouse on raised haunches leaning forward and nibbling a nut or other morsel of food which it holds in its forepaws. The sinuous end of the looped tail, now broken, rests on the left side of the rump. The figure is well-modelled but quite rudimentarily-finished. The pelt is smooth, the ears are worn, the eyes are barely rendered and the head is lightly turned to the left.

22. *Provenance unknown* (BM1975,0310.17); Ht. 25.6 mm. L. 29.7 mm.

A small, plump mouse, on raised haunches, nibbling a nut or other morsel of food which it holds in its forepaws. Only the stub of the tail remains. A well-modelled figure with a corroded surface.

23. *Provenance unknown* (BM1975,0310.18); Ht. 22 mm. L. 32.3 mm.

A tiny mouse, sat back on its haunches, eating a nut or other morsel of food which it holds in its forepaws. The end of the long looped tail rests on the right side of the rump. The figure is well-modelled and simply-finished, with a smooth pelt.

24. *Provenance unknown* (BM1975,0310.19); L. 33.5 mm.

A small mouse on raised haunches leaning forward and nibbling a nut which it holds in its forepaws. The looped tail, now broken, ends on the right side of the rump. A well-modelled but rudimentarily-finished figure with a smooth pelt.

25. *Provenance unknown* (BM 1772,0302.88; *Bronze* 1517); first–second cent. AD; H. 76.2 mm.

A statuette of an Amor (as Autumn) dangling a bunch of grapes in his right hand in temptation of a mouse, which sits, on raised haunches, on a dish held in the left hand.

Other

26. *York* (St John's College, York, History Dept.); surface find of grave goods from disturbed burials at the Mount School site; L. *c.* 45 mm.

A crouched mouse, its muzzle resting on an ovoid nut, berry, fruit or other morsel which it holds in its forepaws and nibbles. Ears and eyes are depicted and the pelt simply rendered by incised dashes. The tail is coiled to form a large circular loop doubtless intended for suspension.

RCHM 1962, 100, xvii pl. 34.

27 *Hayton, East Yorkshire* (PAS FASW-8B6455); MD find; L. 35.5 mm. H. 25.2 mm. Wt. 44 g.

A mouse on raised haunches, leant forward nibbling an ovoid nut or other morsel of food, held in its forepaws. The tail is broken.

Worrell and Pearce 2011, no. 3, 407–8, fig. 4.

28. *Loughor, West Glamorgan* (National Museum and Galleries of Wales, Cardiff, 98.6H/3.155); from the excavations at the Roman auxiliary fort (Site 53, Context 310 = Context Group 4231, Phase 12,), found in the demolition debris (early second cent. AD) of praetorium 3 (Building 3.10); H. 32.1 mm. L. 78.7 mm.

A mouse, with prominent ears and incised eyes, seated on its hind legs and extended, near straight, tail, leaning forward with its muzzle resting on the edge of a relatively large discoid object which it holds in its extended forepaws.

Lloyd-Morgan 1997, 268–9, fig. 100, no. 155.

29. *Provenance unknown* (Paris, Bibliothèque Nationale); L. 34 mm.

A mouse on raised haunches, nibbling a nut or other morsel held in its forepaws, its tail coiled to form a large circular loop.

Babelon and Blanchet 1895, 488, no. 1215; another nine examples (nos 1209–1214, 1216–1218), like 1215 all labelled 'Rat', are probably mice. They are variously described as eating a nut, egg, fruit or cake and measure between 21mm and 48 mm long.

30. *Virunum, Austria* (Landesmuseum für Kärnten); from 1909/10 excavation of temple; H. 32 mm.

A mouse on raised haunches, its tail folded along the ridge of its back, holding and nibbling a large circular cake, nut or fruit (with incised eight-rayed device).

Fleischer 1967, 190, Taf. 130, no. 275.

31. *Köln, Germany* (Landesmuseum Bonn, Inv. Nr. 1020); H. 32 mm.

Mouse, on a flat base, nearly vertical, sitting back on its haunches, holding and nibbling a small morsel.

Menzel 1986, 66, Taf. 81, no. 138.

32. *Xanten (Vetera), Germany* (Landesmuseum Bonn, Inv. Nr. 33748); L. 31 mm.

Crouched nut-nibbling mouse on sub-rectangular base.

Menzel 1986, 66, Taf. 81, no. 139.

33. *Provenance unknown* (Landesmuseum Bonn, Inv. Nr. U 1271); L. 47 mm.

Crouched plump mouse, tail now broken, nibbling a morsel.

Menzel 1986, 66, Taf. 81, no. 137.

34. *Provenance unknown* (Landesmuseum Bonn, Inv. Nr. U 1270); L. 46 mm.

Crouched mouse, with head raised and mouth slightly open, perhaps in anticipation of food, the end of the tail broken.

Menzel 1986, 64–5, Taf. 81, no. 134.

35. *Kastell Oberstimm, Germany* (Prähistorische Staatssammlung München); Second half first cent. AD; L. 52 mm.

Crouched mouse, with curled tail, raised head and punch-textured pelt, holding a fruit, nut or other morsel in its fore-paws. Künzl has noted that the weight of the figure corresponds to one-sixth of a Roman pound prompting the suggestion that this mouse may have been used as a weight.

Künzl 1982, 113; Garbsch 1994, 323–4.

36. *Winterthur, Switzerland* (Kantonsarchäologie Zurich, Fundnr. 5679.1); from the Roman *vicus* at Unteres Bühl, Oberwinterthur, Feld 104/51; associated finds date from the mid-first to second half second cent. AD; L. 40 mm.

A nut-nibbling crouched mouse with prominent looped tail, perhaps a suspension loop since the figure is filled with lead and may have been a steelyard weight.

Kaufmann-Heinimann 1994, 64–5, no. 68, Taf. 56.

37. *Kaiseraugst, Switzerland* (Römermuseum Augst, Inv. 1984.27187-1984.27189); late first or second cent. AD; H. 21 mm. L. 30 mm.; from 1984 excavation in the Roman town, Region 17E, House 2, Room 9, in a wooden box beneath the floor together with several bronze statuettes – Mercury (2), Lar, Hercules, Somnus – interpreted as the contents of a lararium; house burnt down mid-third cent AD.

A small rectangular copper-alloy shelf or stand (163 × 57 mm), regarded as the plinth for the statuette of Somnus (Kaufmann-Heinimann 1998, 133), with four scrolled supports (one lacking) on the underside and the tiny figure of a mouse perched at one end, sitting on its haunches, its tail curled onto its right flank, its upper body leant forward as it nibbles a nut, berry, fruit or other morsel held in its fore-paws.

Kaufmann-Heinimann 1994, 64–5, no. 67, Taf. 56. Kaufmann-Heinimann 1998, 130–134, S67, Abb. 93, 6, Abb. 94.

Copper-alloy lamps

British Museum

38. *Armant, Egypt* (BM1922,0712.10); first cent. AD; L. 90 mm.

A plastic lamp in the form of a crouched mouse, with looped tail, holding the spout in place of food.

Bailey 1996, Q3594.

39. *Egypt* (BM1926,0415.41); third–second cent. BC.
Lamp-lid, hinged, on complete lamp (L. 159 mm.), mouse on raised haunches nibbling a morsel.
Bailey 1996, Q3548.

40. *Provenance unknown* (BM1926,0415.54); second cent. BC.
Lamp-lid, hinged, on complete lamp (L. 183 mm.), mouse elevated on raised haunches, with straight tail, facing nozzle, nibbling a morsel.
Bailey 1996, Q3549.

41. *Kos, Greece* (BM1854,0519.54); first cent. AD; H. 24 mm.
Lamp-lid, mouse on raised haunches with tail and morsel between front paws.
Bailey 1996, Q3734.

42. *Provenance unknown* (BM1814,0704.225); first cent. AD; L. 34 mm.
Lamp-lid, mouse on raised haunches nibbling a morsel.
Bailey 1996, Q3735.

43. *Italy*, probably (BM1824,0454.22); first cent. AD; L. 55 mm.
Lamp-lid, hinged, crouched mouse leaning forward nibbling a morsel.
Bailey 1996, Q3736.

44. *Provenance unknown* (BM1975,0501.3); first cent. BC; L. 33 mm.
Lamp-lid, hinged, crouched mouse nibbling a morsel.
Bailey 1996, Q3750.

45. *Provenance unknown* (BM1814,0704.226); first cent. BC; L. 36 mm.
Lamp-lid, hinged, crouched mouse.
Bailey 1996, Q3748.

46. *Provenance unknown* (BM1975,0501.2); first cent BC; L. 32 mm.
Lamp-lid, hinged, crouched mouse. Hinge loop broken.
Bailey 1996, Q3749.

47. *Konya, Turkey* (BM1876,0510.2); first cent. AD or earlier; H. 30 mm.
Lamp-lid, mouse on raised haunches holding theatre mask (Papposeileinos) in front of face.
Bailey 1996, Q3733.

48. *Tripolitza, Greece*, said to be from tomb (BM1905,1024.4); first cent. AD.
Opposed nozzle lamp (L. 184 mm.), with a crouched nibbling mouse behind and facing both nozzles and a lion-mask on each side of the body.
Bailey 1996, Q3651.

49. *Provenance unknown* (BM1814,0704.205); first cent. AD.
Lamp (L. 157 mm.), with crouched nibbling mouse, with sinuous tail, behind and facing nozzle and a lion-mask on each side of body.
Bailey 1996, Q3641.

50. *Italy* (BM1824,0454.13); first cent. AD.
Lamp (L. 152 mm.), with crouched nibbling mouse, with sinuous tail, behind and facing nozzle.
Bailey 1996, Q3620.

51. *Provenance unknown* (BM1867,0508.386); third–second cent. BC.
Lamp (L. 113 mm.), with crouched mouse, with sinuous tail, behind and facing nozzle.
Bailey 1996, Q3543.

52. *Provenance unknown* (BM1964,0402.1); sixth–seventh cent. AD.
Brass lamp (L. 142 mm.) with domed lid, at the nozzle end of which is perched a mouse.
Bailey 1996, Q3795.

Pottery lamps

British Museum

53. *Provenance unknown* (BM1963,0715.17); first cent. BC.
Mould-made lamp (L. 76 mm.), with crouched mouse behind and facing nozzle.
Bailey 1975, Q608.

54. *Strada Campana, Pozzuoli, Italy* (BM1856,1226.419); AD 40–70.
Mould-made lamp, Loeschke Type 1B (L. 121 mm.), with discus scene showing a wading bird (?stork) holding a balance in its beak. A mouse in the left pan weighs down an elephant in the right pan.
Bailey 1980, Q832.

55. *Pompeii, Italy* (BM1847,1108.7); AD 40–70.
Mould-made lamp, Loeschke Type 1B (L. 122 mm.), with discus scene as No. 54.
Bailey 1980, Q833.

56. *Pozzuoli, Italy* (BM1856,1226.517); AD 100–150.
Mould-made lamp (L. 108 mm.), with crouched mouse behind and facing nozzle.
Bailey 1980, Q1246.

57. *Provenance unknown* (BM1982,1005.2); fifth cent. AD; L. 81 mm.
Lamp in the form of a highly-stylised mouse, the nozzle forming its mouth.
Bailey 1988, Q3314.

Handles, brooches and fittings

58. *Carlisle* (Tullie House Museum and Art Gallery, Acc. no. 1892-187); Ht. *c.* 21 mm.
Amber knife-handle (L. 36 mm.), with finial in the form of a mouse sat back on its haunches nibbling a nut or other morsel of food.
McCarthy *et al.* 1983.

59. *Provenance Unknown* (British Museum, 1814,0704.1018); probably first–second cent. AD; L. *c.* 25 mm.
Copper-alloy knife handle (L. 54 mm.), with finial in the form of a mouse sat back on its haunches eating a morsel.

60. *Provenance unknown* (Landesmuseum Bonn, Inv. nr. 81. 1026); L. *c.*37 mm.
Copper-alloy knife handle (L. 46 mm) in the form of a mouse emerging from a calyx. The mouse crouches, its sinuous tail looped above its back, and nibbles a morsel held in its forepaws, an arrangement which enabled the provision of a small suspension loop.
Menzel 1986, 113, Taf. 117, no. 263.

61. *Ephesus, Turkey*, probably from the sanctuary of Artemis (British Museum, 1909,0620.3); L. *c.*59 mm.
Copper-alloy handle (L. 79 mm.) with inscribed grip (ΥΓΕΙΝΟΥ/ ΚΑΝΠΥΛΙΟΥ/ ΝΕΟΠΟΙΟΥ – 'of Hygeinos Kanpylios, *neopoios* (temple official)') and finial in the form of a crouched mouse, its muzzle resting on a morsel that it holds in its forepaws, its straight tail extended along the handle.
Jackson 1994, 326–8, fig. 6a.

62. *S. W. Asia Minor, probably Ephesus*, part of a grave group (Römisch-Germanisches Zentralmuseum, Mainz Inv. 0.37862); second–third cent. AD; L. *c.*65 mm.
Copper-alloy handle (L. 84 mm.) with inscribed grip, as No. 61, the lightly sinuous tail extended along the handle.
Künzl 2002a, 12–16, Abb. 6, Taf. 1, A5. Künzl 2002b, 75–6, Abb. 101.

63. *Provenance unknown* (on the antiquity market, London, 1993); L. *c.*62 mm.
Copper-alloy handle (L. 85 mm) with inscribed grip, as No. 61.
Jackson 1994, 325–7, figs 5 and 6b.

64. *Provenance unknown* (on the antiquity market, Amsterdam, 2000); L. *c.*75 mm.
Copper-alloy handle (L. 80 mm, the slotted socket broken) with inscribed grip (ΕΛΠΙΔΗ/ ΦΟΡΟΥ/ ΝΕΟΠΟΙΟΥ – 'of Elpidephoros, *neopoios* (temple official)') and finial in the form of a crouched mouse, its muzzle resting on a morsel that it holds in its forepaws, its long, lightly sinuous tail extended along the handle.
Künzl 2001, Abb. 5.

65. *Provenance unknown* (on the antiquity market (ex-Leo Mildenberg Collection), London, 2004); L. *c.*60 mm.
Copper-alloy handle (L. 74 mm, one side of the slotted socket broken) with inscribed grip, as No. 61.
Biers 2004, 71–2, No. 81. Christie's, London, Sale 7017 *A Peaceable Kingdom. The Leo Mildenberg Collection of Ancient Animals*, 26 & 27 October 2004, Lot 246.

66. *Monk Soham, Suffolk* (PAS SF-DFEAD7); probably Roman; L. 18 mm.
A miniature copper-alloy brooch in the form of a crouched mouse, its muzzle at the catch-plate, its tail forming a small loop above the hinge lugs.

67. *Roxby cum Risby, North Lincolnshire* (PAS NLM-A19B05); Roman; L. 20.3 mm. Wt. 5.3 g.
A miniature copper-alloy brooch in the form of a crouched mouse, its muzzle resting on the catch-plate (which gives the impression that it is nibbling a morsel held in its forepaws) and its haunches and broken tail above the hinge lugs. The eyes are probably inlaid with silver, while a sinuous strip of silver beaded wire on the rump was probably intended as the tip of the tail.
Worrell and Pearce 2011, 409–10, fig. 6.

68. *Scawby, North Lincolnshire* (PAS NLM-F3AA42); Roman; L. *c.*15 mm.
A copper-alloy vessel spout in the form of a bull's head (L. 36.9 mm), with a tiny mouse crouched on the beast's neck, behind the horns.

Gems and finger-rings

British Museum

69. *Provenance unknown* (BM1867,0507.63; Gem 2431); first–third cent. AD; 11 × 8 mm.

Sard gem engraved with a fruit-eating mouse, an ear of corn below.

70. *Provenance unknown* (BM1814,0704.1431; Gem 2468); first–third cent. AD; 9 × 10 mm.

Sard gem engraved with a cock standing on a *skyphos* holding a mouse in its beak, by its tail, the mouse clinging to the vessel's rim with its forepaws.

71. *Provenance unknown* (BM1814,0704.1432; Gem 2475); first–third cent. AD; 11 × 9 mm.

Sard gem engraved with a cock holding a mouse in its beak, by its tail; a butterfly above; facing a cornucopia, poppy-heads and an ear of corn.

72. *Provenance unknown* (BM1904,0204.505; Finger Ring 1152; Gem 2644); mid-second–mid-third cent. AD; 11 × 8 mm (gem).

Silver ring set with a sard gem, engraved with an oil amphora containing an olive tree on which perches an owl, a serpent entwined round the stem, an erect mouse on either side, a lizard below.

73. *Provenance unknown* (BM1814,0704.1460; Gem 2577); first–third cent. AD; 15 × 11 mm.

Amethyst gem engraved with a Combination – Silenus, crane, unicorn – with, in the field, a star, an ear of corn, a ?bell, a ?bunch of grapes, a ?mouse, and Greek lettering: ΔΗΠ.

74. *Provenance unknown* (BMOA.9830; Burns Gnostic Gem No. G354; Michel 2001, 572); first cent. AD; 17 × 15 mm.

Magical gem, scarab, of speckled green opaline silica, engraved on flat base with a lizard, lion and mouse.

75. *Snettisham, Norfolk* (BM1986,0401.198); second cent. AD; 10 × 8 mm.

Carnelian gem engraved with a schematic image of a crouched mouse holding a fruit, nut or morsel in its forepaws.

Johns 1997, 198.

76. *Snettisham, Norfolk* (BM1986,0401.196); second cent. AD; 8.5 × 7.5 mm.

Carnelian gem engraved with a schematic image of a crouched mouse holding a fruit, nut or morsel in its fore-paws.

Johns 1997, 196.

Other

77. *Corbridge, Northumberland* (Corbridge Site Museum); ?second cent. AD; 10 × 8 × 4 mm.

A flat oval intaglio of red jasper engraved with the image of a mouse emerging from a nautilus shell. The mouse is shown in stereotypical pose, crouched and holding a nut, fruit or other morsel of food in its forepaws.

Henig 1978, 235 and pl. xiii, no. 392.

78. *Harpenden, Hertfordshire* (PAS BH-58E8E6); first–second cent. AD; L. *c*.11 mm.

Hollow gold finger-ring set with a carnelian intaglio engraved with the image of a crouched mouse on an ear of corn.

79. *London* (LEK95 [341]<173>); third cent. AD; 10 × 14 × 3 mm.; from excavation at Lefevre Walk Estate, Bow, where a 65 m length of the Roman London to Colchester road was revealed, together with roadside strip buildings, burials and grave goods.

A keeled gold finger-ring set with a blue-coloured intaglio engraved with the image of a pair of confronted mice sharing a morsel of food.

Henig 2008, 234, 236, fig. 4.7.2, no. 48.

Miscellaneous

British Museum

80. *Provenance unknown* (BM1772,0320.672; *Vase* F521); 310–300 BC; L. 150 mm.

Black-figured pottery askos (?baby-feeder) in the form of a crouched mouse.

81. *Naukratis, Egypt* (BM1955,0920.155); c. 300 BC.

Rectangular stamp (control mark, W. 32 mm.) on pottery amphora handle, comprising a Greek inscription and the image of a mouse.

Acknowledgements

For information, suggestions and references kindly shared I am most grateful to Catherine Johns, Jenny Hall, Ernst Künzl, Andrew Birley, Rob Collins and Bryan Sitch.

Bibliography

Classical sources

Aristophanes: *Frogs. Assemblywomen. Wealth*, trans. J. Henderson, Loeb Classical Library, London/Cambridge, Mass. 2002.

Homerica: *Battle of Frogs and Mice*, in *Hesiod, the Homeric Hymns and Homerica*, The Online Medieval and Classical Library, http://omacl.org/Hesiod/frogmice.html

Horace: *Satires. Epistles. The Art of Poetry*, trans. H. Rushton Fairclough, Loeb Classical Library, London/ Cambridge, Mass. 1926.

Martial: *Epigrams*, trans. W. C. A. Ker, Loeb Classical Library, 2 vols., London/Cambridge, Mass. 1968.

Pliny: *Natural History*, trans. H. Rackham, W. H. S. Jones and D. E. Eichholz, Loeb Classical Library, 10 vols., London/Cambridge, Mass. 1938–83.

Varro: *On Agriculture*, trans. W. B. Hooper and H. B. Ash, Loeb Classical Library, London/Cambridge, Mass. 1935.

Modern authors

Babelon, E. and Blanchet, J.-A. (1895) *Catalogue des bronzes antiques de la Bibliothèque Nationale*. Paris, Leroux.

Babelon, J. (1928) *Choix de bronzes de la collection Caylus*. Les Trésors du Cabinet des Antiques, Paris and Brussels, Les Éditions G. van Oest.

Bailey, D. M. (1975) *A Catalogue of the Lamps in the British Museum. I, Greek, Hellenistic and Early Roman Pottery Lamps*, London. British Museum.

Bailey, D. M. (1980) *A Catalogue of the Lamps in the British Museum. II, Roman Lamps made in Italy*. London, British Museum.

Bailey, D. M. (1988) *A Catalogue of the Lamps in the British Museum. III, Roman Provincial Lamps*. London, British Museum.

Bailey, D. M. (1996) *A Catalogue of the Lamps in the British Museum. IV, Lamps of Metal and Stone, and Lampstands*. London, British Museum.

Barb, A. A. (1953) *Diva matrix*: a faked Gnostic intaglio in the possession of P.P. Rubens and the iconology of symbol. *Journal of the Warburg and Courtauld Institutes* 16.3/4, 193–238.

Bell, B. (1999) *Minimus: Starting out in Latin*, Joint Association of Classical Teachers. Cambridge, Cambridge University Press.

Bennett, D. and Timm, R. M. (forthcoming) Microfaunal remains from the East Granary, Roman Vindolanda. In A. Birley (2013) *The 2008 Vindolanda Excavation Report, the Granaries*. Bardon Mill, Chesterholm Museum.

Biers, J. C. (2004) *A Peaceable Kingdom: Animals in Ancient Art from the Leo Mildenberg Collection*. Mainz, Verlag Philipp von Zabern.

Dalton, O. M. (1901) *Catalogue of Early Christian Antiquities and Objects from the Christian East in the Department of British and Mediaeval Antiquities and Ethnography of the British Museum*. London, British Museum.

Dunbabin, K. M. D. (2003) *The Roman Banquet: Images of Conviviality*. Cambridge, Cambridge University Press.

Engels, D. (1999) *Classical Cats: the Rise and Fall of the Sacred Cat*. London and New York, Routledge.

Ferguson, J. (1970) *The Religions of the Roman Empire*. London, Thames and Hudson.

Fleischer, R. (1967) *Die Römischen Bronzen aus Österreich*. Mainz, Verlag Philipp von Zabern.

Garbsch, J. (1994) Römischer Alltag in Bayern: das Leben vor 2000 Jahren. In *125 Jahre Bayerische Handelsbank in München 1869–1994*. München, Bayerische Handelsbank.

Henig, M. (1978) *A Corpus of Roman Engraved Gemstones from British Sites*. BAR British Series 8, 2nd edition, Oxford.

Henig, M. (2008) Intaglios from Roman London. In J. Clark, J. Cotton, J. Hall, R. Sherris and H. Swain (eds) *Londinium and Beyond. Essays on Roman London and its Hinterland for Harvey Sheldon*, 226–38. York, CBA Research Report 156.

Izard, K. (1997) The animal bones. In T. Wilmott *Birdoswald. Excavations of a Roman fort on Hadrian's Wall and its successor settlements: 1987–92*, 363–70. London, English Heritage Archaeological Report 14.

Jackson, R. (1990) *Camerton: A Catalogue of Late Iron Age and Early Roman Metalwork*. London, British Museum.

Jackson, R. (1994) The mouse, the lion and 'the crooked one': two enigmatic Roman handle types. *Antiquaries Journal* 74, 325–32.

Johns, C. (1997) *The Snettisham Roman Jeweller's Hoard*. London, British Museum.

Kaufmann-Heinimann, A. (1994) *Die Römischen Bronzen der Schweiz, V: Neufunde und Nachträge*. Mainz, Verlag Philipp von Zabern.

Kaufmann-Heinimann, A. (1998) *Götter und Lararien aus Augusta Raurica. Herstellung, Fundzusammenhänge und sakrale Funktion figürlicher Bronzen in einer römischen Stadt*. Augst, Forschungen in Augst Band 26.

Kozloff, A. P. (1981) *Animals in Ancient Art from the Leo Mildenberg Collection*. Cleveland, Ohio, Cleveland Museum of Art.

Kozloff, A. P. (1986) *More Animals in Ancient Art from the Leo Mildenberg Collection.* Mainz, Verlag Philipp von von Zabern.

Künzl, E. (1982) Was soll die Maus auf dem chirurgischen Instrument? In D. Metzler, B. Otto and C. Müller-Wirth (eds) *Antidoron: Festschrift für Jürgen Thimme*, 111–16. Karlsruhe, Verlag C.F. Müller.

Künzl, E. (2001) Antike Werbegeschenke: Xenia aus Ephesos. In C. Cosma, D. Tamba and A. Rustoiu (eds) *Studia Archaeologica et Historica Nicolao Gudea Dicata,* 213–18. Zalău, Acta Musei Porolissensis Bibliotheca Musei Porolissensis IV.

Künzl, E. (2002a) *Medizinische Instrumente der Römischen Kaiserzeit im Römisch-Germanischen Zentralmuseum.* Mainz/ Bonn, RGZM/ Habelt.

Künzl, E. (2002b) *Medizin in der Antike: Aus einer Welt ohne Narkose und Aspirin.* Stuttgart, Thesis.

Lloyd-Morgan, G. (1997) Objects of copper-alloy and silver, in A. G. Marvell and H. S. Owen-John *Leucarum: Excavations at the Roman Auxiliary Fort at Loughor, West Glamorgan 1982–84 and 1987–88*, 234–73. London, *Britannia* Monograph 12.

McCarthy, M. R., Padley, T. G. and Henig, M. (1983) An amber knife-handle from Carlisle. *Britannia* 14, 267–9 and pl. xxxi, b.

Menzel, H. (1986) *Die Römischen Bronzen aus Deutschland III: Bonn.* Mainz, Verlag Philipp von Zabern.

RCHM (1962) *An Inventory of the Historical Monuments in the City of York, Volume I, Eburacum, Roman York.* London, HMSO.

Rémy, B. (2010) *Les médecins dans l'Occident romain.* Scripta Antiqua 27. Bordeaux, Editions Ausonius.

Shelton, K. J. (1981) *The Esquiline Treasure.* London, British Museum.

Tait, H. (1976) *Jewellery through 7000 Years.* London, British Museum.

Toynbee, J. M. C. (1973) *Animals in Roman Life and Art*, London. Thames and Hudson.

Walters, H. B. (1899) *Catalogue of Bronzes, Greek, Roman, and Etruscan, in the Department of Greek and Roman Antiquities, British Museum*, London, British Museum.

Worrell, S. and Pearce, J. (2011) Roman Britain in 2010. II. Finds reported under the Portable Antiquities Scheme. *Britannia* 42, 399–437.

Yolden, D. M. (1986) Small species – the yellow necked mouse, *Apodemus Flavicollis* in Roman Manchester. In S. Bryant, M. Morris and J. S. F. Walker *Roman Manchester, a Frontier Settlement*, 81–2. Manchester, Greater Manchester Archaeological Unit.

Younger, D. A. (1994) The small mammals from the forecourt granary and the southwest fort ditch. In P. Bidwell and S. Speak *Excavations at South Shields Roman Fort, Volume 1*, 266–8. Newcastle upon Tyne, Society of Antiquaries of Newcastle upon Tyne with Tyne and Wear Museums Monograph Series 4.

Zahlhaas, G. (1996) *Aus der Arche Noah: Tierbilder aus der Sammlung Mildenberg aus fünf Jahrtausenden*, Mainz, Verlag Philipp von Zabern

28

LINDSAY ALLASON-JONES: A BIBLIOGRAPHY

Emma Morris

Notes

Allason-Jones, L. (1979) Two unrecognized Roman surgical instruments. *Archaeologia Aeliana,* 5th Series 7, 239–241.

Allason-Jones, L. (1980) Two Roman Bronzes from County Durham. *Transactions of the Architectural and Archaeological Society of Durham and Northumberland,* Series 5, 47–49.

Allason-Jones, L. (1980) Review of *South Shields, Wallsend, Newcastle and Benwell in the Days of the Roman* by Frank Graham. *Council for British Archaeology Newsbulletin* (Group 3) series 2, 12, 2.

Allason-Jones, L. (1980) A Zoomorphic Spout from Halton Chesters. *Archaeologia Aeliana,* 5th Series 8, 153–154.

Allason-Jones, L. (1980) Antler Macehead from Newsham, Blyth. *Archaeologia Aeliana,* 5th Series 8, 154–155.

Allason-Jones, L. (1981) Two axe-hammers from Northumberland. *Northern Archaeology* II, Part I, 3–5.

Allason-Jones, L. (1981) Vanishing treasures, in *Council for British Archaeology Newsbulletin* (Group 3) series 2, XXV: 6–7.

Allason-Jones, L. and Shorer, P. H. T. (1981) An enamelled stud from West Wharmley. *Archaeologia Aeliana,* 5th Series 9, 347–348.

Allason-Jones, L. (1982) The Saxons are coming. *Muse*: 4.

Allason-Jones, L. and Gillam, J. P. (1982) Roman pottery from Hadrian's Wall Turret 27 A. *Archaeologia Aeliana,* 5th Series 10, 199–200.

Allason-Jones, L. (1984) A temple at Benwell. *Muse*: 5.

Allason-Jones, L. (1984) A first-century bronze torc from Caw Gap. *Archaeologia Aeliana,* 5th Series, 12, 227–228.

Allason-Jones, A. (1984) A lead shrine from Wallsend. *Britannia* 15, 231–232.

Allason-Jones, L. (1985) An eagle mount from Carlisle. *Trans. Cumberland and Westmorland Antiq. and Archaeol. Soc.* 85, 262–66.

Allason-Jones, L. (1986) A Romano-British trumpet brooch from Ushaw Moor. *Durham Archaeological Journal* 2, 41–42.

Allason-Jones, L. (1986) A Roman eagle mount from Carlisle. *Saalburg Jahrbuch,* 42, 68–69.

Allason-Jones, L. (1986) Two medieval mirror boxes. *Archaeologia Aeliana,* 5th Series 14, 179–180.

Henig, M. and Allason-Jones, L. (1986) The Sewingshields finger-ring. *Archaeologia Aeliana,* 5th Series 14, 181–182.

Allason-Jones, L. (1987) Jordanian Archaeology in the Museum of Antiquities. *Society of Antiquaries of Newcastle upon Tyne Newsbulletin* 2, August 1987, 2–3.

Allason-Jones, L. (1987) Metal detecting: a view from the museums. *NEMS News* 15, 8.

Allason-Jones, L. (1988) *Metal detecting: Guidelines prepared for the Museums North Archaeology Panel,* Newcastle upon Tyne, 2pp.

Allason-Jones, L. (1988) Hadrian's Wall goes to Poland, in *NEMS News* 20, 2.

Allason-Jones, L. and Page, H. (1988) New discoveries on Roman Brooches. *Archaeologia Aeliana,* 5th Series 16, 245–250.

Allason-Jones, L. (1989) Nielloed studs. *Arma* 1.1, 10-11.

Allason-Jones, L. (1989) Not to lose sight of our purpose. *NEMS News* 24, 8.

Allason-Jones, L. (1989) Haydon Spa. *Newsbulletin of the Society of Antiquaries of Newcastle upon Tyne* 7 (Dec. 1989), 2.

Allason-Jones, L. (1991) The Aemilia Finger-ring. *NEMS News* 30, 4.

Allason-Jones, L. (1991) The Aemilia Finger-ring.

Archaeology in Northumberland 1990–1, 13.

Allason-Jones, L. (1991) The Aemilia Finger-ring. *Review* (National Art Collections Fund) 87, 126–9.

Allason-Jones, L. (1991) The Aemilia Finger-ring. *Newsbulletin of Society of Antiquaries of Newcastle upon Tyne* X (June 1991): 3–4.

Allason-Jones, L. (1991) The Museum of Antiquities. *Museums Journal* (July 1991): 25.

Allason-Jones, L. (1991) Why Do Finds Research? *Finds Research Group 700–1700 Data Sheet* XIV, 2–3 (republished in *Datasheets 1–24: a consolidated reprint of Datasheets issued by the Finds Research Group between 1985 and 1998*, 1999)

Allason-Jones, L. (1992) Tiger, Tiger. *Arma*, 4.2, 14–7.

Allason-Jones, L. (1992) An intaglio from High Rochester. *Arma*, 4.2, 19–20.

Allason-Jones, L. (1993) Bronze Age axehammer from Felton, Northumberland. *Archaeologia Aeliana,* 5th Series 21, 266–267.

Allason-Jones, L. (1993) Roman objects from Sudan in the Museum of Fine Arts, Boston. *SARS Newsletter* 4 (June 1993), 2–3.

Allason-Jones, L. (1993) The case for BAPLA membership. *Museum Shop and Publishing News* (November 1993), 13–5.

Allason-Jones, L. (1994) A stone head from Walker. *Archaeologia Aeliana,* 5th Series 22, 263–265.

Allason-Jones, L. and Jones. D. M. (1994) Jet and other materials in Roman artefact studies. *Archaeologia Aeliana,* 5th Series 22, 265–272.

Allason-Jones, L. (1995) Trumpet brooch from Healey. *Archaeology in Northumberland 1994–1995*, 24.

Allason-Jones, L. (1995) Research into jet and other materials. *Instrumentum* 1 (June 1995), 12.

Allason-Jones, L. (1995) Bibliography: British contribution to *Instrumentum* 1 (June 1995), 2–11.

Allason-Jones, L., with C. O'Brien and G. Goodrick (1996) Using the World Wide Web: Museum of Antiquities. *Museum Practice* 2, 14–5.

Allason-Jones, L. (1997) Bow brooch from Thornbrough High Barns. *Archaeology in Northumberland 1996–1997*, 10.

Allason-Jones, L. (1998) The Birth of Mithras. *Archaeology in Northumberland 1997–8*: 25.

Allason-Jones, L., with G. Goodrick and C. O'Brien (1998) Using the World Wide Web: an update. *Museum Practice* 9 (3.3), 84–6.

Allason-Jones, L. (1998) Beads of jet and jet-like materials. *Newsletter of the Bead Study Trust* 31, Spring 1998, 6–8.

Allason-Jones, L. (1999) Gilding the black lily. *Roman Finds Group Newsletter* 18, 11–12.

Allason-Jones, L. (2000) A gold Fede-ring brooch from Whinfell Park, Cumbria. *Archaeologia Aeliana,* 5th Series 28, 237–240.

Allason-Jones L. (2002) 'Git in Romeins Brittannie. *In* Sas, K. and Thon, H. (eds) *Schone Schijn.* Limburg, Belgium: Bracelet. Tongeren: 40–42, 150, 151, 199–201.

Allason-Jones, L. (2003) Opinions. *The Archaeologist* 47 (Winter 2003), 30–1.

Allason-Jones, L. (2003) Roman coin hoard found at Long Horsley. *Archaeology in Northumberland 2002–3*, 14.

Allason-Jones, L. (2003) Postscript to 'A Roman coin hoard from Longhorsley' by Abdy, R. *Archaeologia Aeliana* 5th series, 32, 191.

Allason-Jones, L. (2003) Scraping the bottom. *Society of Antiquaries of Newcastle upon Tyne Newsbulletin* No. 35, December 2003, 10.

Allason-Jones, L. (2005) Flint arrowhead from Callaly. *Archaeology in Northumberland* 15 (2005), 49.

Allason-Jones, L. (2005) An unusual exhibition. *Archaeology in Northumberland* 15, (2005), 49.

Allason-Jones, L. (2010) A tale of four paterae. *Archaeologia Aeliana,* 5th Series, 39, 427–432.

Allason-Jones, L. (2011) *Jet, shale and other allied materials* Datasheet 2. Roman Finds Group. Stevenage.

Allason-Jones, L. (2012) Barbara Harbottle 1931–2012. In *Archaeologia Aeliana*, 5th Series, 41, 301–2.

Small finds reports

Allason-Jones, L. (1979) Small finds from the Agricolan Supply Base, Corbridge. *Archaeologia Aeliana,* 5th Series, 7, 61–8.

Allason-Jones, L. (1983) The reports on the silver, bronze, lead, iron, jet and shale, amber, pottery objects, bone objects, flint and stone. In Miket, R. (ed.). *The Roman Fort at South Shields: Excavation of the Defences, 1977–81*, Newcastle upon Tyne, 108–42.

Allason-Jones, L. (1984) The small objects. In Haigh, D. H. and Savage, M. J. D. Sewingshields, *Archaeologia Aeliana,* 5th Series 12, 74–99.

Allason-Jones, L., Bennett, J., and Welsby, D. A. (1984) The finds from Milecastle 54, Randylands. *Archaeologia Aeliana,* 5th Series 12, 228–235.

Allason-Jones, L. (1987) Metalwork. In Heslop, D. H. *The Excavation of an Iron Age Settlement at Thorpe Thewles, Cleveland, 1980–1982.* Cleveland County Archaeology: London: Council for British Archaeology

Research Report 65, 77–82.

Allason-Jones, L. (1988) Ear-ring of gold and garnet. In B. Cunliffe (ed.). *The Temple of Sulis Minerva at Bath* II *The Finds from the Sacred Spring*. Oxford, 21.

Allason-Jones, L. (1988) The inscriptions on Donyatt pottery. In Coleman-Smith, R. and Pearson, T. (eds). *Excavations in the Donyatt Potteries*. Phillimore, 381–86.

Allason-Jones, L. (1988) Objects of copper alloy, iron, and other materials. In Crow, J. An excavation of the North Curtain wall at Housesteads, 1984. *Archaeologia Aeliana*, 5th Series, 16, 89–96.

Allason-Jones, L. (1989) Roman small objects. In Holbrook, N. and Fox, A. Excavations in the Legionary Fortress at Bartholomew Street East, Exeter, 1959. *Proc. Devon Archaeological Soc.* 45, 45–8.

Allason-Jones, L. (1989) Iron nails. In Bishop, M. C. and Dore, J. N. *Corbridge: excavations of the Roman fort and town, 1947–80.* London: Historic Buildings and Monuments Commission for England Monograph 3, D1.

Allason-Jones, L. (1991) The objects of bone, stone and metal. In Haselgrove, C. C., Lowther, P. C. and Turnbull, P. (eds.) Stanwick, North Yorks, Part 3. *Archaeol. Journ.* 147, 37–90 (M1/01).

Allason-Jones, L. with contribution by Ling, R. (1991) Objects of copper alloy. In Holbrook, N. and Bidwell, P. T. *Roman Finds from Exeter.* Exeter: Exeter City Council and the University of Exeter, 242–263.

Allason-Jones, L. with contribution by Greep, S. (1991) Objects of bone and antler. In Holbrook, N. and Bidwell, P. T. *Roman Finds from Exeter.* Exeter: Exeter City Council and the University of Exeter, 266–271.

Allason-Jones, L. (1991) Objects of amber, jet and shale. In Holbrook, N. and Bidwell, P. T. *Roman Finds from Exeter.* Exeter: Exeter City Council and the University of Exeter, 271–274.

Allason-Jones, L. (1991) Small finds of glass and metal. In Smith, C. Excavations at Dod Law West hillfort, Northumberland. *Northern Archaeology* 9 (1988–9), 23–5.

Allason-Jones, L. (1991) Small objects from the western end of mound B. In Welsby, D. A. and Daniels, C. M. *Soba: archaeological research at a medieval capital on the Blue Nile.* London: British Institute in Eastern Africa, 126–162.

Allason-Jones, L. (1991) Small objects from the trial trenches. In Welsby, D. A. and Daniels, C. M. *Soba: archaeological research at a medieval capital on the Blue Nile.* London: British Institute in Eastern Africa, 163–165.

Welsby, D. A. and Allason-Jones, L. (1991) The timber chest. In Welsby, D. A. and Daniels, C. M. *Soba: archaeological research at a medieval capital on the Blue Nile.* London: British Institute in Eastern Africa, 298–300.

Allason-Jones, L. (1993) The small finds. In Gillam, J.P., Jobey, I. M., and Welsby, D. A. (eds). The Roman Bathhouse at Bewcastle, Cumbria. *Archaeol. & Architect. Soc. Cumberland and Westmorland Research Series* No.7, Kendal: 28-31.

Allason-Jones, L. (1993) Small finds. In Casey, P. J., Davies, J. L. and Evans, J. *Excavations at Segontium (Caernarfon) Roman fort, 1975–1979.* York: Council for British Archaeology Research Report 90, 165–210.

Allason-Jones, L. (1995) The Finds. In Haselgrove, C. C. and Lowther, P. (eds). An Iron Age farmsteads at Rock Castle, Gilling West, North Yorkshire. *Durham Archaeol. Journ.* 10, 25 (13–42).

Allason-Jones, L. (1995) The trumpet brooch. In Johnstone, D. A. (ed.). Carronbridge, Dumfries and Galloway: the excavation of Bronze Age cremations, Iron Age settlements and a Roman camp. *Proc. Soc. Antiquaries of Scotland*, 124 (1994), 266–7 (233–91).

Allason-Jones, L. (1996) Roman military and domestic artefacts from Great Chesters. *Archaeologia Aeliana,* 5th Series 24, 187–214.

Allason-Jones, L. (1997) Small finds. In Potter, T. W. and King, A. C. *Excavations at the Mola di Monte Gelato: a Roman and medieval settlement in south Etruria.* London: British School at Rome, 241–256.

Summerfield, J. with contributions by Allason-Jones, L., Bayley, J., Coulston, J. C. N., Davies, J., Edwards, G., Henig, M., Lloyd-Morgan, G., Mould, Q., Price, J., Cottam, S., Riddler, I. and Tomlin, R. S. O. (1997) The small finds. In Wilmott, T. *Birdoswald: Excavations of a Roman Fort on Hadrian's Wall and its successor settlements: 1987–1992.* London: English Heritage Archaeological Report 14, 269–362.

Allason-Jones, L. (1998) The Small objects. In Welsby, D. A. (ed.). *Soba II: Renewed excavations within the metropolis of the Kingdom of Alwa in Central Sudan,* Memoirs of the British Institute in East Africa, No. 15. London, 60–81.

Allason-Jones, L. with a contribution by Price, J. (1999) A catalogue of small finds. In Dore, J. N. and Wilkes, J. J. *Excavations Directed by J D Leach and J J Wilkes on the site of a Roman fortress at Carpow, Perthshire, 1964–7.* Proceedings of the Society of Antiquaries of Scotland 129, 552–561.

Allason-Jones, L. (1999) The jet object. In Halkon, P. and Millett, M. (eds). *Rural Settlement and Industry: studies in the Iron Age and Roman archaeology of lowland East Yorkshire.* Leeds: Yorkshire Archaeological Society,

Roman Antiquities Section and East Riding Archaeological Society, 70.

Allason-Jones, L. (2001) Small finds. In McKay, R. An Investigation of Romano-British Enclosures at Swaythorpe Farm, Kilham. *East Riding Archaeologist* 10, 36–37.

Allason-Jones, L. (2002) 15.2.4 Enamelled flask from Catterick Bypass (Site 433). In Wilson, P. R. *Cataractonium: Roman Catterick and its Hinterland. Excavations and Research, 1958–1997 Part II*. York: Council for British Archaeology Research Report 128, 78–80, fig. 268, pl. 96.

Allason-Jones, L. (2002) The small finds. In Snape, M. and Bidwell, P. (eds). Excavations at Castle Garth, Newcastle-upon-Tyne, 1976–92 and 1995–6: the Excavation of the Roman Fort. *Archaeologia Aeliana*, 5th Series 31.1, 211–233.

Allason-Jones, L. (2002) Copper Alloy. In Cambridge, E., Gates, T., and Williams, A. Berwick and beyond: medieval religious establishments on the north western margin of Berwick-upon-Tweed – problems of identity and context. *Archaeologia Aeliana*, 5th Series, 29: 33–94 (57).

Allason-Jones, L. (2004) The Gold Objects. In Cool, H.EM. *The Roman Cemetery at Brougham, Cumbria, Excavations 1966–7. Britannia* Monograph Series No 21: 101, 122, 188, 198, 204, 214, 263, 473.

Allason-Jones, L. (2004) Appendix 4: A possible 'Hercules' club' earring from Brougham. In Cool, H. E. M. The *Roman Cemetery at Brougham, Cumbria: excavations 1966–67.* London: *Britannia* Monograph Series 21, 473.

Allason-Jones, L. (2006) The small finds. In Millett, M. (ed.). *Shiptonthorpe, East Yorkshire: archaeological studies of a Romano-British roadside settlement.* Leeds: Yorkshire Archaeological Society, Roman Antiquities Section and East Riding Archaeological Society, 220–237, 244.

Allason-Jones, L. (2007) The small finds. in Hanson, W. S. *Elginhaugh: A Flavian fort and its annexe.* London: *Britannia* Monograph 23, 396–443.

Allason-Jones, L. (2008) Appendix A: The Small Finds. In Grogan, E. (ed.). *The Rath of the Synods, Tara, Co. Meath: excavations by Seán P. Ó Ríordáin*. Wordwell and UCD School of Archaeology. Dublin: 107–112.

Allason-Jones, L. (2008) Part 1: The metalwork (excluding brooches and enamelled objects. In Cool, H. E. M. and Mason, D. J. P. (eds). *Roman Piercebridge: excavations by D. W. Harding and Peter Scott 1969–1981*. Durham: Architectural and Archaeological Society of Durham and Northumberland Research Report 7, D11.1–D11.95

Allason-Jones, L. and Large, S. (2008) Part V: the bone objects. In Cool, H. E. M. and Mason, D. J. P. (eds). *Roman Piercebridge: excavations by D. W. Harding and Peter Scott 1969–1981.* Durham: Architectural and Archaeological Society of Durham and Northumberland Research Report 7, D11.137–D11.150.

Allason-Jones, L. (2008) Jet and lignite objects from Grave 5090. In Booth, P., Bingham, A. M. and Lawrence, S. *The Roman Roadside Settlement at Westhawk Farm, Ashford, Kent: excavations 1998–9.* Oxford: Oxford Archaeology, 171–174.

Allason-Jones, L. (2009) Small Finds Report. In Fitts, L. Lease Rigg Roman Fort: the excavations of 1976–80. In Frere, S. S. and Fitts, R. L. (eds). *Excavations at Bowes and Lease Rigg Roman Forts*. Yorkshire Archaeol. Rep. 6. Yorkshire Archaeological Society, Leeds: 273–4.

Allason-Jones, L. with contributions by Henig, M., Griffiths, W. B. and Mould, Q. (2009) The small Finds. In Rushworth, A. *Housesteads Roman Fort: the grandest station: excavation and survey at Housesteads, 1954–95 by Charles Daniels, John Gillam, James Crow and others.* Swindon: English Heritage, 430–487.

Allason-Jones, L. (2010) The small finds. In Dore, J. N. *Haltonchesters: Excavations directed by J. P. Gillam at the Roman Fort, 1960–61.* Oxford: Oxbow Books, 17.

Allason-Jones, L. (2013) The Small Finds. In Wilks, E. M. and Griffiths, F. M., Cadbury Castle, Devon, Reconsidered. *Archaeological Journal* 169 (2012), 254–65 (236–80).

Allason-Jones, L. (forthcoming) Broomholm finds report for excavation report edited A. Rushworth

Allason-Jones, L. (forthcoming) 'Small Finds' in Wallsend excavation report by Daniels, C. M., et al. EH Monograph

Allason-Jones, L. (forthcoming) 'Small Finds' in Camelon excavation report by V. Maxfield, Society of Antiquaries of Scotland Monograph

Allason-Jones, L. (forthcoming) 'Small Finds' in *Excavations in the Aisne Valley* by Haselgrove, C. C., and Lowther, P.

Allason-Jones, L. (forthcoming) 'Small Finds' in Stanwick excavation report by Haselgrove, C. C.

Allason-Jones, L. (forthcoming) 'Jet and shale' in *Archaeotechnology Review* HBMC Monograph

Allason-Jones, L. (forthcoming) Copper Alloy Objects from Castle Terrace, Berwick. R. Charlton

Allason-Jones, L. (forthcoming) Small finds from Newton Bewley, Hartlepool

Allason-Jones, L. (forthcoming) Small finds report on EBC

Allason-Jones, L. (forthcoming) Jet/Shale Objects from Whitby UWWTD Scheme

Journal articles

Allason-Jones, L. (1980) Accessions to the Museum of Antiquities, Newcastle upon Tyne. *Northumbria* 20, 28–9.

Allason-Jones, L. (1984) Were Roman mosaics made at Piercebridge? *Mosaic*: 1–2.

Allason-Jones, L. (1984) Roman ear-rings. *Current Archaeology* 94, 21–2.

Allason-Jones, L. and Osler, A. (1986) The Gosforth (Tyne and Wear) boat [early 20th century rowing boat]. *Northern Archaeology* 7.2, 17–29.

Allason-Jones, L., with C. O'Brien and G. Goodrick (1997) Archaeology, museums and the World Wide Web. *Journal of European Archaeology*, 3.2, Autumn 1995, 33–42.

Allason-Jones, L. (1998) Visions and dreams in Roman Britain. *Archaeologia Aeliana,* 5th Series 25, 21–25.

Allason-Jones, L. (1999) Health care in the Roman North. *Britannia* 30, 133–146.

Allason-Jones, L. (2001) Identification of 'jet' artefacts by Reflected Light Microscopy. *European Journal of Archaeology* 4.2, 233–251.

Masser, P., Allason-Jones, L., Bateson, D., Evans, J. and Willis, S. (2002) Recent work at Drumquhassle Roman Fort, Stirlingshire. *Scottish Archaeological Journal* 24.2, 147–168.

Allason-Jones, L. (2009) The Museum of Antiquities: a retrospective. *Archaeologia Aeliana,* 5th Series 38, 1–21.

Allason-Jones, L. (2009) University museums and outreach: the Newcastle upon Tyne case study. *University Museums and Collections Journal* 2/2009, 27–33.

Allason-Jones, L. and McIntosh, F. (2011) The Wall, a plan and the ancient monuments acts. *Archaeologia Aeliana,* 5th Series 40, 267–276.

Contributions to edited volumes

Allason-Jones, L. (1985) Bell shaped studs? In Bishop, M. C. (ed.). *The Production and Distribution of Roman Military Equipment: Proceedings of the second Roman military equipment research seminar.* Oxford: British Archaeological Report International Series 275, 95–108.

Allason-Jones, L. (1988) "Small finds" from turrets on Hadrian's Wall. In Coulston, J. C. (ed.). *Roman Equipment and the Identity of Roman Soldiers. Proceedings of the Fourth Roman Military Equipment Conference.* Oxford: British Archaeological Report International Series 394, 197–233.

Allason-Jones, L. (1989) Introductory remarks on native and Roman trade in the north of Britain. In van Driel-Murray, C. (ed.). *Roman Military Equipment: the Sources of Evidence. Proceedings of the Fifth Roman Military Equipment Conference.* Oxford: British Archaeological Report International Series 476, 13–24.

Allason-Jones, L. (1991) Roman and Native reaction in Northumberland. In Maxfield, V. A. and Dobson, M. J. (eds). *Roman Frontier Studies: Proceedings of the XVth. International Congress of Roman Frontier Studies 1989.* Exeter: University of Exeter Press 1–5.

Allason-Jones, L. (1992) "Sexing" small finds. In Rush, P. (ed.). *Theoretical Roman Archaeology: Second Conference Proceedings.* Aldershot: Avebury, 22–32.

Allason-Jones, L. (1993) Health care in the Roman North. In Gardner-Medwin, D., Hargreaves, A., and Lazenby, E. (eds.). *Medicine in Northumberland: Essays in the History of Medicine*. The Pybus Society, Newcastle upon Tyne, 24–39.

Allason-Jones, L. (1996) The Actress and the Bishop: Evidence for working women in Roman Britain. In Devonshire, A. and Wood, B. (eds.) *Women in Industry and Technology from Prehistory to the Present Day.* Museum of London, London, 67–75.

Allason-Jones, L. (1996) Coventina's Well. In Billington, S. and Green, M. (eds.). *The Concept of the Goddess*. Routledge, London (reprinted in paperback in 1999), 107–19.

Allason-Jones, L. and Dungworth, D. B. (1997). Metalworking on Hadrian's Wall. In Groenman-van Waateringe, W., Van Beek, B. L., Willems, W. J. H. and Wynia, S. L. (eds). *Roman Frontier Studies 1995. Proceedings of the XVIth International Congress of Roman Frontier Studies.* Oxford: Oxbow Monograph 91, 317–21.

Allason-Jones, L. (1998) The women of Roman Maryport. In Wilson, R. J. A. (ed.). *Roman Maryport and its Setting: essays in memory of Michael G. Jarrett.* Cumberland and Westmorland Antiquarian and Archaeological Society Extra Series XXVIII, Maryport, 105–111.

Allason-Jones, L. (1998) Preface. In Starkey, J. C. M. *Myths and Mirrors: A Report on Ethnographical Collections in the North East of England.* For NEMS, Newcastle upon Tyne, 1.

Allason-Jones L. (1999) What is a military assemblage? In Oldenstein, J. and Gupte, O. (eds). *Spätrömische Militärausrüstung: Proceedings of the Eleventh International Roman Military Equipment Conference, Mainz*. Chirnside: Armatura Press, 1–5.

Allason-Jones L. (1999) Women and the Roman army in Britain. In Goldsworthy, A. and Haynes, I. (eds). *The Roman Army as a Community.* Portsmouth, Rhode Island: *Journal of Roman Archaeology* Supplementary Series 34, 41–53.

Allason-Jones, L. (2001) Material culture and identity. In James, S. and Millett, M. (eds). *Britons and Romans: Advancing an Archaeological Agenda*. York: Council for British Archaeology Research Report 125, 19–25.

Allason-Jones L. (2002) The material culture of Hadrian's Wall. In Freeman, P., Bennett, J., Fierna, Z.T. and Hoffman, B. (eds). *Limes XVIII: proceedings of the XVIIIth International Congress of Roman Frontier Studies held in Amman, Jordan.* Oxford: British Archaeological Report International Series 1084, 821–824.

Allason-Jones, L. (2002) The jet industry and allied trades in Roman Britain. In Wilson, P. and Price, J. (eds). *Aspects of Industry in Roman Yorkshire and the North.* Oxford: Oxbow Books, 125–132.

Allason-Jones, L, (2002) Review of Roman small finds research. In Brooks, C., Daniels, R. and Harding, A. (eds). *Past, Present and Future: the archaeology of Northern England.* Durham: Architectural and Archaeological Society of Durham and Northumberland Research Report 5, 113–119.

Allason-Jones, L. (2004) Mithras on Hadrian's Wall. In Martins, M. and de Boc, G. (eds). *Roman Mithraism: the Evidence of the Small Finds,* Brussels: *Papers of the international conference/ Bijdragen van het internationaal congres, Tienen 7–8 November 2001.* Brussels: Archeologie in Vlaanderen Monografie 4, 183–189.

Allason-Jones, L. and Croom, A. (2004) The family in Roman Britain. In Todd, M. (ed.). *A Companion to Roman Britain.* Oxford: Blackwell, 273–287.

Allason-Jones, L. (2005) Coals to Newcastle. In Crummy, N. (ed.). *Image, Craft and the Classical World: essays in honour of Donald Bailey and Catherine Johns.* Montagnac: M. Mergoil, 181–186.

Allason-Jones, L. (2005) Germs and the Roman army in Britain. In Zsolt V. (ed.). *Limes XIX: Proceedings of the XIXth International Congress of Roman Frontier Studies. Pécs,* 309– 313.

Allason-Jones, L. (2005) Jet and shale objects. In Steiner, M. *Approaches to Archaeological Illustration: a handbook.* York: Council for British Archaeology, 33–38.

Allason-Jones, L. (2006) Catalogue entries. In Hartley, E., Hawkes, J., Henig, M. and Mee, F. (eds). *Constantine the Great: York's Roman Emperor.* York Museums Trust/Lund Humphries. London: nos. 62–8, 70–1, 133, 158.

Allason-Jones, L. (2006) Ancient Words. In Chettle, S. (ed.). *Writing on the Wall.* Arts UK. Newcastle upon Tyne: 12–15.

Allason-Jones, L. (2006) Cultural Foundations: The University Museums. In McCord, N. (ed.). *Newcastle University: Past, Present and Future*. London, 23–6.

Allason-Jones, L. (2008) Finding the significance of finds. In Bidwell, P. *Understanding Hadrian's Wall.* South Shields: Arbeia Society, 41–47.

Allason-Jones, L. (2009) Some problems of the Roman Iron Age in Northern Britain. In Hanson, W. (ed.). *The Army and Frontiers of Rome: papers offered to David J. Breeze on the occasion of his sixty-fifth birthday and his retirement from Historic Scotland.* Portsmouth, Rhode Island: *Journal of Roman Archaeology* Supplementary Series 74, 217–244.

Allason-Jones, L. (2010) Personal appearance. In Allason-Jones, L. and Collins, R. (eds). *Finds from the Frontier.* York: Council for British Archaeology Research Report 162, 78–85.

Allason-Jones, L. (2011) Priests and Priestesses in Roman Britain. In Richardson, J. H., and Santangelo, F. (eds). *Priests and State in the Roman World.* Stuttgart, 429–43.

Allason-Jones, L. (2012) Women in Roman Britain. In Dillon, S., and James, S. L. (eds). *Companion for Women in the Ancient World.* Wiley-Blackwell, 467–477.

Allason-Jones, L. (2012) She said 'emic'. In Duggan, M., McIntosh, F., and Rohl., D. K. (eds). *TRAC 2011: Proceedings of the Twenty First Annual Theoretical Roman Archaeology Conference*. Oxford.

Allason-Jones, L. (2012) Rudge Cup. In Breeze, D. (ed.). *The First Souvenirs: Enamelled Vessels from Hadrian's Wall.* Cumberland and Westmorland Antiquarian and Archaeological Society Monograph. Kendal, 23–36.

Allason-Jones, L. (2012) Hildburgh Fragment. In Breeze, D. (ed.). *The First Souvenirs: Enamelled Vessels from Hadrian's Wall.* Cumberland and Westmorland Antiquarian and Archaeological Society Monograph. Kendal, 61–64.

Allason-Jones, L. (2013) Housesteads *Vicus*: A case study in material culture and Roman life. In Collins, R. and Symonds, M. (eds). *Breaking down Boundaries: Hadrian's Wall in the 21st century.* Portsmouth, Rhode Island: *Journal of Roman Archaeology* Supplementary Series 93, 71–84.

Allason-Jones, L. with J. Harding, R. Johnston, and B. Vyner (2013) Excavation of inner ditch. In Harding, J., (ed.). *Cult, Religion and Pilgrimage: an archaeological investigation at the Neolithic and Bronze Age monument complex of Thornborough, North Yorkshire.* CBA Research Report 174. York: 101–110.

Allason-Jones, L. (2013) Hadrian's Wall as World Heritage: The Museums. In Stone, P., and Brough, D. (eds). *Managing, using and Interpreting Hadrian's Wall as World Heritage*. Springer Briefs in Archaeology. New York, 89–100.

Allason-Jones, L. (2013) Missing people, missing brooches. In Grabher, G. and Schierl, T. (eds). *Relations Abroad. Brooches and other elements of dress as sources for reconstructing interregional movement and group boundaries from the Punic Wars to the decline of the Western Roman Empire. Proceedings of the International Conference from 27th–29th April 2011 in Innsbruck*. IKARUS Band 8. Innsbruck University.

Allason-Jones, L. (forthcoming) Woman, the military and *patria potestas* in Roman Britain. In Bidwell, P. (ed.). *Limes XXI*

Allason-Jones, L. (forthcoming) Zoomorphic brooches: decoration or ideology? In Mazel, S-R. and Stiebel, G. (eds). *Fashion and Ideology*. Chicago University Press.

Allason-Jones, L. (forthcoming) Roman artefacts in Barbaricum north of Hadrian's Wall: The Devil's Causeway in *Archäologie zwiche Römern und Barbaren*

Allason-Jones, L. (forthcoming) Roman military culture, in *The Oxford Handbook of Roman Britain* edited by Louise Revell, Martin Millett and Alison Moore

Books and monographs

Miket, R. and Allason-Jones (1983) *The Roman Fort at South Shields: excavation of the defences 1977–1981*. Newcastle upon Tyne: Tyne and Wear Museums.

Allason-Jones, L. and Miket, R. (1984) *The Catalogue of Small Finds from South Shields Roman Fort*. Newcastle upon Tyne: Society of Antiquaries of Newcastle upon Tyne.

Allason-Jones, L. and Mckay, B. (1985) *Coventina's Well: a shrine on Hadrian's Wall*. Hexham: Trustees of the Clayton Collection, Chesters Museum.

Allason-Jones, L. (1988) *Wał Hadriana* (in Polish, translated by Katarzyna Czarnecka), State Archaeological Museum, Warsaw, 19pp.

Allason-Jones, L. (1988) Commissioning editor of *Recollections* by Maureen Almond and Glyn Goodrick. Flambard Press. Newcastle upon Tyne.

Allason-Jones, L. (1988) Co-ordinating editor of *Prehistory – Who Cares?* By Hannah Lynch. Rennaissance North East. Newcastle upon Tyne.

Allason-Jones, L. (1989) *A Guide to the Inscriptions and Sculptured Stones in the Museum of Antiquities, Museum of Antiquities of the University and Society of Antiquaries of Newcastle upon Tyne*. Newcastle upon Tyne: Department of Archaeology, University of Newcastle upon Tyne.

Allason-Jones, L. and Bishop, M. C. (1988) *Excavations at Roman Corbridge: the hoard*. London: Historic Buildings and Monuments Commission for England.

Allason-Jones, L. (1989) *A Guide to the Inscriptions and Sculptured Stones in the Museum of Antiquities, Museum of Antiquities of the University and Society of Antiquaries of Newcastle upon Tyne*. Newcastle upon Tyne: Department of Archaeology, University of Newcastle upon Tyne.

Allason-Jones, L. (1989) *Ear-rings in Roman Britain*. Oxford: British Archaeological Report 201.

Allason-Jones, L. (1989) *Women in Roman Britain*. London: British Museum.

Allason-Jones, L. (1990) *A Guide to the Inscriptions and Sculptured Stones in the Museum of Antiquities, Museum of Antiquities of the University and Society of Antiquaries of Newcastle upon Tyne*, Newcastle upon Tyne: Department of Archaeology, University of Newcastle upon Tyne.

Allason-Jones, L. (1996) *Roman Jet in the Yorkshire Museum*. York: Yorkshire Museums.

Welsby, D. A. and Allason-Jones, L. (1998) *Soba II: renewed excavations within the metropolis of the Kingdom of Alwa in Central Sudan*, 298–300. London: British Museum.

Allason-Jones, L. (2000) *Roman Woman: everyday life in Hadrian's Britain*. London: Michael O'Mara.

Tolan-Smith, C. with contributions by Allason-Jones. L., Campbell, E., Cook, G., Gidney, L. and Young, C. (2001) *The Caves of Mid Argyll: an archaeology of human use*. Society of Antiquaries of Scotland Monograph Series 20.

Allason-Jones, L. (2005) *Women in Roman Britain, 2nd edition*. York: Council for British Archaeology.

Allason-Jones, L. (2008) *Daily Life in Roman Britain*. London: Greenwood Press.

Collins, R. and Allason-Jones, L. (eds). (2010) *Finds from the Frontier: material culture in the 4th–5th centuries*. York: Council for British Archaeology Research Report 162.

Allason-Jones, L. (ed.). (2011) *Artefacts in Roman Britain: their purpose and use*. Cambridge: Cambridge University Press.

Plate 1. Shoe of a small infant with 'fishnet' uppers and complete tread sole with iron hobnails. Found in the period 3 praetorium. Photo: Elizabeth Greene and the Vindolanda Trust.

Plate 2. A child's 'Fell Boot', the standard military boot worn by children and adults. Found in the period 4 barrack block. Photo: Elizabeth Greene and the Vindolanda Trust.

Plate 3. An infant's shoe with delicate laces holding the shoe to the foot from the period 4 barrack building. Photo: Elizabeth Greene and the Vindolanda Trust.

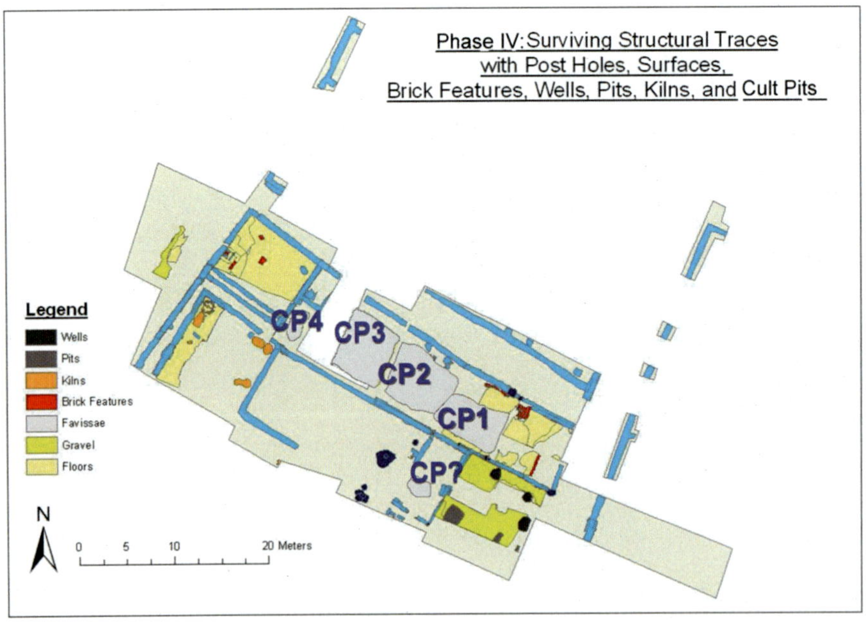

Plate 4: Plan of Phase IV of the site. Room B6 which once housed the altars, lies to the west of the passageway containing cult pits. The brick and clay bases constructed to hold the altars are marked. The southern wall of the mithraeum was discovered north of this. Plan: Stephen Bell/Apulum Project.

Plate 5: Doll's head from the Liber Pater Sanctuary, (66 mm). Photo: Alfred Schäfer/Mariana Egri/Apulum Project.

Plate 6: Bead from Houseseteads (Photo by Nicky Westgate, courtesy of English Heritage).

Plate 7: A red jasper intaglio (18 mm by 13 mm) from Corbridge depicting a satyr, or perhaps Bacchus, contemplating a theatre mask (reproduced by permission of English Heritage).

Plate 8: The combination of Silenus head with elephant mask (red jasper, 13.5 mm by 10 mm) from Corbridge (reproduced by permission of English Heritage).

Plate 9: Dark blue mould-blown ribbed bowl from Blackfriars Street, Carlisle. Photo: Tullie House Museum and Art Gallery Trust, Carlisle.

Plate 10: Pale bluish green ovoid beaker and plaster cast showing part of inscription in Greek letters from Binchester. Photo: J Veitch, Department of Archaeology, Durham University.

Plate 11: Dark blue African head vessel without provenance, thought to be from South Shields or Pompeii. Photo: Society of Antiquaries of Newcastle upon Tyne/Great North Museum.

Plate 12: intact decorated shale bangle from Newstead. © NMS

Plate 13: selection of black stone finds from Camelon. © National Museums Scotland

Plate 14: imported Roman black stone bangles from Traprain Law. © National Museums Scotland.

Plate 15: imported Roman black stone ?handle from Traprain Law. © National Museums Scotland.

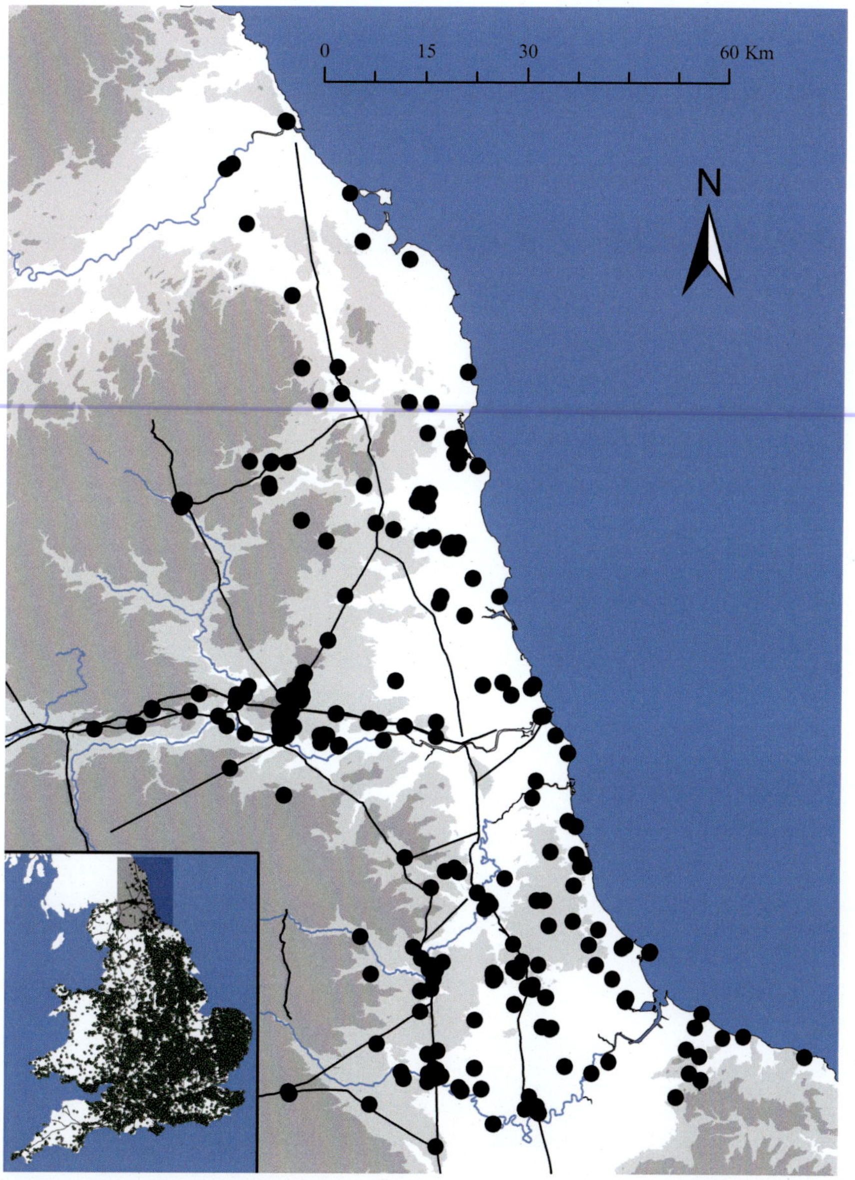

Plate 16: The distribution of Roman objects reported to the PAS from the North East, relative to the 200 m and 400 m contours and the Roman road network. The inset shows the distribution of PAS-recorded Roman objects across England and Wales.

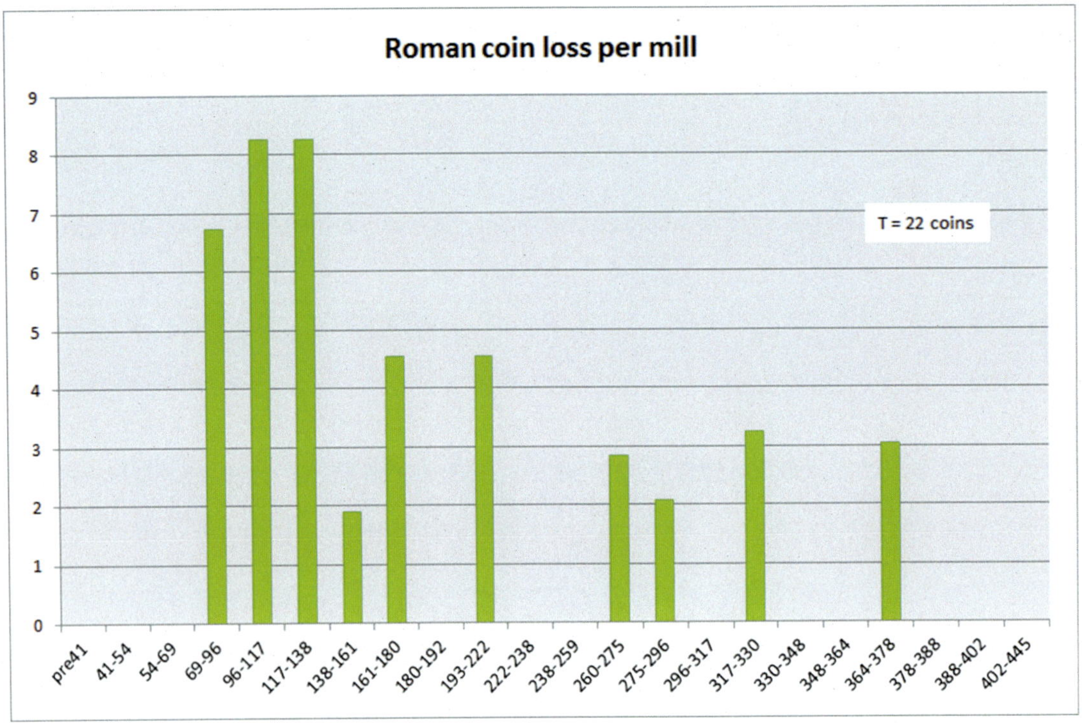

Plate 17: Coin loss analysis of coins from Great Whittington.

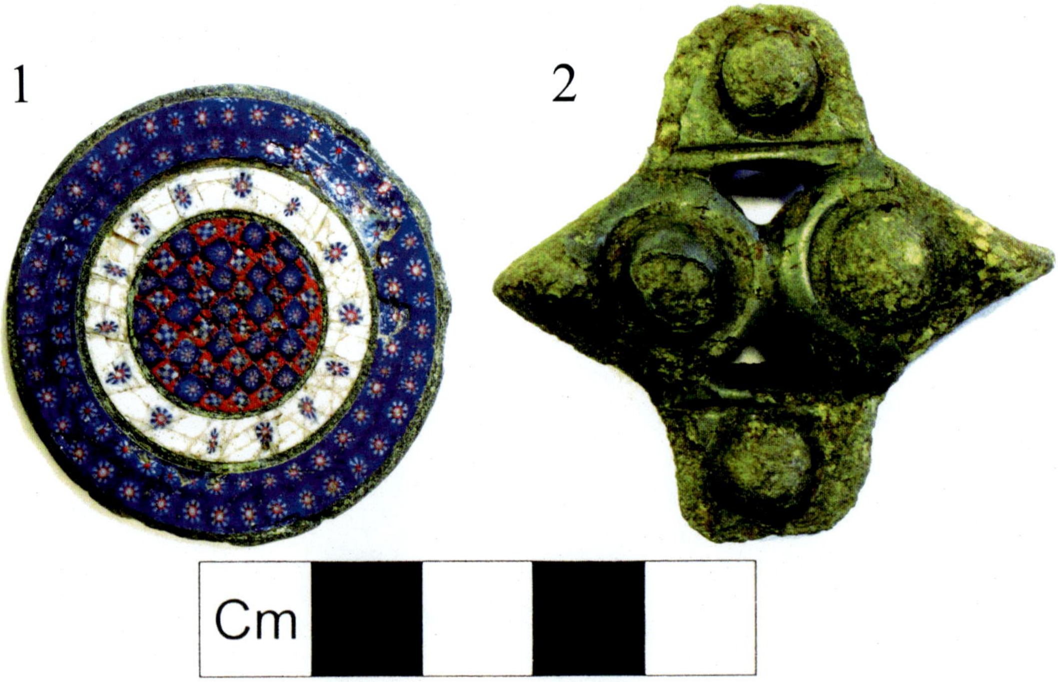

Plate 18: The harness mounts from 1. Glanton parish (NCL-A38DF3) and 2. Whittingham parish (NCL-74DE87).

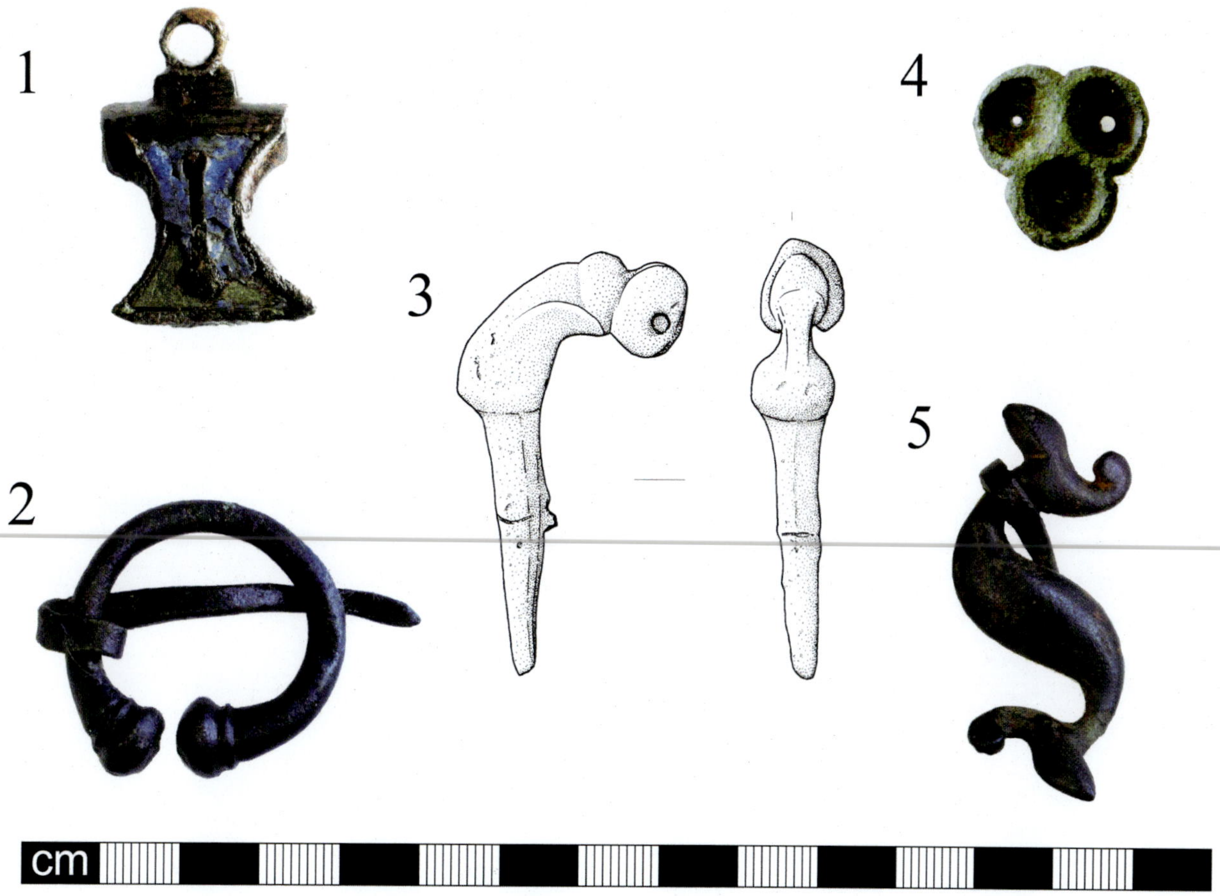

Plate 19: A selection of brooches found around Great Whittington; 1. NCL-1B2CB5, enamelled T-shaped; 2. NCL-BBB6E2, Fowler A3 penannular; 3. NCL-7FD5A4, trumpet-variant; 4. NCL-34AD01, trefoil-cup; 5. NCL-2B2544, dragonesque.

Plate 20: Transcription of the cropmarks of the camps at Moss Side in Cumbria by English Heritage, showing the lines of pits. © English Heritage. NMR.

Plate 21: The current display of the Clayton Collection at Chesters Roman fort.

Plate 22: The fragmentary Etruscan mirror dating to the end of the fourth century BC, donated to the Society of Antiquaries of Newcastle upon Tyne in 1891.

Plate 23: The detail of the mirror, showing Kassandra grasping the column and the capitol atop the column.

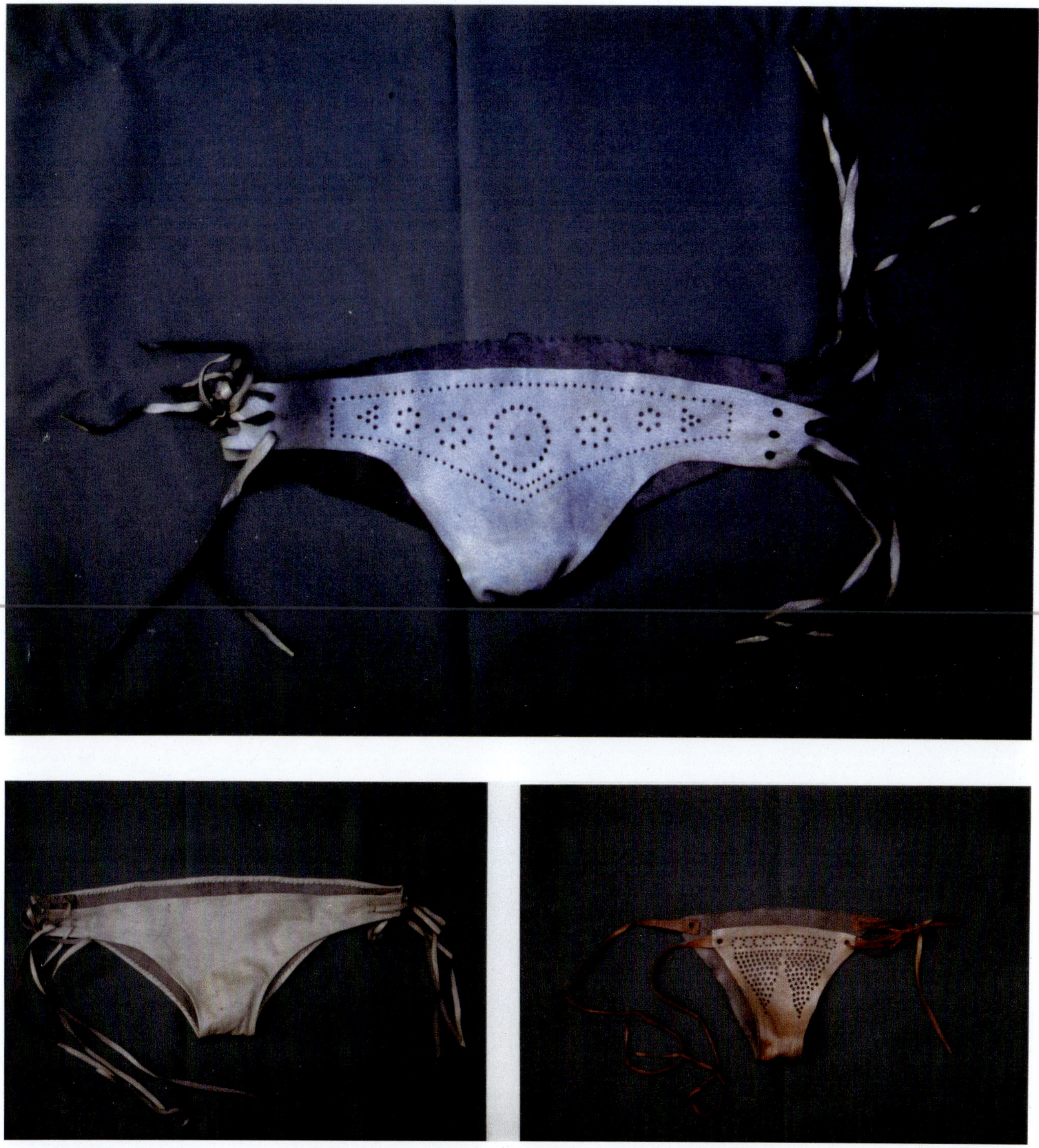

Plate 24: Reconstructions by Olaf Goubitz for the Drents Museum Assen.

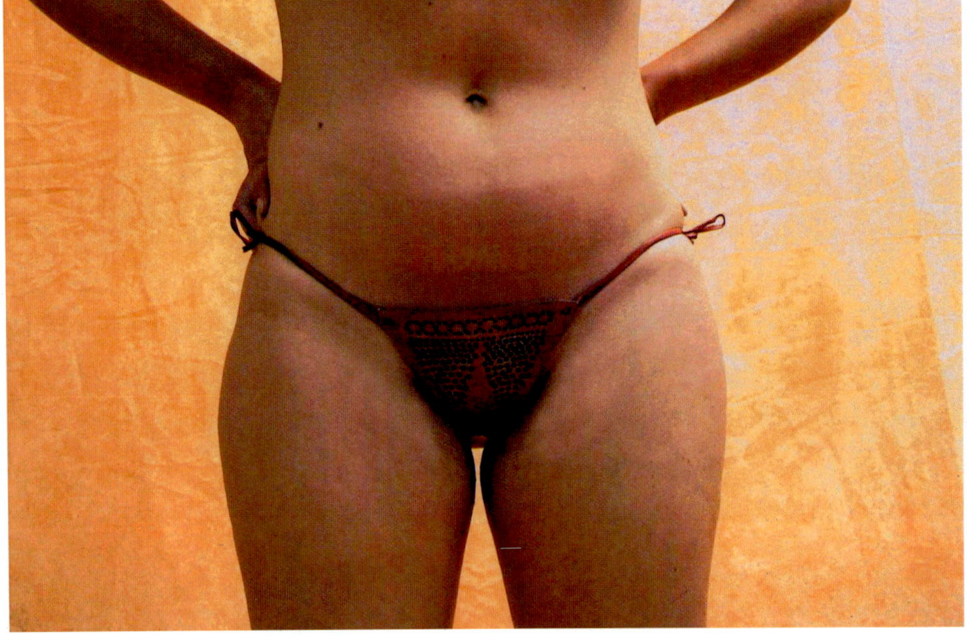

Plate 25: London Wall V-string as worn at the opening of the exhibition '100.000 years sex' Drents Museum Assen 2003 (with permission).

Plate 26: Athletes from the Piazza Armerina, Sicily.

Plate 27: Silver mouse from Stansted Mountfitchet, Cat. no. 1. Photo: British Museum.

Plate 28: Copper-alloy nibbling mouse figure, Cat. no. 5. Photo: British Museum.

Plate 29: Copper-alloy lamp-lid from Konya, Turkey, Cat. no. 47. Photo: British Museum.